Lecture Notes in Computer Science 1839

Edited by G. Goos, J. Hartmanis and J. van Leeuwen

D1584836

Springer
Berlin
Heidelberg
New York
Barcelona
Hong Kong
London
Milan
Paris
Singapore
Tokyo

Gilles Gauthier   Claude Frasson
Kurt VanLehn (Eds.)

Intelligent
Tutoring Systems

5th International Conference, ITS 2000
Montréal, Canada, June 19-23, 2000
Proceedings

Springer

Series Editors

Gerhard Goos, Karlsruhe University, Germany
Juris Hartmanis, Cornell University, NY, USA
Jan van Leeuwen, Utrecht University, The Netherlands

Volume Editors

Gilles Gauthier
Université du Québec à Montréal, Département d'informatique
C.P. 8888, succ. Centre-Ville, Montréal QC, Canada H3C 3P8
E-mail: gauthier.gilles@uqam.ca

Claude Frasson
Université de Montréal, Département d'informatique et de recherche opérationnelle
C.P. 6128, succ. Centre-Ville, Montréal QC, Canada H3C 3J7
E-mail: frasson@iro.umontreal.ca

Kurt VanLehn
University of Pittsburgh, Learning Research and Development Center
Pittsburgh, PA 15260, USA
E-mail: vanlehn@cs.pitt.edu

Cataloging-in-Publication Data applied for

Die Deutsche Bibliothek - CIP-Einheitsaufnahme

Intelligent tutoring systems : 5th international conference ;
proceedings / ITS 2000, Montréal, Canada, June 19 - 23, 2000. Gilles
Gauthier ... (ed.). - Berlin ; Heidelberg ; New York ; Barcelona ;
Hong Kong ; London ; Milan ; Paris ; Singapore ; Tokyo : Springer, 2000
  (Lecture notes in computer science ; Vol. 1839)
  ISBN 3-540-67655-4

CR Subject Classification (1998): K.3, I.2, D.2, H.5, J.1

ISSN 0302-9743
ISBN 3-540-67655-4 Springer-Verlag Berlin Heidelberg New York

Springer-Verlag is a company in the BertelsmannSpringer publishing group.
© Springer-Verlag Berlin Heidelberg 2000
Printed in Germany

Typesetting: Camera-ready by author
Printed on acid-free paper   SPIN: 10722036   06/3142   5 4 3 2 1 0

Preface

ITS 2000 is the fifth international conference on Intelligent Tutoring Systems. The preceding conferences were organized in Montreal in 1988, 1992, and 1996. These conferences were so strongly supported by the international community that it was decided to hold them every two years. ITS'98 was organized by Carol Redfield and Valerie Shute and held in San Antonio, Texas.

The program committee included members from 13 countries. They received **140 papers** (110 full papers and 30 young researchers papers) from 21 countries. As with any international conference whose proceedings serve as a reference for the field, the program committee faced the demanding task of selecting papers from a particularly high quality set of submissions.

This proceedings volume contains **61 papers** selected by the program committee from the 110 papers submitted. They were presented at the conference, along with **six invited lectures** from well-known speakers. The papers cover a wide range of subjects including architectures for ITS, teaching and learning strategies, authoring systems, learning environments, instructional designs, cognitive approaches, student modeling, distributed learning environments, evaluation of instructional systems, cooperative systems, Web-based training systems, intelligent agents, agent-based tutoring systems, intelligent multimedia and hypermedia systems, interface design, and intelligent distance learning. The conference itself was preceded by **seven workshops** on modeling human teaching tactics and strategies, adaptive and intelligent Web-based education systems, applying machine learning to ITS/design construction, collaborative discovery learning in the context of simulations, case-based reasoning in intelligent training systems, learning algebra with the computer (a transdisciplinary workshop), and advanced instructional design for complex safety critical and emergency training. **Three tutorials** highlighted important domains in ITS: ontological engineering and its implication for AIED research, adaptive Web-based educational systems, and animated pedagogical agents.. Finally, **25 papers** from the Young Researcher Track were selected, and **22 posters**.

We would like to thank all the members of the program committee who reviewed conscientiously all the papers which were sent so as to obtain a distributed and equilibrated point of view. We also thank the external reviewers who added their effort to complement the evaluations. A subset of the program committee met in February in Montreal to set up the final list of accepted papers.

The conference was scientifically supported by several prestigious associations. This represents an acknowledgment of the high level of the conference which is now well established. We thank the **American Association for Artificial Intelligence (AAAI)**, the **Association for Computing Machinery (ACM)**, and the special interest groups **SIGART, SIGCUE, and SIGCHI**, the **IFIP TC3 Committee**, the **International Artificial Intelligence in Education (AIED) Society**, and the **Learning Technology Task Force (LTTF)** from **IEEE Computer Society**. They ensured a wide distribution of information regarding the announcement of the conference.

We would like to thank the Université de Montréal and the Université du Québec à Montréal for their support in the organization of the conference. We thank all those many people who gave their time and effort to make the conference a success, all the members of the organizing committee, a fantastic team who regularly spent numerous hours on all the details of the conference, and all the students of the HERON laboratory in Montreal who helped with the practical organization of the conference. Finally, we appreciate the cooperation received from Springer-Verlag during the publication of this volume.

June 2000

Claude Frasson
Gilles Gauthier
Kurt VanLehn

Conference Chair
Claude Frasson (Université de Montréal, Canada)

Program Committee Chair
Kurt VanLehn (Learning Research and Development Center, Pittsburgh, USA)

Program Committee
Marie Michèle Boulet (Université Laval, Canada)
Joost Breuker (University of Amsterdam, The Netherlands)
Peter Brusilovsky (CTE & HCII, Carnegie Mellon University, USA)
Stefano Cerri (Université de Montpellier, France)
Tak Wai Chan (National Central University, Taiwan, R.O.C.)
William Clancey (IHMC, University of West Florida, USA)
Alain Dericke (Université des sciences et techniques de Lille, France)
Pierre Dillenbourg (Université de Genève, Switzerland)
Ben du Boulay (University of Sussex, England)
Isabel Fernandez de Castro (UPV/EHU, Spain)
Carl Fredericksen (McGill University, Canada)
Sylvain Giroux (CRS4, Italy)
Guy Gouardères (Université de Pau, France)
Art Graesser (University of Memphis, USA)
Monique Grandbastien (Université de Nancy, France)
Jim Greer (University of Saskatchewan, Canada)
Denise Gurer (3-Com Corporation, USA)
Danielle Hérin Aimé (Université de Montpellier, France)
Kojih Itoh (University of Tokyo, Japan)
Michelle Joab (Université Pierre et Marie Curie, France)
Lewis Johnson (University of Southern California, USA)
Judith Kay (University of Sydney, Australia)
Ken Koedinger (Carnegie Mellon University, USA)
Susanne Lajoie (McGill University, Canada)
Ruddy Lelouche (Université Laval, Canada)
Alan Lesgold (Learning Research and Development Center, Pittsburgh, USA)
James Lester (North Carolina State University, USA)
Chee-Kit Looi (Kent Ridge Digital Labs, Singapore)
Sandra Marshall (San Diego State University, USA)
Hermann Maurer (University of Graz, Austria)
Gordon McCalla (University of Saskatchewan, Canada)
Riichiro Mizoguchi (Osaka University, Japan)
Claus Moebus (University of Oldenburg, Germany)
Toshio Okamoto (University of Electro-communications, Japan)
Carol Redfield (St. Mary's University, San Antonio, USA)
Jeff Rickel (University of Southern California, USA)
John Self (University of Leeds, England)
Elliot Soloway (University of Michigan, USA)
Daniel Suthers (University of Hawaii, USA)
George Tecuci (George Mason University, USA)
Gerhard Weber (University of Trier, Germany)
Beverly Woolf (University of Massachusets, USA)

ITS Steering Committee
Stefano Cerri (Université de Montpellier, France)
Claude Frasson (Université de Montréal, Canada)
Gilles Gauthier (Université du Québec à Montréal, Canada)
Guy Gouardères (Université de Pau, France)
Marc Kaltenbach (Bishop's University, Canada)
Judith Kay (University of Sydney, Australia)
Alan Lesgold (Learning Research and Development Center, USA)
Vimla Patel (McGill University, Canada)
Elliot Soloway (University of Michigan, USA)
Daniel Suthers (University of Hawaii, USA)
Beverly Woolf (University of Massachusetts, USA)

Organizing Committee Chair
Gilles Gauthier (Université du Québec à Montréal, Canada)

Special Student Track and Poster Session Chair
Roger Nkambou (Université de Sherbrooke, Canada)

Workshops Chair
Esma Aïmeur (Université de Montréal, Canada)

Panels Chair
Stefano Cerri (Université de Montpellier, France)

Publicity Chair
Denise Gurer (3-Com Corporation, USA)

Local Arrangements Chair
Bernard Lefebvre (Université du Québec à Montréal, Canada)

Conference Treasurer & Registration Chair
Michelle Martin (Université de Montréal, Canada)

External Reviewers
Esma Aïmeur
Joseph Beck
Jacqueline Bourdeau
Alexandra Cristea
Aude Dufresne
Claude Frasson
Gilles Gauthier
Gilles Imbeau
Marc Kaltenbach
Tarik Khan
Bernard Lefebvre
André Mayers

Jean-Francois Nicaud
Roger Nkambou

Submitted Papers Repartition

Algeria	1
Austria	2
Brazil	2
Canada	11
Estonia	1
Finland	1
France	10
Germany	6
Greece	3
Hong Kong	1
Japan	13
Korea	1
Mexico	3
The Netherlands	4
New Zealand	3
Portugal	2
Spain	6
UK	10
Ukraine	1
USA	25
Yugoslavia	2

Table of Contents

Invited Presentations

Agent-Based Tutoring Systems

Architectures for ITS

Authoring Systems

Cognitive Approaches

Cooperative Systems

Distributed Learning Environments

Evaluation of Instructional Systems

Intelligent Distance Learning

Intelligent Multimedia and Hypermedia Systems

Instructional Design

Learning Environments

Student Modeling

Teaching and Learning Strategies

Web-Based Training Systems

Poster Papers

Workshops

Adaptive Hypermedia: From Intelligent Tutoring Systems to Web-Based Education

Peter Brusilovsky

Carnegie Technology Education and
HCI Institute, Carnegie Mellon University
4615 Forbes Avenue, Pittsburgh, PA 15213, USA
plb@cs.cmu.edu

Abstract. Adaptive hypermedia is a new area of research at the crossroads of hypermedia and adaptive systems and. Education is the largest application area of adaptive hypermedia systems. The goals of this paper are to provide a brief introduction into adaptive hypermedia and supply the reader with an organized reading on adaptive educational hypermedia. Unlike some other papers that are centered around the current state of the field, this paper attempts, from one side, to trace the history adaptive educational hypermedia in connection with intelligent tutoring systems research and, from another side, draft its future in connection with Web-based education.

1 Introduction

Adaptive hypermedia is a relatively new direction of research on the crossroads of hypermedia and user modeling. One limitation of traditional "static" hypermedia applications is that they provide the same page content and the same set of links to all users. If the user population is relatively diverse, a traditional system will "suffer from an inability to be all things to all people". For example, a traditional educational hypermedia system will present the same static explanation and suggest the same next page to students with widely differing educational goals and knowledge of the subject. Similarly, a static electronic encyclopedia will present the same information and same set of links to related articles to readers with different knowledge and interests. Finally, a static virtual museum will offer the same "guided tour" and the same narration to visitors with very different goals and background knowledge.

Adaptive hypermedia is an alternative to the traditional "one-size-fits-all" approach in the development of hypermedia systems. Adaptive hypermedia systems build a model of the goals, preferences and knowledge of each individual user, and use this model throughout the interaction with the user, in order to adapt the hypertext to the needs of that user. For example, a student in an adaptive educational hypermedia system will be given a presentation which is adapted specifically to his or her knowledge of the subject [10], and a suggested set of most relevant links to proceed further [4]. An adaptive electronic encyclopedia will personalise the content of an article to augment the user's existing knowledge and interests [26]. A virtual museum will adapt the presentation of every visited object to the user's individual path through the museum [30].

2 What Can Be Adapted in Adaptive Hypermedia

A typical *hyperdocument* consists of a set of nodes or "pages" connected by links. Each page contains some local information and a number of links to related pages. Hypermedia systems can also include special navigation tools such as table of contents, index, and map that could be used to navigate to all accessible pages. What can be adapted here are the page (content-level adaptation) and the appearance and behavior of the links (link-level adaptation). In adaptive hypermedia literature they are referred respectively as *adaptive presentation* and *adaptive navigation support*.

The goal of *the adaptive presentation* is to adapt the content of a hypermedia page to the user's goals, knowledge and other information stored in the user model. There could be multiple reasons to use adaptive presentation. Two typical cases in the area of education are comparative explanations and explanation variants. The idea of comparative explanations is to connect new content to the existing knowledge of the student. A page can have one or more hidden comparative explanation fragments that comparing some aspects of new topic with relevant aspects of other topic [15]. For example, "while" loop in C++ language could be compared with the same construct in Pascal. Only students with relevant previous knowledge will (knowledge of Pascal loops in our example) will see the comparison. The idea of explanation variants is to use essentially different variants of explanations for users with different level of knowledge of the topic. A system can store several variants for some parts of the page content. For example, a variant prepared for a medical experts can use extensive Latin terminology, while a variant prepared for novices can use everyday names for illnesses and body parts [2; 17; 34].

The goal of *adaptive navigation support* is to help users to find their paths in hyperspace by adapting link presentation and functionality to the goals, knowledge, and other characteristics of an individual user. It is typically done by one of the following ways:

- Direct guidance: The system outlines visually one of the links on the page showing that this is the best link to follow or generates an additional dynamic link (usually called "next") which is connected to the "next best" page.
- Link sorting: The system sorts all the links of a particular page according to the user model and to some user-valuable criteria: the closer to the top, the more relevant the link is.
- Link annotation: The system augments the links with some form of comments, which can tell the user more about the nodes behind the annotated links. These annotations are usually provided in the form of visual cues. Typical visual cues include icons [7; 12], font colors [5; 10], sizes [20], and types [7].
- Link hiding, disabling, and removal: The system tries to prevent the user from following links that are not relevant for him or her at the moment. There are several ways to achieve it. A link can be hidden by turning a usually underlined hotword into a normal word. It can be disabled so that clicking on the hotword will produce no effect [10]. For a non-contextual link the very anchor (hotword or hotspot) can be removed [5].

A number of interesting forms and applications of adaptive presentation and adaptive navigation support were developed since 1990. A more comprehensive review can be found in [3].

3   From Intelligent Tutoring Systems to Adaptive Hypermedia

Education was always the most popular application area for adaptive hypermedia systems. A number of interesting methods and techniques of adaptive hypermedia were originally developed for in various adaptive educational hypermedia systems. In turn, most of the early research on adaptive educational hypermedia was inspired by the area of intelligent tutoring systems [2; 7; 15; 17; 20; 22; 31] and were born in a trial to combine an intelligent tutoring system (ITS) and an educational hypermedia.

In the early times of ITS, most of these systems provide little or no learning material. The most important duty of an ITS was to support a student in the process of problem solving. It was assumed that the required knowledge is acquired outside of the system, for example, by attending a lecture or reading a textbook. Along with the growth of computer capabilities more and more ITS developers found it reasonable to provide an ITS and a learning material in electronic form in one package. Very soon it became clear that hypertext or hypermedia provides the best option for organizing on-line learning material. A combination of an ITS and a learning material organized as hypermedia was a natural starting point for the research on adaptive educational hypermedia. A number of research groups has independently realized that a hypermedia system coupled with an ITS can offer more functionality than a traditional static educational hypermedia.

Adaptive presentation came first. Adaptive presentation was the natural and the simplest way to make the hypermedia component of the system to use some knowledge about individual students represented in a student model of ITS. A number of adaptive presentation methods and techniques were explored in early projects. In particular, comparative explanations method was used in Lisp-Critic [15] and explanation variants method was used in Lisp-Critic [15], Anatom-Tutor [2], and SYPROS [17].

In our ITS for programming domain ITEM/IP [6] we have explored several adaptive presentation methods including explanation variants. Our goal was to achieve a gradual transformation of the learning material from an explanation-rich textbook to a concise manual. We have developed a simple but powerful technique known as "conditional text". With this technique, all information about that could be presented on a page is divided into several chunks of texts. Each chunk is associated with a condition on the state of user knowledge stored in the user model. When assembling a page for presentation the system selects only the chunks with true condition. This technique is a low-level technique (it requires some "programming" work from the author to set all the required conditions) but it is also very flexible. By choosing appropriate conditions on the knowledge level of the current concept and related concepts represented in the user model we were able to implement several adaptive presentation methods. A simple example is hiding chunks that contain additional explanations if the user's knowledge of the current concept is good enough, or turning on a chunk with comparative explanations if the corresponding related concept is already known. This conditional text technique was later independently developed by Kay and Kummerfeld [21] and De Bra [10] and became quite popular in Web-based adaptive systems.

The work on adaptive navigation support in educational hypermedia was influenced by research on curriculum sequencing. Curriculum sequencing is one of the oldest ITS technologies. The goal of the *curriculum sequencing* is to provide the student with the most suitable individually planned sequence of knowledge units to learn and sequence of learning tasks (examples, questions, problems, etc.) to work with. In other words, it helps the student to find an "optimal path" through the learning material. Early ITS with curriculum sequencing were able to sequence only one kind of learning tasks - problems to for the student to solve [1; 25]. More recent ITS such as ITEM/IP [8], TOBIE [38] and ECAL [14] were able to deal with more rich educational material. The early work on adaptive navigation support in educational hypermedia was simply a trial to apply the ideas of sequencing in a hypermedia context. From the first sight, a dynamic linear sequence of learning tasks produced by a sequencing-based ITS and a static network of educational hypermedia pages looks like two contradictory approaches to organizing access to the learning material. However, these approaches are really complementary. The key is that a typical sequencing engine can do more than just selecting the "next best" task. On the way to the "best", such an engine can usually classify all available tasks into non-relevant and relevant candidates. For example, a task can be considered non-relevant if it was already completed in the past or if it is not ready to be learned due to the lack of prerequisite knowledge and experience. After excluding non-relevant tasks a sequencing engine use some approach to pick up the best of relevant tasks. In a hyperspace of learning material where each learning task is represented by a separate page an ability to distinguish "ready", "not-ready", or "best" tasks is a direct precondition for adaptive navigation support.

In our systems ITEM/PG [6] and ISIS-Tutor [5] we explored several ways of adaptive navigation support. We have used direct guidance in the form of "teach me" button to provide a one-click access to the next best task. We have used adaptive annotation to color-code the links to "ready", "not-ready", and "already learned" tasks. In one of the versions of ISIS-Tutor we have applied adaptive link removal to remove all links to not-ready tasks. From our point of view a sequencing-based adaptive navigation support in educational hypermedia is "best of both worlds". Choosing next task in an ITS with sequencing is based on machine intelligence. Choosing next task in a traditional hypermedia is based on human intelligence. Adaptive navigation support is an interface that can integrate the power of machine and human intelligence: a user is free to make a choice while still seeing an opinion of an intelligent system. From this point of view we can speculate that adaptive navigation support is a *natural* way to add some intelligence to adaptive hypermedia system. It is not surprising that several research groups have independently developed major adaptive navigation support techniques such as direct guidance [42], hiding [10; 31], and annotation [12].

4 Adaptive Hypermedia for Web-based Education

The year of 1996 could be considered a turning point in adaptive hypermedia research. The key factor here is the rapid increase in the use of the Word Wide Web. The Web, with its clear demand for adaptivity, served to boost adaptive hypermedia research, providing both a challenge and an attractive platform.

We know only four Web-based adaptive educational hypermedia systems developed by 1996: ELM-ART [7], InterBook [4], PT [21], and 2L670 [11]. These "classic" systems have influenced a number of more recent systems. The Web platform enabled these systems to live much longer than similar pre-Web systems and influence a number of more recent systems. In particular, ELM-ART gave a start to a whole tree of systems including InterBook, AST, ADI, ART-WEB, and ACE. It is not surprising that all adaptive educational hypermedia systems developed since 1996 are Web-based systems. Examples are: Medtech [13], AST [36], ADI [33], HysM: [23], AHM [32], MetaLinks [27], CHEOPS [28], RATH [19], TANGOW [9], Arthur [16], CAMELEON [24], KBS-Hyperbook [18], AHA! [10], SKILL [29], Multibook [37], ACE [35], ART-Web [41].

The introduction of the Web has impacted not only on the number of adaptive educational hypermedia systems, but also on the type of systems being developed. All the early systems were essentially lab systems, built to explore some new methods, which used adaptivity in an educational context. In contrast, a number more recent systems provide complete frameworks and even authoring tools for developing Web-based courses. The appearance of a number of authoring tools is not only indicative of the maturity of adaptive educational hypermedia, but also a response to a Web-provoked demand for user-adaptive distance education courses.

Existing adaptive hypermedia frameworks such as InterBook, ART-Web, ACE, AHA!, SKILL, MetaLinks or Multibook are getting strikingly close to commercial tools for developing Web-based courses such as WebCT [40] or TopClass [39]. Developers of adaptive hypermedia frameworks are clearly interested in making their systems suitable for handling real Web courses. From another side, developers of commercial course management systems are becoming interested in adaptive and personalized systems. In this situation we could hope that adaptive hypermedia technology that was originally developed inside the area of ITS will soon be used in commercial-strength Web-based systems to deliver thousands of real world courses to students all over the world.

References

1. Barr, A., Beard, M., and Atkinson, R. C.: The computer as tutorial laboratory: the Stanford BIP project. International Journal on the Man-Machine Studies 8, 5 (1976) 567-596
2. Beaumont, I.: User modeling in the interactive anatomy tutoring system ANATOM-TUTOR. User Modeling and User-Adapted Interaction 4, 1 (1994) 21-45
3. Brusilovsky, P.: Methods and techniques of adaptive hypermedia. User Modeling and User-Adapted Interaction 6, 2-3 (1996) 87-129
4. Brusilovsky, P., Eklund, J., and Schwarz, E.: Web-based education for all: A tool for developing adaptive courseware. Computer Networks and ISDN Systems. 30, 1-7 (1998) 291-300
5. Brusilovsky, P. and Pesin, L.: An intelligent learning environment for CDS/ISIS users. In: Levonen, J. J. and Tukianinen, M. T. (eds.) Proc. of The interdisciplinary workshop on complex learning in computer environments (CLCE94), Joensuu, Finland, EIC (1994) 29-33, available online at http://cs.joensuu.fi/~mtuki/www_clce.270296/Brusilov.html
6. Brusilovsky, P., Pesin, L., and Zyryanov, M.: Towards an adaptive hypermedia component for an intelligent learning environment. In: Bass, L. J., Gornostaev, J. and Unger, C. (eds.) Human-Computer Interaction. Lecture Notes in Computer Science, Vol. 753. Springer-Verlag, Berlin (1993) 348-358
7. Brusilovsky, P., Schwarz, E., and Weber, G.: ELM-ART: An intelligent tutoring system on World Wide Web. In: Frasson, C., Gauthier, G. and Lesgold, A. (eds.) Intelligent Tutoring

Systems. Lecture Notes in Computer Science, Vol. 1086. Springer Verlag, Berlin (1996) 261-269

8. Brusilovsky, P. L.: A framework for intelligent knowledge sequencing and task sequencing. In: Frasson, C., Gauthier, G. and McCalla, G. I. (eds.) Intelligent Tutoring Systems. Springer-Verlag, Berlin (1992) 499-506

9. Carro, R. M., Pulido, E., and Rodrígues, P.: TANGOW: Task-based Adaptive learNer Guidance on the WWW. Computer Science Report, Eindhoven University of Technology, Eindhoven (1999) 49-57

10. De Bra, P. and Calvi, L.: AHA! An open Adaptive Hypermedia Architecture. The New Review of Hypermedia and Multimedia 4 (1998) 115-139

11. De Bra, P. M. E.: Teaching Hypertext and Hypermedia through the Web. Journal of Universal Computer Science 2, 12 (1996) 797-804, available online at http://www.iicm.edu/jucs_2_12/teaching_hypertext_and_hypermedia

12. de La Passardiere, B. and Dufresne, A.: Adaptive navigational tools for educational hypermedia. In: Tomek, I. (ed.) Computer Assisted Learning. Springer-Verlag, Berlin (1992) 555-567

13. Eliot, C., Neiman, D., and Lamar, M.: Medtec: A Web-based intelligent tutor for basic anatomy. In: Lobodzinski, S. and Tomek, I. (eds.) Proc. of WebNet'97, World Conference of the WWW, Internet and Intranet, Toronto, Canada, AACE (1997) 161-165

14. Elsom-Cook, M. T. and O'Malley, C.: ECAL: Bridging the gap between CAL and intelligent tutoring systems. Computers and Education 15, 1 (1990) 69-81

15. Fischer, G., Mastaglio, T., Reeves, B., and Rieman, J.: Minimalist explanations in knowledge-based systems. In: Proc. of 23-th Annual Hawaii International Conference on System Sciences, Kailua-Kona, HI, IEEE (1990) 309-317

16. Gilbert, J. E. and Han, C. Y.: Arthur: Adapting Instruction to Accommodate Learning Style. In: Bra, P. D. and Leggett, J. (eds.) Proc. of WebNet'99, World Conference of the WWW and Internet, Honolulu, HI, AACE (1999) 433-438

17. Gonschorek, M. and Herzog, C.: Using hypertext for an adaptive helpsystem in an intelligent tutoring system. In: Greer, J. (ed.) Proc. of AI-ED'95, 7th World Conference on Artificial Intelligence in Education, Washington, DC, AACE (1995) 274-281

18. Henze, N., Naceur, K., Nejdl, W., and Wolpers, M.: Adaptive hyperbooks for constructivist teaching. Künstliche Intelligenz, 4 (1999) 26-31

19. Hockemeyer, C., Held, T., and Albert, D.: RATH - A relational adaptive tutoring hypertext WWW-environment based on knowledge space theory. In: Alvegård, C. (ed.) Proc. of CALISCE'98, 4th International conference on Computer Aided Learning and Instruction in Science and Engineering, Göteborg, Sweden (1998) 417-423

20. Hohl, H., Böcker, H.-D., and Gunzenhäuser, R.: Hypadapter: An adaptive hypertext system for exploratory learning and programming. User Modeling and User-Adapted Interaction 6, 2-3 (1996) 131-156

21. Kay, J. and Kummerfeld, B.: User models for customized hypertext. In: Nicholas, C. and Mayfield, J. (eds.): Intelligent hypertext: Advanced techniques for the World Wide Web. Lecture Notes in Computer Science, Vol. 1326. Springer-Verlag, Berlin (1997)

22. Kay, J. and Kummerfeld, R. J.: An individualised course for the C programming language. In: Proc. of Second International WWW Conference, Chicago, IL (1994), available online at http://www.ncsa.uiuc.edu/SDG/IT94/Proceedings/Educ/kummerfeld/kummerfeld.html

23. Kayama, M. and Okamoto, T.: A mechanism for knowledge-navigation in hyperspace with neural networks to support exploring activities. In: Ayala, G. (ed.) Proc. of Workshop "Current Trends and Applications of Artificial Intelligence in Education" at the 4th World Congress on Expert Systems, Mexico City, Mexico, ITESM (1998) 41-48

24. Laroussi, M. and Benahmed, M.: Providing an adaptive learning through the Web case of CAMELEON: Computer Aided MEdium for LEarning on Networks. In: Alvegård, C. (ed.) Proc. of CALISCE'98, 4th International conference on Computer Aided Learning and Instruction in Science and Engineering, Göteborg, Sweden (1998) 411-416

25. McArthur, D., et al.: Skill-oriented task sequencing in an intelligent tutor for basic algebra. Instructional Science 17, 4 (1988) 281-307
26. Milosavljevic, M.: Augmenting the user's knowledge via comparison. In: Jameson, A., Paris, C. and Tasso, C. (eds.) User Modeling. Springer-Verlag, Wien (1997) 119-130
27. Murray, T., Condit, C., and Haugsjaa, E.: MetaLinks: A preliminary framework for concept-based adaptive hypermedia. In: Proc. of Workshop "WWW-Based Tutoring" at 4th International Conference on Intelligent Tutoring Systems, San Antonio, TX (1998), available online at http://www-aml.cs.umass.edu/~stern/webits/itsworkshop/murray.html
28. Negro, A., Scarano, V., and Simari, R.: User adaptivity on WWW through CHEOPS. Computing Science Reports, Eindhoven University of Technology (1998) 57-62
29. Neumann, G. and Zirvas, J.: SKILL - A scallable internet-based teaching and learning system. In: Maurer, H. and Olson, R. G. (eds.) Proc. of WebNet'98, World Conference of the WWW, Internet, and Intranet, Orlando, FL, AACE (1998) 688-693, available online at http://nestroy.wi-inf.uni-essen.de/Forschung/Publikationen/skill-webnet98.ps
30. Oberlander, J., O'Donell, M., Mellish, C., and Knott, A.: Conversation in the museum: experiments in dynamic hypermedia with the intelligent labeling explorer. The New Review of Multimedia and Hypermedia 4 (1998) 11-32
31. Pérez, T., Gutiérrez, J., and Lopistéguy, P.: An adaptive hypermedia system. In: Greer, J. (ed.) Proc. of AI-ED'95, 7th World Conference on Artificial Intelligence in Education, Washington, DC, AACE (1995) 351-358
32. Pilar da Silva, D., Durm, R. V., Duval, E., and Olivié, H.: Concepts and documents for adaptive educational hypermedia: a model and a prototype. Computing Science Reports, Eindhoven University of Technology, Eindhoven (1998) 35-43
33. Schöch, V., Specht, M., and Weber, G.: "ADI" - an empirical evaluation of a tutorial agent. In: Ottmann, T. and Tomek, I. (eds.) Proc. of ED-MEDIA/ED-TELECOM'98 - 10th World Conference on Educational Multimedia and Hypermedia and World Conference on Educational Telecommunications, Freiburg, Germany, AACE (1998) 1242-1247
34. Specht, M. and Kobsa, A.: Interaction of domain expertise and interface design in adaptive educational hypermedia. Computer Science Report, Eindhoven University of Technology, Eindhoven (1999) 89-93
35. Specht, M. and Oppermann, R.: ACE - Adaptive Courseware Environment. The New Review of Hypermedia and Multimedia 4 (1998) 141-161
36. Specht, M., Weber, G., Heitmeyer, S., and Schöch, V.: AST: Adaptive WWW-Courseware for Statistics. In: Brusilovsky, P., Fink, J. and Kay, J. (eds.) Proc. of Workshop "Adaptive Systems and User Modeling on the World Wide Web" at 6th International Conference on User Modeling, UM97, Chia Laguna, Sardinia, Italy, (1997) 91-95, available online at http://www.contrib.andrew.cmu.edu/~plb/UM97_workshop/Specht.html
37. Steinacker, A., Seeberg, C., Rechenberger, K., Fischer, S., and Steinmetz, R.: Dynamically generated tables of contents as guided tours in adaptive hypermedia systems. In: Proc. of ED-MEDIA/ED-TELECOM'99 - 11th World Conference on Educational Multimedia and Hypermedia and World Conference on Educational Telecommunications, Seattle, WA, AACE (1998)
38. Vassileva, J.: Dynamic CAL-courseware generation within an ITS-shell architecture. In: Tomek, I. (ed.) Computer Assisted Learning. Springer-Verlag, Berlin (1992) 581-591
39. WBT Systems: TopClass, Dublin, Ireland, WBT Systems (1999) available online at http://www.wbtsystems.com/
40. WebCT: World Wide Web Course Tools, Vancouver, Canada, WebCT Educational Technologies (1999) available online at http://www.webct.com
41. Weber, G.: ART-WEB, Trier, University of Trier (1999) available online at
42. Zeiliger, R.: Adaptive testing: contribution of the SHIVA model. In: Leclercq, D. and Bruno, J. (eds.): Item banking: Interactive testing and self-assessment. NATO ASI Serie F, Vol. 112. Springer-Verlag, Berlin (1993) 54-65

Infrastructure for Future Network Learning

Tak-Wai Chan

Dept. of Computer Science and Information Engineering
National Central University, Chungli, Taiwan
chan@src.ncu.edu.tw

Information and communication technology is going to change how, what, who, when, where and why we learn. Unfortunately, we are still uncertain the details how these impacts will bring to future education. Only one thing we are certain: there will be numerous network learning models emerging in the near future. This talk discuss some main ideas of a Grand Project for Excellence: *"Learning technology: social learning and its application, from Taiwan to the World"*, recently launched in Taiwan. Around forty professors across Taiwan are involved in the project. The project actually induces an infrastructure of future network learning from several perspectives: concept, theory, learning model design, and system architecture. This infrastructure provides us an integrated view of how seemingly diversified technologies or concepts converge. For example, within this infrastructure, the roles and implications of terms such as handheld computers, wireless and mobile communication, broadband network, project-based learning, intelligent educational agents in the future network learning can be more intelligible.

Can We Learn from ITSs?

Benedict du Boulay

School of Cognitive and Computing Sciences
University of Sussex
Brighton, BN1 9QH,
U.K.
bend@cogs.susx.ac.uk

Abstract. With the rise of VR, the internet, and mobile technologies and the shifts in educational focus from teaching to learning and from solitary to collaborative work, it's easy (but mistaken) to regard Artificial Intelligence in Education, in general, and Intelligent Tutoring Systems, in particular, as a technology that has had its day — an old solution looking for a new problem. The issues of modeling the student, the domain or the interaction are still very much to the fore, and we can learn much from the development of ITSs.

Despite the changes in technology and in educational focus there is still an ongoing desire for educational and training systems to tailor their interactions to suit the individual learner or group of learners: for example, by being able to deal appropriately with a wider range of background knowledge and abilities; by helpfully limiting the scope for the learner to tailor the system; by being better able to help learners reflect productively on the experience they have had or are about to have; by being able to select and operate effectively over a wider range of problems within the domain of interest; by being able to monitor collaborative interchanges and intervene where necessary; or, most tellingly, by being able to react sensibly to learners when the task they are engaged on is inherently complex and involves many coordinated steps or stages at different levels of granularity. Individualising instruction in an effective manner is the Holy Grail of ITS work and it is taken as an article of faith that this is a sensible educational goal.

This paper explores the question of how much educational difference the "AI" in an ITS system makes compared either to conventional classroom teaching or to conventional CAI methods. One criterion of educational effectiveness might be the amount of time it takes students to reach a particular level of achievement. Another might be an improvement in achievement levels, given the same time on task. So the paper surveys the recent past for ITS systems that have been evaluated against unintelligent versions or against traditional classroom practice and finds cause for optimism in that some of the techniques and solutions found can be applied in the present and the future.[1]

---

[1] This paper is an edited version of [6].

1 Introduction

In many ways Artificial Intelligence in Education is in a state of flux. People sometimes talk of one of its subfields, Intelligent Tutoring Systems, as an outmoded technology that has, in some sense, "failed" [5]. The emphasis today has shifted to exploring the possibilities of newer technologies such as virtual reality and the Internet, and is particularly concerned with learning environments and collaboration. However most of the traditional hard problems still remain — adjusting the environment to meet the needs of the learner(s), determining what to say to learners and when to say it, and so on.

One aspect of the issue of teaching *vs* learning crystalised into the issue of whether the educational system should attempt to model the student [10]. Modelling the student allows, at least in principle, the system to adjust its behaviour or to react to that student as an individual, or at least as a representative of a class of individuals (see [17]). The argument for not modelling the student arises because it is hard — indeed some regard it as inherently impossible — or because it is thought unnecessary. The argument goes that if a learning environment is well-designed and operated by the students within a supportive educational environment, we can rely on the students themselves to manage their own learning without having the system individualise its reactions in any way.

In some ways the heat has gone out of the debate between the modellers and the non-modellers. Although both camps have coexisted throughout the history of Artificial Intelligence in Education, there is a stronger realisation that both approaches have something useful to offer. Indeed both approaches are now sometimes to be found inside a single system, where an ITS of a traditional architecture may be but a single component of a more general, possibly distributed, system offering the learner a variety of learning experiences from which they can choose [14].

This paper examines what has been shown to be of value in ITS work by briefly exploring the question of how much educational difference ITSs make compared either to conventional classroom teaching or to conventional CAI methods (for more detailed reviews see, e.g. [15, 16]). One criterion of educational effectiveness might be the amount of time it takes students to reach a particular level of achievement. Another might be an improvement in achievement levels, given the same time on task.

A problem for computers and education in general is that it gets hijacked from time to time by particular technologies claiming to produce wonderful educational results simply by virtue of that technology — examples include LOGO, hypertext, and now we have the World Wide Web, hypermedia and virtual reality. It is important to separate reasonable from unreasonable claims and expectations.

To the sceptical eye the evidence for the value of ITSs is not yet overwhelming, though the positive trends are clearly visible. The extra individualisation enabled by an intelligent system does indeed produce educational benefits either through faster learning or through better learning.

This paper starts by exploring the issue of the difference between an intelligently designed system and an intelligent system. It goes on to review criteria by which the educational success of an intelligent educational system could be measured. The paper then examines a number of evaluations of actual systems. Finally it briefly surveys some of the educational issues with which ITS research is grappling.

2 Educational value

It is important to acknowledge that non-intelligent but well-designed systems can be educationally excellent. For example, Dugdale [7] offers a telling account of how quite simple programs can generate authentic mathematical activity, discussion and insight, in particular getting students to reflect on strategy and plans rather than simply following procedures. Her examples have simple interfaces and are not internally complex. They essentially invite users to engage in a problem-solving process that involves only a single step at a time and the systems are able to react to the success or failure of that step immediately. For example, Green Globs, displays coordinate axes and a number of points where the task for the student is to provide a function which intersects and then "explodes" as many of the points as possible. In each case the programs provide visual feedback of success or failure and can adjust, within limited parameters, the difficulty of the tasks that they present, e.g. the Green Globs program can choose locations for the points that can be intersected by simple formulae. However the degree of possible individualisation is slight and one would not regard the programs as "intelligent" no matter how educationally successful they are. It is worth stressing that quite small changes in the way problems are presented and represented can make a big difference in the students' success rates, see e.g. [1]. Such findings suggest that intelligent design on its own is inlikely to get it right for all the students in a target population, and that ideally the system itself needs to have some way of adjusting to the background knowledge and learning preferences of the particular student under instruction.

2.1 Criteria for success

Bloom and his colleagues investigated how various factors, such as cues and explanations, reinforcement and feedback, affect student learning taking conventional classroom teaching as the baseline [2]. They found that highly individualised expert teaching, shifts the distribution of achievement scores of students by about two standard deviations compared to the more usual situation where one teacher deals with a classroom of students. They also found that the range of individual differences reduced.

This two standard deviation improvement, or Two Sigma shift, has become a goal at which designers of ITSs aim. A standard method of evaluation of such a system is to compare it with conventional non-computer-based teaching on the same topic, though there have been some comparisons of "smart" and "dumb" versions of the same software.

2.2 Reducing time on task

Smithtown is a discovery environment with which students can explore problem-solving and inductive learning in the domain of microeconomics [20]. The goals of the system are to help students grasp specific economics concepts, such as the notion of "market equilibrium", as well as more general problem-solving skills such as adjusting only one variable at a time when undertaking an experiment.

Shute and Glaser [20] undertook two kinds of evaluation of the system. One was a comparison with a non-computer-based exploration of the same material; the other was an examination of the particular cognitive and learning-style factors that lead to success with this kind of discovery environment. The comparison study was quite small (N = 30) but found that the group using Smithtown improved their pre/post-test scores as much as the classroom based group despite spending about half the time on the material (5 hours vs. 11 hours).

Over a number of years Anderson and his colleagues have produced a variety of tutoring systems for programming and for mathematics in the heart of the ITS tradition (for an overview, see [4]). Their systems attempt to model the student in detail as s/he undertakes complex problem solving so as to be in a position to offer assistance focussed on the point of difficulty and at the most helpful level of generality ("model tracing"), as well as being able to select problems for the student to solve that move him or her optimally through the curriculum ("knowledge tracing").

One such tutor (LISPITS) taught LISP and has been extensively evaluated in terms of its specific educational interaction methodology (e.g. immediate or delayed feedback) as well as in terms of its overall effect on learning gains. For example, novice programmers using LISPITS were compared to a group working on their own with a textbook and to a group working with a teacher in a conventional classroom manner. While all three groups did equivalently well on the post-test, the group who worked with the human teacher finished in about 12 hours, the group who worked with LISPITS finished in 15 hours and the group who worked with the textbook took 28 hours. The authors argue that the intelligent computer-based system was able to produce similar results to a human teacher and achieved this with in only slightly greater time. In another study with slightly more experienced students, there were two groups both of whom took a conventional LISP course. The control group did the exercises with a textbook and a LISP system whereas the experimental group used LISPITS to do the exercises. As before the LISPITS group finished faster, and this time did better on the post-test compared to the non LISPITS group.

2.3 Improving achievement scores

One of Anderson's more recent evaluations concerns a system designed to be used in Pittsburgh High Schools [8]. The Practical Algebra Tutor (PAT) is designed to teach a novel applications-orientated mathematics curriculum (PUMP — Pittsburgh Urban Mathematics Project) through a series of realistic problems.

The system provides support for problem-solving and for the use of a number of tools such as a spreadsheet, grapher and symbolic calculator.

The intelligence of the system is deployed in several ways. Model Tracing, based on representing knowledge of how to do the task in terms of production-rules, is used to keep close track of all the student's actions as the problem is solved and flag errors as they occur, such as misplotting a point or entering a value in an incorrect cell in the spreadsheet. It also adjusts the help feedback according to the specific problem-solving context in which it is requested. Knowledge Tracing is used to choose the next appropriate problem so as to move the students in a timely but effective manner through the curriculum.

Of special note is the way that attention was paid to the use of the Tutor within the classroom. The system was used not on a one-to-one basis but by teams of students who were also expected to carry out activities related to the use of PAT, but not involving PAT, such as making presentations to their peers.

An evaluation was carried out in three Pittsburgh Public High Schools (N > 100). We should note that the evaluation was of the tutor plus the new curriculum against a more traditional curriculum delivered in the traditional manner. Two standardised and two specially prepared tests were used.

The experimental group performed significantly better than the control group on all four tests but did not achieve Bloom's [2] criterion of improving outcomes by two sigma above normal classroom instruction. However they did perform 1.2 standard deviations better than the control on the specially written Representations Test which was designed "to assess students' abilities to translate between representations of algebraic content including verbal descriptions, graphs and symbolic equations".

Table 1. Comparison of PUMP curriculum plus PAT tutor with traditional curriculum and no tutor. Each cell in the first and second columns contains proportion of the post-test correct (standard deviation) and N. The F values in the third column are derived from a between-subjects ANOVA.

	Control Group	Experimental Group	F value and significance	sigma
Iowa Algebra Aptitude	.46 (.17) 80	.52 (.19) 287	$F(2,398) = 17.0$ $p < .0001$	0.3
Math SAT Subset	.27 (.14) 44	.32 (.16) 127	$F(2,205) = 5.1$ $p < .01$	0.3
Problem Situation Test	.22 (.22) 42	.39 (.33) 127	$F(2,186) = 5.3$ $p < .01$	0.7
Representations Test	.15 (.18) 44	.37 (.32) 124	$F(2,183) = 13.4$ $p < .0001$	1.2

(adapted from [8], page 40).

Lesgold, Lajoie and their colleagues have taken a slightly different approach to individualisation in their work on SHERLOCK 1, a tutor designed to teach to airforce technicians the electronic debugging skills needed to operate a complex piece of testgear. In their system all users worked through the same set of problems but the help and other feedback was adjusted to the expertise of user. Various evaluations of this system are cited by Lajoie [9]. For example, the Air Force evaluation was that "technicians who spent 20–25 hours working with Sherlock 1 were as proficient in troubleshooting the test station as technicians who had 4 more years of job experience". In another evaluation a pre/post comparison was made between a group using the tutor and a control group who carried out their normal troubleshooting duties using the real testgear over a twelve day period. The experimental group solved significantly more problems in the post-test than the control group and the quality of their problem-solving methods was more like those of experts.

3   Smart vs. Dumb

Several studies have compared the effectiveness of intelligent and non-intelligent versions of the same program. For instance, Mark and Greer [13] compared the effects of four versions of the same tutor designed to teach the operation of a simulated Video Recorder. The least intelligent version gave simple prompting and allowed the user only a single way of carrying out a task, such as setting the simulated VCR to record for a particular period at a particular time on a particular channel. The most intelligent, and the one providing the most "knowledgeable" teaching offered conceptual as well as procedural feedback, undertook model-tracing to allow flexible ways of carrying out tasks and could recognise and tutor for certain misconceptions. In a comparative evaluation (N = 76), Mark and Greer [13] found that increasing the knowledgeability of the tutor produced a decreasing number of steps, decreasing number of errors and a decreasing time needed for students to complete the post-test. They also found that these gains were not the result of greater time on task in the case of the most knowledgeable tutor.

Shute [17] evaluated a particular method of student modelling (SMART) which forms the individualising component of a tutor named Stat Lady designed to teach elementary statistics, such as data organisation and plotting. Two versions of the tutor were produced. The non-intelligent version worked through the same curriculum for all learners, with fixed thresholds for progress through areas of increasing difficulty and a fixed regime of increasingly specific feedback when repeated mistakes were made. The intelligent version had a more detailed symbolic, procedural and conceptual knowledge representation which enabled it to provide much more focussed remediation as well as to individualise the sequence of problems for the learner to solve by a more careful analysis of the students' degree of mastery of individual elements of the curriculum.

As with Smithtown described above, Shute [17] was interested not just in the comparative performance of the system but also in aptitude-treatment interactions. The unintelligent version of Stat Lady improved students' scores (N = 103) by more than two standard deviations compared to their pre-test scores. Other studies with the unintelligent version did not produce such high learning gains, but did produce as good outcomes as an experienced lecturer [19] or a workbook [18], though Stat Lady subjects showed a significant gain in declarative knowledge compared to workbook subjects. In another study (N = 168) Shute and her colleagues [19] compared the unintelligent version of Stat Lady to a traditional lecture approach. Stat Lady improved pre-post test score differences by about the same margin as the traditional lecture approach (i.e. about one standard deviation) and over the same time on task (about 3 hours). In a similar study (N = 311) Stat Lady was compared with use of a workbook on the same material [18]. Learning gains were generally similar though Stat Lady subjects showed a significant gain in declarative knowledge compared to workbook studies.

A further study [17] was conducted (N = 100) using the intelligent version of Stat Lady. Pre-post test gains were significantly greater than for the unintelligent version, which themselves were high. However there was a cost in that students spent quite a lot more time working with the intelligent version of the system (mean = 7.6 hours) compared the the unintelligent (mean = 4.4 hours). In general high aptitude subjects gained more from Stat Lady than low aptitude subjects.

In a somewhat similar but smaller (N = 26) study, Luckin compared learning outcomes for versions of a tutor for simple ecology covering topics such as food chains and webs [11, 12]. An unintelligent version (NIS) of her system ECOLAB provided a range of activities, perspectives on the domain, traversal through the curriculum and levels of help wholly under the control of the pupils themselves. The intelligent version (VIS) made decisions in all four of these areas for the pupils based on a student model. As with Stat Lady, the intelligent version produced higher pre-post gains than the unintelligent version, with high ability students gaining more than those of low ability. Time on task was the same for both groups; the gains for both groups were maintained at a delayed (10 week) post-test.

4 Conclusions

ITSs have been designed to individualise the educational experience of students according to their level of knowledge and skill. This paper has described briefly some of the evaluations that have been conducted into the educational benefits of this investment in the capability to individualise. Although the evidence is not definitive, there are indications that the extra individualisation enabled by an intelligent system does indeed produce educational benefits either through faster learning or through better learning. There are also indications that high ability subjects are better suited to this kind of treatment. By contrast, it really would be a surprising finding if attempting to match teaching to the learners capability produced *poorer* results than not so matching. However what has not been discussed is whether, in practical terms, the effort needed to produce these intelligent systems is sufficiently paid back through their superior performance.

Acknowledgements

I thank Rosemary Luckin for commenting on a draft of this paper.

References

1. S. Ainsworth, D. Wood, and P. Bibby. Co-ordinating multiple representations in computer based learning environments. In Brna et al. [3], pages 336–342.
2. B. S. Bloom. The 2 sigma problem: The search for methods of group instruction as effective as one-to-one tutoring. *Educational Researcher*, 13(6):4–16, 1984.
3. P. Brna, A. Paiva, and J. Self, editors. *Euroaied: European Conference on Artificial Intelligence in Education*, Lisbon, 1996. Edicoes Colibri.
4. A. T. Corbett and J. R. Anderson. LISP intelligent tutoring system: Research in skill acquisition. In J. H. Larkin and R. W. Chabay, editors, *Computer-Assisted Instruction and Intelligent Tutoring Systems: Shared Goals and Complementary Approaches*, pages 73–109. Lawrence Erlbaum, 1992.
5. F. M. de Oliveira and R. M. Viccari. Are learning systems distributed or social systems? In Brna et al. [3], pages 247–253.
6. B. du Boulay. What does the AI in AIED buy? In *Colloquium on Artificial Intelligence in Educational Software*, pages 3/1–3/4. IEE Digest No: 98/313, 1998.
7. S. Dugdale. The design of computer-based mathematics education. In J. H. Larkin and R. W. Chabay, editors, *Computer-Assisted Instruction and Intelligent Tutoring Systems: Shared Goals and Complementary Approaches*, pages 11–45. Lawrence Erlbaum, 1992.
8. K. R. Koedinger, J. R. Anderson, W. H. Hadley, and M. A. Mark. Intelligent tutoring goes to school in the big city. *International Journal of Artificial Intelligence in Education*, 8(1):30–43, 1997.
9. S. P. Lajoie. Computer environments as cognitive tools for enhancing learning. In S. P. Lajoie and S. J. Derry, editors, *Computers as Cognitive Tools*, pages 261–288. Lawrence Erlbaum, 1993.
10. S. P. Lajoie and S. J. Derry, editors. *Computers as Cognitive Tools*. Lawrence Erlbaum, Hillsdale, New Jersey, 1993.
11. R. Luckin. 'ECOLAB': Explorations in the zone of proximal development. Technical Report CSRP 386, School of Cognitive and Computing Sciences Research Paper, University of Sussex, 1998.
12. R. Luckin and B. du Boulay. Ecolab: The development and evaluation of a vygotskian design framework. *International Journal of Artificial Intelligence in Education*, 10(2):198–220, 1999.
13. M. A. Mark and J. E. Greer. The VCR tutor: Effective instruction for device operation. *Journal of the Learning Sciences*, 4(2):209–246, 1995.
14. J. Mitchell, J. Liddle, K. Brown, and R. Leitch. Integrating simulations into intelligent tutoring systems. In Brna et al. [3], pages 80–86.
15. J. Self. Special issue on evaluation. *Journal of Artificial Intelligence in Education*, 4(2/3), 1993.

17

16. V. J. Shute. Rose garden promises of intelligent tutoring systems: Blossom or thorn? In *Space Operations, Applications and Research (SOAR) Symposium*, Albuquerque, New Mexico, 1990.

17. V. J. Shute. SMART: Student modelling approach for responsive tutoring. *User Modelling and User-Adapted Interaction*, 5(1):1–44, 1995.

18. V. J. Shute and L. A. Gawlick-Grendell. What does the computer contribute to learning? *Computers and Education*, 23(3):177–186, 1994.

19. V. J. Shute, L. A. Gawlick-Grendell, R. K. Young, and C. A. Burnham. An experiential system for learning probability: Stat Lady description and evaluation. *Instructional Science*, 24(1):25–46, 1996.

20. V. J. Shute and R. Glaser. A large-scale evaluation of an intelligent discovery world: Smithtown. *Interactive Learning Environments*, 1(1):51–77, 1990.

Uncertainty, Utility, and Understanding

Eric Horvitz

Microsoft Research, USA
horvitz@microsoft.com

Uncertainty abounds in pedagogy. As such, the effectiveness of intelligent tutoring systems hinges on identifying appropriate actions under uncertainty. I will discuss challenges and opportunities with the use of probabilistic user models in intelligent tutoring systems, drawing key concepts from the broader arena of probabilistic and decision-theoretic user modeling.

Stereotypes, Student Models and Scrutability

Judy Kay

Basser Dept of Computer Science
Madsen F09
University of Sydney
AUSTRALIA 2006
email: judy@cs.usyd.edu.au

Abstract. Stereotypes are widely used in both Intelligent Teaching Systems and in a range of other teaching and advisory software. Yet the notion of stereotype is very loose. This paper gives a working definition of stereotypes for student modelling. The paper shows the role of stereotypes in classic approaches to student modelling via overlay, differential and buggy models.

A scrutable student model enables learners to *scrutinise* their models to determine what the system believes about them and how it determined those beliefs. The paper explores the ways that scrutable stereotypes can provide a foundation for learners to tune their student models and explore the impact of the student model. Linking this to existing work, the paper notes how scrutable stereotypes might support reflection and metacognition as well as efficient, learner-controlled student modelling.

1 Introduction

Stereotype-based reasoning takes an *initial impression* of the student and uses this to build a detailed student model based on default assumptions. This paper explores stereotypes because they constitute a powerful mechanism for building student models and because this form of inference seems to be particularly important for student and user modelling.

We see some rudimentary forms of stereotypic reasoning within a large range of customisable software. For example, many systems offer help which can be customised at one of two levels: beginner or advanced. This usually operates very simply as follows. Users are assumed to be at the beginner level unless they alter the profile settings for help. This means that the default is to assume the user is a beginner.

The form of help offered to a beginner is based on a raft of assumptions about the knowledge and needs of the typical beginner. Similarly, the advanced help is based upon assumptions about typical advanced users. Most systems do not explicitly represent these assumptions. Typically, they reside in the head of the author of the help.

This paper explores the role of stereotypic student models that are *explicit* and *available* to the student.

2 Stereotypes

The use of stereotypes in user modelling began with GRUNDY [26] [27] [28]. Rich defined stereotypes thus:

> A stereotype represents a collection of attributes that often co-occur in people. ... they enable the system to make a large number of plausible inferences on the basis of a substantially smaller number of observations. These inferences must, however, be treated as defaults, which can be overridden by specific observations. [28]:35.

In GRUNDY, the user would give several words of self-description. For example, a user might say they are *athletic*. GRUNDY used this as a *trigger* for a large number of stereotypic inferences about the user. In the case of the athletic person, GRUNDY might infer they were likely to be motivated by excitement, have personal attributes like strength and perseverance, and are interested in sports. Each of these inferences had a rating indicating its strength. From this collection of inferences about the user, GRUNDY recommended books that matched these motivations and attributes. After making recommendations and allowing the user to respond to them, GRUNDY refined the student model by adjusting the rating on each component of the model.

Stereotypes have been explicitly employed in several teaching systems, for example [1] [2] [11] [23]. And the double stereotype was critical to KNOME's construction of user models for the Unix consultant [7] [8]. KNOME reasoned from the user's actions to a classification of their expertise. So, for example, if the user appeared to make competent uses of sophisticated aspects, they were assumed to be expert. In addition, once a user was classified as an expert, KNOME inferred they knew aspects of Unix an expert is likely to know.

Suppose a stereotype M is part of the student modelling in a system which represents a set of components $\{c_j\}$, each of which represents some aspect of the user. For example, one component might represent whether the student knows about *loops* in the programming language, Python.

The stereotype has a set of trigger conditions, $\{tM_i\}$, where each tM_i is a boolean expression based upon components of the student model. Any tM_i may be a single component c_j of the user model or a function of several components, $f(\{c_k\})$. For example, consider a stereotype intended to capture inferences about an expert C++ programmer's knowledge of concepts in Python. One trigger condition might be based on a component which models whether the student is an expert C++ programmer.

The primary action of the stereotype is:

$$if \ \exists \ i, \ tM_i = true \ \rightarrow \ active(M) \tag{1}$$

meaning that when any trigger tM_i becomes true, the stereotype M becomes active.

There is a set of retraction conditions, $\{rM_i\}$. Consider an example of a retraction condition for the C++ programmer stereotype. Suppose, for example, we determine that the student knows neither Python's *while-loop* nor the *if*. Since these constructs are essentially the same in both Python and C++, this condition (that the student does not know Python-while and does not know Python-if) is a retraction condition for the stereotype M.

A stereotype is deactivated when any of the retraction conditions, rM_i, becomes true:

$$\exists\, j,\ rM_j = true\ \rightarrow\ not\ active(M) \tag{2}$$

and finally, the effect of a stereotype activation is that a collection of stereotype inferences $\{sM_k\}$ can be made:

$$active(M),\ \rightarrow\ \{sM_k\} \tag{3}$$

Some triggers may be essential:

$$\exists\, e,\ (tM_e \in \{tM_e\})\ and\ (\ not\ tM_e \in \{rMe\}) \tag{4}$$

meaning that like any trigger, tM_e can activate a stereotype. In addition, if tM_e is known to be *false*, the stereotype is deactivated.

A natural way to think about the stereotype can be based on an agent model. Initially, each stereotype is inactive but waiting for one of its activation conditions to become true. Once it is active, it waits for one of its deactivation conditions to become true.

An important characteristic of stereotypes is that the size of the set of components involved in each trigger function is usually far smaller than that of the inference set.

Rich suggested that another characteristic of stereotypes is that they serve only as default assumptions. These apply only until other, presumably more reliable evidence becomes available. We prefer to generalise this, to allow the possibility of even less reliable sources of evidence. For example, when we ran coaching experiments [18], the student model kept track of cases where the coach had sent advice to a student. We considered this to be a *very* weak form of evidence for the student knowing aspects coached. It would have been quite reasonable to consider it as weaker evidence than a stereotypic inference.

A student modelling system might operate as follows when it needs to know the value of a particular component c_j:

- ask all active stereotypes for information about c_j;
- seek other sources of information about c_j;
- if there is more than one piece of information about c_j, resolve any conflicts about the value of c_j by making assessments of the relative reliability of the information available.

An important characteristic of stereotypic inference is that it is intended to be *statistically* valid. For a population of users who belong to a stereotype M,

$$\forall\, i,\ sM_i \in \{sM_j\},\ p(sM_i)\ >\ p_M \tag{5}$$

where p_M is some probability value that is accepted as the threshold for including an inference in the stereotype. This value p_M is an important defining characteristic of a stereotype. It establishes the standards applied by the designer of the stereotype in deciding which inferences to allow.

Of course, the statistical character of the stereotype means that p_M can give no guarantees for an individual. This means that for an individual, if the stereotype M is active, some of the inferences in $\{sM_j\}$ may well be incorrect. In fact, we would expect that, for a typically large stereotype with many inferences, some of those inferences in $\{sM_j\}$ would probably be incorrect. The whole point of stereotypic inference is that it gives a set of useful *default assumptions* which are generally useful for a population of users. A good set of stereotypes should enable a system to be more effective for *most students*, even if it may be quite ineffective for a small proportion of students.

This statistical character of stereotypes should be distinguished from many other sources of uncertainty in knowledge-based reasoning. For example, we might have an inference:

$$knows(A) \rightarrow knows(B) \qquad (6)$$

meaning that a system can infer from the fact that the student knows A to conclude that they know B. An instance of such an inference might be:

$$knows(loops) \rightarrow knows(variables) \qquad (7)$$

meaning that if a student knows the concept of *loops* in C++, we infer that they know the concept *variables* since it is a *prerequisite*. Suppose that we are uncertain whether the student knows *loops*, perhaps assigning a probability p_{loops} to the truth of the assertion that the student knows *loops*. In that case, the inference about *variables* would also have an associated probability related to p_{loops}.

We can contrast this form of uncertainty from that due to stereotypic inferences (which may also have associated probabilities with each inference). For example, one inference might be

$$active(M) \rightarrow knows(localscope) \qquad (8)$$

which may be the inference that average C++ programmers will understand the notion of *local scope*. We may have written this stereotype after studying the knowledge of many C++ programmers: we may have found that 87% of *average* C++ programmers understood *local scope*. We might then associated a probability .87 with this stereotypic inference. This means that we would expect to find 13% of people who are *average* C++ programmers and for whom this inference does not hold. The complete stereotype M will have many such inferences.

3   Stereotyped Student Models

The stereotypes described above may seem quite unlike the student modelling in most systems. Indeed, aside from the small number of systems mentioned earlier, most systems ostensibly seem to operate quite differently. This section shows the use of stereotypes in most student modelling. This will serve as a foundation for the next section's description of the important role of scrutable stereotypes.

An appealing property of the stereotype is that it should enable a system to get started quickly on its customised interaction with the student. That quick start is often based upon a brief initial interaction with the user or, less commonly, a short period observing the user. For example, a system might ask the user just a few questions. Equally, it might set the student an initial task which is used to assess their level. From this small base of information, the system infers the values of a large number of components of the student model.

Consider the case of a system which teaches Python. If it knows nothing about the student, it would logically have a default initial student model for the *typical person* and this might reasonably set all components of the student model to indicate the student knows no Python concepts. This is the implicit stereotype of the typical beginner's programming book. Equally, it is the implicit stereotype for a classic CAI system.

By contrast, an ITS adapts its teaching to the individual student. So it may begin the interaction with some attempt to construct an initial student model. For example, it might begin by asking the student to indicate their level of knowledge of various programming languages. Suppose the student assesses themself as an expert in C++ but having no knowledge of Python. This can activate a stereotype which assigns the value *known* for the components which model the student's knowledge of the many concepts which are essentially the same in C++ and Python. This represents the intuitive reasoning that a person who is expert in C++ can be expected to know its core concepts and, where these are common to Python, that person should have a conceptual level of knowledge for those concepts in Python. There may be a hundred or more such concepts. For example, these include understanding such notions as *loops, while loops, booleans to control loops* and *nested loops*. So the single question about C++ expertise can have a fanout inference of more than a hundred student model components. If a single question about C++ expertise can be used to infer so much information, a system might quickly begin its customised, highly effective teaching of Python.

A second stereotype can be triggered by the the users claim of no knowledge of Python. This could assign the value *unknown* for components representing the student's knowledge of the detailed syntax and idiom of Python.

Yet another stereotype inference could assign the value *unknown* to those Python concepts which are quite different from anything in C++. It could also set as *unknown*, those Python concepts which clash with knowledge of C++, because there are similar elements but important differences. An example of this is the *for loop* which is a looping construct in both languages but it operates differently in each. The trigger for this stereotype is the user's claimed expertise in C++ combined with their claimed ignorance of Python.

3.1 Novices, Intermediates, Experts and others

We now review some major approaches to representing student models: the overlay, differential and buggy models. We identify the stereotypic inference that occurs in all of these.

The commonest form of student model is the *overlay* which represents the learner's knowledge as a subset of the total domain knowledge modelled. This may be the expert's knowledge. Of course, the notion of an expert domain model is stereotyped: in practice, different experts disagree on some aspects of their domain of expertise.

The differential model is a form of overlay model which represent a subset of domain knowledge. This student model deals only with the aspects that the system intends the student to learn. We might call this *plausibly ideal student*: a stereotype of the sort of student knowledge and skills we might reasonably expect to be achieved after learning with the system. This differs from the overlay on an expert model because it distinguishes those aspects of the expert model the student is expected learn from others. In a sense, it represents aspects of the domain that are within the scope of the teaching system. It captures the system designer's view of knowledge that will have been acquired by the student who learns all the aspects taught by the system.

In contrast to overlay models, buggy student models represent incorrect beliefs that learners may hold. The classic systems in this group were BUGGY [4] and PROUST [20], both of which developed a body of very interesting work on learner's misconceptions and errors. This work can be seen as involving construction of a stereotype model of student errors: it represented a number of the mostly commonly observed errors. Essentially, the buggy student model captures the statistically most common misconceptions. It is not expected that any one learner would have all of them. Indeed, each may be quite uncommon: a relatively common misconception might only be held by 30% of beginners. However, the system represents them because there is an underlying assumption that the system may be better able to understand some of the learner's actions by interpreting them in light of the buggy model. Where a misconception is held by 30% of all beginners, it may be much more common among beginners who are observed to make certain classes of errors.

There is a large literature on differences between novices versus experts, such as [6]. This provides a foundation for constructing stereotypes of beginners and experts in particular domains.

3.2 Building Stereotypic Student Models

Building stereotypes involves defining: the triggers $\{tM_i\}$; the retraction conditions $\{rM_i\}$; the stereotype inferences $\{sM_i\}$; and the threshold probability, p_M, for inferences in the M population.

Hand-crafted Stereotypes. This is a very obvious approach. Nonetheless, it deserves mention because it seems to be so widespread in teaching systems.

Essentially, the designer of the system makes assumptions about the stereotype groups. For example, there may be stereotypes for the beginner and the advanced student. Although this approach may often be ad-hoc, its value and importance should not be underrated. For example, an expert teacher may have built up invaluable stereotypes of typical student knowledge at various stages of their learning. Capturing and encoding this experience in stereotypes could be an important contribution to the body of knowledge of about how to teach effectively.

Another important potential role for handcrafted stereotypes arises in local customisation of systems. for example, an experienced teacher can observe their own students. In addition, that teacher knows the context of the learning activities. So, that teacher is ideally placed to define stereotypes of the individual knowledge, learning goals and common problems for their own students. This is likely to be an important role for stereotypes as ITSs are deployed.

Empirically-based Stereotypes. These approaches do not rely on elicitation of an expert teacher's knowledge of students. Instead, we collect data about students and use this to construct stereotypes. This has considerable appeal where a student works with an online tool such as a spreadsheet. In such cases, it is straightforward to monitor their actions.

For example, we might run empirical studies where users are asked to attempt a task. We then monitor user actions as they attempt the task. If we repeat this experiment over many tasks, we can construct a stereotype which maps from sequences of user actions to the likely task the user was attempting to do. This constitutes a set of stereotypes whose triggers are user actions and each inference set infers both the tasks the user was attempting and the lack of knowledge associated with flawed approaches to tasks. This approach has been applied in Lumiere [16] which can be viewed as a teaching system which gives just-in-time advice, at the time the user needs to learn in order to achieve a task.

More broadly, there is an important role of machine learning in acquiring stereotypes [29] [33] as well as careful study of empirical data to identify stereotypes [32]. There are important potential links between this task and the construction of similar stereotypes for information retrieval and filtering. This goes under various names including community, collaborative, clique-based approaches [24].

Stereotypes Inference. Collection of information for triggering stereotypes comes from three main sources:

- directly elicit information from the student;
- observe the user interacting with the system;
- diagnostic tasks.

The first is very simple and we have already given examples of the student being asked to assess their expertise in a programming language.

The other two are closely linked to each other. For example, in the context of a system which teaches about an operating system, it might be feasible to monitor the student's use of that system. Then, as in the Unix Consultant, use of sophisticated commands might be used to infer expertise. The third method is more common in ITSs. It might ask the student to do set tasks. If the student can do difficult tasks, making effective use of sophisticated commands, this can be used to infer expertise.

4 Stereotypes and Scrutability

Scrutability of stereotypes should mean that a student can scrutinise the system to find answers to questions like the following.

- Am I a beginner?
- What are the implications of being a beginner?
- What would be different if I were an expert?
- How can I let the system model me as a beginner, but have it recognise some of the more advanced things I know?

There seems to be the potential for considerable benefit if learners can explore such issues. Some relate to the possibility of encouraging reflection. This has been described by Goodman, Soller and Linton [13]:

Reflective activities encourage students to analyse their performance, contrast their actions to those of others, abstract the actions they used in similar situations and compare their actions to those of novices and experts.

Others have discussed and explored this notion of the variously described open, accessible or transparent student models and systems. See, for example, [3] [9] [10] [11] [12] [15] [22] [25] [30]. They identify benefits of such approaches in terms of:

- potential learning benefits if access to the model can nurture reflection and metacognition;
- the enhanced learner control over the personal information typically held in a student model;
- the possibility of improving the quality of the student model as learners are able to correct errors in it.

We can expect that the particular case of stereotype-based student modelling would be likely to share these potential advantages.

5 Discussion

We now consider the special relevance of scrutability in association with stereotypes for student modelling.

5.1 Corrections to Stereotype Models

The nature of stereotypes makes them especially important as targets for user access and correction. This is because stereotypes are constructed in terms of their accuracy and utility for a population of users. Equally, there is a corresponding expectation that some inferences sM_k will be incorrect for some users. There are two levels of control associated with stereotypes.

- The whole stereotype: The student can decide that an active stereotype should be deactivated, or vice-versa. So, for example, the student can decide to deactivate the beginner stereotype and possibly choose to activate some other.
- Individual inference level: The student can alter the value any single inference sM_k. For example, the student may be content to have the beginner stereotype active. They might check several of beginner inferences and be happy with these. However, they may see that it makes some incorrect inferences. The student should be able to correct these in their own model.

The first of these could be achieved if we extend the notion of stereotypes as follows: every stereotype has a built-in retraction condition which can be set by the student.

The second can be achieved by regarding the student input as a more reliable source of student modelling information. Then, the set of information about a component c_j could potentially include the inference from the stereotype and the information volunteered by the student. So long as the student modelling system treats the latter as more reliable, we have a simple mechanism for retaining the active stereotype but allowing the student to fine-tune the details.

5.2 Stereotypes, Teaching and Learning Agendas

Typically, a student model represents just those aspects the system needs. Some parts of the student model drive the adaptation of the teaching. Some may assist the system in its interpretation of the student's actions. Yet others represents the core learning goals for the system. We now focus on these.

The student model will typically track the learner's progress: hopefully, the student model will reflect the student's ongoing progress as they learn each of these. Stereotypes can be useful for initialising these aspects of the student model. For example, a few carefully chosen questions or diagnostic tasks might be used to classify the student as intermediate-level and then to infer the initial model, with some of the teaching goals set as *known*. This initialises the system's *teaching* agenda.

Another important potential role for stereotypes relates to the student's own *learning* agenda. In theory this could be modelled separately from the *teaching* goals. This would mean representing both the student's knowledge and whether they *want* to learn each aspect. The default stereotype assumption might set all unlearnt *teaching* goals as *learning* goals. Scrutability of and control over this stereotype would enable the student to tune the *learning* goals.

One important sources of problems for learners can occur when there is a mismatch between the teacher's goals and the learner's appreciation of the overall and, particularly, the current goals [10]. Scrutability of the student model offers the potential to reduce the effect of such problems. As Self notes, [31] student models capture a precise definition of essential state in a teaching system. This is a foundation for individualisation and for shared *understanding* between the learner and the system, with the learner being able to better understand what drives the system.

5.3   Buggy Stereotype as Learning Objects

If a student modelling system makes use of buggy stereotypes, these encode a potentially useful set of information for learners and teachers. Consider the following scenario. A student is classified as a beginner in the domain of Python programming. Suppose they are trying to write a first Python program and they have problems. A clever ITS might diagnose the difficulty. Equally, if there is a good presentation of stereotypic errors by beginners in this task, the student might read this and work out what their problem is. Yet another possibility is that a human teacher might be better able to help the student, aided by this list of stereotypic errors. Just this use was intended for the IDEBUGGY extension of work on BUGGY.

5.4   Individual or Stereotype – Is There a Conflict?

At first glance, one might think that individual and stereotypic student modelling are at odds. In practice, stereotypes can support highly individual student models in two ways. First, a rich collection of stereotypes can ensure that each student will have many active stereotypes at once. The possibility of many combinations of stereotypes leads to a correspondingly large collection of different models, all based purely on stereotypes. Beyond this, if the stereotypes are used as initial default inferences which are refined over time, we can expect each student's model to become more individualised as more data becomes available to refine it.

6   Conclusion

We have defined a stereotype M as:

- triggers, $\{tM_i\}$, which activate a stereotype
- retraction conditions, $\{rM_i\}$, some of which may correspond to the negation of essential triggers, and learner control requires a built-in retraction condition which can be set by the student
- stereotypic inferences, $\{sM_i\}$
- threshold probability for inferences, p_M, which captures the minimum probability of each inference for a population of users matching this stereotype.

The action of a stereotype is to make large numbers of inferences when a trigger becomes *true*. Many student models can be regarded as using stereotypic inferences, although they are often implicitly coded.

Scrutability of student models seems to offer potential benefits in terms of improvements in learning and in the accuracy of the student model. Where student models are based on stereotypic inference, there are even stronger arguments for scrutability since the inferences are only valid in a statistical sense. The elements listed above indicate the aspects which the student might scrutinise to understand the stereotypic reasoning applied in their own student model.

References

1. Boyle, C.: User modeling in the interactive anatomy tutoring system ANATOM-TUTOR. User Modeling and User-Adapted Interaction. 4:1 (1994) 21–45
2. Boyle, C., Encarnacion, A.O.: Metadoc: An adaptive hypertext reading system. User Modeling and User-Adapted Interaction. 4:1 (1994) 1–19
3. Bull, S., Brna, P., Pain, H.: Extending the scope of the student model. User Modeling and User-Adapted Interaction. 5:1 (1995) 44–65
4. Burton, R.R.: Diagnosing bugs in a simple procedural skill. In: Sleeman, D., Brown, J.S. Intelligent Tutoring Systems. Academic Press, London (1982) 157–184
5. Chan, T.W.: Learning companion systems, social learning systems, and the global social learning club. International Journal of Artificial Intelligence in Education. 7 (1996) 125–159
6. Chi, M.T.H., Feltovich, P., Glaser, R.: Categorization and Representation of Physics Problems by Experts and Novices. Cognitive Science. 5:2 (1981) *** pages
7. Chin, D.N.: User Modelling in UC, the UNIX Consultant Proceedings of the ACM SIGCHI Conference on Human Factors in Computing Systems. In: Mantei, M. (ed.): ACM Press (1986) 24–28
8. Chin, D.N.: KNOME: modeling what the user knows in UC. In: Kobsa, A., Wahlster, W. (eds.): User models in dialog systems. (1989) 74–107.
9. Corbett, A.T., Anderson, J.: Knowledge tracing: modeling the acquisition of procedural knowledge. User Modeling and User-Adapted Interaction. 4 (1995) 253–278
10. Crawford, K., Kay, J.: Metacognitive processes and learning with intelligent educational systems. In: Slezak, P., Caelli, T., Clark, R., Perspectives on Cognitive Science, Ablex (1993) 63-77
11. Dimitrova M., Self J.: The interactive maintenance of open learner models. In: Lajoie, S., Vivet, M. (eds.): Artificial Intelligence in Education. (1999) 405–412
12. Fischer, G., Ackerman, D.: The importance of models in making complex systems comprehensible. In: Tauber, M. (ed.): Mental models and Human-computer Interaction 2. Elsevier (1991) 22–33
13. Goodman, B., Soller, A., Linton, F., Gaimari, R.: Encouraging student reflection and articulation using a learning companion. International Journal of Artificial Intelligence in Education. 9 (1998) 237–255
14. Hietala, P., Niemirepo, T.: The Competence of Learning Companion Agents. International Journal of Artificial Intelligence in Education. 9 (1998) 178–192.
15. Höök, K., Karlgren, J., Waern, A., Dahlbeck, N., Jansson, C.G., Lemaire, B.: A glass box approach to adaptive hypermedia. User Modeling and User-Adapted Interaction 6:2-3 Kluwer (1996) 157–184

16. Horvitz, E., Breese, J., Heckerman, D., Hovel, D., Rommelse, K.,: The Lumiere Project: Bayesian User Modeling for Inferring the Goals and Needs of Software Users. Proceedings of the Fourteenth Conference on Uncertainty in Artificial Intelligence. Morgan Kaufmann, San Francisco (1998) 256–265

17. Huang, X., McCalla, G., Greer, J., Neufeld, E.: Revising deductive knowledge and stereotypical knowledge in a student model. User Modeling and User-Adapted Interaction. Kluwer, **1**:1 (1991) 87–116

18. Kay, J., Thomas, R.C.: Studying long term system use. Communications of the ACM. **38**:2 (1995) 131–154

19. Kay, J.: The um toolkit for cooperative user modelling. User Modeling and User-Adapted Interaction. 4:3 Kluwer (1995) 149–196

20. Johnson, W.L.: Understanding and debugging novice programs. Artificial Intelligence. **42**:1 (1990) 51–97

21. Kono, Y. Ikeda, M. Mizoguchi, R.: To contradict is human: student modelling of inconsistency. In: Frasson, C., Gauthier, G., McCalla, G. (eds.): Intelligent tutoring systems. Springer-Verlag (1992) 451–458

22. Morales, R.: Proceedings of the Workshop on Open, Interactive, and other Overt Approaches to Learner Modelling. 9th International Conference on Artificial Intelligence in Education. (1999)

23. Murphy, M., McTear, M.: Learner modelling for intelligent CALL. In: A. Jameson, A., Paris, C., Tasso, C. (Eds.), User modeling: Proceedings of the Sixth International Conference, UM97. Springer Wien Vienna, New York (1997) 301–312

24. Oard, D.W.: The state of the art in text filtering. User Modeling and User-Adapted Interaction. **7**:3 (1997) 141–178

25. Paiva, A., Self, J., Hartley, R.: Externalising learner models. Proceedings of World Conference on Artificial Intelligence in Education. AACE, Washington (1995) 509–516

26. Rich, E.: User modeling via stereotypes. Cognitive Science. **3** (1979) 355–66

27. Rich, E.: Users are individuals: individualizing user models. International Journal of Man-Machine Studies. **18** (1983) 199–214

28. Rich, E.: Stereotypes and user modeling. In: Kobsa, A., Wahlster, W.: User models in dialog systems. Springer-Verlag, Berlin (1989) 35–51

29. Self, J.: In: Lawler, R.W., Yazdani, M.: Artificial Intelligence and Education. **1** (1987) 267–280

30. Self, J.: Bypassing the Intractable Problem of Student Modelling: Invited paper. Proceedings of the 1st International Conference on Intelligent Tutoring Systems. Montreal (1988) 18–24

31. Self, J.: The defining characteristics of intelligent tutoring systems research: ITSs care, precisely. International Journal of Artificial Intelligence in Education. (2000) to appear.

32. Winter, M., McCalla, G.: The emergence of student models from an analysis of ethical decision making in scenario-based learning environment. In: Kay, J. (ed.): User Modeling: Proceedings of the Seventh International Conference, UM99. Springer Wien, New York (1999) 265–274

33. Woolf, B., Murray, T.: A framework for representing tutorial discourse. Proceedings of the International Joint Conference on Artificial Intelligence. (1987)

Life and Learning in the Electronic Village: The Importance of Localization for the Design of Environments to Support Learning[1]

Gordon McCalla

ARIES Laboratory, Department of Computer Science, University of Saskatchewan
Saskatoon, Saskatchewan S7N 5A9, CANADA
mccalla@cs.usask.ca

Extended Abstract

It has been claimed that the world is moving inexorably towards a single global village, spurred by the dominance of television on our lives. Surely it is obvious that globalization can only be accelerated by the rapid spread of information and communications technology (ICT). After all, are we not all neighbours on the internet? Au contraire! It is my thesis that far from being a further stimulus for globalization, ICT will inevitably be mainly a force for *localization*. The very fact that everybody is a neighbour to everybody else on the internet will mandate that each person must restrict their interactions with *almost* everybody (or be overwhelmed). The very fact that an immense amount of information is readily accessible will mean that each person must be very selective in the information they actually access (or be inundated). The consequence will be that each of us will shield ourselves with largely impenetrable barriers to outside interaction, allowing access only to those people and that information that we choose, that synchronizes with our world view. In short there will be no universal global village. Instead, we will each live in our own personal *electronic villages*, each village different from every other village.

How will people learn in such a village? Ensconced as they are in their own local perspectives, people will be unaware of much that is relevant and useful to them. Each person will, however, maintain contact with other people, who in turn will maintain contact with still other people. These contact networks will form *virtual communities* [1], both explicit and implicit. Knowledge will impact a person only when it becomes known within a community in which they participate. While technology will facilitate the spread of this knowledge, fundamentally people will truly learn this knowledge mainly through interaction with other people within a community, who can help ground the knowledge in the context of their shared interests. Thus, the flow of knowledge through society will be relatively slow, moving from community to community, and spreading gradually within communities, as people learn from one another, helped by appropriate technology.

[1] This talk draws on ideas from many research projects carried out in the ARIES Laboratory over the years. I would like to thank my many graduate students and colleagues for their insights and the Canadian TeleLearning Networks of Centres of Excellence and the Natural Sciences and Engineering Research Council of Canada for their funding.

Understanding the interlocking localized notions of personal electronic village and virtual community will be crucial in building environments for learning that are consistent with learning and teaching in cyberspace. In this talk I will look at some of the implications of such localization for learning technology research. I will draw on ideas from my issues paper, appearing in the IJAIEd special issue on "AIEd in 2010" [2], as well as concepts explored in other research projects in the AIEd field, including our own recent work exploring an agent-based peer help environment [3].

References

1. Rheingold, H. (1998). *The Virtual Community: Homesteading on the Electronic Frontier.* accessible at http://www.rheingold.com/vc/book/.
2. McCalla, G. (2000). The Fragmentation of Culture, Learning, Teaching, and Technology: Implications for the Artificial Intelligence in Education Research Agenda in 2010, Int. J. of Artificial Intelligence in Education, 11.
3. Vassileva, J., J. Greer, G. McCalla, R. Deters, D. Zapata, C. Mudgal, S. Grant (1999). A Multi-Agent Approach to the Design of Peer-Help Environments, in S. Lajoie and M. Vivet (eds.), Artificial Intelligence in Education, IOS Press, Amsterdam, 38-45.

Tutoring Diagnostic Problem Solving

Rajaram Ganeshan[1], W. Lewis Johnson[1], Erin Shaw[1] and Beverly P. Wood[2]

[1]Center for Advanced Research in Technology for Education
Information Sciences Institute, University of Southern California
4676 Admiralty Way, Marina del Rey, CA 90292-6695 USA
{rajaram, johnson, shaw}@isi.edu,
http://www.isi.edu/isd/carte/
[2]Professor of Radiology, Pediatrics, Medical Education
Division of Medical Education
Keck School of Medicine, University of Southern California
KAM 211, 1975 Zonal Ave., Los Angeles CA 90089-9024
bwood@hsc.usc.edu

Keywords: agent-based tutoring systems, intelligent agents, learning environments, student modelling, teaching and learning strategies.

Abstract. This paper presents an approach to intelligent tutoring for diagnostic problem solving that uses knowledge about causal relationships between symptoms and disease states to conduct a pedagogically useful dialogue with the student. An animated pedagogical agent, Adele, uses the causal knowledge, represented as a Bayesian network, to dynamically generate a diagnostic process that is consistent with the *best practice* approach to medical diagnosis. Using a combination of hints and other interactions based on multiple choice questions, Adele guides the student through a reasoning process that exposes her to the underlying knowledge, i.e., the patho-physiological processes, while being sensitive to the problem solving state and the student's current level of knowledge. Although the main focus of this paper is on tutoring medical diagnosis, the methods described here are applicable to tutoring diagnostic skills in any domain with uncertain knowledge.

1 Introduction

The motivation for the work described in this paper comes from Adele, an animated pedagogical agent [10] designed to be used for medical education [19]. Adele is being applied to a number of health science curricula, of which undergraduate case-based clinical instruction is a major focus. In a case-based diagnostic exercise, students are presented with a simulated clinical problem. Students are able to examine the simulated patient, ask questions about medical history, perform a physical examination, order and interpret diagnostic tests, and make diagnoses. Adele monitors the student's actions and provides feedback accordingly. Students can ask Adele for a hint or action rationale via a graphical user interface.

Adele's primary emphasis is on the procedural representation of the *best practice* approach to diagnosis and management. Information about the causal relationships between the clinical findings (e.g., an x-ray shows specific lesions) and the hypotheses (i.e., the final and differential diagnoses) is incorporated into the explicitly-authored textual hints and rationales associated with steps in the procedural representation. The rigid distinction between rationales and hints can lead Adele to tell the student *what to do* instead of guiding them through the problem solving process. Evaluations by students have shown this to be the case [19]. Adele cannot effectively guide the student in reasoning about hypotheses because the relationships between hypotheses and findings are not maintained explicitly in her knowledge representation.

This paper presents a different approach to intelligent tutoring for diagnostic problem solving that addresses the problems outlined in the earlier paragraph. In this approach, information about the causal relationships between the clinical findings and the hypotheses is explicitly represented using a Bayesian network. Adele uses the representation to dynamically generate a diagnostic process that is consistent with the *best practice* approach to medical diagnosis. The paper is organized into two main sections. The first section describes the representation of domain knowledge and the student model necessary for tutoring. The second section describes how Adele uses the representation to conduct a dialogue with the student, thus maximizing learning.

2 Representation of Domain Knowledge

2.1 Issues and Related Work

The representation of domain knowledge must support a plausible or correct diagnosis and be teachable. In any diagnostic reasoning process, the main challenges are how to generate and rank the hypotheses based on the evidence and how to select the next best (optimal) evidence-gathering step. The SOPHIE systems [1] for teaching trouble-shooting electronic circuits were the earliest diagnostic intelligent tutoring systems (ITS). SOPHIE III used mathematical constraint based models to represent the behavior of circuit components to do model-based diagnosis [8]. Models are difficult to develop for medical domains because physiological structure and behavior are poorly understood. Medical diagnostic programs operate on heuristic causal relationships between findings (evidence) and abnormal disease states (hypotheses). The causal relationships are captured by rules with certainty factors as in Mycin [20] and Neomycin[3], or causal models[11], or probabilistic causal models [5, 9,16]. A type of probabilistic causal model, the Bayes network, has been used to build commercially viable diagnostic systems in medical domains [9,16]. Our work uses a Bayes network to capture the causal relationships between findings and hypotheses.

Ideally, the selection of the next best evidence-gathering step should ensure that the "value of information" exceeds the cost of gathering evidence [9]. In practice, performing this computation for all possible sequences of observations can be very expensive and hence simplifying assumptions are often made. While such approaches work well for an automated diagnosis program, they are difficult to explain. Clancey

[2] has done extensive protocol analysis of medical experts which indicate that physicians follow an intuitive approach while exploring hypotheses that does not consider costs.

2.2 Representing Relations Between Findings and Hypotheses

Our work uses a Bayesian network representation for the causal relationships between hypotheses and findings. Figure 1 shows a portion of the belief network model for the clinical case (called the "Cough Case") we have developed. Each node in the network

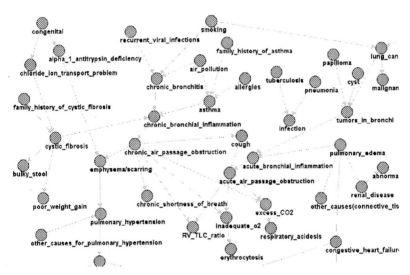

Fig. 1. A portion of a Bayes net for the Cough case

is a random variable that represents some hypothesis (final or intermediate disease state) or possible finding. Each node can take on one or more values. For example, the possible values for the "cough" node are: true or false indicating the presence or absence of cough. A finding can be determined by executing the procedural step associated with it (e.g., ask a patient a question). Steps have costs associated with them which may be monetary, or it may refer to an intangible cost such as time and discomfort to the patient. Causal links connect nodes. A conditional probability table (CPT) associated with the node specifies probability of values for the random variable based on the values of each of its parents. Acquiring these probabilities can be a challenging problem for large networks. However, depending on the particular learning objectives of a case, only a portion of the network might be relevant. Irrelevant portions can be avoided by using an "other miscellaneous causes" node [18] (see Fig. 1). We are losing some diagnostic accuracy but it may be acceptable for pedagogical purposes, since we have the freedom to author the case in such a way that the other causes will be improbable.

2.3   Selecting the Next Evidence-Gathering Step

The Bayes network is used to compute the posterior probability distribution for a set of query variables, given the values of evidence variables.   In our case, the query variables are the possible final diagnoses. Whenever new evidence is obtained, the probabilities of the query variables in the network are updated.   The current implementation uses the JavaBayes engine [4] to perform these updates. Any routine step not already performed that "addresses" a "likely" hypothesis is a valid next step. A hypothesis is "likely" if its current probability >= 0.5.   A step "addresses" a hypothesis when there is a directed causal path between the hypothesis and any finding resulting from the step and at least one of the nodes on this path can affect the probability of the hypothesis given the current evidence.   The set of nodes affecting a query can be determined using algorithms to identify independencies in such networks [6].   Non-routine or expensive steps must meet a higher probability threshold for the hypothesis they address before they can be recommended as a valid next step.   For example, a sweat test provides evidence for or against cystic fibrosis but should be considered only if there is already some evidence for cystic fibrosis (e.g., current probability > 0.6). It is possible that there are no steps available that address likely hypotheses.   In this case, steps addressing unlikely hypotheses will be considered.   In suggesting steps to the student, Adele will suggest lower cost steps before more expensive ones from the set of next valid steps.   Unlike decision-theoretic methods, the approach described here does not guarantee an efficient diagnostic process. However as explained earlier, decision-theoretic methods can be computationally expensive and difficult to explain.

2.4   Modeling the Student's Knowledge

Ideally, the student model should capture all of the knowledge the student is expected to bring to bear on the diagnostic process including the steps (e.g. sweat test) and their associated properties (e.g., cost), the findings associated with the steps (e.g., positive sweat test),   the hypotheses (e.g., cystic fibrosis),   the hierarchical relationships between hypotheses (disease hierarchy), the *causal relationships* between the findings and hypotheses, and the *strengths* associated with these relationships (e.g., a negative sweat test is strong evidence against cystic fibrosis).   However, the current implementation focuses mainly on the causal relationships because the instructional objectives are concerned mainly with the causal mechanisms.   A student's knowledge of each relationship is updated during the tutoring process when the tutor tells the student about it (e.g., as part of a hint) or when the student confirms her knowledge of the relationship by taking a correct action or correctly responding to the tutor's questions. Note that we use the Bayesian network only to represent the domain knowledge and do not use the Bayesian network for modelling the student as in Gertner et al. [7].

3 The Student-Tutor Dialogue

A tutor can convey knowledge to students via an effectively structured dialogue [14, 12, 15, 21]. When the student makes mistakes the tutor can ask questions that will reveal a student's underlying misconceptions, allowing the student to discover her own mistake [15]. Such an approach promotes learning by inducing "cognitive conflict" in the learner [13]. To conduct a coherent dialogue, the tutor needs to maintain a dialogue state, mainly the focus of attention and history of utterances made so far [17]. Clancey [2] notes that people focus on a hypothesis, which guides their actions in the diagnostic process. In this work, the focus of attention is a node in the belief network, which could be a finding or hypothesis. The diagnosis process will be initialized with some initial set of findings - the patient's presenting complaint. Adele's focus is initialized to the most promising finding, i.e., the one that provides the strongest evidence for a hypothesis, and this focus is presented to the student as part of the introduction to the case. The focus of attention is updated as the student and tutor perform actions or make utterances as described in the following sections. This section describes how we have extended Adele's tutoring dialogue by exploiting the causal representation of the Bayesian network to support a detailed probing of a student's actions within the limitations of the interface.

3.1 Hint

Given the current evidence, Adele can determine valid next evidence-gathering steps using the procedures described in the earlier section. When the student asks for a hint, instead of providing the answer directly, Adele can use the opportunity to guide the student through a reasoning process that exposes the student to the underlying physiological processes. For example, at the start of the session the primary finding and current focus is cough. To generate a hint, the agent identifies a path from the current focus to a valid next step (shown by the enclosed box in Fig. 2). Successive hints are generated by traversing this causal path. For example,

> **Student:** *Hint.*
> **Adele***: Chronic air passage obstruction can cause cough.*
> **Student:** *Hint.*
> **Adele:** *Chronic bronchial inflammation can cause chronic air passage obstruction.*

The dialogue state and the student model are both updated after the hint is provided. Hints are generated with respect to what the student knows. For example, if the student model indicates that the student knows that chronic air passage obstruction can cause cough, then the first hint would not be given.

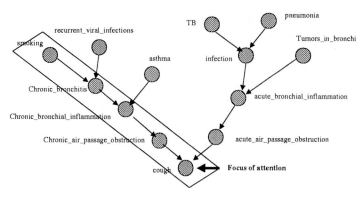

Fig. 2. Hint generation based on focus of attention

3.2 Correct Action

When a student takes a correct action, that is, one that the agent considers a valid next step, the agent can initiate a dialogue to verify the student's reasoning. This dialogue is initiated only if one or more of the relationships involved are "instructionally significant"[1] and if the student has not already been told about the causal relationships involved. For example, assume that the current focus is "chronic air passage obstruction" and the student now takes correct action and asks if the patient smokes. Adele can ask the student about the causal mechanism that leads from smoking to chronic air passage obstruction.

> **Adele:** *Yes. Can you identify the mechanism by which smoking leads to air passage obstruction? Select one from list.*

The possible options (e.g., bronchial inflammation, tumors, infection) are provided to the user in a multiple-choice list dialog box. Adele uses gaze and pointing gestures coordinated with speech to direct the student's attention to objects on the screen such as dialog boxes [19]. If the student correctly identifies the mechanism then the agent utters praise and updates the student model. Otherwise, the agent will point out that the student is wrong and explain the correct mechanism to the student. If the reasoning chain is very long and at least one other link is marked instructionally significant, then this dialogue may be repeated in a recursive fashion.

A correct action can generate evidence that significantly alters the probability of some hypotheses. The probabilistic reasoning process that leads to the change in the probability of a hypothesis in the Bayes net can be quite complicated. Instead of trying to generate an explanation for this reasoning process, we provide a summary that relies on the probability of seeing the evidence assuming that the hypothesis is true. It would be pedagogically beneficial for the agent to intervene and bring this to

---

[1] Certain causal links in the Bayesian network are more pertinent to the instructional objectives of the current case. Links relating to these objectives are marked by the author as being "instructionally significant."

the attention of the student when the student model indicates that the student does not know the relationship between the evidence and hypothesis. For example:

> **Adele:** *Note that the patient experiences significant shortness of breath. This provides strong evidence for chronic bronchitis or asthma.*

If the new evidence causes the probability of the hypothesis in focus to become unlikely, Adele needs to guide the student by shifting the focus to a different node in the network.

> **Adele:** *Notice that a negative sweat test provides strong evidence against cystic fibrosis. Cystic fibrosis is unlikely. You could consider other possibilities. Cough can also be caused by <new focus>.*

A correct action could also cause a shift in the focus because we have exhausted all low cost steps related to the current focus. We need to shift the focus to another branch to pursue other low cost steps. For example, if we finish asking all possible questions leading from "chronic_bronchial_inflammation," we need to shift the focus to "acute_bronchial_inflammation." The assumption here is that the student should be encouraged to ask all relevant questions before proceeding with more expensive steps.

3.3 Incorrect Action

There are three ways in which an action can be incorrect: (1) it can be *irrelevant* to the current case; that is, the action contributes no useful evidence for the current case; (2) it can be a *high cost* step whose probability thresholds are not met; that is, the probability of the hypothesis given the current state of evidence does not support the expensive action -- there are cheaper actions that could have been taken to gather more evidence; or, (3) it can be a *low probability* error; that is, the action provides evidence only for an unlikely hypothesis (probability < 0.5) when there exist more promising hypotheses.

If an action is irrelevant, there is not much the agent can do since it has no way of relating the action to the network. If an action has a high cost or a low probability, it can be related to the network, and there are two possible responses depending on whether or not the action can be related to the current focus.

The "RV_TLC_Ratio", or "lung performance" test in Fig. 3 (bottom node) is an action with a high associated cost. Given the current focus, there are two appropriate next steps that a student might take: she might ask the patient if he smokes, or she might order a lung performance test. Suppose the student orders the lung performance test. Since ordering a test is more expensive than asking a question, the agent points out that there are cheaper actions that will provide evidence for the

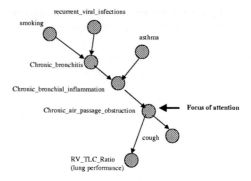

Fig. 3. Incorrect action causally related to focus.

current focus. Our medical collaborators feel that the agent should not intervene too frequently to point out mistakes, so the student is allowed to make a few errors before Adele intervenes. The mistakes are recorded and can be reviewed with the student later.

To illustrate an example of the second case (Figure 4), suppose the student orders a "bronchoscopy."

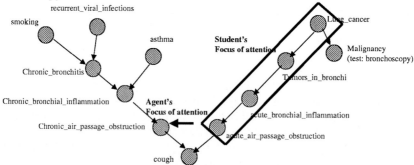

Fig. 4. The student's focus of attention is different from the agent's.

In general, there are two possibilities: (1) the student is under the misconception that the action is somehow related to the current focus (i.e., a bronchoscopy provides evidence for chronic_air_passage_obstruction); or (2) the student has a different focus in mind than the agent – ignoring the agent's hints. The two cases can be distinguished by explicitly asking the student to identify what hypothesis is being pursued. For example:

Adele: I was not expecting you to do this. What hypothesis are you gathering evidence for?

If the student selects the wrong hypothesis to justify the action, the agent will clarify the student's misconception that the action is related to the hypothesis in focus (i.e., that a bronchoscopy does not provide evidence for chronic air passage obstruction)[2]. If the student's focus of attention has shifted to some node along the branch enclosed by the rectangular box then either the hypothesis the student is focussing on is of low probability, or the cost of the action is high. The latter case has already been discussed. If the differing hypothesis is of low probability, the agent will initiate a dialogue to correct the student's misconception about the likelihood of the hypothesis given the current evidence. The agent can ascertain if the student has incorrectly deduced the probability of the hypothesis by asking the student to rank the hypothesis in question with respect to other hypotheses. Once the agent has established the student's misconception about the hypothesis ranking, she can attempt to correct it by asking the student to justify her rationale for the ranking, i.e., identify findings that the student thinks support her misconception. Based on the student's response, the misconception is corrected.

4 Conclusion

By using a Bayesian network to explicitly represent and reason about the causal relationships between findings and hypotheses, Adele can be more effective in tutoring diagnostic problem solving while keeping consistent with a best practice approach. Using a combination of hints and other interactions based on multiple choice questions, Adele guides the student through a reasoning process that exposes her to the underlying knowledge, i.e., the patho-physiological processes, while being sensitive to the problem solving state and the student's current state of knowledge. Effective rationales are generated automatically, although extensions to Adele's language generation capability will be required to make them sound more natural. We have built a complete case focusing on pulmonary diseases in patients who present with a cough as their chief complaint and have conducted informal evaluations of this case with faculty from the medical school at USC. We are planning a more detailed evaluation with students and hope to report on the results of these evaluations at the conference. Although the main focus of this paper is on tutoring medical diagnosis, the methods described here are applicable to tutoring diagnosis in any domain with uncertain knowledge.

Acknowledgements

We would like to thank Jeff Rickel for his insightful comments. Kate LaBore, Andrew Marshal, Ami Adler, Anna Romero, and Chon Yi have all contributed to the development of Adele. This work was supported by an internal research and development grant from the USC Information Sciences Institute.

---

[2] Even if a hypothesis is causally related to a finding, it may not provide any useful evidence if the corresponding variables in the Bayes net are conditionally independent given the current evidence [6].

References

1. Brown, J.S., Burton, R.R., and DeKleer, J.: Pedagogical, natural language and knowledge engineering techniques in SOPHIE I, II and III, in Intelligent Tutoring Systems edited by D. Sleeman and J.S. Brown, Academic Press 1982.
2. Clancey, W. J.: Acquiring, Representing and Evaluating a Competence Model of Diagnostic Strategy, STAN-CS-85-1067, August 1985, Stanford University.
3. Clancey, W. J. & R. Letsinger.: NEOMYCIN: Reconfiguring a Rule-Based Expert System for Application to Teaching, In W.J. Clancey & E. H. Shortliffe (Eds.), Readings in Medical Artificial Intelligence: The First Decade. Reading, MA, Addison-Wesley 1984.
4. Cozman, F.: JavaBayes. http://www.cs.cmu.edu/~javabayes/
5. Gorry, G. and Barnett G.: Experience with a sequential model of diagnosis, *Computers and Biomedical Research*, 1:490-507 1968.
6. Geiger, D., Verma, T., and Pearl, J.: Identifying Independence in Bayesian Networks, Networks, Vol. 20 507-534, 1990.
7. Gertner, A.S., Conati, C. and VanLehn, K.: Procedural Help in Andes: Generating hints using a Bayesian network student model, AAAI 1998.
8. Hamscher, W. C., Console, L., and DeKleer, J.: Readings in Model-based Diagnosis, Morgan Kaufman Publishers, 1992.
9. Heckerman, D., Horvitz, E. and Nathwani, B.: Towards Normative Expert Systems: The Pathfinder Project, KSL-91-44, Department of Computer Science, Stanford University, 1991.
10. Johnson, W.L., Rickel, J., and Lester, J.: Animated Pedagogical Agents: Face-to-Face Interaction in Interactive Learning Environments, International Journal of Artificial Intelligence in Education, (2000), 11, to appear.
11. Patil, R.: Causal Understanding of Patient Illness in Medical Diagnosis, IJCAI, 1981.
12. Pearce, C.: The Mulligan Report, Internal Document, USC/ISI, 1999.
13. Piaget, J.: The Equilibrium of Cognitive Structures: The Central Problem in Cognitive Development. Chicago, Illinois: University of Chicago Press, 1985.
14. Pilkington,R.: Analysing Educational Dialogue Interaction: Towards Models that Support Learning, Proceedings of Workshop at AI-Ed '99 9th International Conference on Artificial Intelligence in Education, Le Mans, France 18th-19th July, 1999.
15. Pomsta-Porayska, K, Pain, H. & Mellish, C.: Why do teachers ask questions? A preliminary investigation, in Proceedings of Workshop at AI-Ed '99 9th International Conference on Artificial Intelligence in Education, Le Mans, France 18th-19th July, 1999.
16. Pradhan, M. Provan, G. M., Middleton, B., and Henrion, M.: Knowledge engineering for large belief networks, Proceedings of Uncertainity in AI, Seattle, WA. Morgan Kaufman, 1994.
17. Rickel, J. and Johnson, W.L.: Animated agents for procedural training in virtual reality: perception, cognition, and motor control, *Applied Artificial Intelligence Journal*, Vol. 13, 343-382, 1999.
18. Russell, S., and Norvig, P. : Artificial Intelligence: A Modern Approach. Prentice Hall, Englewood Cliffs, 1995.
19. Shaw, E., Ganeshan, R., Johnson, W. L., and Millar, D.: Building a Case for Agent-Assisted Learning as a Catalyst for Curriculum Reform in Medical Education, Proceedings of AIED '99, Le Mans, France 18th-19th July, 1999.
20. Shortliffe, E. H.: MYCIN: A Rule-Based Computer Program for Advising Physicians Regarding Antimicrobial Therapy Selection. Ph.D Diss., Stanford University, 1976.
21. Stevens, A., Collins, A. and Goldin, S. E.: Misconceptions in students understanding, in Intelligent Tutoring Systems, Sleeman & Brown, 1982.

LAHYSTOTRAIN: Integration of Virtual Environments and ITS for Surgery Training

José Luis Los Arcos[1], Wolfgang Muller[2], Oscar Fuente[1], Leire Orúe[1], Eder Arroyo[1], Igor Leaznibarrutia[1], Judit Santander[1]

[1] LABEIN. Technological Research Centre. Parque Tecnológico. Ed. 101
48170 Zamudio, Spain
{josel,oscarf,leire,arroyo,igor,jsantander}@labein.es
[2]Fraunhofer-Institut für Graphische Datenverarbeitung. Rundeturmstraße 6
D-64283 Darmstadt, Germany
muellerw@igd.fhg.de

Abstract. Minimally invasive surgery has revolutionised the surgeon's approach by using optical systems to inspect cavities of the human body and by using small instruments to perform surgical procedures. This paper presents the LAHYSTOTRAIN[1] demonstrator a training system for laparoscopy and hysteroscopy, two types of minimally invasive surgery techniques, combining a Virtual Reality Simulator (VRS), which contains virtual anatomical structures and simulates endoscope surgical instruments, a Basic Training System (BTS), that provides web based theoretical training, and an agent-based tutoring system, the Advanced Training System (ATS), oriented to supervise the execution of the practical exercises providing proactive and reactive explanations and emulating the behaviour of some persons involved in the operating theatre like the nurse, assistant surgeon and anaesthetist.

1   Problem Description

The current world-wide used surgical education process on laparoscopy and hysteroscopy generally includes hands-on clinical experience and training on anaesthetised animals, cadavers or plastic models. The traditional model for learning procedural skills follows the rule "see one, do one, teach one". Because of learning by doing operations need a lot of more time, at least 20-25%, this means for the patient a longer time in anaesthesia and so the burden of the patient will be much higher to get

---

[1] LAHYSTOTRAIN (Integration of Virtual Environments and Intelligent Training Systems for Laparoscopy/Hysteroscopy Surgery Training) UE Educational Multimedia (TAP and LdV) project MM 1037 partly supported by the EC is a 30 months lasting project started on September 1998. The partners of the consortium are Fraunhofer IGD (G), Labein (S), Osakidetza (S), Instituto de Engenharia Biomédica (P), Hospital Sao Joao (P), Storz (G) and University Hospital Frankfurt (G). The authors wish to acknowledge the contribution of all members of the project team to the ideas presented in this paper whilst taking full responsibility for the way they are expressed.

complications. On-the-job training proved to be insufficient due to the high risk. Moreover, dissatisfaction with plastic models and the ethical discussion associated with animal experiments led to consideration of alternatives. This is true specially for rehearsing hysteroscopic procedures where it doesn't exists world-wide appropriate training environment at that time. An advanced training system combining virtual reality, web-based learning and agent-based tutoring techniques has the potential to enhance the current education and certification processes by increasing the safety, flexibility and cost-effectiveness. Aim of this paper is to report on the whole experience we have made in the development of LAHYSTOTRAIN demonstrator. In section 2 we describe the application scope and functionalities. Section 3 presents the architecture of the advanced training system. Then we describe the virtual reality simulator (section 4). Finally, section 5 summarises the lessons learned and the conclusions concerning the real applicability of the system.

2   Application Scope and Functionality

The LAHYSTOTRAIN training system is addressed to an heterogeneous collective composed of expert and novice surgeons, resident and medical students. It admits two types of users: surgeons, called trainees, and medical instructors. *Trainees* use the system to train and recycle in the execution of Laparoscopy and Hysteroscopy procedures/pathologies. Depending on the background and skills of the trainees, they are grouped in four categories: Expert Surgeons, Novice Surgeons, Residents and Medical Students. *Medical Instructors* are in charge of controlling and supervising the trainees evolution. They are able to set-up new exercises and consulting information related with the domain (such as initial patient conditions, list of phases, tasks and actions which make up each procedure, and pre-defined patient complications) and with the trainee data base (like user profile, didactic paths and last sessions evolution). Training in LAHYSTOTRAIN is carried out in two temporal consecutive phases:

- *Acquisition of theoretical knowledge* related to pathologies, complications, instruments and equipments. This training phase implemented in the BTS [1] can be completed remotely (for those people don't having access to a training centre or a hospital in which the ATS is installed) or locally in the opposite case. The basic training course is intended to give novice surgeons, by means of a web-based multimedia environment, the basic knowledge on laparoscopic and hysteroscopic procedures before proceeding with the VR advanced training. The LAHYSTOTRAIN Web based training can make a strong contribution to the existing training efforts because the target audience is geographical and timely scattered. Additionally, since surgery is a field of constant evolution, it is easier to update the didactic contents in this environment rather than on a printed support.
- *Acquisition of practical skills* previous to real interventions. During this phase the trainee interacts with the ATS (see figure 1). He has to execute correctly at the VR simulator the interventions proposed by the Tutor. During the execution of each exercise he is guided by the *Assistant* (pedagogical agent) who provides proactive and reactive explanations. Proactive assistance consists in the generation of explanations about different aspects of the procedures the surgeons have to carry on. These explanations are only provided when the user request for them to get

specific information. The list of actions which compose an intervention, the consequences of execution an action at the simulator, the safest path to an organ or an expert demonstration are some examples of pro-active explanations. Reactive assistance consists in the generation of explanations whenever the user makes a mistake, or something anomalous is happening at the VR simulator. The aim of these explanations is, depending on the expertise level of the trainee, to provide hints and information not only about the mistake or the anomalous situation, but also about its possible causes and remedy strategies. Reactive explanations suppose an interruption in the trainee execution of the session, which could disturb his/her training process. To avoid this situation, LAHYSTOTRAIN allows the trainee to select the intrusion level (low, medium, high) of the system. For instance, in low intrusion level, instead of interrupting the trainee operation, it stores all the session events in order to build a final debriefing at the end of the session. This final debriefing includes information like session success or not, trainee incorrect actions, violations, complications detected, description of the trainee misconceptions, and recommended actions. The *Tutor*, another pedagogical agent, is in charge of managing the whole training process: rostering and registering student information, acquiring trainee performance data and generating and executing the session Instructional Plan proposing different training lessons and exercises according to the user's expertise. This plan is constructed based on the information about the current trainee stored in the User Model. The Tutor modifies dynamically this plan adapting it to the trainee's performance during a training session. Finally, three behavioural agents, *Assistant Surgeon, Nurse and Anaesthetist*, reproduce and emulate the behaviour of some persons involved on the operating theatre. Surgeons must learn their individual role in the team as well as how to co-ordinate their actions with their team-mates.

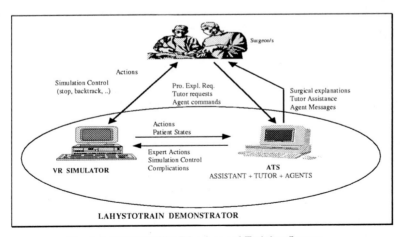

Fig. 1. LAHYSTOTRAIN Advanced Training System

The domain scope (pathologies and complications) covers in the BTS all subjects considered by the ESHRE (European Society of Human Reproduction and Embryology) laparoscopy and hysteroscopy competence levels. The ATS, in addition to the theoretical exercises, contains a set 12 practical exercises with the more frequent and complicated pathologies. Surgical procedures have been broken down into a number of self-contained steps, tasks and phases [2]. Some of these need to be performed in order while for others this is not essential. A complete set of event graphs, showing the required actions ordering and used to monitor user progress through the operative procedure and to provide accurate feedback, have been created. The ATS system is designed to allow the human instructor to edit new exercises selecting the pathology, the virtual patients and the introduction of pre-programmed complications. The main innovative approaches of the system are the following ones:

- *VR simulator Patient and instruments models.* LAHYSTOTRAIN uses MRI images to generate 3D patients models. A semi-automatic process to generate the models and assigning textures is being investigated within the project.
- *VR Simulator using force feedback sensor devices.* Force feedback at surgical instruments in an essential element to recreate a realistic training environment. LAHYSTOTOTRAIN allows the simultaneous use of 2 surgical instruments with force feedback as well as a positioning device for the optics.
- *ATS Team Training covering all phases of the intervention.* The correct execution of laparoscopy and hysteroscopy interventions implies working in collaboration with other people in the operation theatre (assistant surgeon, nurse and anaesthetist). In LAHYSTOTRAIN some exercises are performed by two surgeons at the same time (one with the instruments and the other with the camera). During the intervention they have to communicate with the nurse (for surgical instruments) and the anaesthetist for controlling the patient state. In addition to that, LAHYSTOTRAIN also trains in the initial intervention phases (patient setting up, equipment connection, etc.) that are also very important for successful conclusion of it.
- *ATS Pedagogical and Behavioural Agents.* LAHYSTOTRAIN uses Pedagogical Agents with physical appearance to guide the trainee during the training session execution. Two specialised Pedagogical Agents have been created: Tutor, expert in curriculum planning and supervision, and the Assistant, expert in the pathologies considered in the demonstrator.

3   Architecture of the Advanced Training System

The architectural design of the LAHYSTOTRAIN ATS demonstrator is shown in figure 2. It is composed of two systems the VR simulator and the ATS. The ATS system contains six subsystems represented as rectangles: Assistant, Tutor, Assistant Surgeon, Nurse , Anaesthetist , Student and User Interface and one data base, the Session Log, represented as a cylinder. Two of the subsystems are pedagogical agents, that is, agents whose aim is to teach something related to the considered pathologies (Assistant Agent) or to control the training process (Tutor Agent). The other three agents are behavioural agents emulating the behaviour of some of the personnel involved in the operating theatre. The Assistant is in charge of controlling the evolution of the training exercise.

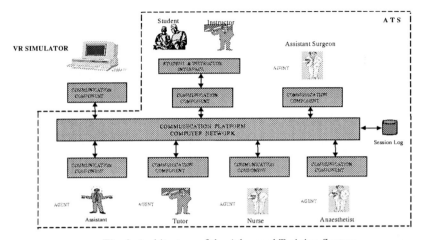

Fig. 2. Architecture of the Advanced Training System

This means that, on the one hand, it has to receive from the VR Simulator all relevant information (trainee actions, patient states) about the trainee operation, and on the other hand, the Assistant has to send to the VR Simulator commands to manage its evolution (stop, continue, backtrack, etc.), expert operations and the introduction of complications. This implies a fully integration of the ATS (Assistant) with the VR Simulator as it is shown in figure 1. The Student and Instructor Interface provide some functionalities to allow the communication with the demonstrator end-users. The Student Interface allows to ask for different types of explanations related to the current exercise as well as to call the Assistant or Tutor when needed. It also allows to establish communication with the behavioural agents. The Instructor Interface has icons to edit/create new exercises, to manage the trainees data-base, to analyse the last training sessions and to a assign an instructional plan to a user or group of users. The communication among subsystems is implemented by means of sockets.

The User Model it is divided into two folders: static (not updated during the training session) and a dynamic one. The static folder contains informations about his preferences (i.e. tutor intrusion level, preferred media to present explanations), personal details (name, age, hospital, identification code), experience level and previous theoretical background, etc. The dynamic folder includes the trainee performance, exercises carried out, errors made and pathology and instrument knowledge. At the end of each exercise the demonstrator updates the user model using the information stored during the training session. Finally, the Session Log stores all relevant events during the execution of an exercise (detected discrepancies, trainee errors, explanations requested generated by the system, user actions) as well as information related to the general development of the training session. The *Assistant* pedagogical agent contains the modules represented in figure 3. The *Simulator Interface* receives messages related to the actions performed by the surgeon at the VR Simulator as well as the variables describing the patient state and possible complications.

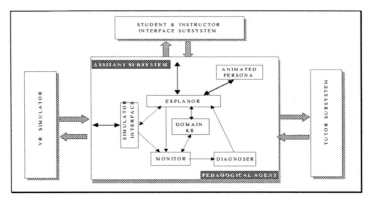

Fig. 3. Assistant Pedagogical Agent

These simulation data are passed to the *Monitor* which is in charge of recognising the actions performed by the surgeon and detecting discrepancies with respect to the expected behaviour. The Monitor loads the procedural model from *Domain* module represented by event graphs containing the optimal sequence of phases, tasks and actions and the possible correct alternative ways of performing each intervention. For monitoring a normal procedure we follow the so-called situated plan attribution approach [3]. The primary functions performed by the Monitor are to recognise the actions executed by the surgeon, generate the expected actions and goals with respect to the current patient state, match the interpreted surgeon actions against the expected procedure, determine achievement of operational goals, detect discrepancies when comparing trainee actions with expected actions and goals and classify detected discrepancies (superficial errors). The *Diagnoser* subsystem receives the superficial errors detected by the Monitor and tries to infer their causes (deep errors). It has been implemented as a rule-based system with two different phases: hypothesis generation and validation.

The *Explanor* is the main Assistant module charge not only of generating the content and structure of an explanation, but also of managing a dialogue with the end-users (trainees). Explanations are composed by on-line and off-line information, and adapted to the user necessities. They use different types of medias (animated persona, texts, graphs, sounds, videos, etc.) to present the information in the most suitable way and can interrupted by the user in order to request for additional information, clarifications, or examples. An explanation is composed by a set of interactions: Response, Demonstration, Warning, Notification, Information, Remedy and Restoration. Depending on the type of user, his expertise and preferences and the cause and type of error detected, The Explanor selects the set of interactions which composes the explanation. Examples of types of explanation provided by LAHYSTOTRAIN are: "Where is an organ?", "What is that?" while pointing at an anatomical structure, "Where am I", "Show me how to get an organ", "Next action/phase/task", "Operation objective", "How to use a surgeon instrument", "When to use it", etc. Finally, the *Animated Persona* [4], when selected by the Explanor, presents in a human-like (see figure 4) the explanations requested by the trainee. For example, he can demonstrate actions, use gaze and gestures to direct the student's attention, show how to use a surgical instrument, guide the trainee in the execution of an intervention and communicate through spoken dialogue by sending a messages to the person's text-to-speech module.

Fig. 4. Tutor and Assistant Animated Personas

The structure of the *Tutor* pedagogical agent can be seen in figure 5. Its main function is to supervise and manage the trainee sessions.

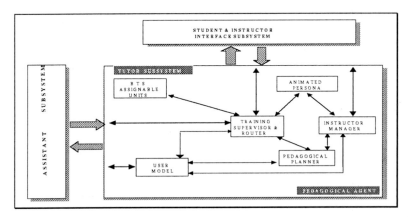

Fig. 5. Tutor Pedagogical Agent

The main module is the *Training Supervisor* which analyses the trainee's behaviour and performance during a session evaluating its errors and performance in the execution of Assignable Units (AU) and replanning the training session if necessary (surgeon serious errors, changes in its expected performance, trainee request or changes in the time period assigned to the session). The *Pedagogical Planner* establishes at the beginning of each training session or when requested by the Training Supervisor the Instructional Plan (IP) for the student. It defines the IP taking into account the pedagogical knowledge and the information contained in the *User Model*, the available time selected by the student for the training session and the estimation of the time necessary to complete each AU. The IP is structured in three levels. The first level corresponds to the *Instructional Objectives* -skills an cognitive capabilities that the Tutor wants to transmit to the student-. The second level contains *Instructional Strategies* -types of student activities assigned by the Tutor to reach a fixed Instructional Objective-. The last level corresponds to the *Tutor Objectives* (TO) which are detailed assignments the trainee has to carry during a training session-. The Behavioural Agents (Assistant Surgeon, Nurse and Anaesthetis*t*) are implemented as reactive agents [5]. They are composed (see figure 6) of five main modules: *Agents*

Manager which obtains the simulation variables from the VR Simulator and allows to perform actions in the virtual environment, the *Perception Module* that monitors messages from the other software components, identifies relevant events and maintains a snapshot of the state of the patient. Input messages to this module can be of two types: VR Simulator Actions and Communication messages addressed through the User Interface or the Animated Persona (oral commands). The *Reasoning Engine* purpose is to interpret the input received from the Perception module, process this information and generate the appropriate interventions. To do that, it contains a task representation specifying the actions to be carried out in the intervention. Finally, the *Action Control* module decomposes the interventions selected by Reasoning Engine into a sequence of lower-level actions (VR Simulator actions or communication messages to the trainee) that are sent to the other software modules.

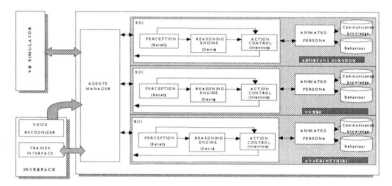

Fig. 6. Behavioural Agents

The Animated Persona uses a very simple *behaviour space* [4] consisting of a reduced set of animation sequences and utterances (happy, clap, passing instruments, boring, etc.) created with Poser and Microsoft Agent SDK. The physical aspect of the behavioural agents it shown in figure 7.

Fig. 7. Behavioural Agents: Nurse, Anaesthetist and Assistant Surgeon

The next figure presents two states of the *Student Interface,* during the intervention and when he requests a "Next Step" explanation. On the interface left side we can see the pedagogical agents Assistant and Tutor. The Assistant can explain orally the next step to perform showing at the same time a video from a real intervention or an animation taken from the VR Simulator. At the bottom side are located some buttons that provide additional explanations like: "Next Action" of the current procedure, "Why?" to carry on that action and "What For?".

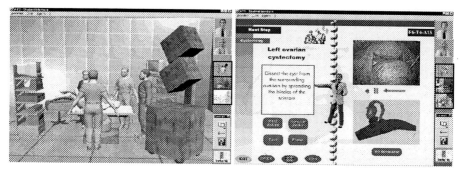

Fig. 8. Student Interface

4 Virtual Reality Simulator

The Virtual Reality (VR) simulator [6] provides the realistic surgical environment in which training on the various hysteroscopical and laparoscopical interventions is possible. Similar to a real hysteroscopy/laparoscopy the trainee is able to use surgical instruments interacting on the anatomical region of interest -the virtual situs-. The VR simulator consists of a graphics workstation, two tracking/haptic devices needed for the simulation of two surgical instruments and a tracking device for the simulation of a virtual endoscope. The virtual environment (VE) provides virtual instruments (endoscope/surgical instruments) and the virtual situs.

- *Virtual instruments (endoscope/surgical instruments)*: Not using a real endoscope and other surgical instruments the instrumentation has to be simulated. An intuitive handling of surgical instruments is provided in which its 3-D geometry is generated with input data available from 2-D construction plans provided by Storz. These representations have been integrated in the *VR Simulator* preserving shape and function of the instruments.
- *Virtual Situs*: The VE requires a realistic 3-D representation of the abdominal region. Input data for the generation of the virtual situs are Computer Tomography (CT) or Magnetic Resonance (MR) scans as well as video sequences of laparoscopic/hysteroscopic procedures. The data is collected at the hospitals involved in the project. Based on this image data a virtual situs has been reconstructed suitable for real-time simulation.

Finally, the different aspects of the simulation require data models with several levels of detail. Within LAHYSTOTRAIN have been generated three models: visualization model, collision detection model and deformation model.

5 Conclusions

This paper has presented the LAHYSTOTRAIN prototype oriented to train surgeons performing Laparoscopy and Hysteroscopy procedures. We have described its functionalities and architecture. The potential value of surgical simulation is its cost to benefit ratio and its ability to impact the morbidity and mortality rates of practising and future surgeons. At present the development costs for inmersive simulation are too high and there is few experimental data available proving the transfer of training knowledge into a surgical environment. We plan to evaluate the efficiency of the training system by means of three pilot experiences that will be carried out at the hospitals involved in the project (Hospital Sao Joao, University Hospital Frankfurt, Osakidetza) with different user groups: experienced and novice surgeons, residents and medical students. It is expected that LAHSYOTRAIN will overcome some of the current drawbacks of traditional training methods providing a safe, flexible and cost effective environment for teaching, maintaining and assessing endoscopic skills.

Acknowledgements

The work described in this paper has been undertaken with the support of the EC Educational Multimedia Joint Call project MM1037 and Comision Interministerial de Ciencia y Tecnología (CICYT) project reference TIC98-1730-CE

References

1. Barros, A., Marques, R., Monteiro, M.P.,Marques de Sá, J.P., Padilha, A., Bernardes, J.: Web Training in Laparoscopy and Hysteroscopy. Proc. of European Medical and Biological Conference EMBEC '99. Vienna. Published by the International Federation for Medical & Biological Engineering. Volume 37, Supplement 2, Part I. (1999) 696-697.
2. Billinghurst, M.; Savage, J.; Oppenheimer, P.; Edmond, C.: The Expert Surgical Assistant. In: Sieburg, H., Weghorst, S., Morgan, K. (eds.). Health Care in the Information Age, IOS Press and Ohmsha, (1996) 590-607.
3. Hill, R. W., Johnson, W. L. Situated Plan Attribution: Journal of Artificial Intelligence in Education, vol. (6) 1. (1995) 35-66.
4. Johnson, W. L. and Rickel, J.W.: Animated Pedagogical Agents: Face-To-Face interaction in Interactive Learning Environments. International Journal of Artificial Intelligence in Education 11 (2000), to appear.
5. Rickel, J. and Johnson, W. L.: Virtual Humans for Team Training in Virtual Reality. Proc. of the Ninth Wolrd Conference on AI in Education. IOS Press. (1999)
6. Voss G., Bockholt U., Los Arcos J.L., Muller W., Oppelt P., Stähler J.: LAHYSTOTRAIN Intelligent Training System for Laparoscopy and Hysteroscopy. Westwood J.D, Hoffman H.M., Mogel G.T. (eds): Proceedings of Medicine Meets Virtual Reality. IOS Press, Amsterdam (2000) 359-364.

Active Learner Modelling

Gordon McCalla, Julita Vassileva, Jim Greer and Susan Bull

ARIES Laboratory, Dept. of Computer Science, University of Saskatchewan, Saskatoon, Saskatchewan S7N 5A9, Canada.
{mccalla, jiv, greer, bull} @cs.usask.ca

Abstract. It is common to think of a "learner model" as a global description of a student's understanding of domain content. We propose a notion of learner model where the emphasis is on the modelling process rather than the global description. In this re-formulation there is no one single learner model in the traditional sense, but a virtual infinity of potential models, computed "just in time" about one or more individuals by a particular computational agent to the breadth and depth needed for a specific purpose. Learner models are thus fragmented, relativized, local, and often shallow. Moreover, social aspects of the learner are perhaps as important as content knowledge. We explore the implications of fragmented learner models, drawing examples from two collaborative learning systems. The main argument is that in distributed support environments that will be characteristic of tomorrow's ITSs, it will be literally impossible to speak of a learner model as a single distinct entity. Rather "learner model" will be considered in its verb sense to be an action that is computed as needed during learning.

1. Introduction

It is still common parlance in intelligent tutoring systems (ITS) to speak of a "learner model", meaning a single global description of a student to be used by an ITS to judge understanding of deep domain content. In this paper we propose an alternative notion of learner model where the emphasis is on the activity and context of modelling, rather than on the global description. Focusing on the activity of learner modelling, we show how the model can be a function used to compute relevant information about one or more learners as needed depending on the purpose, learners involved and available resources. This approach lends itself to the kind of learner modelling often needed in systems coordinating many learners who communicate with one another, who form pairs or groups for learning activities, and who form opinions about one another, thus participating in some form of peer assessment. In such a setting there is no one monolithic learner model associated with each learner. Rather the knowledge

·This research has been partially funded by the Telelearning Network of Centers of Excellence under Project 6.28.

about a learner is distributed among agents who interact with that learner (teachers, other learners, software applications, web-based software agents, etc.) In future, as borders of learning environments disappear and learning environments span the web, many applications and people will hold learner model information about a learner.

Thus learner modelling is the process of assembling and summarizing fragmented learner information from potentially diverse sources. This information can be raw data recorded by a web application, partially computed learner models inferred by an ITS, opinions about the learner recorded by a teacher or peers, or a history of learner actions. The key to making sense of this widely distributed information is the ability to interpret multi-modal information from multiple heterogeneous relevant sources and integrate this just-in-time into a learner model of appropriate granularity. Integration introduces many new requirements for the learner modelling process. In this paper we discuss the implications of this sort of learner modelling.

2. Examples: I-Help and S/UM

We have chosen to illustrate our approach in two systems: I-Help and S/UM.

2.1 I-Help

I-Help provides a student with a matchmaking service to find an online peer to help with a problem [1]. The most recent implementation is based on the Multi AGent Architecture for Adaptive Learning Environment (MAGALE) [2], which uses a decentralized approach in system design and an economic infrastructure to trade knowledge resources. The MAGALE architecture comprises individual personal agents representing each user, and manages a variety of learner models. These models are created and updated by a variety of diagnostic agents. A diagnostic agent can be contacted by another agent to request knowledge about some particular learner. This happens either periodically, or when information from this model is needed. In addition, each personal agent creates models of peers, whose agents the agent has encountered through a help interaction (see Figure 1).

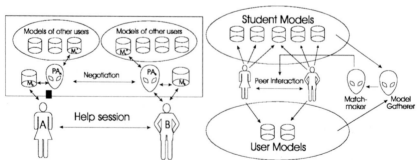

Fig. 1. I-Help: each personal agent maintains a model of its own learner and others encountered

Fig. 2. S/UM: each user maintains their user model, and contributes to student models of numerous peers

2.2 S/UM

S/UM [3] also offers a matchmaking service to students, but its focus differs from I-Help. S/UM is concerned with matching learners who may offer or wish to receive feedback on some aspect of their work, or who may want to collaborate or cooperate in their learning. The aim is to arrange partnerships to promote reflection through peer interaction and peer modelling. A major goal is that the feedback *givers* should also benefit, by reflecting while evaluating a peer. The additional relationship of cooperation in S/UM concerns a double feedback/help situation: X helps Y on A; Y helps X on B. Collaboration takes its usual sense of two learners working together on a common problem or task. Peer interactions may take place either on-line or off-line.

The S/UM architecture focuses on student and user models used by a 'model gatherer' and the matchmaker. The single modeller-modellee relationship does not hold: representations are constructed from self-evaluation by the model's owner–i.e. the modeller is also the modellee [4]; and by contributions from peer modellers after peer interaction [3]. The model gatherer organises these model fragments, generating an appropriate synopsis of model contents from the multiple information sources (e.g. more weight to recent entries and assessments from competent peers). This synopsis may be of interest to the model's owner for reflection; to the matchmaker for finding suitable partners; to peers who may browse information about potential partners. A single student model may comprise many entries from different peer sources, and a single learner may contribute to any number of peer models (see figure 2).

3. Integration in Learner Modelling

As illustrated in the above systems and many others, it is often inconvenient, unproductive, or computationally difficult to maintain a single consistent global model about each learner. In I-Help learner models are derived as needed according to the person or people being modelled, the agent who is modelling, and the end use or purpose of the model [5]. In S/UM learner models are aggregated for presentation to peer viewers. We believe this emerging trend of deriving learner models from distributed model fragments will increase as learners interact with more widely distributed learning resources and applications on the Web. Continuous contact between learners and technology will allow for fine-grained tracking of learners' activities under different circumstances and by different modelling agents. The problem for learner modelling will be making sense out of too much knowledge, rather than trying to make do with too little [6]. Thus the need for integrating learner model fragments will grow, and the ideal of maintaining a single monolithic learner model for each learner will be seen as less desirable (and likely intractable).

We believe the fragmented, distributed learner model will have a significant impact on learner modelling research. The main question is how to manage the information:

- how to find the agent who has a relevant model depending on the context and the purpose for which the model is needed;
- how to make sense of possibly inconsistent or even contradictory data;
- in general how to interpret models created by other agents.

The focus is shifted from the model itself to the process of modelling, i.e. the learner model is thus not so much a noun as a verb. The learner model is computed "just in time" [7] and only makes sense in the context of who is being modelled and for what.

For clarification we introduce a simple notation. We can think of a learner model as a function: *learnerModel (a, L, p, r)*, where:

a is the agent doing the modelling,

L is the set of learners participating in the modelling activity,

p represents the purpose of the model, and

r corresponds to the computational resources (time, space, etc.) which are available at the time the model is being created.

It may also be useful to think of *learnerModel* as a **method** of the agent doing the modelling. From this viewpoint, the notation might be: *a.learnerModel(L, p, r)*.

It is important to note that this notation has no ambition of broad generality, nor do we intend to make a contribution to computational mathetics [8]. There is some overlap of our approach and the notion of runnable learner models. Indeed our learner model function implies that the learner model is a computation. The distinction is that our approach permits the computation to work on partially computed learner models drawn from diverse sources in addition to just-in-time computation with raw data.

4. The Different Purposes of Learner Modelling

Learner models can have a variety of purposes. They form a set of partially computed models describing fragments of knowledge about learners. The aggregate of **all** such *fragmented* models, if such a thing could be computed, would be the complete and definitive model of all learners associated with a system. We not only believe this aggregate could be very hard to compute, but we also believe it is not necessary for most purposes. We now investigate the various purposes of learner modelling.

4.1 Reflection

learnerModel(a: learner's personal agent; *L*: learner and other relevant learners; *p*: to find out how the learner is viewed; *r*: might not need real time response)

Making the contents of learner models accessible to students can be used to promote *reflection* on the target domain [9-11]. With the broader information in fragmented models in multi-user systems, such reflection may concern not only domain content, but may also be focused on other issues, e.g. "how do other learners view me?"

"How do other learners view me?" may refer to social issues such as helpfulness in I-Help, perhaps to assist someone in rethinking their attitude to the group; or for learners to compare their performance with their peers in S/UM. They may wish to see how well they are doing compared to the average student, or they may wish to view possibilities attainable by high achievers [12]. Students may also reflect on reactions of others who have viewed their work, leading to better understanding of difficulties. Finally, helpers may also benefit by reflecting on their own knowledge or the helpee's knowledge, when giving feedback.

4.2 Validation

learnerModel(*a*: modelling agent; *L*: the learner whose model is validated, the agents whose models are used for comparison; *p*: to confirm some of the beliefs in the initial model created about the learner, to leverage others, to add new beliefs; *r*: will probably take place off line, so lots of time and resources)

Learners can make use of various learner model viewpoints to confirm or deny opinions/knowledge. This could be used to confirm domain knowledge, and also to find out other people's opinions about a person's social characteristics. *Validation* is probably a special kind of reflection, distinguished by the learner starting with an opinion, rather than with a blank request. In I-Help validation would take place by direct agent interactions; in S/UM, it occurs through learner requests for feedback.

With so many distributed user models, questions of validity and consistency arise. Ensuring global consistency seems impossible and unnecessary. However, if each person, component or agent maintains its own models and is indifferent to how other agents model the same users, there is no advantage to multiple models. If an agent can communicate with other agents about its models, it can benefit from their experience, extend and validate its model (see also [13]). This is easier when agents are validating models created for the same purpose, with a similar modelling function. It is harder with data collected by an agent for a different reason, with a different function.

4.3 Matchmakers

learnerModel(*a*: matchmaking agent; *L*: learner and potential partners; *p*: to find appropriate peer; *r*: must complete in "real time" (I-Help) / need not complete in "real time" (S/UM))

In both I-Help and S/UM the system finds a ready, willing and able partner for a particular learner and learning need. Locating a suitable partner is handled by an agent we call the *matchmaking* agent.

Depending on the matchmaking agent *a* and the purpose *p*, the modelling function *learnerModel* may differ and different features *L* of the learner and potential peer helpers may be relevant for matching. For example, matching with the purpose of finding a peer helper may use the models of the potential helpers' knowledge and social characteristics (helpfulness, class ranking, eagerness) only, or it could also use the helper's and helpee's preferences. Matching with the purpose of finding partners in a collaborative project (p_1) may be done by another agent, a_1 which uses the same user characteristics *L*, but a different modelling function, *learnerModel*$_1$, which searches for knowledge and social characteristics which complement each other.

The modelling function *learnerModel* may depend on the agent who does the modelling, *a*, as will usually be the case, since it is easier to design smaller matchmaking agents specialized for one modelling function and purpose only. However, in the general case, there can be also more complex agents, able to create models of other agents for different purposes and with various alternative modelling functions.

4.4 Negotiation

learnerModel(a_1: helpee's personal agent; *L*: learners known by the agent; *p*: to obtain a fair price for help; *r*: must complete in "real time")

learnerModel(a_2: helper's personal agent; *L*: learner associated with the help request; *p*: to obtain a fair price for help; *r*: must complete in "real time")

In I-Help two personal agents can interact and *negotiate* for various reasons. This can be part of the matchmaking process [14], but can also occur between agents for other reasons, such as knowledge sharing where agents can acquire information directly from other agents so that one or both can work "better".

In this case we have 2 agents performing the modelling. They are personal agents involved in negotiation, let's say a_1 and a_2. a_1 develops a model of user L_2 and a_2 develops a model of user L_1. The purposes p_1 and p_2 of modelling may be identical (in the case of MAGALE, to better predict the reaction of the opponent in negotiation), or may differ. The same applies to the modelling functions. However, in a more general and complex case, when for example two agents are negotiating about the models of their users, the purposes / functions may be completely different.

Various versions of I-Help have been deployed to experiment with reflection, validation, matchmaking and negotiation. To achieve real time response we have computed minimal and partial models, with both content and social dimensions. Other "proof of concept" experiments in negotiation [14], supporting the helper [15] and visualizing models [16] have shed more light on these functions in use. S/UM emphasizes reflection and larger scale models of content. We aim to integrate the S/UM and I-Help approaches in a distributed environment, to further illuminate these issues. Other "classical" purposes of learner modelling e.g. diagnosis, assessment, context adaptation are also consistent with this active, procedural view of modelling.

5. What Processes and Techniques are Needed to Learner Model?

With this perspective of learner modelling as distillation and integration of fragments of data and models, the important activity changes from model building to model management. The focus expands from diagnosis of behaviour and representation of learner information to retrieval of appropriate model fragments and their integration to suit the purpose. Thus learner modelling consists of several processes, including:

- retrieval - gathering suitable data, processes, learner model fragments from various sources that would be relevant to the learners and purposes of the learner modelling process.
- integration - aggregating and abstracting learner model fragments (and possibly additional raw data) into coarser-grained, higher-level learner model fragments. Integration across all possible information about a learner might result in a single monolithic learner model. However, computational resources would likely preclude such comprehensive integration, and the purpose of the modelling would rarely require a monolithic learner model.
- interpretation - using the result of learner modelling for some purpose. The result of the learner modelling/integration process is a knowledge structure

that is to be interpreted by applications requiring learner model information. These processes will necessarily be idiosyncratic to the purpose required. We will focus on retrieval and integration in this section. Many of the interpretation issues have already been covered in the discussion of purposes in section 4.

5.1 Retrieval

Since there are multiple models of various aspects of every learner, developed by different agents with different purposes under different resource constraints, it would be helpful to make use of all this information when a learner modelling need arises. How can one retrieve an appropriate model or collection of models? If several candidate models are available, which should be chosen? What should be done if candidates have contradictory contents? Two criteria will likely be most relevant in retrieving models: who created the model (a) and for what purpose (p). E.g. if an agent a_0 (of learner L_0) wants to learn the qualities of learner L_1 with respect to programming in C++, it will ask other agents that a_0 trusts and that know something about L_1. From these it will select agents who have models developed with the same purpose, i.e. evaluation of L_1's knowledge in C++. This means only users who have interacted with L_1 in the context of C++ will be queried. Another criterion, which can be considered as supplementary to the first, and will probably be more difficult to implement, is to look for agents with a similar modelling function ($a.learnerModel$). In this way an agent may seek models developed by trusted agents, or agents with similar evaluation functions. Finally, the time resources under which the model was created could regulate retrieval. A model created in a rush might be less adequate than one developed over a longer period of time and with more computational resources.

5.2 Integration

We use the term "integration" in a broad sense, more like "mediation" introduced in information systems [17], to denote the integration of diverse and heterogeneous information sources, achieved by abstracting away representational differences and integrating individual views into a common model. This integration captures the requirement for combining learner model fragments into coherent explanations. In its most complete sense, this process is complex, domain dependent, and resource intensive. Fortunately it is often only necessary to get an approximation of a learner's cognitive or social state derived from a few bits of raw data. Sometimes all that is needed is to confirm that a new bit of evidence is consistent with prior inferences.

Integration involves aggregation and abstraction of data and partial models. It demands that a domain ontology has been chosen and model elements are tagged according to that ontology. Integration of information is even more difficult than retrieval, as it requires interpretation and summarization of data retrieved from the model fragments to be integrated. This interpretation depends on the agents that created the model fragments, and moreover on the models of these agents created by the agent performing the integration, on their modelling functions and on the purposes of modelling. Suppose agents a_1, a_2 and a_3 had each created a model of L_0's eagerness, and L_4 wants to aggregate this information. L_4's agent (a_4) will interpret information from each of the three agents depending on its model of L_1 and L_2 and L_3's evaluation functions (i.e. how capable are they of accurately judging L_0's eagerness). Figure 3 shows how this integration might occur.

To achieve aggregation we must be able to represent and reason about a modeller's objectivity and priorities (expressed in the modelling function *learnerModel*). We must also be able to represent circumstances under which modelling is done. This is different from *p* (the purpose for which the model was created). Here we are more interested in the interpersonal relationship between modeller and modellee at the moment the model was created: whether they were in a cooperative or adverse relationship, close or distant, whether the modeller was observer or collaborator, whether they had common or different goals, as well as the general result of the situation (positive or negative, success or failure). This implies that complex reasoning may happen during integration. The good news is that global integration will rarely (if at all) be required. Integrating learner models will be done mostly by various agents (*a*) with a certain purpose (*p*), for a small subset of partial goal-related models (*L*), and under certain time constraints (*r*). In a narrow context this can be feasible.

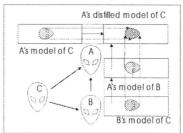

Fig. 3. Integration in A's model of C

Many AI techniques can possibly enter into the retrieval and integration processes:

- *belief revision*, to be able to incorporate new evidence into models personal agents keep about their learner. This belief revision is entirely local to the personal agent doing it, however, and will be done in the context of end use. The big issue will be whether to just add information without interpretation, and then put it together when there is an end use, or to have a separate belief revision process run occasionally like a garbage collection algorithm.

- *knowledge representation*, to capture both social and content knowledge. For many purposes knowledge will only need to be fairly shallow, so perhaps many of the deep KR problems can be avoided. Semantics will necessarily have to be procedural, in the sense that final meaning is totally relative to the procedures using the knowledge. A consistent ontology would simplify the representation process. Unfortunately, the likelihood of fine-grained ontologies remaining consistent across the diversity of applications and knowledge sources we envision would be small. The ability to merge, abstract and reason about ontologies will thus become important issues.

- *information retrieval and information filtering*, that is getting knowledge from the environment when needed, often very quickly.

- *knowledge externalization*, that is putting knowledge into a form that can be easily understood by the learner(s) or end users. This may vary from learner to learner and from one end use to another. Techniques for *knowledge visualization* will be useful here [16].

- *data mining* techniques to find patterns within and between agents' models and raw data.
- *group modelling techniques*, to find characteristics shared among many personal agents [18]. This will need to be retrieved by means of agent-agent negotiations, and will support collaborative styles of learning.
- *Bayesian belief networks* [19], useful for integrating multi-modal, multi-source evidence and propagating beliefs using a well-defined process.

Despite the daunting list of techniques and apparent complexity of learner modelling, we believe learner model computation to be tractable in many circumstances.

6. Conclusion

This paper argued for a revised view of "learner model" as a computation (the verb sense of "model"), rather than a data structure. We argued that in the new distributed computational architectures such a view will not only be useful, but necessary. Learner modelling will be a fragmented activity, performed on demand as a function of the people being modelled, purpose of modelling, and resources available. Learner modelling will occur for many reasons, extended from the traditionally narrower focus on diagnosis and assessment. For many purposes learner modelling computations will compute social as well as content aspects of learners. This should be easier than in the past given the vast amount of information that will be available about learner interaction in the emerging information technology intensive world.

These revised ideas about learner modelling will shift the learner modelling research agenda. Techniques such as retrieval, integration, and interpretation will be much more important. Many interesting research issues surrounding these techniques will have to be explored. In a fragmented, distributed, and universally accessible technological environment, learner modelling will increasingly be viewed as essential to building an effective system, but will also increasingly be seen to be tractable as new techniques emerge. Nevertheless, as our experiments have already shown, it will not be necessary to resolve all of these issues in order to usefully learner model.

References

1. Greer, J., McCalla, G., Cooke, J., Collins, J., Kumar, V., Bishop, A. and Vassileva, J. (1998) The Intelligent HelpDesk: Supporting Peer Help in a University Course, Proceedings ITS'98, San Antonio, Texas, LNCS No1452, Springer Verlag: Berlin pp.494-503.
2. Vassileva J., J. Greer, G. McCalla, R. Deters, D. Zapata, C. Mudgal, S. Grant (1999) A Multi-Agent Approach to the Design of Peer-Help Environments, in S. Lajoie and M. Vivet (eds.) Artificial Intelligence and Education, IOS Press: Amsterdam, 38-45.
3. Bull, S. (1997) A Multiple Student and User Modelling System for Peer Interaction, in R. Schäfer & M. Bauer (eds) ABIS-97: 5 GI-Workshop, Adaptivität und Benutzermodellierung in interaktiven Softwaresystemen, Universität des Saarlandes, Saarbrücken, 61-71.
4. Bull, S. (1998) 'Do It Yourself' Student Models for Collaborative Student Modelling and Peer Interaction, in B.P. Goettl, H.M. Halff, C.L. Redfield & V.J. Shute (eds) Intelligent Tutoring Systems-ITS98, Springer-Verlag, Berlin Heidelberg, 176-185.

5. Vassileva, J.I., Greer, J.E., McCalla, G.I. (1999) Openness and Disclosure in Multi-agent Learner Models, in Proceedings of Workshop on Open, Interactive, and Other Overt Approaches to Learner Modelling, International Conference on AIED, Le Mans, France.

6. McCalla, G.I. (2000) The fragmentation of culture, learning, teaching and technology: implications for artificial intelligence in education research agenda in 2010. Int Jnl of AIED.

7. Kay, J. (1999). A Scrutable User Modelling Shell for User-Adapted Interaction. Ph.D. Thesis, Basser Department of Computer Science, University of Sydney, Sydney, Australia.

8. Self, J. (1990) Theoretical foundations for intelligent tutoring systems, Int Jnl of AIED 1(4).

9. Bull, S. & Pain, H. (1995) "Did I say what I think I said, and do you agree with me?": Inspecting and Questioning the Student Model, in J. Greer (ed), Proceedings of World Conference on AI in Education, AACE, 501-508.

10. Dimitrova, V., Self, J. & Brna, P. (1999) The Interactive Maintenance of Open Learner Models, in S.P. Lajoie & M. Vivet (eds), Artificial Intelligence in Education, IOS Press.

11. Paiva, A., Self. J. & Hartley, R. (1995) Externalising Learner Models, in J. Greer (ed), Proceedings of World Conference on AI in Education, AACE, 509-516.

12. Kay, J. (1997) Learner Know Thyself: Student Models to give Learner Control and Responsibility, in Z. Halim, T. Ottmann & Z. Razak (eds), Proceedings of International Conference on Computers in Education 1997, AACE, 18-26.

13. Maes, P. (1994) Agents that Reduce Work and Information Overload, Communications of the ACM 37(7), 31-40.

14. Mudgal, C., Vassileva, J. (to appear) An Influence Diagram Model for Multi-Agent Negotiation, Proceedings of International Conference on Multi-Agent Systems, Boston.

15. Kumar, V., McCalla, G., Greer J. (1999) Helping the Peer Helper. S. Lajoie and M. Vivet (eds.) Artificial Intelligence and Education, IOS Press, Amsterdam, 325-332.

16. Zapata-Rivera, J.D. & Greer, J., (this volume), Inspecting and Visualizing Distributed Bayesian Student Models.

17. Wiederhold, G. & Genesereth, M. (1997) The Conceptual Basis for Mediation Services, IEEE Expert.

18. Hoppe, H.-U. (1995) The use of multiple student modelling to parameterise group learning, in J. Greer (ed), Proceedings of World Conference on AI in Education, AACE, 234-241.

19. Reye, J. (1999) Student Modelling based on Belief Networks. Int Jnl of AI in Education, 11.

Training Teams with Collaborative Agents

Michael S. Miller, Jianwen Yin, Richard A. Volz, Thomas R. Ioerger, John Yen

MS 3112
Department of Computer Science
Texas A&M University
College Station, Texas 77843-3112
{mmiller, jianweny, volz, ioerger, yen}@cs.tamu.edu

Abstract. Training teams is an activity that is expensive, time-consuming, hazardous in some cases, and can be limited by availability of equipment and personnel. In team training, the focus is on optimizing interactions, such as efficiency of communication, conflict resolution and prioritization, group situation awareness, resource distribution and load balancing, etc. This paper presents an agent-based approach to designing intelligent team training systems. We envision a computer-based training system in which teams are trained by putting them through scenarios, which allow them to practice their team skills. There are two important roles that intelligent agents can play; these are as virtual team members and as coach. To carry out these functions, these agents must be equipped with an understanding of the task domain, the team structure, the selected decision-making process and their belief about other team members' mental states.

1 Introduction

An integral element of large complex systems is that a team of humans is needed to manage them. Teams demand that the members be competent not only in their individual skills, but also in anticipating the needs of the team as if it were an entity by cooperating with other team members to act effectively. Teams can induce a large amount of stress on members that can lead to tragic consequences such as the shooting down of an Iranian airliner by the USS Vincennes. Stressors such as sensor overload, fatigue, time pressure, and ambiguity contributed to this accident [1]. In order to better manage these factors teams train together to be able to perform together effectively.

In heterogeneous teams, that is teams that require specialists in order to function, team members must not only be able to perform their own unique functions, but they must also be able to act as a cohesive part of the team. A team member may or may not be familiar with the functions of other team members but is competent within his own domain. In order for the team to become competent, the team members must practice together [2]. Team training is normally done using simulations of the system or the actual system with all of the human team members participating. When an intelligent tutoring system is added, it is typically in the role of training an individual to be able to understand his individual tasks before taking part in the team. In order to train teams it would be useful to expand an ITS so that it can support team activities.

In our approach, partial teams can be simulated using computed-based agents to represent team members and thus teach a trainee necessary team skills such as situational awareness, group decision-making, and communications efficiency without having to involve the entire human team for all training sessions.

By building computer-based simulation environments, trainees can be run through simulated scenarios, providing a type of hands-on experience. Intelligent agents serving as virtual team members can provide significant cost-savings through partial team training. However, significant challenges exist in developing such *intelligent team training systems* (ITTS). First, for agents to participate in the simulation (and provide believable interactions) as virtual team members, they must have an understanding of the team structure and the collaboration process, requiring multi-agent belief reasoning. Second, in order to diagnose problems with teams and provide dynamic feedback (e.g. coaching), things such as distributed plan recognition and interpreting individual's action in terms of their beliefs about their teammates must be done.

We envision a computer-based training system in which teams are trained by putting them through scenarios, which allow them to practice their team skills. Our proposed approach to training teams is to use an intelligent multi-agent based system that has a knowledge-based foundation. This ITTS allows the human trainee to build an understanding of his role within the team. The trainee is able to learn which other team members the trainee must monitor and when or where the trainee can provide support to the other team members without interrupting them in the performance of their duties. This also called a *shared mental model*, which is thought to be a key to effective teamwork [3]. Mistakes that the trainee makes can be caught by a coaching agent that can either use other virtual team agents to correct the trainee or directly interact with the trainee as a tutor within the system.

2 Teamwork

Our definition of a team is a group of entities (humans or agents) that are working together to achieve a goal that could not be accomplished as effectively (or at all) by any one of them alone [4]. Team members play unique roles, which may require unique skills and resources. Our focus is on teams that are hierarchical, with a clear chain-of-command and leadership or authority roles. Teams are also heterogeneous in that individual team members have different roles and responsibilities within the team. All teams have to deal in one way or another with sharing information and distributed decision-making (also called cooperation or collaboration) [5].

3 Team Training

In team training, the focus is not on each individual's skills (which are typically learned beforehand), but on optimizing interactions, such as situational awareness, communications efficiency, and the effectiveness of team decision-making [6]. Intelligent agents can help extend these methods to build Intelligent Team-Training Systems. There are two important functions that intelligent agents can play in such systems. First, we can have agents that can substitute for other team members. This allows for partial team training, which could provide huge cost savings, and allows for either individuals or sub-teams to train without the need for the rest of the team. A second major role is for a knowledge-based agent to play the role of coach [7]. This eases the burden of a human instructor from having to monitor both the trainee and the other virtual team members in the simulation. To carry out their roles, these agents must be equipped with an understanding of the task domain, the team structure, the selected decision-making processes and their belief about other team members' mental states.

4   Other Agent Based Teams

The agent-based teams that exist in the literature are focused on allowing rational agents to work together on a common goal. Such agents have a shared mental model of what each agent is able to contribute to the team. This shared mental model is a simplified model of the mental states of all the other members on the team. Agents must be able to query and establish team goals that the agents collaborate upon in order to achieve a shared goal that they would otherwise be unable to achieve.

A teamwork model must provide support for reasoning about team goals, plans, and states. It must also represent the roles and responsibilities of individual team members as this relates to other team members. Information needs of team members need to be fulfilled by the team by finding out who best can answer those needs. In the approaches listed below such information needs are not yet examined.

In the SharedPlans approach each agent maintains individual plans and shared plans [5]. Individual agents accomplish plans that require cooperation between such agents by building shared plans. Other team-based agents build on this foundation to construct general models of teamwork. COLLAGEN [8] uses a plan recognition algorithm in order to reduce communications during collaboration between a human and an agent. Using attention, partial plans, and clarification enables COLLAGEN-based agents to interact with humans in an intelligent fashion. COLLAGEN is an implementation of the SharedPlans theory.

The approach that STEAM uses is to find *joint intentions* between agents and create a hierarchy of joint intentions so that the agents can monitor other agents' accomplishments or failures in achieving these shared intentions [9]. Both systems provide a model of teamwork into which domain specific knowledge and agents can be added. STEAM is designed to be domain independent in its reasoning about teamwork. It is based on the *joint intentions* framework by Levesque [10]. STEAM also provides for capabilities to monitor and repair team plans.

PuppetMaster addresses the issue of reporting on student interactions within a team for use by an instructor [11]. A top-down approach is used to reduce unnecessary details and be able to recognize actions at the team level. The focus of PuppetMaster is not on the individual student's behavior but as an aid to an instructor to recognize team failures.

5   CAST – Collaborative Agents for Simulating Teamwork

We describe a computational system for implementing an ITTS called CAST, for *Collaborative Agent architecture for Simulating Teamwork*. We focus on humans as a part of the virtual team. We wish to model the individual's beliefs and actions within the context of the team. We also wish to automate the training process and allow individuals to practice alone without needing a large support staff to setup and monitor the exercise. We assume that a good description can be provided of the actions that a team and its members will be able to perform. Therefore, we assume that the team has a plan of what needs to be accomplished in the performance of the team mission, and we know who are the team members and what their roles will be.

We want to enable an individual new to the team to become a part of the team by increasing his situational awareness, showing him who or what to monitor, and how best to respond to the actions and requests of his fellow team members. The team exists in a domain in which each team member plays a specific role and responses need to be well rehearsed in order to overcome any difficulties that the team may encounter. We can best illustrate what such a team looks like with the following brief example.

6   An Example Team Domain

The NASA Mission Control Center consists of a team that is arranged in a hierarchical manner with clearly delineated roles for each team member. The Flight Director (FD) oversees 10 disciplines which each monitor functions on the Space Shuttle. These stations are manned continually during a Space Shuttle mission, which typically lasts less than 10 days. During scheduled events all relevant disciplines are fully staffed. During down times, such as when the astronauts are sleeping, only lighter staffing needs are required.

To examine the operation more closely, consider the PROP (Propulsion Systems Officer). The PROP is responsible for the operation of the Space Shuttle Orbital Maneuvering System (OMS) and Reaction Control System (RCS). These secondary engines are used for orbital corrections, docking operations, and the De-orbit burn. The PROP is assisted by the OMS/RCS Engineering Officer (OREO) and the Consumables Officer (CONS) as a sub-team [12]. The PROP knows the functions and duties of his sub-team members but instead typically focuses on interacting with the other disciplines. The PROP uses his sub-team to fulfill his requirements for information and allows them to manage their respective sub-systems.

The PROP officer is also in a vertical chain of command leading up to the Flight Director. The Flight Control Room (FCR) provides each FCR team member a headset with separate channels dedicated to different disciplines and needs. The sub-team members such as the OREO and CONS officers sit on consoles in a separate room from the FCR called the Multipurpose Support Room (MPSR).

As an example scenario during the launch stage, the FD asks the PROP officer for a status check to see if the discipline is ready for launch. The PROP officer checks with his sub-team. Each sub-team member checks his own console and reports to the PROP officer. The PROP officer reports back to the FD that they are ready for launch. This is a simple example but shows the need for monitoring the needs of the team and having a situational awareness as to what functions each individual should be performing. Individuals are aware of what the team goals are and what their responsibilities and needs are in order to fulfill the team goals.

In order for the MCC team to be able to train as a team, the resources of the MCC at Johnson Space Center must be dedicated to running a training simulation. This can involve not only the MCC team members, but also astronauts in the Space Shuttle Trainer (which is located in a different building), building and computer support personnel, and the resources of the actual FCR. When such a training task is in progress no other work can be done with the facilities. Such team training is not done when a space shuttle is in flight. This will become a problem when resources must also be used for monitoring the International Space Station.

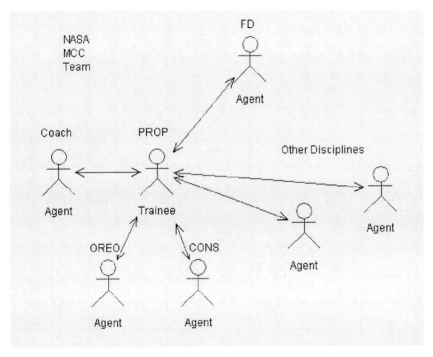

Fig. 1. A subset of the NASA MCC Team

7   The CAST Architecture

The approach we take in CAST is to model the team interactions of team members using Petri Nets. We propose to use a model of teamwork and reasoning agents with beliefs about the team and themselves in order to construct the ITTS. The virtual team agents must also be able to interact with human trainees and communicate with a human counterpart. The explicit representation of goal hierarchies and intentions will be important for diagnosing problems with team behavior and providing useful feedback for coaching and evaluation.

7.1 Challenges in Developing an ITTS

An agent-based, team-centered ITS for training teams has certain challenges to overcome in order to be an effective training tool. First, the virtual team members have to generate reasonable interactions for human team members. Humans must be incorporated in the ITTS initially as one or more trainees, and eventually as other team members in order to allow sub-teams to practice among themselves. Second, the coaching agent should be "non-intrusive" by passively monitoring and interpreting all actions and interactions of the trainee instead of announcing itself as a coaching agent and asking the trainee about his intentions and reasons. And last, understanding the actions of an individual on a team is more complicated because their decision-making explicitly involves reasoning about the other members of the team (e.g. their beliefs, roles, etc.), and their actions may be implicitly in support of a team goal or another agent.

7.2 Components of CAST

The ITTS will have four major components. Intelligent agents are used to represent individual team members. The individual team members incorporate a model of teamwork in order to help identify points of communications and shared goals. The state of a simulated world within which the training will occur must be maintained. To be useful the simulation should also be able to interface into an existing simulation, or integrate into an actual system. This last approach is the one planned for use with the MCC NASA domain. A coaching agent also maintains a user model of the trainee and acts when appropriate to tutor the trainee on understanding his role as a team member.

7.3 Elements of a Knowledge-Based Model of Teamwork

An ITTS agent must reason not only about its goals and capabilities, but also about the goals of the team and other team members and about commitments or shared responsibilities. This requires what is known as *belief reasoning*, which we simulate in CAST.

First, we use the team-description language MALLET [13] to provide a framework for modeling teamwork. Second, we encode this model of actions and interactions of a team into a representational structure using *Petri Nets*. Third, we use an *Inter-Agent Rule Generator* (IARG) to determine the interactions that will take place among the agents. Fourth, we incorporate a coaching agent to be able to detect when the trainee fails to act as a member of the team and provide feedback to the trainee to enable him to act appropriately.

7.4 MALLET: A Multi-Agent Logic Language for Encoding Teamwork

The ontology underlying our framework is based on the BDI model [14] (Belief represents the knowledge of the agent, Desire represents the general goals of the agent, and Intention represents the selected plans of the agent). The purpose of using an ontology is to identify the general concepts and relationships that occur in teamwork across multiple domains, and give them formal definitions that can be used as the basis of a team-description language with predicates with well-specified meanings. MALLET is a language based on predicate logic that allows the encoding of teamwork. Being a logic-based language, MALLET provides a number of pre-defined terms that can be used to express how a team is supposed to work in each domain such as Role (x), Responsibility (x), Capability (x), Stage (x), etc.

7.5 Petri Net Representation of MALLET

The actions and interactions of a team can be encoded in *Petri Nets*, which are a natural representation for actions, synchronization, parallelism, etc. Petri Nets have previously been suggested as an appropriate implementation for both intelligent agents and teamwork [15]. Petri Nets are particularly good at representing actions in a symbolic/discrete framework. They can represent the dependence of actions on pre-conditions in a very natural way, i.e. via input places to a transition. The effects of the chosen action simply become output places in the Petri Net. We use an algorithm to transform descriptions of roles in MALLET into Petri Nets, including beliefs, operators, and goals, etc. We use a Petri Net for each role on the team, with beliefs specific to that agent.

7.6 IARG algorithm

The IARG (Inter-Agent Rule Generator) algorithm is used to detect information flow and generate team interactions. IARG uses both offline and online components. An agent analyzes the Petri Nets of all the other agents using the IARG algorithm in order to derive information flow and identify propositions that other agents need to know. We can define information flow as a 3-tuple: *<Proposition, Providers, Needers>*. *Proposition* is a truth-valued piece of information. *Providers* is the set of roles that can provide the information (i.e. perhaps has the responsibility of achieving and/or maintaining it). *Needers* is the set of roles that need this information. An agent is said to need a piece of information in the sense that the proposition maps onto an input place of a transition in the Petri Net corresponding to an action that that agent can execute to carry out one of its responsibilities. We believe that using a belief representation for handling communications can serve as the shared mental model that a team maintains. This can then reduce the *explicit* communications needed between team members by instead promoting *implicit coordination* among team members. The information flow computed by the IARG algorithm can be used to generate communications for information exchange.

8 Development of a Coaching Agent

An advantage of our approach in CAST is that a coaching agent can use the model of teamwork within CAST to facilitate user modeling and the detection of errors between team members. User models [16] exist in single-user training systems in order to detect [17] and correct errors [18] in the trainee's domain knowledge. In a traditional ITS, an overlay approach is often used, in which the user's actions are compared to those that would be generated by an expert, to identify discrepancies between the student's (user) model, and the expert model (typically involving trigger or production rules for deciding what to do). However, understanding the actions of an individual on a team is more complicated because their decision-making explicitly involves reasoning about the other members of the team (e.g. their beliefs, roles, etc.), and their actions may be implicitly in support of a team goal or another agent.

Our approach in CAST is to model team members as maintaining simplified models of the mental states of all the other members on the team. To avoid issues of computational complexity with belief reasoning (e.g. via modal logics), we use Petri Nets as an approximate representation of these mental states. Then when a team member needs to decide what to do, they can not only reason about what actions would achieve their own goals, but they can reason about the state and needs of others. In particular, we focus on two effects: by making teamwork efficient through anticipating the actions and expectations of others (e.g. by knowing others roles, commitments, and capabilities), and by information exchange (knowing who to ask for information, or providing proactively just when it is needed by someone else to accomplish their task).

The coaching agent focuses on observing an individual's activities within the context of the team goals. Actions that each virtual team member takes depend on beliefs those agents hold regarding the goals and state of the other agents. Actions that a trainee takes also depend on his beliefs as to what needs to be done at that time in order to achieve the team goals. But beyond these actions, we can attempt to detect and properly classify whether a trainee has failed to act because of either inaction on the trainee's part, or an assumption by the trainee that it was another's responsibility, or a failure to properly monitor another team member. We also use the individual's model of teamwork to support the user model. We can infer the state of the team mode for the trainee based on observed actions, and we can map incorrect actions to problems with the trainee's representation of the other team members in the trainee's model of the team that would explain them, and from there back to the team/domain knowledge. Finally, the coaching agent will provide corrective feedback based on an appropriate pedagogical model (e.g. dynamically through hints during the scenario, and/or through after-action reviews).

9 Conclusions

The CAST system is currently being implemented as a distributed system in JAVA and RMI. We are using the domain of the NASA MCC to demonstrate this approach. We believe that this system can be a useful complement to traditional approaches in training teams. The agent-based teamwork model can not only be used to implement virtual team members in an intelligent team training system, it can also serve as the "expert teamwork model" for a coaching agent to assess the actions and the performance of a team being trained.

An ITTS cannot replace an actual human team. But it can reduce the time and overall cost of training individuals in a team staff for domains such as control centers and other team-centered applications. An eventual goal is to run the ITTS system in parallel with real-time operations in order to allow agent-based virtual team members to follow, monitor, and advise the actual human team members as they perform their duties.

10 Acknowledgements

This research was partially supported by GANN fellowship grant P200A80305 and seed funds from the Texas Engineering Experiment Station for the Training System Sciences and Technology Initiative.

References

1. Cannon-Bowers, J. A., Salas, E.: Making Decisions Under Stress: Implications for Individual and Team Training. American Psychological Association, Washington, DC (1998)
2. Van Berlo, M. P. W.: Systematic Development of Team Training: A Review of the Literature. Tech. Rep. TM-96-B010, TNO Human Factors Research Institute, Soesterberg, The Netherlands (1996)
3. Blickensderfer, E., Cannon-Bowers, J. A., Salas, E.:Theoretical Bases for Team Self-correction: Fostering Shared Mental Models. In: Beyerlein, M., Johnson, D., Beyerlein, S., (eds.): Advances in Interdisciplinary Studies of Work Teams. JAI Press, Greenwich, CT (1997) 249-279
4. Cohen, P. R., Levesque, H. J.: Teamwork. Nous, vol. 25, no. 4 (1991) 487-512
5. Grosz, B., Kraus, S.: Collaborative Plans for Complex Group Action. Artificial Intelligence, vol. 86, no. 2 (1996) 269-357
6. Salas, E., Driskell, J. E., Huges, S.:Introduction: The Study of Stress and Human Performance. In: Driskell, J. E., Salas, E., (eds.): Stress and Human Performance. Lawrence Erlbaum Associates, Inc., Mahwah, NJ (1996) 1-46
7. Mengelle, T., DeLean, C., Frasson, C.: Teaching and Learning with Intelligent Agents: Actors. In Intelligent Tutoring Systems '98, San Antonio, Texas (1998) 284-293
8. Lesh, N., Rich, C., Sidner, C. L.: Using Plan Recognition in Human-Computer Collaboration. In Seventh Int. Conf. on User Modeling, Banff, Canada (1999) 23-32
9. Tambe, M.: Towards Flexible Teamwork. Journal of Artificial Intelligence Research, vol. 7, no. 1 (1997) 83-124
10. Levesque, H., Cohen, P., Nunes, J.: On Acting Together. In American Association for Artificial Intelligence (AAAI '90), Boston, MA (1990) 94-99
11. Marsella, S. C., Johnson, W. L.: An Instructor's Assistant for Team-Training in Dynamic Multi-Agent Virtual Worlds. In Intelligent Tutoring Systems '98, San Antonio, Texas (1998) 465-473
12. Schmitt, L. J.:Prop Position. In: (eds.): Shuttle Prop, JSC-17238. NASA, Houston, Texas (1998) I.1.1-1 - I.1.1-13
13. Yin, J., Miller, M. S., Ioerger, T. R., Yen, J., Volz, R. A.: A Knowledge-Based Approach for Designing Intelligent Team Training Systems. In Proceedings of the Fourth International Conference on Autonomous Agents, Barcelona, Spain (2000)
14. Rao, A. S., Georgeff, M. P.: Modeling rational agents within a BDI Architecture. In 2nd International Conference on Principles of Knowledge Representation and Reasoning, Cambridge, MA (1991) 473-484

15. Coovert, M. D., McNelis, K.:Team Decision Making and Performance: A Review and Proposed Modeling Approach Employing Petri Nets. In: W.Swezey, R., Salas, E., (eds.): Teams: Their Training and Performance. Ablex Pub Corp, (1992)
16. Wenger, E.: Artificial Intelligence and Tutoring Systems. Morgan Kaufmann Publishers, Inc., Los Altos, California (1987)
17. Horvitz, E., Breese, J., Heckerman, D., Hovel, D., Rommelse, K.: The Lumiere Project: Bayesian User Modeling for Inferring the Goals and Needs of Software Users. In 14th Annual Conference on Uncertainty in Artificial Intelligence, Madison, WI (1998) 256-265
18. Baffes, P. T., Mooney, R. J.: Using Theory Revision to Model Students and Acquire Stereotypical Errors. In 14th Annual Conference of the Cognitive Science Society, Bloomington, IN (1992) 617-622

Evaluating an Animated Pedagogical Agent

Antonija Mitrovic and Pramuditha Suraweera

Intelligent Computer Tutoring Group
Department of Computer Science, University of Canterbury
Private Bag 4800, Christchurch, New Zealand
tanja@cosc.canterbury.ac.nz, psu16@student.canterbury.ac.nz

Abstract. The paper presents SmartEgg, an animated pedagogical agent developed for SQLT-Web, an intelligent SQL tutor on the Web. It has been shown in previous studies that pedagogical agents have a significant motivational impact on students. Our hypothesis was that even a very simple and constrained agent, like SmartEgg, would enhance learning. We report on an evaluation study that confirmed our hypothesis.

1 Introduction

Computers and Internet access are available in most schools today and offer a wealth of information to students. However, the access to computers does not guarantee effective learning, as many students lack the abilities to find their way through a vast amount of accessible knowledge. Students need guidance, either from human or computerized tutors. Recently, there have been several research projects that concentrate on the development of animated pedagogical agents, lifelike creatures that inhabit learning environments. Experiments have shown that such agents significantly increase student motivation and perception of their learning. Here we present SmartEgg, an animated pedagogical agent for SQLT-Web, and the initial evaluation of it.

We have developed SQL-Tutor, a standalone system for the SQL database language [9,10]. The system has been used by senior computer science students and has been found easy to use, effective and enjoyable [11]. Recently, SQL-Tutor was extended into a Web-enabled system, named SQLT-Web, and our initial experiences show that students find it equally enjoyable and useful [12]. SQLT-Web has been used only by local students. We plan to have SQLT-Web widely accessible soon, in which case students outside our university may find some aspects of the system more difficult to grasp. Therefore, we have started exploring possibilities of providing more feedback, and providing it in a manner that would motivate students.

We discuss animated pedagogical agents in section 2. Section 3 introduces SQL-Tutor and the Web-enabled version of it. We present SmartEgg in section 4, focusing on its implementation, behaviour space and communication with SQLT-Web. Section 5 presents the results of the initial evaluation, followed by discussion and conclusions.

2 Animated Pedagogical Agents

Animated pedagogical agents are animated characters that support student learning. They broaden the communication channel by using emotive facial expressions and body movements, which are very appealing to students. Pedagogical agents are extremely important for student motivation, as they provide advice and encouragement, empathize with students, and increase the credibility and utility of a system. Several studies have investigated the affective impact of agents on student learning and revealed the *persona effect*, "which is that the presence of a lifelike character in an interactive learning environment - even one that is not expressive - can have a strong positive effect on student's perception of their learning experience" [6]. Experiments have shown that students are much more motivated when the agent is present, tend to interact more frequently and find agents very helpful, credible and entertaining.

Animated pedagogical agents may be presented as cartoon-style drawings, real video or 3D models. Most agents are fully bodied, and use facial expressions and body movements to communicate emotions. An agent may exist within the learning environment, i.e. be immersed into the learning environment, move through it and manipulate objects within. It is also possible for an agent to exist in a separate window. Agents may adhere to the laws of physics, or may be stylised to emphasize emotions. Agents' behaviour may be specified off-line, manually. Ideally, behaviour should be generated online, dynamically, so as to correspond to the changes in the learning environment.

Herman the Bug [7] is an animated pedagogical agent for the *Design-A-Plant* learning environment, in which children learn about plant anatomy and physiology by designing plants for specific environments. Herman is a 3D model, immersed into the learning environment, capable of performing engaging actions, such as diving into plant roots, bungee jumping, shrinking and expanding.

Adele (Agent for Distance Education – Light Edition) [5] is an autonomous agent that facilitates distance learning. The agent is used with a simulated environment in which students solve problems. Adele consists of three components: a reasoning engine, which monitors student's actions and generates appropriate pedagogical responses to them, an animated persona that runs in a separate window, and a session manager, which enables multiple students to use the system concurrently.

Steve (Soar Training Expert for Virtual Environments) [4] is a human-like animated agent that cohabits a virtual reality environment and helps students learn to perform procedures. Being a 3D model immersed in a simulation, Steve can perform not only the pedagogical functions common in intelligent educational systems, but also can demonstrate actions by manipulating objects in the simulated environment. Multiple Steve agents can inhabit the environment, thus giving a possibility to teach team tasks.

PPP Persona [3] guides the learner through Web-based material by pointing to important elements of Web pages, and providing additional auditory comments. There are five different characters, three of which are video-based, and the remaining two are cartoon characters. AlgeBrain [1] is a Web-based intelligent tutoring system that teaches students how to solve algebraic equations. The pedagogical agent used is a cartoon-like drawing that appears in a separate window.

Three architectures have emerged for online generation of agent behaviour [4]. The *behaviour sequencing approach* is based on a behaviour space, which is a library of predefined primitives (actions, speech elements etc). In an instructional session, the behaviour of an agent is assembled on-line from the primitives, by a behaviour sequencing engine. The behaviour space of Herman the Bug consists of 30 animated segments of the agent performing various actions, and of 160 audio clips and songs [6]. These actions are combined at runtime by the emotive-kinaesthetic behaviour sequencing engine [7].

The second architecture is the *layered generative approach*, where animations are generated in real time. This is the architecture Steve is based on, and it is especially suitable for immersive environments, but it requires a much higher rendering computation load. Finally, the *state machine compilation approach* composes behaviour out of primitives, but generates a state machine, so that the behaviour of an agent can adapt at run time to student actions. Andre, Rist and Muller [2] describe a presentation planner, which develops a navigation graph from given goals. A navigation graph contains all presentation units with associated durations and transitional information.

3 An Intelligent SQL Tutor

SQL-Tutor is an Intelligent Teaching System (ITS) that helps students to learn SQL [9,10]. It is designed as a problem-solving environment and as such is not intended to replace classroom instruction, but to complement it. We assume that students are already familiar with the database theory and fundamentals of SQL. Students work on their own as much as possible and the system intervenes when the student is stuck or asks for help.

The standalone version of the system consists of an interface, a pedagogical module that determines the timing and content of pedagogical actions, and a student modeller that analyses student answers. There is no domain module, as usual in ITSs, which can solve the problem being posed to a student. The system contains definitions of several databases, implemented on the RDBMS used in the lab. SQL-Tutor also contains a set of problems for specified databases and the ideal solutions to them. In order to be able to check the correctness of the student's solution, SQL-Tutor uses domain knowledge represented in form of constraints, as described in [11]. Student solutions are compared to the ideal solutions and the domain knowledge.

At the beginning of a session, SQL-Tutor selects a problem for the student to work on. When the student enters the solution, the pedagogical module (PM) sends it to the student modeller, which analyses the solution, identifies mistakes (if there are any) and updates the student model appropriately. On the basis of the student model, PM generates an appropriate pedagogical action (i.e. feedback). When the current problem is solved, or the student requires a new problem to work on, the pedagogical module selects an appropriate problem on the basis of the student model.

SQL-Tutor uses Constraint-Based Modelling (CBM) [13] to form models of its students. CBM is a computationally efficient student modelling approach, which reduces the complex task of inducing student models to simple pattern matching. The strength of CBM lies in domain knowledge, represented in the form of state constraints, which contain the basic principles of a domain.

We have recently developed SQLT-Web, a Web-enabled version of SQL-Tutor [12]. The basic philosophy remains the same, but SQLT-Web is capable of dealing with multiple students. It has been developed in a programmable CL-HTTP Web server [8]. All pedagogical functions (student modelling, generation of feedback and selection of problems) are performed on the server side. The system communicates to the student's Web browser by generating HTML pages dynamically. The server stores all student models at the same place, thus allowing a student to access the system from any machine.

4 SmartEgg: an Animated Pedagogical Agent for SQLT-Web

SmartEgg is an animated pedagogical agent developed by our group for SQLT-Web. It is a cartoon-like character that gives feedback on student actions. As the agent was developed for a fully functional ITS, it was possible to have SQLT-Web to generate student models and appropriate feedback. Therefore, our agent has to perform much simpler tasks in comparison to agents discussed in the previous section.

The agent explains system's functions, provides feedback on student's actions and informs students about additional ways of getting help or background information. The project is still in its initial phases, and so far the agent presents all information in textual form. In the later phases, we plan to broaden the types of available feedback, including audio, and to extend agent's functionality.

I will look at your solution and tell you how good it is. I am pretty good at guessing how much detail you need, but you may also ask for a specific type of message directly.

Fig. 1: Introduction to SmartEgg

SmartEgg is implemented as a Java applet, by using the animation toolkit of Adele [5]. An appropriate character was developed (illustrated in figure 1), and thirty-eight frames were sketched to define the gestures. The animation toolkit swaps frames and uses techniques such as morphing to perform animations. Currently, there are 14 gestures that SmartEgg can perform, requiring two to five frames each. The library of gestures consists of presentation gestures (e.g. pointing), reactive gestures (used to present feedback) and idle-time gestures (e.g. waiting for a solution).

The required behaviours were developed next. Behaviour is a sequence of several gestures. The behaviours of our agent are pre-specified, and not dynamically generated. The SmartEggs's behaviour space consists of three main categories of behaviours: introductory, explanatory and congratulatory. *Introductory behaviours* accompany initial interactions, introducing the system's functions and describing levels of feedback to new users. Feedback messages from SQLT-Web are delivered to students using *explanatory behaviours*. For each type of feedback, there is a set of behaviours the pedagogical agent can perform. *Congratulatory behaviours* are an attempt to motivate users. SmartEgg congratulates the student when a correct answer is submitted and displays disappointment after an incorrect submission.

SmartEgg follows a predefined set of rules when selecting an appropriate behaviour from its behaviour space. This procedure is based on the student's interactions with SQLT-Web. Each distinct state (e.g. login, solving a problem, logout) is assigned three different behaviours to ensure variation in the agent's appearance.

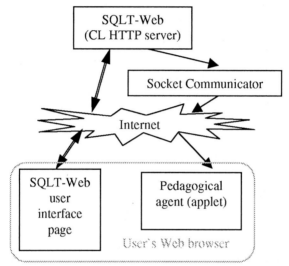

Fig. 2: Architecture of SQLT-Web with pedagogical agent

Finally, the applet persona was incorporated with SQLT-Web. The pedagogical agent's Java applet and the server are required to exchange messages in order for the agent to receive the feedback text and know the actions performed by the user. This was achieved by implementing a Java socket connection between the server and the applet. The agent consists of a dedicated thread of execution that waits to receive messages from the server. For each received message, the agent selects an appropriate behaviour by using the behaviour selection rules, which is then carried out by the animated persona. Figure 2 illustrates the architecture of SQLT-Web and the pedagogical agent.

5 Evaluation of SmartEgg

Our goal when developing SmartEgg was to increase the motivation of students by presenting feedback in an engaging way. We started with a hypothesis that the existence of a simple animated pedagogical agent would enhance students' perception of the system (as reflected in the students' subjective ratings of the system), and would support learning, resulting in better understanding and application of the underlying knowledge. Both gains would come from the motivational impact of the agent. Earlier studies [1,3,4,7] have shown that pedagogical agents have such effects on students; however, in these cases, the agents were much more sophisticated than SmartEgg. Here we set to determine whether even a very simple and constrained agent would enhance learning.

5.1 Experimental Setting

In October 1999 we performed an evaluation study, which involved second year students enrolled in an introductory database course. The students used the system in a 2-hour lab session and were randomly assigned to a version of the system with and without the agent (the agent and the control group respectively). SQLT-Web and SmartEgg conveyed exactly the same information to the students, as we wanted to determine the impact of the agent's existence on students' learning.

The study started with a pre-test, consisting of three multi-choice questions. After that, students interacted with the system. The problems and the order in which they were presented were not identical, as students were allowed to select problems by themselves, or let the system to select appropriate problems based on their student models. After working with the system, students completed a post-test consisting of three multi-choice questions of the same difficulty as the ones in the pre-test. They also filled a user questionnaire, the purpose of which was to evaluate the students' perception of SmartEgg and SQLT-Web.

5.2 System/Agent Assessment

The questionnaire consisted of 16 questions based on the Likert scale with five responses ranging from *very good* (5) to *very poor* (1). Students were also allowed to put free-form responses. Out of 26 students who participated in the study, 22 completed questionnaires.

The analysis of the responses revealed that the students liked SmartEgg. When asked to rate how much they enjoyed the system, the average rating for the agent group was 4.5 and for the control group 3.83 (Table 1). The majority (60%) of the agent group students chose option 5, compared to only 33% of the control group. The difference is significant (t=1.79, p=.03).

Both groups were equally comfortable with the interface, in the terms of how much time it took to learn it, and the ease of using the interface. The students were also asked to rate the amount learnt from the system. Both groups chose similar values, the means being 3.8 for the agent group and 3.92 for the control group. This result was expected as both groups received identical feedback.

However, when asked to rate the usefulness of feedback, the mean for the agent group was 4.8 and for the control group was 4.09. The majority (80%) of the students who used the agent rated the system as very useful (option 5), and only 42% of the control group chose the same option. As both versions of the system presented the same problem-based messages, it is clear from the findings that the students who used the agent found it easier to comprehend the feedback from the system. The difference in rating the usefulness of feedback is significant (t=2.15, p=.015). The written comments were also very positive.

	Mean		Standard deviation	
	Agent group	Control group	Agent group	Control group
Enjoyment rating	4.50	3.83	0.71	1.03
Time to learn interface (min)	11.00	10.83	10.22	9.25
Ease of using the interface	4.10	3.73	0.74	1.01
Amount learnt	3.80	3.92	0.79	0.67
Usefulness of feedback	4.80	4.09	0.42	1.04

Table 1: Mean responses for system/agent assessment

5.3 Learning Efficiency and Effectiveness

All actions students performed in the study were logged, and later used to analyse the effect of the agent on learning (Table 2). The students in the agent group spent 55.9 minutes interacting with the system, and the control group subjects averaged 49.6 minutes. As the agent group spent more time with the system, they attempted and solved more problems.

The agent group took fewer attempts to solve problems (30.9 compared to 32.56 attempt needed by the control group). In order to establish whether the knowledge level of the students may have affected this, we looked at the proportion of problems that were solved in the first attempt and found them to be similar for both the groups (5.1 for the agent group and 4.56 for the control group). This finding was consistent with our expectations, as the students did not get any direct help from the system before submitting initial solutions. Therefore, the students in both groups have comparable knowledge of SQL (this is also justified by the pre-test performance, discussed in section 5.4). Furthermore, students in both groups required a similar number of attempts to solve problems that could not be solved in the first attempt (when problem-specific hints were provided). The number of problems successfully solved per unit of time was similar for both groups. Students who used the agent recorded on average 0.27 correct answers per minute and the control group managed 0.22.

	Mean		Standard dev.	
	Agent	Control	Agent	Control
Total interaction time (mins)	55.90	49.63	17.30	26.70
No. of attempted problems	14.00	11.56	5.27	6.49
No. of solved problems	11.60	10.94	4.35	6.36
Total no. of attempts to solve the problems	30.90	32.56	14.13	23.97
Problems solved in the first attempt	5.10	4.56	2.60	2.73
Problems solved per time (problem/min)	0.22	0.27	0.07	0.21
Attempts to solve problems that could not be solved in the first attempt (attempts/problem)	2.90	2.91	1.61	1.34

Table 2: Means of interaction analyses

The average number of attempts taken to solve problems that were not solved in the first attempt was very similar: the agent group required 2.90 and the control group 2.91 attempts. As both versions of the system offered the same feedback, students from both groups required the same number of attempts.

In order to establish the effect of the agent on the student's learning over time, we plotted the average number of attempts taken to solve the ith problem for each group. To reduce individual bias, the problems solved by less than 50% of the participating population were discarded (Fig. 3). Although no substantial trends can be seen, the agent group required 0.2 fewer attempts to solve each problem than the control group.

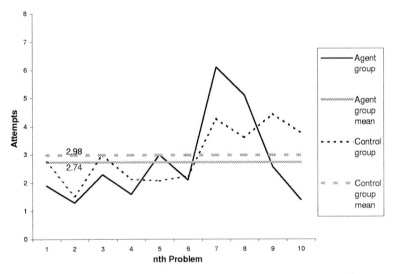

Fig. 3: The mean number of attempts taken to solve the ith problem

5.4 Pre- and Post-Tests

Pre- and post-tests consisted of three multi-choice questions each, of comparable complexity. The marks allocated to questions were 1, 5 and 1 respectively. Nine out of ten students in the agent group and fourteen out of sixteen in the control group submitted valid pre-tests, the results of which are given in Table 3. The mean scores in the pre-test for the two groups are very close, suggesting that the two groups contained students of comparable knowledge.

Although participation in the pre-test was high, only four students from both groups sat the post-test[1]. Three of these students had used the agent, and a definite increase in their performance and confidence can be seen from the results of the post-test (4.33 and 2 for the agent and control group respectively). However, as the numbers involved are small, unbiased comparisons on the mean performances cannot be made.

Question	Agent group	Control group
1	0.33	0.14
2	2.56	2.50
3	0.67	0.71
Total	3.56	3.36

Table 3. Means for the pre-test

6 Discussion and Future Work

This paper presented SmartEgg, an animated pedagogical agent for SQLT-Web, an intelligent SQL tutor on the Web. Previous works on pedagogical agents have shown that they significantly increase motivation, resulting in longer interaction times and higher quality of learning.

In contrast to other discussed pedagogical agents, which required large teams of animators, pedagogues and programmers, SmartEgg was developed by a team of two people in a short period of time. Our initial hypothesis was that even a very simple agent would reveal the persona effect. In order to test the hypothesis, we performed an initial evaluation study in which two groups of students interacted with SQLT-Web and SmartEgg in a two-hour session. The students sat pre- and post-tests; all their actions were logged and finally the students filled a user questionnaire. Various analyses of the data collected in the evaluation study were performed, which showed a significant increase of motivation in the agent group. The students who interacted with the agent spent more time with the system, and solved more problems in fewer attempts than the students in the control group. We acknowledge the low number of students involved in the study, and will perform a much wider study to confirm the results from this initial evaluation.

---

[1] Some students did not log off properly, and have not even seen the post-test, which was administered on a separate Web page.

At the moment, SmartEgg provides textual information only. We plan to add verbal comments in the next phase, as it has been shown that more expressive agents are perceived to have greater utility and clarity [6]. Also, we plan to develop dynamic generation of behaviours. The behaviours would depend on the context of the feedback message, thus enabling SmartEgg to make a higher impact on students. Another future plan includes using the agent to provide support for self-explanation. This support would be in terms of dialogues with a student, where the agent prompts questions to guide the student.

Acknowledgements

This work was supported partly by the University of Canterbury research grant U6242. We are grateful to the Centre for Advanced Research in Technology for Education (CARTE) for providing the source code for the animation toolkit of Adele. We appreciated the stimulating environment in ICTG and the comments of its members. Our thanks go to Nenad Govedarovic for the initial drawing of SmartEgg, and the COSC205 students for their time and suggestions.

References

1. Alpert, S., Singley, M., Fairweather, P. Deploying Intelligent Tutors on the Web: an Architecture and an Example. *Int. J. AI in Education*, 10 (1999) 183-197.
2. Andre, E., Rist, T., Muller, J. WebPersona: a Life-Like Presentation Agent for Educational Applications on the WWW (1997). P. Brusilovsky, K. Nakabayashi, S. Ritter (eds) *Proceedings of workshop on Intelligent Educational Systems on the WWW, AI-ED'97*.
3. Andre, E., Rist, T., Muller, J. WebPersona: a Life-Like Presentation Agent for the World-Wide Web. (1998). *Knowledge-based Systems*, 11(1) (1998), 25-36.
4. Johnson, W.L. Pedagogical Agents. Invited paper, *ICCE'99* (1999).
5. Johnson, W.L., Shaw, E., Ganeshan, R. Pedagogical Agents on the Web. *Workshop on WWW-based Tutoring, ITS'98* (1998).
6. Lester, J., Converse, S., Kahler, S., Barlow, S., Stone, B., Bhogal, R. The persona effect: Affective Impact of Animated Pedagogical Agents, *Proc. CHI'97* (1997) 359-366.
7. Lester, J., Towns, S., FitzGerald, P. Achieving Affective Impact: Visual Emotive Communication in Lifelike Pedagogical Agents (1999). *Int. J. AI in Education.* 10 (1999).
8. Mallery, J.C. A Common LISP Hypermedia Server. *Proc. 1st Int. Conf. On the World Wide Web* (1994).
9. Mitrovic, A. A Knowledge-Based Teaching System for SQL. *Proc. ED-MEDIA'98*, T. Ottmann, I. Tomek (eds.) (1998) 1027-1032.
10. Mitrovic, A. Experiences in Implementing Constraint-Based Modeling in SQL-Tutor. *Proc. ITS'98* (1998) 414-423.
11. Mitrovic, A., Ohlsson, S. Evaluation of a constraint-based tutor for a database language, *Int. J. Artificial Intelligence in Education*, 10 (3-4) (1999).
12. Mitrovic, A., Hausler, K. An Intelligent SQL Tutor on the Web. Tech. Report TR-COSC 04/99, Computer Science Department, University of Canterbury (1999).
13. Ohlsson, S.: Constraint--based Student Modeling. In: Greer, J.E., McCalla, G.I. (eds.): *Student Modeling: the Key to Individualized Knowledge--based Instruction*. NATO ASI Series, Vol. 125. Springer-Verlag, (1994) 167-189.

Multi-Agent Negotiation to Support an Economy for Online Help and Tutoring

Chhaya Mudgal and Julita Vassileva

University of Saskatchewan, Computer Science Department,
Saskatoon, Saskatchewan S7N 5A9, Canada
{chm906, jiv}@cs.usask.ca

Abstract. We have designed a computational architecture for a "learning economy" based on personal software agents who represent users in a virtual society and assist them in finding learning resources and peer help. In order to motivate users to participate, to share their experience, offer help and create on-line learning resources, payment is involved in virtual currency and the agents negotiate for services and prices, as in a free market. We model negotiation among personal agents by means of an influence diagram, a decision theoretic tool. In addition, agents create models of their opponents[1] during negotiation to predict opponent actions. Simulations and an experiment have been carried out to test the effectiveness of the negotiation mechanism and learning economy.

1. Introduction

The Internet provides a variety of options for on-line training, tutoring and help, from access to FAQs and multi-media teaching materials, to more interactive forms like discussion forums, on-line tutoring, collaboration or peer-help sessions. The creation of high quality teaching materials is associated with significant costs, which usually have to be paid by those who benefit directly from them, i.e. the learners. There is a potential for a rapidly growing market of on-line training and there has been a significant increase in the number of commercial vendors in this area. A number of universities are already offering on-line degrees, and charge significant fees (still, somewhat lower than the costs of traditional university education).

However, still the most on-line training materials appear informally; collaboration and help happen spontaneously. University lecturers post their course outlines, lecture notes and course readings / materials on-line as an additional source of information for their students. People facing problems in a certain area search for a newsgroup related to the area and send their question there, hoping for someone competent to answer it. People ask their colleagues, personal acquaintances and friends for help. This is a huge pool of knowledge and expertise, which is not formally valued in organizational or commercial form and which is used only randomly, occasionally and scarcely. Our goal is to provide an infrastructure that motivates the usage of this

---

[1] We will use the word "opponent" to denote the other agent in negotiation, though we don't
imply necessarily an adversary or strongly competitive negotiation

knowledge. We hope to achieve this by creating a marketplace for learning resources, i.e. an e-commerce environment for trading with intangible goods (advice, help, teaching or tutoring). This economy encompasses information exchange, which happens both asynchronously and asynchronously. For example, the use of on-line resources like web-pages, FAQ entries, or the use of e-mail to ask a question and provide advice can be viewed as asynchronous information exchange, since they don't imply that both sides (the learner and the helper/ tutor are present and involved in interaction in the same time). Synchronous information exchange involves both sides in a real-time, live contact -- for example, in an on-line help session via some chat tool, telephone, or collaboration environment.

The basic assumption in the design of a learning economy model is that resources like effort and time spent to provide help or to create teaching material have inherent costs. To take them into account, these resources should be made tradable. Thus paying the helper/tutor may motivate a user to get online and help another user. In this paper we focus on a synchronous information exchange since it is related with more immediate motivational need. However, the approach encompasses asynchronous information exchange too.

Maes et al. [6] proposed to help consumers in e-commerce applications in the search of goods, price comparison, negotiation or bidding by providing them with personal agents / assistants. We believe that this is even more important in trading with knowledge resources, since users have to be able to concentrate on their work or learning rather than thinking about how to get a better deal. The free market infrastructure for learning resources that we propose is based on personal agents representing individual users in a distributed (web-based) learning environment. The personal agents form an economic society designed to motivate the students who are knowledgeable to help their fellow students by receiving payment in a cyber pseudo currency.

2. Multi-Agent Based Learning Economy

I-Help provides a student of a university course with a matchmaking service to find a peer-student online who can help with a given question/problem [3,4]. The most recent implementation of I-Help is based on Multi AGent Architecture for Adaptive Learning Environment (MAGALE[2]), described in [12], which ensures an economic infrastructure for trading with help. MAGALE is a society of agents trading with knowledge-resources. The users who possess knowledge resources become sellers and the users who seek for help or advice, tutoring or teaching materials on a specific topic become buyers. The buyer is ready to pay some amount of virtual (or real) currency in order to achieve the goal of getting knowledge while the seller of the resources is ready to give advice in exchange for money, thus achieving the goal of accumulating currency. Like any market system, in MAGALE (and respectively in its implementation, I-Help) the price of a good depends on the demand and the importance of that good to the buyer. A detailed description about the requirements for the economic model in MAGALE can be found in [5].

---

[2] The name MAGALE is introduced to distinguish the more general architecture from I-Help, which is an application

Various pricing models have been incorporated in e-commerce systems. The most common are "post and charge", "pay-per-use" and "auction". "Post and charge" is applied in I-Help for paying for asynchronous resources, such as web materials, FAQ items, or answers in a discussion forum. One can post an answer to a question in I-Help's discussion forum and people who read it would be charged to pay a certain price. A similar model is implemented in the Marketplace for Java Technology Support [10], a community where people buy and sell technical support (the forum is operated by HotDispatch, Inc).

The "pay-per-use" model implies paying a certain rate for a unit of usage time of the resource, for example paying for a telephone call. This can be an appropriate mechanism when the duration of the service is connected with costs and it can not be fixed or agreed upon in advance. This is an appropriate model of payment for the various forms of synchronous knowledge transfer that are supported in I-Help (chat, phone-communication or collaboration). The duration of a help session implies costs to the helper, who is asked to interrupt some current task. It is hard to say in advance what duration will be required since it depends on the question, on the ability of the helper to explain, and on the helpee's ability to understand. Therefore, it is appropriate to deploy this payment method in synchronous help allowing both sides to interrupt the session when they feel that it doesn't make sense for them to continue.

The "auction" model, where several agents are bidding for goods [6] is appropriate when there is a big demand and short supply. It allows the resource to be allocated to a consumer who values it most. This could be an appropriate model in the case where synchronous information exchange (e.g. help request) is required by many users and there are few knowledgeable users on-line to provide help. This model has not been applied in I-Help yet, but it could be.

The auction model is, in fact, a way of collective negotiation of the price for a resource, where the main factors that determine the price are the demand and the supply. The other two models don't imply per se a mechanism for determining the price - they assume that there is a price that is agreed upon in advance. The price can be established centrally by a component that analyses the state of the market at the moment or it can be negotiated between the agents who participate in the deal [13]. The advantage of negotiation is that it allows for including multiple factors (preferences, priorities) in the price calculation depending on the specific buyer and seller, i.e. the agents can compromise some of their preferences and settle on the most suitable price for both parties.

The price of a learning resource depends on many factors. Of course, the supply and demand (e.g. how many competent helpers are currently on line and how many people are requesting help) play a major role. However, many other factors can play a role, for example, whether the help is urgently needed or not, whether the potential helper minds being interrupted, whether the helper and the person asking for help (the helpee) are already involved in a social relationship. For example, the helper might not want to be interrupted in principle, but would make an exception for a friend. Therefore, a negotiation mechanism is appropriate as a way to dynamically determine the price, especially for synchronous information exchange.

We have proposed a negotiation mechanism for the personal agents in MAGALE that determines the price for synchronous information exchange (e.g. on-line peer help in I-Help) using the "pay per use" payment model. This mechanism mimics the process of human negotiation in a buyer-seller situation, by representing it as an iterative decision making process. It also allows the negotiator to anticipate the opposing party's actions and takes into account the personal risk attitude towards money of the user represented by the agent. The purpose of negotiation is to find the best deal for the user independently on whether the user requires help or is playing the role of a helper.

3. Negotiation Mechanism

The MAGALE architecture underlying I-Help consists of personal agents representing the users/ students. The agents maintain user models containing information about the user's goals, knowledge and preferences [3]. When the students in the class need help their agents contact a centralized matchmaker who knows which users (i.e. personal agents) are online. These agents negotiate with each other about the price (the payment rate per unit of help time) and when a deal is made they inform their user. If the user agrees to help, a chat window opens for both sides and the help session starts. The agents make decisions on behalf of their users about the price to offer to strike a better deal. During negotiation each agent decides how to increase or decrease the price depending on the user's preferences, such as the urgency of the user's current work, importance of money to the user and the user's risk behavior.

3.1 Decision Theoretic Approach to Negotiation

We have developed a novel negotiation approach, using influence diagrams, which is based on decision theory and on modelling the opponent agent. Negotiation in a buyer-seller context can be viewed an iterative process in which the agents make offers and counteroffers based on their preferences. Modelling negotiation as iterative decision making supports the dynamics of the situation, e.g. it allows the negotiating agents to change their preferences and their beliefs about the likelihood of uncertainties.

In open multi-agent systems (i.e. the systems in which new agents dynamically enter or leave) there is a high degree of uncertainty about the current state of the market (i.e. the demand/supply ratio), or the preferences of the opponent. An influence diagram is a graphical structure for modelling uncertain variables and decisions. It explicitly shows probabilistic dependence and flow of information [8].

An influence diagram is a directed acyclic graph with three different kinds of nodes: decision nodes, chance nodes and a value node. These nodes are represented as squares, circles, and diamonds respectively. The decision nodes represent choices available to the user, the chance nodes carry probabilistic information corresponding to the uncertainty about the environment and the opponent, and the value node represents the utility, which the agent wants to maximize. Arcs into random variables indicate probabilistic dependence and the arcs into a decision node specify the information available at the time of making decision. Evaluating the diagram gives an optimal solution for the problem. Influence diagrams provide a means to capture the nature of the problem, identify important objectives, and generate alternative courses of action. A decision model based on an influence diagram can deal with multiple objectives and allows tradeoffs of benefits in one area against costs in another. A good introduction to influence diagrams and methods to evaluate them can be found in [8,9].

The negotiation protocol is based on decision theory and is a straightforward iterative process of making offers and counteroffers. So, during negotiation the agent can be repeatedly in state *Offer* or *Counter-offer*. The final state will be *Accept* or *Reject*. Similar to [13], we use "negotiation strategy" to denote the actions an agent takes in every iteration depending on its preference model. In our model once the agent is in a final state, it cannot retreat back from it. The negotiation mechanism takes into account the preferences of the user, which usually depend in the domain of the negotiation context. The preferences include:

- the *maximum price* of the buyer (i.e. how much the helpee is willing to pay),
- the *urgency* of the current goal (to get help for the buyer, or the seller's current task, which she has to interrupt in order to help),
- the *importance* that either agent attaches to *money*, and
- the user's risk behavior (a risk-averse or a risk-seeking person).

We have incorporated utility to model the way in which the decision-maker values different outcomes and objectives. Each agent in I-Help can be a buyer or seller of help. The utility for the buyer (helpee) and the seller (helper) for the actions *accept*, *reject* and *counter-propose* vary according to their risk behavior.

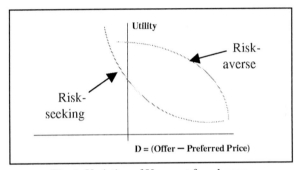

Fig. 1. Variation of U_accept for a **buyer**

It is important to note that money importance and risk-behavior are two different entities and they are set by the user in the user preference model. The risk behavior of the user instructs the personal agent about the increase or decrease in the price offers to be made. A risk-seeking person will try to counter-propose an offer rather than accepting. A risk-averse person will accept whatever minimum price he/she is offered and will refrain from counter proposing in fear of losing. The agent calculates the utility values of the action alternatives that it has at any time during negotiation. The utility of actions depends upon the money that the seller gets and the buyer has to pay. It also varies with the specified risk behavior of the user. For instance, as shown in the Figure 1 the utility of accepting an offer for a risk-averse buyer increases much slower as the difference between the offered price and the preferred price decreases. That means that as long as the offer price of the seller comes closer to the preferred price of the agent (buyer), it will be more willing to accept the offer, since there is not significant growth in utility if it continues to counter-propose. For a risk-seeking agent, the utility continues to grow fast in this case, since it is willing to take the risk of counter-proposing, hoping to get a price even lower than the preferred price.

Risk behavior also affects the increment and the decrement of the buyer and the seller. For a risk-averse buyer, if the urgency of the current task is very high and the importance of money is also high, it will start by offering a price, which is near to the maximum price it is willing to pay. A risk-seeking buyer will start from a very low price and will try to get the lowest price possible. For a risk-seeking seller the utility of accepting an offer increases if it gets more money than its minimum price. The functions the agents use to increase or decrease their offers and counteroffers as a buyer and as a seller are defined as follows:

For Buyers
If max_price > std_price then
    Offered price := std_price – Δ
Else
    Offered price := max_price – Δ

For Sellers
If min_price > std_price then
    Offered price := min_price + Δ
Else
    Offered price := std_price + Δ

where std_price is the market price provided by the matchmaker. It is calculated based on the current situation of the market of help on this topic and on the difficulty of the topic, thus providing some measure for the actual worth of the resource. For both the buyer and the seller the values of Δ should not exceed their preferred prices, R. Δ is determined as follows (x is the offered price):

For Buyers
If urgency = very urgent then
If risk_behavior = risk seeking then
    $\Delta := 1 - e^{-x/R}$ $x > R$
If risk_behavior = risk averse then
    $\Delta := 1 - e^{-x/R}$ $x < R$

For Sellers
If urgency = very urgent then
If risk_behavior = risk seeking then
    $\Delta := \sqrt{min\_price}$
If risk_behavior == risk averse then
    $\Delta := \log(min\_price)$

We use an influence diagram that has a conditional node representing the uncertainty about the other party (see Figure 2). The outcomes of this node are the probabilities that an opponent can be in any of the states *accept*, *reject* and *counter-offer*, because at every step the agents have to choose between these three actions. They do so by calculating the maximum expected utility for the actions, which are represented as the possible choices for the decision node in the influence diagram. In any practical application of negotiation there are multiple objectives involved and there is a tradeoff between one over the other. Before the decision is made the factors that are already known to affect the decision (deterministic nodes) are taken into account as they affect the actions to be made. The node corresponding to the opponent's action can be considered conditional since nothing is known about the opponent at the beginning of the negotiation. We can either treat the outcomes of the opponent node as equally likely or replace the equal likelihood of the opponent's actions with the outcome of a model of the opponent using a probabilistic influence diagram.

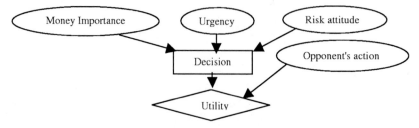

Fig. 2. Influence Diagram for the decision model

3.2. Modeling the Opponent

One of the basic ingredients of a negotiation process is the correct anticipation of the other side's actions. In a dynamic environment e.g. in a market place where the situation is changing all the time and new buyers and sellers keep on entering and leaving the system, it is very costly for agents to create and maintain models of the other participants in the environment. In the I-Help system the environment is dynamic and since the agents represent real users, it is hard to predict the actions of the opponent agent on the basis of its past behavior (since the user's preferences which participate in the agent's negotiation strategy can change in the meantime). It is unlikely that the user will be willing to share preferences with other users (or their agents) before or during the negotiation process. However, it is useful for an agent to model the opponent's behavior during the negotiation session, since this can help predict the opponent's reaction. It is important to note that we are not doing recursive or nested agent modeling. Agents initially have no knowledge about each other. After the first round of offers made the agent starts using the opponent's response to infer a model of the opponent's preferences and to predict the possible reaction of the opponent to the counteroffer that the agent is about to make.

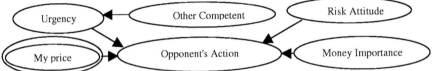

Fig. 3. Probabilistic influence diagram representing the opponent's model

An appropriate tool for this purpose is a probabilistic influence diagram. Figure 3 shows the model of the opponent represented as a probabilistic influence diagram. The oval nodes are conditional and the double-circled node is deterministic. The conditional probability distribution of the conditional nodes over the outcomes is assessed on the basis of the first offer. The probability distribution for the "Opponent's action" node can be calculated by performing reductions over the nodes. For instance, performing arc reversal from the "Money Importance" node to the "Opponent's Action" node makes "Money Importance" a barren node. Hence, it can be removed from the diagram and a new conditional probability distribution is calculated. Conditional predecessors of the nodes (if any) are inherited. In a similar way the diagram can again be simplified by using arc reversal and barren node removal, which finally gives the probability distribution for the Opponent's Action node. If the next move of the opponent does not match with the predicted action, Bayes' update rule is used to update the probability distributions. More information about probabilistic influence diagrams can be found in [9].

4. Evaluation

First we evaluated the proposed negotiation mechanism in an environment, where agents represented only themselves, i.e. no real users were involved. In this way we were free to vary the negotiation parameters and generate a lot of experimental data.

The purpose was to evaluate the results of the negotiation method only. The results [7] showed that the proposed negotiation approach achieves a better deal for the agent that uses it compared to other negotiation approaches, for example, one based on step-wise decreasing (for seller) / increasing (for buyer) of the offered price. We carried out a further experiment, which showed that if the agents are bluffing, i.e. offering help at much higher price than their preferred price, the acceptance percentage of their negotiation is low. Agents who are more reasonable get a good deal maximum number of times.

In order to evaluate the principal usefulness of an economic model to motivate users a version of I-Help was developed, using the simple rate increment / decrement negotiation method that was the basis for comparison in the simulation-based evaluation. This system was applied in a 3rd year undergraduate computer science class at the University of Saskatchewan. In the end we "cashed" the accumulated virtual currency in small souvenirs, i.e. the people who have helped most received rewards. Initially there seemed to be an enthusiasm among the students about the system, however, consequently there turned out to be very little usage, which didn't allow us to draw any conclusions about the efficiency of the economy or the planned control measures. There were several different reasons for this failure, which can be grouped in two classes: social and technical. Perhaps one of the "social" reasons was the inadequacy of the reward (maybe students are more motivated by marks?). Another reason might have been the quality of help received from peers. Along with the personal agent-based peer help system, the class was using a discussion forum, in which students participated much more actively. Informal interviews showed that students preferred to look in the forum since the instructor was monitoring it and was replying to the more important / interesting questions. Presumably the quality of answers / hints received from the instructor was higher than those provided by peers. A third reason is that good students seemed to be more motivated to post answers on the publicly visible place. In this way they could impress their classmates and the instructor (which could potentially help them get a better mark in the end). Obviously, an ongoing social recognition is an important factor, which has to be taken into account.

There were also technical reasons: the most important one was the slow response time of the system, especially off campus, due to slow network connections during this period. It must be pointed out that the slow response was completely due to reasons independent on the implementation of the system or the negotiation mechanism. A second reason might have been an inappropriate interface design, which made interaction with the personal agent somewhat cumbersome. A third reason might have been fact that the 3rd year students knew each other very well, had established multiple ways of interacting with one another in class and in the labs and hence they did not find any need to login to the system to get help. The reasons for us choosing this class were purely pragmatic: the implementation required the least adaptation effort, because the domain representation and student modelling components were already developed.

Generally, the experiment gave some answers and opened many new questions to investigate. Our inability to obtain strong (whether positive or negative) evaluation results taught us a good lesson: that introducing such advanced mechanisms makes sense only when the basic technology works reliably (with respect to network speed, response time and user interface design). Another lesson we learned is that the right user group and social situation should be selected very carefully before trying to test and evaluate such system. We hope that if the proposed market economy model is utilized in distance learning or a very large first year class where students don't know each other and have no other incentives to be helpful to each other, it will prove to be successful. Currently we are testing an improved version of the system in a large introductory computer science class; the data available so far shows that the system is being used vigorously.

This experiment also shows that there are sometimes unexpected difficulties in testing such complex distributed multi-agent systems, due to very basic "low-level" problems, completely unrelated to the proposed technology. It seems that new evaluation methodologies are needed which would allow evaluation without the need of developing of stable nearly ready for marketing system.

5. Related Work and Discussion

To our best knowledge, there is currently no other work in the area of market economy based distributed systems that support human learning. A learning economy has been proposed by Boyd [1], but it was based on the barter (exchange) model and has not been implemented. IBM has proposed an economy for trading information resources [2], however this proposal assumes that the resources are ready documents and it focuses mainly on pricing models that are appropriate for them. The most closely related work to ours is in the field of multi-agent negotiation in e-commerce [13]. In [13] negotiation and modelling the opponent is realized by using a Bayesian network where the agents have store the relevant information about each other, while in our approach negotiation is modelled as an influence diagram i.e. as a decision process. In addition, our agents do not share information about each other's priorities and model each other to predict the actions of the opponents and thus to optimize their decisions.

Our approach opens some interesting research avenues in student / user modelling to be pursued further. There are multiple models about each user in the system. They are created by different agents, contain different (but also sometimes overlapping) information, are created under different circumstances. More research on these issues will help to find the benefits and pitfalls of distributed user-modelling [11].

More research is needed on analyzing the global behavior of a system based on individual negotiations between agents, like ours. Especially in an educational system, it is very important to predict and be able to control the overall behaviour that emerges as a result of interaction of personal agents and users. We have proposed an economic model [5], which provides a variety of options to control the economy from outside to ensure desirable distribution of learning resources. However, it will be hard to design an experiment to test the benefit of these measures, since the system is very complex - so many factors come to play, that it is hard to attribute success or failure even to a group of factors. New methods, possibly borrowed from sociology, will be needed to evaluate such systems.

6. Conclusion

We have developed an original approach for negotiation among personal agents based on decision theory and influence diagrams. By use of probabilistic influence diagrams agents are able to model their opponents during the negotiation process and thus to predict better their actions. Experiments on a simulation showed the effectiveness of the proposed negotiation mechanism [7]. An attempt has been made to evaluate the benefits of the proposed economy as a basis for the peer help environment I-Help in a third level university class. Our experience showed that such experiments have to be designed very carefully to keep complexity and technical issues under control and in the same time to be able to answer some interesting research questions. Probably new evaluation methodologies for distributed agent based systems on the Internet will be necessary.

Acknowledgement. This research has been partially funded by the Telelearning Network of Centers of Excellence under Project No. 6.28.

References

1. Boyd, G. 1997. Providing Real Learning with Virtual Currency. Proceedings of the International Conference on Distance Education, Penn State University, June 1997.
2. Greenwald A.and J.Kephart 1999. Shopbots and Pricebots. in Proceedings of IJCAI '99. Stockholm, on line at: http://www.research.ibm.com/infoecon/researchpapers.html
3. Greer, J., McCalla, G., Cook, J., Collins, J., Kumar, V., Bishop, A. and Vassileva, J. (1998) The Intelligent HelpDesk: Supporting Peer Help in a University Course, Proceedings ITS'98, 494-503.
4. Greer, J. McCalla G., Collins J., Kumar V., Meagher P., Vassileva J. (1998) Supporting Peer Help and Collaboration in Distributed Workplace Environments, *International Journal of AI and Education*, 9.
5. Kostuik, K., Vassileva, J. Free Market Control for a Multi-Agent Based Peer Help Environment. Workshop on Agents for Electronic Commerce and Managing the Internet-Enabled Supply Chain, Seattle, Autonomous Agents' 99, Washington, May 1, 1999
6. Maes, P., Guttman, R., Moukas, G., Agents that Buy and Sell. Communications of the ACM. March 1999- Volume 42, Number 3, 81-83.
7. Mudgal, C., Vassileva, J. (to appear) An Influence Diagram Model for Multi-Agent Negotiation, in Proceedings of International Conference on Multi-Agent Systems, ICMAS'2000, 7-12 July 2000, Boston, MA.
8. Shachter, R., Evaluating Influence Diagrams. Operations Research. Volume 34, No 36, 1986, 871-882.
9. Shachter, R., Probabilistic inference and influence diagrams. Operations Research. Volume 36, No.4, 1988, 589-604.
10. Marketplace for JavaTM Technology Support. available on-line at http://www.hotdispatch.com/sun
11. McCalla, J, Vassileva, J., Greer, J., Bull, S. (2000) Active Learner Modelling, this volume.
12. Vassileva J., Greer J., McCalla G., Deters R., Zapata D., Mudgal C., Grant S. A Multi-Agent Approach to the Design of Peer-Help Environments, in Proceedings of AIED'99, 1999, 38-45.
13. Zheng, D., and Sycara, K. Benefits of Learning in Negotiation in Proceedings of Fifteenth National Conference on Artificial Intelligence, 1997. 36-41.

The Collaborative System with Situated Agents for Activating Observation Learning

Toshio OKAMOTO and Toshinobu KASAI

Graduate School of Information Systems, The University of Electro-Communications,
1-5-1 Chofugaoka, Chofu, Tokyo, 182-8585, JAPAN
okamoto@ai.is.uec.ac.jp

Abstract. This study focuses on modality of externalized knowledge-acquisition on problem solving via "Learning by Observing" and "Learning by Teaching/Explaining". Among the learning effects expected by collaborative learning, we can suppose meta-cognition/distributed cognition such as reflective thinking, self-monitoring and so on. We propose the architecture of the intelligent collaborative system with situated agents for activating observation learning, which is a kind of virtual collaborative learning environment. The situated agents are embedded in this system, who have the different roles to make a real student activate observation learning. Each of the situated agents behaves dynamically based on the "Student Model" which represents the understanding state of a real student, and "Transforming Process Model" which stands for the converting process from internal state into external state for a level of acquired knowledge. A real student is expected to acquire any meta-knowledge via the interaction among situated agents in the collaborative learning environment. A facilitator agent who is a kind of a situated agent manages these Models and controls the other situated agents' behavior. Moreover, it can identifies a real student's bugs/faults occurred in the converting operations.

1 Introduction

Nowadays, the studies of collaborative learning environments with plural learners such as CSCL(Computer Supported Collaborative Learning) as well as group learning are rapidly increasing, taking influence of the new idea, that is "Learning is caused by interactions among several learners and the outside world, and they are inseparable."[3, 4]. In such a collaborative learning environment, two kinds of learning effects are expected. One is knowledge understanding by reflection that is invoked/facilitated by giving explanation to the other learners. Another is to modify/adapt self-knowledge and thinking ways by observing the other learners' behavior. This learning modality is called "Learning by Teaching" and "Learning by Observing", and a higher cognitive ability is expected as self-monitoring/evaluation for understanding objects there. More or less, many studies that aim to facilitate these learning effects are being done pervasively.

The purpose of this study is to realize the situated agents system for activating observation learning with the function for supporting an interaction among learners, taking into consideration of a situated context in a collaborative learning environment. So far, we have developed the CALE(Companion Agent Learning Environment)based on the framework of a multi-agent architecture in a collaborative learning environment[5]. With this CALE project (embedded one computer companion agent), we expected the acquisition of deeper knowledge with reflective thinking by observation learning[1, 2]. In this study, we have developed newly "CollaboRative sYstem with SiTuated Agents for activating observation Learning (CRYSTAL)". So, we introduce the theoretical mechanism of this system here. A companion agent is also called a situated agent because of emphasizing situated cognition in this system.

2 What Is a Situated Agent?

The process of interaction includes complicated learning modality such as reflective thinking, self-monitoring and so on. Especially, the action of "observing" needs sensitive awareness/interests for the other companions' behavior/thinking ways as well as understanding a problem to solve/discuss along the situated context. So, the collaborative learning is necessarily based on situated context and it requires knowledge-sharing in order to achieve the common goal. In this sense, we define a companion agent as a situated agent. In this study, we try to build the interactive learning environment accompanied with three pseudo-companion agents who play the different roles in terms of the situated context, that is a virtual group learning.

3 The Outlines of "Crystal"

Here, we describe the system configuration of CRYSTAL firstly. We show its conceptual figure in Fig. 1. In CRYSTAL, a *novice agent* and an *advanced agent*, co-existing as situated agents share a learning space and study collaboratively with a *real learner*. The novice agent has problem-solving knowledge which is poorer than a real learner's one. This agent can behave like a tutee, as a situated one which owns the activating strategy to make a real learner acquire problem-solving knowledge through "learning by teaching". Along such a strategy, this agent tries to make a real learner notify problem-solving knowledge which has not been acquired yet and make him explain.

The *advanced agent* has problem-solving knowledge which is smarter than a real learner's one. This agent can behave like a tutor, as a situated one which owns the activating strategy to make a real learner acquire problem-solving knowledge through "Learning by Observing". Along this strategy, this agent tries to make a real learner observe his right solving way of problem. It provides so-called modeling process for a real learner.

These situated agents decide the action plan adaptively according to each activating strategy based on two kinds of models. One is "Student Model" which represents the understanding state of a real learner. Another is "Transforming Process Model" which represents the converting process from internal state into external state for a level of acquired knowledge. It stands for the quality of applied rules to evaluate a certain understanding level on which a real learner

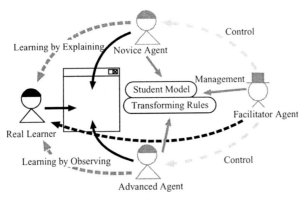

Fig. 1. The conceptual figure of CRYSTAL

is expected to achieve. The *facilitator agent* controls those situated agents' behavior by managing these models. The *facilitator agent* has also the role of a supervisor and a coordinator so as to make correction of a learning flow in the situation where each of the situated agents can't decide any action plan. Furthermore, a facilitator agent has the function to detect bugs/faults in a real learner's converting rules by Transforming Process Model. Then he points out it to him.

4 How to Decide an Action Plan for Each Situated Agent

Each situated agent has the function to decide an action-plan in reference to five kinds of information-sources, which consist of 1) Student Model, 2) Transforming Process Model, 3) Learning Effect Value of a real learner, 4) Consistency Value of Action for each situated agent and 5) Mental Load Value of a real learner.

4.1 Representation of Learning State

EXPLICIT KNOWLEDGE AND IMPLICIT KNOWLEDGE. We introduce both concepts of *Explicit Knowledge* and *Implicit Knowledge* required to represent "Student Model" and "Transforming Process Model".

We define *Explicit Knowledge* and *Implicit Knowledge* as follows. *Explicit Knowledge* is "Knowledge which a real learner is aware of at present", and *Implicit Knowledge* is "Knowledge that a real learner is not aware of at present, but can be made aware of by chance". Namely, the first one is a kind of meta-knowledge which a learner can apply for solving a given problem. On the other hand, the second one is the just observed knowledge which is expressed or explained in problem solving by another person. Therefore anyone can not warrant whether this knowledge is useful or not for a real learner.

In Fig. 2, we show the relationship between *Explicit Knowledge* and *Implicit Knowledge* used in this study, which is the philosophical root of our system.

When a real learner observes any behavior of the others in a collaborative learning environment, new knowledge is added to his/her Mental State as *Implicit Knowledge* in this system. If he could utilize this knowledge correctly for

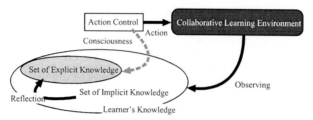

Fig. 2. Explicit Knowledge and Implicit Knowledge

solving a problem, then the system regards he could acquire *Explicit knowledge*, because he could succeed in converting from *Implicit Knowledge* into *Explicit Knowledge* through any mental operations in his brain. However, if he could not utilize this knowledge correctly, then the system regards he failed to acquire *Explicit Knowledge*. The mental converting operation with which the learner converts *Implicit Knowledge* into *Explicit Knowledge* is called "externalized reflection". If this knowledge is alive/conscious knowledge for problem-solving, the conversion process from *Implicit Knowledge* into *Explicit Knowledge* is called transforming of knowledge with symbolization/verbalization.

THE REPRESENTATION SCHEME OF THE STUDENT MODEL.

We try to represent *Explicit Knowledge* and *Implicit Knowledge* by introducing nine modal predicates. Also, we try to represent a learner's understanding state by introducing these modal predicates. We will explain the representation scheme for each as followings.

1. Explicit Knowledge
   - (Negative) Knowledge to Explain $(Neg_-)ExS_A(Knowledge)$
     This means ; an Agent A (doesn't have)/ has $Knowledge$: can explain how to solve a problem.
   - (Negative) Knowledge to Indicate $(Neg_-)ExP_A(Knowledge)$
     This means ; an Agent A (doesn't have)/ has $Knowledge$: can point out faults/bugs.
   - (Negative) Knowledge to Apply $(Neg_-)ExT_A(Knowledge)$
     This means ; an Agent A (doesn't have)/ has $Knowledge$: can apply.
2. Implicit Knowledge
   - Direct Explanation $ImT_A(Knowledge)$
     This means ; some situated learner explained $Knowledge$ to agent A directly.
   - Explanation Observation $ImS_A(Knowledge)$
     This means ; agent A observed some situated learner who had explained $Knowledge$ to another agent.
   - Application Observation $ImK_A(Knowledge)$
     This means ; agent A observed that some situated learner had applied $Knowledge$.

[Some situated learner means either a real learner or a situated agent.]

Modal predicates in *Explicit Knowledge* have the following set/logical-relation.

$$ExS_A(Knowledge) \supset ExP_A(Knowledge) \supset ExT_A(Knowledge)$$

$$Neg\_ExT_A(Knowledge) \supset Neg\_ExP_A(Knowledge) \supset Neg\_ExS_A(Knowledge)$$

TRANSFORMING PROCESS MODEL. "Transforming Process Model" which we define, represents the converting process from internal state into external state for a level of acquired knowledge. As we stated above, *Explicit Knowledge* as an external state is knowledge which a real learner really used correctly (applied, pointed out and/or explained). On the other hand, *Implicit Knowledge* as an internal state is knowledge which a real learner observed in the collaborative learning environment. Therefore, we can regard that the process of knowledge acquisition in our research framework is to convert *Implicit Knowledge* into it Explicit Knowledge. Naturally, each real learner has his/her own conversion rules from *Implicit Knowledge* into *Explicit Knowledge*. In this converting process, transportable/representational thinking with verbalization (or symbolization) and conceptualization is expected through symbolic operation among a real student and situated agents. In this study, we regard these converting/transporting rules as the "Transforming Process Model" of a real learner. In short, we can ask ourselves for "When should a real learner observe some kind of situation?", "What kind of knowledge can he/she acquire?" under a transportable form. It is very beneficial to model this transforming process of an individual real learner and make a real learner observe some situation according to a transportable form from an intelligent system's research point of view. So, we need to control each situated agent's behavior in order to make a real learner experience more meaningful situation according to a transportable form. By modeling this transportable form, the system can extract a real learner's bugs/faults occurred in this collaborative learning environment. In the following, we explain the modeling method of a transportable form.

THE MODELING TECHNIQUES OF TRANSFORMING PROCESS. Modeling of transforming process is executed when the system regards new valid information obtained by diagnosing a real learner's response as *Explicit Knowledge*. That is, modeling of transforming process is done for either of two cases below.

1. The case in which affirmative *Explicit Knowledge* is gathered
2. The case in which information on negative *Explicit Knowledge* is gathered

Elicitation of transportable form is done by inductive reasoning (there are a positive example and a negative example). Here, each example is a set of *Implicit Knowledge* which was acquired before and *Explicit Knowledge* which is acquired just now. As a result of it, transportable form is modeled in the following scheme.

$$P_1 \wedge P_2 \wedge \cdots \wedge P_n \Rightarrow EXPL_A(Knowledge)$$

Here, one of the modal predicates on *Explicit Knowledge* exists on the right side, and there is a set of modal predicates on both of *Implicit Knowledge* and *Explicit Knowledge* on the left side. However, any modal predicate which exists on the right side does not come to the left side.

Elicitation of transportable form applies the technique of Version Space which represents $P_1, P2, \cdots, P_n$ as nodes. The way of modeling is how the system computes a contradiction value for each node in the version space in accordance with the past examples, and adopts the node which has the lowest contradiction value. The computation of a contradiction value is shown in the following.

The weight of example i

$$W_i = 1.0 - 0.2(i-1), \quad (i = 1,2,3,4,5)$$

The contradiction value of node n on example i

$$C_{ni} = \begin{cases} W_i & (\text{example } i \text{ is contradictory for node } n.) \\ -W_i & (\text{example } i \text{ is not contradictory for node } n.) \end{cases}$$

The contradiction value of node n

$$C_n = \sum_{i=1}^{l} C_{ni} \quad (\text{in this version, } l = 5)$$

In the following, we give an example of transportable form which was modeled by the above way.

$$ExP_A(Knowledge) \wedge ImT_A(Knowledge) \wedge ImK_A(Knowledge)$$
$$\Rightarrow ExS_A(Knowledge)$$

This formula means "if agent A has already a certain knowledge to indicate, then he/she can get its knowledge to explain through the experience of explanation and application".

4.2 The Learning Effect Value for a Real Learner

From educational point of view, we must consider a learning effect of a real learner in this system. Here, we discuss how to evaluate a learning effect. A real learner seems to understand essentials of knowledge, when he/she feels some knowledge to be meaningful/useful to solve a problem under a certain situation. Standing on this aspect, we set up the table of learning effect value for a real learner as Table 1.

Here, we show the learning effect value as $Ef(Cond, Act)$. $Cond$ is the understanding state of a real learner (located horizontally in Table 1). Act means some situation which a real learner experiences, as shown in the rows of Table 1. When several modal predicates exist in the same knowledge, the system adopts the highest modal predicate. Each value in Table 1 means the expected values of learning effect for each condition by an experienced teacher. This value ranges from 0 to 2. The larger this value is, the more learning effectiveness is expected. That is the strategic coordinating knowledge in order to optimize a real learner's achievement/motivation.

Table 1. The table of the learning effect value for a real learner

	ObK	ObS	ObT	AcT	AcP	AcS
ExS	0	0	0	0	0	0
ExP	0	1	1	0	0	2
ExT	0	1	1	0	2	2
Neg_ExT	1	1	1	1	0	0
Neg_ExP	0	1	1	2	1	0
Neg_ExS	0	1	1	2	2	1
NoInf	0	0	0	1	1	1

ObK : a real learner observes that a situated agent applied knowledge.

ObS : a real learner observes that a situated agent explained knowledge to another situated agent.

ObT : a situated agent explains knowledge to a real learner.

AcT : a real larner applies knowledge.

AcP : a real learner points out knowledge.

AcS : a real learner explains to a situated agent.

$NoInf$: there is no information in Student Model.

4.3 The Consistency Value of Action for Each Situated Agent

In this study, it is important to maintain a situated agent's action consistently. That is, if a situated agent behaves inconsistently (e.g., a situated agent can solve the problem in some situation, but can't solve the same problem in another situation), then a real learner will be compelled to suspend his thinking under the same situation. This will lead to decrease his/her motivation of learning and will confuse a real learner's thinking schema. So, in order to avoid such a situation, we introduce the idea of "Consistency Value of Action" (show in Table 2). This value represents the degree of consistency between some actions which a situated agent experienced in the past and some actions which he/she takes now by applying the same knowledge. The values in brackets in Table 2 represent the consistency of the actions which a situated agent is not allowed to do.

Table 2. The consistency value of action for Novice Agent and Advanced Agent

Novice Agent				Advanced Agent			
	(Not)AcS	(Not)AcP	(Not)AcT		(Not)AcS	(Not)AcP	(Not)AcT
ExS	(-1) 0	(-1) 0	(-2) 0	ExS	(-2) 0	(-2) 0	(-2) 0
ExP	(0) -1	(-1) 0	(-1) 0	ExP	(-1) 0	(-2) 0	(-2) 0
ExT	(0) -1	(0) -1	(-1) 0	ExT	(-1) 0	(-1) 0	(-2) 0
ImT	(0) -2	(0) -1	(0) 0	ImT	(-1) 0	(-1) 0	(-2) 0
ImS	(0) -2	(0) -1	(0) -1	ImS	(-1) 0	(-1) 0	(-2) 0
ImK	(0) -2	(0) -2	(0) -1	ImK	(0) -1	(-1) 0	(-1) 0
NoInf	(0) -2	(0) -2	(0) -1	NoInf	(0) -1	(-1) 0	(-1) 0

Here, we represent this value as $Cs(Cond, Act)$. $Cond$ means the understanding state of each situated agent (located horizontally in Table 2). Act means the situation which each situated agent experiences (shown on the rows in Table 2). These values in Table 2 mean that some action will have any contradiction with the previous behaviors for a small value, and are set up by the system designer. The value ranges from -2 to 0, and -2 stand for the maximum of a contradiction degree. By utilizing this consistency value of action, Novice Agent will be inclined to take more often the same action such as making a real learner explain its knowledge. It means Novice Agent is always inferior to a real learner for its knowledge state. Therefore, this system is designed so that Novice Agent should be inferior for the function of knowledge acquisition in order to have a real learner teach Novice Agent how to solve. On the other hand, Advanced Agent will decide any action which makes a real learner observe his way of problem solving. It means Advanced Agent is always superior to a real learner for its knowledge state. Therefore, our system is contrived so that Advanced Agent should be superior for the function of knowledge acquisition in order to have this agent teach a real learner how to solve. Moreover, we suppose to define implicitly Novice Agent's characteristic as a situated learner who doesn't have an ability to learn smoothly, and Advanced Agent's one as a situated learner who has an ability to learn smartly.

4.4 The Mental Load of a Real Learner

As an applied field of this study, we have chosen the liner operations in liner algebra. In consideration of the features in this domain, we can get a desired solution by repeating some steps of applying problem-solving knowledge. For this kind of problems, if the system controls a situated agent's action by only both parameters of the learning effect value and the consistency value of actions, then some misbehaved issues seem to arise. That is, Novice Agent must ask a real learner to explain every step of problem solving. Because the learning effect value of a real learner at such a situation is set up highly as shown in Table 1. This situation will increase a real learner's mental load up. Therefore, we try to introduce Mental Load Value here in order to evade repetitions of such a question. We define Mental Load Value *load* as follows;

When S steps passed from a real learner's last explanation,

$$load = \begin{cases} S - 4 & (S \leq 3) \\ 0 & (S > 3) \end{cases}$$

4.5 The Flow of Action-Selection for Each Situated Agent

We mention how each situated agent decides the next action according to the method of evaluation stated previously. In the following, we show the decision-flow to lead agent A to an appropriate action, utilizing a set of problem-solving knowledge $OP = \{O_1, O_2, \cdots, O_N\}$.

1. Agent A enumerates a set of possible actions $ACT = \{Ac_1, Ac_2, \cdots, Ac_M\}$ by using the dialogue model. Then it generates a set of situations $COND = \{C_1, C_2, \cdots, C_M\}$ which a real learner can experience with action ACT.
2. Agent A picks out $Neg\_expl(Op)$, $Op \in OP$ from the negative knowledge in Explicit Knowledge in Student Model and generates a set Neg_EXPL. If $Neg\_EXPL = \phi$, go to 5 with $Modal = COND$.
3. Agent A scans the transition states of "Transforming Process Model" which have affirmative Explicit Knowledge in the conclusion part. Here, we express each the taken model as LS_{Ex}, and its contradiction value as Val_{Ex} ($Ex \in \{ExS, ExP, ExT\}$). If there is no Transforming Process Model, go to 5 with $Modal = COND$.

4. Agent A computes Total Contradiction Value VAL_{Ex} for each LS_{Ex} and finds out LS_{Ex} which has the lowest value. Then, we express a set of modal predicates existing in the conditional part of LS_{Ex} as $Modal = \{M_1, M_2, \cdots, M_L\}$. The expression of computing Total Contradiction Value is $VAL_{Ex} = Val_{Ex} \cdot N$. Here, N is the number of the negative knowledge existing at the same level with Ex (e.g., the Neg_ExS, when $Ex = ExS$.) in the set of Neg_EXPL.

5. Agent A alters all modal predicates in the set of Modal from $Im*$ and $Ex*$ to $Ob*$ and $Ac*$. Then, it computes Action Appropriate Value App_k for each element of $Comp = \{Co_1, Co_2, \cdots, Co_K\} = Modal \cap COND$, and adopts the action plan $Co_{k'}$ which has the highest value. In the following, we show the expression of computing Action Appropriate Value.

$$App_k = \sum_{i=1}^{N}(Ef(RS_i, Co_k) + Cs(A_i, Ac_m)) + L_k$$

Here, RS_i stands for the understanding state of a real learner for the problem-solving knowledge O_i, and A_i stands for the understanding state of agent A for O_i. The value of L_k is as follows.

$$L_k = \begin{cases} load & (Co_k = ExS) \\ 0 & (Co_k \neq ExS) \end{cases}$$

In such a way, each situated agent can decide the most appropriate action according to the learning state of a real learner.

5   Dialogue Example

We show the dialogue example between a real learner and situated agents in Fig. 3. This dialogue starts from the situation where Novice Agent gives a real learner a certain problem. At this time, a real learner is forced to solve this problem, and then Novice Agent and Advanced Agent try to observe his problem solving process. A real learner can choose either mode of "answering" or "asking". In this example, he/she chooses the mode of "answering".

Concerning the above dialogue, the knowledge of (step-1) and (step-2) is explicit one, but the knowledge explained by Advanced Agent remains still implicit one for Real Learner at this stage. After a real learner could solve the same kind of problems by him/herself, we can regard it as explicit knowledge.

6   Conclusion

In this study, we introduced four main concepts which are 1) situated agents, 2) implicit knowledge and explicit one, 3) transportable form, 4) transforming process model, and 5) modal predicates.

In particular, we described the modeling method for the learning state of a real learner in details, which makes each situated agent decide/choose the most appropriate action-plan. The modeling of a real learner's understanding state became feasible by introducing concepts of *Explicit Knowledge* and *Implicit Knowledge*, and by applying the idea of modal predicates. Also, we contrived theoretically the mechanism by which the system examines a real learner's

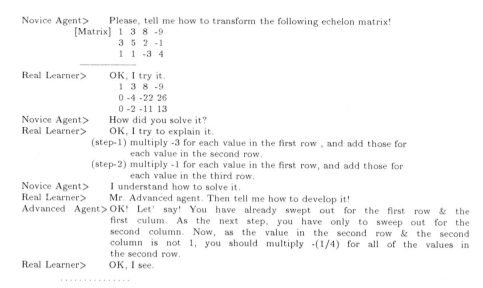

Fig. 3. The example of dialogue between Real Learner and Situated Agents

transportable form (for conversion process) and models it by Transforming Process Model. In the near future, we are going to examine the learning effectiveness for this system from the educational point of view. Especially, we must evaluate how each agent facilitates a real learner's observation learning and appropriateness of behavioral model (validity of the rule base) of each agent. Moreover, we need to examine effectiveness of observation learning for different tasks. Anyhow, this research aims to explore the mechanism for enhancing highly interactivity based on the architecture of multi-agents. However, the psychological effect of observation learning, especially psychological functionality of transforming process from implicit knowledge to explicit knowledge would not be specified under the practical experiment by this present system.

References

1. Aizenstein,H., Chan,T.W., Baskin,A.B., "Learning companion systems : Using a reading companion for text-based tutoring", Department of Veterinary Science (1989)
2. Chan,T.W., Chung,I.L., Ho,R.G., Hou,W.J., Lin,G.L., "Distributed Learning Companion System WEST Revisited", ITS'92 pp.645-650 (1992)
3. Dillenbourg,P., Self,J., "Designing Human-Computer Collaborative Learning", Computer Supported Collaborative Learning, NATO ASI series Vol.F-128, Berlin: Springer-Verlag, pp.245–264(1994)
4. Inaba,A., Okamoto,T., "Negotiation Process Model for Supporting Collaborative Learning", IEICE, Vol.J80-D-II, No.4, pp844-854(1997)
5. Kasai,T., Okamoto,T., "Construction of an Intelligent Learning Environment embedded Companion Agent: About a Function of Supporting an Enhancement of Recognizing Ability about a Companion Agent's State" JSISE, VOL.14, No.3, pp38-47(1997)

Should I Teach My Computer Peer?
Some Issues in Teaching a Learning Companion

Jorge A. **RAMIREZ URESTI**

School of Cognitive and Computing Sciences, University of Sussex, Brighton
BN1 9QH, U.K. +44 (1273) 678524
jorgeru@cogs.susx.ac.uk
http://www.cogs.susx.ac.uk/users/jorgeru/

Abstract. This paper describes work carried out to explore the role of a learning companion as a student of the human student. A LCS for Binary Boolean Algebra has been developed to explore the hypothesis that a learning companion with less expertise than the human student would be beneficial for the student in her learning. The system implemented two companions with different expertise and two types of motivational conditions. Results from a empirical evaluation suggested that subjects interacting with a less capable companion (weak) have a trend of more improvement than subjects interacting with a more capable companion (strong). Finally, the experiment also suggested that learning companions might be confusing for students if they try to resemble human behaviour, i.e. if they do not perform as they are told.

1 Introduction

Recent research on Intelligent Tutoring Systems (ITSs) is exploring the benefits of having human students collaborate with computerized agents. The issues being studied range from the external representation of such agents [14] to the selection of their internal characteristics [8]. Among all of these systems, Learning Companion Systems (LCSs) extend the traditional model of ITSs by adding computerized agents whose aim is to provide a peer for the human student. This kind of agent is called a *Learning Companion* [3].

In principle the learning companion (LC) could take any role that a human peer could take. Being the student of the human student is a role which has recently started to be explored in LCSs [5,9]. The rationale for such a selection of role is that by teaching the LC, the student should be able to reflect on her own knowledge and thus learn more effectively.

This paper describes work carried out to study this role: a LC as a student of the human student. A LCS for Binary Boolean Algebra has been developed to explore the hypothesis that a LC with less expertise than the human student would be beneficial for the student in her learning. The system was empirically evaluated in a study with 32 subjects. The results of the evaluation suggested that subjects interacting with this kind of LC have a trend of more improvement than subjects interacting with a more capable LC.

2   The LC as a Student

Work in LCSs has increased in the last few years but much remains to be done to explore the full capabilities and possibilities opened up by the inclusion of a LC in an ITS [4]. From all the issues surrounding LCSs, one of the most important is perhaps the question of the expertise level that the LC should possess in order to be of educational value to the student interacting with it. Most systems developed so far have dealt with this issue in one way of another but Hietala and Niemirepo [8] have been the only ones to design their system in order to study explicitly the expertise of LCs.

2.1   Expertise

Students in Hietala and Niemirepo's experiments faced a LCS which provided four LCs. They classified LCs as *weak* or *strong* based on their expertise. A weak LC was one with minimal expertise whereas a strong LC had almost an expert-like expertise. Their results showed that, in general, students preferred to collaborate with strong LCs rather than with weak LCs. Hietala and Niemirepo's interest was in studying which level of expertise would motivate students to collaborate with these agents. In this sense, their results were successful as a LC with a strong expertise proved to be motivating for the student. However, was this expertise the most beneficial for the student to learn?

Subjects in Hietala and Niemirepo's experiments were, in general, more comfortable with a strong LC at the end of the interaction, when tasks got harder. This was a very effective way to complete the task on hand, by asking someone who knows more for the answer. However, this is perhaps the main disadvantage of having a strong LC: if it is almost an expert in the domain, it could be easily confused with a tutor. And even worse, if the LC would answer or would do anything the student directs it to, the student could end up by asking the LC to do all work. There is therefore, a possibility that this use of the strong LC may encourage in the students a passive attitude towards learning and, thus, hamper their learning. On the other hand, subjects in Hietala and Niemirepo's work used weak LCs mainly at the beginning of the interaction. Most probably this was because LCs were not labelled with their expertise level and, therefore, students had to search for the most suitable LC. Collaboration with the weak LC was then due to a search rather than to a real desire to collaborate with it — although, it must be said, some subjects preferred collaboration with weak LCs. In general, the weak LCs were not perceived as good enough for serious tasks. However, weak LCs could have potentially benefited students more than collaborating with strong LCs. A weak LC may allow students to explain and teach to it.

Research has found evidence to support the notion that Learning by Teaching can be a facilitator for learning. Students who teach other students learn more and better [7, 10]. A student who needs to teach other people will have to revise, clarify, organize and reflect on her own knowledge in order to be able to teach, i.e. the student will need to master the knowledge. A weak LC should in principle be helpful for the student to learn by teaching [12]. Work in LCSs has recently started to explore the role of a LC as a student of the human student [5, 9]. The results of this work are not encouraging as students did not benefit from using these systems. The most probable reason for the failure of these LCSs was that they permitted students to perceive teaching the LC as a passive activity. However, despite the failure of those LCSs, recent work on Teachable Agents has shown that students find teaching a virtual human agent interesting [1]. This agent captured the students attention and motivated them to teach it. Teaching it was an active enterprise as students had to research and study beforehand. In consequence, the students in the experiments with this system showed high learning gains. Also, recent work by Scott and Reif [15] has found that students who coached (taught) a computer tutor benefited as much as those subjects who had personalized tutoring from expert teachers.

Therefore, given the work done so far, the hypothesis of the experiment described in this paper is that *a LC less capable than the student (weak) would be helpful to the student in her learning if she can be encouraged to teach it.*

2.2 Motivation

The weak LCs in the work of Hietala and Niemirepo were regarded by subjects as disappointing, lazy and irritating. This is perhaps the main disadvantage of weak LCs: that students would find them a nuisance and may decide not to use them anymore. Besides, as reported in a study by Nichols [11], the 'knowledge-hungry' characteristic of these agents could discourage students to collaborate with them. Subjects facing these kinds of agent found them uncomfortable to teach. This effect may have been in part due to the effort needed to teach another person or, in this case, a computerized agent. In consequence, given the negative image that students could have of a weak LC, if teaching a LC is an important aim of a LCS, the student should be motivated in some way to collaborate with it. Unfortunately, in contrast with the work of Hietala and Niemirepo, the expertise of the LC cannot be employed as the motivational factor if the LC is required to possess a predefined expertise level. In the work reported in this paper, the system implemented two types of LCs: one with a weak expertise and the other with a strong expertise. Therefore, a different form of motivation had to be found.

On the other hand, as has been discussed before, strong LCs have been found to encourage students to collaborate with them but there is also a possibility that students would direct these kind of LCs to perform all the work. Therefore, the students interacting with strong LCs should be motivated to work by themselves and not to take a passive attitude towards learning.

3 The System

3.1 LECOBA

A **LE**arning **CO**mpanion system for binary **B**oolean **A**lgebra (LECOBA) was developed to explore the hypothesis that a less capable LC would be helpful to students in their learning by encouraging them to teach it. The system implemented two types of LC: one with a little less knowledge than the student (weak) and the other with a little more expertise (strong). LECOBA also had two types of motivational condition: Motivated and Free. The Motivated condition strongly encouraged the student to either collaborate with the weak LC or work more by herself. This motivation was achieved using a series of scores. In contrast, in the Free condition, the student was mildly encouraged to interact with the LC. The encouragement was just by reminding the student that collaborating with the LC would be beneficial for her.

A screen dump of LECOBA is shown in Fig. 1. The figure shows the system at the moment when the student and the LC are beginning to work on a problem. The windows shown here are: 1) the tutor's window at the top left corner, 2) the LC's window at the top middle of the screen, 3) the student's window at the top right corner, 4) a tool for the student to solve problems ("Simplification Tool") at the bottom left corner, and 5) a window for the student to give suggestions to the LC ("Student - Suggestion") near the middle of the screen. Figure 1 also displays the score mechanism used to motivate the student. In each one of the tutor's, LC's and student's windows there is a score whose value ranges from 0% to 100%. The scores in the LC's and student's windows are based on the performance of each respective learner. Scores were designed to challenge the student to interact more with the LC or to work more by herself. The challenge is to obtain the maximum score in the 'Total Score' at the tutor's window. This score is determined not only by the student's performance, but also by the LC's performance. The LC's performance can be improved mainly by teaching the LC, specially for the weak LC. The student's performance improves as a mixture of her own work and her involvement in the problem resolution when the LC is working. While the 'Total Score' has not reached its maximum value, students will continue studying the same topic in the curriculum. A more detailed description of the system can be found in [13].

3.2 Teaching Window

The student has the opportunity to teach to the LC via a window called the *Teaching Window* (Fig. 2). The Teaching Window is based on the idea of inspectable student models [2]. It presents to the student the LC's understanding of the domain at a specific moment during the interaction — i.e. its 'student model'. The objective is to let the student see exactly what the LC knows when trying to solve a problem. In the figure, the LC's knowledge is represented by a series of buttons and menus — each button with its corresponding menu. The first four buttons and their menus are enabled. These represent the boolean rules which the learners have studied so far. Rules are ordered by the priority that the LC will try to apply them to a boolean expression. For instance, rule OROX is labeled as 1st, this means that this rule is the first one which the LC will try to use when solving a problem. Rule ANOO is the last one the LC would consider. The order in which the LC uses rules can be changed by clicking on their corresponding buttons and then swapping position with another rule. The menus

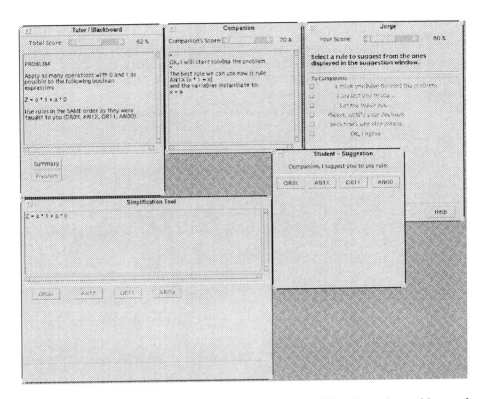

Fig. 1. LECOBA. Students are solving a problem, the LC is solving the problem and the user is about to give a suggestion to the LC.

allow the student to tell the LC how to use a rule. She can tell it to use rules in a specific mode or not to use them at all.

To teach the LC students must change its knowledge to make it more suitable for the task. Students can enable, disable, change the order, and modify the way in which rules are used by the LC. All of these changes are recorded while the student is performing them in the Teaching Window. They are considered as 'explanations' which the student is giving to the LC. Once the student has taught the LC, it automatically modifies its behaviour to immediately reflect its new understanding of the domain based on the student's teaching.

The Teaching Window can be seen as a reflection tool for the student. It encourages her to reflect on her own learning before deciding what to teach to the LC. When teaching the LC the student will need to modify its knowledge in a way she considers to be better to solve the current problem. To select the LC's new knowledge the student will need to understand why the LC is using that particular combination of rules or heuristic. In order to try to understand the LC's knowledge, she will first need to think about her own knowledge of the domain, i.e. what knowledge does she use to simplify expressions and why.

Fig. 2. The Teaching Window in LECOBA.

4 Results on Teaching a LC

LECOBA was empirically evaluated using a 2x2 factor, between-subjects design. There were two independent variables: expertise and motivation, and one main dependent variable: learning gain. This design enabled the use of the system under four different conditions: Condition 1 (Weak/Motivated), Condition 2 (Strong/Motivated), Condition 3 (Weak/Free) and Condition 4(Strong/Free).

Thirty two (32) undergraduate engineering students in their first and second years took part in the experiment. They attended two sessions of 1 hour each. The first session consisted of a pre-test, a demo of LECOBA and interaction with the system. In the second session subjects started immediately using LECOBA. This was followed by a post-test and a questionnaire to measure the students' perception of LECOBA as a tool for their learning. The time for the tests was of 15 minutes and of 30 minutes per session for using LECOBA. All the subjects were requested to start the interaction with LECOBA from the beginning of the curriculum. The sessions were logged by the system.

4.1 Was the Weak LC Best for Learning?

In general subjects improved their performance in the post-test after the interaction with LECOBA. On a scale from 0 to 100 the average improvement was of 11.79 points. The pre- and post-test scores of subjects were used as a measurement to see if they had learnt from the interaction with LECOBA. A two-way mixed-design Analysis of Variance (ANOVA) was run after determining that its assumptions had been met. The effect of the expertise and of the motivational condition were not statistically significant, neither their interaction. However, there was a highly significant effect of the tests (pre and post) on the subjects ($F(1, 28) = 16.87, p << 0.01$). In other words, there was a very marked difference on the scores of the pre- and the post-tests. Unfortunately, this difference cannot be only attributed to the level of the LC's expertise or to the motivational condition as they were not significant. Regardless of the type of condition to which subjects were assigned, they learnt some new concepts from the interaction with LECOBA as well as having revised existing knowledge. Although there was not a significant difference in the learning gain between the four conditions, some trends could be detected which allow for conclusions based on the expertise and on the motivational condition.

Condition 1 (Weak/Motivated) could be said to have a trend of being the most beneficial for the subjects' learning. It had a very low dispersion of the learning gain, i.e. learning under this condition was similar for all subjects in the condition. And it was the condition where subjects improved most, though not significantly. Besides, subjects in this condition were the ones who taught and made suggestions to the LC significantly more than in any other condition — these were their main activities. These two activities may account for some of the improvement of the subjects in this condition given that a small positive correlation between the learning gain and the number of teaching incidents and suggesting incidents was found. Therefore, this trend in Condition 1 of subjects improving consistently, more than in the other conditions, and teaching and making suggestions to the LC gives some support to this work main hypothesis: that a weak LC would help the student to learn by teaching it.

On the other hand, Condition 4 (Strong/Free) seems to have a trend of being the worst condition for learning. It had the most consistent learning of all the four conditions, but it also had the worst improvement. Therefore, subjects in Condition 4 had a consistent low improvement. Besides these results, when the tests were analyzed for improvement in the understanding of BBA concepts, subjects in this condition were the only ones with a trend of low beneficial effect on their understanding of simplification strategies. Some subjects even showed a negative effect on their learning of the strategies. They did not practice them enough as they preferred to solve problems by themselves and not to collaborate with the LC. Taking also into consideration the number of teaching and suggesting incidents, there were very few as there was little need for these actions given the high expertise of the strong LC. From all of these results it could be concluded that subjects in Condition 4 were the ones who least benefited from the interaction with LECOBA.

4.2 Reactions from the Interaction with the LC

Suggestions. A very interesting result of the experiments was the subjects' reactions to the LC's answer when it was given a suggestion. The LC was programmed to try to behave in a human-like way. It accepted or rejected suggestions as follows: the more it knew about a simplification rule, the less probable it would accept the suggestion (unless it was the same rule). This attempted to model the following human behaviour: the more a person knows about a concept, the less probable it is that he will accept a suggestion which contradicts his belief in this concept.

Mainly with the strong LC, but sometimes with the weak LC as well, subjects were confused to read that the LC was rejecting their suggestion. If the LC was strong, they were more amazed to read that the LC was telling them that they were wrong and that it would not follow the suggestion given. Subjects did not like this rejection of their suggestions very much. Usually when receiving this kind of comment from the LC they made an expression of disbelief. Some tried to suggest the same or a different rule again and some to teach it. In any case, subjects were expecting the LC to accept the suggestion that it had been given. They were not prepared to be rejected by a machine. Eventually they got used to this kind of behaviour of the LC. This reaction towards the LC is a good example of the plausibility problem [6]: users of a LCS may not be prepared to deal with a LC who reacts as a human peer might do.

Teaching. Another interesting result, also related to the plausibility problem, was the reaction of subjects towards the 'learning' capabilities of the LC. The LCs in LECOBA were programmed to 'not understand' some of what was being taught to them depending on their expertise: the more a LC knew, the more it would understand the student's teaching. This behaviour was trying to emulate human behaviour: the more a person knows about a domain, the more probable it is that he would understand when others are teaching this subject to him.

Subjects interacting with the weak LC were very annoyed to observe that the LC did not 'learn' all the concepts that had been so carefully taught to it. As the weak LC had low expertise, it would frequently 'not understand' what had been taught to it. This inability of the LC to understand may have discouraged some subjects to interact more frequently with the weak LC. However, it is not difficult to imagine a human student who has weak knowledge of a domain and that due to this low knowledge does not easily understand what is taught to her. Subjects were just not prepared to deal with a LC that would not understand everything that was taught to it.

Another issue arose because subjects had to teach the same thing to the weak LC several times, as it did not understand all that was taught to it. This fact made subjects reluctant to teach the LC. When subjects had to teach the LC they should have taught it the complete heuristic they were learning at the current level. The logs of interaction revealed a trend of complete teaching during the initial problems of the interaction. However, after some teaching incidents, students started to diminish the quality of their teaching until just the rule needed for the current step was taught to the LC. This low quality teaching was mostly carried out with the weak LC and mostly by those subjects in Condition 3 (Weak/Free); subjects in Condition 1 (Weak/Motivated) maintained good quality teaching. Once students noticed that the LC was not learning quickly they started to teach only one rule instead of the complete heuristic. This combination of teaching all the strategy and having to teach it again and again may have been detrimental to the perception of the weak LC and of the teaching process. It may also explain why the weak LC was described in the post-test as not very exciting and annoying.

5   Conclusion

The experiments with LECOBA showed that subjects who faced the weak LC and who were strongly motivated to interact with it had a trend of most learning gain, though the differences were not significant. On the other hand, subjects who interacted with a strong LC and who were mildly motivated had a trend of worst learning, though again the difference in learning gains were not significant. So, in general, these results give some support to the conclusion that students may benefit more from interacting with a weak LC than from interacting with a strong LC.

LECOBA allowed a passive attitude to teaching in the Free motivation and strongly encouraged teaching in the Motivated condition. As a result, teaching the weak LC was performed significantly more often with the strong motivation than with the mild motivation. Teaching in LECOBA was also not an action which permitted a passive attitude. Evidence suggests that it was so demanding when facing the weak LC that the high effort required might have been a reason for subjects in the Free condition to markedly decrease their teaching. But more importantly, the results give also some support to the claim that subjects who are strongly motivated to teach the weak LC benefit most from the teaching interaction. The benefits related to teaching could not have occurred with the strong LC as it does not lend itself for teaching.

Finally, the replies of the LC to the teaching and suggestions offered by the student were confusing for her. Subjects expected the LC to learn immediately everything that had been taught to it and to accept without question the suggestions given to it. The users of the system were not prepared to deal with a LC which reacted as a human peer might do. Future LCSs could explore the reaction of students and the effect on their learning when 1) they face LCs that behave and can be answered as if they really were human peers, and 2) when they face LCs which behave and are treated as 'dumb' computer agents performing exactly as they are told, i.e. accepting the users input without questioning it. Judging by the work so far in LCSs, the first scenario is envisaged as the one where subjects would benefit most from the interaction with a LC. But, as demonstrated with LECOBA, the second scenario might surprisingly be more beneficial if it is found more credible by students.

Acknowledgements

The author wishes to thank Benedict du Boulay and the reviewers for commenting on a draft of this paper, and *Consejo Nacional de Ciencia y Tecnología* (CONACYT) of México for their financial support.

References

1. Sean Brophy, Gautam Biswas, Thomas Katzlberger, John Bransford, and Daniel Schwartz. Teachable agents: Combining insights from learning theory and computer science. In Susanne P. Lajoie and Martial Vivet, editors, *Artificial Intelligence in Education*, pages 21–28. IOS Press, 1999.
2. Susan Bull, Helen Pain, and Paul Brna. Mr. Collins: A collaboratively constructed, inspectable student model for intelligent computer assisted language learning. *Instructional Science*, 23:65–87, 1995.
3. Tak-Wai Chan. Integration-Kid: A learning companion system. In J. Mylopolous and R. Reiter, editors, *Proceedings of the Twelfth International Conference on Artificial Intelligence (IJCAI-91)*, volume 2, pages 1094–1099. Morgan Kaufmann Publishers Inc., 1991.
4. Tak-Wai Chan. Learning companion systems, social learning systems, and the global social learning club. *Journal of Artificial Intelligence in Education*, 7(2):125–159, 1996.
5. Tak-Wai Chan and Chih-Yueh Chou. Exploring the design of computer supports for reciprocal tutoring. *International Journal of Artificial Intelligence in Education*, 8:1–29, 1997.
6. Benedict du Boulay, Rosemary Luckin, and Teresa del Soldato. The plausibility problem: Human teaching tactics in the 'hands' of a machine. In Susanne P. Lajoie and Martial Vivet, editors, *Artificial Intelligence in Education*, pages 225–232. IOS Press, 1999.
7. Sinclair Goodlad and Beverly Hirst. *Peer Tutoring: A Guide to Learning by Teaching*. Kogan Page, London, 1989.
8. Pentti Hietala and Timo Niemirepo. The competence of learning companion agents. *International Journal of Artificial Intelligence in Education*, 9:178–192, 1998.
9. Y. Jun. Linear kid: A mathematical software designed as a computer-based peer tutoring system. In *Electronic Proceedings of the Second Asian Technology Conference in Mathematics (ATCM'97)*, 1997.
10. Donald Michie, Andrew Paterson, and Jean Hayes-Michie. Learning by teaching. In *2nd Scandinavian Conference on Artificial Intelligence 89*, pages 307–331. IOS Press, 1989.
11. David Nichols. Issues in designing learning by teaching systems. In P. Brusilovsky, S. Dikareva, J. Greer, and V. Petrushin, editors, *Proceedings of the East-West International Conference on Computer Technologies in Education (EW-ED'94)*, volume 1, pages 176–181, 1994.
12. Jorge Adolfo Ramírez Uresti. Teaching a learning companion. In Gerardo Ayala, editor, *Proceedings of the International Workshop "Current Trends and Applications of Artificial Intelligence in Education"*. The Fourth World Congress on Expert Systems, pages 83–89, ITESM, Monterrey, México, 1998.
13. Jorge Adolfo Ramírez Uresti. The LECOBA learning companion system: Expertise, motivation, and teaching. In Linda Baggott and Jon Nichol, editors, *Intelligent Computer and Communications Technology (PEG99)*, pages 193–201. University of Exeter, England, July 1999.
14. Jeff Rickel and W. Lewis Johnson. Virtual humans for team training in virtual reality. In Susanne P. Lajoie and Martial Vivet, editors, *Artificial Intelligence in Education*, pages 578–585. IOS Press, 1999.
15. Lisa Ann Scott and Frederick Reif. Teaching scientific thinking skills: Students and computers coaching each other. In Susanne P. Lajoie and Martial Vivet, editors, *Artificial Intelligence in Education*, pages 285–293. IOS Press, 1999.

WHITE RABBIT – Matchmaking of User Profiles Based on Discussion Analysis Using Intelligent Agents

Marc-André Thibodeau, Simon Bélanger, Claude Frasson

Université de Montréal
Département d'Informatique et de Recherche Opérationnelle
C.P. 6128, succursale Centre-ville
Montréal, Canada H3C 3J7

{thibodea,belanger,frasson}@iro.umontreal.ca

Abstract. The White Rabbit system intends to enhance cooperation among a group of people by analyzing their conversation. Each user is assisted by an intelligent agent which establishes a profile of his or her interests. Next, with its autonomous and mobile behavior, the agent will reach the personal agents of other users to be introduced and presented to the ones that seem to have similar interests. A mediator agent is used to facilitate communication among personal agents and to perform clustering on the profiles that they have collected. Conversation between users takes place in a chat environment adapted to the needs of the system.

1   Introduction

In a large business or a large-scale research center, it is extremely common to see significant problems in coordination and cooperation. The resulting mismanagement generally leads to considerable drops in productivity. The fact is that when a large number of people work in the same organization, everybody is not aware of all the available resources or even of the other projects underway in the organization. Sometimes, different groups of people will work on similar, even identical projects, consequently reinventing the same ideas and concepts, or else develop many times the same components instead of combining their efforts and sharing their knowledge. Similarly, resources like experts or past realizations could be used in a profitable way but are not, because of the ignorance of their existence.

This is the problem we are trying to solve. The approach we chose is the use of intelligent agents to discover the similar interests held among a group of people working in a particular domain with the intent to put them in relation and enhance their level of cooperation. The agents analyze conversation between users through a chat interface to build up for each of them a precise profile of their interests. Once these profiles are built, they will be used to categorize users who will finally be introduced to each other when they are classified in a similar category (or cluster).

First, this article presents research advances in the particular domain of intelligent agents for matchmaking by presenting two similar systems. Next, the White Rabbit system's prototype is explained in detail. It ends analyzing and discussing both the results obtained as well as the future directions that the system may take.

2 Matchmaking Using Agents

This section compares the White Rabbit system with two similar systems developed at the Massachusetts Institute of Technology : Yenta and Butterfly. This discussion highlights White Rabbit's characteristics.

2.1 Yenta vs. White Rabbit

Yenta is a matchmaking system designed to find people with similar interests and encourage communication between them [1]. This system is composed of a set of decentralized agents that group into categories to represent the user's similar interests. These categories can then be used to make presentations and enable users to exchange messages with people that are part of the same cluster, i.e. having common interests.

Many agent systems already implemented use a centralized architecture by which an agent serves one or many people at a time. However, such an architecture presents notable disadvantages :

- It is difficult to apply a centralized architecture to large-scale systems. Shardanand and Maes [2] claim that the communication problems which arise through such a system are generally of a quadratic order of complexity.
- A centralized server presents only one location where an accidental breakdown can have severe consequences for a system that has to be reliable and available at all times.

Consequently, future perspectives tend to show that agent systems will use a larger number of agents communicating with one another. This is the approach used by Yenta and the one that we also used for White Rabbit. However, we improved this architecture by adding a mediator agent, which facilitates the communication between the agents, and provides a single rally-point for clustering.

The main idea for Yenta's clustering consists in an algorithm similar to the hill-climbing algorithm [1]. Once clusters are built, they can be used in different ways. The most important one consists in realizing matchmaking by doing presentations of similar users. This way, the system helps the user to find the expert he or she needs since the expert's interests, if he or she is represented by an agent of the system, are grouped in the same categories as other users. White Rabbit uses a completely different clustering algorithm, but its use of the clusters found is similar, allowing the user to explicitly ask to be presented to another member of the same cluster and thus facilitating the discovery of an expert.

2.2 Butterfly vs. White Rabbit

Butterfly is another project underway at MIT which presents a lot of similarities with White Rabbit. Butterfly is an intelligent agent system which analyzes conversation over IRC (Internet Relay Chat) in order to suggest to users some discussion channels that may be of interest to them [3]. In order to do that, it samples the conversations going on into the different discussion groups available and builds, for each user, a profile of his interests. The analysis by agents of real-time discussion is precisely one of White Rabbit's functions. However, the role of these agents is different. White Rabbit has to form clusters of users with similar interests itself, like Yenta. Instead, Butterfly suggests to users groups that already exist and that have been explicitly created by those users. It has consequently no clustering function to fulfill.

For White Rabbit, we chose to build our own chat system possessing the conversation control capacities and the organization we needed, instead of using the already existing IRC.

The user's profile of interests used by Butterfly is simply based on a vector of terms associated to positive and negative weights. The actual version of Butterfly uses fixed constants to represent « low », « normal » and « high » levels of interest (e.g. −50, 100, 200). However, more varied weights could be used if the profiles were learned. White Rabbit uses information retrieval techniques to attribute weights to the different concepts that are part of the profile. The way in which the agents learn the user's profiles in White Rabbit will be described in the next section. One important disadvantage of Butterfly is the fact that it forces the user to explicitly declare his interests to the system and that the profile obtained offers little flexibility. This demands heavy participation of the user who will eventually put the system aside and won't use it anymore. Automated learning of the profile's weights solves this problem.

3 The White Rabbit System

Up to now, the project led to the development of a prototype for the discussion analysis agent system. This section presents this prototype's architecture and explains how its different components work.

3.1 The System's Architecture

First, we will present White Rabbit system's global architecture. You can see this architecture in figure 1. Figure 2 shows a personal agent's architecture in its environment.

The system is made of six principal sections.

- The chat server that organizes the flux of messages through the network;
- A user interface dedicated to both the user and administrator of the system. It allows the user to send and receive messages and to consult and modify his profile. It allows the administrator to observe and adjust the parameters of the clustering process and to change the knowledge base;
- A personal agent for each user that performs the message content analysis and the presentation service;
- The Voyager layer giving White Rabbit's agents their mobility and autonomy;

- The PC^2 knowledge base where different knowledge keywords and links between them are located;
- A mediator agent attached to the server and dedicated to the clustering process and the facilitation of communication between agents.

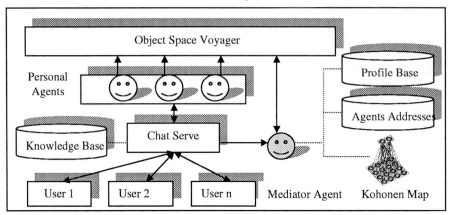

Fig. 1. White Rabbit's general architecture

3.2 User Profile

The whole system works around this essential component. The user profile contains all relevant information about the user's interests in the chosen domain which will allow agents to discover similarities and consequently to perform an appropriate clustering of users. So it is important that the agent traces a correct portrait of the user it represents.

The approach we adopted for building profiles is based on the PC^2 knowledge representation developed during the ALICE project, a knowledge extraction system also underway at University of Montreal. This model consists in forming a knowledge (or concepts) graph of keywords to which are linked users via their publications, reports, and projects they are involved in. Concepts are linked to one another by links that have a semantic signification. For example, two concepts can be linked together by similarity links if they are similar or else by specialization links if one is general and "uses" the more specific one. This way, the whole knowledge domain is represented by a graph.

3.3 Learning Module

As we just mentioned, the learning module is the one that modifies the user profile's weights to make it more and more accurate and realistic. At this moment, this process is made of two steps. We will propose one more during discussion. The first step consists in a preliminary acquisition of information about the user through a questionnaire. The first time he or she uses the system, the user is invited to fill it in and by doing this to give the system keywords reflecting his interests (projects, realizations, expertise). This information is used by White Rabbit to constitute a basic profile for the user. The second step is the one of analyzing discussion. It consists in extracting domain keywords from messages the user sends and then in updating the profile by increasing weights of associated concepts, following a sigmoid function (1)

$$f(x) = \frac{1}{1+e^{-x}} .$$
(1)

where f(x) is the new weight and x is the keyword's « importance ». The keyword's importance is the number of occurrences of this keyword, modified according to some factors like the similarity degree between concepts, the declarations of interest from the user, etc. The sigmoid function is frequently used in neural networks for computing the values of updates for the link's weights between units (or neurons). It has the property to vary strictly between 0 and 1 and to have a slow increase for low x-axis values, then a high increase for medium values and finally slow again for high values on the x-axis.

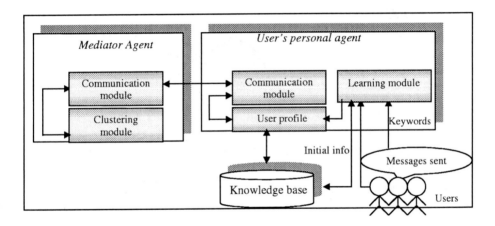

Fig. 2. A personal agent architecture

Furthermore, since knowledge is represented in a PC^2 form, it becomes possible to update weights of all concepts linked to the keyword discovered by following simple heuristics. For example, all concepts similar to the one found may have their weights modified in the same direction and following the same function, proportionally to the similarity degrees associated to similarity links of the knowledge graph. Consequently, following discovery of a few keywords only, the agent's learning module can possibly update the weights of all knowledge in the profile. As we will see, this is very important for our clustering algorithm, Kohonen Maps [4], to work well.

On top of discovering keywords during conversation, the personal agent performs a verification of the profile periodically to allow the user to validate or else invalidate one or more of his profile's interests . When a keyword's weight increases over a predetermined threshold, the agent asks the user if he or she is really interested in the associated concept. Weight is then adjusted according to the answer received. This allows the dynamic correction of errors that may have been introduced in the profile during analysis.

So, this second step is done in a totally automatic way, asking only for a minimal user participation who just has to answer the agent's periodical questions. This constitutes an important advantage over the Butterfly system presented earlier. Indeed, Butterfly forces the user to explicitly declare his interests and the weights obtained are rigid, permitting the system no flexibility to adapt itself or to correct its errors. In this case, the user must correct himself the errors made by the system by modifying his profile explicitly during discussion. In fact, the user builds his profile himself and Butterfly doesn't update it in any way. White Rabbit's discussion interface still allows the user to accelerate learning of his profile by making such explicit declarations, but he or she is in no obligation to do it for his profile to be learned. In the same way, the first learning step (through a questionnaire), is only aimed at simplifying the agent's task of rapidly building a representative profile of its user's interests.

3.4 Communication Module

The communication module allows the system's agents to talk, listen and move to each other. It is entirely based on the ObjectSpace Voyager's technology [5].

Two of White Rabbit's aspects demonstrate autonomy and mobility of its agents. First is the discussion analysis of a user by it's personal agent. Indeed, after having analyzed and updated its client's profile, the agent goes to another machine connected to the network to meet one of its colleagues. This one is the mediator agent which must analyze the user profiles and determine in which cluster they are classified and consequently to which group the corresponding users are assigned. The mediator agent gives the personal agent the result of clustering, and finally, the latter returns to its source machine and continues analyzing its client's discussion.

The second important evidence of mobility happens when the user asks to be presented to a second user who is a member of the same cluster, as determined by the mediator agent. At this moment, the requesting client's agent (A) will use its autonomy to move to and meet the agent associated to the client to be presented (B). Then, agent A will have the possibility to ask for more information from agent B. If the agent B's client accepts the request, then, agent B will give to agent A the personal information (real name, email, project description, etc.) on his client that was not set to « private ». A user can set any or all of his personal information to « private » to control what others have access to, maintaining privacy. This is the presentation step following the clustering process.

These two situations demonstrate the strength achieved by the mobility and autonomy of our agents, which allows a considerable reduction of the number of transmitted messages in the network. This way, risks of network overload or lack of resources are greatly reduced, even when the number of personal agents (and equivalently, the number of users) is high.

3.5 Clustering Module

Like we mentioned earlier, the clustering algorithm we used is the Kohonen Map [4] and constitutes an interesting aspect of our system. Indeed, this algorithm invented in 1982 by Teuvo Kohonen, professor at University of Helsinki, Finland, proved for many years to be efficient, being applied to a lot of different domains like medicine [6], physics [7] and seismology [8]. Kohonen Maps are a type of neural network that performs an « unsupervised » learning, i.e. requiring no examples or « good answers » in feed-back, contrary to back-propagation neural networks. Since neurons learn in a competitive way, there is no goal to reach nor errors to minimize. So this type of neural network is ideal when output values are not known or hard to measure, as is the case with clustering.

Kohonen Maps are composed of two distinct layers: the input layer and the projection layer (or Kohonen layer). Each neuron present in the input layer represents an attribute, or a dimension of the input data. Each of the input units is connected to all neurons in the projection layer. And finally, each of these connections has an associated weight, generally a number between 0 and 1 so a neuron of the projection layer possesses a vector of weights, each element of this vector corresponding to an input data's attribute. With this vector, each neuron has the possibility to compute its activation level (or simply activation). The activation is defined by the Euclidean distance given by equation (2).

$$a = \sqrt{\sum_{i=0}^{n} (weight_i - input_i)^2} \ . \tag{2}$$

We can see that a neuron that possesses a weight vector similar to the activation levels vector of the input nodes will have a low activation level and vice versa. The projection layer's node having the lowest activation is called the "winner". In our case, each node of the projection layer corresponds to a cluster. The number of nodes in the projection layer thus determines the number of different clusters in which profiles can be classified. This number can be changed to better suit the number of profiles in the system at a given moment.

But before being used to perform clustering, the network has to be trained. During this training, each input data is presented to the network and activation levels are computed as explained earlier. For each such input, the weight vectors of the winner node and its neighbors are adjusted in a way to approach the input vector. Equation 3 is used to compute the weights variations.

$$\delta w_i = -\alpha (weight_i - input_i) \tag{3}$$

where α is the learning rate which decreases linearly during the training process and δw is a weight adjustment value.

In our system, the Kohonen Map is found in the mediator agent which receives user profiles brought by the personal agents. When a profile is brought, it is first added to a base containing all the profiles. These profiles are then converted one by one into weight vectors that will then be used for activation values of the input units of the neural network. This conversion is trivial, since a user profile makes the correspondence between each keyword in the knowledge base and a real number (the weight), which means that each weight value of the profile can be simply assigned to one input unit of the neural net. The network is trained by making a few passes through the set of profiles in the base. This training leads to the adjustment of the weight values of connections, after which time weights are locked. A cluster is then determined for each profile by computing activation levels and determining the winner for each of them. Finally, the determined clusters are communicated to all personal agents to allow them to update their user's interface.

Consequently, persons categorized in the same cluster have profiles that are similar and are then listed on each member's interface (see section 3.6, figure 3, right part). This allows them to greatly reduce the research space when searching for individuals sharing the same interests. And one can easily imagine the time savings it represents in a large company, with hundreds or thousands of employees.

3.6   Discussion Environment

We have developed our own discussion environment for the users of White Rabbit instead of using an existing interface like IRC. We wanted to have a discussion environment that allowed us to easily integrate all the discussion analysis and clustering functions we wanted to implement. We also wanted to restrict in some way, through the interface, the discussion in the chosen interest domain. So we have implemented a simple chat environment allowing many people to converse and agents to do their work in an efficient way (figure 3).

The interface allows a user to create and maintain a profile, to visualize it, to discuss and specify, if he or she judges necessary, the type of messages he or she sends (explicit interest declaration, restriction formulations, etc.), to adjust his agent's activity level, to know the list of users considered having similar interests by the system, to ask for the presentation of one or many of them and to receive and answer questions asked by his personal agent. To insure confidentiality, the user must choose a pseudonym as well as a password to open an existing profile. The profiles and the knowledge base are stored on the server machine.

4   Discussion and Results

White Rabbit is basically a system designed to answer to the needs of a small to medium sized community like the one of a research center, an organization or a company. Consequently, we have not focused on problems related to the system scalability. Instead, we have emphasized the efficiency of the agents work, i.e. by carefully choosing the knowledge representation, by implementing well-known and well-tested learning, clustering and communication algorithms, by making the interface graphical and user-friendly and by using state-of-the-art technologies like the Voyager architecture and the most recent Java version. The prototype implemented is portable on all platforms and aims at forming a solid basis for the development of a useful application, easy to transfer to industries as well as to the different scientific communities. It is also this practical aspect that lead us to chose the real-time discussion analysis instead of user email analysis for example. Indeed, this last alternative would have posed serious problems in a real working environment in terms of accessing information and confidentiality [9].

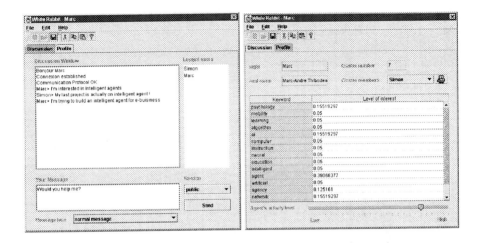

Fig. 3. White Rabbit's discussion (left) and profile management (right) interface

Basic tests have been conducted to verify the prototype's efficiency. The first conclusion is the major importance of the knowledge base quality in the quality of the user clustering results. In fact, this process' quality depends directly on the links between concepts of the base that allow agents to build a correct representation of the user's interests. If the knowledge graph is incomplete and is not representative of reality, the agent's learning is inefficient and consequently the clustering step loses all sense. To facilitate the construction of the knowledge base, White Rabbit will eventually be integrated with the ALICE system. This system is composed of a graphical editor which easily allows a knowledge graph in PC^2 form to be built. We are presently working at collecting statistical data relative to the knowledge base's size, to the number of users and to other different parameters having an impact on the clustering quality and the user cooperation improvement that should result.

One more function we propose to add to our system in our future works is a third learning step consisting in asking for a feed-back to the user about the clustering produced. This way, the user should be able to easily correct the system by giving it an appreciation of its work. The user would have his profile adjusted according to this appreciation without having to determine himself the causes of his bad classification. Possibilities would be to use a back-propagation neural network to automatically adjust profile weights or, more simply, to use heuristics.

5 Conclusion

In brief, White Rabbit tries to evolve in a system that is applicable to real industrial problem solving. It uses well-known and efficient artificial intelligence techniques to reach this goal. The analysis made by its intelligent agents gives the user a maximum of freedom by asking him as little participation as possible. White Rabbit is really an intelligent agent system where agents are autonomous and move across the network using the Voyager agent architecture, contrary to many existing agent systems. We are convinced that intelligent agents have a real potential and we are confident that their use will answer a lot of actual and future needs of industries and researchers.

References

1. Foner, L. (1997) Yenta: A Multi-Agent, Referral-Based Matchmaking System, in *Proceedings of the First International Conference on Autonomous Agents (Agents '97)*, Marina Del Rey, CA, USA.
2. Shardanand U., Maes P. (1995) Social Information Filtering: Algorithms for Automating Word of Mouth, in *proceedings of the CHI '95 Conference.*
3. Van Dyke, N.W., Lieberman, H., Maes, P. (1999) Butterfly: A Conversation-Finding Agent for Internet Relay Chat, in *Proceedings of the 1999 International Conference on Intelligent User Interfaces.*
4. Kohonen, T. (1988) *Self-Organization and Associative Memory*, Springer-Verlag, Berlin.
5. ObjectSpace Inc. (1999) Overview of Voyager: ObjectSpace's Product Family Computing.
6. Silipo N., Bortolan G., Marchesi C. (1997) Supervised and unsupervised learning for diagnostic ECG classification, in *Proceedings of the 18th Annual International Conference of the IEEE Engineering in Medicine and Biology Society.*
7. Bemudez, J.L., Piras, A., Rubinstein, M. (1996) Classification of lightning electromagnetic waveforms with a self-organizing Kohonen map, in *13th International Wroclaw Symposium on Electromagnetic Compatibility.*
8. Musil, M., Plesinger, A. (1996) Discrimination between local micro-earthquakes and quarry blasts by multi-layer perceptrons and Kohonen maps in *Bulletin of the Seismological Society of America.*
9. Foner L. (1996) A security Architecture for Multi-Agent Matchmaking, in *The Second International Conference on Multi-Agent Systems* at Keihanna Plaza, Kansai City, Japan.

Applying Patterns to ITS Architectures

Vladan Devedzic

University of Belgrade, FON - School of Business Administration, Department of Information
Systems, POB 52, Jove Ilica 154, 11000 Belgrade, Yugoslavia
devedzic@galeb.etf.bg.ac.yu

Abstract. The concept of patterns has received surprisingly little attention so far from the designers of ITS architectures. This paper is an attempt to bring more light on this important concept and to describe the benefits that patterns can bring to the field of ITSs. The paper concentrates on two issues: a) how to use well-known design patterns from the general field of software design for development of ITSs; and b) the process of discovering patterns in existing ITS architectures. The last part of the paper discusses the benefits of using patterns in ITS architectures and the relation of patterns to some other important design issues of ITSs, like using interoperable software components and ontologies.

1 Introduction

Designing the architecture of an Intelligent Tutoring System (ITS) involves a large measure of art. This is true not only for the interface design, but also for the system's architecture as a whole. However, relying only on the designer's artistic expression and knowledge of instructional theories can result in fragile systems, maintenance problems, and even chaotic design. What is needed as well is a firm and stable engineering backbone around which the rest of the system's architecture should be built.

That backbone is not easy to provide. To a large extent, ontological engineering of ITSs can help build solid architecture [9], [13]. Using well-founded teaching and learning strategies as the basis for ITS architectures is important, too (e.g., [7]), and so is the knowledge of ITS models, both traditional and new (e.g., [1], [11]). Experience of other ITS designers and architectures of other successful ITSs also facilitates fundamental design decisions in developing a new system [10], [12].

One additional approach to a more systematic design of ITS architectures is the use of *patterns*. In software engineering, patterns are attempts to describe successful solutions to common software problems [16]. Software patterns reflect common conceptual structures of these solutions, and can be applied over and over again when analyzing, designing, and producing applications in a particular context. Patterns exist in several phases of software development. The software patterns community has first discovered, described and classified a number of *design patterns* [8]. More recent developments have also identified many patterns related to other phases and issues of software development, like *analysis patterns* [5] and *patterns for software architectures* [18].

Knowledge of patterns and using them definitely brings more engineering flavor to the field of ITSs. It is also important to stress that it does not mean abandoning learning theories, teaching expertise, curriculum structuring, or instruction delivery as the cornerstones of any ITS system. Using patterns is just taking more care about AIED *systems* themselves, especially about the way we develop them.

2 Problem Statement

This paper has three main objectives:
- to show how design patterns, being an established technology in the general field of software engineering, can be applied to ITS design and development;
- to show how patterns can be discovered in existing ITS architectures; such patterns are implicitly present in the architectures, and most ITS designers have used them without thinking in pattern-oriented way.
- to increase the ITS community's awareness of patterns and of benefits that patterns can bring to ITS developers.

In short, the idea is to show *what* does it mean to use design patterns in ITS development, *how* to use them, and *why* should ITS developers care about it.

3 Applying Patterns to ITS Design

Software designers have discovered dozens of patterns so far. They are all collected in different *pattern catalogues*, in which each pattern is described using some previously adopted, uniform and consistent template. For example, some well-known catalogues of design patterns can be found in [4], [8], [17]. Within the catalogues, patterns are classified so that it is possible to talk about families of related patterns. The classification helps designers find their way around the catalogues and also find the candidate patterns to be used in solving specific design problems.

3.1 Related Work

In the literature on ITS design and development, only some vague and implicit reminiscences of using patterns can be found. Some examples include [11], [14], and [21]. In contrast to these examples, patterns have been used explicitly in developing software that supports *GET-BITS*, a previously developed framework for building ITSs [3]. Whereas the GET-BITS framework itself has been discussed in detail elsewhere [2], [3], this section illustrates how patterns have been applied to develop different components of GET-BITS. Specifically, the example described below shows how one of the most common design patterns, known under the name *Composite* [4], [8], has been used in GET-BITS to represent part-whole hierarchies.

3.2 Using the Composite Pattern

The Composite pattern has been applied in several components of GET-BITS (see the *Known uses* subsection below). For the purpose of illustrating the use of the Composite pattern from the ITS perspective, the pattern is described here using a modified version of the pattern-description template from [8].

Classification and intent. Composite is a structural pattern. Its intent is to compose objects into tree structures to represent part-whole hierarchies. It lets clients treat individual objects and compositions of objects uniformly.

Motivation. Lesson presentation planner of an ITS may decide to build an agenda of the topics to be presented during the lesson. Complex topics can be divided into simple elements, like concepts, text, graphics, and the like, or into a sequence of subtopics (simpler topics). Each subtopic in turn can be further subdivided into a lower level sequence of simple elements and other subtopics, producing an agenda like in the following example:

1. Topic 1
   Text
   Graphics
   Concept A
   1.1. Subtopic 1.1
   1.2. Subtopic 1.2
        Text
        Concept B
        1.2.1. Subtopic 1.2.1
        1.2.2. Subtopic 1.2.2
2. Topic 2
        . . .

A simple implementation could define classes for simple elements, such as text and graphics, plus additional classes for subtopics as containers of simple elements. But in that case, the code using these classes would have to treat simple and container objects differently, which would be inefficient from the design point of view. Instead of that, the Composite pattern shows how to use recursive composition so that clients don't have to make this distinction. Moreover, using Composite makes it easier to achieve any desired depth of subtopics nesting.

Structure. The key to the Composite pattern is an abstract class that represents *both* primitive elements (concepts, text, and graphics) and their containers (subtopics). Fig. 1 shows the general structure of the Composite pattern, using the standard UML notation for object-oriented design [6].

Participants and collaborations. The abstract class *Component* in Fig. 1 corresponds to the contents to be presented during the lesson in our example. It is responsible for providing common interface to all objects in the composition, both simple (concepts, text, and graphics) and complex (topics and subtopics), like the example *Add* and *Remove* functions in Fig. 1. It also defines the interface for accessing the child components of a complex object (a topic or a subtopic), e.g. the functions *Operation* and *GetChild*. The concrete classes *Leaf* (corresponding to simple contents of a lesson in our example) and *Composite* (corresponding to topics and subtopics) are derived from *Component*. The *Leaf* class represents leaf objects in the composition and has no children. It defines behavior for primitive objects in the composition. The *Composite* class implements child-related functions from the *Component* interface, stores child components, and defines behavior for components having children. A client object (e.g., a lesson presentation planner) interacts with any object in the composition through the common interface provided by the *Component* class. The client's requests are handled directly by *Leaf* recipients, and are usually forwarded to child components by *Composite* recipients.

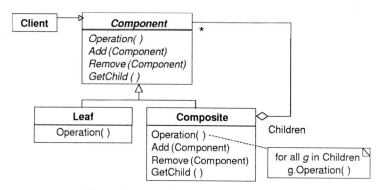

Fig. 1. Structure of the Composite pattern

Applicability. Typical situations in which the Composite pattern can be applied in ITS design include representing part-whole hierarchies of objects (such as composing topics, lessons, and curricula), and those when it should be possible to treat all objects in the composite structure uniformly by a client (such as a lesson presentation planner or curriculum composer).

Consequences. Using the Composite pattern lets designers define hierarchies consisting of both primitive and composite entities, makes the client simple, also makes it easier to add new kinds of components, but can make the design overly general because it is hard to restrict the components in such a design.

Implementation. There are many things to consider when implementing the Composite pattern [8]. Due to space limitations, only one of them will be mentioned here. That one is extremely important for ITS designers. It is related to child to parent references in a composite structure. Maintaining such references can make the design much more efficient, since it simplifies traversal and management of the composite structure. For example, having appropriate references from graphics objects to topics of a lesson is essential, especially when a graphics object can be presented during more than one topic presentation.

Known uses. The Composite pattern is used explicitly in the GET-BITS framework's lesson presentation planner and remedial actions planner (which is a part of the student's knowledge examination and assessment), as well as in topic representation and curriculum composer. The GET-BITS-based FLUTE system, developed as an ITS for teaching formal languages [2], is a concrete ITS within which such planners are used. In the design of Eon tools [14] and SimQuest [21], there are implicit signs of the presence of the Composite pattern, although the authors of these tools don't talk about it directly.

Related patterns. Composite is often used with the patterns called Chain of Responsibility, Iterator, and Decorator (see [8] for details of these patterns). These patterns were also extensively used in the design of the GET-BITS framework.

4 Discovering Patterns in Existing ITS Architectures

Nobody should *invent* patterns. They are rather *discovered from experience* in building practical systems. I describe here how I have discovered a simple, concrete ITS-architectural pattern and outline the pattern discovery process I have used. The entire section is written subjectively, and that's on purpose. I don't claim that this is the only way to discover patterns in ITS architectures, nor I can say that the process I have used is optimal or that it guarantees success. My intents were to try discovering some patterns, to describe them in the way patterns for software architectures are usually described, and to see how strong is the support for them in existing ITSs and on-going projects.

4.1 Pattern Discovery Process

In the beginning, it was a matter of intuition. I just had a feeling that different ITS architectures hide several common principles and solutions, regardless of the ITS models used in building specific systems. The patterns I have discovered describe what I believe that were the guiding principles and driving forces that have led ITS designers to develop architectures of their systems the way they did. More precisely, I was trying to *extract* patterns from known examples, systems, architectures, designs, learning and teaching styles, strategies, etc.

The issues that have been really important to me were:

- Are there common solutions in the architectures of different ITSs and their parts, and if so - what are they?
- What has led the designers to apply such solutions in the versions of their systems that I have considered?

In the course of answering the above questions, I have analyzed different ITS architectures that have been described in all the conference and workshop proceedings of ITS and AIED conferences since 1997, as well as in the IJAIED journal's volumes 8 through 11. I have also consulted the proceedings of some other relevant conferences and workshops, and some journals other that IJAIED that publish ITS/AIED-related papers. The relevant numbers are shown in Table 1. I am aware of the fact that I might have missed some other important work on ITS architectures.

Table 1. Statistics about the ITS-architectural patterns discovered so far

Total number of patterns discovered	7
Total number of papers analyzed	66
Total number of papers found to support some pattern(s) that have been discovered	42
Number of papers that support individual patterns	5-12

4.2 An Example of Discovering a Pattern in ITS Architectures

The ITS-architectural pattern considered here is *very simple*, but also quite sufficient to describe the main issues of patterns and the pattern discovery process. Note that, generally, patterns need not necessarily be something complex and very sophisticated - on the contrary, many software patterns are quite simple (see [8], [5], [18]). What is definitely *not* simple is the pattern discovery.

The pattern described here is related to layered architectures of ITSs. Fig. 2 shows two different, layered ITS architectures. Vassileva has proposed creating *application agents* associated with applications, tutors, coaches, and learning environments, Fig. 2a [22]. Such application agents would represent specific applications (e.g., learning environments) in much the same way personal agents represent their users. Just like personal agents have knowledge of their users' goals, plans, and resources, an application agent should have knowledge of the corresponding application's goals, plans, resources, and actions. This way, the application agent mediates communication of its application with the user and other entities in the external world, just like the personal agent does the same on behalf of its user. The application agent appears as extracted from its application in order to perform that role. The result is quite a symmetric situation.

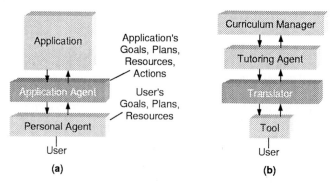

Fig. 2. a) Introducing the application agent [22] b) Using translator in a plug-in component architecture [15]

The *translator* layer in Ritter's plug-in tutor architecture [15] has a similar role, Fig. 2b. It mediates communication between a commercial, off-the-shelf tool (such as Microsoft Excel) and the tutoring agent. Such a translator provides students with the ability to work with industry-standard software, while still getting intelligent guidance from the tutor. This is very different from tightly integrated ITSs developed with traditional tools.

A common detail in both of the above architectures - a pattern - is an *inserted layer* that provides a new or specific functionality. The abstract structure of the pattern is shown in Fig. 3. In the literature that has been analyzed in search for ITS-architectural patterns, 12 different architectures that use this pattern have been found. These architectures have been developed in various ITS/AIED subject areas, such as student modeling, pedagogical agents, ontologies, collaborative learning systems, and so on. Some examples (other than the two mentioned above) include [1], [9], [19] and [20]. Apart from these 12 architectures, traces of this pattern can be seen in some other systems as well. If similar (but different) patterns also count, then more than 20 different ITS architectures that have been analyzed support this pattern.

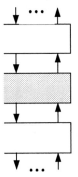

Fig. 3. The pattern's structure

It is important to stress that the designers of different ITS architectures have used this pattern probably without being aware of it and without thinking in the pattern-oriented way. They were just applying it as a natural solution of the problems like introducing a new functionality into a layered architecture, better decoupling of two adjacent layers, the need to bridge domain-specific and domain-independent layers, and the like. Essentially, all of them have *implicitly* used the pattern from Fig. 3 in their architectures. The following section describes the pattern and its driving forces *explicitly*.

5 The Inserted Layer Pattern

One typical way of describing a pattern is specifying the *context* where the pattern is useful, the *problem* that the pattern addresses, the *forces* that drive the process of forming a solution, and the *solution* that resolves those forces [5]. Specifying the solution often involves showing a *diagram*, and sometimes the pattern's *variants* are also described and pointers to *related patterns* are given [8], [18]. Most of these "parts" of a pattern are usually shown in the form of simple statements.

All patterns have names. Naming a newly discovered pattern is never easy, since the name itself has to reflect the pattern's purpose, the way it is applied, and still be common enough to represent generalized solution of a certain typical problem. The name I have given the pattern from Fig. 5 is *Inserted Layer*. Some patterns have alternative names. Good alternative names for the Inserted Layer pattern are *Slot* and *Decoupler*. The pattern's description is as follows.

Context. A layered ITS architecture. The layers can be functional modules, autonomous agents, or parts of a larger module.

Problem. Either of the following:

- a new functionality is needed in the ITS or the architecture must be adapted to a new requirement (e.g., [1]);
- the architecture of the ITS must clearly differentiate between domain-dependent and domain-independent layers (e.g., [9], [20]);

- translation between adjacent layers of the ITS architecture is necessary (e.g., [11], [15], [19]);
- mediation or negotiation between the layers or the educational agents is required (e.g., [7], [22]).

Forces. Either of the following:
- existing layers should be better decoupled (e.g., [22]);
- the knowledge and operational levels in the architecture should be clearly distinguished (e.g., [5], [20]);
- component-based, plug-in design needs, and interoperability between ITSs (e.g., [11], [15]).

Solution. Insert a new layer to implement and encapsulate the new functionality. Check the trade-offs caused by the addition of the new layer (such as satisfying the new requirement vs. possibly increasing the overhead, and increased modularity and reusability vs. the necessary changes of the existing functional layers).

Diagram. See Fig. 3.

Variants. Sometimes the inserted layer either only receives some input from an adjacent layer, or it only sends some output to it, but not both. Putting the inserted layer on top of all the other layers instead in between some of them is possible, but that's another pattern. In some cases, the inserted layer and some of the other functional layers can share some knowledge, data, and other resources (e.g., the student model, a common ontology, simulation parameters, and other resources; see [11], for an example).

Related patterns. 12 other, already known patterns have been found to resemble Inserted Layer. Some of them (Bridge, Facade, Mediator, Adapter, and Proxy) are described in [8].

6 Discussion and Conclusions

During the analysis of ITS architectures that has been conducted in search of patterns, six other patterns have been discovered along with Inserted Layer. They have got the names Top, Cascade, T-join, Cross, Multiplexer, and Store. They will be all described in the forthcoming larger paper.

A structured collection of interrelated patterns is often called a *pattern language* [16]. Pattern languages cover particular domains and disciplines, and provide specialists with vocabularies for talking about specific problems. The seven ITS-arhitectural patterns that have been discovered represent the core of a pattern language for ITS architectures. Such a pattern language can help ITS developers communicate better, especially if new patterns continue to accumulate in that language over time.

As for using well-known patterns such as general design patterns, it is of primary importance to ITS developers to understand that patterns do not require knowledge of specific programming tricks or languages. They only require little extra effort in order to understand the recurring nature of solutions to specific problems, recognize instances of such problems in building ITSs, and find a suitable way to apply already known solutions. The pay-off is definitely much larger that the extra effort: increased flexibility, modularity, and reuse of ITS software, reduced development time, and efficient, elegant, and effective design solutions.

Discovering patterns in ITS-related issues like ITS architectures is not a kind of search for *new* modeling and design solutions. It is more like *compiling* what we already know. Patterns enable us to see what kind of solutions ITS/AIED researchers and developers *typically* apply when faced with common problems. By discovering useful patterns, describing them in an appropriate way, and creating pattern catalogues, we are actually unveiling common structures of frequently arising problems and are representing the knowledge of their contexts, solutions, driving forces and trade-offs in the form of explicit statements. Once we have such explicitly represented knowledge and experience, we can get a valuable feedback - we can use the patterns intentionally and systematically in other systems and applications, i.e. for further developments. In that sense, AIED/ITS patterns and pattern languages can be understood as many small tools for modeling and developing ITSs, and a catalogue of AIED/ITS patterns would be a toolkit. Knowledge of patterns lets us design our systems better.

References

1. Abou-Jaoude, S., Frasson, C.: Integrating a Believable Layer into Traditional ITS. In: Lajoie, S.P., Vivet, M. (eds.): Artificial Intelligece in Education. IOS Press, Amsterdam / OHM Ohmsha, Tokyo (1999) 315-324
2. Devedzic, V., Debenham, J.: An Intelligent Tutoring System for Teaching Formal Languages. In: Goettl, B.R., Halff, H.M., Redfield, C.L., Shute, V.J. (eds.): Lecture Notes in Computer Science, Vol. 1452. Springer-Verlag, NY (1998) 514-523
3. Devedzic, V., Radovic, D., Jerinic, Lj.: The GET-BITS Model of Intelligent Tutoring Systems. Int. J. of Continuing Eng. Education and Life-Long Learning, Special Issue on Intelligent Systems/Tools in Training and Life-Long Learning (2000) forthcoming
4. Design Patterns Home Page: http://st-www.cs.uiuc.edu/users/patterns/patterns.html (2000)
5. Fowler, M.: Analysis Patterns: Reusable Object Models. Addison-Wesley, Reading, MA (1997)
6. Fowler, M., Scott, K.: UML Distilled: Applying the Standard Object Modelling Language. Addison-Wesley, Reading, MA (1997)
7. Frasson, C., Martin, L., Gouarderes, G., Aimeur, E.: LANCA: A Distance Learning Architecture Based on Networked Cognitive Agents. In: Goettl, B.R., Halff, H.M., Redfield, C.L., Shute, V.J. (eds.): Lecture Notes in Computer Science, Vol. 1452. Springer-Verlag, NY (1998) 594-603
8. Gamma, E., Helm, R., Johnson, R., Vlissides, J.: Design Patterns: Elements of Reusable Object-Oriented Software. Addison-Wesley, Reading, MA (1995)
9. Ikeda, M., Kazuhisa, S., Mizoguchi, R.: Task Ontology Makes It Easier To Use Authoring Tools. Proceedings of The Fifteenth International Joint Conference on Artificial Intelligence. Nagoya, Japan (1997) 193-200
10. Johnson, W.L., Rickel, J., Lester, J.C.: Animated Pedagogical Agents: Face-to-Face Interaction in Interactive Learning Environments. Int. J. of Artificial Intelligence in Education 11 (2000) to appear
11. Koedinger, K.R., Suthers, D.D., Forbus, K.D.: Component-Based Construction of a Science Learning Space. Int. J. of Artificial Intelligence in Education 10 (1999) 38-56
12. Lester, J.C., Towns, S.G., Fitzgerald, P.J.: Achieving Affective Impact: Visual Emotive Communication in Lifelike Pedagogical Agents. Int. J. of Artificial Intelligence in Education 10 (1999) 87-102
13. Mizoguchi, R., Bourdeau, J.: Using Ontological Engineering to Overcome Common AI-ED Problems. Int. J. of Artificial Intelligence in Education 11 (2000) to appear

14. Murray, T.: Authoring Knowledge-Based Tutors: Tools for Content, Instructional Strategy, Student Model, and Interface Design. The J. of the Learning Sciences 7 (1998) 5-64
15. Ritter, S.: PAT Online: A Model-Tracing Tutor on the World-Wide Web. Proceedings of the Workshop "Intelligent Educational Systems on the World Wide Web". Kobe, Japan (1997) 11-17
16. Schmidt, D., Fayad, M., Johnson, R.E.: Software Patterns. Comm. of The ACM 39/10 (1996) 37-39
17. Schmidt, D.: Design Patterns and Pattern Languages. http://siesta.cs.wustl.edu/~schmidt/patterns.html (2000)
18. Shaw, M.: Patterns for Software Architectures. In: Coplien, J., Schmidt, D. (eds): Pattern Languages of Program Design. Addison-Wesley, Reading, MA (1995) 453-462
19. Shaw, E., Ganeshan, R., Johnson, W.L., Millar, D.: Building a Case for Agent-Assisted Learning as a Catalyst for Curriculum Reform in Medical Education. Proceedings of the Workshop "Animated and Personified Pedagogical Agents". Le Mans, France (1999) 70-78
20. Tecuci, G., Keeling, H.: Developing Intelligent Educational Agents with Disciple. Int. J. of Artificial Intelligence in Education 10 (1999) 16-35
21. van Joolingen, W., King, S., De Jong, T.: The SimQuest Authoring System for Simulation-Based Discovery Learning. In: du Boulay, B., Mizoguchi, R. (eds.): Artificial Intelligence in Education. IOS Press, Amsterdam / OHM Ohmsha, Tokyo (1997) 79-86.
22. Vassileva, J.: Goal-Based Autonomous Social Agents: Supporting Adaptation and Teaching in a Distributed Environment. In: Goettl, B.R., Halff, H.M., Redfield, C.L., Shute, V.J. (eds.): Lecture Notes in Computer Science, Vol. 1452. Springer-Verlag, NY (1998) 564-573

Andes: A Coached Problem Solving Environment for Physics *

Abigail S. Gertner[1] and Kurt VanLehn[2]

[1] The MITRE Corporation, Bedford, MA 01730
[2] LRDC, University of Pittsburgh, Pittsburgh, PA 15260

Abstract. Andes is an Intelligent Tutoring System for introductory college physics. The fundamental principles underlying the design of Andes are: (1) encourage the student to construct new knowledge by providing hints that require them to derive most of the solution on their own, (2) facilitate transfer from the system by making the interface as much like a piece of paper as possible, (3) give immediate feedback after each action to maximize the opportunities for learning and minimize the amount of time spent going down wrong paths, and (4) give the student flexibility in the order in which actions are performed, and allow them to skip steps when appropriate. This paper gives an overview of Andes, focusing on the overall architecture and the student's experience using the system.

1 Introduction

This paper is an overview of problem solving in Andes – an Intelligent Tutoring System for introductory college physics. Andes interacts with students using *coached problem solving* [12], a method of teaching cognitive skills in which the tutor and the student collaborate to solve problems. In coached problem solving, the initiative in the student-tutor interaction changes according to the progress being made. As long as the student proceeds along a correct solution, the tutor merely indicates agreement with each step. When the student gets stuck or makes an error, the tutor helps the student overcome the impasse by providing hints that lead the student back to the correct solution path.

The fundamental principles underlying the design of Andes are: (1) encourage the student to construct new knowledge by providing hints that require them to derive most of the solution on their own, (2) facilitate transfer from the system by making the interface as much like a piece of paper as possible, (3) give immediate feedback after each action to maximize the opportunities for learning and minimize the amount of time spent going down wrong paths, and (4) give the student flexibility in the order in which actions are performed, and allow them to

---

* This research was supported by ARPA's Computer Aided Education and Training Initiative under grant N660001-95-C-8367, by ONR's Cognitive Science Division under grant N00014-96-1-0260, and by AFOSR's Artificial Intelligence Division under grant F49620-96-1-0180. The authors would like to thank the members of the Andes group.

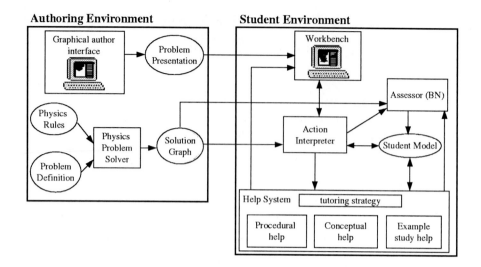

Fig. 1. The Andes System Architecture

skip steps when appropriate. This paper gives an overview of the system that we designed following these principles, focusing on the overall architecture and the student's experience using Andes. Several of the modules that Andes comprises are described in other papers and so we will not discuss them in detail here. In particular, we will not talk at all about the Self-Explanation coach or the Conceptual help system, which are described in [4, 5] and [1] respectively.

The following section provides a brief summary of the Andes architecture and implementation. Section 3 gives an example of the typical student interaction with Andes while solving a problem. In Section 4, we describe the underlying system for providing feedback and help. Finally, in Section 5 we present some of the work we have done to evaluate Andes with students.

2   Andes system overview

The Andes project began in September 1995, and is a collaboration between the University of Pittsburgh and the US Naval Academy. Andes is implemented in Allegro Common Lisp and Microsoft Visual C++ and runs on Pentium PCs under Windows 95.

Andes has a modular architecture, as shown in Figure 1. The left side of Figure 1 shows the authoring environment for creating new problems. Prior to run time, a problem author creates both the graphical description of the problem, and the corresponding coded problem definition. Andes' problem solver uses this definition to automatically generate a model of the problem solution space called the *solution graph.*

The right side of the figure shows the run-time student environment. The Workbench is the graphical interface with which the student studies examples and solves physics problems. The Workbench communicates with the Action Interpreter, which looks up the student's entries in the solution graph and provides immediate feedback as to whether the entries are correct or incorrect. More detailed feedback is provided by Andes' Help System [12]. Both the Action Interpreter and the Help System refer to the student model to make decisions about what kind of feedback and help to give the student. The central component of the student model is a Bayesian network that is constructed and updated by the Assessor, and provides probabilistic estimates of the student's mental state [3]. The student model also contains information about what problems the student has worked on, what interface features they have used, and what help they have received from the system in the past.

3 Solving problems with Andes: an example

One of the principles underlying the design of Andes was that the interface ought to be as much like a piece of paper as possible, so as to facilitate fading of tutorial support as students become more familiar with the physics domain, and the eventual transfer from solving problems with Andes to solving problems on paper. We attempted to keep the number of structured entry fields to a minimum, since every piece of structure in the interface might serve as scaffolding to the student, on which they could become dependent. As a result, the interface initially appears quite simple, consisting of two main entry panes (Figure 2), in which students can draw diagrams (upper left) and enter equations (lower right), as well as the variable definitions pane, located above the equation pane, and the hint window, below the diagram pane on the left.

3.1 Drawing diagrams

When a problem is first opened, the diagram pane contains a statement of the problem and a (read-only) picture of the problem situation. The lower part of the pane is initially blank. This area is provided for the student to perform a *qualitative analysis* of the problem before they begin working out the quantitative solution (in fact, some problems only ask for the qualitative analysis and do not require the student to write any equations). This type of qualitative reasoning is an important part of physics problem solving. It is used by expert physicists both in talking about simple physics problems [2] and when discussing real-world research results [10]. In addition, requiring qualitative reasoning in solving problems has been found to uncover students' misconceptions better than allowing students to use algebraic reasoning alone [11, 8].

Students use the drawing tools to the left of the diagram pane to enter elements of a free body diagram such as force vectors. The student can also draw motion vectors such as velocity and acceleration. To draw a vector, the student clicks and drags the mouse in the diagram pane, rotating the vector until it points in the desired direction and then releasing the mouse. Other items that can be included in a diagram include coordinate axis systems, angles between

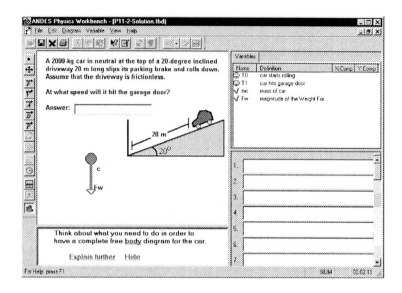

Fig. 2. The Andes problem solving interface

vectors and axes, and the radius of a circular path. All of these are drawn with the mouse using the tools on the left of the screen.

After the student has drawn an item in the diagram window using the mouse, a dialog box appears in which the student must enter information defining the object they have just drawn. This departure from the "piece of paper" principle is necessary so that Andes can give appropriate feedback based on not just what the student drew (eg. a vector pointing straight up) but also what they *meant* by that entry (eg. a normal force exerted by the driveway on the car).

3.2 Variable definitions

Another significant way that the Andes interface differs from a piece of paper is in the definition of variables and how they are used in equations. When a student is solving a physics problem on paper, she can start out right away by writing down an equation, such as $F = m*a$ without explicitly stating what F, m, and a refer to. Andes, on the other hand, requires all quantities to be defined explicitly before they may be entered in equations. This enforces a systematic approach to problem solving which can greatly reduce the number of careless mistakes students make.

Variables may either be defined by assigning a label to an item in the diagram, or by using a special purpose variable definition menu. Certain quantities (such as scalar quantities like speed) cannot be drawn in a diagram, so the variable menu must be used to define variables for these quantities. Using the variable menu involves choosing the type of quantity to be defined and then filling in a dialog box similar to the ones for diagram entries.

Whether a variable was defined as a diagram entry or using the variable menu, after it has been defined it will appear in the variable definitions pane. This pane lists all defined variables with their definitions and, for vectors, the names of their components.

3.3 Entering equations

Equations are entered in the text fields in the lower right pane of the Workbench, a single equation per line. There is no structured equation editor in Andes. Students use a conventional syntax for entering equations (operators *, /, +, and -; ^ for exponentiation; _ for subscripts). Students can enter anything they want into the equation field and Andes will attempt to parse it and determine whether it corresponds to a correct equation [6]. There may be more than one possible parse for an equation, in which case Andes will look up whether any of the parses represents a correct equation.

Variables in equations must first be defined so that they are listed in the variable pane. If Andes finds tokens in the equation that can only be interpreted as undefined variables, it displays an error message listing those tokens. If the equation cannot be parsed for some other reason, it displays an error message informing the student that it could not interpret the entry. Otherwise, Andes gives simple correct/incorrect feedback on the equation entry.

4 Feedback and help

As illustrated in Figure 1, the Action Interpreter is the central module of Andes. It is responsible for getting student input from the Workbench, recording the input in its databases, and returning feedback to the Workbench which includes information about whether the student's action was correct or incorrect, as well as hints and help messages to be displayed. The following sections describe how the Action interpreter and related modules do their jobs.

4.1 The student model

Modeling a student in an ITS involves a great deal of inherent uncertainty regarding not only the student's *beliefs* and *goals*, but also the level of *knowledge* that she has about the domain. There is additional uncertainty in Andes since the student is not constrained to perform actions in a particular order. This means that even if Andes has not observed the student performing a certain action, it cannot assume that the student doesn't know *how* to perform that action because the student may intend to perform it in the future. To address these multiple sources of uncertainty, Andes' student model combines information about the current state of the problem solving process with long-term assessment of the student's knowledge of physics in a probabilistic representation using Bayesian networks [3].

Each physics problem is represented by a separate Bayesian network. As a student moves from one problem to the next, Andes' assessment of her general physics knowledge is updated and used to initialize the model for the next problem. Thus the modeling of *problem-specific* knowledge about each problem is related through the *domain-general* assessment of physics knowledge that the problems have in common.

The Bayesian network for each problem is constructed from a data structure called a *solution graph* which represents alternative solution paths for each problem, including some that involve "buggy" rules and thus represent typical incorrect student solutions. Andes' Bayesian networks may have anywhere from around 100 to over 200 nodes, depending on the complexity of the problem. Using a network that represents the entire solution space for the problem means that the student model always has estimated probability values, even for steps that haven't been explicitly observed. This supports the Andes design principle of allowing the student maximum flexibility in performing solution steps in any order and skipping steps.

Bayesian networks provide us with a principled framework for combining all of the different sources of uncertainty about the student's problem-solving processes. For example, if a given fact may be derived in two different ways, and a student is observed to know the fact, the Bayesian network provides a straightforward way of sharing the credit for that knowledge between the two alternative derivations. Furthermore, if one of the derivations is known to be less likely than the other (e.g., because it depends on a rule that the student probably does not know), then the credit will be apportioned accordingly – giving more weight to the derivation that the student is likely to know.

The Action Interpreter interacts with the Bayesian network in two ways. First, when Andes observes the student performing an action that corresponds to a node in the Bayesian network, the value of that node is clamped to True, and the network is updated to reflect the new evidence. Second, when Andes needs to respond to the student in a way that depends on some aspect of her current knowledge or mental state, the Action Interpreter queries the Bayesian network to find out the current probabilities associated with the relevant nodes. This can be used for resolving ambiguities in determining the student's current goal, as well as for determining the appropriate level of help to give for part of the problem.

4.2 Immediate feedback

When a student makes an entry in Andes, the workbench always responds with immediate flag feedback by changing the color of the entry – green for correct and red for incorrect. This feedback is generated using information from the solution graph. Here, we will describe how the feedback is generated for diagram entries and variable definitions. Feedback for equation entries is more complicated, and is described in some detail in [6].

Each student entry may reflect several different pieces of information, as represented by the multiple fields of the dialog boxes for defining diagram entries.

For example, the definition of a force vector includes fields for the type of force, the object it is acting on, the agent of the force, and its direction. When the student enters a definition, the Action interpreter looks at the information in the solution graph to see if any quantity exists there with exactly the same features as the student's entry. If it finds such an entry, the dialog box disappears and the entry turns green on the screen. If no matching quantity is found, the Action Interpreter has to determine what part of the entry is incorrect. To do this, it attempts to determine what the student was most likely to have been trying to enter, and then finds the features that differ between that intended entry and the actual entry.

Finding the most likely intended entry is done using a combination of matching features and probabilities. The solution graph quantity with the most features in common with the student's entry, and the highest probability in the Bayesian network, is selected as the intended entry. This entry is then compared to the student's entry to finds those features that differ between the two. Andes then turns red only the fields in the dialog box corresponding to the mismatched features. This gives the student specific feedback on what part of their entry was in error.

4.3 What's wrong with that?

As noted earlier, one of the design principles for Andes was to encourage *constructive*, as opposed to passive, learning. Therefore, Andes gives away as little information as possible unless the student asks for it. In the case of errors, Andes always starts by giving flag feedback. This feedback is accompanied by a hint or error message only in the case of simple syntactic errors. For all other errors, the student is expected to attempt to fix the problem on her own if she can.

If the student is not able to fix an erroneous entry on her own, she can select the entry and ask "what's wrong with that?" using a menu, and Andes will respond with a short hint intended to point the student toward the feature of her entry that was incorrect. For example, if the entry was an acceleration vector labeled 'a' whose direction was incorrect, the hint might say "think about the direction of 'a'."

When a non-specific hint is given, there will also be a link labelled "Explain Further" in the hint window, which the student can click on to get more information. Clicking repeatedly on "Explain Further" will eventually result in a hint that explicitly tells the student how to fix their entry. For example, the bottom-out hint for the direction of the acceleration vector might be "The direction of 'a' is horizontal and to the left."

4.4 Procedural help

Procedural help is the part of Andes' help system that is responsible for generating a hint when the student gets stuck and asks for help [7]. Hints are generated based on the state of the student model at the time the student asks for help. To produce a hint, Andes first selects a node in the solution graph that will be the topic of the hint. The topic node should represent a proposition that is relevant to what the student has been doing recently and that the student is likely to want to address next. The hint topic node is selected by first identifying a goal node in the solution graph that is likely to be the reason for the student's most recent action, and then following a path from that goal to find a node representing an action that the student has not yet done and, according to the Assessor, probably does not know about (this procedure is described in more detail in [7]).

Once a hint topic node has been selected, the hint template belonging to the proposition the node represents is instantiated with the contextually relevant information from the problem to generate an English string to be displayed to the student. As in the case of the "what's wrong with that" hints, the initial hint given for a particular topic node will be quite general, to encourage students to recover from the impasse on their own. Students can then click on a link to get successively more specific hints until they are able to continue solving the problem.

5 Evaluations of Andes

Andes' development has been carried out in conjunction with an ongoing series of formative evaluations, which were used to assess the usability of the interface, suggest new features, and evaluate the effectiveness and clarity of hints and help messages. Prototype versions of the system have been used by students at the US Naval Academy every semester since the Fall of 1996. Additionally, several more in-depth user studies were carried out at the University of Pittsburgh during that time.

At the Naval Academy, students taking the introductory physics course were asked to use Andes to do some of their homework. To do this, each student had to download the Andes installation file from the local network, install it on their personal computer in their dorm room, and start using on their own after just a short demonstration. Right away, this required us to implement an easily used installation program, to make sure that the Andes interface was simple enough that students could get up and running without much help, and to include extensive on-line help files that they could access while they were using the program.

We used several methods for getting information from students during these formative evaluations. First, they were encouraged to enter comments in a special dialog box as they worked with Andes. We found that students did not enter comments very often, but when they did we were able to bring them to the attention of the instructors who would quickly address the student's question or concern. Second, students filled out a questionnaire about their experience using the program. These questionnaires turned out to be not very informative because students did not give much detailed information about what they would like to see changed in the system. Third, they communicated frequently with their instructors about problems they were having using the system. This was extremely important as it allowed the instructors to develop a very complete overall view of the problems people were having and what we could do to fix them. Finally, all student activity within Andes is recorded in log files which the students were prompted to upload each time they exited the program. These log files, including students' comments as well as a complete record of every action performed on the interface, provided a wealth of information to guide us in improving the system. Log files were also used by the instructors to get a better sense of what a student had been doing when they came in for extra help.

At the University of Pittsburgh our approach in evaluating the system was to record a small number of sessions with students using Andes, and to have the students "think out loud" as they worked with the program. We could then identify significant events in the session records where students failed to learn something due to a flaw in Andes' help, and rank them according to frequency and importance. We used these events as targets for improving the system and tested our changes by performing the same actions on the new version of Andes and seeing if the help it gave had improved. In this way, we were able to fix many of the major problems students had both with the interface design and the help system.

In the Fall of 1999 we performed a summative field evaluation of Andes at the Naval Academy. Andes was used for four weeks by 173 students in eight sections of the Naval Academy's introductory physics course. At the end of this time, they were given a midterm exam covering material that was taught by Andes (and by instructors during course lectures and sections). The students' performance on the midterm was compared to a control group of 162 students whose sections did not use Andes. The results of this comparison were encouraging. Students who used Andes performed 2.9 percent (1/3 of a letter grade) better on average than students who did not use Andes ($p \leq 0.033$). This compares favorably with other successfully evaluated tutoring systems. For instance, the PUMP Algebra Tutor had an effect size[1] of 0.3σ on standardized math tests [9], whereas Andes effect size was 0.2σ on the normal exam used by the whole course. Although the PUMP Algebra Tutor also had an effect size of approximately 1.0σ on tests designed for its content, we did not use such tests in our evaluation of Andes.

Perhaps more interestingly, when the Andes results are broken down by the students' major, we see that the effect of Andes for humanities majors was the largest (7.3 percent), with the effect for science majors next largest (3.9 percent). In the case of the engineering students (who were also taking a course on statics concurrently) there was actually a small (1.3 percent) negative effect for Andes. Thus, Andes appears to be most effective with students who are most likely to need help learning physics.

6   Conclusions

In this paper we have provided an overview of the Andes system, showing how we were guided by the four design principles listed in the Introduction. We have

---

[1] Effect size is calculated as the difference between the score of the experimental group and the score of the control group, divided by the standard deviation of the control.

learned a great deal in the process of developing and deploying Andes, both about designing an ITS to teach complex problem-solving skills and about the integration of such a system into an existing instructional environment. Future work on this project should continue to yield many more insights (see [13] in this volume).

References

[1] P. L. Albacete and K. A. VanLehn. The conceptual helper: An intelligent tutoring system for teaching fundamental physics concepts. In *Proceedings of the Fifth International Conference on Intelligent Tutoring Systems*, 2000.

[2] M. Chi, P. Feltovich, and R. Glaser. Categorization and representation of physics problems by experts and novices. *Cognitive Science*, 5:121–152, 1981.

[3] C. Conati, A. S. Gertner, K. VanLehn, and M. J. Druzdzel. On-line student modeling for coached problem solving using Bayesian networks. In *Proceedings of UM-97, Sixth International Conference on User Modeling*, pages 231–242, Sardinia, Italy, June 1997. Springer.

[4] C. Conati and K. VanLehn. Teaching meta-cognitive skills: implementation and evaluation of a tutoring system to guide self-explanation while learning from examples. In *In ¿ Proceedings of AIED 99, 9th World Conference of Artificial Intelligence and Education, Le Man, France*, 1999.

[5] C. Conati and K. A. VanLehn. Further results from the evaluation of an intelligent computer tutor to coach self-explanation. In *Proceedings of the Fifth International Conference on Intelligent Tutoring Systems*, 2000.

[6] A. S. Gertner. Providing feedback to equation entries in an intelligent tutoring system for physics. In *Proceedings of the 4th International Conference on Intelligent Tutoring Systems*, San Antonio, August 1998.

[7] A. S. Gertner, C. Conati, and K. VanLehn. Procedural help in Andes: Generating hints using a Bayesian network student model. In *Proceedings of the Fifteenth National Conference on Artificial Intelligence*, Madison, WI, 1998.

[8] J. I. Heller and F. Reif. Prescribing effective human problem-solving processes: Problem descriptions in physics. *Cognition and Instruction*, 1(2):177–216, 1984.

[9] K. R. Koedinger, J. R. Anderson, W. H. Hadley, and M. A. Mark. Intelligent tutoring goes to school in the big city. In J. Greer, editor, *Proceedings of the 7th World Conference on Artificial Intelligence and Education*, pages 421–428, Charlottesville, NC, 1995.

[10] A. Van Heuvelen. Learning to think like a physicist: A review of research-based instructional strategies. *American Journal of Physics*, 59(10):891–897, 1991.

[11] A. Van Heuvelen. Overview, case study physics. *American Journal of Physics*, 59(10):898–907, 1991.

[12] K. VanLehn. Conceptual and meta learning during coached problem solving. In C. Frasson, G. Gauthier, and A. Lesgold, editors, *Proceedings of the Third International Conference on Intelligent Tutoring Systems ITS '96*, pages 29–47. Springer, 1996.

[13] K. VanLehn, R. Freedman, P. Jordan, R. C. Murray, R. Osan, M. Ringenberg, C. Rosé, K. Schulze, R. Shelby, D. Treacy, A. Weinstein, and M. Wintersgill. Fading and deepening: The next steps for andes and other model-tracing tutors. In *Proceedings of the Fifth International Conference on Intelligent Tutoring Systems*, 2000.

A Collection of Pedagogical Agents for Intelligent Educational Systems

Ruddy Lelouche

Département d'informatique, Université Laval, Québec G1K 7P4 CANADA
Tel.: (418) 656 2131, ext. 2597   Fax: (418) 656 2324
Ruddy.Lelouche@ift.ulaval.ca

Abstract. This paper presents an original modelling of the tutoring knowledge in an intelligent educational system based on a collection of interacting agents, in particular in a problem-solving domain. After a brief description of the knowledge modelling and a generic functioning framework for ITSs in problem-solving domains, we introduce the tutoring knowledge modelled as pedagogical agents. We show how these agents interact with one another and with the student, and discuss tools which may help optimise decisions about how an agent takes control or fulfils a given pedagogical function. To illustrate our point of view, we then present and comment on a tutoring dialogue in detail, using as background a problem-solving exercise. Such a interactive-agent-oriented model should both facilitate the implementation of the tutoring knowledge in an intelligent educational system and help improve the student's comprehension through better pedagogical interactions.

Introduction

For several decades, computers have been used in the development of educational systems. In particular, IA-based systems have evolved, being successively called intelligent computer-assisted instruction (ICAI) systems, intelligent tutoring systems (ITSs), or more lately interactive learning environments (ILEs). In the first projects, research has been focused more on the domain knowledge representation than on the tutoring knowledge: in many first experimental systems, pedagogical procedures were integrated into the domain knowledge [3]. However, interest for an explicit representation of tutorial knowledge has been continuously growing: concepts like student model [4], pedagogical diagnosis [14] and tutoring expertise [11] have been widely discussed since their introductions into the ICAI world. Most AI representation paradigms have been used: production rules, networks, frames, etc. More recently, the multi-agent-system concept was adapted to ITSs, giving way to an agent-based approach to represent the pedagogical knowledge and its use for tutoring [12]. In that context, while working on a specific ITS, Lelouche and Morin also conducted their reflections about how to help the system to generate simple and meaningful pedagogical interactions and the tutoring knowledge to be as general and portable as possible. They thus came up with the concept of *know-how domains* or KH-domains, in which the student should acquire, besides domain theoretical elements, some kind of problem-solving skills. They then applied the KH-domain concept to ITSs [10], yielding KH-ITSs (SCHOLAR [2], although an ICAI system, was not a KH-ITS: there was no or little problem-solving involved). The goal of this paper is to generalise their work to other kinds of intelligent educational systems (IESs), in particular to ILEs and computer-supported collaborative learning (CSCL), and to emphasise the system–student interactions and the agent–agent interactions in such systems.

We first recall how knowledge is defined and structured in a KH-domain and how generic operating modes can be based on that structure (section 1). Next, we introduce our tutoring knowledge model using the concept of pedagogical agents (section 2), and examine some of their general characteristics (section 3). We then give excerpts of a tutoring session in cost-engineering based on our approach, including some examples of student-related knowledge involved in agent interactions (section 4).

1 Knowledge representation and operating modes

1.1 Domain knowledge and problem-solving knowledge

We deal here with the knowledge to be acquired by the student. In the particular case of KH-domains, the domain to be taught clearly encompasses both domain theoretical elements and practical problem-solving skills. We therefore think that knowledge to be taught in a KH-ITS or in a KH-ILE ought to be divided in the same way.

In a KH-domain, we restrict the name *domain knowledge* (DK) to that part containing all theoretical and factual aspects of the knowledge describing the domain to be taught. Although its structure can be varied, DK typically may include concepts, entities, relations, possible use restrictions, objects, semantic networks, facts, rules, etc. This is very similar to what is often called *declarative knowledge* (note that rules are ambiguous in that respect). By opposition, the *problem-solving knowledge* (PSK), specific to KH-domains, henceforth to KH-ITSs and KH-ILEs, contains all computational and inferential dynamic *processes* used to solve a problem, i.e. a practical situation based on DK [8]. PSK is very close to the more usual *procedural knowledge*, although some declarative concepts are part of PSK (see 4.2).

1.2 Generic operating modes

In most educational systems, depending on what he wants to do, the student can use it in either of two ways: either to augment or improve his knowledge, or to check the correctness of what he thinks he has learnt. These correspond to two fundamental *pedagogical missions* of the system. In the former case, the knowledge the student wants to acquire or improve goes obviously *to the student*. In the latter case, the student provides *to the tutor* the knowledge that he wants to be assessed. It is worth noting that the "tutor" role may be played either by the system (ITS or ILE with mixed-initiative control) or by another student (collaborative learning or peer-help context). But we contend that the basic student's goal is fundamentally the same.

Besides, like that of a human tutor in a KH-domain, the objective of a KH-ITS or ILE is to help the student master the knowledge in both DK and PSK. Therefore, for whichever reason the student wants to use the system, the involved knowledge may be either essentially factual and theoretical (DK) or essentially practical and applied to a problem (PSK). As a result, these orthogonal considerations yield altogether four distinct *generic operating modes*, briefly presented in table 1 (see details in [13]).

Certainly, these operating modes do not imply that learning involves only some transfer of knowledge. Indeed, it takes place in an environment which is situated, must keep the student motivated, etc. But we consider these as being *modalities* or *constraints* of learning rather than a learning goal per se; other examples of such modalities are collaborative learning [15], peer help [7; 17], teacher training, taking an exam, etc. This is why, in table 1, we deal with a *tutor* and a *learner* rather than with a system and a student, which would be unduly restrictive: in a collaborative environment, a human student may alternatively act as learner or as tutor. Thus, in any operating mode, some tutoring activities have to take place, so that the selected mode may help the student attain his goal while *simultaneously* coping with the imposed modalities or constraints. In particular, to facilitate the student's learning and motivation, some activities may involve interactions usually associated with another operating mode, i.e. trigger a temporary *mode shift*. This brings us to the tutoring knowledge.

Learner's goal		To learn new material	To assess his learning
Knowledge destination		Learner	Tutor (human or system)
Main type of knowl- edge in- volved	Domain knowl- edge	*Domain-presentation mode:* The learner asks the tutor some information about a domain element; the tutor reacts by transferring to the learner the required information or knowledge.	*Domain-assessment mode:* The tutor basically prompts the learner to develop a domain element; the learner thus expresses his understanding of that element.
	Problem -solving knowl- edge	*Demonstration mode:* The learner asks the tutor to solve a practical problem or to show him a given resolution step while he solves such a problem.	*Exercising mode:* The tutor prompts the learner to solve a practical problem; the learner then solves it step by step, showing his understanding of the required problem-solving knowledge and associated domain knowledge.

Table 1: Operating modes in a KH-ITS.

2 Tutoring knowledge as pedagogical agents

2.1 Definition and purpose of the tutoring knowledge

Tutoring knowledge (TK) contains all tutoring entities enclosed in the system. It is not directly related to DK or PSK, for it is not to be learned by the student. Instead, it is there to help the student understand, assimilate, and master more efficiently the knowledge included in DK and PSK [5]. Because of its reusability, we expect TK to be the same for a variety of KH-domains, for a given type of educational system.

The main system activities using TK are thus:
- ordering and formatting the topics to be presented to the student;
- monitoring a session, i.e. triggering the various tutoring processes according to the tutoring goal and the student's actions; such monitoring may imply giving explanations, asking questions, changing the type of interaction, etc.;
- in a KH-domain, while the student is solving an exercise, monitoring the student's problem-solving activities as required by the student or the tutoring module;
- in a collaborative environment, monitoring the activities of the student playing the tutor's role at that instant, as above;
- continuously analysing the progress of the student(s).

2.2 Introduction of pedagogical agents

Because of its dynamic nature, like PSK, TK will be made of process-like entities. However, the tutorial processes are not predetermined, because of the need for adaptive reactions to the students' actions (acting as a learner, a companion, a helper, a tutor, etc.). Moreover, to keep their attention and cope with the various modalities and constraints, the tutoring module must be able to use a variety of stimuli, of ways to present a topic, and of explanations. This is why the concept of *pedagogical or tutoring agent*, able to interact and cooperate with a student, is appropriate to model TK.

As we see it, the goal of every tutoring agent is to perform a given *tutoring function* for the student's benefit. Some of these functions are: to present or to explain a subject element, to give an example, to answer a student's question, to evaluate the student's answer to a system-asked question, to diagnose a student's behaviour. A tutoring function is ultimately defined by its specification, i.e. the data that it processes or on which it operates, and the output that it provides as a result. To each agent we may thus initially associate one tutoring function and to each tutoring function one interaction with a student (the unique student in a standalone ITS).

Some examples of agents in a KH-domain environment may thus be the following, named after the function they are expected to perform [13]: *domain presenter, domain assessor, problem solver, exerciser, question asker, problem selector, topic chooser, problem step solver*, or *explanation provider*.

3 More about pedagogical agents

3.1 Interactions between pedagogical agents: types of agents

As "tutoring" and "agent" suggest, the ultimate purpose of tutoring agents is to *communicate with the student(s)* in order to efficiently fulfil their respective tutoring function, as part of the system pedagogical mission. However, for software engineering reasons, we shall modularise complex tutoring functions into simpler ones.

As a result, supposing that each system agent is still specialised in a particular tutoring function, it may have to count on other agents specialised in different functions, then used as *service functions*, to perform its own tutoring function and produce its expected "pedagogical output". An agent may thus be put forward either by a student's action/behaviour or by a higher level function performed by another agent. For the same reason, the result of an agent's action may be used either by a student or by the higher level agent that used it.

In the case of a KH-environment, we then have three types of agents.
- *Tutoring agents* (TA) interact with a student and perform real tutoring functions. Examples are the problem solver, the domain presenter, the domain assessor, and the exerciser, each in charge of one operating mode (in a collaborative environment, the operating mode at a given time is not necessarily the same for all students).
- *Service agents* perform functions on behalf of other agents; they may interact with a student or not. The problem selector, the topic chooser and the question asker are service agents: their sole action cannot be a student-related tutoring function.
- Finally, *mixed agents* may be triggered in either way depending on the circumstances. Such are the problem step solver and the explanation provider.

The four tutoring agents (TAs) may also help one another, in particular when *mode shifts* take place (see 3.3). Our division of pedagogical agents in three categories is very close to that used for agents in the cognition-based architecture [1].

3.2 Scope of agents

When a pedagogical agent takes control, both the scope of the subject matter covered and the level of the data processed by that agent must be kept under control, at a lower level than that of the task of the relieved agent. Therefore, the function performed by an agent may be associated to an *abstraction level*, defined by the level of the entities on which it operates. This abstraction level is also that of the agent's output, the result of its action. Our approach is in fact close to Tambe's [16].

We conjecture that the notion of agent *scope*, based on the abstraction and complexity levels, will or can be used as a general foundation to circumvent the possible problem of infinite recursive transfers of control between agents [9]. Indeed, since each agent fulfils a lower-scope function than the previous one, control must eventually be taken by an agent which will itself do the job for which it intervened initially.

3.3   A variety of agents for a variety of stimuli

In a classroom, a teacher must keep his students' attention and motivation to facilitate their learning; a way to do so is to vary the *stimuli*. Similarly, a tutoring system should use a sufficient variety of stimuli; a way to do so is to have pedagogical agents create these stimuli on demand for every stimulus type of the system. This approach will incrementally augment the system capabilities as new agents are developed, and will allow it to run, maybe in a degraded way, even if not all stimuli-related agents are available; this approach is thus worthwhile even for one student.

That endeavour for variety can be more interestingly applied to the *pedagogical behaviours and tactics* employed by the tutor or the environment setting (e.g. for collaborative learning), to the explanations provided, and even to the generic functioning modes. Indeed, when the system as a whole is to change its type of interaction, it will use another main TA, normally associated to another operating mode. This is the *mode shift* principle, discussed in detail in [13].

With such a variety, it becomes easy for a teacher, henceforth for the tutoring module of an IES, to vary its tutoring tactics rather than giving a monotonous page-turning-type lecture (would bore the student). For example, in the domain-assessment mode, if the student has difficulty answering a question, the ITS may give him various hints and clues, e.g. by showing him a solved problem, by presenting him a paragraph of theory, or even by asking him another theoretical question, naturally having a narrower — and expectedly easier — scope than the initial one (see 3.2). All these possible hints or clues will then be provided by as many possible other agents.

3.4   How an agent takes control

If an IES is to vary the types of its interactions with the student, it should also be able to make wise decisions about what interaction(s) to choose and when to apply it (them). One way to do so is to keep track of the various interactions that have occurred during the current session. But a still better way would be building and maintaining a student model [4] for every student involved. Building a student model is obviously one of the deepest and longest-term means of keeping track of a student's evolution: a student model is an incremental interpretation of that student's behaviour, of the current state of the that student's knowledge, of his learning profile and possibly his learning preferences. In such a way, an IES can thus use its students' models to guide its interactions, which may become very efficient when enough appropriate data about the students has been gathered into the student models. How an agent "reasons" to takes control is more detailed in 4.5, following the dialogue examples.

4   An application domain example

In this section, we want to give a more concrete flavour to our work. Our application domain is cost engineering [6], which consists of mathematical and computational tools for the engineer to evaluate the worth of engineering projects, and to act appropriately in order to optimise the cost-effectiveness of his decisions.

4.1 Separation between domain knowledge and problem-solving knowledge

Cost engineering is a KH-domain. It is thus modelled as two parts (see 1.1). The domain knowledge DK is essentially modelled as concepts and relations, while PSK is modelled as processes and subprocesses (see details in [13]).

In the *domain knowledge, concepts* are entities like investment, investment duration, present and future values, compounding period, interest rate, or annuity. They are linked by *relations* like *kind of, part of,* or numerical relations. For example,

$$F = P \times (1 + i)^n \qquad (1)$$

is a quaternary relation $R(F, P, i, n)$ which, given the present value P of an investment over n periods at rate i, expresses the future value F of that investment. Such relations, or formulæ like (1), lead to the notion of *factor*, a pedagogical concept:

$$\Phi_{PF,i,n} = (1 + i)^n = F/P \qquad\qquad \Phi_{FP,i,n} = (1 + i)^{-n} = P/F$$

Factors like $\Phi_{PF,i,n}$ or $\Phi_{FP,i,n}$ allow us to distinguish their algebraic definition from their possible uses in the application domain. Similarly, there exists a factor $\Phi_{AP,i,n}$ to convert a periodic series of identical amounts A into a unique present value P.

The *problem-solving knowledge* is modelled as various domain-specific processes and subprocesses that may be used to solve various types of cost-engineering problems. Rather than presenting them *in abstracto*, let us move directly to the problem to be solved, and we shall explain the processes used to solve that problem.

4.2 A problem-solving example

Let the exercise to be solved be as follows (e.g. as presented to the student):

> *Determine the present value of a five-year annuity of $1,000 starting at the end of year 1, plus an extra revenue of $500 at the end of year 3, plus an expense of $1,500 at the end of year 4. The annual interest rate is assumed to be 10%.*

The normal processes used by an engineer, a human tutor, or a good student to solve this exercise are the following:

1. *Identify and instantiate the given problem data:*
   - annual interest rate $i = 10\%$;
   - ($n_1 = 5$)-year annuity $A_1 = 1,000$;
   - future value amount $F_2 = 500$ at end of year $n_2 = 3$;
   - future value amount $F_3 = -1,500$ at end of year $n_3 = 4$.

2. *Identify and instantiate the expected result:* some present value P equivalent to the sum of all above amounts.

3. *Build a temporal diagram:* this diagram thus shows the data identified above and the result P sought after (bold arrow). Note that the composition of a time diagram is declarative, although by its very nature and purpose it is part of PSK.

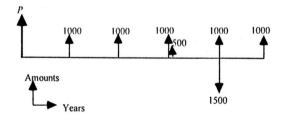

The solving process basically consists in adding all the arrowed amounts together to get their equivalent present value P. However, because of the interest over time, these amounts cannot be added directly. We must thus decompose that activity.

4. *Choose a common reference date* towards which all the amounts will be moved prior to their final addition. Here, the simplest date is the present moment, year 0.

5. *Deal with each element individually:*
   a. The annuity is a series of five annual $1,000 amounts. Using the Φ_{AP} factor above, we may compute their present value directly: $P_1 = 1,000 \times \Phi_{AP,10\%,5}$.
   b. Since the amount of $500 at the end of year 3 must be moved back three years, its present value is $P_2 = 500 \times \Phi_{FP,10\%,3}$.
   c. Similarly, the expense of $1,500 must be moved back four years, but with an opposite sign. Then its equivalent present value is $P_3 = -1,500 \times \Phi_{FP,10\%,4}$.

6. *Add the obtained present values:* $P = P_1 + P_2 + P_3$

7. *Replace all factors by their numerical values*, by computing them or from a table:

$$P_1 = 1,000 \times \Phi_{AP,10\%,5} = 1,000 \times 3.79079 = \$3,790.79$$
$$P_2 = 500 \times \Phi_{FP,10\%,3} = 500 \times 0.75131 = \$375.66$$
$$P_3 = 1,500 \times \Phi_{FP,10\%,4} = -1,500 \times 0.68301 = -\$1,024.52$$
$$P = P_1 + P_2 + P_3 = 3,790.79 + 375.66 - 1,024.52 = \$3,141.93$$

and, therefore, the expected answer is $3,141.93.

4.3 Tutoring session excerpts based on that problem

We now try to illustrate the generation and development of tutorial processes by the tutoring agents in TK. To mimic the session progress, we assume the interactions are conducted in natural language; the corresponding dialogue is shown in italics, with the student's input preceded by **. To visually distinguish them from the dialogue, we indent our explanations; moreover, only the major intervening agents are mentioned.

For our sample session, we assume that we have a one–student KH–ITS, that the student, a female, has selected the exercising mode, and that the system has given her the cost-engineering problem shown and solved in 4.2 (using the normal solving steps). For the first excerpt, we suppose that the student has correctly identified and named the problem data and the expected results (processes 1 and 2); she is beginning to draw the temporal diagram (process 3). The session might then proceed as follows.

> The tutoring agent A, a problem-solving assessor, is in control of the exercising mode and monitors the student's actions.

** *Where should I put the arrows of the annuity? In columns 0 to 4 or 1 to 5?*   (D1)

> The student does not understand how to position annuity arrows in a temporal diagram. Among other alternatives, A elects to give her a short theoretic reminder (shift to a domain-presentation mode interaction), provided by tutoring agent B, a domain presenter.

Remember what you learnt about annuities. By default (like here), the arrows are placed at the end of their respective years. Therefore, the first arrow will be placed at the end of the first year (column 1), and so on.   (D2)

** *OK, I think I understand now.*   (D3)

> The student claims she understands the pedagogical output provided by B. Control thus returns to agent A and to the standard exercising mode.

[...]   (D4)

Let us skip a few steps. For the second excerpt, suppose now that the student has finished drawing the temporal diagram, and has correctly moved the appropriate amounts towards year 0 (process 5). She is thus adding them together (process 6).

** *We have 1000 * FAP(0.10, 5) + 500 * FFP(0.10, 3) + 1500 * FFP(0.10, 4).*   (D5)

> The student has correctly understood how to calculate the annuity and the $500 income, but she mistakenly adds the $1,500 expense (see process 5c).

Almost...   (D6)

> This time, the student is asked a domain question (temporary shift to a domain-assessment interaction). This is done by another agent, C, a domain assessor.

... What did you learn about the difference between incomes and expenses?   (D7)

** *I don't understand where my error is.*   (D8)

> The theoretical domain question failed. Agent A', another problem-solving assessor, then gives as a clue to the student a short mathematical question (of narrower scope).

For example, if you receive $5,000 and spend $1,500, how much will you have?   (D9)

> The interaction produced by agent A' is associated with the exercising mode.

** *$3,500.*   (D10)

> The student correctly answered the question of agent A', which returns a success acknowledgement. But agent C takes control back and elects to rephrase its own question.

So, what is your deduction upon this clue?   (D11)

> The student applies it to the initial problem.

** *I think I got it: + 1500 * FFP(0.10, 4) should be – 1500 * FFP(0.10, 4).*   (D12)

> The student has understood. But her answer is local, i.e. she has not integrated it into the complete answer. So agent A comes back at the highest level.

You are right. Now you can formulate the complete answer.   (D13)

** *1000 * FAP(0.10, 5) + 500 * FFP(0.10, 3) – 1500 * FFP(0.10, 4).*   (D14)

> The student has given the expected complete computation layout (process 6).

Very good.   (D15)

> The dialogue would then proceed with the numerical computation (process 7).

4.4   Roles of tutoring agents in that excerpt

There are several agents intervening in the above dialogue.

- Agent A, a *problem-solving assessor*, is in control of the exercising mode. It globally drives the solution of the problem, monitors and assesses the student's actions. To help her, it lets other agents take some subtask in charge when needed.
- Agent B, a *domain presenter*, intervenes to present a domain element.
- Agent C, a *domain assessor*, "interrupts" A to ask the student a theoretical question. Since she is unable to answer it, C lets agent A' help her resolve this impasse.
- Agent A', another *problem-solving assessor*, takes over agent C to ask the student a problem-solving question. Its small exercise is completely different from the A-supervised problem at hand, and of much narrower scope.

Figure 1 summarises the student–agent and agent–agent interactions taking place in the above examples. The involved agents have triggered various tutoring processes: ask a question, answer a student question, make a decision regarding the type of interaction to enable, temporarily change that type of interaction, all while monitoring the whole session in order to keep track of the student's progress and to understand and influence its evolution throughout the problem-solving session.

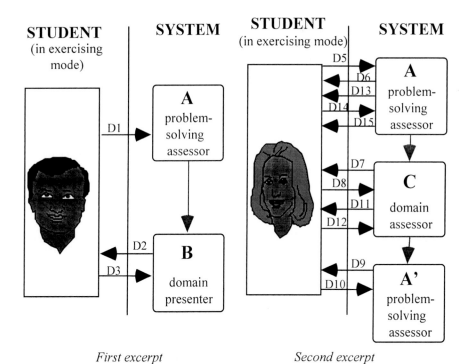

First excerpt   *Second excerpt*

Figure 1: Diagram of the agent interactions.

4.5 Student-related knowledge involved in agent interactions

In general, a pedagogical agent (not necessarily a TA, see 3.1) may refer to various types of *contextual knowledge elements* to decide to intervene and generate a terminal student–system interaction, or to let another pedagogical agent take control. Such are:

- the student's current knowledge state (or the current state of the student model),
- the student's primary goal (expressed by his choice of the leading tutoring mode),
- the session log (information on the student's knowledge and the past interactions),
- the points where the student stumbled,
- the student's motivation and physical state (tired, in good shape, etc.),
- possibly the learning theory advocated by the system, if there is one.

Conclusion

In this paper, we presented how tutoring knowledge can be modelled in terms of tutoring agents. We first presented, in a KH-IES, the division of the knowledge to be learned into DK and PSK, and the four generic operating modes defined upon this division. We then introduced the tutoring knowledge TK, partly common to all IESs, through an agent-based approach, and we gave some KH-domain examples. We then gave some general rules regarding the interactions between our agents and with the students, their respective scope in an interactive context, their variety, and how an agent takes control to fulfil a given function. We then presented a cost–engineering problem and its solution, which we used in a tutoring session integrating these notions.

Since this paper is essentially AI-oriented and in the long run aimed at building more cost-effective systems by reusing components (here agents), it does not deal with educational problems like learning theories or assessment. But, owing to its flexibility, our approach could be used for experimenting with and testing various learning theories or tutoring strategies. However, on the AI side, we do think that the various concepts regarding pedagogical agents presented should help an ITS designer to take a systematic approach to model the knowledge to be acquired, and later to devise a relatively easy and efficient way to model the tutoring knowledge required to fulfil the pedagogical mission(s) of his system. Moreover, the pedagogical agent concept might be extended to more general agents, e. g. to deal with the maintenance of the student model, to take care of the interface management, to manage the various modalities of learning implemented in the system; etc. Certainly, much progress still has to be made to reach a complete model. However, we think that our approach, being simple and systematic, is a promising one for modelling the tutoring knowledge in an IES.

References

[1]   Arcand J.-F. & S.-J. Pelletier (1996) "Cognition-based multiagent architecture". In *Intelligent Agents II: Agent Theories, Architectures and Languages* (M. Wooldridge, J. P. Müller & M. Tambe, eds.). Proc. *IJCAI'95 Workshop (ATAL)*, Montreal, Canada, August 1995. LNAI 1037, Springer (Berlin), p. 267-282.

[2]   Carbonell J. R. (1970) "AI in CAI: an artificial intelligence approach to computer-aided instruction". *IEEE Trans. on Man–Machine Systems*, vol. MMS-11, no. 4, p. 190–202.

[3]   Clancey W. J. (1983) "GUIDON". *Journal of Computer-Based Instruction*, vol. 10, no. 1, p. 8–14.

[4]   Fletcher J. D. (1975) "Modeling of learner in computer-based instruction". *Journal of Computer-Based Instruction*, vol. 1, p. 118–126.

[5]   Gagné D. & A. Trudel (1996) "A highly flexible student-driven architecture for computer-based instruction". In *Intelligent Tutoring Systems* (C. Frasson, G. Gauthier & A. Lesgold, eds.), Proceedings of the *Third International Conference, ITS'96*, Montréal, Canada, 12-14 June 1996, p. 66–74. LNCS 1086, Springer (Berlin).

[6]   Galibois A. (1997) *Analyse économique pour ingénieurs*, 2nd edition. Éditions AGA (Sainte-Foy, Canada).

[7]   Greer J., G. McCalla, J. Collins, V. Kumar, P. Meagher & J. Vassileva (1998) "Supporting peer help and collaboration in distributed workplace environments". *International Journal of Artificial Intelligence in Education*, vol. 9, pp. 159-177.

[8]   Kowalski R. (1979) *Logic for Problem Solving*. North-Holland (Berlin).

[9]   Lelouche R. & J.-F. Morin (1997a) "Use of abstraction and complexity levels in intelligent educational systems design". Proc. of the 15th *Internat. Joint Conf. on Artificial Intelligence* (IJCAI-97), Nagoya, Japan, 23–29 August 1997, p. 329-334.

[10]   Lelouche R. & J.-F. Morin (1997b) "Knowledge types and tutoring interactions in an ITS in a problem-solving domain". Proc. 10th *Florida Artificial Intell. Research Symposium* (FLAIRS-97) — Spec. Track on ITSs, Daytona Beach, FL. 10–14 May 1997, p. 62–66.

[11]   Macmillan S.A. & D.H. Sleeman (1987) "An architecture for a self-improving instructional planner for intelligent tutoring systems". *Computational Intelligence*, vol. 3, no. 1.

[12]   Masthoff J. F. M. (1997) *An agent-based interactive instruction system*. Ph.D. thesis, University of Technology Eindhoven (Netherlands), 222 pages, ISBN 90-386-0319-3.

[13]   Morin J.-F. (1998) *Conception of an intelligent tutoring system in cost engineering: knowledge representation, pedagogical interactions, and system operation*. Master Thesis, Dép. Informatique, Univ. Laval (Québec, Canada).

[14]   Ohlsson S. (1987) "Some principles of intelligent tutoring". In *AI and Education: Learning Environments and Intelligent Tutoring Systems* (R. Lawler & M. Yazdani, eds.). Ablex Publishing (Norwood, NJ).

[15]   Suthers D. & D. Jones (1997) "An Architecture for Intelligent Collaborative Educational Systems". In *Artificial Intelligence in Education*, Proc. *8th World Conf., AIED 97*, Kobe (Japan), 20-22 August 1997, p. 55-62. IOS Press (Amsterdam).

[16]   Tambe M. (1995) "Recursive agent and agent-group tracking in a real-time dynamic environment". *Proc. of the First Intern. Conf. on Multiagent Systems (ICMAS 95)*, San Francisco, CA, June 1995.

[17]   Vassileva J., J. Greer, G. McCalla, R. Deters, D. Zapata, C. Mudgal & S. Grant (1999) "A multi-agent design of a peer-help environment". In *Artificial Intelligence in Education*, Proc. of the *9th Intern. Conf., AIED 99*, Le Mans (France), 19-23 July 1999, p. 38-45. IOS Press (Amsterdam).

DT Tutor: A Decision-Theoretic, Dynamic Approach for Optimal Selection of Tutorial Actions

R. Charles Murray* and Kurt VanLehn

Intelligent Systems Program & Learning Research and Development Center
University of Pittsburgh, Pittsburgh, PA 15260
{rmurray,vanlehn}@pitt.edu

Abstract. *DT Tutor* uses a decision-theoretic approach to select tutorial actions for coached problem solving that are optimal given the tutor's beliefs and objectives. It employs a model of learning to predict the possible outcomes of each action, weighs the utility of each outcome by the tutor's belief that it will occur, and selects the action with highest expected utility. For each tutor and student action, an updated student model is added to a dynamic decision network to reflect the changing student state. The tutor considers multiple objectives, including the student's problem-related knowledge, focus of attention, independence, and morale, as well as action relevance and dialog coherence. Evaluation in a calculus domain shows that DT Tutor can select rational and interesting tutorial actions for real-world-sized problems in satisfactory response time. The tutor does not yet have a suitable user interface, so it has not been evaluated with human students.

1 Introduction

Tutoring systems that coach students as they solve problems often emulate the turn taking observed in human tutorial dialog [7, 15]. Student turns usually consist of entering a solution step or asking for help. The tutor's main task can be seen as simply deciding what action to take on its turn. Tutorial actions include a variety of action types, including positive and negative feedback, hinting, and teaching. The tutor must also decide the action topic, such as a specific problem step or related concept. DT Tutor's task is to select the optimal *type* and *topic* for each tutorial action.

How to select optimal tutorial actions for coached problem solving has been an open question. A significant source of difficulty is that much of the useful information about the student is not directly observable. This information concerns both the student's cognitive and emotional state. Compounding the difficulty, the student's state changes over the course of a tutoring session.

Another complication is that just what constitutes optimal tutoring depends upon the tutorial objectives. A tutor's objectives normally include various student-centered goals and may also include dialog objectives and action type preferences. Furthermore, the tutor may have to balance multiple competing objectives.

DT Tutor uses decision-theoretic methods to select tutorial actions. The remainder of the Introduction describes the basis of our approach, DT Tutor's general architecture, and prior work. Subsequent sections describe DT Tutor in more detail, a preliminary evaluation, future work and conclusions.

* Research supported by ONR's Cognitive Science Division, grant number N0014-98-1-0467.

1.1 Belief and Decision Networks

Probability has long been the standard for modeling uncertainty in diverse scientific fields. Recent work with belief network (equivalently, Bayesian network) algorithms has made modeling complex domains using probabilistic representations more feasible. Unfortunately, belief network inference is still NP-hard in the worst case. However, many stochastic sampling algorithms have an *anytime* property that allows an approximate result to be obtained at any point in the computation [4].

DT Tutor represents the tutor's beliefs about the student's problem-related knowledge using a belief network obtained directly from a *problem solution graph*, a hierarchical dependency network representing solutions to a problem [2, 11]. Nodes in the graph represent (1) problem steps, and (2) domain rules licensing each step. Problem steps include the givens and every goal and fact along any path towards the solution. We currently model incorrect steps as errors. Arcs represent dependence between nodes. For instance, knowledge of a step depends on knowledge of both its antecedent steps and the rule required to derive it. In belief network form, the nodes represent the tutor's beliefs about problem-related elements of the student's cognitive state and arcs represent conditional dependence between the elements.

Nodes within a belief network represent variables whose values are fixed. However, a student's mental state and the problem solution state change over the course of a tutoring session. To represent variables that change over time, it is more accurate to use a separate node for each time. *Dynamic belief networks* (DBNs) do just that. For each time in which the values of variables may change, a new *slice* is created. Each slice consists of a set of nodes representing values at a specific point in time. Rather than fixed time intervals, slices can be chosen so that each corresponds to the student model after a student or tutor action. Nodes may be connected to nodes within the same or earlier slices to represent the fact that a variable's value may depend on concurrent values of other variables (*synchronic* influences) and on earlier values of the same and other variables (*diachronic* influences). The evolution of a DBN can be represented while keeping in memory at most two slices at a time [10].

Decision theory extends probability theory to provide a normative theory of how a rational decision-maker should behave [13]. Utilities are used to express preferences among possible future states of the world. To decide among alternative actions, the *expected utility* of each alternative is calculated by taking the sum of the utilities of all possible future states of the world that follow from that alternative, weighted by the probabilities of those states occurring. Decision theory holds that a rational agent should choose the alternative with the maximum expected utility. A belief network, which consists entirely of *chance* nodes, can be extended into a decision network (equivalently, an influence diagram) by adding *decision* and *utility* nodes along with appropriate arcs [13]. For tutoring systems, decision nodes could represent tutorial action alternatives, chance nodes could represent possible outcomes of the actions, and utility nodes could represent the tutor's preferences among the possible outcomes.

A *dynamic decision network* (DDN) is like a DBN except that it has decision and utility nodes in addition to chance nodes. DDNs model decisions for situations in which decisions, variables or preferences can change over time. Just as for DBNs, simple algorithms exist to represent the evolution of a DDN while keeping in memory at most two slices at a time [10].

1.2 General Architecture

Our basic approach is to use a DDN to implement most of the intelligent, non-user-interface part of DT Tutor. The DDN is formed from dynamically created decision networks. These networks are called *tutor action cycle networks* (TACNs) because they each represent a single cycle of tutorial action, where a cycle consists of

- deciding a tutorial action and carrying it out,
- observing the next student action, and
- updating the student model based on these two actions.

TACNs consist of three slices, as illustrated in Figure 1. A TACN is used both for deciding the tutor's action and for updating the student model. When deciding the tutor's action, slice 0 represents the tutor's beliefs about the student's current state.

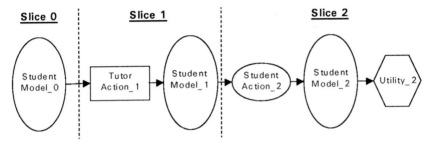

Fig. 1. Tutor action cycle network, high-level overview

Slice 1 represents the tutor's possible actions and the influence of those actions on the tutor's beliefs about the student. Slice 2 represents the student's possible actions and the influence of those actions on the tutor's beliefs about the student. In other words, slice 0 represents the current student state and the other slices represent predictions about the student's state after the tutor's action and after the next student action. Slice 2 also includes the utility model since most of the outcomes in which the tutor might be interested concern the final effects of the tutor's current action.

The DDN update algorithm calculates the action with maximum expected utility. The tutor executes that action and waits for the student to respond. When the tutor has observed the student's action, the student model update phase begins.

The tutor clamps the student's action and updates the network. At this point, the posterior probabilities in *Student Model*[1] represent the tutor's current beliefs about the student. It is now time for another tutorial action selection, so another TACN is created. Posterior probabilities from *Student Model*, of the old TACN are copied as prior probabilities to *Student Model*, of the new TACN. The old TACN is discarded. The tutor is now ready to begin the next phase, deciding what action to take next.

With this architecture, the tutor not only reacts to past student actions, but also anticipates future student actions and their ramifications. Thus, for instance, it can act to prevent errors and impasses before they occur, just as human tutors often do.

---

[1] For sub-network and node names, a numeric subscript refers to the slice number. A subscript of n refers to any appropriate slice.

1.3 Prior Work

Although probabilistic reasoning is become increasingly common in tutoring systems and AI in general, we believe this is the first application of a DDN to tutoring. Probabilistic reasoning is often used in student and user modeling. In particular, Bayesian networks are used in the student models of Andes [2], HYDRIVE [16] and other systems [12]. However, even with a probabilistic student model, other systems select tutorial actions using heuristics instead of decision-theoretic methods. Reye [19] has suggested the use of a decision-theoretic architecture for tutoring systems and the use of dynamic belief networks to model the student's knowledge [20, 21].

2 Detailed Solution

This section describes TACNs in more detail, along with their implementation to form DT Tutor's action selection engine.

2.1 Major TACN Components and Their Interrelationships

Figure 2 provides a closer look at a TACN. The student model includes components to represent the student's knowledge state (sub-network *Knowledge Network$_n$*), the student's problem completion status and focus of attention (sub-network *Relevance Network$_n$*), and the student's emotional state (nodes *Morale$_n$* and *Independence$_n$*). Tutor and student actions are represented by two nodes each: one for the action *topic (Tutor/Student Topic$_n$)* and another for the action *type (Tutor/Student Type$_n$)*. Tutorial action relevance and coherence are represented by the *Relevance$_1$* and *Coherence$_1$* nodes respectively. The utility model (*Utility$_2$*) represents the tutor's preferences.

In Figure 2, the Knowledge and Relevance Networks are shown as large rounded rectangles. Each arc into or out of these sub-networks actually represents multiple arcs to and from various sub-network nodes. For instance, there is a diachronic arc from each *Knowledge Network$_0$* node to the corresponding *Knowledge Network$_1$* node.

Student Knowledge Network. For each problem, a Knowledge Network is created from the problem solution graph to represent the tutor's beliefs about the student's problem-related knowledge.

Within the Knowledge Network, each node has possible values *known* and *unknown*. Rule nodes represent the tutor's belief about the student's knowledge of the corresponding rule. Problem step nodes represent the tutor's belief about the student's potential to know the corresponding step given the student's current rule knowledge. At the beginning of a problem, the nodes representing the givens and the problem goal are clamped to *known*, since these are given in the problem statement. The student's potential knowledge of the remaining problem steps depends upon the student's knowledge of the rules required to complete each problem step in turn.

Influences on Knowledge Network nodes include (1) synchronic influences to model the interdependence of the student's problem-related knowledge, and (2) diachronic influences between corresponding nodes in different slices to model the stability of the student's knowledge over time. The tutor can also influence *Knowledge Network$_1$* nodes directly, with an influence depending on the tutor action type. For in-

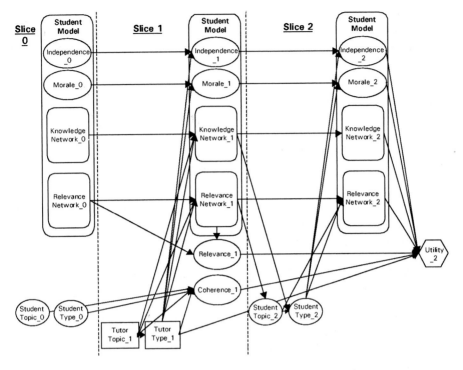

Fig. 2. Tutor action cycle network in more detail

stance, if the tutor teaches a domain rule, there is normally a greater probability that the rule will become *known* than if the tutor hints about it.

Student Relevance Network. Like the Knowledge Network, the Relevance Network is a belief network created from the problem solution graph. It represents the tutor's beliefs about the student's problem solving progress and problem-related focus of attention. The representation of the student's focus of attention is used to select relevant tutorial actions and to predict the topic of the student's next action.

Rule nodes have possible values *relevant* and *irrelevant*, where *relevant* means that the rule is part of the student's focus of attention. If the tutor addresses a rule directly, the rule becomes *relevant* with a probability dependent on the tutor action type. For instance, teaching a rule is more likely than hinting to make a rule *relevant*.

Problem step nodes have possible values *complete, not ready, ready*, and *relevant*. Completed step nodes have the value *complete*. If a step node is not *complete* and if it has any synchronic step node parents that are not *complete*, its value is *not ready*, meaning that it is not ready to be completed until its parent steps have been completed (but this does not preclude the student from completing it anyway – e.g., by guessing). Otherwise, a step node has some distribution over the values *ready* and *relevant*. Such nodes represent the frontier of the student's work within the problem space, possible next steps and thus potentially the focus of the student's attention. The value *ready* means that a step is ready to be completed since all of its parent steps have been completed. The value *relevant* means that not only is the step ready to be completed, but it is also part of the student's focus of attention. For instance, a step is likely to be *rele-*

vant if the tutor addresses it (e.g., with a *hint*) or if the student makes an error on it. Steps that are *relevant* at some point in time become a little less *relevant* with each passing time slice. This is to model *relevance aging*: steps that were *relevant* slowly become less *relevant* as the student moves on to other topics.

When there are multiple steps that could be *relevant* by virtue of being the next uncompleted step along a solution path, DT Tutor assumes a depth-first bias to decide how likely the various steps are to be part of the student's focus of attention: When applying a rule produces multiple *ready* steps, students usually prefer to pick one and complete work on it before starting work on another. Such a bias corresponds to a depth-first traversal of the problem solution graph and is consistent with both activation-based theories of human working memory [1] and observations of human problem solvers [18]. However, a depth-first bias is not absolute. At any given step, there is some probability that a student will not continue depth-first.

To model depth-first bias, when a step first becomes *ready* or *relevant* because the last of its outstanding parent steps has become *complete*, that step becomes *relevant* with high probability. This is because with a depth-first bias, having just completed the step's parent, the student is likely to continue working with the step itself. Relevance aging helps to model another aspect of depth-first bias: preferring to continue with more recently raised steps. When the student completes or abandons a portion of the solution path, steps that were recently highly *relevant* but that are still not *complete* have had less relevance aging than steps that were highly *relevant* in the more distant past, so the more recently raised steps remain more *relevant*.

Student Emotional State. Human tutors consider the student's emotional or motivational state in deciding how to respond [5, 14]. Concern for student morale is likely to be one reason why tutors tend to give negative feedback subtly, to play up student successes and downplay student failures, etc., while maximizing the student's feeling of independence is likely to be one reason why tutors tend not to intervene unless the student needs help, to minimize the significance of the tutor's help, etc. [15]. Such behaviors cannot be explained in terms of concern for the student's knowledge and the problem solving state alone.

The student's emotional state is modeled with the $Morale_n$ and $Independence_n$ nodes. Each of these nodes has possible values *level 0* through *level 4*, with higher levels representing greater morale or independence. Both tutor and student actions influence these nodes with an influence dependent on the action type. In addition, diachronic influences model the stability of the student's emotional state over time.

Tutor Action Nodes. The $Tutor\ Type_t$ alternatives include fairly fine distinctions to model some of the subtlety that human tutors exhibit when working with students. These alternatives include *prompt, hint, teach, positive feedback, negative feedback, do* (do a step for the student), and *null* (no tutor action).

$Tutor\ Topic_t$ can be any problem-related topic, so there is an alternative for each rule or step node in the problem solution graph. The value *null* is also supported to model (1) a tutor action with a type but no topic (e.g., general *positive feedback*), and (2) no tutor action at all, in which case $Tutor\ Type_t$ is *null* as well.

Student Action Nodes. First, the values of the student action nodes in slice 0 are simply the values of the student action nodes in slice 2 of the previous TACN, except for the very first TACN, in which they both have the value *null*.

Student Topic$_n$ can be any step in the problem solution graph. It can also be *null* to model either no student action at all (in which case *Student Type$_n$* is *null* as well) or a student action with a *null* topic (e.g., a general *impasse* or an *error* which the tutor cannot interpret as an attempt at a particular step). *Student Topic$_2$* is influenced by the relevance of the steps that are most likely to be the topic of the student's next action – i.e., by *Relevance Network$_1$* step nodes that are *ready* or *relevant*.

Student Type$_n$ has possible values *correct, error, impasse*, and *null*. *Impasse* means that the student does not know what action to take – for instance, when the student asks for help. *Null* is used to model no student action. *Student Type$_2$* is influenced both by the student action topic and by the student's knowledge of that topic – i.e., by *Student Topic$_2$* and by the *Knowledge Network$_1$* step nodes.

Utility Model. Node *Utility$_2$* is actually a structured utility model consisting of several nodes to represent tutor preferences regarding the following outcomes:

1. Student rule knowledge in slice 2 (rule nodes in *Knowledge Network$_2$*)
2. Student problem step progress in slice 2 (step nodes in *Relevance Network$_2$*)
3. Student independence in slice 2 (*Independence$_2$*)
4. Student morale in slice 2 (*Morale$_2$*)
5. Tutor action type in slice 1 (*Tutor Type$_1$*)
6. Tutor action relevance in slice 1 (*Relevance$_1$*)
7. Tutor action coherence in slice 1 (*Coherence$_1$*)

2.2 Implementation

DT Tutor was implemented using software developed at the Decision Systems Laboratory, University of Pittsburgh: GeNIe, a development environment for graphical models, and SMILE$^©$, a platform independent library of C++ classes for reasoning with graphical probabilistic models. From the problem solution graph structure, DT Tutor creates a TACN with default values for node outcomes, prior probabilities, conditional probabilities, and utilities. An optional file can be loaded to specify any prior probability or utility values that differ from the default values. After creating the initial TACN, DT Tutor recommends tutorial actions, accepts inputs representing actual tutor and student actions, updates the network, and adds new TACNs to the DDN as appropriate. We have not yet developed a suitable graphical interface for students, so a simple text interface was created for evaluation.

While DT Tutor will work with most any problem solution graph, for the initial implementation we selected the domain of calculus related rates problems for two reasons. First, the number of steps per problem is non-trivial without being too large, so results obtained should be generalizable to other real world domains. Second, Singley [23] developed an interface for this domain with the purpose of reifying goal structures. We assume an extension to Singley's interface that makes all problem solving actions observable. This makes it easier to determine the student's current location in the problem solution space and thus to model the student's current focus of attention and predict the student's next action.

3 Evaluation

The goals for evaluation were to evaluate whether DT Tutor's approach can be used to select actions within reasonable space and time that are not only optimal but that also correspond to some of the more interesting behaviors of human tutors.

3.1 Evaluate Tractability

One of the major challenges facing Bayesian models for real world domains is tractability in terms of both space and time. A number of measures were taken to reduce space requirements [see 17] which were then considered tractable since the tutor was able to successfully perform the tests described below.

It is important to provide real-time responses in order to keep the student engaged. With an early version of the Andes physics tutor [2], students tolerated response times of up to 40 seconds. However, considering both (1) the variety of domains for which ITSs might be constructed, and (2) ever-improving computer hardware and algorithms for evaluating probabilistic models, no exact response time requirement can be determined. Rather, it is more important to begin to evaluate how such systems will scale.

Test results are shown in Table 1. Both of the approximate algorithms using 1,000 samples returned responses for both problems well within the tolerated limit, as did the exact algorithm for the smaller of the two problems. Response times for the approximate algorithms grew linearly in the number of samples and in the number of nodes. The approximate algorithms using 10,000 samples and the exact algorithm on the larger problem did not return responses quickly enough, and in any case, faster response times are desirable. Fortunately, a number of speedups are feasible, as discussed in [17]. In addition, the *anytime* property of the approximate algorithms could be used to continually improve results until a response is required. For many applications, including this one, it is sufficient to correctly rank the optimal decision alternative. When only the rank of the optimal decision alternative was considered, the approximate algorithms using 1,000 samples were correct on every trial.

Table 1. Action selection response times

Algorithm	Response time mean (range)	
	Problem A[a]	Problem B[b]
Exact: Clustering [9]	108 (107-109)	11 (11-12)
Approximate:		
Likelihood Sampling [22]		
1,000 samples	12 (12-13)	8 (7-8)
10,000 samples	106 (104-110)	64 (62-66)
Heuristic Importance [22]		
1,000 samples	12 (12-13)	8 (7-8)
10,000 samples	104 (101-106)	64 (60-66)

Note. Response time is the number of seconds required to determine the optimal tutorial action. Mean and range are over 10 trials. All tests were performed on a 200MHz Pentium MMX PC with 64MB of RAM. The algorithms were tested with Cooper's [3] algorithm for decision network inference using belief network algorithms.

[a] 10-step problem, 185-node TACN. [b] 5-step problem, 123-node TACN.

3.2   Evaluate Tutorial Action Selections

DT Tutor's decision-theoretic representation guarantees that its decisions will be optimal given the beliefs and objectives it embodies. Therefore, besides a sanity check of the implementation, the purpose of this part of the evaluation was to find out whether DT Tutor's approach and choices about which outcomes and objectives to model were sufficient to endow the tutor with some of the more interesting capabilities of human tutors. While detailed results would be too lengthy to report here [see 17], testing showed that DT Tutor is indeed capable of selecting rational tutorial actions that correspond in interesting ways to the behavior of human tutors. Notable behaviors included the following:

- DT Tutor did not provide help when it believed the student did not need it. Human tutors foster their students' independence by letting them work autonomously [14].
- When the student was likely to need help, DT Tutor often intervened *before* the student could experience failure. Human tutors often provide help proactively rather than waiting for a student error or impasse [14, 15].
- As the student moved around the problem space, DT Tutor adapted to support the student's current line of reasoning, assuming a depth-first topic bias.
- All other things being equal, DT Tutor preferred to address rules rather than problem-specific steps. Effective human tutoring is correlated with teaching generalizations that go beyond the immediate problem-solving context [24].
- DT Tutor considered the effects of its actions on the student's emotional state as well as the student's knowledge state. Human tutors consider both as well [14].
- DT Tutor prioritized its actions based on current beliefs and objectives. Likewise, human tutors prioritize their actions based on the student's needs and tend not to waste time addressing topics that the student does not need to know [15].

4   Future Work and Conclusions

We still need to develop a graphical interface or embed DT Tutor's action selection engine within an existing ITS and evaluate it with human students. Efficiently obtaining more accurate probability and utility values would be beneficial as well. However, an encouraging result from prior research is that Bayesian systems are often surprisingly insensitive to imprecision in specification of numerical probabilities [8] and may be accurate enough to infer the correct *decision* even if some of their assumptions are violated [6], so that precise numbers may not always be necessary.

This research has shown that a decision-theoretic approach can indeed be used to select tutorial actions that are optimal, given the tutor's beliefs and objectives, for real-world-sized problems in satisfactory response time. The DDN representation handles uncertainty about the student in a theoretically rigorous manner, balances tradeoffs among multiple objectives, automatically adapts to changes in beliefs or objectives, and increases the accuracy of the information upon which the tutor's decisions are based. By modeling not only the student's problem-related knowledge but also the student's focus of attention and emotional state, DT Tutor can select actions that correspond to some of the more interesting behaviors of human tutors.

References

1. Anderson, J. R. (1993). *Rules of the Mind*. Lawrence Erlbaum Associates.
2. Conati, C., Gertner, A., VanLehn, K., & Druzdzel, M. (1997). On-line student modeling for coached problem solving using Bayesian networks. *6th International Conference on User Modeling*, pp. 231-242.
3. Cooper, G. F. (1988). A method for using belief networks as influence diagrams. *Workshop on Uncertainty in Artificial Intelligence*, pp. 55-63.
4. Cousins, S. B., Chen, W., & Frisse, M. E. (1993). A tutorial introduction to stochastic simulation algorithms for belief networks. *AI in Medicine 5*, pp. 315-340.
5. del Soldato, T., & du Boulay, B. (1995). Implementation of motivational tactics in tutoring systems. *Journal of Artificial Intelligence in Education 6(4)*, pp. 337-378.
6. Domingos, P., & Pazzani, M. (1997). On the optimality of the simple Bayesian classifier under zero-one loss. *Machine Learning 29*, pp. 103-130.
7. Graesser, A. C., Person, N. K., & Magliano, J. P. (1995). Collaborative dialogue patterns in naturalistic one-to-one tutoring. *Applied Cognitive Psychology 9*, pp. 495-522.
8. Henrion, M., Pradhan, M., Del Favero, B., Huang, K., Provan, G., & O'Rorke, P. (1996). Why is diagnosis in belief networks insensitive to imprecision in probabilities? *Twelfth Annual Conference on Uncertainty in Artificial Intelligence*.
9. Huang, C., & Darwiche, A. (1996). Inference in belief networks: A procedural guide. *International Journal of Approximate Reasoning 15*, pp. 225-263.
10. Huang, T., Koller, D., Malik, J., Ogasawara, G., Rao, B., Russell, S., & Weber, J. (1994). Automated symbolic traffic scene analysis using belief networks. *Twelfth National Conference on Artificial Intelligence*, pp. 966-972.
11. Huber, M. J., Durfee, E. H., & Wellman, M. P. (1994). The automated mapping of plans for plan recognition. *Tenth Conference on Uncertainty in Artificial Intelligence*, pp. 344-350.
12. Jameson, A. (1996). Numerical uncertainty management in user and student modeling: An overview of systems and issues. *User Modeling and User-Adapted Interaction 5(3-4)*, pp. 103-251.
13. Keeney, R., & Raiffa, H. (1976). *Decisions with Multiple Objectives*. Wiley.
14. Lepper, M. R., Woolverton, M., Mumme, D. L., & Gurtner, J.-L. (1993). Motivational techniques of expert human tutors: Lessons for the design of computer-based tutors. *Computers as Cognitive Tools* (pp. 75-105). Lawrence Erlbaum Associates.
15. Merrill, D. C., Reiser, B. J., Merrill, S. K., & Landes, S. (1995). Tutoring: Guided learning by doing. *Cognition and Instruction 13(3)*, pp. 315-372.
16. Mislevy, R. J., & Gitomer, D. H. (1996). The role of probability-based inference in an intelligent tutoring system. *User Modeling and User-Adapted Interaction 5(3-4)*.
17. Murray, R. C. (1999). A dynamic, decision-theoretic model of tutorial action selection. Unpublished MS Thesis, University of Pittsburgh. http://www.isp.pitt.edu/~chas/
18. Newell, A., & Simon, H. A. (1972). *Human Problem Solving*. Prentice-Hall, Inc.
19. Reye, J. (1995). A goal-centred architecture for intelligent tutoring systems. *World Conference on Artificial Intelligence in Education*, pp. 307-314.
20. Reye, J. (1996). A belief net backbone for student modeling. *Intelligent Tutoring Systems, Third International Conference*, pp. 596-604.
21. Reye, J. (1998). Two-phase updating of student models based on dynamic belief networks. *Fourth International Conference on Intelligent Tutoring Systems*, pp. 274-283.
22. Shachter, R. D., & Peot, M. A. (1990). Simulation approaches to general probabilistic inference on belief networks. *Uncertainty in Artificial Intelligence*, pp. 221-231.
23. Singley, M. K. (1990). The reification of goal structures in a calculus tutor: Effects on problem solving performance. *Interactive Learning Environments 1*, pp. 102-123.
24. VanLehn, K., Siler, S., Murray, C., Yamauchi, T., & Baggett, W. B. (in press). Human tutoring: Why do only some events cause learning? *Cognition and Instruction*.

Experimenting Features from Distinct Software Components on a Single Platform

Marilyne Rosselle and Monique Grandbastien

Loria - UHP Nancy I University
Campus Scientifique - B. P. 239,
54506 Vandoeuvre lès Nancy CEDEX, France
`Marilyne.Rosselle@loria.fr` and `Monique.Grandbastien@loria.fr`

Abstract. This paper addresses the issue of building research scenarios with existing or forthcoming research prototypes for educational purposes. It defines an Experimentation Space allowing the cooperation of several software components. First it presents the general architecture and the properties which are required from each component to run on the experimentation platform. Then a case study showing several existing prototypes in Geometry cooperating on the platform is described. Lastly implementation problems and choices are discussed.

1 Introduction

Research in IES (Intelligent Educational Software) such as ITSs (Intelligent or Interactive Tutoring System) and ILEs (Intelligent or Interactive Learning Environments) used to develop entire systems from scratch. Time and resources were spent on software design and implementation. Despite huge efforts, the resulting prototypes could not provide all the required features. However we have noticed a growing interest in architectures and frameworks for inter-operable and component-based systems ([2, 3, 10, 9, 11]). Moreover, several international initiatives have been launched to promote standards for describing, implementing and retrieving educational components on the Web (IEEE P1484: Learning Technology Standards Committee [1], ISO/IEC JTC1 Information Technology Subcommittee SC36 on Learning Technology, ARIADNE [2], *etc.*).

All categories of products would benefit from a component based approach since all kinds of products require features that are not yet implemented in a single existing piece of software. But for building research scenarios, *i.e.* experimental settings for observing students using rich and innovative learning environments and for confirming or dis-confirming research hypothesis, it is be the only affordable approach as the experimental setting will perhaps not be reused.

Our research aims at providing an experimental space for researchers in Cognitive Sciences and Didactics. This experimental space should enable them to build the educational environments they need by using the features of several

---

[1] http://grouper.ieee.org/P1484/

[2] http://ariadne.unil.ch

existing educational components on a single platform. Taking such a component based approach for building rich and innovative learning environments requires specific properties from the components. Two complementary approaches are investigated. On which conditions is it possible to slightly modify existing components in order to allow them to cooperate with others across a single platform? Which guidelines and requirements should be observed by future designers in order to avoid any change for allowing inter-operability?

In both cases, we need to answer the four following questions. (1) What properties should a piece of IES own to allow its cooperation with other prototypes? In others words, what is necessary to add or modify in an existing prototype to allow its cooperation with other prototypes? (2) How to share domain knowledge between several prototypes? (3) How to manage graphic interfaces produced by prototypes? (4) How to articulate prototypes that cooperate?

For the first question, Ritter and Koedinger defined in ([10]) the following properties for a prototype so that it could cooperate with another prototype: prototypes should be "script-able, scrutinise-able and trace-able". With regard to the sharing of knowledge needed by several software, Macrelle and Desmoulins ([6]) proposed a solution using macro-definitions. With regard to the management of graphic interfaces by the various prototypes, we need an additional property of prototypes: they must be able to export their interfaces, we can then combine them via a virtual graphic interface.

In this paper, we focus our presentation on articulating the execution of several prototypes. We started from a case-study in the domain of geometry. This domain was selected for several reasons. Firstly, there are several available prototypes and products ([1,4,8]) that provide the user with some of the needed features (*i.e.* drawing a figure, checking figure correctness with respect to an exercise statement, developing a proof, supporting the learner in writing a proof). Secondly some of these prototypes were designed within our research team or in neighbour teams, so theirs authors were available for advice in programming code changes. Third geometry is a well formalised domain that gave birth to many different machine representations for geometrical objects and concepts; thus it is a good field for experimenting translators from one representation to another one. Last but not least, we started a partnership with researchers working on geometry didactics who are interested in such a platform. From this case-study we draw conclusions and begin the design of a set of guidelines and requirements for plugging educational software components in our experimentation space.

The paper is organised as follows. We start with a global presentation of the platform and of its service components. Then we show how a component can be integrated into the platform and used for a scenario. Implementation choices are described. We conclude on several further developments on which we are currently working.

2 Definition of the Experimentation Space

2.1 General Presentation

To allow prototypes to cooperate in a single environment, we propose an "Experimentation Space" (see Fig 1). In Fig. 1, we have three prototypes P1, P2

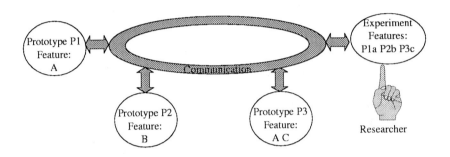

Fig. 1. Experimentation Space

and P3 providing features A, B and C. The objective of the Experimentation Space is that for the user, *i.e.*the researcher, everything occurs as if he had on his machine all the features chosen in the several prototypes (here the feature 'A' of P1, feature 'B' of P2 and feature 'C' of P3).

For example, in geometry, prototype P1 (in Fig. 1) is for drawing and moving geometrical figures (CABRI [4]), prototype P2 is for finding and writing a geometrical proof (MENTONIEZH [8]), and prototype P3 is for drawing a figure and for finding a proof (CHYPRE [1]). With these three prototypes, the researcher can built up an experimentation including the drawing of a figure, the search for a proof and the writing of the proof found.

2.2 Components Presentation

The Experimentation Space is a computerised environment including service components (see Fig. 2) that handle:

- articulation of features of the various prototypes in a scenario, it is the scenario manager. A scenario is composed of several elementary tasks. Each task involves a given feature.
- share of knowledge that is useful to various prototypes, it is the knowledge manager. The knowledge manager handles domain knowledge translation.
- management of graphic interfaces of the various prototypes within a virtual graphic interface (implemented on the target machine, *i.e.* the machine on which runs the experimentation) by the various prototypes, it is the (graphic) interface manager. It handles the common interface unification.

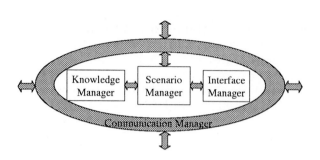

Fig. 2. Software Components of the Experimentation Space

- management of communications between the various prototypes, scenario, knowledge and interfaces manager.

This Experimentation Space supports the cooperation between prototypes. It makes it possible to bring solutions to the questions previously mentioned. Interface Manager and Knowledge Manager are both examples of service components that the Experimentation Space should provide.

3 Integrating an Educational Piece of Software

If we want to give birth to the Experimentation Space we have previously defined, we should explain how to use it. Therefore we build up a set of properties that future designers should take into account.

3.1 Identify Prototype properties and characteristics

To be integrated into the Experimentation Space, each prototype publishes the four following informations: (1) its abilities or features that can be scripted, (2) its pieces of knowledge that may be scrutinised or communicated, (3) its observable-events that can be traced, (4) its graphic interface components that can be exported.

Therefore, in order to link up with the Experimentation Space, the ideal piece of education software needs to have the following properties: as seen in ([10]) and in our introduction, it should be: script-able, "scrutinise-able", trace-able (or record-able) and "interface-export-able".

The three first properties were identified (and named) by Ritter and Koedinger in [10]. It should be *script-able i.e.* it provides a mechanism (a kind of script) that allows the Experimentation Space to launch, to stop and to undo functions, methods or procedures and to recover the results (*e.g.* some Microsoft applications which can be scripted via DDE and some Macintosh applications which can be scripted via APPLE-script). It should be *scrutinise-able i.e.* it allows the Experimentation Space to read critical variables, states or registers. It should be *traceable i.e.* it allows the Experimentation Space to keep traces of the user interactions with the software interface. It should be *"interface-export-able" i.e.* it may be able to give his graphic interface to the Experimentation Space, so that the Experimentation Space can operate on it.

3.2 Integration

We propose for each prototype the five following characteristics. (1) its features (especially those that can be scripted) together with their launch access points, (2) its pieces of knowledge: domain knowledge that can be scrutinised or transfered to another prototype and interaction knowledge *i.e.* observable-events that can be traced, (3) its graphic interface components (such as windows), (4) its host machine, and (5) its host operating system.

Knowing that, we can initialise the Experimentation Space. Through a dialog box we fill a form for each prototype to publish what it offers to the Experimentation Space (knowledge, features, etc.). Filling such a form for existing pieces of intelligent educational software may require some additional work. There are two cases of prototype integration within the Experimentation Space.

The first one is the ideal case *i.e.* the educational software is script-able, scrutinise-able, trace-able and interface-export-able. The definition of the prototype characteristics is easy and so is their publication in the Experimentation Space form. Future pieces of education software should have these properties.

The second one occurs when the educational software is not script-able and/or scrutinise-able and/or trace-able. In this case properties to ensure the script-ability, scrutinise-ability and trace-ability should be added to the prototype before integrating the prototype. This needs slight code changes that should be performed by the authors. In the other cases (i.e. if no such services can be added) the prototype integration depends on several others parameters.

The first parameter is the granularity of features and knowledge that should be published. It depends on the way the software is programmed. If knowledge and features granularity is fine and if the needed pieces of knowledge and features are easily reachable, we have to add access points to the software component. Then we publish them and make the necessary links to access knowledge or to run features. If the granularity is large we cannot publish so many things. For example we can only launch the whole software and wait for its result; thus there is only one thing to be published.

The second parameter is the existence of observable-events generated by the software. If observable-events exist, we only have to choose those that we want to keep (parameterisation). If they do not exist, we need to build them up.

3.3 Defining an Experiment Using Prototype Features

Now that we know how to add a prototype into the Experimentation Space, we should illustrate the design of an experimentation. We have chosen geometry as an application domain. We first define the exercise we implement inside the experimentation. Secondly, we define the scenario we use. Thirdly, we decide which Access Point we need to the different features of the different prototypes involved. And Fourth, we launch the built scenario.

A Geometry Exercise

We aim the learner to perform a complete geometry exercise including figure drawing, proof finding and proof writing. To do that we selected two pieces of educational software.

The first one is TALC, written in Prolog. It allows us to set an exercise statement. It provides a graphic interface to draw a figure (through CABRI). It checks the correctness of a learner's figure with respect to an exercise statement. The TALC features we would like to launch are the tree following ones: (1) Loading the exercise statement (load_statement), (2) Running the drawing figure module (drawing_figure), (3) Running the check figure module (check_figure).

The second one is MENTONIEZH, written in Prolog. It helps the learner to solve and justify a geometrical proof exercise, but provides no graphic interface to draw a geometry figure. It first asks the learner to analyse the exercise statement. Then the learner has to find the proof. And last he has to write out his proof. The MENTONIEZH features we would like to launch are the four following ones: (1) Loading an exercise statement (load_statement), (2) Running the analysing statement module (analysing_statement), (3) Running the finding proof module (finding_proof), (4) Running the writing proof module (writing_proof).

Features identified here are used in next section to build a scenario.

Building a Scenario

In the example the scenario is designed to manage a complete single geometry exercise. Here we only describe the parts of the Scenario Manager algorithm that relates to TALC and MENTONIEZH.

```
1       choose an exercise statement
2       launch the tool for drawing and manipulating the figure
3       launch the validation of the figure
4       launch the tool for analysing the exercise statement (and
            validating this analysis)
5       launch the tool for helping the learner to find a proof
6       launch the tool for validating the proof
7       launch the tool for writing out the proof text
```

Steps 1, 4, 5, 6, 7 are done with MENTONIEZH. Steps 2, 3 are done with TALC. Steps 1, 3, 4, 5, 6, 7 finish when the following step begin. Steps 2 runs until the end of the exercise.

Choosing Feature Access Points

Here the pieces of software were not built to co-operate. As they run on the same machine, we are not dealing with network communication problems.

As it is now, TALC is monolithic. Therefore the only thing we can launch is TALC itself. However it is written with prolog predicates and each of the previously cited features corresponds to a prolog predicate. Therefore with little modification we should be able to launch each of these predicates separately.

In the same way, MENTONIEZH is monolithic. Therefore the only thing we can launch is MENTONIEZH itself. However it already defines modules. Each module is reachable. Therefore with little modification Dominique Py (MEN-TONIEZH' author) should be able to launch each of these modules separately. For this implementation we take TALC and MENTONIEZH as they are now. TALC uses an exercise statement expressed in CDL (a predicate-based language) and MENTONIEZH uses an exercise statement expressed in HDL (another predicate-based language). Therefore TALC publishes the 'CDL_statement' attribute and the 'launch' method, while MENTONIEZH publishes the 'HDL_statement' and 'HDL-CDL_macro-text' attributes and the 'launch' method. As the features included in TALC and MENTONIEZH cannot be run independently, we have to modify the previous algorithm in the following way: We decide to add steps to tell the user what he has to do with each piece of software. This solution does not allow us to check that the learner has done what he has to do, but it allows us to test the Experimentation Space. For example step 1 of the Scenario (described before) is modified as follows:

```
A1      display the instructions:  Choose an exercise statement
            and indicate that you are ready to continue
A2      launch Mentoniezh
A3      wait for the ''ready event''
```

Note that during this step, the feature choice is done within the subject (learner or teacher) activity, because the prototype doesn't separate features and therefore it does not allow to make this feature choice directly.

Executing a Scenario

During the scenario execution, steps are active the one after the other. During one step, a prototype feature is run. Therefore the prototype is active. But when the step is over, the question is should we stop the prototype or not? For example, when the user has drawn a geometrical figure, the drawing tool may still be running to allow the user to use it later. But when the correctness tool has given a "success" feedback, there is no need to let it continue to run. Therefore, we identified at least two kinds of behaviour for a scenario Step: the prototype is stopped at the end of the step or it is stopped at the end of the whole scenario.

3.4 Implementation Choices

We implemented our Experimentation Space in Java. The communication level is implemented with JacORB [3], a middleware that follows the CORBA [7] standard. The Experimentation Space is being tested on PC (Windows95) and Unix (Solaris) platforms. Hereafter we describe some of our implementation choices.

Managing Graphic Interfaces

In the implementation of the current scenario the chosen prototypes are run on the same machine. This case is simpler than the general one. The prototypes have not been designed to export their interface. Therefore the only possible solution in this case is to display two separate windows on the same screen one for TALC, one for MENTONIEZH. Moreover to tell the user what he has to do

---

[3] http://www.inf.fu-berlin.de/ brose/jacorb/

with each piece of software we need a third window. We call it an instruction window. The role of the Interface Manager here is only to activate the windows that are useful in one step of the Scenario.

In the general case, we aim to use a virtual graphic interface that we represent here by the "including window" in which we can organise the display of the other windows. Therefore the necessary features for our Interface Manager are the five following ones: (1) to activate a window, (2) to de-activate a window, (3) to create an including window (e.g. for a piece of software), (4) to organise the windows, (5) to assign an identifier to a window (e.g. useful to activate it). Therefore the implemented Interface Manager contains the following methods: Activate_window, De-activate_window, Create_including_window, Organise_windows and Assign_Window_ID (identifier).

Managing Knowledge

TALC needs an exercise statement expressed in CDL (Classroom Description Language). MENTONIEZH needs an exercise statement expressed in HDL (Hypothesis Description Language).

We call them CDL_statement and HDL_statement.

To make TALC and MENTONIEZH cooperate require using the same exercise statement. Macrelle and Desmoulins in [6, 5] have shown that HDL is translatable into CDL. Therefore we have decided to enter the exercise statement in HDL (with MENTONIEZH), and then to translate it to CDL. To perform this translation we use the Macro-Definition Interpreter together with the HDL to CDL macro-text. In this case MENTONIEZH language is the source language for the translation. Therefore we have decided to publish the HDL to CDL macro-text via MENTONIEZH.

For knowledge sharing, we use the Macro-definition interpreter as service component. It publishes three attributes (In_statement, Out_statement and Macro-Text) and a method (Interpret).

Implementation of the access points to prototype features

When initialising the Experimentation Space, each piece of software and service is included in a CORBA object as servers.

When each object is started, each object initialises CORBA services and creates an object 'implementation' is created.

For example when we start the MENTONIEZH CORBA Object and make all the necessary initialisations, then an implementation of the MENTONIEZH Object is created (we call it M_Impl). From this moment on, M_Impl waits for a client request. The client in this case is Scenario Manager. When it is started, it initialises CORBA services. Then it binds each CORBA object (e.g. it binds MENTONIEZH CORBA Object). From this moment on, a proxy of each bound CORBA object is created (e.g. the proxy for MENTONIEZH is created: M_Proxy).

Here is the detail of step A2. To launch MENTONIEZH, the Scenario Manage, written in java, uses the M_Proxy together with MENTONIEZH publication in an IDL. Then CORBA directs the M_Proxy behaviour. It makes the request to M_Impl. A return value is then sent back to M_Proxy that receives it. Then

M_Proxy sends back the method result to Scenario Manager etc. So CORBA technology enables us to easily implement the Scenario Manager.

4 Summary and Future Trends

The objective of this article was to define a platform supporting inter-operation between pieces of software, which provides help in teaching and learning (Intelligent Educational Software). This platform, called Experimentation Space, was applied in the geometry domain to manage cooperation between TALC and MENTONIEZH.

We endeavoured to make it as general and portable as possible, using existing standards where we could. Compared with [3, 11] our approach embeds existing prototypes (or components) into CORBA objects. This allows us to use the communication facilities available with CORBA object bus instead of using a specific communication component.

In addition we increase the list of properties that a piece of educational software should possess to cooperate with the Experimentation Space: It should be scripted, scrutinised, traced and interface-exported. It should be scripted *i.e.* it provides a mechanism that allows us to launch, to stop and to undo functions, methods or procedures and recover the results. It should be scrutinised *i.e.* it allows us to reach critical variables, states or registers. It should be traced *i.e.* it allows us to keep traces of the user interactions with software interface. It should be interface-exported *i.e.* an other Software Component should catch its graphic interface, display it, etc.

The theoretical and practical trends of this research work are the following ones: Concerning cooperation and connectivity aspects, first we aim to validate the proposals via the implementation of other prototype components. Secondly, we aim to validate the proposals via the experimentation of the Experimentation Space on separate machines. And thirdly we aim to evaluate the efficiency, the ease of use and the complexity of the applications built by using the Experimentation Space. Concerning knowledge sharing aspects, we aim to implement the aggregation of interface events to build up interaction knowledge. Concerning interface integration aspects, we define the desirable characteristics of a user interface. And finally, concerning the definition of a minimal set of objects that must be shared, we aim to define a taxonomy. We have yet identified the following elements: exercise statement and data, learner's exercise solution, (constructions, interfaces events and reasoning) history and learner's conjecture. We need to precise and extend this taxonomy.

This Experimentation Space constitutes a basis for future additions and developments of software components. It should be useful to exploit the complementarity of existing software as well as to increase incrementally the features of educational software. We hope this will help ensure that the achievements in a given domain are perennial and better evaluated and that, in turn, the research is better validated. It should contribute to make educational software more user-friendly for both researchers (to test and validate ideas) and end-users (*i.e.* teachers or learners). The joint use of complementary features would make it possible to offer richer environments to teachers and learners.

References

1. Philippe Bernat. *Conception et réalisation d'un environnement interactif d'aide à la résolution de problèmes. CHYPRE : un exemple pour la démonstration en géométrie.* PhD thesis, Université Henri Poincaré, 1994.
2. Brant A. Cheikes, Marty Geier, Rob Hyland, Frank Linton, Linda Rodi, and Hans-Peter Schaefer. Embedded Training for Complex Information Systems. In Henry M. Goettl, Barry P. anf Halff, Carol L. Redfield, and Valerie J. Shute, editors, *4th International Conference, ITS'98, Intelligent Tutoring Systems, San Antonio, Texas, USA*, volume 1452 of *LNCS*, pages 36–45. Springer, august 1998.
3. Kenneth R. Koedinger, Daniel D. Suthers, and Kenneth D. Forbus. Component-Based Construction of a Science Learning Space. In Henry M. Goettl, Barry P. anf Halff, Carol L. Redfield, and Valerie J. Shute, editors, *4th International Conference, ITS'98, Intelligent Tutoring Systems, San Antonio, Texas, USA*, volume 1452 of *LNCS*, pages 166–167. Springer, august 1998.
4. Jean-Marie Laborde and Franck Bellemain. Cabri-Géomètre II, logiciel et manuel d'utilisation, 1994.
5. Marilyne Macrelle. HDL to CDL Macro-Definition Set. Technical report, LORIA-UHP, 1998.
6. Marilyne Macrelle and Cyrille Desmoulins. Macro-Definitions, a Basic Component for Interoperability between ILEs at the Knowledge Level: Application to Geometry ILEs. In *4th International Conference ITS'98, Intelligent Tutoring Systems*, volume 1452 of *LNCS*, San Antonio, Texas, USA, August 1998. Springer Verlag.
7. Robert Orfali, Dan Harkey, and Jeri Edwards. *Instant CORBA*. Wiley Computer Publishing, New York, 1997.
8. Dominique Py. Geometry Problem Solving with Mentoniezh. *Computers in Education*, 20(1):141–146, 1993.
9. Steven Ritter, Peter Brusilovsky, and Olga Medvedeva. Creating more versatile intelligent learning environments with a component-bases architecture. In Henry M. Goettl, Barry P. anf Halff, Carol L. Redfield, and Valerie J. Shute, editors, *4th International Conference, ITS'98, Intelligent Tutoring Systems, San Antonio, Texas, USA*, volume 1452 of *LNCS*, pages 554–563. Springer, august 1998.
10. Steven Ritter and Kenneth R. Koedinger. An Architecture for Plug-in Tutor Agents. *Journal of Artificial Intelligence in Education*, 7(3/4):315–347, 1996.
11. Dan Suthers and Dan Jones. An Architecture for Intelligent Collaborative Educational Systems. In Ben Du Boulay and Riichiro Mizogushi, editors, *AIED'97, International Conference on Artificial Intelligence in Education, Kobe, Japan*. IOS Press, 1997.

Using Student Task and Learning Goals to Drive the Construction of an Authoring Tool for Educational Simulations

Brendon Towle

KnowledgePlanet.com
5900 Hollis Street, Suite A
Emeryville CA 94608
510-768-2433
btowle@knowledgeplanet.com

Abstract. Learning by doing simulations remain difficult to construct, yet are appropriate training mechanisms in domains where the learning goals involve learning how to make decisions in a complex evolving environment. The learning goals that occur in such an environment are described. Using those learning goals as a basis, an architecture which allows students to achieve those learning goals is described, and then an authoring tool which allows non-programmers to create simulations which address those learning goals is presented. Finally, the results of applying this authoring tool to several domains are discussed, and directions for future work elucidated.

1 Introduction

In many industry training and educational applications, a learning by doing simulation is an appropriate training mechanism. These simulations allow trainees or students to acquire the knowledge they need in an authentic context, thus situating the learning appropriately [1], while allowing them to make the mistakes that are often necessary for learning [9]. For example, training power plant unit operators how to transition from a regulated to a deregulated environment requires that they learn how to analyze the factors of a changing environment in order to make power production decisions based on the potential profit to the company. This is a complex training problem, and one that is likely to recur across companies and locations, thus making it an ideal application for a training simulation.

However, accurate simulations of complex worlds are, by definition, complex, and the development of complex software is a time and money intensive process. Further, the people who are most able to build the simulations (programmers) are the least likely to understand either the domain to be taught or the educational principles involved. One possible solution to this problem is to provide an authoring tool or set of tools that would allow domain experts without programming expertise to build the sort of software alluded to above. Previous research in this area includes the work of Drake [3] and Towne [13], as well as work done under the direction of Schank [7]. Additionally, Murray [8] gives a critical review of many additional projects in this area. This paper describes one approach to creating such authoring tools, as well as one tool that arose from this approach and the results of using that tool.

2 Task/Learning Goal Architectures: Easing the Authoring Burden

One way of easing the burden of the author of an ILE is through a three-part method of developing an authoring tool. First, define a generic task that has educational ramifications, such as managing a complex system in the world. Second, define a set of learning goals that are consistent with that task, such as learning how to make decisions in that system. Finally, design an authoring environment around those constraints.

This approach (or slight variants of it) has been the approach taken by Schank and his students in building a set of tools for Goal-Based Scenarios (GBS) [10], and is the approach used in the tool described in this paper. The major advantage to this approach is that the authoring tool can allow for the creation of much more complex software than would be otherwise possible given the available resources, because it is optimized for a particular task and set of learning goals. The major drawback is that the resulting tool is substantially limited in the types of simulations that can be produced; a tool designed to produce investigation scenarios, for example, [2], cannot then be used to produce rote performance scenarios [5]. This paper describes the construction of an authoring tool for complex simulations, the Crisis Management Tool (CMT), which was built using this approach.

2.1 Learning to Manage a Complex System

The CMT was built around the task of managing a complex system. This could be anything from managing the emergency first aid at the scene of an auto accident to controlling the financial management of a power plant. I have defined the essential features of this task as follows:

- The simulated world is changing as time passes, in accordance with some set of causal relationships in the world;
- The student is taking actions in the simulated world, which can have the effect of changing the evolution of the world;
- The world can be changing both in response to student actions and independently of them.

This task description covers an extremely wide variety of tasks, such as the ones described above, but simultaneously excludes a wide variety of tasks, such as a wide variety of diagnosis and recommendation tasks.

Learning Goals in Management Simulations
Given this task description, then, the next step in the approach is to define the learning goals that will be associated with this task. In the CMT, the nature of the educational task is to learn how to manage the environment so as to accomplish a specified set of

goals, as opposed to simply learning the nature of the causal relationships within the domain. While the nature of these goals in different domains is very different, all of them fall into several general categories. Within the "how-to" category, I have identified four main classes of learning goals:

- Learning how to solve common problems in the domain, usually by applying a stock solution;
- Learning how to avoid common mistakes in the domain;
- Learning how to solve problems in the domain where no stock solution exists, usually by analyzing and evaluating the choices; and
- Learning which problems in the domain must be given a high priority.

In proposing an architecture specifically aimed at handling these learning goals, it is important to know what these goals are, exactly, so as to be able to demonstrate how the architecture supports these authoring goals.

Naturally, these learning goals are not the only ones that can arise in the task of managing a complex system. I have found that the learning goals which arise in this task but do not involve "how-to" learning can be further categorized, and these categories are:

- Understanding the causal mechanics involved in a system;
- Knowing the important vocabulary and concepts in a system; and
- Understanding the typical decisions in a domain.

An in-depth discussion of the details of each of these sets of goals, and how the two sets of goals differ is out of the scope of this paper; see [12] for further details.

3 An Authoring Tool for How-To Simulations of Complex Scenarios

In the previous section, I described the characteristics of the decision-making process that students undertake in complex scenarios, and described what sorts of things are available for the student to learn in these scenarios. Given these characteristics, it is possible to define a tool that will allow for the construction of these how-to simulations.

3.1 The Crisis Management Architecture

Above, I said that the essential features of the task facing the student are:

- The simulated world is changing as time passes, in accordance with some set of causal relationships in the world;
- The student is taking actions in the simulated world, and these can have the effect of changing the evolution of the world;
- The world can be changing both in response to student actions and independently of them.

The Crisis Management Architecture is a predefined set of objects and relations between them that allows authors to build a simulated world that satisfies these criteria. In order to show how these objects fit together, I will first describe the student's interaction with a generic Crisis simulation, then I will describe the set of objects which allow the student to take action, and finally I will describe the set of objects that cause the world to change, both in response to student actions and independently.

In creating simulations within the architecture, it is important to note that authors are not given any flexibility in terms of the components of their simulation. The architecture provides a fairly rigid definition of the objects in the world, and how those objects interact, and those are the only options that are given to authors in constructing their simulations.

Student Interaction With a Crisis Simulation

To illustrate the student interaction with a Crisis simulation, I will give examples from Fire Commander, the first Crisis simulation. In Fire Commander, the student is given the task of directing the firefighting teams at the scene of a house fire. First, the student sees a movie designed to capture her attention and introduce the situation. Then, she is presented with a graphical representation of the firefighting scene, showing the firefighters, civilians, and fires. From this scene, she can choose which one of the firefighting teams to direct. When she has chosen a team to direct (for example, the hose team), she then sees the set of things that team can do at the current time (for example, enter the dining room, enter the kitchen, or spray the house from outside). When she chooses one of these actions, she will then see the action being taken in the simulated world, and then see any consequences of that action, both by seeing a movie of the action and consequences, and by seeing the display of the firefighting scene change. Then, she can choose a team to direct, and the process repeats.

At any time, she can ask questions of expert firefighters, who will give her suggestions about how to approach the problems at hand. This questioning process takes her into a form of hypermedia help system called an ASK system [4], which allows her to continue asking questions on related topics until she is satisfied.

Architectural Components That Cause the World to Change

The Crisis Architecture uses four main components to represent the state of the world and changes to that state: *variables, events, effects,* and *world facts*. Further, the architecture supports the student in observing and inquiring about the world by the use of *media items* and *questions*.

Variables are simply the state variables of the system under simulation, as defined by the author. There are several types of variables supported by the architecture: numeric, enumerated, computed, and list-valued. These different types of variables allow authors to think about the domain in terms of the domain, instead of in terms of the architecture.[1] From the firefighting example, a variable might be the state of the fire in the living room, or the location of the hose team.

---

[1] For example, an author in a firefighting scenario could choose to define the states of the fire as {extinguished, small content fire, large content fire, fully involved fire, extensions fire} as opposed to {1, 2, 3, 4, 5}.

Events are the architectural representation of what happens in the world, and are implemented as a forward-chaining rule engine. An event has four main components: the set of world facts that define when the event should happen, the set of effects that take place when the event does happen, the set of media items that should be displayed to the student when the event happens, and the set of questions that the student should be allowed to ask after the event happens. From the firefighting example, an event might be that the fire in the living room grows to fully engulf the room.

World facts come in two flavors: simple and complex. Simple world facts are simple statements about the world that can be either true or false: the value of the variable "Living Room FIre" is greater than medium, for example, or the student just took the action "Send the Hose Team into the Living Room". Complex world facts are boolean combinations of either simple or complex world facts. This boolean nesting allows authors to construct expressions of arbitrary complexity.

Effects are the representation of the changes to the world, and essentially represent all of the various changes that can happen to the different types of variables. In addition to a specification of the change that should happen, effects can also include a media item to present to the student when that effect happens. Each type of effect has its own representation; a typical representation would be an ordered tuple of the form {variable, change-type, value}, such as {Living Room Fire, Add, 1}.

Media items are simply the architecture's reference to the multimedia resources which will be displayed to the student.

Questions are the conceptual inquiries that will be presented to the student, and consist of three main components: the actual text of the question, the set of followup questions that should be presented after the student asks the question, and the media item(s) that answer the question.

Architectural Components That Allow the Student to Take Action

The primary components of the Crisis Management Architecture that allow the student to take action in the simulated world are *situations* and *actions*. Situations are the architectural representation of those parts of the world which the student can act upon, and actions are the architectural representation of the things that the student can do about any given situation.

The major components of a situation are: the text used to describe that situation to the student, the actions that the student can take about that situation, a set of world facts describing when the situation should be presented to the student, and a set of questions that the student can ask in deciding what to do about that situation.

The major components of an action are: the text used to describe that action to the student, the effects that action has on the world when it is taken, a set of world facts which describe when that action cannot be presented to the student, and a set of questions that the student can ask in evaluating that action.

Collectively, the components mentioned here allow for all of the actions described in the architectural overview: students can choose between situations, take actions about those situations, observe the results of their actions, and ask questions about both the results and what to do next.

How The Architecture Supports the Learning Goals

Since this architecture was designed to support a particular set of learning goals, it is important to demonstrate how students can achieve the learning goals within the context of the architecture. Tthe four types of learning goals that were defined as the primary targets of the Crisis Management Architecture were: solving common problems, avoiding common mistakes, analyzing and evaluating decisions, and prioritizing problems appropriately.

The first and second types of learning goal are addressed by simply giving the student three related opportunities: the opportunity to attempt to solve the problem, the opportunity to watch the attempted solution succeed or fail, and the opportunity to ask questions about why the solution succeeded or failed, with answers given by experts in the domain. By situating these opportunities in a relevant context, the CMT gives the student a much better chance to retain this knowledge appropriately, and gives the student a more motivating way to learn it [1].

The third learning goal is also addressed by giving students the opportunity to solve problems, but in conjunction with the opportunity to ask questions about what to do and how to think about the problem, with answers again given by experts in the domain. Again, the student has been motivated to want to solve the problem (by virtue of the structure of a Goal-Based Scenario), and again the problem solving is situated in a real context.

The fourth learning goal is addressed in the same manner. The student is given the opportunity to choose which problems should be addressed first. If these choices are poor, the outcome of the simulation will be less than optimal (by definition). The student is then given the opportunity to ask questions of experts about why things happened the way they did, and can then discover which problems should have been addressed first.

Finally, all of these goals are further addressed by a reflection component built into the architecture. After a student has finished the scenario, either by choosing to exit, or by satisfying any of the success or failure criteria defined by the author, she is presented with the opportunity to review their actions. The system uses that as a further opportunity to engage the student in a dialogue about what should have been done, via the built in ASK system.

3.2 The Crisis Management Tool: Instantiating the Architecture

The essential mechanisms by which the CMT supports the creation of simulations within the architecture are as follows:

- The CMT includes code which defines all the classes of objects in Crisis simulations, how they relate to each other, and the processing that needs to occur to make the simulation work.
- The CMT provides authors with a set of graphical editors, all of which work in the same way. These graphical editors allow authors to define a population of objects within their simulations by use of standard GUI mechanisms (drag and drop, selection from dialog boxes, etc.).
- The CMT provides authors with a set of debugging and exploring mechanisms that they can use to confirm that their simulation works as expected, and that the required educational opportunities are available to the student.

The CMT also provides authors with a rich set of mechanisms to build a customized interface to their simulation, but a complete discussion of those mechanisms is outside the scope of this paper; again, see [12] for further details.

Object Definitions and Graphical Editors

One of the design goals of the CMT was that authors not have to write a single line of code in order to design and build their simulations. To accomplish this goal, the CMT defines all of the classes of objects mentioned in the architecture overview, and how they relate to each other. For example, the CMT includes the code that defines how world facts associated with actions cause those actions to be unavailable to the student if the world facts are true, the code which causes situations to be available to the student when their world facts are true, the code which maintains the list of state variables, and so forth.

The inclusion of this code frees the author from most of the programming requirements that would normally be associated with building a simulation. However, the author still has the task of creating all of the situations, actions, events, and so forth that make the simulation work.

To allow the author to do that, the CMT provides a set of graphical editors, one for each type of object in the simulation. All of the objects in the CMT are defined as slot and filler structures, with strong restrictions on the type of object that can be used as a filler. Because of this, each graphical object editor can provide a GUI widget for each slot, and that widget can produce the right editor. For example, the editor for a situation has a standard scrolling list interface widget associated with the actions slot, and this scrolling list has buttons to allow the author to create a new action, add an existing action, and so forth. When the author clicks on the button to add a new action, the CMT pops up a new action editor window, and knows that when the author finishes that editor, it should be associated with the previous situation. Similarly, when the author clicks on the button to add an existing action (or actions), the CMT pops up a selectable scrolling list containing all of the existing actions. The fact that all of the editors share the same set of basic slot editors and buttons aids in ease of use; once an author has learned how to use one, he has learned them all.

Debugging/Exploring Mechanisms

It is an unfortunate fact of life that computer programs don't work as expected when first written. Because of this, the CMT includes a set of three different tools which allow authors to explore how their simulations function, and fix them: the data checking facility, a Simulation Analyzer, and an ASK System Analyzer. Each of these tools allows authors to inspect their simulations in a different way. Unfortunately, a detailed discussion of these tools is outside of the scope of this paper; see [12] for the details.

4   Results: The CMT in Practice

The CMT was used by 13 different project teams to build 13 distinct simulations over a two-year period. Each of these simulations was a complete prototype, although the simulations were not used in classroom settings; however, some of the simulations were used as business demonstrations. (This magnitude of use corresponds to Murray's category 2 of degree of use—a tool that is a completely functional prototype, and has been used to create multiple functioning prototypes [8].)

Authors were given 1-2 hours of instruction in the use of the tool at the beginning of their project, and then another hour or so of instruction in the use of the interface builder at the time they began to build the interface. Very little additional instruction was necessary to allow authors to complete their simulations.

Of the 13 different teams, 12 were able to complete their projects in the timeframe allotted, which differed from team to team; some of the teams were given 6 weeks as a part time project, while others were given 4 months full time. All 12 of these projects were functional standalone software, although obviously the projects built in 4 months were more fully developed. Some of these projects were built before the interface editor was completed, and the interface code for these was built by hand, but the projects that were built with the interface editor were completed start to finish without the authors needing to write a single line of code. These projects varied widely in their interface appearance and their educational domains, showing that the CMT does indeed provide a domain independent environment for authoring educational simulations.

In conclusion, I have described an authoring tool for the creation of complex management simulations. Although it is clear that the tool does work, the effectiveness of the resulting simulations is a question in need of further research. Additionally, it would seem that using the tool itself as a teaching mechanism, allowing students to build simulations of a domain in order to learn about that domain, might be a fruitful area of further research.

Acknowledgements
This paper describes work done under the direction of Roger Schank, whose vision was a driving influence on the work. Many people aided in the construction and design of the CMT, but the comments of Alex Kass and Michael Wolfe were particularly helpful. Edwin Bos and Clark Quinn provided helpful comments on an earlier draft of this paper, as did two anonymous reviewers.

References

1. Brown, J. S., Collins, A., Duguid, P.: "Situated Cognition and the Culture of Learning." Educational Researcher 18 (1989) 32-42
2. Dobson, D.: Authoring tools for investigate-and-decide learning environments, Northwestern University. (1998)
3. Drake, L.: The Instructional Simulation Builder. (demo) International Conference on the Learning Sciences, Evanston, IL, Association for the Advancement of Computing in Education. (1996)

4. Ferguson, W., Bareiss, R., Birnbaum, L., Osgood, R.: ASK Systems: An Approach to the Realization of Story-Based Teachers. Institute for the Learning Sciences, Tech Report 22. (1992)
5. Guralnick, D. A.: An Authoring Tool for Procedural-Task Training, Northwestern University. (1996)
6. Interational Fire Services Training Association: Essentials of Firefighting, Third Edition. Stillwater, OK, Fire Protection Publications, Oklahoma State University. (1992)
7. Korcuska, M., Kass, A., Jona. M.Y.: Design Choices for Learning-by-Doing Software: When to Choose Advise. International Conference on the Learning Sciences, Evanston, IL, Association for the Advancement of Computing in Education. (1996)
8. Murray, T.: "Authoring Intelligent Tutoring Systems: Analysis of the state of the art." International Journal of AI and Education 10(1). (1999)
9. Schank, R. C.:. Explanation Patterns. Hillsdale, NJ, Lawrence Erlbaum Associates. (1986)
10. Schank, R. C.: Goal-Based Scenarios, Institute for the Learning Sciences, Tech Report 36. (1992)
11. Shlick, A. (Wauconda IL Fire Department). Personal communication with author. (1996)
12. Towle, B.: Authoring Tools for Learning How to Manage Complex Scenarios, Northwestern University. (forthcoming)
13. Towne, D. M.: Learning and Instruction in Simulation Environments. Englewood Cliffs, NJ, Educational Technology Publications. (1995)

Using an ITS Authoring Tool to Explore Educators' Use of Instructional Strategies

Shaaron Ainsworth[1], Jean Underwood[1&2] and Shirley Grimshaw[1]

1 *ESRC Centre for Research in Development*, Instruction & Training, School of Psychology, University Park, University of Nottingham, Nottingham, NG7 2RD, UK.
2 Division of Psychology, Nottingham Trent University, Burton Street, Nottingham, NG1 4BU, UK.
Email: sea, jdu, skg@psychology.nottingham.ac.uk.

Abstract. REDEEM is an ITS authoring environment that creates simple ITSs from existing domain material. In this paper, we report on an exploratory study which examined how authors used the REDEEM tools to create ITSs that matched their views on instruction. Four authors were asked to describe a class of children learning primary mathematics and then use REDEEM tools to create ITSs that they thought appropriate for these students. The results of the study showed that although all the authors tended to analyze the class in the same way, they had very different approaches to how they should be taught. We report on the inter-author and intra-author differences in the number and composition of teaching strategies and the application of these strategies to individual children. We conclude that the REDEEM environment can cater for different instructional goals.

1. Introduction

REDEEM is an ITS authoring environment used to create simple ITSs from existing domain material. The ITS tools take extant Computer Based Training (CBT) and allow teachers or subject matter experts (SMEs) to overlay their instructional expertise. The REDEEM shell uses this knowledge, together with its own default teaching knowledge, to deliver the courseware adaptively. REDEEM ITSs are limited by the domain content of the CBT and have a small number of tutorial actions. But, a teacher can use REDEEM to create an ITS from CBT in substantially less time than that reported for other ITS authoring tools [9] at around two hours per hour of instruction [1]. REDEEM therefore represents one solution to the problem of providing the power of an ITS without overwhelming investment in time or expertise.

REDEEM is a relatively unusual authoring tool. Unlike other systems such as RIDES[6], Eon [8] it does not help users to construct the domain material. Nor, does it have the specific and indepth knowledge of the domain as systems such as Diag [11] or Demonstr8[3] do. Instead, it aims to create simple ITSs that reflect teachers' pedagogic goals with relatively little authoring. Given its unusual design and aim, it is very important to evaluate and hopefully validate this approach to ITS construction.

Evaluation of an authoring tool is complex with many different metrics required for a complete analysis (see.[7]). Essentially however these are based upon two dimensions – how effectively does the resulting ITS teach students and how effectively do the tools support an author in construction of the ITS? Our current evaluations focus on the latter of these two goals. We concentrate first upon 'author-centered' evaluation because, until it has been demonstrated that REDEEM allows authors to develop the ITSs they require, we can not sensibly evaluate the impact of those ITSs on students' learning outcomes. In previous work we have examined the issue of usability of the tools [1]. We now turn to a more fundamental question - Do teachers use the functionality that REDEEM provides? If all teachers view courses and students in the same way then REDEEM is redundant. Rather than provide teachers with tools to create ITSs that reflect their own pedagogic preferences, we should instead provide the 'right' ITS.

ITSs constructed and run under REDEEM vary along two key dimensions – "what they teach" and "how they teach it". In the former case, the ITS shell varies through the CBT material, supplements it with additional questions and feedback, suggests reflection points and supports integration into the classroom by the use of non-computer based tasks. In the latter case, REDEEM varies factors including the degree of student control, position and amount of testing, help provision and response to student error to adapt its teaching style to students' needs. Previously, we discussed how authors use REDEEM to create different sequences through material for their students [2]. Here we consider their instructional strategies. This paper reports on an exploratory study that examines the ITSs created by four users. By so doing, we hope to show that REDEEM can be used to produce ITSs that differ substantially from author to author and argue that this validates the claim that authors can and will create ITSs that reflect their (implicit or explicit) pedagogic theories.

A second and no less important goal is to consider if the design of REDEEM supports the functionality that teachers require. Most ITS authoring environments aim to trade-off the complexity of authoring decisions with the power and flexibility of the resulting ITS (e.g. [10]. This is particularly true of REDEEM as it is aimed at authors with little experience in the development of computer-based learning environments. Ideally, the way that REDEEM allows authors to describe how they prefer to teach students will result in an ITS with many different strategies. However, if all authors make very similar decisions about a teaching strategy, then choice in this dimension is redundant and may become hard-coded into future systems. This should allow the development of systems that are quicker or simpler to use or can be used to 'free up' time to describe other authoring decisions.

2. Authoring with REDEEM

The ITS authoring tools require users to provide descriptions of course content, student characteristics and teaching strategies. In order to illustrate how REDEEM ITSs created in this study varied the instructional strategies for different children, it is helpful to consider how the second and third decisions of these are authored. Fuller descriptions of the complete authoring process can be found in [5]

Assuming authors have either described a course or been provided with a pre-described course, they can customise it to their class by developing teaching strategies for individual children or groups of children. They use three tools to do this; student categorisation, teaching strategy development and relating student categories to teaching strategies. The first two tasks could be performed in any order, but relating strategies to students must come last. It is possible to revise these decisions.

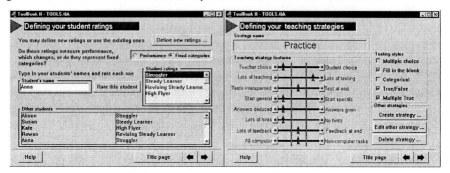

Fig. 1. The student characteristics tool **Fig. 2.** Defining teaching strategies tool

Authors begin to consider student characteristics by defining a set of categories which will be used by the shell to determine which teaching strategy and what material a student receives. These categories can be based upon any factors that teachers consider important such as previous experience of the course, aptitude in the topic, learning style or degree of literacy. Figure 1 provides an example of one teacher's decisions, where the categories chosen are based upon a combination of function (revision or first exposure) and perceived ability. If teachers choose to select performance-related categories, then the validity of student placement within categories can be evaluated against a student's performance in the ITS shell. If this is the case, then the shell will automatically change the category as the overall standard of the student (as defined in the shell's student model) changes. Teachers must create a minimum of one category (e.g." My Class") but there is no upper limit on this number. For example, a teacher may create as many categories as children although previous studies show that this is unlikely to occur [12]. Having created the categories, teachers then enter the names of their students and associate them with one of these categories. It is possible to change categories and students at any time.

Different teaching strategies are created by manipulating dimensional sliders of eight components of instruction. Teachers are free to use previously developed strategies, edit them or develop new ones (Figure 2). These dimensions were developed by a combination of interviewing teachers and the research literature on aptitude by treatment interactions. They do not represent an end-point of design and this research is aimed at determining which ones teachers found most and least useful. The position and meaning of each slider can be found in table 1. The final stage in the process is to simply relate teaching strategy to student category.

Table 1. Dimensions of teaching strategies in REDEEM

	Slider Left	Slider Centre	Slider Right
Student choice	No student choice	Choice of section	Choice of any page
Lots of teaching	Offer no tests	One test limit per page	All tests available
Position of ?s	Test after each page	Test after each section	Test after course
General to Specific	Prefer general pages first		Prefer specific pages first
Answers deduced	Right answer given when no further answers	Right answer given upon second error	Right answer given upon error
Help Given	Help on request	Help on error	No help
Summarise	Summarise after section and ?	Summarise after section	No summary
Non-computer task	No non-computer tasks	Non-computer tasks after section	All non-computer tasks after page

3. Study One

Four educators were recruited, one SME and three teacher practitioners (TPs). The SME was a teacher trainer with 20 years experience in primary mathematics. The TPs were classroom teachers who had not previously developed computer-based material. They were asked to create an ITS from a course 'Understanding Shapes' which is aimed at children of 7-11 years and focuses on mathematical concepts such as vertices and symmetry. The material covers around six hours of teaching and includes text, graphics, sound, and animation. To compare the educators' decisions, it was necessary for them to author for the same group of learners. As there was no class of children with which all the authors were familiar we created a simulated class of 7-year old girls. Vignettes were developed describing each child's performance in mathematics over the last year. The vignettes manipulated familiarity with the course and mathematical aptitude. The profiles were developed from records of children unknown to the participants and vetted by a local headmaster. Each author was provided with descriptions such as these for seven children. They were then free to define student ratings and to develop as many teaching strategies as they required.

4. Results

The first issue that will be considered is how teachers saw the virtual class. Four authors were asked to develop scales and rate the class of seven children using them. Table 2 shows the resulting categorization. Although no author saw any of the other authors' ratings, each author created five categories of students. It is apparent from the names they give the categories and the way they group the students that two of the authors were mainly concerned with the students perceived ability in maths (TP2 and SME) whereas the other two authors combined ability characteristics with familiarity with the course to determine their student ratings (TP1 and TP3). However, it can be seen from Table 2, that the resulting order of the student categories is very similar across the authors.

Table 2. Students in author-defined categories

Name	TP1	TP2	TP3	SME
Alison	to L1 unfamiliar	group 5	a	very low
Susan	L1 unfamiliar	group 4	b	low
Sally	L1 unfamiliar	group 4	b	middle
Anne*	L1 familiar	group 3	revising b	middle
Lucy	L2 unfamiliar	group 2	c	high
Emma	L2 unfamiliar	group 1	c	high
Kate*	L2 familiar	group 2	revising c	very high

Key. Students are ordered from the least to the most mathematically proficient. Those marked with an asterisk were identified as revising the course.

Each participant authored a number of different teaching strategies: TP1 created five and she assigned each of these to at least one group of children, TP2 authored five strategies which she also used at least once, TP3 created six and used five of them for this class and SME developed three and used two of them for the class. Furthermore, it can be seen from table 3, that the authors used REDEEM to create many different strategies. There are 8 dimensional sliders each of which can be placed in one of three positions. In total, 20 of these 24 slider positions were used by the authors. This is surprisingly high given that this is just one course for a single age-group of students. The wide use to which the sliders were put suggests that we have achieved our goal of identifying dimensions of teaching strategies that authors consider important to differentiate instruction.

When we examine the content of the authors' decisions, we can see that there are marked differences between the authors. Individually, the number of dimensional ratings used by each author were 19 for TP1, 13 for TP2, 17 for TP3 and 12 for SME. The SME differs from the other authors in that she was the only author to use a single teaching strategy for more than one group of students. Incidentally, this does not mean that these groups of students received the same ITS because the material covered by each of these groups was different. As she only created two strategies, she is limited to a maximum of 16 possible slider locations. The other three authors all used five teaching strategies for the class, one for each of the five defined student groups, so the variations between them are due more to differences in how finely they differentiated their teaching strategies across the class. TP2 used just five additional dimensional ratings above the minimum of eight whereas TP1 used an additional eleven. The reasons for these differences between authors or what the effects of these differences on learning within the class might be are outside the bounds of this study. However, such differences are interesting as they point to ways of using REDEEM as a means of exploring different conceptions of teaching.

Table 3. Strategies created by authors given by position of dimensional sliders and student categories 1 = Left, 2 = Middle, 3= Right

TP1	SC	LT	PQ	GS	AD	H	S	NT	Groups
Low Unfam	1	2	1	1	2	1	2	3	to L1 unfam
Mid Unfam	1	3	1	1	2	2	2	3	L1 unfam
Mid Fam	2	2	1	1	1	2	2	1	L1 fam
High Unfam	1	3	2	1	2	2	2	3	L2 unfam
High Fam	3	3	3	2	1	2	2	1	L2 fam
TP2	SC	LT	PQ	GS	AD	H	S	NT	Groups
Group 5	1	2	1	1	1	1	1	2	group 5
Group 4	1	2	1	1	1	1	1	2	group 4
Group 3	1	2	1	1	1	2	2	2	group 3
Group 2	1	2	2	1	1	2	2	2	group 2
Group 1	3	3	2	2	1	2	2	2	group 1
TP3	SC	LT	PQ	GS	AD	H	S	NT	Groups
Strategy a	1	2	1	1	3	1	2	2	a
Strategy b	2	3	2	1	2	2	2	2	b
Strategy c	3	3	2	2	1	2	2	2	c
Revising b	2	3	2	1	1	2	2	1	revising b
Revising c	3	3	2	2	1	2	2	1	revising c
SME	SC	LT	PQ	GS	AD	H	S	NT	Groups
Control	1	3	1	1	2	2	1	3	very low, low, middle
Low control	2	3	2	1	2	1	2	3	high, v. high

Key. SC Student choice, LT Lots of teaching, PQ Position of questions, GS General to Specific, AD Answers deduced, H Help Given, S Summarization, NT Non-computer task

An alternative way of examining the data reveals a slightly different picture. In this case, the class is taken as the unit of analysis and the number of children who receive each position of the teaching dimensions is summed. Therefore with four authors and seven children there is a maximum of 28 entries for each cell. This analysis allows us to examine whether just one aspect of a dimension is used for all of the student groups or whether there is a more even distribution where each dimensional rating is used for at least one student group.

It can be seen from figure 3 that the teaching dimension most consistently used in just one location is "General to specific" which is used in "Prefer general" just over 80% of the time and "Ignore this dimension" in the remaining cases. A future research question is to compare this to the authoring of other courses to determine if this result is a characteristic of the particular course used in this study or a more general preference.

The second most consistently used dimension is "summarization". This was used in position 2, "summarize after section" 75% of the time and in position 1, "summarize after section and page" 25% of the time. Even in the cases where it was used in position 1, the authors were not always happy with the decision and suggested changing it upon review. This slider is a plausible candidate for assumption into the REDEEM architecture - i.e. hard coding the decision to summarize after section in the ITS shell. However, caution is warranted as again it may be a characteristic of the course (the relative size of sections and number of questions authored) which causes its relative lack of differentiation. Further authoring with other courses for other age groups is underway that will help clarify this.

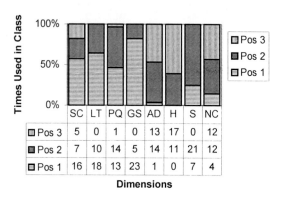

	SC	LT	PQ	GS	AD	H	S	NC
▨ Pos 3	5	0	1	0	13	17	0	12
▨ Pos 2	7	10	14	5	14	11	21	12
▨ Pos 1	16	18	13	23	1	0	7	4

Dimensions

Fig. 3. Use of each of the teaching dimensions collapsed across author and class

Five of the remaining dimensions were used in two positions fairly consistently (Lots of Teaching, Position of Questions, Answers Deduced, Help Given and Non-Computer Based Tasks). In most cases, the third dimensional rating was almost never used. This may be due to the nature of the course and task. The Student Control dimension is probably the most differentiated as although it had one fairly strong home position (All teacher control), the other two dimensions were represented fairly equally. We now turn to consider whether these results are based on differences **between** the way that authors use the strategy dimensions (inter-author differences) or whether they are based on differences **within** an author's use of teaching strategies for their class (intra-author differences).

It is apparent that use of the teaching dimensions varied between authors in the study. For example, only two of the dimensions of "Lots of Teaching" were used (this determines how much time a student spends in questions versus exploration of new material) position 1(10/28 times) and position 2 (18/28 times). This distribution is very similar to "Help Given" (whether students receive no help, help on error or help on error and request) which again was used in only two positions - position 2(11/28 times) and position 3 (17/28 times). However, these total scores hide variation in inter-author and intra-author differences. For "Help Given", the authors apply two facets of the dimension fairly equally (more intra-author difference), whereas for "Lots of Teaching", each author had a strong preference for one position of the slider but did not always agree on that position (more inter-author difference).

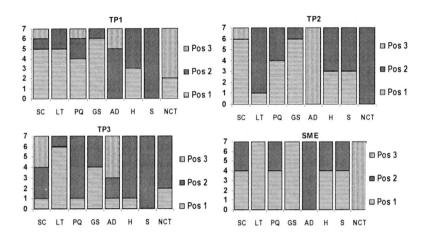

Fig.4. Authors assignment of teaching dimensions to their classes

Marked inter-author differences but less intra-author differences are also observed in use of non-computer based tasks. Two authors used only one facet of the dimension (but each selected different ones) whereas the other two authors used two positions of the slider. In this case the difference between the author strategies can be explained on the basis of their student categories. If they took account of familiarity when creating categories they used strategies without non-computer tasks. Student control, which was the dimension that is most differentiated across authors is revealed by this analysis to combine inter-author and intra-author differences. TP1 and TP2 used this slider primarily in position 1 (all teacher control), TP3 only uses position 1 once and then uses positions 2 and 3 equally, and SME uses positions 1 and 2 equally. It suggests that some educators believe that (for this age of children) there is an appropriate level of student control whereas others believe that this decision is best made on a case by case basis. The authors strong but differing views on the role of student control are very interesting, particularly as the degree of student control has often been considered as a defining feature of an ITS (*e.g.*[5]).

A final source of variation in the design of the ITSs is differences in how the authors treated each of the students - there may be some types of students where there is much higher agreement than others. To illustrate this we scored each dimension for every child by the degree of agreement between the authors. There were four authors so the only possibilities are complete agreement, where all authors select the same dimensional rating (4,0,0) scored 4, or levels of partial agreement; three authors agree (3,1,0) scored 3, two sets of authors agree with each other (2,2,0) scored 2 and the least agreement (2,1,1) scored 1. These were then summed for each child to give a maximum score between 8 and 32. These data can be seen in Figure 5.

It is apparent that there were variations in how the authors treated the different children. The major source of disparity is whether authors took account of familiarity with the course when developing strategies. Anne and Kate are the two students who were identified as 'revising' in the student profiles. These students generated the least agreement as two authors created revision strategies and two did not. Although it would be unwise to over interpret this data, there also seems to be more agreement between authors with lower performing students. This suggests more concordance amongst teachers about how to support learning for children of lower aptitude/experience than children with higher aptitude/experience in that domain.

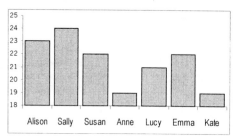

Fig. 5. Agreement on the choice of teaching strategies by four authors

5. Conclusions

This investigation forms part of our ongoing evaluation of the REDEEM authoring environment. The analysis of the way that authors constructed teaching strategies from the different dimensions confirms that the tools are being used nearly to their full extent as 20/24 of the possible options were selected by authors in this study. This is striking given the limited nature of the underlying course and the few authors who took part in the study. Two dimensions were identified as having limited differentiation, "General to Specific" and "Summarization". These are candidates for inclusion in the REDEEM architecture if future studies find that they are rarely used. The other dimensions were used in a more differentiated fashion with the majority being used in two positions fairly regularly and only Student Control and to a lesser extent Non-Computer Based Tasks having substantial use in all three. We are currently exploring courses aimed at different populations (secondary school students and naval recruits) and different topics (biology and electricity) to establish whether these will produce similar pattern teaching strategies.

Another interesting outcome of this study is the difference between the authors. Although all the educators tended to see that class similarly, they differed in how they developed and then assigned teaching strategies. One author, the SME, used two strategies whereas all the other authors used five strategies. These total figures hide more subtle differences. The SME, for example, used 12 dimensional ratings in her two strategies whereas TP2 used only one more in five different strategies. TP2 seems more inclined to a model of 'home' positions on the dimensions which she tweaks for individual students whereas the SME has more even distribution across the dimensional ratings. Finally, we can see that some of the learner profiles in this study led to more agreement about the appropriate teaching strategy than others. Revising children caused the most disagreement with two authors developing strategies specifically for them and two not. There also appeared to be a trend for less concordance amongst authors for children with more experience/aptitude.

These results lead us to further studies. One is to repeat this experiment using more authors to explore the use of an ITS authoring tool for capturing views of teaching. This research is underway with students training to be teachers of primary mathematics. A second set of studies will explore whether these differences in strategies described and developed under REDEEM impact on the learning experiences of students. Studies of the impact of REDEEM on learning outcomes with naval trainees are also underway and should help to answer this question.

Acknowledgements

This research was supported by the ESRC Centre for Research in Development, Instruction and Training We would like to thank Nigel Major, Sue Cavendish, Iona Bradley, Sue Hewes, Ruth Guy-Clarke Ben Williams and David Wood

References

1. Ainsworth, S.E., Underwood, J.D., Grimshaw, S.K: Formatively evaluating REDEEM – an authoring environment for intelligent tutoring systems. In: Lajoie, S. Vivet, M. (eds.): A.I. in Ed.. Amsterdam: IOS Press. (1999) 93-100
2. Ainsworth, S.E., Grimshaw, S.K. Underwood, J.D: Teachers implementing pedagogy through REDEEM. Computers and Ed. (1999) 171-181
3. Blessing, S. B:. A programming by demonstration authoring tools for model tracing tutor. Int. Journal of A.I. in Ed., 8(3-4), (1997). 233-261
4. Elsom-Cook, M: Guided discovery tutoring and bounded user modelling. In Self, J: (eds.) *A.I. and Human Learning*: London: Chapman and Hall. (1988) 165-178
5. Major, N., Ainsworth, S.E., Wood, D.J.: REDEEM: Exploiting symbiosis between psychology and authoring environments, Int. Journal of A.I. in Ed., 8(3-4), (1997) 317-340
6. Munro, A., Johnson, M. C., Pizzini, Q. A., Surmon, D. S., Towne, D. M., Wogulis, J. L.: Authoring simulation centred tutoring with RIDES Int. Journal of A.I. in Ed., 8(3-4), (1997) 284-316
7. Murray, T.: Expanding the knowledge acquisition bottleneck for intelligent tutoring systems. Int. Journal of A.I. in Ed., 8(3-4), (1997) 222-232
8. Murray, T. Authoring knowledge based tutors: Tools for content, instructional strategy, student models and interface design. Journal of the Learning Sciences, 7(1), (1998) 5-64
9. Murray, T. (1999). An overview of the state of the art in ITS authoring tools In: Lajoie, S. Vivet, M. (eds.): A.I. in Ed.. Amsterdam: IOS Press. (1999) 9
10. Sparks, R., Dooley, S., Meiskey, L. Blumenthal, R: The Leap authoring tool: Supporting complex courseware authoring through reuse, rapid prototyping and interactive visualizations. Int. Journal of A.I. in Ed., 10, (1999) 75-97
11. Towne, D. M.: Approximate reasoning techniques for intelligent diagnostic instruction. Int. Journal of A.I. in Ed., 8(3-4), (1997) 262-283.
12. Underwood, J., Cavendish, S., Lawson, T.: The Sustainability of Learning Gains: An investigation of the Medium-Term Impact of Integrated Learning Systems on Pupil Performance. Coventry: NCET (1996)

Is What You Write What You Get?:
An Operational Model of Training Scenario

Yusuke Hayashi[1], Mitsuru Ikeda[1], Kazuhisa Seta[1],
Osamu Kakusho[2], and Riichiro Mizoguchi[1]

[1] The Institute of Scientific and Industrial Research, Osaka University
8-1, Mihogaoka, Ibaraki, Osaka, 5670047, Japan
{hayashi, ikeda, seta, miz}@ei.sanken.osaka-u.ac.jp
[2] Faculty of Economics and Information Science, Hyogo University
kakusho@humans-kc.hyogo-dai.ac.jp

Abstract. To meet the needs for large-scale, high-quality learning contents, needless to say, we have to sharpen authoring tools. Authoring process can be roughly divided into two phases, a composing phase and a verification phase. A great deal of effort has been made on the support in the former phase. What seems to be lacking, however, is that in the latter. An ontology-aware authoring tool we have been developing has a function called "Conceptual level simulation. " This supports authors in the latter phase by showing the behavior of learning contents not only as a sequence of concrete behavior but also as structured and abstract behavior along the design intention. Ontology lays the foundation for the function by explicating operational and conceptual semantics of a training scenario.

1. Introduction

Contents-oriented research comes to attract considerable attention in information engineering field. The trend has been accelerated with broad diffusion of multimedia and internet technologies. In the research field on educational systems, the transitions from story-board type to knowledge-based type, from individual type to collaborative type and from tutoring type to learning environment type, are symbolic of the trend. Large-scale, high-quality learning contents are becoming one of the critical needs of technetronic society. To meet the needs, needless to say, we have to sharpen our tools to produce high-quality learning contents in a large scale, because the quality of the learning contents depends not only on the author's ability but also on authoring tool's performance. In fact, many researchers address this issue from a variety of viewpoints [6].

Authoring process can be roughly divided into two phases, a composing phase and a verification phase. Existing authoring tools support both phases of authors' work to a some extent. However, compared with the support performance for the former phase, one for the latter does not seem very helpful to the author. A typical support function for the latter is to provide a behavior-level test bed where authors can examine their learning contents step by step along the control structure. In general, of course, it is helpful and absolutely necessary. However, it is not very helpful to resolve the logical drawback of learning contents. On analogy of programming, it could be described as "semantic-error debugging. " Shapiro explains the hardness of debugging [7]:

A program is a collection of assumptions, which can be arbitrarily complex; its behavior is a consequence of these assumptions; therefore we cannot, in general, anticipate all the possible behaviors of a give program.

This is true in case of authoring of learning contents as well. The key to lightening the hardness of debugging is to shift the load to maintain the design assumptions from authors to authoring tools. To realize this, new functions of an authoring tool to be developed include

- A framework for authors to describe design assumptions including design intention of learning contents.
- A function to show the behavior of learning contents not only as a sequence of concrete behavior but also as structured and abstract behavior along the design intention.

We call the latter as "conceptual-level simulation. "Our idea is that the structured information generated based on author's design intention will lighten the author's major debugging load to compare what he/she thinks (design intention) with what he/she gets (behavior). We use the term "design intention" to prevent confusion of it with more general term "design rationale". Generally, design rationale includes reasons behind design decisions, justification for them, other alternatives considered, the trade-offs evaluated, and the argumentation that led to the decision [3]. Intuitively, design intention is a part of design rationale: limited to reasons behind a design decision and justification for it. Reasons behind concrete learning contents are represented as a hierarchical structure of instructional goals. Justifications for the structure are teaching strategies or pedagogical principles used for hierarchical arrangement of the goals. The benefits of using design intention is that authors can enjoy services to record, maintain, or access their "design intention" behind learning contents and it can thus improve reuse and maintenance of the contents.

An ontology [5] plays an important role to embody the above idea. One of the most important roles of ontology is to lay the theoretical foundation for educational system development process. It maintains continuity from authors conceptual understanding of an educational task including design intention to the computational semantics of educational systems [1]. It provides human friendly vocabulary/concepts for authors to describe the learning contents along with design intention. For the authoring tools, on the other hand, it specifies the operational semantics of the learning contents. This operationality enables the conceptual-level simulation of learning contents. Based on this idea, we have developed an ontology-aware authoring tool SmartTrainer/AT[2, 4].

2. Ontology-Aware Authoring Tool

2.1 Composing a Model

Basically, an ontology is a set of definitions of concepts and relationships and a model is a set of instances of them. Roughly speaking, the role of an ontology is to direct the authors towards the correct model. Our idea is that an ontology-aware authoring tool can help authors to reduce the problems of authoring caused by unintentional error and to improve the quality of the product. Our research on SmartTrainer/AT is an embodiment of this idea. We have developed a training task ontology and incorporated it into SmartTrainer/AT as fundamental knowledge source to yield the intelligent functions to support the authoring process.

The authors' task is to write a "training scenario" for SmartTrainer that is a training system engine we have developed. At the appropriate phase of authoring process, the author is required to clarify his/her own idea from the three fundamental viewpoints listed below.

– What type of learner the scenario of the teaching material is designed for?
– What educational effect the teaching material is supposed to bring about?
– How to achieve it?

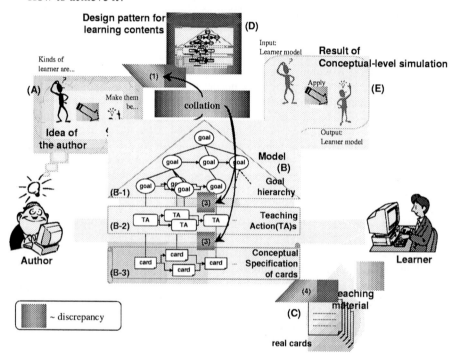

Fig. 1. An overview of authoringprocess

Fig.1 shows how the idea (A) is embodied in the teaching material (C). The model (B) can be regarded as a representation of design process. An ontology provides vocabulary and concepts, axioms necessary to describe the model. Firstly, an author describes the idea (A) clearly as a topmost, abstract and instructional goal. Then he/she repeats the expansion of the super-goal into relatively concrete sub-goals until a sequence of the sufficiently concrete goals (B-1) is specified. Secondly, he/she designs a sequence of teaching actions (B-2) which are expected to attain the goals (B-1). Thirdly, he/she embodies the actions (B-2) in a sequence of conceptual specification of cards (B-3).

In (B-1) there are two kinds of instructional goals: a goal for diagnosis[1] (D-goal) and a goal for teaching/learning (T/L-goal). A D-goal is to identify the state of a learner. The structure of the D-goals behind a training scenario implies the classification of the learners assumed by the author. By analyzing the structure, we can know the type of the learner supposed by the author at a certain context of the training scenario. A T/L-goal is to make educational effects on learners. Thus, the author can clarify the last two of the three viewpoints discussed above while describing the model (B-1) using two kinds of goals. The D-goal represents the type of the learner to whom the teaching material is designed for and the T/L-goal represents the educational effect the teaching material is supposed to bring about. At the bottom two levels (B-2) and (B-3), the teaching scenario is characterized from the third viewpoint: "how to achieve it. " The author clarifies how to attain the goal in (B-1) by selecting an appropriate teaching action for the goal (B-2) and specifying the target topics and the level of learner intended for the card (B-3). When the author is very active in referring the ontology, the rationality of the training scenario designed is expected to be quite high. In addition, reusability and sharability of training scenario is also expected to be high, as we have discussed, because an ontology-aware authoring tool stores not only concrete teaching material (C) but also the design intentions and rationale behind it as a model (B) based on the ontology.

2.2 Conceptual-Level Simulation

As we have seen in the previous section, an ontology-aware authoring tool is expected to be able to bridge the potential conceptual gap between ideas (A), and presentations (C), and suppress the unintended error caused by the gap. Models (B) play the important role as a pivot between ideas (A) and presentation (C): as conceptual representation of ideas or as the design intention behind presentation. Needless to say, the error cannot be suppressed completely and there happen to be discrepancies (1)..(4) during design process as shown in Fig.1. To resolve the - and be close to perfection, it is very important to identify the location of the discrepancies that are not realized by the author during the design process. However, everyone knows the "debugging" is difficult to do and requires huge efforts, because of the conceptual gap between what he/she thinks during composing phase (A) and what he/she observes during verification phase (C). If it is possible for the authoring tool to bridge the gap, the cost of "debugging" can be reduced considerably. As we have discussed, ontology-aware authoring tool knows the model (B) to bridge the gap and can provide the information about the difference between what an author writes and what he/she gets. It can be a good cue to identify the discrepancies. The function of our ontology-aware authoring tool is called conceptual level simulation (E) which shows the behavior of the training scenario. Conceptual-level simulation can demonstrate the behavior of the training scenario from various viewpoints, along the structure of the design model and may expose the three categories of problems caused by discrepancies (1)..(3) to the author's eye. In the case of forth one, it is rather helpless

---

1 In the research area of ITSs, the term "diagnosis" implies the intelligent reasoning process to identify the cause of a wrong answer. However, diagnosis process adopted in SmartTrainer is rather simple. It carries out diagnosis based on simple association patterns of wrong answers with erroneous knowledge.

to resolve the problem caused by discrepancy (4) because conceptual-level model is too abstract to evaluate the quality of real contents. In this section, firstly, we briefly summarize a debugging aid of conventional programming environments. Then, in contrast with it, we will discuss the advanced feature of debug support function of our ontology-aware authoring tool.

2.2.1 Debugger

A debugger of conventional programming environments provides the various functions for authors to enable them to observe the complex behavior of the programs in a systematic manner, such as tracing the process flow, displaying the change of variable, and setting for a break-point of execution. Programmers need to interpret the program behavior, compare it with the design intention, identify and resolve bugs if exist.

2.2.2 Verification Support Function in an Ontology-Aware Authoring Tool

In an ontology-aware authoring tool, the design intention remains in an operational form. This means that tools and authors can interpret the behavior of the product from the common viewpoint and enables the tools to provide useful information for authors to interpret it and identify the problems of design. We call the model with operational form of design intention as a conceptual-level model. "Conceptual-level simulation" is a function that simulates the behavior of the conceptual-level model in various levels of abstraction.

As shown in Fig. 1(E), the conceptual-level simulation shows the behavior of a training scenario as the change of a learner model. We call the learner model which is turned to an input and an output of the conceptual-level simulation as a 'pseudo-learner.' In other words, it is a kind of personification of a stereotyped learner in author's mind while he/she is authoring the training scenario. Of course, it is very different from the real learner because we assume its stable and non-autonomous learning behavior. In addition, the pseudo-learners' understanding does not depend on the quality of concrete contents in teaching material. This means that a pseudo-learner always succeed in learning what a training system teaches as long as the teaching activities are reasonable from educational principle prescribed in training task ontology.

Fig. 2 explains the role of the pseudo-learner in training scenario verifying. It is an ideal situation but almost impossible for authors to be able to examine whether the teaching material has the intended educational effect on all the real learners as shown in Fig. 2 (A). In Fig. 2 (B), by observing the changes taken place in pseudo-learners instead of the real learners, the author can examine whether the conceptual-level model of the teaching material is reasonably designed or not. One might think pseudo-learners supposed in a training scenario could be intractably numerous. It is true if we enumerate them all at once. When verifying, however, the number of the pseudo-learners is not necessarily large, because the author tends to concentrate at a local context of a training scenario. For example, Fig. 3 shows an example of a structure of D-goals, which are represented by a black diamond, and T/L-goals, which are represented by a white rectangle. The example is small because it includes only two steps of a diagnosis. However, training scenarios generally has a complex and large structure of goals. Real learners taking the training would have a long history of learning along the structure. It is intractable to trace all the possible paths in the

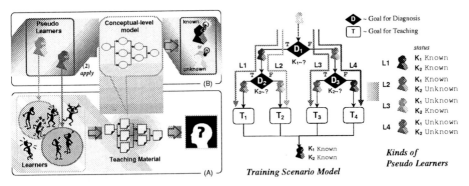

Fig. 2. The role of the pseudo-learner in conceptual level simulation

Fig. 3. Goal structure and kinds of pseudo-learner

structure. This is a problem that large software generally has. Common way to solve such a problem is to divide the problem into a set of tractable ones. Well-accepted principle behind this way is called modularity. Our goal hierarchy in a model plays a similar role to modular structure of software. Authors verify the model step by step along the goal hierarchy. Goals that the author concentrates in each step represent the necessary and sufficient local context and include tractable number of the pseudo-learners.

The purpose of the conceptual-level simulation is to show "which part of the training scenario" adds "what type of an educational effect" to "what type of a learner" systematically. The two kinds of instructional goals play the important role to realize the purpose: D-goals and T/L-goals mainly concerns the classification of learners and the educational effect of the teaching activities, respectively. In the following, we will see how the authoring tool interprets the training model and simulates its behavior briefly.

Classification of learners. The purposes of training scenarios are to characterize a learner in terms of understanding status, grade and ability and to teach him/her in a way well adapted to his/her characteristics. D-goals are largely concerned with the former. Fig.3 shows a correspondence of a structure of D-goals to the classifications of learner. Learners are classified into four kinds of pseudo learner and four pseudo learners L1,.., L4 represent the kinds of pseudo learners. For example, L1 are characterized as the pseudo learners who understand both two knowledge units, K1 and K2, based on the two D-goals D1 and D2. The four different T/L-goals, T1,..T4, are set for L1,..,L4 respectively. This enables ontology-aware authoring tools to provide authors with basic information to verify whether the pseudo learner is appropriately characterized by the training scenario.

Effects on learners. Goals for education is to teach knowledge to a learner or to develop his/her skills in a way well adapted to his/her characteristics. Educational effect of the instructional goal and the necessary conditions to achieve the goal are specified as abstract axioms in the training task ontology. After an author specified the goal as a component of the model, the conceptual-level simulator can simulate the behavior of the goal. Intuitively, it adds the educational effects of the goal to pseudo-learner's status if the necessarily condition of the goal is satisfied. In Fig. 3, the four education goals T1,.., T4 represented by white rectangles are defined. If the training model is well designed, the all the pseudo-learner will understand knowledge units K1 and K2 at the end of the training scenario as shown in Fig. 3. On the other hand, if more than one of pseudo-learners cannot understand both K1 and K2, there might be some problems in the training scenario.

3. An Example of the Conceptual-Level Simulation

In this chapter, we will take an example to explain the conceptual-level simulation. SmartTrainer/AT is an ontology-aware authoring tool for a substation operator training system SmartTrainer. A training scenario in SmartTrainer consists of a variety of grain sizes of modules. Typical ones are "backbone stream", which is a sequence of questions along the workflow and a "rib stream", which is a treatment of a learner's erroneous answers to questions in a backbone stream. The goal of SmartTrainer is to help learners to master all the operations in workflow implemented in the backbone stream by giving necessary knowledge in the course of instruction in the rib stream.

A small example of a training scenario is shown in Fig. 4. A question2 (1) of a backbone stream is connected with a ribstream (4) by a treatment (2) based on a diagnosis (3). Diagnosis (3) represents the diagnosis of a learner's incorrect answer of selecting option 1 to the question and ribstream (4) is set up as a treatment for the diagnosis. The purpose of the ribstream is to teach a missing knowledge according to the diagnosis and it is represented by the top goal of a goal hierarchy (4-1) as design intention. An upper goal of the goal hierarchy is expanded into a series of subgoals. In this case, the top goal "Improve Knowledge" is expanded into a series of subgoals "Notice An Error", "Acquire A Correct Knowledge" and "Grasp A Principle" and furthermore the goal "Acquire A Correct Knowledge" is expanded into "Understand A Correct Knowledge" and "Resume The Question". A sequence of teaching actions (4-2) is designed to attain those goals, for example, the teaching action "Teach-Topic" is expected to attain the goal "Understand a correct knowledge". Finally, the sequence of teaching actions embodied in a sequence of card specification (4-3) where the topics to be referred and the level of learner intended are specified.

Let us next show the conceptual level simulation with a pseudo learner who selects an option1 to the question2. Firstly, SmartTrainer/AT specifies the status of the pseudo learner according to a diagnosis and then applies ribstream to it. In this case, it assumes the pseudo learner does not know about the topic "64 Relay" based on a diagnosis (2). When the teaching action "Teach Topic" of a ribstream (4) is applied to the pseudo learner, a status of the pseudo learner is changed by the goal "Understand A Correct Knowledge". The change when "Understand A Correct Knowledge" is realized by "Teach-Topic" is shown in a conceptual level model on the right side of Fig. 4. This model means that the status of the learner is changed from before-status (a), where the pseudo learner does not know about the topic "64 Relay", to after-status (b), where it does.

Let us assume an author wants to examine the case that the pseudo learner is at the novice level. In the following scenario, we also assume that the task ontology prescribes that an average novice learner does not completely master a topic "Relay" prerequisite to the topic "64 Relay"

When an author does the conceptual level simulation of the pseudo learner's behavior, SmartTrainer/AT shows two problems in the teaching scenario. The author is expected to notice that one is caused by a lack of T/L-goal and the other is by a lack of D-goal. The right of Fig. 4 indicates the former case with a conceptual model. In this case, the pseudo learner (e) does not fill the condition for understanding the topic "64 Relay" (c) because he does not master a knowledge (d) prerequisite to it. Thus, the understanding status of the topic "64 Relay" cannot be changed by the goal. The situation is represented as the status of the pseudo learner (f). In the latter case, the goal "Grasp A Principle" cannot be attained by the pseudo learner because the training task ontology prescribes that the principled knowledge is beyond the limits of novice learner's understandability. A proper way to resolve this problem is to add a new D-goal to classify learners according to the levels of mastery and set the goal "Grasp A Principle" only for advanced learners.

Our conceptual level simulator displays these results in the window as shown in Fig. 5. The simulation monitor window (W1) consists of three panes. The left pane (w1-c) shows a progression of a pseudo learner's learning in the training scenario, which consists of a backbone-stream and rib-streams with a goal structure. A node represents a question, a goal or a teaching activity and a link represents control flow or relation between goals. The top right pane (w1-s) shows the knowledge status of the pseudo learner. The hierarchical classification of pseudo learners is displayed in the bottom right pane (w1-p).

As we have mentioned before, Problems in a training scenario are caused by discrepancies (1)..(4) shown in Fig. 1. The problems are shown to authors as either the unachieved D-goals or T/L-goal. For example, in pane (w1-c), an author is supposed to focus on a problem of training scenario shown as an icon (G1) "Improve Knowledge". The icon means that there exist some learners who are not able to

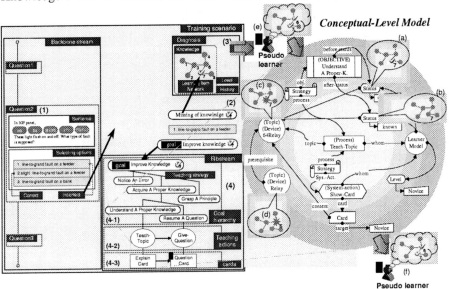

Fig. 4. An example of a training scenario

achieve the goal specified. At this situation, pseudo-learners have hierarchical structure as shown in w1-c, where a pseudo-leaner A is expanded into three pseudo-learners A-1, A-2, A-3. The learners who are imposed the goal are represented by a pseudo-learner A. The gray icon of pseudo learner A means that the goal could not be attained by some learners represented by it. The learners who cannot attain the goal are represented by pseudo-learner A-2. Pane w1-s displays the knowledge status of pseudo learner A-2 currently selected in w1-c. It shows a knowledge unit K1, which is expected to be taught, is not acquired by the learner after actions are executed under the goal (G1).

The author can reason the cause of the problem in the training scenario by means of getting down into specifics of its behavior along the goal hierarchy from top to bottom in the same way he/she have designed it. The problem can be resolved by adding new goals or correcting the erroneous goals. The author may ask SmartTrainer/AT for a further detailed information about the execution of goal (G1) by double clicking it. Then the goal is expanded into a sequence of subgoals as shown in w2-c. The author can observe the goal closely in W2 and find that the unachievement of (G1) is caused by unachievement of (G2) "Understand A Proper Knowledge" and (G3) "Grasp A Principle". As we have mentioned before, the former problem (G2) is caused by a lack of a T/L-goal a prerequisite topic. The author can reason the cause from the facts that the topic "Relay" has not been taught before and is a prerequisite to the target topic "64 Relay" of the goal (G2). Similarly, the latter problem (G3) is caused by a lack of a D-goal to classify levels of mastery. By

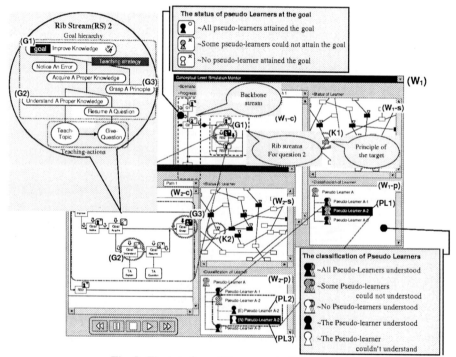

Fig. 5. The interface of the conceptual simulation

observing that a novice pseudo learner (PL3) does not attains the goal but an expert one (PL2) does as shown in w2-c, the author can reason that the problem can be resolved by adding a D-goal to classify the two pseudo-learners. In this manner, SmartTrainer/AT provides useful information for authors to identify and resolve the problems in the model.

4. Conclusion

An ontology-aware authoring tool has functions to effectively reduce the number of the problems which arise during the course of learning contents design. However, there still may remain some problems passed over in the design phase. The conceptual-level simulation helps authors to resolve those problems in verification phase before the training scenario is delivered to the real learner. It simulates the behavior of the conceptual-level model of learning contents in various levels of abstraction and provides good cue to identify the problems.

The conceptual-level simulation of learning contents is enabled by having operational semantics specified by the training task ontology. The most important role of the ontology is to maintain the continuity from authors' conceptual understanding of learning contents to the operational semantics of them. The implication of "ontology-awareness" and "operationality of the learning contents" is deep. To arrange the best collaboration between authors and tools, it is quite important to create an environment for authors to describe the model easily and for tools to operate the model systematically. One of the most important merits introduced by ontological engineering is that an ontology enables human to share the model with computers. We believe that this issue is important in enabling the efficient production of large-scale, high-quality learning contents which will be critical needs of this new millennium.

Acknowledgements Special thanks to Yoshiyuki Takaoka and his colleagues in Toko Seiki Company for helpful suggestions and providing me with the materials.

References

1. Bourdeau, J., and Mizoguchi, R.: Ontological Engineering of Instruction: A Perspective; Proc. of AIED-99, Le Mans, France, pp. 620-622, 1999.
2. Ikeda, M., Hayashi, Y., Jin, L., Chen, W. Bourdeau, J., Seta, K., and Mizoguchi, R.: Ontology More Than a Shared Vocabulary; Proc. of Workshop on "Ontologies for Intelligent Educational Systems", AIED-99, Le Mans, France, pp. 1-10, 1999.
3. Lee, J.: Design Rationale Systems: Understanding the Issues; IEEE Expert, vol. 12, no. 3, May/June, pp. 78-85, 1997.
4. Lai Jin, Weiqin Chen, Yusuke Hayashi, Mitsuru Ikeda, Riichiro Mizoguchi, Yoshiyuki Takaoka, Mamoru Ohta: An Ontology-aware Authoring Tool, ~ Functional structure and guidance generation ~, AIED-99, Le Mans, France, 1999, pp. 85~92.
5. Mizoguchi, R., Sinitsa, K., and Ikeda, M.: Task Ontology Design for Intelligent Educational/Training Systems; Proc. of Workshop on "Architectures and Methods for Designing Cost-Effective and Reusable ITSs", ITS'96, Montreal, pp. 1-21, 1996.
6. Murray, T.: Authoring Intelligent Tutoring Systems: An analysis of the state of the art; International J. of Artificial Intelligence in Education, Vol. 10, pp. 98-129, 1999
7. Shapiro, E.: Algorithmic Program Debugging; The MIT Press, 1982.

Designing for Collaborative Discovery Learning

Wouter R. van Joolingen

Graduate School of Teaching and Learning
University of Amsterdam
Wibautstraat 2-4
1091 GM Amsterdam
The Netherlands
Wouter@ilo.uva.nl

Abstract. In this paper a general design is introduced for collaborative discovery learning. Starting from the properties of learning processes involved in discovery learning, an analysis is made how they can be supported by collaboration, and how new types of instructional support can be created from the interaction between collaborative support measures and the specific learning processes involved in discovery learning. This is elaborated into a generic architecture for collaborative discovery learning environments.

1   Introduction

In modern views on teaching and learning, the view on the learner as an active agent in the learning process is becoming increasingly important. *Constructivist* (Jonassen, 1991) views of learning see knowledge and learning as dependent of context, person and social situation. This active role of the learner is stressed in *discovery* learning and *collaborative* learning. In *discovery* learning (De Jong & Van Joolingen, 1998) learners engage in a domain by performing experiments with a *discovery learning environment* representing the domain and hypothesizing and inferring domain knowledge from those experiments. The basic assumption behind discovery learning is that through experimenting learners will construct their own knowledge by building upon their existing knowledge base, using the information they gather from the discovery environment. Discovery environments are often based on computer simulations that offer a safe and flexible way of representing the domain in a form that the learner can play and experiment with it.

In *collaborative* learning, learning is seen as a *social* process in which meaning, information and knowledge are negotiated between learners (Van der Linden, Erkens, Schmidt and Renshaw, in press). In collaborative settings learners discuss, argue and engage in shared activities in order to create understanding and representations of knowledge. Collaborative learning environments support collaboration activities between two or more learners like discussion and construction of knowledge representations.

In both collaborative learning and discovery learning, it is an accepted phenomenon that learners need to be supported in the processes of learning. In discovery learning support is needed for specific discovery processes like hypothesis generation, experiment design etc. (De Jong & Van Joolingen, 1998). In collaborative learning environments support is often directed at the structure of the argumentation or the construction of communicative actions (e.g. Veerman & Treasure-Jones, in press). These kinds of support can enhance learning with these environments by structuring the learning process and providing the learners with cognitive tools expanding the learner's possibilities of performing complex learning processes and strategies.

This paper deals with learning environments that combine discovery and collaborative learning. In these environments learners work together in small groups on a discovery task, for instance discovering the laws of physics in a mechanical system. In combining collaboration and discovery interaction between the two tasks will occur, providing new opportunities for supporting the learner. The paper will provide a short overview of the two kinds of learning and explore the possible problems and mutual enhancements that occur when combining discovery and collaboration into one learning environment. The paper will conclude with some issues on the *architecture* of learning environments for collaborative discovery.

2   Discovery Learning

The main goal of a discovery learning activity is to obtain and/or construct knowledge about a domain by performing experiments and inferring rules and properties of the domain from the results of those experiments. Research on discovery learning has shown that learners can experience a range of problems that can prevent successful learning. Discovery learning requires learners to act in the same manner as scientists when discovering the properties and relations of the domain that is simulated, using processes that are very similar to the processes of scientific discovery (Klahr & Dunbar, 1988; de Jong & Njoo, 1993; Van Joolingen & de Jong, 1997). Learners need to generate hypotheses, design experiments, predict their outcome, interpret data and reconsider hypotheses (Van Joolingen & de Jong, 1998) in order to construct knowledge about the domain. With each of these learning processes, problems can arise. Learners can fail to state testable hypotheses (Van Joolingen & de Jong, 1991), design uninformative experiments (e.g. Mynatt, Doherty, & Tweney, 1977) or interpret experimental results badly (Klahr & Dunbar, 1988).

In order to make discovery learning successful, learners can be supported from within the learning environment. The learning environment can contain *cognitive tools* that can be directed at the support of one or more learning processes (Van Joolingen, 1999; Lajoie, 1993). Cognitive tools can offer support to the learner in several ways. The theoretical frameworks describing discovery learning are well-established and can be applied to analyze the learning processes and support them. Current research in discovery learning aims at finding new ways of support, creating a learning dialogue between the learning environment and the learner and at establishing the conditions under which profitable learning processes take place. Cognitive tools play a role in supporting and provoking these learning processes.

3 Collaborative Learning

The basic idea behind collaborative learning is that it is beneficial for learners to work together on learning tasks and by communicating about the task enhance learning (Plötzner, Dillenbourg, Preier and Traum, 1999). Collaboration in itself can have a valuable contribution to learning. For instance, in a review study, Springer, Stanne and Donovan (1999) report that learning together in small groups increases the performance of learners in Science, Mathematics, Engineering and Technology. They find that group learning contributes to higher academic achievement, more favorable attitudes and increased persistence of learning.

Collaborative learning is "in the air" as Van der Linden, *et al.* (in press) put it. They mention, when discussing process oriented research into collaborative learning, several factors that seem to make collaboration effective:

- *Maintaining common ground* – participants need to be aware of the task goal and stay in common focus.
- *Co-responsibility, equality and mutuality* – participants need to have a significant role and be responsible for the learning task as a whole.
- *Mutual support and criticism* – seems to be a central vehicle in collaborative learning, making two or more learners reach higher goals than they can reach individually.
- *Verbalization and co-construction* – discussion and argumentation stimulate explicit formulation of knowledge, which in its turn helps students with the performance of cognitive processes.
- *Elaboration* – students learn from providing others with elaborate help.
- *Tuning in cognitively and socially* – learners are more at one level of understanding than a teacher and a learner. Therefore it is thought that communication within a group of learners can be more effective than teaching.

Supporting collaboration with computer-based tools will aim at improving one or more of these factors, for instance, communication tools may help learners to make their thoughts explicit, or allow learners to negotiate on the common task (Veerman & Treasure-Jones, in press). Some factors in collaborative learning can be supported more or less independently from the structure of the task at hand. For instance, tuning in socially will be task-unrelated, but most of the factors can benefit from explicit knowledge about the task structure. Verbalization can be supported by a tool that lets learners edit their contributions before sending them to their fellow learners, a task-related editor may provide learners with task-specific terms to verbalize their thoughts. In the following section we discuss how task specific support for *discovery learning* may interact with and enhance means of support for communication.

4 Interaction Between Collaboration and Discovery

The functions that determine success for supporting discovery and collaborative learning overlap to a considerable extent and may result in mutual reinforcement. This close relationship may be exploited in several ways. On the one hand the *discovery behavior* displayed by learners may improve under influence of collaboration. On the other hand, collaboration, and especially the communication that underlies it, may benefit from information that can be extracted from the discovery process. In this section we will explore how this can come to life and how existing technology can be put into action to make this happen.

Verbalization, making one's thoughts explicit plays an important role in both discovery and collaborative learning. In discovery learning a number of cognitive tools aim at provoking explicit performance of learning processes. Well-known examples are the hypothesis scratchpad (Van Joolingen, 1993) and a monitoring tool (Veermans & Van Joolingen, 1998). Other examples include goal posting tools (Singley, 1990) that lets learners make their learning goals explicit. Collaboration needs and provokes explicit communication about one's cognitive processes, as vehicle for creating common ground and for exchanging ideas on how to perform the learning task. As discovery learning itself needs explicit performance of learning processes, a genuine question is whether collaboration in itself contributes to discovery, in the sense that learners in a collaborating group improve on performing crucial learning processes like hypothesis generation and experiment design. This means that from the perspective of a discovery learning environment communication in collaboration can serve as an instructional measure or cognitive tool.

4.1 Using Task Knowledge to Support Communication

The previous section discussed how collaboration in itself can contribute to performing learning processes in discovery learning. In the current section, it is discussed how collaboration can be supported by using knowledge about the task at hand, in casu the discovery of domain properties and relations. We do this by elaborating an example in which a well-known tool for supporting collaborative knowledge creation and show how this tool could profit from including knowledge about discovery learning in generating support for learners.

The example is centered around *Belvedere* (Suthers, Toth & Weiner, 1997) which offers learners a structure for constructing scientific arguments. Learners can synchronously work together in constructing an argumentation structure consisting of hypotheses, evidence and links between them. The links indicate whether some specific evidence supports or disconfirms a specific hypothesis. This example was chosen because the structure of hypotheses and evidence clearly matches common processes in discovery learning where forming hypotheses and gathering evidence is a major activity.

Belvedere itself contains an *advisor* for supporting learners who are constructing arguments. This advisor analyses the argument *structure* and suggests directions for further extension of the argument. For a general tool like Belvedere it would be virtually impossible to use the *contents* of the argument, because hypotheses and evidence are strongly domain related. In a general tool, using the content in advice on the argument would mean that from a single line of text referring to some evidence, an inference should be made whether the evidence supports or rejects a hypothesis. This is impossible, due to the fact that, at least within the current status of technology, it is not possible to reconstruct the original evidence from a short reference to it.

This situation is different when we may do more assumptions about the task at hand. In discovery learning with computer simulations we can define the realm of investigation and assume that all statements made on an argumentation diagram refer to events and concepts related to the simulation. It becomes possible to derive whether some evidence really supports a hypothesis and hence an advisor can use this information to adapt its support to the actual progress made by the learners.

Support aimed at the content of the interaction can be provided on the basis of a theory on discovery learning (Van Joolingen and De Jong, 1997) that describes hypotheses as statements on *relations* between *variables* and experiments as *manipulations* of variables together with the results or *effects* of these manipulations. The theory describes discovery as a search process in two related spaces (based on work by Klahr & Dunbar, 1988), a hypothesis space and an experiment space. Van Joolingen and De Jong (1997) describe how the structure of the two search spaces can be used to determine whether evidence matches hypotheses, how various pieces of evidence relate to each other and how various hypotheses relate to each other. Examples of propositions that can be derived are: "this experiment supports/rejects this hypothesis", "experiment A can be compared with experiment B" and "hypothesis A is more precise than hypothesis B". In supporting single learners engaged in simulation-based discovery this technique was applied by Veermans and Van Joolingen (1998).

It is possible to use this technique in conjunction with an argument-building tool like Belvedere. If the elements in Belvedere would refer to elements present in the simulation environment, i.e. evidence would refer to experiments and hypotheses would be expressed in the sense defined in the theoretical framework by Van Joolingen and De Jong (1997), then the tool developed by Veermans and Van Joolingen (1998) can analyze the evidence relationships in the argumentation diagram and provide advice and feedback on the *content* of the diagram.

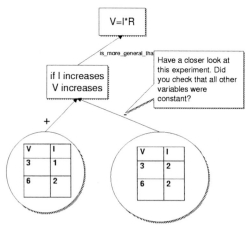

Figure 1 Example of feedback that is enabled by integrating discovery support in a collaborative tool.

Figure 1 displays an example of feedback that becomes possible when we apply this technique. The diagram is a fictitious diagram that learners could have constructed in a learning environment on electricity. Rectangles are hypotheses, ellipses represent evidence. The callout displays feedback that, in order to be generated, would require an analysis of experiments in the way described above. An interesting question is how to present this feedback. Simply stating that a certain evidence relationship is correct or not probably is not enough or may even be disadvantageous for learning. Probably a better way for support is attracting a learner's attention to troublesome evidence relations and stimulating learners to investigate such a relation further.

In this section we have shown that the combination of tools for supporting collaboration and application of task related knowledge, in our case a theory about discovery learning can form a new generation of supportive cognitive tools for collaborative learning. In principle the technique can be combined with many different kinds of collaborative tools. The two kinds of interaction between collaboration and discovery learning illustrate the need for a tight integration between the discovery environment and the collaborative tools. Until now this integration is not seen very often. In many cases collaborative environments consist of communication tools only, like a chat channel or discussion list, or of collaborative tools added to a task environment, but linked only loosely to the task execution. A thesis would be that there is something to be gained in increasing integration. In the following section an architecture is presented that allows such a tight integration, without sacrificing generic design of collaborative tools.

5   An Architecture for Collaborative Discovery

The goal of the architecture presented here is to provide a context in which collaborative tools can be designed independently of the specific subject domain of the discovery environment, but ensure a tight integration with the task environment. Koedinger, Suthers and Forbus (1998) sketch a component-based architecture of a *Science learning space*. The architecture presented here aims to be a bit more general and to outline some basic issues in the conceptual and technical designs of environments for collaborative discovery.

5.1   Basic Ingredients

The basic ingredients this architecture are: *frames of reference, collaborative tools*, and *experimentation space*.

Frame of reference. In collaboration environment two or more learners will perform a discovery task together by doing experiments, interpreting the results and sharing thoughts. Collaborative components included in the environment can use elements from the simulation environments. For instance, on a shared whiteboard allowing learners to construct and argument, it is possible to refer to an experiment done with the simulation, or to a hypothesis stated on a hypothesis scratchpad. These references to elements can improve the discussion, because learners can make themselves absolutely clear which elements they mean, other participants can replay the reference (for instance replaying the experiment), read the remarks that a learner has made about it and decide to add a new contribution to the discussion. An important ingredient for such a setup is a common *frame of reference*: the collaboration tools must be able to interpret the experimental results and hypotheses stated in the simulation environment, at least, they need to know what to do with it. For instance, an experiment can be executed, meaning that the simulation will be set up according to the experiment's initial conditions, will be started and manipulations during the experiment run will be replayed. Elements that are referred to can be accessed in multiple ways. An experiment can be run, but also viewed as text, a table, or a graph. This means that the internal description of the experiment must be decoupled from the view, for we cannot expect collaborative tools to manage all possible views on the experiment, or any other element from the discovery environment. A way of realizing this would be using XML-descriptions for the content of elements in the discovery environment, and components providing interfaces and viewers to access, manipulate and view these elements.

Collaborative tools. Discussion forums, chat channels, whiteboards are all tools that can support collaboration in one or another way. Within the architecture discussed they get an added responsibility. They must act as a component that on the one hand manages the interactions between learners, and supporting them in their communication, and, on the other hand, must be able to communicate with other components within the architecture. They must be able to receive, manage and operate on elements described in the agreed language of the frame of reference, and communicate with any component that is used to manipulate any element. The collaborative tools themselves must act as a component and provide an interface for sending and retrieving references and structures that can be used by other components, for instance to generate feedback.

Experimentation space. The experimentation space represents the task domain in which the discovery learning is taking place. It is a generator of elements that is reasoned about, but must also be able to accept elements from elsewhere. For instance when two learners discuss experiments and in that discussion construct a new experiment, they may do this in some collaborative tool. This new experiment must be imported fluently into the experimentation space.

The experimentation space is also the main provider of information to construct a frame of reference. It contains the definitions of variables in the domain and usually also a domain model. This information can be used to construct the terms that will be accepted by other components of the complete environment. A first version of such a frame of reference has been constructed in the SimQuest environment, in the form of a *simulation context* (Van Joolingen, King, & De Jong, 1997). This simulation context is constructed based on information in the simulation model and directs all the information traffic in and out of the simulation. An extension of this context can be a basis for generating frames of reference for domains represented by the experimentation space.

Collaborative scenarios. For *synchronous* collaboration, it is essential that the experimentation space is available to all participants in the same view. Collaboration tools may have a different view for each learner. In a *synchronous* setting, a session must be *initiated* by a learner, who hosts a session and invites others to join. When another learner joins, the experiment space will be shared between the learners, they can take turns in operating the application and specific collaboration tools such as a whiteboard and a chat facility become available. Figure 2 displays the architecture for a synchronous setting. The architecture elements are converted to real components. The initiator masters the experimentation space, made available to other learners by dedicated client software. The communication between them is enabled by the common frame of reference.

In *asynchronous* collaboration learners work on their own and may have their own copy of the experimentation space to do this. However, apart from this, collaboration channels are present. This time they do not depend on timing. Learners can import and export onto collaboration tools that are available, like a newsgroup/discussion list or a whiteboard. The collaboration tools communicate with the server to retrieve and post the contributions by learners. Learners can log in and out as they like, and on logon they will be updated with new contributions since their last session.

Elements in a discussion only have meaning if they are viewed and used within the same context as where they were created. This means that a server must hold reference to the frame of reference and be able to supply the correct versions of the experimentation space with the elements themselves. Figure 3 displays an architecture for an asynchronous configuration.

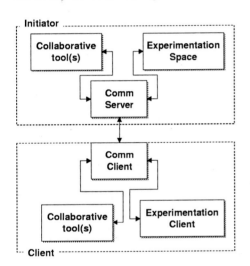

Figure 2 Architecture for synchronous collaboration

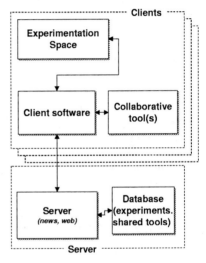

Figure 3 An architecture for asynchonous collaboration

6   Conclusion

In this paper we presented a view on combining collaborative learning and discovery learning. The aim was to show how we can benefit from theoretical knowledge on discovery learning to enhance the added value that collaboration can have and, vice versa, how collaboration in itself can serve as support for the processes of discovery that learners can engage in. The current paper outlines how a mutual gain can be created from combining collaborative and discovery learning by increasing the mutual awareness in tools supporting either type of learning. Adding knowledge about discovery to collaborative tools can enhance collaborative tools to adapt themselves or give feedback on their contents. On the other hand can collaborative processes take the role of cognitive tools for discovery learning in making learning processes explicit. Of course the examples given in the paper are only a small part of what becomes possible in combining two powerful paradigms of learning.

In the latter part of the paper we show how a theory of discovery learning can help to *design* an architecture for communicative support for discovery learning. A central place is taken by a common frame of reference that supports the communication between the different components in the architecture. Using this reference frame components can be designed independently of each other and still work together smoothly. This is important in providing learners with the feeling that they work in a consistent environment.

In the approach a number of research questions are raised:

- *What is the minimum support needed for learners to let collaboration have a genuine contribution to the discovery process?* In other words, does just collaborating between learners already have an effect, or is some basic support needed from within the discovery environment? The target is to minimize support and to maximize learning gain
- *What are the properties of the frame of reference?* Exactly what properties have to be defined in the frame of reference? SimQuest's simulation context (Van Joolingen, King & De Jong, 1997) provides a starting point, but elements stemming from the collaborative nature of the environment should also get a place, like the identity of the person making a certain contribution.
- *How to interweave support into collaboration?* Especially in collaboration, instructional support should be quite unobtrusive. The communication between learners is usually more important than information generated by the learning environment. Issues are what to present, and also how to use supportive information in constraining the learners, rather then directing them explicitly.
- *What are the properties of a model of collaborative discovery learning?* Models of discovery learning base themselves on theories of scientific discovery (e.g. Klahr & Dunbar, 1988). We are only at the beginning of modeling these aspects in a form that they can be useful for *supporting* learners engaged in collaborative discovery.

Collaborative tools as addressed in this paper can help to realize some of the factors of collaborative environments mentioned by Van der Linden *et al.* (in press). The mere presence of a frame of reference can help learners in maintaining common ground and provide them with a dedicated language to verbalize their thoughts. On-line analysis of the communication and generating supportive information can create germs of mutual discussion and criticism. The further exploration of the links between collaboration and discovery can give rise to the next generation of intelligent learner support in constructive learning environments.

References

Jonassen, D. H. (1991). Objectivism versus constructivism: Do we need a new philosophical paradigm? *Educational Technology Research & Development, 39*, 5-14.

Jong, T. de, & Joolingen, W.R. van (1998). Discovery learning with computer simulations of conceptual domains. *Review of Educational Research, 68* 179 - 201.

Jong, T. de, & Njoo, M. (1992). Learning and Instruction with computer simulations: learning processes involved. In E. de Corte, M. Linn, H. Mandl & L. Verschaffel (Eds.), *Computer-based learning environments and problem solving* (pp. 411-429). Berlin, Germany: Springer-Verlag.

Joolingen, W.R., van & Jong, T. de (1993). Exploring a domain through a computer simulation: traversing variable and relation space with the help of a hypothesis scratchpad. In D. Towne, T. de Jong & H. Spada (Eds.), *Simulation-based experiential learning* (pp. 191-206). Berlin, Germany: Springer-Verlag.

Joolingen, W.R. van, & Jong, T. de (1997). An extended dual search space model of learning with computer simulations. *Instructional Science, 25*, 307-346.

Joolingen, W.R. van, King, S., & Jong, T. de (1997). The SimQuest authoring system for simulation-based discovery environments. In B. du Boulay & R. Mizoguchi (Eds.), *Knowledge and media in learning systems* (pp. 79-87). Amsterdam: IOS.

Joolingen, W.R. van (1999). Cognitive tools for discovery learning. *International Journal of Artificial Intelligence and Educatio,. 10 ,*385-397.

Klahr, D., & Dunbar, K. (1988). Dual space search during scientific reasoning. *Cognitive Science, 12*, 1-48.

Koedinger, Suthers Forbus, (1998). Component-based construction of a science learning space. *In B.P. Goetl, H. M. Halff, C.L. Redfield, V.J. Shute (Eds.) Intelligent Tutoring Systems, 4th International Conference, San Antonio, TX USA.* (pp. 166-175). Berlin: Springer.

Lajoie, S.P. (1993). Cognitive tools for enhancing learning. In S. P. Lajoie & S.J. Derry (Eds.), *Computers as cognitive tools* (pp. 261-289). Hillsdale, NJ: Erlbaum.

Linden, J. van der, Erkens, G. Schmidt, H., & Renshaw, P. (in press). Collaborative Learning. *In P.R.J. Simons, J. van der Linden & T Duffy (Eds.), New Learning*. Dordrecht: Kluwer.

Mynatt, C.R., Doherty, M.E., & Tweney R.D. (1977). Confirmation bias in a simulated research environment: An experimental study of scientific inference. *Quarterly Journal of experimental Psychology, 29*, 85-95.

Plötzner, R. Dillenbourg, P., Preier, M., & Traum, D. (1999). Learning by explaining to oneself and to others. In *P. Dillenbourg (Ed.), Collaborative learning, cognitive and computational approaches* (pp. 103-121). Amsterdam: Pergamon.

Singley, M.K. (1990). The reification of goal structures in a calculus tutor: effects on problem solving performance. *Interactive learning environments 1,* 102-123.

Springer, L., Stanne, M.E., Donovan, S.S. (1999). Effects of small-group learning on undergraduates in science, mathematics, engineering and technology: a meta-analysis. *Review of Educational Research, 69*, 21-51.

Suthers, D., Toth, E., & Weiner, A. (1997). An Integrated Approach to Implementing Collaborative Inquiry in the Classroom. *Computer Supported Collaborative Learning (CSCL'97),* December 10-14, 1997, Toronto.

Veerman, A. L., & Treasure-Jones, T. (in press). Software for problem solving through collaborative argumentation. *In J. Andriessen & P. Coirier (Eds.) Foundations of argumentative text processing*. Amsterdam: AUP.

Veermans, K. & Joolingen, W.R. van (1998). Using induction to generate feedback in simulation-based discovery learning environments. *In B.P. Goetl, H. M. Halff, C.L. Redfield, V.J. Shute (Eds.) Intelligent Tutoring Systems, 4th International Conference, San Antonio, TX USA.* (pp. 196-205). Berlin: Springer.

An Analysis of Multiple Tutoring Protocols[1]

Byung-In Cho[1], Joel A. Michael[2], Allen A. Rovick[2], Martha W. Evens[1]

[1] Department of Computer Science, Illinois Inst. of Technology,
10 W. 31st Street 236–SB, Chicago, IL 60616, U.S.A.
chobyun@charlie.iit.edu. evens@iit.edu
http://www.csam.iit.edu/~circsim
[2] Department of Physiology, Rush Medical College
1750 W. Harrison St., Chicago, IL 60612, U.S.A.
{jmichael,arovick}@rush.edu

Abstract. The tutoring protocol controls the interaction between the tutor and the student in a tutoring session. Our goals are to understand human tutoring so that we can emulate it better and to discover which tutoring protocol gives the best results in teaching causal reasoning. We used C5.0 to analyze a set of human tutoring transcripts to discover how and when human tutors switch protocols. In order to understand which students prefer which protocols, we compared the students' performance using CIRCSIM-Tutor with their responses to a questionnaire about the program.

1 Introduction

Determining effective tutoring strategies may be the most important and hardest issue in intelligent tutoring systems. The tutoring protocol controls the interaction between the tutor and the student in a tutoring session. Moore [9] identified three types of interaction: student-content, student-teacher, and student-student. In traditional classroom teaching (student-teacher) interaction is normally immediate. Much educational research supports the belief that immediate feedback increases a sense of excitement and spontaneity [2], [10], [15]. Our colleagues, Joel Michael (JAM) and Allen Rovick (AAR) believe, however, that immediate feedback is not always the best choice. They feel that they can do a better job of tutoring if they ask the student to make predictions first, because the improved student model allows them to plan a tutorial strategy that targets the student's misconceptions [8].

[1] This work was supported by the Cognitive Science Program, Office of Naval Research under Grant No. N00014–94–1–0338, to Illinois Institute of Technology. The content does not reflect the position or policy of the government and no official endorsement should be inferred.

We are building an intelligent tutoring system called CIRCSIM-Tutor designed to help medical students learn to solve cardiovascular problems. Our system is based on the study of human tutoring sessions carried out by JAM and AAR. The tutors had decided to use the following protocol they had designed for our intelligent tutoring system in their human tutoring sessions: collect predictions first and tutor afterwards, in order to provide us with examples of the kind of tutoring they wanted the system to produce. We discovered in the analysis described here, however, that the tutors did not always follow the protocol. Sometimes the tutor did not wait until the student finished the predictions. If the student started out with poor predictions then the tutor immediately began to guide the student in the right track with hints or explanations. So, in fact, they changed the tutoring protocol to best fit the student's needs at the time.

In this paper we analyze a subset of those human tutoring transcripts to discover how and when the tutors switch protocols. We used the machine learning program C5.0 [13] to find more rules that govern this change in tutoring. We also wanted to find out how the students feel about the issue of immediate feedback. To do so we analyze the students' performance using CIRCSIM-Tutor and their responses to a questionnaire about their view of CIRCSIM-Tutor. Our goals are to understand human tutoring so that we can emulate it better and to discover which tutoring protocol gives the best results in teaching causal reasoning.

1.1 Planning

The first and most important capability of an Intelligent Tutoring System is dynamic planning. The planner must be able to decide what and how to teach next. It must have a dynamic planning capability; it must be able to generate plans, monitor the execution of the plans, and generate new plans. It must be able to replan when necessary [17]. Finally, the planner must be adaptive. It must customize its tutoring plans for each student [5], [16], [17].

Planners select and sequence the subject matter. Curriculum Planning is concerned with selecting the next problem [1]. Instructional Planning selects and sequences the material to be tutored. Discourse Planning controls the actual presentation of material to the students [4].

1.2 CIRCSIM-Tutor

The domain of CIRCSIM-Tutor is cardiovascular physiology. CIRCSIM-Tutor assists students to reason about the qualitative, causal responses of the human circulatory system when the blood pressure is perturbed. The system asks the student to enter predictions in the Prediction Table [12] indicating how the perturbation affects seven important physiological variables at three different stages of the response, and then it initiates a tutorial dialogue to remedy any errors. Table 1 shows a prediction table for the perturbation "Increase Venous Resistance to 200% of normal." The three stages are the Direct Response (DR): the immediate change in the variables induced by the perturbation; the Reflex Response (RR): the change induced by the response of the central nervous system to the change in blood pressure; and the Steady State (SS): the long term balance between the effects of the perturbation and the effects of the negative feedback. We ask the student to predict the qualitative change from the values before the perturbation to the new steady state. The primary variable is the first variable in the DR column of the Prediction Table that is affected by the current perturbation. Therefore the student should identify and predict the primary variable first.

Table 1. The Prediction Table of the Procedure "Increase Venous Resistance to 200% of Normal" with Correct Answers

Physiological Variable	DR	RR	SS
Inotropic State (IS)	0	+	+
Central Venous Pressure (CVP)	–	–	–
Stroke Volume (SV)	–	–	–
Heart Rate (HR)	0	+	+
Cardiac Output (CO)	–	+	–
Total Peripheral Resistance (TPR)	0	+	+
Mean Arterial Pressure (MAP)	–	+	–

(+: Increased, –: Decreased, 0: unchanged)

2 Tutoring Protocols

Instructional planning determines the content and sequence of the subject matter to be taught in a single procedure. One of the important features of the tutorial planning process is the tutoring protocol. The tutoring protocol defines the overall communication between the tutor and the student. We want to be able to compare the effects of different protocols or to change the protocol during a session.

2.1 Tutoring Protocol 3

Khuwaja described three tutoring protocols that he found used in human tutoring sessions [6]. In Tutoring Protocol 1 the tutor ignores the sequence of the student's predictions and explores the student's response at each point in problem solving. Here the tutor provides immediate feedback for each student prediction and response. In Tutoring Protocol 2 the tutor insists that the student follow the preferred prediction sequence but does not correct the values of the variables until all predictions have been made. In Tutoring Protocol 3 the tutor makes sure that the student chooses the primary variable (DR) first and predicts its change correctly before asking the student to predict the remaining variables in any order. In RR and SS the students are free to start with any variable and to make predictions in whatever sequence they choose.

2.2 A new tutoring protocol

We have accumulated over 60 transcripts of human tutoring sessions. Our domain experts JAM and AAR carry out keyboard-to-keyboard tutoring using a program, CDS [7], that establishes communications between two computers using modems. In this study we made a detailed analysis of a set of tutoring sessions to see how the tutors used the tutoring protocols. Most sessions contain only one procedure and are one hour long. We chose to study the nine sessions that involved two procedures and lasted up to two hours, so we could observe changes in behavior over time. In four sessions the tutor started with the Centrifuge procedure in which the primary variable is CVP. In five sessions the tutor started with the Alpha-adrenergic procedure in which the primary variable is TPR.

```
Tutor (Problem)
   Tutor (DR)
      Prediction & Tutoring (Primary Variable)
         Prediction (Primary Variable)
         Tutoring (Primary Variable)
      Prediction & Tutoring (Rest of the prediction ta-
                     ble variables)
         If not "sequence violation"
               Then Prediction (Variable X)
                     Tutoring (Variable X)
               Else give a sequence hint
   Tutor (RR)
      Prediction & Tutoring (Prediction table variables)
         If not "sequence violation"
               Then Prediction (Variable X)
                     Tutoring (Variable X)
               Else give a sequence hint
   Tutor (SS)
      Prediction & Tutoring (Prediction table variables)
         Prediction (Variable X)
         Tutoring (Variable X)
```

Figure 1. Tutoring Protocol 4

The results of the analysis of protocol use in the tutoring sessions were a complete surprise to us. The tutors planned to use Protocol 3. This means that the tutor analyzed the student's prediction results and then planned the tutoring strategy based on these results. Sometimes, however, the tutor does not wait until the student finishes the predictions. If the student starts with poor predictions then the tutor starts to guide the student in the right track with hints or explanations. We named this new protocol, Protocol 4. According to our analysis of the transcripts, when the tutor used immediate feedback they also enforced a particular tutoring sequence. In Protocol 4 (see Figure 1) the tutor considers the student's prediction sequences. The student must follow a prediction sequence that the tutor thinks correct. The tutor explores the student's response at each point in problem solving. Therefore the tutor provides immediate feedback for each student prediction and response.

Each tutoring session in our transcripts can be divided into prediction phases and tutoring phases. The structure of the Prediction Table, shown in Figure 1, divides the problem into three stages - DR, RR, and SS. In each stage the tutor performs two common operations. During the first operation "Prediction", the student predicts whether a physiology variable will increase (go up, +, up,...), decrease (go down, −, down, ...), or stay the same (unchanged, 0, stay, ...). During the second operation "Tutor", the tutor starts a dialogue to remedy any prediction errors.

In Protocol 4, like other protocols, the primary variable is predicted and taught first. The rest of the variables should be predicted and taught in the sequence defined by the problem. If the student does not follow the sequence, the tutor gives a sequence hint about the prediction order based on the causal reasoning to be followed. Otherwise, the tutor gives instant feedback for the predicted variable.

3 Analysis of Human Tutoring Transcripts

We used C5.0 [13], which is an upgraded version of the decision tree induction program C4.5 [11], to produce the rules that describe when our domain experts switched tutoring protocols. In this experiment we had 44 cases (the number of tutoring phases recorded in the 18 procedures studied), each with 11 attributes.

3.1 Attributes

The first three attributes in Table 2 are related to the discussion about the basic concept. The basic concept involves the effects of the centrifuge in the Centrifuge procedure, or the Alpha-adrenergic Receptors in the Alpha-adrenergic procedure.

Table 2. Attributes for Rule Extraction

attribute	value	remark
Discussion Type	T, S	Tutor-Primary / Student-Explanation
Discussion Success	S, U	Satisfied / Unsatisfied
Discussion Length	continuous	How many turns in the discussion
Primary Error	continuous	Wrong answers for a primary variable
Prediction Score	continuous	(right - wrong) prediction
Remediation	continuous	Correct answers in the total answers
Sequence Error	continuous	Sequence error in Protocol 4
Pre-Prediction Score	continuous	Previous stage, (right - wrong) prediction
Pre-Remediation	continuous	Previous stage, correct answers in the total answers
Pre-Sequence Error	continuous	Previous stage, sequence error in Protocol 4
Current Stage	dr, rr, ss	Current stage

The students often had difficulty in determining the primary variable. Therefore tutoring frequently began with a discussion of the relationship between the basic concept and the primary variable. Thirteen of the eighteen procedures started with a discussion of the basic concepts. The Discussion Type (DT) in Table 2 is T if the tutor started the discussion to remedy a wrong primary variable prediction. It is S if the student began the discussion with a request for an explanation. The Discussion Success (DS) indicates whether the discussion was successful or not, that is, whether the tutor is satisfied with the student's responses at least 50% of the time. The Discussion Length (DL) indicates the number of turns in the discussion counting from the start to the turn in which the student gave the right answer for the primary variable. The Primary Error (PE) is a count of the number of wrong answers entered for the primary variable. The number of primary errors reflects the comprehension of the procedure. The Prediction Score (PS) indicates how many right or wrong answers were made in the prediction phase. The score we used was the number of right answers minus the number of wrong answers. The value of the Remediation (RM) attribute is the percentage of correct answers among the total answers given by the student in that stage. The Sequence Error (SE) attribute represents the number of sequence errors during Protocol 4. The Pre-Prediction Score, Pre-Remediation, and Pre-Sequence Error: These attributes represent the Prediction Score, Remediation, and Sequence Error from the previous stage. The Current Stage (CS) indicates the stage on which the student is now working.

Table 3. The Summary of Human Tutoring Sessions K30 - K38

Tutor	Session	DR							RR			SS		
		DT	DS	DL	PE	PS	RM	SE	PS	RM	SE	PS	RM	SE
AAR	K30 CVP	-	-	-	0	1	0	-	3	0.22	-	1	0.25	-
	K30 TPR	T	U	19	3	3	0.44	-	5	0	-	3	0	-
	K31 TPR	S	U	28	5	-1	0.3	-	-3	-	-	=		
	K31 CVP	-	-	-	2	-	).2	0	=			=		
	K32 TPR	S	S	4	1	5	0.28	-	3	0.25	-	5	0	-
	K32 CVP	T	S	13	2	7	0	-	7	0	-	5	0.4	-
	K33 CVP	-	-	-	0	7	0	-	1	0	-	5	0.5	-
	K33 TPR	T	S	13	1	1	0.5	-	3	0.5	-	7	0	-
	K34 CVP	T	U	5	1	1	0.125	-	-1	-	-	=		
	K34 TPR	S	U	4	1	-	).45	0	=			=		
JAM	K35 CVP	-	-	-	1	1	0	-	3	0.4	-	1	-	-
	K35 TPR	S	U	14	1	-	).17	0	-	0.25	0	-	)	0
	K36 TPR	S	U	14	1	1	·	-	=			=		
	K36 CVP	T	S	7	1	7	)	0	1	0.33	-	=		
	K37 CVP	-	-	-	0	-1	0	-	7	1	-	3	0	-
	K37 TPR	S	S	10	0	3	0.1	-	5	0	-	7	0	-
	K38 TPR	T	U	17	1	-2	·	-	-	0.25	2	=		
	K38 CVP	T	S	11	1	-	).17	1	1	0.75	-	3	0.33	-

CVP: Centrifuge Procedure
TPR: Alpha-adrenergic Procedure

Table 3 summarizes sessions K30 - K38, which are the input to the rule induction program. "=" means the transcript does not have the stage data. "-" means that the data is not available. For example, the "K30 CVP" procedure did not include a discussion about the basic concepts. A white cell indicates that Protocol 3 was in use and a shaded cell indicates that Protocol 4 was in use in that stage.

3.2 Switching Rules

The rules extracted by C5.0 do not classify all cases correctly; there is an error rate of 9.1 %. The switching rules are:

```
If Discussion Success = S
   If Remediation <= 0.5
      If Current Stage = ss
         If Prediction Score <= 1
            then switch from Protocol 3 to Protocol 4

If Discussion Success = U
   If Primary Error > 2
      If Prediction Score <= -2
         then switch from Protocol 3 to Protocol 4

If Discussion Success = U
   If Primary Error <= 2
      If Pre-Remediation > 0.35
         If Current Stage <> rr
            then switch from Protocol 3 to Protocol 4

If Discussion Success = U
   If Primary Error <= 2
      If Pre-Remediation <= 0.35
         If Discussion Type = T
            If Current Stage = rr
               then switch from Protocol 3 to Protocol 4

If Discussion Success = S
   If Remediation > 0.5
      then switch from Protocol 4 to Protocol 3

If Discussion Success = S
   If Remediation <= 0.5
      If Current Stage = dr
         If Pre-Sequence Eerror <= 1
            If Pre-Prediction Score <= 1
               then switch from Protocol 4 to Protocol 3
```

Examing these rules we see that two important factors determined whether the tutor switches the protocol from Protocol 3 to Protocol 4. The occurrence of a discussion about the basic concepts of the procedure at the very beginning of a procedure is an important factor in protocol switches. For example, the protocol switch is likely if the student asked for some explanation before the prediction and did not understand that explanation right away, or if the tutor asked some question about the basic concepts to remedy the student's wrong primary variable prediction, but the student replied with unsatisfactory answers. The other important factor, which makes the tutor switch the protocol from Protocol 3 to Protocol 4, is the student's performance scores. One score is the prediction score and the other is the number of primary variable errors. However, if the student performed well in the previous stage then the tutor did not switch but gave some hints about the primary variable.

On the other hand, the tutor went back from Protocol 4 to Protocol 3 under the opposite conditions. If the student made a good performance in the previous stage and there was a satisfying discussion about the basic procedure concepts then the tutor switched back to Protocol 3.

4 Some other important characteristics of tutoring protocols

We found some by-product rules during the analysis of human transcripts. We wondered how long the tutor keeps a given protocol. The tutor always starts a procedure with Protocol 3. However, after switching the protocol, the tutor sticks with the Protocol 4 to the next stage or next procedure.

Student initiatives also affect protocol switches. A student initiative means any student contribution to the dialogue that is not an answer to a question asked by the tutor [3], [14]. In Protocol 3, sometimes our tutor met with a simple student initiative that requires only a short response from the tutor. In the prediction phase, for example, the student may ask a simple question [3] or the student could not answer in more than one minute. In these cases, the tutor gives a simple hint [18] and sticks with the current protocol. In particular, if the student performed well in the previous stage, but starts with poor predictions, then the tutor does not switch protocols but gives hints about the current stage.

5 Which students prefer immediate feedback?

Who prefers immediate feedback? Which students feel a lack of instant feedback during the prediction phase in Protocol 3? We can imagine the situation intuitively. Sometimes the student may want to know whether the current prediction is correct or not. The variables in the prediction table are causally related. Therefore if the student is not sure of one variable then the uncertainty may affect the following variables. In order to discover how the students feel about the protocol issue we compared the students' performance using CIRCSIM-Tutor with their answers to a questionnaire asking about their view of CIRCSIM-Tutor.

This data came from an experiment that was performed by forty-eight first year students at Rush Medical College, in November 1998. The system presented four cardiovascular procedures to be solved. The system was designed to use Protocol 3, which means no immediate feedback and discard the prediction sequence except for the primary variable.

After using CIRCSIM-Tutor the students answered a questionnaire that asks the students' view of the system. The questionnaire had ten questions and employed a five point Likert scale. Question 8 "I would prefer that the system always tell me about my mistakes immediately" asked the student's opinion about the tutoring protocol.

Seven students answered that they would prefer immediate feedback and six of them (86%) made poor predictions while using the program. We defined a poor/good prediction result to mean that the student's prediction score on four procedures was under/over the average prediction result of all students. Which students do not ask for immediate feedback? Twelve students answered that they prefer the current protocol, Protocol 3, which does not give feedback immediately, in the questionnaire and eight of them (67%) made good predictions when using the program. The analysis results suggest that the students who made poor predictions are eager to know their mistakes immediately.

6 Conclusion

In this study we carried out a detailed analysis of tutoring sessions to see how the tutors used the tutoring protocols. Two important factors that determined whether the tutor switches the protocol are the discussion about the basic concepts of the procedure and the student's performance scores. If the student did not perform well then the tutor responded immediately. The tutor did not wait until the student finished the predictions but started to tutor the student in the right track. However, when the tutor met a simple student initiative the tutor did not change the protocol but gave some hints. If the student performed well in the previous stage, giving good predictions and a satisfactory discussion about the basic procedure concepts, then the tutor switched back to Protocol 3.

In order to find out which protocol the students prefer we also analyzed the result of the CIRCSIM-Tutor experiment and the questionnaire. The analysis results say that the students' protocol preference is closely related to their performance using CIRC-SIM-Tutor. Students who are doing well are comfortable waiting for feedback while most students who are doing badly want immediate feedback.

We plan to enable CIRCSIM-Tutor to switch protocols. Then we will carry out a controlled experiment to find out which protocol improves the students' learning outcomes.

References

1. Cho, B., Michael, J., Rovick, A., and Evens, M.: A Curriculum Planning Model for an Intelligent Tutoring System. Proceedings of 12th International Florida Artificial Intelligence Research Symposium. Orlando, FL. (1999) 197–201

2. Cuffman, D. and MacRae, N.: Faculty Development Programs in Interactive Television. Proceedings of the 1996 Mid-South Instructional Technology Conference. Track 2: Distance Learning. (download:1999.12.30.) http://www.mtsu.edu/~itconf/proceed96.html

3. Freedman, R.: Degrees of Mixed-Initiative Interaction in an Intelligent Tutoring System. In: Haller, S. and McRoy, S. (eds.): Working Notes of AAAI97 Spring Symposium on Mixed-Initiative Interaction, Stanford, CA. (1997) 44-49

4. Freedman, R.: Atlas: A Plan Manager for Mixed-Initiative, Multimodal Dialogue. AAAI '99 Workshop on Mixed-Initiative Intelligence, Orlando. FL. (1999) 107-114

5. Katz, S., Lesgold, A., Eggan, G., Girdin, M., and Greenberg, L.: Self-adjusting Curriculum Planning in Sherlock II, Lecture Notes in Computer Science: Proceedings of the Fourth International Conference on Computers in Learning (ICCAL '92). Berlin: Springer Verlag. (1992) 343-355

6. Khuwaja, R. Rovick, A., Michael, J., and Evens, M.: A Tale of Three Tutoring Protocols: The Implications for Intelligent Tutoring Systems. Proceedings of Golden West, Las Vegas, Nevada, June 9-12 (1994) 109-118

7. Li, J., Seu, J., Evens, M., Michael, J., and Rovick A.: Computer dialogue system (CDS): A system for capturing computer-mediated dialogue. Behavior Research Methods, Instruments, & Computers, 24(4) (1992) 535-540

8. Michael, J., Rovick A., Evens, M., Shim, L., Woo, C., and Kim, N.: The uses of multiple student inputs in modeling and lesson planning in CAI and ICAI programs. In I. Tomek (editor), Computer Assisted Learning. Berlin: Springer Verlag. (1992) 441-452

9. Moore, M.: Three types of interaction. American Journal of Distance Education. Volume 3 Number 2 (1989) 1-6

10. Moore, M. and Kearsley, G.: Distance Education: A Systems Perspective. Wadsworth, Bermont, CA. (1996)

11. Quinlan, J.: C4.5: Programs for Machine Learning. Los Altos, CA: Morgan Kaufmann (1993)

12. Rovick, A. and Michael, J.: The predictions table: a tool for assessing students' knowledge. American Journal of Physiology 263 (Advances in Physiology Education 8) (1992) S33-S36

13. RuleQuest. RuleQuest Research Pty Ltd. (download:1999.9.8.) http://www.rulequest.com/download.html

14. Shah, F, and Evens, M.: Student Initiatives and Tutor Responses in a Medical Tutoring System. In: Haller, S. and McRoy, S. (eds.): Working Notes of AAAI97 Spring Symposium on Mixed-Initiative Interaction, Stanford, CA. (1997) 138-144

15. Travers, A. and Decker, E.: New Technology and Critical Pedagogy. Radical Pedagogy, Volume 1: Issue 2, Summer (1999)

16. Wilensky, R., Chin, D., Luria, M., Martin, J., Mayfield, J. and Wu, D.: The Berkely UNIX Consultant Project (CSD-89-520). (download:1998.6.4.) http://sunsite.berkeley.edu:80/Dienst/UI/2.0/Describe/ncstrl.ucb%2fCSD-89-520?abstract.

17. Woo, C.: Instructional Planning in an Intelligent Tutoring System: Combining Global Lesson Plans with Local Discourse Control, Ph. D. Dissertation, Illinois Institute of Technology (1991)

18. Zhou, Y., Freedman, R. Glass, M. Michael, J., Rovick, A., and Evens, M.: Delivering Hints in a Dialogue-Based Intelligent Tutoring System, Proceedings of the Sixteenth National Conference on Artificial Intelligence (AAAI-99), Orlando. FL. (1999) 128-134

Understandable Learner Models for a Sensorimotor Control Task

Rafael Morales[1,*], Helen Pain[1], and Tom Conlon[2]

[1] Division of Informatics, University of Edinburgh,
80 South Bridge, Edinburgh EH1 1HN, UK.
{R.Morales,H.Pain}@ed.ac.uk

[2] Moray House Institute of Education, University of Edinburgh,
Holyrood Road, Edinburgh EH8 8AQ, UK.
tomc@education.ed.ac.uk

Abstract. We discuss the implications of making learner models that can be inspected by learners within the context of a sensorimotor control task—that of balancing a pole hinged to a cart. We argue that the requirement of producing models that are comprehensible by learners limits the options of modelling strategy, constrains model structure and calls for further refinement of model contents. We discuss the issues of modularity of model contents, modality and interactivity of model presentation, and present results from a preliminary evaluation of a graphical interface to learner models for pole balancing.

1 Introduction

Inspectability of learner models as a design goal has been advocated for imposing beneficial constraints on learner modelling, like avoiding crude classifications of learners; for encouraging accountability, understandability, and acceptability of learner models; and for adopting a learner-centred perspective [6, 11, 23]. This paper presents a case study of building learner models that can be shown to learners, and understood. The task used as illustrative domain is balancing a pole hinged to a cart; a domain rather different to those inspectable learner models have been previously built for, such as second language acquisition [2, 6, 7, 8], use of a text editor [11], application of engineering procedures [5] and algebraic problem solving [21]. Pole balancing is a sensorimotor control task that has been heavily used as a test domain for machine learning techniques—e.g. [4, 18]. It is appealing because it is relatively simple and facilitates quick construction of fairly individualised learner models [20].

We evelute the feasibility of making learner models in this domain inspectable by the learners. Careful selection of a modelling strategy is required for learner models to be presentable to learners in a way that facilitates their understanding, and further refinement of model contents may be necessary to improve model comprehensibility. Next section outlines the task of pole balancing and summarises our approach to building learner models in this domain, and in Sections 3, 4 and 5 we discuss isues of modularity of model contents, modality and interactivity of model presentation. Section 6

* Supported by CONACYT and the Instituto de Investigaciones Eléctricas, Mexico, under scholarship 64999/111091.

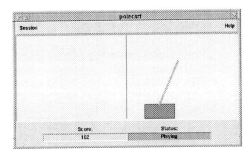

Fig. 1. Graphical user interface to the pole and cart. A position of the cart on the right (left) half of the track/window is taken to be positive (negative). An inclination of the pole to the right (left) of the vertical is considered positive (negative).

describes an informative study carried out to assess the comprehensibility of a graphical interface to the learner models. Section 7 comes back to the potential benefits of building inspectable learner models and discusses some obstacles to making them more understandable to learners. Finally, Section 8 presents our conclusions.

2 From Traces of Behaviour to Learner Models

The task of pole balancing involves controlling a simulation of a rigid pole hinged to a cart that in turn is mounted on a straight rail of finite length (Fig. 1). The device can be controlled only by applying (or not) a force to the cart of fixed magnitude and parallel to the rail but with a choice of left or right direction. User input is restricted to pressing arrow keys: ↑ to start a new control trial, ← to push the cart to the left, and → to push the cart to the right. The system saves a trace of every control trial per learner containing records of the form (*pole and cart state, action*) which associate each user action in the control run with a state of the pole and cart. After merging several control trials per learner, while taking into account factors related to learners (e.g. reaction time) and the task (e.g. symmetry of the pole and cart system), a final set of records is produced that better describes the correspondence between states of the pole and cart and user actions [20]. These records are the raw material for generating a model of the strategic knowledge employed by each learner when performing the task.

Constructing a learner model from a collection of input-output records can be seen as a classification task. From this perspective, the application to learner modelling of machine learning techniques for classification looks quite attractive and straightforward (yet cf. [24]), with a number of alternatives available: rule discovery, decision trees, Bayesian and neural networks, case-based reasoning, etcetera [19]. Every technique will impose a particular structure upon the resulting model, and the criterion for selecting a specific technique in this case is the production of models structured in a way that facilitates their inspection, understanding, and possible modification by apprentices of pole balancing who are mostly unfamiliar with knowledge representation techniques.

left 960 317 if $a \leq -0.110277$.
left 789 263 if $\dot{a} \leq -0.13729$ $a \leq 0.047092$.
right 357 20 if $x \leq 0.869831$ $a \geq 0.286856$.
right 693 74 if $\dot{a} \geq -0.218725$ $a \geq 0.151792$ $x \leq 1.42121$.
right 179 25 if $a \geq 0.104776$ $\dot{a} \geq -0.725516$ $\dot{a} \leq 0.325668$ $x \geq 0.356233$ $\dot{x} \leq 2.38745$.
right 566 143 if $a \geq -0.055733$ $\dot{a} \geq 0.141926$ $x \leq 0.534309$.

Fig. 2. Angles (a) are measured in radians (clockwise direction is positive), angular velocities ($\dot{a}$) in radians per second, cart positions (x) in metres, and cart velocities ($\dot{x}$) in metres per second. The two integers in between each rule's action and preconditions are the number of cases correctly and incorrectly classified by that rule, respectively.

Morales and Pain [20] chose production rules because they are easy to interpret in operational terms, have a symbolic character[1] and simple structure that resembles familiar rules of thumb, and support modularity of representation [3, 16]. Furthermore, production rules have been used effectively in modelling human skill acquisition and performance [1]. In an empirical study involving thirty subjects, supervised rule induction with RIPPER [9] produced learner models containing between four and sixteen rules ($\bar{x} = 10.9, s = 3.4$), with the number of preconditions per rule varying from two to four ($\bar{x} = 2.6, s = 0.5$). An example of a learner model from that study is given in Fig. 2.

Models like this provide useful information for a number of purposes: to predict which direction the learner will push, if any; to simulate the behaviour of the learner; and to discover similarities and differences with other learner's strategy through statistically comparing their models' predictions [20]. Combinations of positions and velocities where the learner's reaction is markedly different from that of an expert can be discovered by comparing the model to a set of rules representative of expertise. The common feature among these different uses of a learner model is, nevertheless, that they do not require for it to be understandable by the learner. In fact, they do not require human intervention at all, since all is needed is for the computer system to be able to process the model. Things can be quite different when it comes to human processing of the models though, particularly when these humans are the learners being modelled.

3   Presenting Models in the Right Modality

Rule preconditions in Fig. 2 are expressed in numerical terms. Although they are very accurate, they are also quite difficult to correlate to the behaviour of the pole and cart on the screen. A different choice of units—for example, degrees instead of radians, or millimetres instead of metres—does not alleviate the problem, because it is not a problem of units but one of *modality*[2]: the lack of consistency in the way the task (Fig. 1) and the learner model (Fig. 2) are presented makes the latter difficult to comprehend despite experience with the former.

---

[1] Greer et al. [15], on the other hand, present an interesting example of how learner models based on Bayesian networks can be opened to learner inspection.

[2] We use the term *modality* to imply a combination of language and medium, without attempting to give a more precise definition of it. For a deeper discussion of modality, see [22].

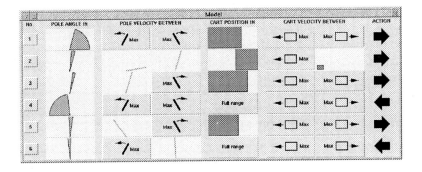

Fig. 3. Graphical presentation of a refined version of the learner model shown in 2, with preconditions of rules mutually exclusive (Section 4).

A different approach to presenting the learner model is illustrated in Fig. 3. Here the model is presented graphically, in a table-like format in which every row represents a rule; actions are represented by arrows, resembling the arrow keys used to command actions in the interface to the simulator; and rule preconditions are represented by arcs, boxes, and animations of the pole and cart moving with different velocities (every pair of animations denoting the range of velocities defined by the velocities of the animations)[3]. It can be seen that task and model are presented now in the same (graphical) modality. Consequently, much less translation is necessary, the cognitive load on the learner being reduced in this way, and previous experience with the task should better support their understanding of the model.

The issue of consistency between the modalities in which the tasks in the domain and the learner models are presented have not been raised explicitly in previous research on inspectable learner models, where matching of modalities for domain and model presentation varies. In cases of second language learning as the application domain, written natural language has been the modality of choice both for presenting the tasks and the models [2, 6, 8]. In a similar way, de Buen et al. [5] employ mathematical notation, specialised technical terminology and natural language to convey engineering concepts and procedural steps, both during task and model presentation. In contrast, Cook and Kay [11] present their models of users of the SAM text editor using a mixture of text and diagrams (conceptual trees) that differs from the textual interface of the editor itself. Paiva et al. [21] describe language selection as a major difficulty for externalising learner models, although the early example they provide shows the learner model in a logic-based language that is closer to the model's internal representation than to the language in which the task (simplification of algebraic equations) is presented.

The relevance of matching the modalities in which task and model are presented may vary among domains. Sharing modality may be more important in domains that involve the acquisition of sensorimotor skills, like pole balancing, than in domains with

---

[3] The graphical presentation contains also textual and iconic representations, which are introduced to improve the clarity of the presentation and to diminish the overwhelming effect of too many fast animations.

demands on higher cognitive abilities. In the latter cases, it may be more important for task and model to share more structural properties of their representations, or even a deeper but recognisable set of abstractions, without regards for superficial details of presentation. Individual learners have different preferences of modality and different degrees of representational competence [10, 12] which should be recognised as well.

4 Increasing the Modularity of Models

Rules in Fig. 2 are presented in order of importance; i.e. a rule is supposed to fire only on states of the pole and cart that satisfy its preconditions but do not satisfy the preconditions of any rule above it. This ordering has the potential benefits of reducing the number of rules in the model and simplifying their preconditions. However, rule firing is not determined entirely by each rule's preconditions but also by the preconditions of all other rules with higher priority (as if every rule has the negated preconditions of all previous rules). That makes the role of every rule but the first one harder to comprehend.

Fig. 3 contains a refined version of the model presented in Fig. 2, with the preconditions of all rules modified to make them mutually exclusive. Both models are equivalent, yet each rule in Fig. 3 can be understood independently of any other rule. Hence the new model profits more from the modularity of production rules [3, 16].

The issue of modularity has not been explicitly discussed in the context of previous research on inspectable learner models. Although distinct components that may favour a modular design can be observed in all models and their presentations—grammatical rules, description of general tendencies, answers to exercises and their evaluation, specific and more general comments, communicative goals and capabilities, knowledge components, user properties, beliefs and reasoning rules—their use does not intrinsically guarantee modularity, as our example using production rules clearly illustrates.

5 Providing Interactivity

Giving learners improved access to their models (as above) does not guarantee that they will pay any attention to their models nor understand them. Learners should feel they are able to interact with their models, through means of exerting influence over their construction, content or structure, as opposed to merely observing them. Most researchers dealing with participative learner modelling have provided means for learners to interact with their models, varing from browsing and direct editing [2, 5, 6, 11, 21], to mechanisms for discussing and negotiating their contents [8, 13].

Our system gives learners direct control over the content of their models by enriching their presentation with editing facilities. Learners can modify the preconditions of any rule either by directly manipulating their graphical presentation or by dragging sliders on a graphical scale; change the resulting action of every rule as they wish, by clicking a button on the mouse; and add, delete, and alter the order of rules in their models (reordering is still important because independence among rules is not guaranteed after learners' editing of their models).

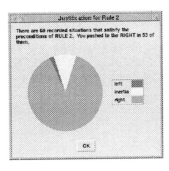

Fig. 4. Justification of a rule.

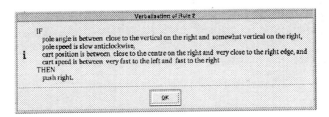

Fig. 5. Example of rule verbalisation. Learners are warned that they should regard the textual description of a rule as a complement to, but not a substitute for the graphical description.

Information about the number of cases correctly and incorrectly classified by each rule is stored in the learner model and can be displayed on request to justify the existence and relevance of every rule (Fig. 4). This simple move makes the accountability of the models more apparent to learners, so it is expected for it to increase model acceptability. Learners can also ask for a short execution of the learner model with initial conditions that trigger a chosen rule, as well as for an explanation of the rule in natural language, the latter being an *if... then* template filled with translations of the rule's preconditions and action (Fig. 5). This facilities for justification, execution and verbalisation of rules offer the possibility of immediate feedback to learners on changes to their models.

6 Informative Study

The ease of understanding such a graphical interface was evaluated. Eleven postgraduate students took part in the study, which consisted of three stages. Firstly, each participant was requested to provide some basic background information via a short questionnaire. The second stage consisted in playing with the simulator of the pole and cart for about nine minutes. The third stage required reviewing the graphical presentation of a fictitious strategy for controlling the pole and cart (Fig. 6) and answering a questionnaire about it. Instructions and questionnaires were handed out in printed form to the

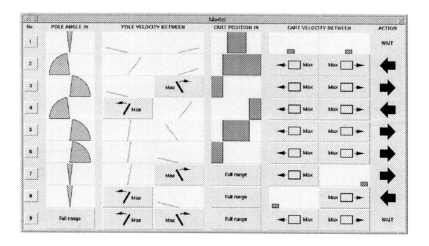

Fig. 6. The fictitious strategy for controlling the pole and cart.used in the study.

participants at the beginning of each stage and, whereas human intervention was kept to a minimum, the participants were allowed to ask for clarification of any aspect of the program and printed material. They were given as much time as they wished to answer the questionnaires, and they spent between 35 and 75 minutes reviewing the fictitious strategy and answering questions about it.

The questions in the second questionnaire were organised in increasing order of difficulty, from simple questions that tested understanding of the arrow-notation for actions to a final question aimed at testing understanding of the strategy as a whole. Every completed questionnaire was evaluated by the first author, who wrote a model answer for each question, which he then compared to each participant's response. For example, the model answer for the question 'Try to provide a description, in your own words, of the overall strategy defined by the rule set' (Q14) was

> The strategy is a "natural" one, with a touch of laziness. That means doing nothing if both pole and cart are centred and moving slowly; pushing in the direction of pole falling if it accelerates, but not if the cart is moving fast in the same direction. In general, the idea is to try to revert to a centred position as long as the cart is not too close to an edge (with the pole falling rather quickly towards it) or the pole is not falling too quickly (the cart being anywhere).

An example of an answer taken as correct is

> If the pole is well balanced and the cart is moving slowly in the centre of the screen , do nothing. If the pole is pointing off to the left, is not falling rapidly to the right and the cart is not on the far left, push left. If the pole is pointing to the right and the cart is not on the far right push right. If the pole is upright falling right and the cart is not travelling fast right, push right. Similarly if it is falling left, not going fast left, push left. Otherwise do nothing. (Participant 6)

The results, summarised in Table 1, suggest that question difficulty increased as expected. The questions were weighted according to their number of right answers[4], and scores calculated for each participant by summing the weights of all correct answers and penalising for incorrect ones. It can be seen that three participants scored less than 50% (2.92), four between 50% and 75% (4.38), and four over 75%—the maximum possible score being 5.85 (100%).

Table 1. Answers to the questions about the graphical presentation of a strategy for controlling the pole on a cart. A period (.) indicates a correct answer; 'X' indicates an incorrect answer; '?' indicates an answer that could be regarded as partially (in)correct; and 'N' indicates no answer.

Question		P1	P2	P3	P4	P5	P6	P7	P8	P9	P10	P11
On actions	Q1	.	X	.	.	.	.	.	.	.	.	.
	Q2	.	X	.	.	.	.	.	.	.	.	.
On cart position	Q3	.	X	X	.	.	.	.	.	.	.	.
	Q4	?	X	X	.	.	.	.	?	?	.	.
On pole angle	Q5	.	X	?	.	.	.	.	?	?	.	X
	Q6	.	X	N	.	.	.	?	X	?	.	.
On pole velocity	Q7	?	X	X	?	.	?	X	?	?	X	.
	Q8	?	X	X	.	.	?	.	?	?	?	?
On cart velocity	Q9	?	X	X	.	.	.	?	?	?	X	.
	Q10	.	X	?	.	.	.	.	.	?	?	.
	Q11	?	X	X	.	?	.	?	?	X	.	.
On whole rules	Q12	?	?	X	.	?	.	?	?	?	?	.
	Q13	.	?	X	.	?	.	?	?	?	X	.
On whole strategy	Q14	?	N	N	N	N	.	N	.	N	?	N
Score per participant		4.00	0.46	0.68	4.79	4.39	5.29	3.31	3.53	2.59	3.27	4.47

7 Discussion

From the responses to the questionnaire, and doubts expressed during the study, it became clear that the participants' main problem was to interpret the ranges of velocities represented by the animations. In addition, they frequently got confused by the short executions of the strategy, what made evident their low confidence on their interpretation of the presentation of the strategy. This results suggest three means of facilitating a better understanding of the graphical presentation of a strategy, all of them implemented in the current system: (1) provision of complementary explanations in natural language; (2) rewriting of the printed material; and (3) making explicit the action being executed at each moment in the short executions of the learner model.

---

[4] The probabilities of right (p_r) and wrong (p_w) answers were estimated (using Laplace estimate) and weights calculated as $\omega_r = p_w$ and $\omega_w = p_r$ (doubtful answers were considered half-right answers).

Despite the limitations of the study (e.g. size, subjective evaluation of correctness), the results obtained suggest that learners are able to achieve a reasonable understanding of their models. Some obstacles to comprehensibility of the models exist, however:

- Sets of rules with no explicit rationale (e.g. in terms of goals) may be inherently difficult to comprehend, no matter how small they are—this relates to the *opacity* of sets of rules discussed by Barr and Feigenbaum [3].
- The refined version in Fig. 3 of the model presented in Fig. 2 contains the same number of rules, but unfortunately that is not always the case. In fact, although half of the refined versions of the models obtained in our empirical study contain no more rules than the original models, a couple of refined versions were up to 1.6 times bigger.
- Graphical presentations in this context are more natural than numerical presentations, but they can be too concrete and less intuitive than correspondent expressions in natural language. The explanations produced by our system are, however, no more than simple verbalisations of rules preconditions and actions.
- Presenting ranges of angles by arcs, and ranges of positions by boxes appear to be straightforward choices. In contrast, the clarity of presenting ranges of velocities using animations is less obvious.

8 Conclusions

This case study has focused on producing learner models that are designed to be studied, and understood, by the learners. A number of reasons justify why the models so constructed should be easy to comprehend by learners: they are presented in a consistent modality, profiting from previous experience in the domain task; they are modular, allowing understanding of each component independently of others; and they can be reviewed and edited interactively, in an attempt to make their presentation more enticing. Qualitative verbalisations of the rules and short executions of the model focused on any rule are also provided. Each learner model is supported by data, which is displayed graphically in order to justify the existence and relevance of every component of the learner model, making the accountability of the models more apparent to learners, with the aim of increasing their acceptance of the models.

The results of an informative study suggest that learners can understand the graphical interface to learner models. The study also exhibited a number of factors that can affect the comprehensibility of the models and its graphical presentation. Despite the fact that further research is necessary to fully appraise the suitability of our approach, we are confident this paper gives convincing support for the claim that learners can comprehend a carefully designed presentation of their learner models, at least in the context of a sensorimotor control task.

References

[1] Anderson J.R.: Rules of the Mind. Lawrence Erlbaum Associates (1993)

[2] Ayala G., Yano Y.: Learner models for supporting awareness and collaboration in a CSCL environment. In: Frasson C., Gauthier G. (eds.), Intelligent Tutoring Systems (ITS'96), vol. 1086 of Lecture Notes in Computer Science. Springer-Verlag (1996) 158–167

[3] Barr A., Feigenbaum E.A. (eds.): The Handbook of Artificial Intelligence, vol. I. Pitman, London (1981)

[4] Barto A.G., Sutton R.S., Anderson C.W.: Neuronlike adaptive elements that can solve difficult learning control problems. IEEE Transactions on Systems, Man and Cybernetics **SMC-13** (1983) 834–846

[5] de Buen P.R., Vadera S., Morales E.F.: A collaborative approach to user modeling within a multi-functional architecture. In: Kay [17] (1999) 291–293

[6] Bull S.: See yourself write: A simple student model to make students think. In: Jameson A., Paris C., Tasso C. (eds.), User Modeling (UM'97). Springer Wien New York (1997) 315–326

[7] Bull S., Brna P., Pain H.: Extending the scope of the student model. User Modeling and User-Adapted Interaction **5** (1995) 45–65

[8] Bull S., Pain H.: "Did I say what I think I said, and do you agree with me?" inspecting and questioning the student model. In: Greer [14] (1995) 501–508

[9] Cohen W.W.: Fast effective rule induction. In: Prieditis A., Russell S. (eds.), Machine Learning (ML'95). Morgan Kaufmann (1995)

[10] Conlon T.: Alternatives to rules for knowledge-based modelling. Instructional Science **27** (1999) 117–146

[11] Cook R., Kay J.: The justified user model: A viewable, explained user model. In: Proceedings of the Fourth International Conference on User Modeling . Hyannis, MA (1994) 145–150

[12] Cox R., Brna P.: Supporting the use of external representations in problem solving: the need for flexible learning environments. Journal of Artificial Intelligence in Education **6** (1995) 239–302

[13] Dimitrova V., Self J., Brna P.: The interactive maintenance of open learner models. In: Lajoie S.P., Vivet M. (eds.), Artificial Intelligence in Education (AIEd'99). IOS Press (1999) 405–412

[14] Greer J.E. (ed.): Proceedings of the Seventh World Conference on Artificial Intelligence in Education. Washington, DC (1995)

[15] Greer J.E., Zapata-Rivera J.D., Ong-Scutchings C., Cooke J.E.: Visualization of Bayesian learner models. In: Morales R., Pain H., Bull S., Kay J. (eds.), Proceedings of the Workshop on Open, Interactive, and Other Overt Approaches to Learner Modelling. Le Mans, France (1999) 9–13

[16] Hayes-Roth F.: Rule-based systems. Communications of ACM **28** (1985) 921–932

[17] Kay J. (ed.): User Modeling (UM'99). Springer Wien New York (1999)

[18] Michie D., Chambers R.A.: BOXES: An experiment in adaptive control. In: Dale E., Michie D. (eds.), Machine Intelligence, vol. 2. Oliver and Boyd, Edinburgh (1968) 137–152

[19] Mitchell T.M.: Machine Learning. McGraw-Hill (1997)

[20] Morales R., Pain H.: Modelling of novices' control skills with machine learning. In: Kay [17] (1999) 159–168

[21] Paiva A., Self J.A., Hartley R.: Externalising learner models. In: Greer [14] (1995)

[22] Pineda L., Garza G.: A model for multimodal representation and inference. In: Paton R., Neilsen I. (eds.), Visual Representations and Interpretations. Springer (1999)

[23] Self J.A.: Bypassing the intractable problem of student modelling. In: Proceedings of ITS'88. Montreal, Canada (1988) 18–24

[24] Sison R., Shimura M.: Student modeling and machine learning. International Journal of Artificial Intelligence in Education **9** (1998) 128–158

Using Meta-Cognitive Conflicts to Support Group Problem Solving

Patricia Azevedo Tedesco[1]* and John Self *

* Computer Based Learning Unit
University of Leeds
Leeds – LS2 9JT
UK
Phone: +44 113 2334626
E-mail: {patricia,jas}@cbl.leeds.ac.uk

Abstract: The emphasis on building collaborative/co-operative environments has brought the issue of conflicts to light. The inevitability of conflicts in group interactions, as well as their role as promoters of *reflection* and *articulation* has generated a significant amount of research on the subject. In this light, we have built a computational framework for the detection and mediation of *meta-cognitive* conflicts. In order to make mediation more effective, we have considered group and individual models, the history of the interaction and model of the task. This approach is exemplified by the implementation of *MArCo*.

1. Introduction

The emphasis on building collaborative/co-operative environments has brought the issue of communication to light. Without a means to share ideas, etc. we cannot work together. As evidence shows [1,2,3], conflicts happen through dialogue, and are inevitable to group problem solving. Moreover, they can also be beneficial to it [1].

If well employed, conflicts can be a tool to articulate solutions, to avoid groupthink and to increase group productivity. However, conflicts that escalate to the personal level will probably weaken group cohesiveness, thus hindering further interactions.

The inevitability of conflicts and their potential to help increase group productivity has generated a lot of research in different areas (Sociology, Psychology, Education, Distributed Artificial Intelligence, etc). In the Educational scenario, there are different lines of work that tackle conflicts as an important part of group problem solving, and as a vehicle of cognitive change. For instance, Joiner's work [4] presents a model of conflicting interactions based on Doise and Mugny's theory of socio-cognitive conflicts [5]. As a result of his analysis, he has pointed out some issues to be

---

1 Sponsored by CAPES-Brazil

considered in Computer Supported Collaborative Learning Environments (CSCLE) design. Other authors (for example, see [6,7]) have also investigated conflicts in CSCL interactions, aiming at analysing the ongoing collaboration process.

The issue of conflicts has been considered from various perspectives. However, there is no research that aims at using conflicts to foster *productive interactions* in *computer-based environments*. Moreover, in spite of the models of conflicting interactions in Distributed Artificial Intelligence (DAI) there is not an executable model of *meta-cognitive* conflicts that would allow a CSCW/CSCL system to detect their occurrence and take action to provoke *reflection* and *articulation*.

In this paper, we will present a computational model of *Meta-Cognitive* conflicts (encountered in group planning), with a practical example of its use. The model is based on our categorisation of conflicts in such a situation.

This paper is organised as follows: section 2 describes our classification of *Meta-Cognitive Conflicts* and the computational model generated from that; section 3 presents our computer system, *MArCo*, describing its architecture and giving an example of its usage. Section 4 presents our conclusions and ideas for further work.

2. The Classification and Modelling of *Meta-Cognitive* Conflicts

In order to reach the goal stated above, we investigated the types of conflicts that occur in group interactions. As a result of the empirical investigation described below (for further details, see [8]), we arrived at the classification of conflicts presented in section 2.2. The model derived from these findings is shown in section 2.3.

2.1 The Empirical Investigation

The main goal of the investigation was to find out what kind of *Meta-Cognitive* conflicts occur between peers in group planning interactions. For this experiment, we chose a PERT/CPM problem. PERT/CPM graphs [9], allow us to build a network model of a project, given the activities that compose it along with their duration.

The experiment was carried out with three pairs of students. Two were of postgraduates, and the third was formed by one MEd student and an undergraduate.

None of the subjects had prior knowledge about PERT/CPM. Upon arrival, they were given information sheets about the technique. Subjects' questions (about the technique or the vocabulary) were answered before they started solving the problem.

Each pair was given pen and paper, and asked to build a common problem solution. Their dialogue was tape-recorded and later transcribed. The observer only intervened in the discussion when explicitly asked to clarify some doubt.

Besides yielding the conflict categorisation described on section 2.2 (as well as the computational model), the experiment also gave us a good insight into the sorts of dialogue moves people use when talking about *Meta-Cognitive Conflicts*.

2.2 The Conflict Categorisation

From our point of view, conflicts are the last stage of a three-phase process:
- We start with a *difference of views* – when agents have different views about something, but have not yet communicated them to each other;
- After that we have a *disagreement* – where the agents inform each other about their inconsistent views, but a discussion over them does not follow;
- Finally, we have a *conflict* - if the agents involved also try to convince the other about their own points of view.

By distinguishing between *disagreements* and *conflicts* we want to ensure that the *mediator* will only intervene when there is potential for *reflection* and *articulation*. Let us now present our categorisation of the conflicts in group planning interactions:
- *Non task-related or social conflicts* are related to the social roles and positions of the group members. A conflict about group leadership is classified in this category.
- *Task-related conflicts* can be further divided into:
    - ❖ *Belief conflicts* are about the domain under discussion. They relate to the two lower levels of the DORMOBILE framework [10] – namely *Domain* (facts) and *Reasoners* (rules of inference in the domain). Belief Conflicts have been extensively investigated (e.g. [11]);
    - ❖ *Contextual conflicts* relate to defining what exactly is the problem being solved. In fact, *Contextual Conflicts* are a specialisation of *Belief Conflicts*. Contextual beliefs represent constraints of the problem. For example, when planning the release of a toy for Christmas sales, the belief that the toy has to be ready by November is contextual. The distinction between the two types of conflicts is also due to the evidence (see [12]) that significant parts of group problem solving dialogues are about establishing the model of the problem.
    - ❖ *Meta-Cognitive conflicts* correspond to the two upper levels of the DORMOBILE framework (*Monitoring* and *Reflection*). They can be divided into:
        - *Reflectors Conflicts:* "How do we choose our intentions/goals/orderings?"
        - *Intention Conflicts:* "Which steps do we take to solve the problem?"
        - *Ordering Conflicts:* "How do we organise our steps?"
        - *Goal Conflicts:* which can be divided into
            - ⇒ Goal Definition Conflicts: "What are we trying to achieve?"
            - ⇒ Goal Achievement Conflict: "Have we achieved it?"

Having described our categorisation, we will now present a computational model of Conflicts. More examples of the conflicts can be found in [8].

2.2 A Computational Model of Conflicts

Based on our empirical investigation, as well as on some existing *DAI* models of conflicting interactions (e.g. [13,14,15,16]) we have built a *Belief-Desires-Intentions (BDI)* conflict model. The choice of a *BDI* approach was mainly due to the mapping that can be drawn between the levels of the DORMOBILE and the mental states.

The attitudes towards the problem-solving process (*collaboration* and *co-operation*) influence the changes on the plan being built. In the *co-operation* case, where the task is split in different parts, the incidence and scope of conflicts can be much smaller than in the *collaboration* case. Thus, let us define these two attitudes:

Suppose that two agents, x and y, are trying to achieve a goal p together. Agent x is considered engaged in a *one-way collaboration* with y when:

$$One\_way\_Collab (x\ y\ p) = def [Bel (x\ \Diamond p) \wedge Bel (x(Bel\ y\ \Diamond p))] \wedge [Intend(x\ strategy_x(p)) \wedge Expects(x\ Intend(y\ strategy_y(p)))]$$

In this case, x believes that p will eventually be true, and that y has the same belief. Also, x intends to provide part of the problem's solution, and expects y to provide the rest. However, it might be the case that y is not engaged in the *collaboration*.

If both parties are engaged in the process, we have a *mutual collaboration* case, defined below:

$$M\_Collab(x\ y\ p) = def\ One\_way\_Collab (x\ y\ p) \wedge One\_way\_Collab (y\ x\ p)$$

The *co-operative* case is defined in a similar way. The distinction between the cases is that in the collaborative case, there is an interleaving of $strategy_x(p)$ and $strategy_y(p)$ to form the problem solution, whereas in the co-operative case, $strategy_x(p)$ and $strategy_y(p)$ complement each other.

Let us now analyse a definition of strategies. We define a strategy to be a consistent ordered set of intentions to achieve a goal. This set is built according to the *Context* of the problem. To make matters clearer consider example 1:

```
Example 1: Suppose that agent x has the following
problem: it has to go shopping, and has to get some
food from the supermarket, a book, some clothes and has
to be back home by 12. So, let
A = {go to the Market}
B = {get clothes}
C = {get the book},
be the steps it intends to accomplish in its trip.
So, Set_of_Intentions = {A, B, C}
Goal = {Be back home by 12 with shopping done}
Context = {book store is the farthest, mall is close to
supermarket}
Due to relative distances of each place, x decides to
do A, B, and C, according to the following ordering:
Ordering_Relation = {<C, B>, <C, A>, <B, A>}
```

In our model, a strategy is defined as:

Strategy (Agent Goal) = *{Agent, Set_of_Intentions, Ordering_Relation, Context, Goal}*. The *Ordering_Relation* is a set of pairs of intentions $<i_1, i_2>$, where i_1 comes before i_2 in the strategy being built.

Thus, in Example 1, x's strategy to go shopping is represented as follows:

Strategy(x, be home by 12 with shopping) = {x, {A, B, C}, {<C, B>, <C, A>, <B, A>},{book store is the farthest, mall close to supermarket}, {Be home by 12}}

A *task-related conflict* about a sentence *s* is defined as:[2]

Task-related conflict (x y s) = def Bel_conflict(x y s) ∨ Context_conflict(x y s) ∨ M_c conflict(x y s).

A *Belief Conflict* is defined as:

Bel_Conflict (x y s) = def [Bel (x s) ∧ Bel (x (Bel y ¬s)) ∧ Intend (x ◊(Bel y s))]

Let us make a distinction between *conflicts* and *mutual conflicts*. *X* is in conflict with *y* about *s* (Conflict (x y s)) if *x* believes that *y* has got a different view about *s*, and intends to convince *y* to adopt his/her view. However, *x*'s beliefs about *y* may be wrong, and thus the conflict situation might generate confusion. On the other hand, *mutual* conflicts (corresponding to the notion presented in section 2.2) have more potential for *reflection* and *articulation*. A *mutual conflict* is defined below:

Mutual_Conflict(x y s) = def Conflict(x y s) ∧ Conflict(y x s).

The distinction between conflicts and mutual ones is due to the fact that they require different mediation strategies. It is also valid for all the conflict types in this section. For instance, a Mutual Belief_Conflict is defined as:

Mutual_Bel_Conflict(x y s) = def Bel_Conflict(x y s) ∧ Bel_Conflict (y x s). [3]

A *context_conflict* is a special case of a *belief conflict* as mentioned in section 2.2. Now, let us define *Meta-Cognitive* conflicts:

M_c conflict (x y s) = def Intention_Conflict(x y s) ∨ Ordering_Conflict(x y s) ∨ Goal_Conflict(x y s). ∨ Ref_Conflict(x y s)

And an intention conflict is defined as:

Intention_Conflict (x y s) = def [Intend (x s) ∧ Bel (x (Intend y ¬s)) ∧ Intend (x ◊(Intend (y s)))]

Now, suppose that *x* and *y* have the following strategies:

Strategy (x,goal) = {x, Set_of_Intentions, OR_x, Context, goal}
Strategy (y,goal) = {y, Set_of_Intentions, OR_y, Context, goal}

Then an *ordering conflict* is defined as follows:

Ordering_Confict (x y $<i_1\ i_2>$) = *def* ($<i_1\ i_2>$ ∈ OR_x ∧ Bel(x,($<i_1\ i_2>$ ∉ OR_y)) ∧ Intend (x $<i_1\ i_2>$ ∈ OR_y)

As defined on section 2.2 a goal conflict can be of two types: (1) a *Goal Definition* :

Goal-def_Conflict (x y p) = def [Goal (x p) ∧ Bel(x (Goal (y ¬p))) ∧ Intend (x ◊(Goal(y p)))];

---

[2] For the sake of simplicity, we are dealing here with the *2-student* case. However, the definitions presented can be generalised for *n-student* case.

[3] Due to questions of space, from now on, we will present only the conflict definitions, leaving the *mutual* cases for the reader.

and (2) a *Goal Achievement* conflict, defined as follows: Suppose that x and y had previously agreed on a goal p, and, at a given instant t, x believes that p is true (goal achieved) and y does not. Thus,

Goal-ach_Conflict $(x\ y\ p)=$ def Bel_Conflict $(x\ y\ p) \wedge$ goal $(\{x,y\},p)$ at instant t.

Where *goal ({x,y}, p)* means that x and y have previously agreed on goal p. A reflector_conflict is defined as:

$$Ref\_Conflict\ (x\ y\ s) = def\ [Reflector(x\ s) \wedge Bel\ (x\ (Reflector(\ y\ \neg s))) \wedge Intend$$
$$(x\ \Diamond(Reflector(\ y\ s)))]$$

3. The Conflict Model Put to Use – the *MArCo* System

MArCo's (Artificial Conflict Mediator, in Portuguese) reasoning mechanism is based on the conflict model presented. The domain chosen for its implementation is PERT-CPM graphs, also used in our experiment. *MArCo* has a Java-based distributed interface, which hosts the interaction between the group members. The interface (Fig. 1) communicates with a Prolog server and is divided into three regions:

1. The *Graph Region* – has a graph window where the group builds its common graphical solution. The *Logic and Constraints Window (LCW)* provides a tool for the discussion of constraints and goals of the problem being solved. Terms in the *LCW* use logical and time sequencing operators found on the menus beside it.
2. The *Active Members Window* –when a group member logs onto a discussion, its identification goes to the *active members' window*.
3. The *Dialogue Region* - to facilitate the analysis of the dialogue and the mapping of the utterances onto *BDI* attitudes, we have adopted a dialogue game approach [18]. Thus, each contribution to the dialogue is made by a *dialogue move* plus its contents (expressed either in the graph window or in the *LCW*). It also contains the *Dialogue Record (DR)* window, where the history of the interaction is kept.

Once a member finishes her/his utterance, s/he presses *Submit*. The contribution is then sent to the *DR* and to the Prolog Server, which has three processes communicating – a *dialogue processor*, that receives utterances, maps them onto the *BDI* attitudes, and calls the *maintainer* to update group and individual models (GM and IM, respectively), and the *mediator*. Fig. 2 shows *MArCo*'s architecture.

MArCo's mediator observes the dialogue looking for conflicts and acts if necessary. It uses three levels of mediation. On the simplest level, it only informs the group that some sort of conflict has occurred (as shown in Fig. 4). In the next level, the *mediator* informs the group that a conflict has occurred and then checks if any of the participants is saying something inconsistent with her/his (or the group) model. If that is the case the *mediator* asks the respective member to elaborate on this "change of mind", attempting to provoke reflection. In the third level the system also suggests actions that can lead to more refined solutions (e.g. build up solutions involving more members of the group). In order to do so, it draws on the group characteristics, a model of strategic changes and a model of the task.

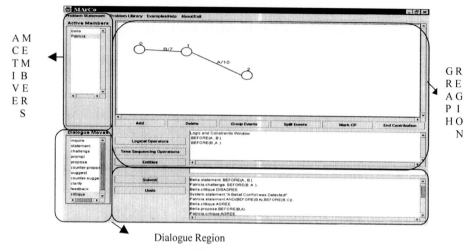

Dialogue Region

Fig. 1. *MArCo*'s Interface.

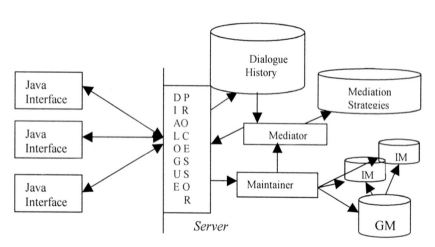

Fig. 2.- *MArCo*'s Architecture.

3.1 An Example of MArCo's Usage

This section shows an interaction using *MArCo*. The problem discussed is shown in Fig. 3. At the beginning, the GM and the IM for both agents (P-IM and B-IM) are empty. The IM consists of four sets of attitudes: *Domain Beliefs*, *Intentions*, *Goals* and *Reflectors*. Whilst the first three directly represent the strategic components, *Reflectors* account for meta-attitudes. The GM consists of the same sets of attitudes, plus a set of group member's characteristics (leader, follower, outspoken, shy, reflector, actor) that are assigned to group members according to the quantity and type of their contributions. Both the IMs and GM are updated as the interaction flows.

In (I)(Fig. 4), after Bella's utterance is passed to the dialogue processor, it is mapped onto attitude (bel_dom (Bella, BEFORE (A, B))), before the *Maintainer* is called. It adds the new attitude to B-IM, and then looks for inconsistencies within B-IM. If it finds any, a Belief Revision is carried out in B-IM. When this is done, the *Maintainer* checks if any new beliefs can be derived. We have used *modus ponens* as the inference rule for this operation.

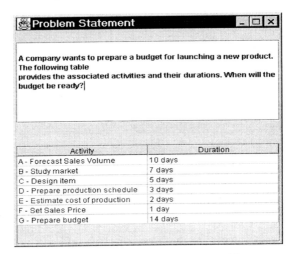

Fig. 3. A Sample PERT-CPM Problem.

Patricia's following move is a *challenge*, which implies her disbelief in the previous statement (a belief in its negation) and a belief in BEFORE (A, B). Consequently, the *Maintainer* updates P-IM, by bel_dom (Patricia, not(BEFORE (A, B))) and bel_dom (Patricia, BEFORE (B, A)).

By analysing the history of the dialogue, the *mediator* finds a *disagreement* (represented in the dialogue by a *statement* followed by a *challenge* about the same focus), and asserts:

disagreement ([Patricia, Bella], Before(B,A), [B,A], bel_dom),

meaning that a bel_dom disagreement between the two agents, with focus ([B,A]), has occurred. At this point, B_IM and P_IM contain the following beliefs:

- B_IM: bel_dom(Bella, BEFORE(A,B))
- P_IM:bel_dom(Patricia, not(BEFORE(A,B))), bel_dom(Patricia, BEFORE(B,A))

Excerpt (II) in figure 4 shows the follow up from (I), where Bella disagrees with the last utterance. Then the Maintainer updates B-IM by:

bel_dom (Bella, not(BEFORE (B,A))).

At this point, the *mediator* detects another *belief disagreement*, and thus asserts:

disagreement ([Bella, Patricia], not(BEFORE (A,B)), [A,B],bel_dom).

Upon detecting a disagreement, the mediator checks if there has been another disagreement of the same kind, involving the same agents and focus. If that is the case, a conflict is detected and an intervention is generated. In this case, the *mediator* has just pointed out that a belief conflict was detected, as shown in figure 4.

In (III) Patricia offers further information about activities A and B. Bella then agrees with it, thus settling the conflict, and bringing the IM's to the state shown below.

- B-IM: bel_dom(Bella, (BEFORE(B,A))), bel_dom(Bella,(BEFORE(B,C)))
- P-IM: bel_dom(Patricia,   not(BEFORE(A,B))),   bel_dom(Patricia, (BEFORE(B,A))), bel_dom(Patricia,(BEFORE(B,C))).

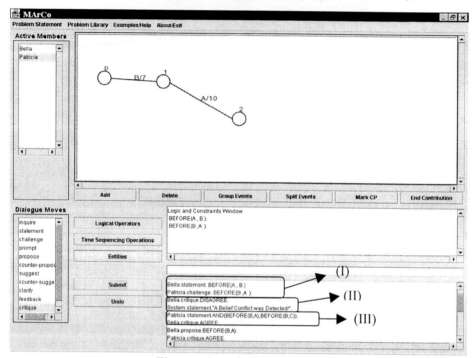

Fig. 4. A Sample Interaction.

4. Conclusions and Further Work

In this paper we have explored the idea that it is possible to use conflicts that occur during group problem solving to provoke *reflection* and *articulation* of the solution being built. In order to show that the idea is feasible, we have built an artificial *mediator*, capable of detecting conflicts and taking action whenever necessary.

In order to build the mediator, we first classified the conflicts in group problem solving situations. The classification served as a basis for a computational model of conflicts, and gave us insight on how mediate conflicting situations.

To illustrate these ideas, we have built a computer system, *MArCo*, containing the artificial *mediator*. It bases its reasoning on the history of the interaction, individual and group models, as well as on the strategic changes triggered by the conflicts.

We intend to compare the usage of the *mediator* with three different levels of mediation. Our hypothesis is that the more informed the mediation, the more useful it will be. With the feedback obtained from this comparative study, we will refine our models, aiming at extending them to different domains.

References

1. Putnam, L.L.: Conflict in Group Decision-Making. In: Hirokawa, R.Y. and Poole, M.S. (eds.): Communication and Group Decision-Making, Sage Publications, (1986), 175-196
2. Easterbrook, S.M., Beck, E.E., Goodlet, J.S., Plowman, L., Sharples, M. and Wood, C.C.: A Survey of Empirical Studies of Conflict. In Easterbrook, S. (ed.):(1992) in *CSCW: Cooperation or Conflict?*, Computer-Supported Cooperative Work series, Diaper, D. and Sanger, C. (eds.) Springer-Verlag, (1992) 1-68
3. Robbins, S.P., Organizational Behaviour: Concepts, Controversies and Applications, London, Prentice-Hall, (1996)
4. Joiner, R.: The Negotiation of Dialogue Focus: An Investigation of Dialogue Processes in Joint Planning in a Computer Based Task. In: Claire O'Malley (ed.): *Computer Supported Collaborative Learning*, Nato ASI Series, (1995) 203-222
5. Doise, W., and Mugny, G.: *The Social Development of the Intellect*, International Series in Experimental Social Psychology, vol. 10, Pergamon Press, (1984)
6. Barros, B. and Verdejo, M.F.: An approach to Analyse Collaboration when Shared Structured Workspaces are Used for Carrying Out Group Learning Processes. In: Lajoie, S.P. and Vivet, M. (eds.), *Proceedings of the IX International Conference in Artificial Intelligence in Education (AIED'99)*, (1999) 449-456
7. Quignard, M. and Baker, M.: Favouring Modellable Computer-Mediated Argumentative Dialogue in Collaborative Problem Solving Situations. In: Lajoie, S.P. and Vivet, M. (eds.) *Proceedings of the IX International Conference in Artificial Intelligence in Education (AIED'99)*, (1999) 129-137
8. Tedesco, P. and Self, J.A:. *Towards a computational model of meta-cognitive conflicts: a preliminary investigation.* Technical Report 98/28, Computer Based Learning Unit, University of Leeds (1998).
9. Winston, W.L: *Operations Research – Applications and Algorithms*, Second Edition, PWS-Kent Publishing Company (1991)
10. Self, J.A.: Dormorbile: a Vehicle for Metacognition. In T.W. Chan and J. A. Self (eds.) *Emerging Computer Technologies in Education,* Charlottesville AACE (1995)
11. Gärdenfors, P: Belief Revision: An Introduction. In Gärdenfors, P. (ed.): *Belief Revision,* Cambridge Treats in Theoretical Computer Science 29, Cambridge University Press, (1992), 1-28
12. Ferguson,G., Allen, J., and Miller, B.: TRAINS-95: Towards a Mixed Initiative Planning Assistant. In *Proceedings of the Third Conference of Artificial Intelligence Planning Systems (AIPS-96),* Edinburgh, Scotland, (1996) 70-77
13. Galliers, J.R.: A Theoretical Framework for Computer Models of Cooperative Dialogue, Acknowledging Multi-Agent Conflict, PhD Thesis, Open University (1989)
14. Jennings, N.R.: Controlling Cooperative problem Solving in Industrial Multi-Agent Systems Using Joint Intentions. In *Artificial Intelligence*, volume 75, (1995) 195-240
15. Grosz, B.J., and Kraus, S.: Collaborative Plans for Complex Group Action. In *Artificial Intelligence*, 86, (1996) 269-357
16. Parsons, S.D., Sierra, C.A., Jennings, N.R.: Agents that reason and negotiate by arguing. In *Journal of Logic and Computation*, vol. 8 (3), (1998), 261-292
17. Pilkington, R. M.: Dialogue games in support of qualitative reasoning. In Journal of Computer Assisted Learning: Special Issue on Qualitative Reasoning. 14, (1998), 308-320

LeCS: A Collaborative Case Study System

Marta C. Rosatelli[1], John A. Self[2], and Marcello Thiry[3]

[1] Department of Computing and Statistics, Federal University of Santa Catarina
Cx.P. 476, Florianópolis-SC, 88040-900, Brazil
martacr@inf.ufsc.br
http://www.inf.ufsc.br/~martacr/english/index.html
[2] Computer Based Learning Unit, University of Leeds
Leeds, LS2 9JT, UK
jas@cbl.leeds.ac.uk
[3] University of Vale do Itajaí, Campus São José
Rodovia SC 407, km 4, São José-SC, 88122-000, Brazil
thiry@sj.univali.br

Abstract. Research on Intelligent Tutoring Systems has much to contribute to distance learning applications. Recently the distance learning area has experienced an increasing demand for the development of applications that make use of the new information and communication technologies (e.g., the web) as the medium for delivering courses. Intelligent distance learning can supply this demand and also provide real-time support to the distance learning process through the incorporation of ITS techniques. In this paper we describe LeCS – a collaborative case study system. LeCS supports web-based distance learning from case studies, allowing collaborative learning between a group of learners that is geographically dispersed. It provides the necessary tools to carry out the case solution development and accomplishes functions that altogether assist the learning process.

1 Introduction

As a result of the possibilities allowed by the new technologies we observe a rapid growth in computer-based applications for distance learning. Most of the systems developed focus on providing tools for the teachers to design distance courses (e.g., WebCT, Lotus LearningSpace) and/or on the distance course management (e.g., [1]). However, we believe that providing real-time support to the distant learners might be of greater relevance from an educational point of view.

In [2] we proposed a World Wide Web (web)-based distance learning from case studies model that allows a group of learners to work on a case study at a distance. This model consists of an application of the case method to distance learning that makes uses of Intelligent Tutoring Systems (ITS) elements.

In this sense, research on ITS has much to contribute to distance learning applications. Recently the distance learning area has experienced an increasing demand for the development of applications that make use of the new information and communication technologies (e.g., the web) as the medium for delivering courses. Intelligent distance learning can supply this demand and also provide real-time support to the distance learning process through the incorporation of ITS techniques. Thus, the work presented in this paper, besides introducing the case study element that is particularly novel in ITS research, shares characteristics with other approaches used in the area: agent-based ITSs (e.g., [3]), work on collaboration (e.g., [4]), and work on supporting the problem solving process at a distance (e.g. [5]).

In this paper we describe LeCS (Learning from Case Studies) – a collaborative case study system that can be characterised as an intelligent distance learning system. LeCS supports web-based distance learning from case studies and allows collaborative learning from case studies between geographically dispersed learners. It provides tools to carry out the case solution development and accomplishes functions that assist the learning process.

The paper is organised as follows. Section 2 gives an overview of LeCS. Section 3 details LeCS architecture. Section 4 describes the current stage of LeCS implementation and the next stages of tests. Section 5 presents our conclusions.

2 LeCS Overview

LeCS is a collaborative case study system that supports learning from case studies in distance education. The learning scenario for LeCS is a group of learners that is geographically dispersed, enrolled in a distance course, on a discipline where the case method is applied (e.g., engineering, medicine, business, etc.) [6].

Learning from case studies is an educational method, typically used in the business schools to train the students in disciplines that contain open-ended problems, which present complex, realistic situations, and that demand cognitive flexibility to cope with them. The case method is used when the situated nature of cognition in the learning process and/or learning in ill-structured domains is required [7]. The method application in the traditional classroom consists roughly of presenting a case study that introduces a problem situation to a group of learners who are supposed to discuss the case and find a solution to it. The role of the case instructor is to guide the process by which the group of learners explore the case and develop the case solution.

LeCS was developed based on the recommendations derived from an empirical qualitative study that we carried out with pairs of subjects [2]. The aim of this study was to help provide support to the case study activity over the web with: (1) the use of text based/graphical hypermedia resources to present a case study and to lead the learner through the system use; (2) the use of tools to carry out discussions and group activities; (3) the combination of both off-line and on-line case study activities, as they usually take longer than other learning activities. Thus, in this empirical study we simulated a learning scenario where a pair of subjects at a distance were provided with a collaborative learning environment and required to collaborate in order to solve a case study.

The collaborative learning environment was based on Habanero [8], a collaborative system that includes a client, a server, and a set of applications. Among those we used the browser, the chat, and the collaborative text editor. The browser was used to access the web pages that presented the case study contents and the steps of the approach to guide the case solution development. The text editor was used to answer the questions posed in the steps. The chat was where the case discussion took place.

LeCS provides a similar set of tools for working collaboratively on a case study solution and in addition accomplishes functions that altogether support the learners during the development of this solution. The tools are a browser, a chat, a text editor, and a representational tool. The support LeCS provides is achieved by representing the solution path taken by the learners and by making interventions regarding certain aspects of the case solution development: the time the learners spend on each step of the Seven Steps approach [9]; the learners degree of participation in the case discussion; the misunderstandings the learners might have about the case study; the coordination of the group work; and the accomplishment of the steps activities.

Figure 1 shows LeCS user interface which displays a *pull down menu,* and the following areas starting from the upper left, clockwise: *participants list, browser, solution graphical representation, text editor, chat* and *system interventions.*

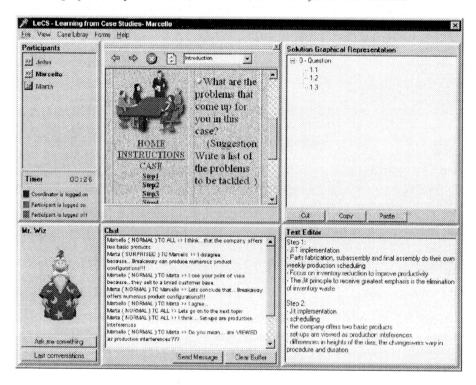

Fig. 1. LeCS User Interface

2.1 Web-Based Distance Learning From Case Studies

Web-based distance learning from case studies is our model of how the learning from case studies method can be supported in a computational environment, in a distance learning context. Such a model is embedded in LeCS design.

LeCS design is based on the Seven Steps Approach [9]. This approach can be described as a methodology that proposes that the case study solution be developed step-by-step. It guides the case solution development, splitting it into parts that, from a computational point of view, have a manageable grain size of information. In that way the system is able to reason about each part that is added to the case solution as the learners proceed towards the case solution. The outcomes of each step can be represented by the system so that it is capable to interact with the learners, providing support and feedback during the case solution process.

Each step of the approach has its own goal and suggests an activity to be carried out by the learners in order to achieve such goal. In order to demand from the learners the accomplishment of the activities we have associated each step to a question. Those questions were chosen from a set of examples used by case study instructors in the traditional classroom [10]. In order to choose the appropriate questions to each step, the categories were matched to each step goal and required activity.

Table 1 presents an overview of the steps sequence, stating each step goal, exemplifying the activities, and the questions associated with each of them.

Table 1. The Seven Steps approach (adapted from [9]), activities and questions

The Seven Steps	Activities	Questions
Step1. Understanding the situation	Relate	What do you think are the relevant pieces of information presented by the case?
Step2. Diagnosing problem areas	List problems	What are the problems that come up for you in this case?
Step3. Generating alternative solutions	List solutions	Would you please list the alternative solutions to the problems?
Step4. Predicting outcomes	List outcomes	Can you tell what can happen as a result of each action?
Step5. Evaluating alternatives	List pros and cons	Can you list the pros and cons of each outcome?
Step6. Rounding out the analysis	Choose	What is your choice among the alternative solutions?
Step7.Communicating the results	Present the case solution	What is your answer to the question posed by the case?

2.2 LeCS Dynamics

LeCS includes a server that hosts sessions and a client that interacts with sessions. A session is associated with a group of students working collaboratively on the solution of a case study. The clients run on the students' machines and therefore there are as many clients running as the number of participants on a session. The server can run on one of the students' machine or alternatively on another machine. LeCS was implemented in the Delphi language.

To begin working with LeCS the learners have to register in order to join a session, i.e., they register as a member of a certain group that will work on a given case study. As a result, among the case studies included in the case library (the set of cases modelled in the system), a particular case study is enabled, whereas the others are disabled during the session. Also, the set of pages and questions relative to each of the Seven Steps are made available.

The group of learners should also choose one of its members to be the group coordinator. The coordinator is responsible for filling in the forms with the group joint answers to the step questions. In this way the contributions gleaned from the various participants regarding the step answers are integrated into the joint answers. The forms are then disabled to all the group members except the coordinator. However, at any time during the solution process the group can change its coordinator.

After joining the session the learners start working by browsing the web pages that include the instructions for how to proceed to use the system, the case study contents, and the steps of the approach. Thus, in all the steps described in section 2.1 the following procedure takes place:

- First, the learners individually answer the question posed in the step. This usually is carried out off-line, asynchronously, using the text editor tool. In this phase, individual *learning* takes place.
- Then, the learners work collaboratively and discuss to reach a consensus in order to have a group joint answer to the step question. The starting point for the discussion is the differences or similarities between their individual answers. These can be copied from text editor and pasted into the chat in order to be made available to the group. This *collaborative learning* phase is carried out on-line, in a synchronous mode.
- Once the group reaches an agreement about what to respond to the present question, the group coordinator fills in the form with the *step answer*. This step answer represents the accomplishment of the activity demanded in the step. The system reasoning is based on this group answer rather than on the individual ones.
- After that, the group move on to the next step, where the previous procedure (individual learning, collaborative learning, and group agreement on an answer) takes place again. By proceeding sequentially through the steps, the learners will be guided to the case study solution.

2.3 LeCS Functions

The support LeCS provides to the learners during the case solution development consists of the solution representation presented on the user interface and the different kinds of interventions it makes. Below we describe those functions.

LeCS dynamically generates a knowledge representation, a tree data structure [11], of the case solution as developed so far by the learners, according to the Seven Steps approach. The input for the generation of this tree are the components sentences with which the group coordinator fills in the forms. The root of the solution tree corresponds to the question posed by the case. The levels of the tree represent each of the Seven Steps. Each node on a given level refers to a component sentence of the joint group answer to that step question. At a given step, the system adds one level to the tree, generating it from the expansion of the nodes on the previous level. The tree final state is represented then for all (ideally) alternative solutions that can be generated through the Seven Steps approach.

The links between the nodes (arcs) are made by LeCS using a rule-based algorithm that define our heuristics to build the solution tree. It compares the sentences on a given level with the sentences on the previous level in order to determine how the link between a node to its parent node is obtained. The comparison is made based on keywords, which are selected by the system from the sentences on the higher level that is being compared [12].

The solution tree graphical representation is displayed to the learners on LeCS user interface. All the group participants see the same representation. The graphical elements in this window are editable by the learners when they disagree with the system reasoning represented in the tree (e.g., when the link made between a node to its parent node is not what the learners meant in their textual answer). The aim of this graphical representation is to make the learners aware of the solution path taken by the group and to facilitate choosing the best envisaged solution.

In addition, LeCS makes different kinds of interventions during the solution process development that, in a certain way, resembles the procedures of the case instructor in the traditional classroom. Such interventions concern:

- *Timing*: LeCS intervenes when the group exceed the time limits established for the solution regarding collaborative learning (on-line work). This control is made at every step.
- *Participation*: LeCS identifies a low degree of participation in one or more learners during the case discussion and makes interventions inviting the learner(s) to participate. This is accomplished through the monitoring of the learners contributions in the chat per step.
- *Case-Specific Utterance Patterns*: The interventions that LeCS makes regarding case-specific utterances are based on the system knowledge about the case study, which is represented as constraints [13] in LeCS domain knowledge base. This kind of representation is appropriate to the identification of case-specific utterance patterns that characterise a learner misunderstanding the case study contents. In order to initiate the intervention LeCS checks among the sentences of the group joint answer to the step questions (which in a final analysis are case-specific utterance patterns already extracted from the case discussion dialogue) for any violations of the constraints that were modelled. When a violation is found LeCS intervenes stating to the group the correct sentence. The constraints are modelled based on an analysis of the case study text from the point of view of the case instructor, regarding what kind of misunderstandings it could originate. Figure 2 shows the user interface LeCS provides for the case instructor modelling a case study.

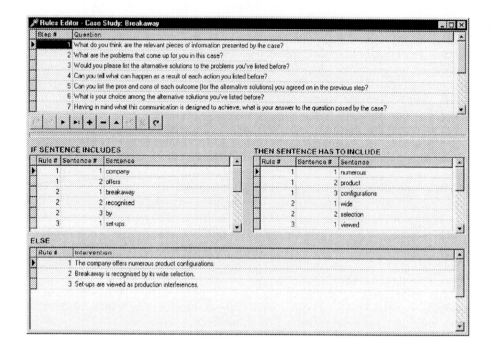

Fig. 2. LeCS user interface for the case instructor modelling a case study

- *Group Coordination*: In order to allow the coordination of the group activities through the Seven Steps by LeCS, when starting a session, the group should define a co-ordinator who will be in charge of filling in the forms with the group joint answers to the step questions. Thus, once the coordinator fills in the form of a particular step question, and then moves on to the next step, LeCS "knows" in which step the group should be working on. That is, the group coordination is done based on the group coordinator actions. He/she in a certain way defines to LeCS the pace in which the group proceeds in the solution development. If any of the learners tries to access a page different to the one that the group is currently working on, LeCS intervenes, warning the learner that the group is working on another step.
- *Jumping a step*: Despite the fact that we do not constrain the learners in the sense of requiring them to complete all the steps, LeCS intervenes notifying the group if they jump a step during the solution development.

3 LeCS Architecture

LeCS agent-based architecture is organised in a federated system. The agents' communications are based on an Agent Communication Language (ACL) [14]. The messages exchanged among the agents use the KQML (Knowledge Query and Manipulation Language) format [15]. Figure 3 shows the agent-based architecture and communications structure used, which establishes that the communications does not happen directly between agents, but rather through a *facilitator*. The facilitator is a special program (implemented as a agent) that keeps the information about each agent on the system and is responsible for routing the messages, working as a broker. In addition, two local databases are implemented: in the first one the facilitator stores all the necessary information in order to route messages; in the second one it logs all the exchanged messages. LeCS architecture includes three classes of agents: interface agents, information agents, and advising agents. There is one information agent and one advising agent running on a session, but as many interface agents as many participants logged on.

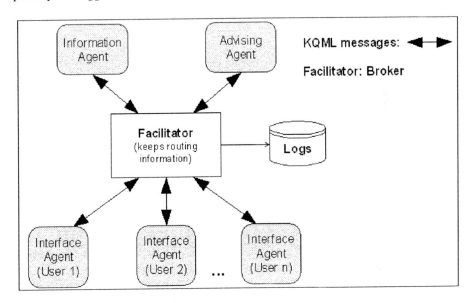

Fig. 3. LeCS agent-based architecture

Interface Agent. The interface agent can be characterised as an animated pedagogical agent [16] (cf. Figure 1). All the system interventions are presented through this agent. Besides, the interface agent stores information about the individual users: what is typed in the text editor, the number of contributions in the chat, the current step he/she is working on, the answer to each step question, and the time spent on each step (these last two are functions accomplished just by the interface agent of the group coordinator). Based on this information, the interface agent generates the interventions about timing, and participation. A resources database contains additional information: the agent's address, the name by which it is known, and its network mapping. A history database is implemented to log everything the interface agent does, including the communications with the user and the other agents. The information agent and the advising agent also have these same kinds of databases.

Information Agent. The information agent deals with the domain and the pedagogical knowledge. Both the interface and the advising agents can access the information agent. The information this agent stores is divided into two different categories: didactic material and knowledge bases. Didactic material consists of HTML pages, images, and text. The knowledge bases refer to the domain and to the representation of the case solution developed. This agent also stores the chat interactions.

Advising Agent. While the information agent has knowledge bases and databases access features, the advising agent has engines to reason about the user actions, and to recognise situations where some support is needed. The advising agent executes the algorithm to generate the solution tree representation with the information provided by the interface agent, and returns the representation to this agent. It controls the violations of the constraints with the information provided by the information agent. When applicable it generates an intervention about the learners' misunderstanding the case study, and send the request of an intervention to the interface agent. It also generates and requests interventions to the interface agent concerning the coordination of the group work and the jumping of a step.

4 Implementation and Evaluation

The first stage of LeCS implementation is concluded. Based on the recommendations of the empirical study that we carried out [2] we implemented a first prototype of the system. The next stage is to test LeCS with pairs of subjects in an experiment along the same lines of this empirical study. The intention is to test the system performance and the effectiveness of its tools and functions, particularly the case solution graphical representation, having the previous experiment as a parameter of comparison. Then, after making the necessary adjustments, the following stage is to test LeCS with more than one group of learners working simultaneously rather than only a pair of subjects at a time. The final evaluation stage is to use LeCS in a real distance learning context.

5 Conclusion

In this paper we described LeCS, a collaborative case study system that can be characterised as an intelligent distance learning system. LeCS implements web-based distance learning from case studies, supporting a group of learners working collaboratively on a case study at a distance. We introduced LeCS by presenting an overview of the system. We detailed our web-based distance learning from case studies model, explaining how a group of distant learners work with LeCS and what are the functions that LeCS accomplishes to provide support to the distant learners. Then, the LeCS agent-based architecture was described, showing its communications framework and kinds of agents. Finally LeCS current stage of implementation and evaluation was outlined.

Acknowledgments

This research was sponsored by CNPq-Brazil and received financial support from CAPES-Brazil.

References

1. Preston, J.A., Shackelford, R.: A System for Improving Distance and Large-Scale Classes. In: Proceedings of Third Annual Conference on Integrating Technology into Computer Science Education. ACM Press, New York, NY (1998) 193-198
2. Rosatelli, M.C., Self, J.A.: Supporting Distance Learning from Case Studies. In: Lajoie, S.P, Vivet, M. (eds.): Artificial Intelligence in Education. IOS Press, Amsterdam (1999) 457-564
3. Shaw, E., Ganeshan, R., Johnson, W.L., Millar, D.: Building a Case for Agent-Assisted Learning as a Catalyst for Curriculum Reform in Medical Education. In: Lajoie, S.P, Vivet, M. (eds.): Artificial Intelligence in Education. IOS Press, Amsterdam (1999) 509-516
4. Mühlenbrock, M., Tewissen, F., Hoppe, H.U.: A Framework System for Intelligent Support in Open Distributed Learning Environments. International Journal of Artificial Intelligence in Education 9 (1998) 256-274
5. Greer, J., McCalla, G., Cooke, J., Collins, J., Kumar, V., Bishop, A., Vassileva, J.: The Intelligent Helpdesk: Supporting Peer-Help in a University Course. In: Goettl, B.P., Halff, H.M., Redfield, C.L., Shute, V.J. (eds.): Intelligent Tutoring Systems. Springer-Verlag, Berlin (1998) 494-503
6. Christensen, C.R., Hansen, A.J.: Teaching with Cases at the Harvard Business School. In: Christensen, C.R., Hansen, A.J. (eds.): Teaching and the Case Method: Text, Cases, and Readings. Harvard Business School, Boston, MA (1987) 16-49
7. Shulman, L.S.: Toward a Pedagogy of Cases. In: Shulman, J.H. (ed.): Case Methods in Teacher Education. Teachers College Press, Columbia University, New York, NY (1992) 1-30
8. NCSA: The NCSA Habanero Users Guide. Available at http://havefun.ncsa.uiuc.edu/habanero/Docs/ index.html (1998)
9. Easton, G.: Learning from Case Studies. Prentice Hall, London (1982)
10. Meyers, C., Jones, T.B.: Promoting Active Learning: Strategies for the College Classroom. Jossey-Bass Publishers, San Francisco, CA (1993)
11. Russell, S.J., Norvig, P.: Artificial Intelligence: A Modern Approach. Prentice Hall, Englewood Cliffs, NJ (1995)
12. Rosatelli, M.C., Self, J.A.: An Empirical Qualitative Study on Collaborating at a Distance to Solve a Case Study. Technical Report 98/27, Computer Based Learning Unit, University of Leeds (1998)
13. Mitrovic, A., Ohlsson, S.: Evaluation of a Constraint-Based Tutor for a Database Language. International Journal of Artificial Intelligence in Education 10 (1999) 238-256
14. Genesereth, M.R., Ketchpel, S.P: Software Agents. Communications of the ACM 147 (1994) 48-53
15. Labrou, Y., Finin, T.: A Proposal for a New KQML Specification. Technical Report CS-97-03, Computer Science and Electrical Engineering Department, University of Maryland Baltimore County (1997)
16. Lester, J.C., Converse, S.A., Stone, B.A., Kahler, S.E., Barlow, S.T: Animated Pedagogical Agents and Problem-Solving Effectiveness: A Large-Scale Empirical Evaluation. In: du Boulay, B., Mizoguchi, R. (eds.): Artificial Intelligence in Education. IOS Press, Amsterdam (1997) 23-30

"Today's Talking Typewriter"
Supporting Early Literacy in a Classroom Environment

Frank Tewissen, Andreas Lingnau, H. Ulrich Hoppe

Dept. of Computer Science and Education, University of Duisburg, Lotharstr. 65,
D-47048 Duisburg, Germany
{tewissen, lingnau, hoppe}@informatik.uni-duisburg.de

Abstract. In this paper we present a specific phonics based approach to supporting early literacy. The application system is cooperative and embedded in a "computer-integrated classroom". It provides an interactive writing environment using a visual palette of letters associated with icons and synthetic speech feedback for the writing results. Ongoing developments enhance the intelligent support modules for the initiation of partner or group work and for the provision of context sensitive individual help.

1 Introduction

Today, early learning in primary schools is often characterized by learner-controlled work in rich and pleasant environments. The foundations of such rich and stimulating learning environments along with less teacher-centered classroom activities are rooted in the general ideas of modern pedagogy (e.g. [5]). Children work in different partner and group constellations in classroom environments that present a choice of different activities, tasks, and cooperation modes. Children select from these "menus", i.e. they choose the task that they want to carry out during a day. Teachers prepare these rich environments, assist, and manage the distributed and cooperative activities in the classroom.

Our project "Networked Interactive Media In Schools" (NIMIS, cf. [8]), as part of the European ESPRIT subprogram "Experimental School Environments", aims at supporting early learning in primary schools by augmenting the classroom physically, media-wise, and procedurally using networked digital media. So far, it is the most complete and consequent implementation of the idea of a "Computer-integrated Classroom" or CiC (cf. [2] for a first notion) that we have developed (see figure 1). As for the content of learning, the project is targeted at supporting literacy-oriented activities in the age group of 5-8 year old children.

Based on an integrated desktop environment for young children, three applications have been developed in the NIMIS project. One application ("T'rrific Tales") aims at supporting collaborative story telling in a cartoon format. A second application ("Teatrix", see [9]) aims at promoting collaborative acting in 3D scenarios. In the following we focus on a third application, "Today's Talking Typewriter" (T³). T³ provides a phonics-based learning environment for the acquisition of initial reading and writing skills by enabling children to freely and flexibly compose their own words. The T³ application and all NIMIS applications are embedded in distributed classroom activities, i.e. they are not designed as stand-alone tools but as customizable and user-adaptive tools in a collaborative setting.

2 Environment

The three different NIMIS classrooms aim at supporting scenarios that are common in the existing practice of the primary schools associated to the project. They envisage a smooth interplay of human and computer-mediated interaction. Environments and software have been designed following this rationale. The NIMIS software is flexible and usable in a variety of modes (by individuals, pairs or larger groups). Intelligent support can be easily plugged in as appropriate. The design also accounts for both teachers and pupils changing locations without losing the current context.

Fig. 1. In a NIMIS CiC: first graders and teachers in action

2.1 Embedment

Hardware and furniture in the NIMIS classrooms have been specially designed or selected under the consideration of existing classroom culture. A big interactive and height-adjustable screen replaces the chalkboard. Pen-based input facilities (interactive LC-displays integrated in special tables) provide intuitive interfaces for the children. The computers as such are almost invisible (covered or placed in a separate chamber), information technology is a means and not the subject of learning in this CiC framework.

Development of software applications for early learning needs to take into account open forms of learning and interacting, and the varied roles of teachers and learners in different contexts. We believe that the suitability and usability of educational software for in-classroom use is a central quality criterion. Based on this premise, we think that the development of computer support for rich collaborative scenarios should consider some central demands in a certain order of priority. It should

- be conceived as an integrated set of tool-like interactive applications conceptually embedded in existing classroom activities,
- be easily customizable by the teachers,
- have flexibly adjustable and robust cooperation modes,
- provide individual intelligent feedback, and
- provide intelligent support for group and partner work.

From a conceptual perspective, the tool character of an application is the first and most important design aspect. The software has to present itself similar to real physical learning material: ready to use, easy to use, and adaptable to the concrete context of usage. The design of software, hardware, and furniture ("roomware" cf. [11]) must be subordinate to curricular goals, and not vice versa.

3   Reading through Writing

T³ takes up and extends a well known method "Lesen durch Schreiben" ("Reading through Writing", henceforth abbreviated RtW), propagated mainly by J. Reichen (cf. [10]). This method is used in Switzerland and currently becomes more and more popular in Germany, too. The most important benefit of this method is, that children acquire reading and writing skills at their own pace, applying already existing knowledge about letters, phonemes, vowels, etc. Independent of the different stages of cognitive development of the children in a class, each child can immediately start to write words or even small sentences. I.e., the starting point is a synthetic activity with letter symbols, before acquiring the analytic skill of reading. In contrast to traditional approaches in which all children in one class learn one letter at a time, all phonetically necessary letters are provided from the very beginning. Letters are presented in a uniform way and associated with images that represent familiar objects. Without explicitly training reading skills, after an individually varying amount of time each child starts to read without any further external guidance. I.e., the synthetic activity of writing triggers the analytic activity of reading.

The RtW method has one important premise: it is restricted to languages with a regular phonetic spelling, like German, Turkish, or most of the Roman languages (except French). In a first phase, any phonetically correct spelling would be accepted. The phonetic regularity of the language guarantees that the deviation from the orthographically correct spelling is not too big and a later smooth transition is possible. An example from German would be the phonetic spelling "fogl" for the word "Vogel" (bird) in standard form. The transition to standard form would deal with general principles like the frequent f/v alternative and the identification of almost unpronounced e's. For English and French, the potential differences between phonetic and standard spelling are probably too big to successfully apply the method.

3.1 T³ Usage

The method in computerized form follows in its general interactions and support functions the non-computerized usage. Figure 2 shows typical RtW activity frames and associated support actions. According to the RtW method, children start to write words and later simple sentences by composing each word from single letters.

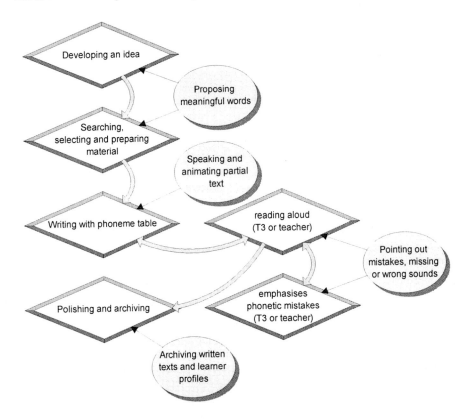

Fig. 2. Activity diagram of the usual RtW practice and means for support. The diagram consists of activity frames (*diamond shapes*), attached changes of activities (*thick arrows*), and descriptions of support actions (*elliptical shapes*)

The basic tool which is used by the children to recognize, write, and remember the shape of letters is a table made up by characters and images ("phoneme table", see figures 3 and 4). Children have to be sure about the word associated with the presented images and its pronunciation before they can start using the table. Each phonetically important letter is listed on the table with its upper and lowercase variants, accompanied by an image representing an object that begins with this letter.

Each phoneme in a word to be written is now checked against the phoneme-table. If an appropriate sound is found, the image itself or the associated letter is dragged from the table and dropped into a working window. This workspace replaces the normal paper material that would be used without computer support. Combined with pen-based input facilities, the handling is very natural (similar to magnetic letters or stamps). For example the children might be searching for an "i" sound. By scanning through the table they may find an image of an island. Once they recognize, that "island" starts with the sound "i" (which is also true for the German "i" in "Insel") they know that they have to copy the symbol, i.e. the letter right beside the image to represent this specific sound. Then, T3 provides the option to listen to the "product", i.e. the written word spoken by an artificial speaker (see 3.2).

Fig. 3. Visualization of a letter and the associated images that represent the variants of a German sound. In this case the images of the apple and the ant are standing for the short and long pronunciation of the letter "a"

Additionally, T³ allows teachers to prepare "theme pages" (cf. figure 4). Theme pages are composed of background images and prepared text in the writing workspace which stimulate children to chose words from a specific field (e.g. seasonal pictures etc.). With a simple click on the images, the corresponding word is spoken and transferred to the workspace. Children can compare the pronunciation of the correct word to the pronunciation of their own writing. Additionally, prepared words from theme pages enable more elaborate forms of intelligent support (see section 4).

3.2 Audible Feedback

One of the most important features of T³ is, to provide almost immediate audible feedback on the children's writing products. In the non-computerized classroom practice, the feedback cycle starts with an exact pronunciation of the writing provided by the teacher. Using T³, children can press the "speak" button whenever they wish to hear the complete text or a single word that they were most recently working on. T³ uses a Text To Speech (TTS) system to provide this kind of phonetic feedback. TTS systems are designed and implemented for speaking and emphasizing correctly written texts including punctuation in different languages. The requirements for a TTS system used by young children is different. Results of writing processes in T³ are initially single words which are in general not spelt correctly (e.g., often vowels are omitted). To adapt this to the built-in capabilities of the TTS system, T³ places a filter between the external representation of the word and the speech synthesis. It adds a minimal vocalization and modifies TTS parameters, like stress, speed, pitch or dynamic volume so as to pronounce the words in a phonetically correct way.

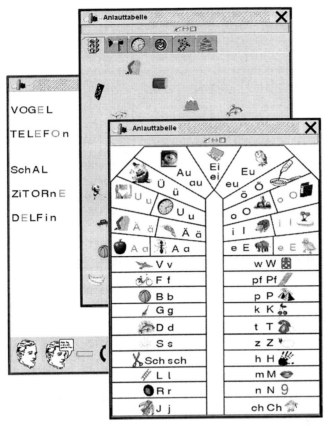

Fig. 4. Main parts of T³'s user interface. The German phoneme table using different colors for consonants, short, and long vowels (*on the right side*), a theme page with the visual representation of prepared words (*window in the middle*), and the result of a child in the writing workspace (*on the left*)

4 Intelligent Support

T³ supports learners and teachers in three different ways:

1. In the sense of model-based design, the T³ scenario is based on an explicit assessment of "traditional" classroom procedures. (The result of such an analysis has already been shown in figure 2.) A fundamental principle of NIMIS' design philosophy is that the application and its support functions should integrate seamlessly with these procedures without getting in the way. There is, e.g., a special supervisor's desktop which allows teachers to observe the current classroom scenario and even to provide new task material individually without disrupting ongoing learning activities.

2. T³ provides individualized support in two different modes with respect to how feedback is presented in the environment.

3. Following recent suggestions (cf. [4],[12]), T³ also aims at providing stimuli and support for collaborative activities.

The latter two will be further explained and elaborated.

4.1 Individualized Support

The external embedment and presentation of intelligent feedback to the user can vary from changes inside the same environment the user is interacting with (e.g. changes in the user's workspace) to using virtual creatures which act as an interface between the user and the machine. In the NIMIS project we follow two different approaches of the visualization and integration of intelligent support.

The first approach is more implicit in that it conveys feedback by modifying the environment rather than initiating an explicit dialogue with the user on a separate communication level. Although this is internally based on an agent architecture, help agents do not appear externally. The technical communication with internal intelligent agents is based on the same principle of shared activity spaces as the person-to-person communication. The help mechanism is controlled by predefined rules which are triggered by modifications in the external environment (cf. [6]). We believe that, following this implicit approach for the T³ application, we gain the additional feature of intelligent support without losing the explorative ILE character of the software. Currently, intelligent support follows this approach.

In the explicit approach, animated or personalized agents appear as artificial creatures that can talk to the user through speech synthesis or canned phrases (cf. [9]). Although the presence of these creatures may be more distracting as in the implicit scenario, we hope to find positive motivational effects when children work with such externalized agents. While the implicit approach will be the first choice for T³'s intelligent support, the explicit approach (i.e. using visual virtual creatures) will be evaluated in specially prepared test-cases, too. Which kind of initiative is more suitable for the children in the age group addressed here (an active, agent-triggered or a passive, user-triggered initiative) is still an open question.

First implementations of intelligent support are based on domain knowledge, i.e. on expert rules to judge the correctness of written words. Words are treated as correct or incorrect with respect to their phonetic correctness. Typical German mistakes in the beginning are, e.g.,

- missing vowels (e.g. "Bll" instead of "Ball"),
- mixing up of phonetically similar consonants (e.g. "Bur" instead of "Buch", German for book),
- missing "h" and double consonants to emphasize long and short vowels (e.g. "Bal" instead of "Ball").

The RtW learning process requires a dynamically changing notion of correctness which should be based on a model of students' individual achievements and competence. E.g., slight phonetic differences would not be considered in the initial phase of the learning process (i.e. with low competence). Orthographic errors only play a role if phonetic writing works correctly.

Figure 5 gives an impression of how implicit feedback in the T³ environment looks like. Here the mistake is easy to detect (omission of vowel), but the judgement and the kind of feedback is based on the learning history with the T³ application.

$$\text{BII} \Rightarrow \text{B II}$$

Fig. 5. Visualization of an error. The system detected the goal word "Ball" and highlights the missing "a" by simply moving the existing characters and generating a gap

4.2 Support for Collaboration

The current version can optionally be used in a collaborative mode, in which children share their writing spaces. To stress the distinction between vowels and consonants, the phoneme table can be split so that one ore more children keep the consonants while one child gets the vowels ("jigsaw" design, cf. [1]). The children can agree on a word to be written and compose it collaboratively from the phoneme table. In such a scenario, one child acts as a "vowels advocate" who takes the responsibility for the vowels in a word.

Ongoing extensions of the T³ application will implement and provide intelligent support for the initiation of partner or group work. For example, a module that supervises the networked activities in the classroom might find out that children had similar problems related to a certain word (see figure 6).

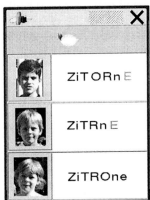

Fig. 6. Visualization of the classmates' solutions for the German word "Zitrone" (citron)

Depending on the individual settings for an application instance, the system will now give the hint, that a couple of other children have written the same word. Now, the child can select and hear one of the other variants, or select a word to work with, or decide to ask a child for help on this specific word. This will lead to a collaboration outside the system (i.e. meet with the child at one workplace) or inside the system within a shared workspace and further intelligent support. The underlying architecture for these support features follows the example described in [7].

5   Implementation

T³ and the NIMIS desktop environment are completely written in Java and use a general Java-based XML format for all persistent data. Collaborative modes are based on a generic Java toolkit for coupled objects, called MatchMaker. The former C++ version has already been used in applications of the approaches presented in [7] and [3]. The new Java based version of MatchMaker now provides a high level API to access object-wise coupling and flexible dynamic remote method invocation based on Java's RMI and Reflection mechanism (cf. [13]).

The phonetic feedback is provided by a commercial text-to-speech (TTS) system that has been interfaced to Java. Before T³ submits the text to the TTS it is parsed through a Prolog based converting algorithm. The Prolog interface and MatchMaker also serve as the gateway to the intelligent support architecture and its modules. This significantly simplifies the integration of further modules and the adjustment of existing algorithms to the special needs of young children.

6   Experiences and Perspectives

T³ is in everyday use in the CiC of a primary school in Duisburg since August 1999. Both the environment and the T³ application are used in normal curricular activities for one hour each day in a class of first-graders. Handling and integration in the (also non-computerized) classroom activities turned out to be easy and robust. Children and teachers are satisfied with the quality of feedback provided by T³. The teachers are able to set up and maintain the environment alone. Technical support is only provided when new software versions are installed.

The application is still going through design and re-design phases, mainly based on the children's and teachers' feedback. The following features are currently being prepared for practical use:

- integration of a visual three dimensional head (showing the movement of the mouth to increase the number of easily distinguishable characters)
- systematic use of synchronous collaboration modes in the classroom (accompanied by interviews and observations for evaluation purposes)
- visualization and smooth integration of intelligent analysis results
- suggestion of pairs or groups for collaboration (controlled by teacher)

Teachers appreciate that T³ relieves them from the mechanical work of reading aloud written results of the children on request. Furthermore, the added value lies in the increased freedom of the teacher to support children with special needs of many kinds. For the children, the application presents itself as an interactive learning tool to experiment with. Preliminary observations indicate that children use the computerized feedback more often than the teacher's feedback in a normal classroom situation. This may be interpreted as an indicator of a more explorative way of learning.

7 Acknowledgements

Parts of this work refer to the Esprit project No. 29301, "NIMIS". We thank our NIMIS partners, namely from CBLU Leeds, INESC Lisbon and MediaWorld Bad Lippspringe, for the good and constructive cooperation, and especially the teachers and pupils of the associated German primary school "GGS Kirchstraße" for constructive discussions and creative input.

References

1. Aronson, E., Balney, N., Stephan, C., Sikes, J. & Snapp, M. (1978). The jigsaw classroom. Beverley Hills CA: Sage.
2. Hoppe, H.U., Baloian, N. & Zhao, J. (1993). Computer support for teacher-centered classroom interaction. In Proc. of ICCE 1993, Taipei, Taiwan.
3. Hoppe, H.U., Gaßner, K., Mühlenbrock, M. & Tewissen, F. (2000). Distributed Visual Language Environments for Cooperation and Learning: Applications and Intelligent Support. To appear in Special Issue in the Group Decision and Negotiation Journal, vol. 9, no. 3.
4. Hoppe, H.U. & Plötzner, R. (1999). Can Analytic Models Support Learning in Groups? In Dillenbourg, P. (ed.). Cognitive and Computational Approaches, Pergamon 1999, Amsterdam, Netherlands.
5. Montessori, M. & Hunt, J. McV (contr.) (1989). The Montessori Method. Paperback reissue edition, Schocken Books.
6. Mühlenbrock, M. & Hoppe, H.U. (1999). Computer Supported Interaction Analysis of Group Problem Solving. In Proc. of CSCL 1999, Stanford: CA.
7. Mühlenbrock, M., Tewissen, F. & Hoppe, H.U. (1998). A Framework System for Intelligent Support in Open Distributed Learning Environments. In International Journal of Artificial Intelligence in Education, vol. 9.
8. NIMIS, Esprit funded i3 Project (No. 29301) (1998). Networked Interactive Media In Schools. http://collide.informatik.uni-duisburg.de/Projects/nimis/
9. Prada, R., Machado, I. & Paiva, A. (2000). TEATRIX: Virtual Environment for Story Creation. To appear in Proc. of ITS'2000, Montreal, Canada.
10. Reichen, J. (1991). Lesen durch Schreiben. (German teacher's guide to "Reading through Writing"), Heinevetter Lehrmittel Verlag.
11. Streitz, N., Geißler, J. & Holmer, T. (1998). Roomware for Cooperative Buildings: Integrated Design of Architectural Spaces and Information Spaces. In Proc. of CoBuild 1998, Darmstadt, Germany.
12. Supnithi, T., Inaba, A., Ikeda, M., Toyoda, J. & Mizoguchi, R. (1999). Learning Goal Ontology Supported by Learning Theories for Opportunistic Group Formation. In Proc. of AIED 1999, Le Mans, France.
13. Tewissen, F. (1998). Java MatchMaker Online Documentation. http://collide. informatik.uni-duisburg.de/Software/Docs/JavaMatchMaker/, Dept. of Computer Science and Education, University of Duisburg.

An Adaptive, Collaborative Environment to Develop Good Habits in Programming

Aurora Vizcaíno[1], Juan Contreras[2], Jesús Favela[3], Manuel Prieto[1]

[1]Computer Sciences Department
Universidad de Castilla-La Mancha. Escuela Superior de Informática
Ronda de Calatrava 5, 13071 Ciudad Real, Spain
{ avizcaino, mprieto}@inf-cr.uclm.es
[2]Telematics Department
Universidad de Colima, México
juancont@ucol.mx
Computer Sciences DepartmentCICESE, México
favela@cicese.mx

Abstract. In this paper we discuss how computer supported collaborative learning (CSCL) can be deployed to develop new skills and habits in students at university level. These considerations led to the development of an adaptive environment to develop good programming habits. We start by describing the difficulties in teaching and learning programming and more concretely, in making students good programmers. Afterwards, we explain why group work is an adequate approach to learn programming. Next HabiPro, an environment that trains students in Programming is described. The principal features of this system are: It is adaptive: depending on the group features the environment proposes different pedagogic methodologies and different exercises. The tool promotes collaboration and interaction among the students. The pedagogic methodologies are based on reflection, observation, and relation. Finally, we present our conclusions and discuss future work.

1. Learning and Teaching Programming

Programming is a subject which is normally taught in the first year of a Computer Science, Computer Engineering degree, or other degrees related to information technology.

Programming is characterised by being more practical than theoretical. It is a topic that must be learnt "by doing" rather than memorising.

Many researchers indicate that the information that is received but isn't used during the learning process, is difficult to remember when we need it [8].

In a procedural topic, like programming, resolving practical exercises is even more necessary than in a declarative topic like, for instance, history. "Procedural learning requires theoretical learning, but not in all cases. To sum up, the application of practical or operative activities and/or the use of information is implied [2].

In procedural learning students must practice, learn from their mistakes and use abilities such as observation, reflection or relation. But students are not used to this type of learning.

Working in a group or using new technology can help students to develop skills and to learn procedures. This paper explains on what occasions collaboration can improve learning, and why group work is favourable in learning programming. Afterwards, HabiPro, an adaptive and collaborative environment to train student in programming is presented.

The contents of this paper are organised as follows: Section two explains why collaboration is useful in learning programming, section three presents HabiPro a tool to develop good habits in programming. The next sections describe the structure, adaptability, and use of HabiPro. Section seven presents results obtained from experiments carried out with HabiPro and finally we present our conclusions and future work.

2. Collaboration in Learning Programming

At our university there is a large number of students that give up or fail programming. Last year, of the 339 students who were registered, only 131 students went to the exam and of them, 90 passed. Concerned about this, we asked programming students and teachers why, in their opinion, programming has an high degree of failures.

The students' answers were very diverse, but all of them agreed that they only had a few hours of laboratory practice. They also agreed that when they were at home it was more difficult to do the exercises because when they made a mistake they didn't know how to continue because the books didn't have the answers.

On the other hand, the teachers agreed that programming is a very abstract topic and on many occasions they don't know how to explain topics like recursion or data structures.

Another reason why teachers think students don't write good programs is because students do not think about the possible solutions to the problem, and which of them is the best. Pupils try to solve the problem as quickly as possible without thinking if her/his solution is good.

When we studied the answers we thought that a distributed and collaborative tool could be a solution to several of the presented problems so we decided to develop HabiPro. The current methods of teaching programming include lecturing, and laboratory sessions in which the students reinforce what they have learned in lectures by developing small programs of their own. A further way of assisting students is to provide computerised aids that are designed specifically for the novice [9].

Computer networks permit students to be connected, although they are in different places, so a distributed environment permits students to work in a group and solve exercises from their homes.

Collaborative learning has many advantages such as the interchange of ideas among the students, or an increase of the motivation to learn. There is a substantial body of empirical evidence demonstrating the positive effects of social interaction for learning [11], [10], [6]. As the results of these studies emerged, it became apparent that computer use can constitute a particularly valuable context for social interaction [3].

So currently there are many learning programs based on collaborative learning. But is collaborative learning good in all situations?

When people begin to learn programming, apart from buying a book about the language that they are using, on many occasions they also attend courses and if they have access to Internet, they join message lists, or news and work groups where they can ask questions or advice from other programmers.

So the students look for the experience and collaboration of other people. This shows that in programming learning collaborative techniques are often used because students join together to write programs and to take advice about their doubts in a spontaneous and natural way.

3. What is HabiPro?

HabiPro (Habits of Programming) is a pedagogical and collaborative software designed to develop good programming habits. It doesn't try to teach programming but to develop in the novice students skills such as observation, reflection or structure, which are necessary to become good programmers.

The interface of the application has two windows (Fig. 1). One of them is a chat window that permits communication among students. And the second one is a shared window (work window) where students must collaboratively solve a problem.

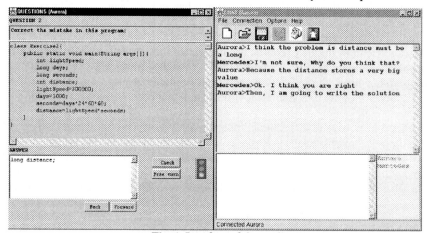

Fig. 1. Interface of the application

The work window can present four types of exercises:
- Finding the mistake: Students must find a mistake in a program. All programmers at some time must find the mistake because the program doesn't work. It is convenient for novice students to be in the habit of thinking and predicting which is the mistake or mistakes that don't permit the program to work correctly. In these types of exercises the most frequent mistakes made in Java programming are shown.

- Put a program in the correct order. With this exercise we try to help students to learn to structure a program and reflect on the order in which the sentences should be.
  To solve the exercises the screen is divided into two parts. In the first one the disarranged program appears. When the students choose a sentence it is automatically put into the second window. At the end, students check if they have ordered the program correctly. In this case, the program is presented with comments and indenteds. The visualisation of a perfectly ordered program helps the students to realise that the presentation of a program aids a better understanding of what the program does.
- Predicting the result: This exercise also attempts to show the importance of creating programs which are easy to understand (with comments and with significant names of variables) even for other people. At the beginning, programs without comments and variables with random names will be shown to the students and they must guess what the program does. Next, a similar program will be shown but in this case the program will have adequate comments and significant names of variables so that students can see that in the second case it is easier to trace a program.
- Completing a program: Students must write one sentence that is omitted. In this exercise we try to make sure that there are different solutions. The system only accepts the best solution. So students learn that normally a problem can be solved using different techniques but in many cases one solution is better than the rest. They must try to find this solution. For instance, the system shows a program where students must declare a variable. It is possible to use an integer but perhaps only a byte is really necessary, so students can learn it is important to save memory when possible.

When a group proposes a solution, if it is incorrect the system shows four types of 'help'. This assistance has two goals: first, to help the group to find the solution, and second, to obtain information about the group. The following explains how HabiPro achieves both goals.

The first type of assistance gives clues to the student about how they can solve the problem. So they must think about and reflect on the solution. This type of help is situated at the beginning to try to influence students to choose it (first button).

The second help button shows the solution and an explanation of it because the problem is solved with that technique.

The third one shows a similar example of the problem that students have to solve, and its solution. In this case students must use the techniques of comparing and observation to detect which part of the example looks like their problem and relate the solution in the example to their own problem.

The last one shows only the solution to the problem.

The choice of the type of help gives information about the group motivation and their willingness to learn. If a group frequently chooses the help button that only shows the solution, this indicates that their motivation is very poor because they aren't interested in knowing why that is the correct solution. On the other hand if other groups prefer to use clues or compare the example with the problem this indicates that the group likes thinking about the solution and that the group is active. If a group prefers to see the solution with an explanation it is because the students are interested in knowing "the reason why things are as they are". In this way, the solution is not only a tool of assistance for the group, but also for the system itself. The system is able to detect each group's characteristics depending on the type of assistance chosen.

4. Structure of the System

HabiPro has a client-server architecture (Fig. 2). The client and the server are divided into two parts. Those of the client are formed by:

- Interface: A chat window where students write possible solutions to the problem. A shared work window of the type WYSIWIS (What You See Is What I See). And a small window where the information about the other users appears are the windows that the system presents to the users.
- A collaborative component, which gives collaboration awareness to the students. This part is very important in non-presence collaboration where students lack some advantages like eye contact or knowing the companion's emotional state by her/his tone of voice. For this reason a window is added indicating how many students are connected, their names and if it is possible, their photo. It also shows the frequency with which each person takes part in the conversation in order for the students to know who they are working with and which people are participating most.
- Collaboration awareness and emotional state during the collaboration process are important topics that are currently being researched. Systems to detect the emotional state of companions are currently being designed [5].
- Student memory: In this part all actions performed by the student are stored. Part of this information will be sent to the server and the rest will be used to produce statistics about the progress and the participation of each student.
- Communication component: This allows the sending of messages to the server and the reception of messages from the server.

The server architecture is composed of three parts:

- The communication part: This permits a group of students to be connected, and to be able to send and receive messages. The main functions of these components are:

  - ➢ Connection: Each time the server detects that a client wants to connect, the server has to create a new communications channel and to tell the connected clients that a new client is connected.
  - ➢ Disconnection: When a client abandons the application the server informs the rest of the clients who has disconnected.Send control events and messages to the clients.

- Specific database: The database stores the exercises, solutions and aids (clues, explanations, and examples) that HabiPro proposes to the group. If we want to use the application to teach other topics, it is necessary to change the information in the specific database for the new information related to the new topic.

- Group model: This is an essential part of the system. "A model of cooperative problem-solving should predict what forms of cooperation can exist and ideally what interactive learning mechanisms they trigger" [1].

  The group model is based on the model proposed by Ana Paiva [7]. The more we know about someone, the more we know his/her necessities and preferences. In the same way, the more information the group model has about the people with whom it interacts, the more precise it is in determining what exercises are needed. The group model represents and characterises the group. The group model may include two types of information: One of them relates to pedagogical aspects, and the second relates to social aspects. This is because when a group is learning, apart from knowing what knowledge the group has, it is important to also know the characteristics and preferences of the group.

  The information stored in the group model will be used to adapt the system to the group.

  In relation to pedagogical aspects, the group model stores theses points:

  ➢ What abilities the group has. This information is obtained from the exercises done by the group.
  ➢ What type of exercises the group prefers. After each exercise each student must indicate, his or her opinion about the degree of difficulty of the exercises and if s/he thinks the exercise is interesting, boring, etc, by filling in a brief questionnaire.
  ➢ What mistakes the group has made. These are obtained from the mistakes made in solving the exercises.

In relation to social aspects, it is important to know the degree of motivation of the students and with what frequency each person collaborates:

➢ Motivation: The system has four different types of help (explained in the second point). Depending on the type of help chosen, HabiPro can suppose the degree of group motivation.
➢ Participation: Using the conversation in the chat window HabiPro checks how many times each student takes part in the conversation. If the same student always takes part perhaps there was a leader of the group, or maybe the rest of the group are passive people. This is important information if the system is to succeed in allowing everybody to take part in solving a problem.

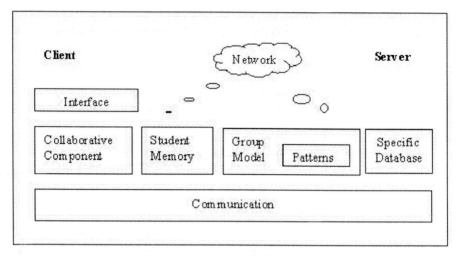

Fig. 2. Architecture of the HabiPro

5. Why HabiPro is Adaptive?

The group model has stored different social and pedagogic patterns. Each pattern has characteristics that describe behaviours. The patterns also contain a list of exercises, types of clues and pedagogic techniques.

While the group is working with HabiPro the group model compares the new information with the characteristics in the patterns and tries to classify the group in a pattern. Once the group is classified, the pattern indicates which exercises and work methodology is the most adequate for a group with a type of specific behaviour. For instance, a group could have a pedagogic pattern with the follow characteristics:

- Mistakes: The group can't find the mistakes in the problems.
- Preferences: Exercises that involve filling in the program.
- Frequent Solution chosen: Solution without explanation.

For this type of pattern the group model proposes:
⇒ To show low level exercises.
⇒ Not allowing the group to choose help without explanation with out letting a certain amount of time elapse.
⇒ To show some "finding mistakes exercises" adding some clues in order to aid students to find the mistakes.

And the same group could have a social pattern with these characteristics:
- Participation: Only one or two people take part.
- Motivation: Low

This pattern proposes five activities that HabiPro can use to increase motivation and participation:

⇒ HabiPro activates the rotator turn system, so that all students must take part in the work.
⇒ Presenting more attractive exercises.
⇒ The system produces personality questions, indicating the name of the person who must answer.
⇒ The system gives points to the person who writes the correct solution (like a game).
⇒ By showing statistics, which demonstrate the performance of other groups that worked with is system, thus the group can compare this with their own performance.

The group model in this case is not only the representation of the characteristics of the group, it is also the component that permits the system to be adaptive.

6. Evaluating HabiPro

Several versions of HabiPro have been implemented and tested. Experimenting with these versions has allowed us to establish the more adequate number of people that can work using HabiPro, and observe what social protocols are used by the students in order to come to an agreement, or give solutions.

Firstly, a version with free floor protocol was tested. Twenty-three students divided into different sizes of groups (in order to research in which groups collaboration was better) had to solve twenty exercises. Each student used a computer, and they interchanged ideas via the chat.

When students agreed about a solution one of them had to write the solution in the answer window and if the solution was correct, the system automatically showed all group students the next exercise.

This version presented a problem: Some students wrote the solution without consulting with their colleagues, so if the answer was correct all the students advanced to the next exercise, although some of the group members did not understand why the solution was as it was. This fact produced a feeling of anger and frustration in the other members of the group. The same students proposed a solution to the problem: The system should only accept a solution when it was proposed by all the students (each student has to write the solution in the answer window). Currently, a version with this feature is being implemented and we hope to test it soon.

The second version has a turn protocol. Only the student whose turn it is can write the solution in the answer window. A student can take a turn until another student asks for it. The turn protocol facilitated communication because students did not have to spend time deciding who would write the answer.

In this version, the interface shows a traffic light that tells the student if she/he has a turn (green light) or if she/he hasn't it (read light). So, the person who has the green light knows that he has to write the answer in the adequate window.

We could prove that the turn protocol is also convenient for collaboration, because if one student did not collaborate his/her companion could give a turn to this person and in this way motivate his/her collaboration.

The experiments were done with groups of different sizes: five groups formed of two students, three groups of three and one group with four people.

When students finished solving the exercises they filled in a form where they answered some questions and they could also express opinions about the experience.

The group with four companions agreed that it was very difficult to work with so many people, and in many cases no one took part in the activities. On the other hand, the groups with three members solved less exercise that the groups with two members, this could be because the groups with three people spent more time in communication, and the negotiation was more difficult than in groups with two members.

We can conclude that HabiPro woks efficiently with groups with two members, or a maximum of three. With more people collaboration decreased and communication was more difficult.

We can also observe that adding a turn protocol increases the performance and facilitates collaboration.

7. Conclusions

Collaborative learning has many advantages but before applying collaboration in a topic we must study whether the topic is really adequate to be handled in a collaborative environment.

In this paper we have explained why programming is a field which can be learned by using collaborative techniques.

HabiPro, a tool for developing good programming habits in the novice students has been presented and its main characteristics such as adaptive techniques and methods to teach the student to think have been explained.

Creating adaptive collaborative systems is more difficult than creating individual adaptive systems because apart from the pedagogical aspects, we must also take into account aspects related to social relations and group dynamics.

8. Future Work

When a set of people work or study in a group a figure usually appears who influences in the group, sometimes voluntarily and other times involuntarily. This figure is the leader, who can influence the group positively or negatively. If we can insure that the leader's influence is good we can help learning to be more efficient.

We want to add a virtual student in HabiPro. This virtual agent must collaborate with the group, and perhaps on some occasions it could carry out the roll of leader.

The virtual student is a software student who can control communication. For instance when a person doesn't take part in the conversation, the virtual student can say to him/her: "What do you think about this?". Also the software student can propose correct answers when the rest of the members in the group have proposed wrong ideas.

The student's virtual knowledge could be similar to the knowledge of a teacher or an expert, but it is better for learning if students work with a student although it is "virtual" one than with a teacher. This is because when somebody tries to collaborate with somebody who has a higher status (a boss, teacher...), it is not collaboration but obligation, so the motivation is less than in the case where the members of a group belong to the same status. Collaboration is more likely to occur between people of a similar status than between a boss and his/her employee, or between a teacher and a pupil [4].

Currently we are carrying out an experiment that will allow us to know and limit the language that students use in the communication process in order to know the discourse universe that the virtual student must have.

References

1. Baker, M. "The roles of models in Artificial Intelligence and Education Research: a prospective view". International journal of Artificial Intelligence in Education, 1999.
2. Castañeda Yánez, M. 1995. "Análisis del aprendizaje de conceptos y procedimientos". Editorial Trillas.
3. Crook, C. "Computers and the Collaborative Experience of Learning". London: Routledge.
4. Dillenbourg, P.; "Introduction: What Do You Mean By Collaborative Learning?". In Collaborative Learning. Cognitive and Computational Approaches. Edited by Pierre Dillenbourg. Elservier Science, 1999.
5. García, O.; Favela, J.; Machorro, R. "Emotional Awareness in Collaborative Systems". In Proceedings 5th International Workshop on GroupWare. Cancún, Mexico, September, 1999.
6. Light, P.; Littleton, K.; Messer, D.; Joiner, R. "Social and communicative processes in computer-based problem solving". European Journal of Psychology of Education, 9 (1), 93-109. 1994.
7. Paiva, A. "Learner Modelling for Collaborative learning Environments". In Boulay, B., Miyoguchi, R.(Eds.). Artificial Intelligence in Education. pp 215-222. IOS Press.Pg 215-222, 1997.
8. Schank, R.; Kass, A. "A Goal-Based Scenario for High School Students". Communications of the ACM. Vol 39, N° 4. 1996.
9. Smith, P.A.;Webb G. F. " Evaluation of Low-Level Program Visialization for Teaching Novice C Programmers". In proceedings of ICCE'99, 7th International Conference on Computers in Education. Chiba, Japan, November, 1999.
10. Teasley, S.; Roschelle, J. "Constructing a joint problem space: The computer as a tool for sharing knowledge". In Computers as Cognitive Tools (pp 229-257). S. P. Lajoie & S.J. Derry (Eds.). Hillsdale, NJ: Lawrence Erlbaum Associates. 1993.
11. Tudge, J.; Rogoff, B. "Peer influences on cognitive development: Piagetian and Vigotskian perspectives". In Interaction in Human Development (pp. 17-40). M.H. Bornstein & J. S. Bruner (Eds.). Hillsdale, MJ: Lawrence Erbaum Associates. 1989.

A Reflective CSCL Environment
with Foundations Based on the Activity Theory

Grégory Bourguin, Alain Derycke

Laboratoire TRIGONE, Institut CUEEP,
Université des Sciences et Technologies de Lille, 59655 Villeneuve d'Ascq, France
Email : {gregory.bourguin;alain.derycke}@univ-lille1.fr

Abstract. Users need more evolving CSCL systems allowing them to co-construct their groupware environment. As a response to this problem, this paper presents how we are trying to define more foundational relationships between human and computer sciences. Starting from studies of the contribution of human science to CSCW, we present some approaches similar to ours. We finally present DARE, our new meta-groupware. DARE takes elements coming from both human and computer sciences defining a boundary abstraction with its conceptual model. Its design is mainly rooted in Activity Theory and advanced software design strategies like open implementation. DARE particularly emphasises on co-construction and expansiveness properties of human activity and may be defined as more than a meta-groupware, but as a reflective groupware.

1 Introduction

In the last years we have made an important effort in research and development for Computer Supported Collaborative Learning (CSCL) and for new education and training modes based on openness and distribution of learning activities [1][2][3]. We have accumulated a lot of experiences and have been involved (and are still involved) in the real uses, with some small to medium user population scales (more than 1000 users cumulated) in more than five different sites. Different social and pedagogical experiments have clearly proved the value of CSCL for better education and training and for the socialisation of distance learners.

From our experiences, we have drawn the conclusion that a traditional design process based on a first phase of intensive user requirement gathering and analysis, and done before the modelling and implementation phases, cannot achieve our goals about flexibility and adaptability to specific needs. The observation of advanced educational actors (pedagogical designers, tutors) shows that they proceed with a light planning of their activities: they start with an initial pattern, but during the process, which can last a long time, they adopt an opportunistic behaviour, revising and evolving their instructional strategies and learning activities according to the learners reactions and progresses. It clearly appears that they need more evolving CSCL systems allowing them to co-construct the groupware environment at run-time, not only between the educational agents (such as teachers, course planners, tutors, system administrators…), but also with the learner group. This should allow the learners to be engaged in a more reflective practice in their learning processes.

Our aim is to take advantage of the re-engineering effort for our second generation of integrated CSCL system in order to push more deeply the contribution of the human science applied to the CSCW field. This requires first that we give our understanding of the contribution of human sciences and our choice to ground our work on the emergent Activity Theory (part 2), and secondly, to show how we have taken this into account in designing a new meta-groupware which we call DARE (part 3).

2 CSCW system design and Human Science

2.1 An Overview

The Humanisation of Technology. The impact of human science, in Human Computer Interaction (HCI) or CSCW, can be drawn from the work of L. Suchman [4]. The benefit from this work was the intrusion of new approaches based on contributions of the anthropology: ethnography and ethnomethodology.

In order to summarise most of the contributions of human science we can break them down into two major levels:

- The different fundamental disciplines or knowledge domains which compose the human science itself, sociology, anthropology, political science and cognitive psychology. These disciplines provide a general framework for thinking about sociotechnical systems and some paradigms for analysis and theorisation;
- The levels of the theories or of the world interpretations, provided by advances in knowledge at the upper level. We would like to mention, for the CSCW field: the Activity Theory, situated action theory, structuration theory, adaptive structuration theory…

We can observe the same evolution in the design of learning environments. For example, there is the contribution of J. Lave [5] taking its roots in the Vygotsky theoretical work and in the anthropocentric approaches close to those of Suchman.

Contribution from the Anthropology. Ethnomethodology, and also but less prominent, ethnography, have become of great interest to the CSCW community, especially in Great Britain and North America. These kinds of sociological enquiry have proven their interests in the analysis and design of CSCW systems, taking more systematically into account the real nature of the human fieldwork, and its relationships with the context and the situation.

In spite of its great interest, ethnography is not really efficient for providing articulation between analysis, user requirements in a social context, and the design process itself. Another criticism is that the requirements identified through ethnography are often constraints for the system design rather than functional requirements [6].

The case of ethnomethodology is different. Its purpose is greater than providing "tools" for observation. The aim of the ethnomethodology is not to provide new methods for ethnology, but a conceptual framework for revealing and understanding everyday social action. However and until now, with the exception of Dourish and Button [7], ethnomethodology has only found its place in the first (analysis) and last (criticisms) steps of the design process of CSCW systems.

The Activity Theory. Activity Theory (AT), is another strong contribution of human science that has a wide audience in the fields of HCI, CSCW and also in the educational technology field. AT has its foundation in the soviet cultural historical school of psychology founded by L. Vygotsky, A. Leont'ev and A. Luria. AT is characterised by a combination of (a) objective, (b) ecological, (c) socio-cultural perspectives on human activity [9]. It has been identified as a hot issue for HCI and CSCW over the 10 last years, due to contributions from Engeström [10], Kuutti [11][12] or Bodker [13]. For example, for Kuutti [14] the concept of activity is seen as a basic unit of analysis for CSCW research.

Progressively AT has emerged as a body of concepts whose aim is to unify the understanding of human activity, providing a bridge towards other approaches, or even merge [16], over time, with some like distributed cognition [15]. However we would like to emphasise the contribution of Engeström [10] [17], which defines a simple structural model of the concept of activity, expressing the mediation between the subject (the individual or the subgroup) and the object (the motive of activity) through the tool (material or intellectual). By virtue of its simplicity, this model may favour the sharing of a common understanding between computer scientists, software designers, social scientists, or even with the user community; see [18] for an application to distributed learning. This model has been used with extensions from Kuutti [11] to replace human activity modelling or analysis in the framework of the organisational context "in the large" and to introduce the concept of "expansiveness". Expansiveness corresponds to the dynamic construction of activity. Extensions have also been introduced by Bardram [19], these concerning the design of dynamic co-operative work activities.

2.2 More Foundational Relationships

There are some recent approaches for CSCW systems design trying to take account of the contribution of the human sciences more deeply in the design process:

The first approach [20] is rooted into the contribution of human science for CSCW with a particular emphasis on the AT framework and the involvement of end user into the design process through participatory design strategy and the *designing by doing* philosophy. Bodker has proposed a conceptual framework for designing activities of CSCW systems. The idea of an opened development platform for this purpose is similar to our aim to provide a meta-groupware allowing user co-construction of their collaborative environments.

The second approach, the *technomethodology* as proposed by Dourish and Button [7], is capitalised on the analysis and design of CSCW systems based on the contribution of ethnomethodology. For them, ethnomethodology "can take a foundational place in the very notion of system design rather than simply being employed as a resource in aspects of the process such as requirements elicitation and specification". The *technomethodology* which particularly emphasises the *accountability* concept is the new approach where contributions of the social scientists and computer science are more than exchanges, but also relationships that are more than practical. This presents similarities with our approach proposed below, even if ours focuses on AT.

3 DARE : a Reflective Groupware

This part presents the design properties of DARE, an environment for groupware support. Even if "DARE" signifies Distributed Activities in a Reflective Environment and has been designed to support multiple activities in an organisational context (reusing parts of our first framework [3]), we will only focus here on how it helps supporting one of them by emphasising on *co-construction* and *expansiveness* properties of activity [14].

DARE is a reflective-groupware. It modestly tries to fill in the *great divide* [21] between human and computer science by taking elements coming from these two domains for its design. Roots of this model are coming from AT that has already been introduced as an interesting foundation for groupware design.

3.1 Activity Theory and the Conceptual Architecture

We will not expose here all the AT because there is a large literature about the subject [14][8][22] and we do not believe possible to summarise it here. However, we would like to present some key elements we found essential to understand DARE's philosophy. First and according to Kuutti, we consider activity as our basic unit of analysis. Secondly, activity is mediated by artefacts and we use Engeström's *basic structure of activity* model to create our conceptual model. Finally, we accept that elements appearing in this model are creating a situation that influences activity and that these elements are subjects to evolutions because activity always modifies its situation in a reflective fashion.

Using Engeström's *basic structure of activity*, the concepts we will use for our conceptual model are the object (the motive of activity), the subject (because the object cannot be realised if no subject is working for that), the community (a set of subjects sharing the same object), the tool (mediating the subject and object relationship ; anything used in the transformation process), the rules (mediating the subject-community relationship ; explicit and implicit laws, accepted practices...) and the division of labour (mediating the community-object relationship ; explicit and implicit organisation of a community). One must remember that all the mediating components are carrying with them the history of the relationship.

For our design, we have decided to synthesise the two last concepts in only one named role, because a role can be 'given' to a subject. The role includes rules because it determines what it means to be a member of this community. The rules it represents strongly influence actions that a subject may perform during activity by defining an evolving set of rights. Finally, the role mediates the community-object relationship by determining what each role has to do, this corresponding to the division of labour.

Bedny [22] mentions that task is the basic component of activity. According to Leont'ev [23], task's definition is as follow : task is *"a situation requiring realisation of a goal in specific conditions"*. Activity starts with an initial situation given in the task. This situation is transformed by task performance and concludes with a final state that can't be predicted. For our design, we accept that the support for activity is created according to a given explicit task defining the object of activity, the tools to be used and the roles. However, activity tends to modify this task until the end.

Based on these foundations, our belief is that we have to offer to users a system helping them to create, share and evolve an activity according to their emerging needs. We are aware that the introduction of a computer system mediating the activity will inevitably modify it. This is why this mediating system has to be considered as another artefact that will certainly be modified by users according to their emerging work practices.

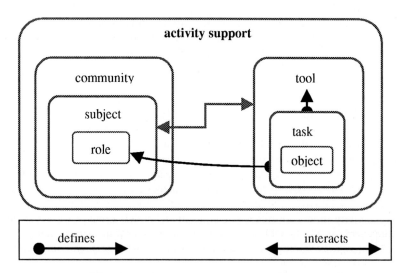

Fig. 1. Activity support-task, a reflective system

We define Activity Support (AS) as a task instance. AS is the support offered by DARE for the activity, so defined to make a distinction with the full activity that DARE is engaged in. Fig. 1 shows how artefacts (tools and roles) are parts of the AS described in the corresponding task. A subject is a member of a community. He plays a role and interacts with tools. Some of these tools enable manipulation of the task itself. Modification affecting task implies direct consequences on AS. The context has to be shared by actors and is the result of interactions. This is why we consider task itself as an artefact accessed and modified by subjects according to their role.

3.2 Open Implementation and Meta Object Protocol

Usually, CSCW systems are offered to users with a specific task that has been constructed thanks to a task analysis in specific conditions. This task is supposed to correspond exactly to the task the user wants to perform. Unfortunately, breakdowns often appear and sometimes rejection of the system generally due to a shift between system's embedded task and the user's one (or the representation he has constructed). If the user is unable to understand the task the system really implements, or to adapt it to its one, the system will certainly not be used.

In our model, we have defined that task contains a representation of the AS. This representation is causally connected to the elements constituting AS. Our meaning is to allow users to access to the representation contained in the task in order to help them in understanding the real task behind the system and, if needed, to modify it.

This corresponds exactly to the *open implementation* approach described by Kiczales [24]. Kiczales discusses the limits of the *black-box abstraction* broadly used in software engineering domain. He argues that the black box has to be opened to allow users to understand the implementation strategy that relies under the system and/or to allow them to chose the strategy that better fits their needs. For us, the black box is the CSCW system and the strategy is the underlying task. Open implementation approach has already been used in CSCW by Dourish with Prospero [25], a toolkit for CSCW designers. One main difference between Prospero and our system is that Prospero is rooted in ethnomethodology as DARE is inspired from AT and directly addresses end users.

An existing technique for open implementation is *computational reflection* [26] that helps in providing system interfaces for examination and modification (introspection and intercession), in other words, providing a meta-interface. Computational reflection has already been used in CSCW domain by Tolone [27] and Dourish [28] demonstrating how reflective computing can help to support flexible environment taking into account more user and context oriented concerns. Following these recommendations, we have used *Meta Object Protocol* [29] (M.O.P.) technique to implement DARE.

M.O.P. defines a meta-level description of the system allowing examination and manipulation of the system during its own execution while maintaining a causal connection between them. Our meaning is to apply those concepts in order to create a reflective system based on task and activity. We have mentioned before that task has to be a part of AS and may be accessed by subjects in introspection and/or intercession. Task defines AS, and then, accessing to it corresponds to a meta-activity (cf. Fig. 2) in which subjects are able to modify their own working context according to their role.

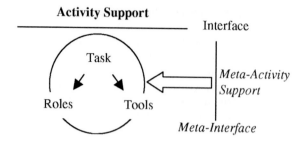

Fig. 2. Activity & Meta-Activity Support

M.O.P. uses object oriented programming techniques. In languages implementing M.O.P. like Smalltalk or Java, meta-level corresponds to the classes and execution to their instances. In DARE, everything concerning task is mapped in term of class and activity in term of instance. This correspondence task / class and activity / instance takes advantages of the reflective and inheritance properties of the languages that are used (Distributed Smalltalk and Java). This allows reusing and refining any task or elements.

3.3   Tailorability in DARE : a Component Approach

It is clear now that one of our aims, accordingly to AT, is to allow subjects to define or transform their own activity by managing themselves their own mediation rules and artefacts. Open implementation and M.O.P. have helped in creating a system as flexible as needed to do so. However, we do not believe that subjects will develop from scratch and themselves the required tools (e.g. a whiteboard). The challenge is then to allow subjects to integrate new tools in their environment without stopping it, but simply passing to its meta-level. The role of the system is to compose and articulate needed tools in an integrating environment that carries the persistence of the co-operation. Once a tool has been brought in AS, subjects adapt it to their needs by defining relationships between it and existing roles.

Recent state of the art shows that many people are actually working to create tailorable CSCW systems. Sandkhul [30] shows how "CSCW research is currently shifting towards the integration of different existing tools into comprehensive CSCW systems". It must be noted that the same evolution is done in the field of the educational software with the emergence of the concept of "Educational Object Economy" which combines a digital library of reusable, interoperable software components [31]. Moreover, it seems to be clear that it is impossible to create a 'ready to use' CSCW system containing all tools that may be needed. Finally, Activity Theory demonstrates that needs about tools are emerging from practices.

A solution to achieve tailorability may reside in the component paradigm. Our position is enforced by the growing interest for component technologies as ActiveX and JavaBeans in software engineering domain. However, one can notice that components are usually brought into the system by developers. Our approach differs by allowing subjects themselves to integrate tools in their environment when they need it during AS execution. This approach can be considered closed to those developed by Hummes [32] for the building of collaborative applications dedicated to the tele-tutoring processes.

In such an approach, components are linked together with glue like a scripting language for example. In DARE the glue is the activity itself because each component constitutes a tool. Using meta-level functions, like introspection, subjects are able to create links between roles and integrated components, determining how the tool will be used during activity. However this is not a simple problem: as subjects are able to bring themselves components in AS, these components will certainly not be designed for DARE. Moreover, subjects may want to integrate components that have not been designed to be integrated !

In DARE, each component and then AS tool, is a Java Applet. That way, any Applet found on the Web by a user may become a tool in a more or less elegant fashion, depending of the Applet openness. This is done specifying Applet's URL and parameters and using a dynamic encapsulation mechanism based on CORBA. Using Java introspection mechanism, subjects are able to describe co-operative actions applicable by each role. One can notice that this is done thanks to meta-level tools that are Applets too and that are managed in the same way. Then in DARE, subjects can modify, according to their role, even the meta-level tools and their dedicated mediation rules, this corresponding to a real co-operative meta-activity.

4 Conclusion

Some different approaches have raised in the CSCW research domain trying to define more foundational relationships between human science and system design. For example, we can notice the work of Dourish and Button with technomethodology [7], which is based on ethnomethodology. This approach copes with the design of systems, as an opposition of coping with the design of one dedicated system. This is exactly what we have been working for, except that our approach is rooted in AT.

The design of systems addresses meta-system design. This paper has presented how we have used a simple model and mechanisms coming from AT to design a meta-groupware that helps users to define their own activities. However, AT teaches us that activity is reflective in the sense that it is co-constructed and expansive. This is why DARE is more than a meta-groupware but a reflective groupware allowing users to access the meta-level of their activity during its execution. Finally, as DARE constitutes the fusion of AT and advanced software design strategies, it takes advantages of an inheritance-specialisation mechanism allowing to reuse activity patterns and to co-adapt them as needed.

The first version of DARE is actually in testing phase and further work concerns the user interface. The main problem is to offer to end-users an interface allowing easy understanding and use of AS and its meta-level that are cohabiting in the same environment. Another problem that we are actually solving concerns the component approach for the tailorability provided to the end-users. We are using a meta-level description of structures of nested and interconnected JavaBeans components (for components that are not really "activity aware") and Enterprise JavaBeans like components (for co-operative "activity aware" components), this using an XML extension close to the Bean Mark-up language provided by IBM [33].

During the following months, DARE is going to be used for experimentation in CSCL domain. The main idea is to provide to users (students and teachers) a bootstrap CSCL activity and to study how they use DARE reflective properties to adapt, evolve and co-construct this CSCL environment. This possibility allowing self-organisation inside a learner group and co-construction of the collaborative learning activities [1] is seen for us as an important contribution to self reflection activities. This is really valuable for the development of the learner meta-cognitive skills [34].

References

1. Derycke, A. Kaye, A.: Participative modelling and design of collaborative learning tools in the CO-LEARN project. In G. Davis, B. Samways (eds), IFIP, Teleteaching 93 Conference, Trondheim, August 20-25,North-Holland, Amsterdam (1993) 191-200
2. Derycke, A.: Integration of the learning processes into the Web: Learning Activity Centred Design and Architecture. Webnet'98 conference, invited conference, Orlando, FL, (1998)
3. Viéville, C.: An Asynchronous Collaborative Learning System on the Web. *The Electronic University*, Springer Verlag, " ", the CSCW series (1998) 99-113
4. Suchman, L.: *Plans and Situated Actions.* Cambridge University Press, Cambridge, UK (1987)
5. Lave, J. Wenger, E.: Situated learning: legitimate peripheral participation. Cambridge University Press, Cambridge, UK (1991)
6. Sommerville, I. Bentley, R. Rodden, T. Sawyer, P.: Cooperative systems design. In The Computer Journal, vol. 37, N°5 (1994) 357-366.
7. Dourish, P. Button, G.: On "Technomethodology": foundational relationships between ethnomethodology and system design. *Human-Computer Interaction,* volume 13, Lawrence Erlbaum Associates, (1998) 395- 432
8. Nardi, B. A.: *Context and consciousness: activity theory and human-computer interaction,* B. A. Nardi (Ed.), Cambridge, Massachusetts: The MIT Press (1996)
9. Kaptelinin V.: Activity Theory: Implications for Human-Computer Interaction. *In [8].* (1996) 103-116.
10. Engeström, Y.: *Learning by expanding: an activity-theoretical approach to developmental research.* Orienta-Konsultit Oy, Helsinki (1987)
11. Kuutti, K.: Notes on systems supporting "Organisational context" – An activity theory viewpoint, COMIC European project, deliverable D1.1 (1993) 101-117
12. Kuutti K.: Activity Theory as a Potential Framework for Human-Computer Interaction Research. *In [8]* (1996) 17-44
13. Bodker, S.: Activity Theory as a challenge to system design. In *Information systems Research: Contemporary Approaches and Emergent Traditions,* Nissen, H; Klein, H. Hirschheim, R. (eds), Elesevier Science Publishers, BV (North Holland), (1991) 551-564
14. Kuutti, K.: The concept of activity as a basic unit of analysis for CSCW research. Proceeding of the second ECSCW'91 conference, Kluwers Academics Publishers, (1991) 249-264
15. Salomon, G.: *Distributed Cognition,* Cambridge University Press, Cambridge, UK (1993)
16. Nardi, B. A.: Studying Context : A Comparison of Activity Theory, Situated Action Models, and Distributed Cognition. *In [8]* (1996) 69-102.
17. Engeström, Y. Brown, K. Christopher, L. Gregory, J.: Coordination, cooperation and communication in the courts. In Cole, M. Engeström, Y. Vasquez, O. (eds) Mind, Culture and Activity, Cambridge University Press, Cambridge, UK (1997)

18. Lewis, R.: Apprendre conjointement : une analyse, quelques expériences et un cadre de travail. Proceedings of Hypermedia et Apprentissage, Poitiers, France (1998) 11-28
19. Bardram, J. Designing for the dynamics of cooperative work activities. Proceedings of the ACM CSCW'98 conference. ACM Press (1998) 89-98
20. Bødker, S. Christiansen, E. Thüring, M.: A conceptual toolbox for designing CSCW applications, in Proceedings of Int. workshop on the design of Cooperative systems, Juan-les-Pins, France (1995) 266-284
21. Bowkers, G; Leigh Star, S. Turner, W. Gasser, L.: *Social science, technical systems and cooperative work: beyond the great divide.* Lawrence Erlbaum Associates, "Computer, cognition and work" series (1997)
22. Bedny G., Meister D.: *The Russian theory of activity, Current Applications to Design and Learning,.* Lawrence Erlbaum Associates Publishers (1997)
23. Leont'ev, A. N.: Leont'ev, A. N.: *Activity, consciousness, and personality.* Englewood Cliffs, NJ: Prentice-Hall (1978)
24. Kiczales G.: Beyond the black box: open implementation, IEEE Software, January, (1996)
25. Dourish P.: *Open Implementation and Flexibility in CSCW Toolkits*, Ph.D. Thesis, University College London (1996)
26. Maes P.: *Computational Reflection*, Ph.D. Thesis, V.U.B, Brussels (1987)
27. Tolone W. J.: *Introspect : A meta-level specification framework for dynamic, evolvable collaboration support*, Ph. D. Thesis, University of Illinois at Urbana-Champaign (1996)
28. Dourish P.: Meta-level Architectures and CSCW : Designing for Change, Position Paper for CSCW'92 Tools and Technologies Workshop, Toronto (1992)
29. Kiczales G., Bobrow D.G., Des Rivieres J.: *The Art of the Metaobject Protocol*, MIT Press (1991)
30. Sandkuhl K., Nentwig L., Manhart S., Lafrenz P.: Redesigning CSCW-System for Network Computing, Experience from the HotCon Project, http://www.computer.org/proceedings/euromicro-pdp/8332/8332toc.htm (1998)
31. Roschelle, J, Kaput, J. Stroup, W. M Kahn, T. Scalable Integration of educational software : exploring the Promise of Component Architecture. http://www-jiime.open.ac.uk/98/6/roschelle-01.html (1998)
32. Hummes, J. Kohrs, A. Merialdo, B.: Software Components for Co-operation: a Solution for the "Get help" Problem. Proceeding of COOP'98 conference, INRIA, http://eurecom.fr/~hummes/docs/COOP98/coop98-submitted.html/ (1998)
33. Codella, C. Dillenberg, D. Ferguson, D. Jackson, R. Mikalsen, T. Silva-Lepe, I.: Support for Entreprise JavaBeans in Component Broker. In IBM Systems Journal. vol. 37. n°4. (1998) 454-474
34. Sherry, L.: "Issues in Distance Learning." International Journal of Educational Telecommunications 1, no. 4 (1966) 337-365

How Can We Form Effective Collaborative Learning Groups?
— *Theoretical justification of "Opportunistic Group Formation" with ontological engineering* —

Akiko Inaba, Thepchai Supnithi, Mitsuru Ikeda, Riichiro Mizoguchi, and
Jun'ichi Toyoda

I.S.I.R., Osaka University, 8-1 Mihogaoka, Ibaraki, Osaka, 567-0047 Japan
inaba@ai.sanken.osaka-u.ac.jp,
http://www.ai.sanken.osaka-u.ac.jp/index-e.html

Abstract. Our research objectives include constructing a collaborative learning support system that detects appropriate situation for a learner to join in a collaborative learning session, and forms a collaborative learning group appropriate for the situation dynamically. In this paper, we describe a system of concepts concerning learning goals expected to attain by learners through collaborative learning process with justification by the learning theories. With the ontology, it will be possible to compare and synthesize the learning theories to design the collaborative learning settings.

1 Introduction

Many researchers on educational technology have extended the field of study from stand-alone learning environment to group collaborative learning environment. Although advantages of collaborative learning over individual learning are well known, the collaborative learning is not always effective for a learner. Educational benefit that a learner gets through the collaborative learning process depends mainly on interaction among learners. The interaction is partly influenced by relations among members of learning group, which suggests that how to form an effective group for the collaborative learning is critical to ensure educational benefit to the members.

Our research objectives include constructing a collaborative learning support system that detects appropriate situation for a learner to join in a collaborative learning session, and forms a collaborative learning group appropriate for the situation dynamically. To fulfill these objectives, we have to consider the following:

1. How to detect the appropriate situation to start a collaborative learning session and to set up the learning goal,
2. How to form an effective group which ensures educational benefits to the members of the group, and
3. How to facilitate desired interaction among learners in the learning group.

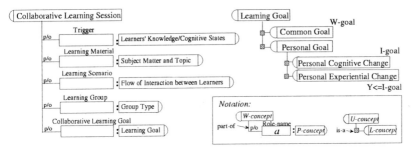

Fig. 1. Collaborative Learning Ontology

We have discussed item 1 in our previous papers[11, 12], and this paper focuses on item 2. When we have clarified item 2 and extracted the desired interaction in the group, we would consider item 3.

There are many theories to support the advantage of collaborative learning. For instance, Observational learning[2], Constructivism[18], Self-regulated learning[10], Situated learning[15], Cognitive apprenticeship[6], Distributed cognition[20], Cognitive flexibility theory[21, 22], Sociocultural Theory[24, 25], Zone of proximal development[24, 25], and so on. If we select a theory from these and form a learning group based on the theory, we can expect effective collaborative learning with the strong support of the theory. However, it is difficult to understand all theories because these theories are derived from a wide research area including pedagogy, sociology and psychology. Moreover, we can expect different educational benefits based on these learning theories, and observe various kinds of interaction between learners through collaborative learning process. Due to the diversity, it is difficult to list the learning theories effective to gain a specific educational benefit for a learner, and to compare the theories to form a suitable collaborative learning group for the learner.

Therefore, we have been constructing a system of concepts to represent collaborative learning sessions mentioned in these learning theories[12, 23]. We call the system of concepts "Collaborative Learning Ontology". In this paper, we focus on "Learning Goal Ontology" which is a part of the Collaborative Learning Ontology. The concept "Learning Goal" is one of the most important concepts for forming a learning group because each learner joins in a collaborative learning session to attain a learning goal. The Ontology will be able to make it easier to form an effective learning setting and to analyze the educational functions of a learning group.[16, 17]

2   Structure of Collaborative Learning Ontology

There are many factors to characterize a collaborative learning session. When should the learners start a collaborative learning session? What subject matter should they learn in the session? How should the session progress? Who should join in the session? What educational benefit should be expected for each learner through the session?

We picked up concepts to represent a collaborative learning session through a survey of learning theories and studies on collaborative learning. As a result, we set up five primitive concepts to characterize the session: trigger, learning material, learning scenario, learning group, and learning goal. Fig. 1 shows the conceptual structure of collaborative learning ontology.[1] The concept "trigger" means the desired situation for each learner to start a collaborative learning session. The concept "learning material" means the subject matter, learning topics, and problems to be addressed in the session. The concept "learning scenario" means how the collaborative learning session progresses; for example, a learner demonstrates how to solve a problem and another learner observes it, and then they exchange their roles. The concept "learning group" means a group type and each learner's role in the session. Here, we focus on the concept "learning goal". The concept "learning goal" can be specified as two kinds of goals: "common goal" as a whole group and "personal goal" for each learner. The concept "personal goal" can be specified as two kinds: the goal represented as a change of a learner's knowledge/ cognitive states, and the goal attained by interaction with other learners.

3 Learning Goal Ontology

As Fig. 1 shows, the collaborative learning ontology has three kinds of goals: one common goal and two kinds of each member's personal goals. In this section, we distinguish among the three goals and identify the goals with justification based on learning theories.

3.1 Classification of Goals for Collaborative Learning

A learner will join in a collaborative learning session to attain learning goals. We classify the goal of the first person (I), that of the first person to interact with the second person (You), and that of the whole group as I-goal, $Y{\Leftarrow}$I-goal, and W-goal, respectively. I-goal, which is described as G:I, represents what a learner is expected to acquire through the collaborative learning session. $Y{\Leftarrow}$I-goal, which is described as G:$Y{\Leftarrow}$I, represents the means to attain I-goals. Both I-goals and $Y{\Leftarrow}$I-goals

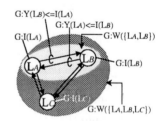

Fig. 2. Learning Goal Ontology

are personal goals for a learner. W-goal expresses the situation being set up to

---

[1] Notation: the schemata define the W-concept and the U-concept. The W-concept has entity a, which is an instance of the concept P-concept, as a part. The entity a plays a specific role (Role-name) in the W-concept. The concept P-concept has a semicircle on the right sides. It means the concept is defined in other schema. The L-concept is a specification of the U-concept, and the U-concept is a generalization of the L-concept.

Table 1. I-goals

I-goal	Definition	Src.
Acquisition of Content-Specific Knowledge	To add new knowledge concerning the target domain to existing schemata, to understand it, and then to (re) construct knowledge structure.	[2, 4, 5, 7, 8, 19]
Accretion		
Tuning		
Restructuring		
Development of Cognitive Skill	To get knowledge concerning cognitive skills such as diagnosing and monitoring, to practice them, and then to refine them.	[3, 18, 20]
Cognitive stage		
Associative stage		
Autonomous stage		
Development of Metacognitive Skill	To get knowledge concerning metacognitive skills for observing self-thinking process, diagnosing it and regulating or controlling of self-activity, to practice them, and then to refine them.	[10, 18]
Cognitive stage		
Associative stage		
Autonomous stage		
Development of Skill for Self-Expression	To get knowledge concerning the skills for externalizing self-thinking process and presenting the learner's self-perspectives, to practice them, and then to refine them.	[4, 21, 22]
Cognitive stage		
Associative stage		
Autonomous stage		

attain $Y \Leftarrow$ I-goals and we describe the goal as G:W. W-goal is a common goal characterizing the whole group.

Fig. 2 represents learning goals in a group where three learners: L_A, L_B and L_C are participating. Learner L_A has an I-goal which is attained through this collaborative learning session and this goal is described in the Fig. 2 as G:I(L_A). Both L_B and L_C have I-goals, and they are represented as G:I(L_B) and G:I(L_C) respectively. G:Y(L_B)$\Leftarrow$I(L_A) is a $Y \Leftarrow$ I-goal between L_A and L_B observed from L_A's viewpoint. In other words, it means the reason why L_A interacts with L_B. Concerning this interaction between L_A and L_B, there is also a $Y \Leftarrow$ I-goal observed from L_B's viewpoint. That is, it is the reason why L_B interacts with L_A. This $Y \Leftarrow$ I-goal is represented as G:Y(L_A)$\Leftarrow$I(L_B). Both G:I(L_A) and G:Y(L_B)$\Leftarrow$I(L_A) are personal goals of L_A. G:W(L_A, L_B) is a W-goal of the learning group (L_A, L_B). G:W(L_A,L_B,L_C) is a W-goal of the learning group (L_A, L_B, L_C).

3.2 Identification of Learning Goals

In this section, we identify goals for collaborative learning for each of the three categories based on learning theories. Tab.1 shows the I-goals. We can expect learners to acquire not only new knowledge concerning problems they solve, but also cognitive skills, meta-cognitive skills, and skills for self-expression through the collaborative learning session. The process to acquire a specific knowledge includes three qualitatively different kinds of learning[19]: Accretion, Tuning, and Restructuring. Accretion is to add new information to a learner's preexisting schemata, and to interpret the information in terms of relevant preexisting schemata. Tuning is to understand the knowledge through applying the knowl-

286

Table 2. Y⇐I-goals

Y⇐I-goal	Definition	Src.
Learning by Observation	Learning indirectly by observing other learners' learning processes	[2]
Learning by Self-Expression	Learning by externalizing self-thinking process, such as self-explanation and presentation.	[4]
Learning by Teaching	Learning by teaching something he/she already knows to other learners	[7,8]
Learning by being Taught	Learning directly by being taught by other learners	[7,8]
Learning by Apprenticeship	Learning by observing other learners' behavior and then imitating it.	[6]
Learning by Practice	Learning by applying knowledge or skill to a specific problem	[15]
Learning by Diagnosing	Learning by diagnosing other learners' learning or thinking processes	[5]
Learning by Guiding	Learning by demonstrating knowledge or skill to other learners and guiding the learners	[6]
Learning by Reflection	Learning by rethinking and observing the learner's self-thinking process.	[20-22]
Learning by Discussion	Learning by discussion with other learners	[18,20]

Table 3. W-goals

	W-goal	Definition	Src.
M-PR	Setting up the situation for Peer Tutoring [PT]	Setting up the situation where a learner teaches something to another learner.	[7,8]
	Setting up the situation for Anchored Instruction [AI]	Setting up the situation where a learner diagnoses another learner's problem and then solve it (Problem-based Learning)	[5]
M-SR	Setting up the situation for learning by Cognitive Apprenticeship [CA]	Setting up the situation to learn knowledge or skill as an apprentice	[6]
	Setting up the situation for sharing (Meta-) Cognitive function between learners [SC]	Setting up the situation to share cognitive or meta-cognitive function between learners based on Sociocultural Theory	[24,25]
	Setting up the situation for sharing Multiple Perspectives [CF]	Setting up the situation to evoke a learner's reflective thinking based on Cognitive Flexibility theory.	[21,22]
PR=SR	Setting up the situation based on Distributed Cognition [DC]	Setting up the situation where full participants, whom knowledge bases are different each other, discuss problems	[20]
	Setting up the situation based on Cognitive Constructivism [CC]	Setting up the situation where full participants discuss problems	[18]
CW	Setting up the community for Legitimate Peripheral Participation [LPP]	Setting up the the community of practice for peripheral participant	[15]
	Setting up the situation for Observational Learning [Ol]	Setting up the situation to share other learners' learning processes	[2]

Note: [**] means an abbreviation for the W-goal.
e.g., The W-goal "Setting up the situation for Peer Tutoring" is abbreviated as "PT".

edge to a specific situation. Restructuring is to reconstruct the learner's knowledge structure. Concerning development of skills, there are also three phases of learning: Cognitive stage, Associative stage, and Autonomous stage[1, 9]. Cognitive stage involves an initial encoding of a target skill into a form sufficient to permit a learner to generate the desired behavior to at least some crude approximation. Associative stage is to tune the target skill through practice. Errors in the initial understanding of the skill are gradually detected and eliminated. Autonomous stage is one of the gradual continued improvements in the performance of the skill.

The learner is expected to achieve these I-goals through interaction with other learners. Tab.2 shows the Y⇐I-goals. For example, to achieve the I-goal "Acquisition of Content-Specific Knowledge (Accretion)", some learners could take the Y⇐I-goal "Learning by being Taught[7, 8]", while some learners could take another Y⇐I-goal "Learning by Observation[2]".

Tab.3 shows the W-goals. The W-goals are classified into three kinds (*i.e.*, M-PR, M-SR, and PR=SR) and one exceptional W-goal (CW) according to their structures. Next section, we describe the conceptual structure of a W-goal and each kind of W-goals.

4 Conceptual Structure of W-goal

To form a learning group means to pick up learners who join in the group as members and to assign a specific role in the group to each member. The formation should have rationale supported by learning theories. The structure of learning goals expresses the rationality. A W-goal, which is a learning goal as a whole group, provides the rationale for the interaction among the members. It means that a W-goal specifies a rational arrangement of Y⇐I-goals. Fig. 3 shows a typical representation for the structure of a W-goal. It would be more easily to understand a learning theory by preparing the structure to represent the theory and filling in each component of the structure with suitable concepts according to the theory.

To describe the specification, we classify the members into two kinds of role-holders: the members who play Principal Role (PR-members) and the members who play Secondary Role (SR-members). Each role is defined as follows:

Principal Role (PR): the most important role in a collaborative learning session. A PR-member is expected to gain main educational benefit through the session. PR is usually played by the learner who first proposed to have the collaborative learning.

Secondary Role (SR): a supporting role for the PR. A SR-member helps the PR-member attains his/her I-goal. The body of specification of a W-goal is the rational arrangement of the goals for interaction among the PR-members and the SR-members. A W-goal has two kinds of goals of interaction as follows:

SR⇐PR-goal: a Y⇐I-goal which means how and for what purpose the PR-member interacts with the SR-member.

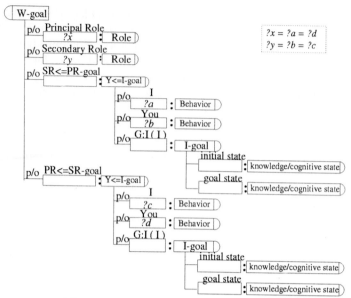

Fig. 3. Conceptual Structure of a W-goal

PR⇐SR-goal: a Y⇐I-goal which means how and for what purpose the SR-member interacts with the PR-member. In the collaborative learning session, all members of learning group are expected to get some educational benefits. So, the SR-member also has an I-goal, and the PR⇐SR-goal should be effective to attain the I-goal.

The entities of these goals refer to the concepts defined in the Y⇐I-goal Ontology. The conditions, which are proper to each W-goal, can be added to the concepts, if necessary. Each of the Y⇐I-goals referred to by SR⇐PR-goal and PR⇐SR-goal consists of three components as follows:

I: a role to attain the Y⇐I-goal. A member who plays "I role" (I-member) is expected to attain his/her I-goal by attaining the Y⇐I-goal.
You: a role as a partner for the I-member.
G:I: an I-goal which means what the I-member attains.

We classify the W-goals into three kinds of W-goals and an exceptional W-goal: M-PR, M-SR, PR=SR, and CW. The following classification of the W-goals depends on the number of the components PR and SR.

M-PR: The W-goals of M-PR type can have plural PR-members and single SR-member.
M-SR: The W-goals of M-SR type can have plural SR-members and single PR-member.
PR=SR: The W-goals of PR=SR type have only one role for members. In this type W-goal, each member joins in a collaborative learning session on an equal footing: they have the same I-goal, and the same Y⇐I-goal is expected for among the members. So we can regard each member as either PR-member or SR-member.

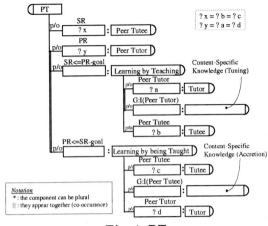

Fig. 4. PT

Fig. 4 represents the W-goal "Setting up the situation for Peer Tutoring (PT)" as an example of the M-PR type W-goal using the structure shown in Fig. 3. According to the theory of Peer Tutoring, main educational benefit by Peer Tutoring is that a learner understands a knowledge more deeply by explaining the knowledge to another learner[7,8]. A learner, who explains the knowledge, is expected to gain the main benefit, and the benefit corresponds to the I-goal "Acquisition of Content-Specific Knowledge (Tuning)[19]". So, the PR is "Peer Tutor", SR⇐PR-goal is "Learning by Teaching", and G:I(Peer Tutor) is "Acquisition of Content-Specific Knowledge (Tuning)" in Fig. 4. On the other hand, "Peer Tutee", who is the partner of "Peer Tutor", is expected to acquire a new knowledge by being taught from the member who plays "Peer Tutor". The SR is "Peer Tutee", PR⇐SR-goal is "Learning by being Taught", and G:I(Peer Tutee) is "Acquisition of Content-Specific Knowledge (Accretion)".

The members solve problems and perform assigned tasks in the collaborative learning session. They are expected to get a few educational benefits as secondary effects through the session[14]. For example, a member could develop his/her cognitive skills (*i.e.,* educational benefit), while he/she solves a problem in physics (*i.e.,* assigned task) with other members. In the M-PR type W-goal, the SR-member mainly solves a problem with the PR-

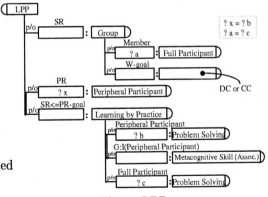

Fig. 5. LPP

member's help. The PR-member is expected to gain an educational benefit from the experience of helping other member. On the other hand, the PR-member mainly solves a problem with the SR-member's help in the M-SR type W-goal. The role of main problem-solver should be assigned to single member, and the role of helper can be assigned to multiple members. For example, in the situation of Peer Tutoring we mentioned above, the role of main problem-solver is "Peer Tutee" (SR) who wants to get a new knowledge to perform assigned tasks, while the role of helper is "Peer Tutor" (PR)[7, 8]. So, the number of members who play "Peer Tutee" should be single, the number of members who play "Peer Tutor" can be multiple, and the W-goal "PT" is identified as the M-PR type.

A W-goal(W_i) can have a group, which has another W-goal(W_j), as the component SR of the W-goal(W_i). We call the W-goal(W_i) "CW-goal" which means a composite W-goal. Fig. 5 shows the structure of the CW-goal "Setting up the situation for Observational Learning (OL)[2]" as an example. A learning group to attain the CW-goal "OL" has a member as an observer (i.e., its component PR). The observer requires a group as an object to observe meaningful interaction. The group is identified as SR.

Each W-goal can be expressed by a set of Y⇐I-goals and I-goals. We can identify a group formation to start an effective collaborative learning session with these goals.

5   Conclusion

We have discussed learning goal ontology which will be able to make it easier to form an effective learning setting and to analyze the educational functions for a learning group. By considering the personal and common goals, we have identified three kinds of learning goals; I-goal, Y⇐I-goal and W-goal. In this paper, we described each learning goal ontology, and the conceptual structure of a W-goal. With the ontology, it is possible to compare and synthesize the learning theories to design the collaborative learning settings.

We have been developing a multi-agent system, which we call "FITS/CL", to support collaborative learning dynamically based on the idea of "Opportunistic Group Formation (OGF)"[11, 12, 23]:

> *Opportunistic Group Formation* is a function to form a collaborative learning group dynamically. When it detects the situation for a learner to shift from individual learning mode to collaborative learning mode, it forms a learning group each of whose members is assigned a reasonable learning goal and a social role which are consistent with the goal for the whole group.

In FITS/CL, each agent should have an ability to realize the following functions:

1. Setting up appropriate learning goal for a learner,
2. Forming learning group to enable the learner to attain the learning goal, and
3. Negotiating with other agents to reach an agreement: a formation of collaborative learning group that each member of the group can get educational benefit.

It is hard to realize the function 2 for the agents, even if each agent can realize the function 1 based on its learner model. Our learning goal ontology is useful for the function 2. By representing group formation suggested by many learning theories using the learning goal ontology, the agents can form a learning group according to learning theories. The agents only look for the W-goals which include a specific I-goal as their component. Concerning the function 3, the agents cannot negotiate or reach an agreement if there is no criterion for the educational benefit. Our learning goal ontology enables the agents to infer educational benefit before the collaborative learning session starts, and justifies the agent's proposal by learning theories.

Future work includes identification of learner's role appeared in collaborative learning session and description of conditions to select a learner appropriate for each role.

References

1. Anderson,J.R. (1982) Acquisition of Cognitive Skill, Psychological Review, 89(4), 369-406.
2. Bandura, A. (1971) Social Learning Theory, General Learning Press.
3. Bransford, J. D. et al.(1990) Teaching thinking and content knowledge, In: Dimensions of thinking and cognitive instruction, Erlbaum. 381-413.
4. Chi, M.T.H. et al.(1989) Self-Explanations, Cognitive Science, 13, 145-182.
5. CTGV (1992) Anchored instruction in science education, In: Philosophy of science, cognitive psychology, and educational theory and practice. SUNY Press. 244-273.
6. Collins, A. (1991) Cognitive apprenticeship and instructional technology, In: Educational values and cognitive instruction, Erlbaum.
7. Cooke, N.L. et al.(1983) Peer tutoring, Special Press.
8. Endlsey, W.R. (1980) Peer tutorial instruction. Educational Technology
9. Fitts, P.M. (1964) Perceptual-Motor Skill Learning, In: Categories of Human Learning, Academis Press. 243-285.
10. Flavell, J. H. (1976) Metacognitive aspects of problem-solving, In: The nature of intelligence. Erlbaum. 231-235.
11. Ikeda, M. et al.(1995) Ontological issue of CSCL Systems Design, Proc. of AI-ED 95, 234-249.
12. Ikeda, M. et al.(1997) Opportunistic Group Formation, Proc. of AI-ED 97, 166-174.
13. Inaba, A. et al.(1999) The Learning Goal Ontology for Collaborative Learning. http://www.ai.sanken.osaka-u.ac.jp/~inaba/LGOntology/
14. Inaba, A. et al.(1997) The Intelligent Discussion Coordinating System for Effective Collaborative Learning, AIED 97: Workshop Notes IV, 26-33.
15. Lave,J. et al.(1991) Situated Learning, Cambridge University Press.
16. Mizoguchi, R. et al.(2000) Using Ontological Engineering to Overcome Common AI-ED Problems, IJAIED, 11, to appear
17. Mizoguchi,R. et al.(1997) Roles of Shared Ontology in AI-ED Research, Proc. of AI-ED 97, 537-544.
18. Piaget, J. et al.(1971) The Psychology of the Child, Basic Books.
19. Rumelhart, D.E. et al.(1978) Accretion, Tuning, and Restructuring, In: Semantic factors in cognition. Erlbaum. 37-53.
20. Salomon, G. (1993) Distributed cognitions, Cambridge University Press.
21. Spiro, R. J. et al.(1988) Cognitive flexibility. Proc. of the 10th Annual Conf. of Cognitive Science Society, Erlbaum. 375-383.
22. Spiro, R. J. et al.(1995) Cognitive flexibility, constructivism, and hypertext. http://www.ilt.columbia.edu/ilt/papers/Spiro.html
23. Supnithi, T. et al.(1999) Learning Goal Ontology Supported by Learning Theories for Opportunistic Group Formation, Proc. of AIED99.
24. Vygotsky, L.S. (1929) The problem of the cultural development of the child, II. Jl. of Genetic Psychology, 36, 414-434.
25. Vygotsky,L.S. (1930) Mind in Society, Harvard University Press. (Re-published 1978)

Limitations of Student Control:
Do Students Know When they Need Help?

Vincent Aleven and Kenneth R. Koedinger

HCI Institute
School of Computer Science
Carnegie Mellon University
Pittsburgh, PA 15213

aleven@cs.cmu.edu, koedinger@cs.cmu.edu

Abstract Intelligent tutoring systems often emphasize learner control: They let the students decide when and how to use the system's intelligent and unintelligent help facilities. This means that students must judge when help is needed and which form of help is appropriate. Data about students' use of the help facilities of the PACT Geometry Tutor, a cognitive tutor for high school geometry, suggest that students do not always have these metacognitive skills. Students rarely used the tutor's on-line Glossary of geometry knowledge. They tended to wait long before asking for hints, and tended to focus only on the most specific hints, ignoring the higher hint levels. This suggests that intelligent tutoring systems should support students in learning these skills, just as they support students in learning domain-specific skills and knowledge. Within the framework of cognitive tutors, this requires creating a cognitive model of the metacognitive help-seeking strategies, in the form of production rules. The tutor then can use the model to monitor students' metacognitive strategies and provide feedback.

1   Introduction

Intelligent tutoring systems would not be *that* if they did not provide intelligent help and feedback to learners. The intelligent hint messages and feedback help students reduce unproductive time and thereby to learn more efficiently [Anderson, *et al.,* 1989; McKendree, 1990]. Also, the tutor's explanations, if read carefully, may help students to bridge gaps in their knowledge. Some systems also provide unintelligent, or low cost help, in the form of on-line dictionaries [Shute and Gluck, 1996], or a Glossary [Aleven, *et al.,* 1999].

The common wisdom in the field of intelligent tutoring systems holds that by and large, the system should let students control and organize their own learning

Acknowledgments: This research is sponsored by an NSF grant to the Center for Interdisplinary Research on Constructive Learning (CIRCLE), a research center located at the University of Pittsburgh and Carnegie Mellon University.

processes; the system should intervene as little as possible [Burton and Brown, 1982] and help should be given on request only. The underlying assumption is that the student herself is a better judge of when help is needed than the system, which does not have much bandwidth to access a students' thoughts, and may not have a complete enough domain model to account for all observed strategies. Thus, in many systems, the help messages are given primarily when the student requests help, for example in Belvedere [Paolucci, *et al*, 1996] and Sherlock [Katz, *et al*, 1998].

Recognizing the need for help is a (metacognitive) skill in its own right. It requires that students monitor their own progress and understanding. For example, it requires that students judge whether an error is just a slip and easily repairable, and when an error is due to a lack of knowledge or the result of guessing. Such metacognitive skills are very important, for example, they mediate learning from examples [VanLehn, *et al.*, 1992]. There is evidence that such skills are not mastered by all. There are individual differences with respect to students' metacognitive skills, for example, the abilty to explain examples [Chi *et al*, 1989] or the ability to make productive use of optional on-line tools in a computer tutor [Shute and Gluck, 1996]. Therefore, it is not clear that placing control in the hands of the learner is always the best strategy. There is evidence that higher-ability students do better in (non-intelligent) computer-based environments that offer a greater degree of learner control, whereas lower-ability students do better in more structured environments [Recker and Pirolli, 1992]. Also, students with higher prior ability are better able to judge their need for help after errors than students with lower prior ability, in an intelligent tutoring system with on-demand help [Wood and Wood, in press]. These studies suggest that higher-ability students have better metacognitive skills. This means that emphasizing learner control in intelligent tutoring systems may lead to the unfortunate situation that those who need help the most, are the least likely to receive it in time.

Thus, there is ample reason further to study whether the users of intelligent tutoring systems have the metacognitive skills necessary to take advantage of the help facilities that these systems offer. We studied students' use of two types of help facilities of the PACT Geometry Tutor. In this paper, we discuss our findings and the implications for the design of intelligent tutoring systems.

2   Intelligent and Unintelligent Help in the PACT Geometry Tutor

The PACT Geometry tutor is an integrated part of a complete high school course for geometry, developed with guidance from a mathematics teacher. This curriculum emphasizes geometry problem solving (as opposed to proof), including the use of geometry for real-world problems, following guidelines from the National Council of Teachers of Mathematics [NCTM, 1989].

The PACT Geometry Tutor is a cognitive tutor [Anderson, *et al.*, 1995]. It supports guided learning by doing: It monitors students as they solve geometry problems, and provides hints and feedback. It employs a cognitive model of the skills of an ideal student, represented as production rules. The tutor uses the model, in a process called *model tracing,* to assess students' solutions and to generate hints. The cognitive model is also the basis for student modeling. The tutor maintains estimates of the probability that the student masters each skill in the model, using a Bayesian algorithm called *knowledge tracing.* The information in the student model is used to select appropriate problems and to advance the student to the next section of the curriculum at appropriate times.

In most problems in the PACT Geometry Tutor, students are given a description and a diagram, and are asked to calculate unknown quantities, such as angle measures or segment measures (see Figure 1, window top left). In addition, students must provide an explanation of each solution step, by indicating which geometry theorem or definition justifies it. They can select "reasons" from the tutor's Glossary window, which lists important geometry theorems and definitions, shown in the middle in Figure 1. When students enter a numeric answer or explanation, the tutor tells them whether it is correct or not.

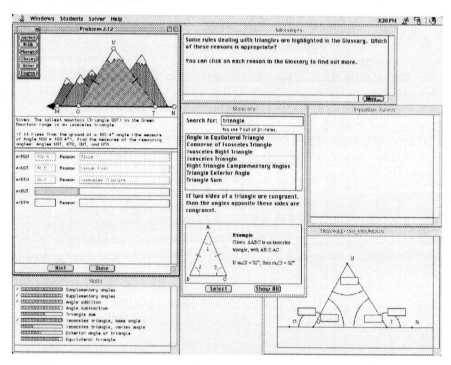

Fig. 1: The PACT Geometry Tutor

The tutor provides intelligent help in the form of on-demand hints and unintelligent, or low-cost, help in the form of a Glossary of geometry knowledge. For each relevant geometry rule, the Glossary contains a description and a short example, as can be seen in Figure 1. Students can search and peruse the Glossary at will. The Glossary was introduced in the PACT Geometry tutor in an attempt to get students to pay more attention to the rules of geometry (as the reasons behind their actions) and thereby improve their understanding [Aleven, *et al.*, 1999]. Also, the Glossary is much like low-cost sources of information that students are likely to encounter in the real world, such as their own bookshelf, the library, the world-wide web, etc. Teaching students to take advantage of such resources is an important goal in its own right.

The tutor provides intelligent help in the form of on-demand hints. The hints usually have multiple levels, each with increasingly more specific advice. The hints are designed to encourage a general metacognitive strategy: When you do not know something, use an available resource, such as the Glossary, to look it up. Look at what kind of problem you are dealing with, and then look at Glossary rules that are relevant to that kind of problem. For example, if the problem involves a triangle, such as the problem shown in Figure 1, look for rules dealing with triangles (see Table 1, level 1). The next hint highlights a small number of relevant geometry rules the Glossary (Table 1, level 2). Further hints explain which Glossary rule could be used and how it applies to the problem. The last hint of each sequence (the "bottom out hint") makes it clear what the unknown quantity is, usually by stating an expression, or an equation, (Table 1, level 7).

When students request a hint, this counts as an error, with respect to the tutor's knowledge tracing. That is, the tutor's estimate of the student's mastery of the relevant skill

1. In this problem, you have Triangle OUT. What do you know about triangles that enables you to find the measure of Angle OUT?

2. Some rules dealing with triangles are highlighted in the Glossary. Which of these reasons is appropriate?

   You can click on each reason in the Glossary to find out more.

3. The sum of the measures of the three interior angles of a triangle is 180 degrees.

   Angle OUT is an interior angle in a triangle. You know the measures of the other two interior angles: Angles UOT and OTU.

4. Can you write an equation that helps you find the measure of Angle OUT?

5. The sum of the measures of Angles OUT, UOT, and OTU equals $180°$. So you have:

   $m\angle OUT + m\angle UOT + m\angle OTU = 180$

6. In the previous hint, you saw that:

   $m\angle OUT + m\angle UOT + m\angle OTU = 180$

   You can replace $m\angle UOT$ by 79 and $m\angle OTU$ by 79. Also, you can use a variable (say, x) instead of $m\angle OUT$. This gives:

   $x + 79 + 79 = 180$

7. Find the measure of Angle OUT by solving for x:

   $x + 79 + 79 = 180$

   You can use the Equation Solver.

Table 1: A hint sequence generated by the PACT Geometry Tutor.

is debited. This was done for two reasons: The theory behind knowledge tracing requires that a hint request is treated as evidence that the student has not mastered the given skill. Also, debiting the skill estimate makes it less likely that students complete problems simply by asking for a hint on each step.

Given these tutor facilities, a rational help-seeking strategy may be to try to avoid the penalty that results from errors or hints, and use the Glossary as a first line of defense:

For a step that has not been worked on previously:

If one can find the answer or reason with reasonable certainty (relying on one's memory, not the tutor's help), then enter it.

If one is not sure, use the Glossary: extract a search cue, type the search term into the Glossary, evaluate the rules that are listed.

If all else fails, ask for intelligent help.

After an error:

If one understands what went wrong, then correct the error, without using help.

If one is not sure, use intelligent help.

3   Evaluation Study

In the Spring of 1998, we conducted a study to evaluate the PACT Geometry tutor. The study took place in a suburban school in the Pittsburgh area, in the context of a geometry course based on the PACT Geometry curriculum. Thus, the data pertain to normal use of the tutor in a school. Since the goal of the study was to evaluate the effect of reason-giving, two versions of the PACT Geometry tutor were used: a reason version, which is

	Rate of Glossary use		Rate of Glossary use prior to first attempt		Success rate
	All use	Deliberate use only	All use	Deliberate use only	
Answer Steps	2.7%	2.0%	1.4%	0.8%	54%
Reason Steps	43%	15%	36%	12%	55%

Table 2: Rate of Glossary use, as compared to the success rate. The rate of Glossary use is the percentage of steps for which the Glossary was used. The success rate is the percentage of steps where students got the answer right, without errors or hints.

the version described above, and an answer only version, in which students were not required to provide reasons for their answers. In this paper, however, we present the data for both groups of students together.

The study involved 53 students, enrolled in the course, 41 of whom completed the study. All students participated in four activities: they had classroom instruction, they solved problems on the tutor (they spent 500 minutes, on the average, working on the tutor unit that deals with the geometric properties of angles), and they took a pre-test, and a post-test. The pre-test took place before students started to work on the tutor, the post-test afterwards. The tests involved problems of the same type as those in the tutor curriculum, and included transfer problems as well. The results indicate that there was a significant improvement in students' test score, attributable to their work on the tutor, in combination with classroom instruction [Aleven, *et al.*, 1999].

4   Use of Unintelligent Help

We analyzed the protocols of students' sessions with the tutor, in order to learn more about their strategies for help use. The protocols, collected automatically by the tutor, contain detailed information about the students' and tutor's actions. We were interested in finding out whether the students followed the strategy for help use, outlined above. We found the following:

- Students used the Glossary on 43% of the explanation steps and used it on 2.7% of the numeric steps (see Table 2). By "step" we mean a subgoal in the problem, or (equivalently) an entry in the tutor's answer sheet, shown on the top-left in Figure 1.
- On numeric answer steps, students used the Glossary about as often in response to errors as they used it before a first attempt at entering a solution (1.3% v. 1.4% of all steps, see Table 2).
- There is little evidence that the students used the Glossary for the more difficult skills, at least not prior to their first attempt at entering a numeric answer. For numeric answer steps, the correlation between Glossary use (prior to first attempt) and skill difficulty was 0.29. Skill difficulty was measured as the success rate for the skill, a measure of performance with the tutor.
- On 0.33% of steps (47 out of 14094), students were apparently able to take advantage of the Glossary to find a correct numeric answer, without errors or hints. In these steps, students went to the Glossary before a first attempt at answering, looked at a Glossary rule that could be applied to solve the step, and perhaps looked at other Glossary items, and then entered a correct answer.

Thus, for numeric steps, the evidence is that students did not follow the strategy for help seeking outlined above. If students followed this strategy, they would consult the Glossary when they anticipated that a step was beyond their capability. They would therefore not make many errors without first consulting the Glossary. But students did not use the Glossary much at all on numeric steps (2.7%) and correctly completed only 0.33% of answer steps with apparent help from the Glossary. They made many errors without first consulting the Glossary: The rate of Glossary use is far below the error rate (see Table 2). The rate of Glossary use is even lower when we count only the steps where the students used the Glossary in a *deliberate* manner. We defined deliberate use as meaning that the student inspected at least one Glossary item for more than 1 second. It is obviously not possible to read and interpret a complete Glossary item in such a short time. However, one second might be enough to recognize as relevant a description that one has read before.

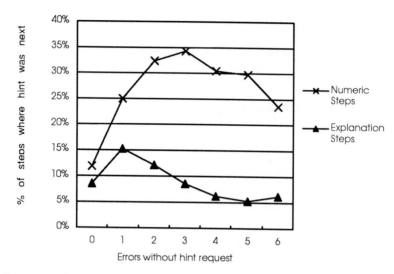

Fig. 2: Frequency of help use after *N* errors without help—that is, given that a student had made *N* errors on a step without asking for help, how often was the next action on that step a help request and not another attempt at answering?

Further, if students followed the desired help-seeking strategy, the bulk of Glossary use would occur before a first attempt at entering a step. After that attempt, students could use intelligent help without penalty. Also, students would use the Glossary primarily for more difficult skills. These predictions were not borne out by the data, as shown above. Students used the Glossary primarily to enter explanations (43% of steps). This can in part be explained by the fact that students could enter explanations by selecting from the Glossary. Much of the Glossary use for explanation-giving appears to be rapid selection, but we also saw a considerable amount of deliberate use (see Table 2).

5   Use of Intelligent Help

We also analyzed the student protocols with respect to students' use of the tutor's on-request hints. We found that:

- The students used the intelligent help facility on 29% of the answer steps and 22% of the explanation steps.

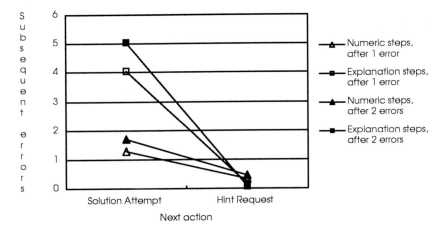

Fig. 3: Subsequent errors on a step, given that the student had already made 1 or 2 errors on that step without asking for a hint, and then attempted another solution ("solution attempt") or asked for a hint ("hint request").

- Students used help before their first attempt at answering on 12% of the answer steps and 9% of the explanation steps.
- When the students requested help, they requested to see all hint levels (i.e., they asked for more help until they had seen the bottom out hint) on 82% of answer steps and 89% of explanation steps.
- When students made an error, and if they have not asked for help already, then it is was more likely that they would attempt another answer than that they would ask for help, as Figure 2 indicates. This is so regardless of how many errors the student had made already. For example, after making three errors on a numeric step without asking for a hint, students asked for a hint only 34% of the time.

As before, we ask to what extent students followed the help-seeking strategy described above. If students followed the strategy, they would ask for intelligent help in two kinds of situations: when they made an error that they could not fix quickly, and on steps where they had little idea how to proceed. The overall rate of hint use, (29% for numeric steps, 22% for explanation steps), is consistent with this. A close up view of the data reveals however that students often waited too long before requesting a hint, that is, they made too many errors without asking for a hint. According to the desired strategy for help use, students should not make more than one or two errors on a step, before asking for a hint. However, if this was what really happened, the help use graph in Figure 2 would be (close to) 100% after 2 or 3 errors without a hint. Clearly it is not. Further, the fact that students requested to see the bottom out hint in 82% or 89% of all steps with help, indicates that the intermediate-level hint messages were not effective. In short, while there is some evidence that students follow the desired help-seeking strategy, there is significant room for improvement.

We also investigated the immediate effects of the tutor's hints. We found that after one or two errors were made on a step, asking for a hint helped to reduce both the number of subsequent errors on the same step (see Figure 3) and the amount of time spent to complete the step (see Figure 4). This is evidence that intelligent help aids performance, as was found also in other studies [Wood and Wood, in press; Anderson, *et al.*, 1989; McKendree, 1990].

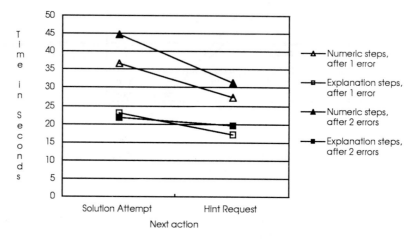

Fig. 4: Time to complete the step, given that the student had already done one of the following four things: made 1 or 2 errors without asking for a hint, and then either asked for a hint ("hint request") or entered another solution ("solution attempt").

6   Discussion and Conclusion

Student control is often regarded as a good thing in intelligent tutoring systems. Many systems provide help only on students' request. Thus, the students must decide when and how to use the help facilities, which requires that they make judgments about their own knowledge (self-monitoring) and that they are able to judge when they can benefit from help. But are they able to do so? In order to evaluate the assumption that student control is beneficial, we assessed students' help-seeking strategies in a representative intelligent tutoring system, the PACT Geometry tutor. This tutor provides intelligent help in the form of on-demand hints, and unintelligent help in the form of a Glossary.

The data indicate that students did not use the Glossary very much, contrary to our expectation that they would use it regularly to help with difficult steps. This is surprising, especially if one considers that the students may have been able to avoid errors by using the Glossary and generally seem to be quite aware that the more errors they make, the more problems the tutor will assign. So why would they pass up a source of free help?

This probably says something about the metacognitive skills of the given student population, ninth graders (15-year olds) in a suburban high school. They may not have sufficient metacognitive skills to judge when they can benefit from Glossary lookup. They may not be very good in judging the difficulty of steps, or at monitoring their own knowledge and understanding. Also, they may not have learned the general strategy to look up things that they do not know. Further, students may lack the mathematical reading ability to interpret the information in the Glossary: statements of definitions and theorems, illustrated with examples. It takes considerable effort to read a rule (even one that has been discussed in class before) and evaluate how it can be applied to the problem at hand.

Students used the tutor's intelligent help facilities far more frequently than they used the Glossary. But they often waited long before asking for a hint, not taking multiple errors on a step as a signal that it is time to ask for a hint. Also, they did not seem to benefit much from the intermediate hint levels. In the vast majority of cases in which they asked for help (82% of numeric steps, 89% of explanation steps), students repeated their help request until they reached the bottom out hint. It may be that in most of these cases, students quite deliberately did not read the intermediate hint levels and read only the bottom out message, which as mentioned pretty much hands them the correct answer. Such hint abuse is undesirable. Learning from being given only the right answer (i.e., the bottom out hint), just as learning from examples, requires that the student constructs an explanation of why the right answer is right. [Anderson, et al., 1989]. The intermediate hint levels may be helpful in this regard. An alternative explanation for the high percentage of bottom out hints is that students find it difficult to read and interpret the tutor's hint messages, just as they seem to find it difficult to interpret the information in the Glossary. In sum, the data indicate that students do not have the necessary metacognitive skills, nor the required mathematical reading ability, to take maximum advantage of on-request help, or the tutor's on-line Glossary.

The tutor should provide more support. It should not always leave it up to the students to judge when they can benefit from using the tutor's on-line help facilities. Rather, the tutor should help students to *learn* to develop effective metacognitive help-seeking strategies (see also [Wood & Wood, in press; Recker and Pirolli, 1992; Conati and VanLehn, 1999]). Further, it should provide support for the interpretation and application of mathematical rules listed in the Glossary.

In order to tutor at the metacognitive level, a cognitive tutor needs a model of the metacognitive strategy to be taught. The model presented in this paper may serve as a starting point, although further study may indicate that it needs to be refined. Within the framework of cognitive tutors, the model could be implemented as a production rule model and be used for model-tracing. It may be useful also to take into account information in the student model to assess whether a student might be over-using or under-using the help facilities, as suggested by Wood and Wood [in press].

For example, with a model of metacognitive strategy in place, the tutor could do much more to help students learn to make effective use of the Glossary. As mentioned, the Glossary is representative of many sources of low-cost help that students will encounter in the real world. Glossary lookup skills learned with the tutor may transfer to the use of the World-Wide Web, for example. Using a model of metacognitive skill, the tutor will be able to help the students in finding relevant information in the Glossary and evaluating how that information applies to the current problem. When students type a search cue into the Glossary, the tutor could check whether the search will be productive and if not, it could provide feedback and advice. If the tutor is to help students evaluate how a rule in the Glossary applies to the problem at hand, a mapping step needs to be added to the tutor interface, that lets the student point out how a rule is instantiated in the current problem, that is, which geometric objects in the problem (angles, etc.) correspond to objects mentioned in the rule and what conclusions follow. The tutor could provide feedback.

Further, the metacognitive tutor could help students to use the tutor's on-demand intelligent help more appropriately, like the strategy tutor agent proposed in [Ritter, 1997]. For example, it could help the student learn that it is often best to try to use a low-cost source of help before using a source of high cost help. When a student asks for a (high-cost) hint without first using the (low-cost) Glossary, the tutor could interpret this as evidence that the student does not master the desired metacognitive strategy. It could provide feedback saying "Instead of asking for a hint, you might use the Glossary in order to figure this out. It is better to use the low cost help (the Glossary) before you use high-cost help (the tutor's hint messages)." Similarly, if the student did not ask for help when this would seem appropriate, (e.g., after making two or more errors on a step), the tutor could provide feedback, saying: "Usually, when the going gets tough like this, it means that there is a piece of geometry knowledge that you have not mastered yet. It is good to ask for a hint." (As a first step, we have modified the PACT Geometry tutor so that it initiates help after two errors. According to the data presented in this paper, this will reduce the number of errors students make and save them some time.) Similarly, the tutor could protest when a student abuses hints, going straight for the bottom out hint without paying attention to the intermediate levels. When this happens, the tutor could for example require that the student explain the bottom out hint, by constructing a mapping with a Glossary rule. These forms of feedback at the metacognitive level may help students to balance the use of help and errors, which in one study was shown to be an important indicator of success, especially for lower-ability students [Wood and Wood, in press].

To conclude, in order to for intelligent tutoring systems to be truly adaptive, they should help students to develop effective metacognitive skills. The potential payoff is great, since these skills will help students learn in other domains as well. They will help them to become not just better geometrists, or mathematicians, but better learners.

References

Aleven, V., K. R. Koedinger, and K. Cross, 1999. Tutoring Answer Explanation Fosters Learning with Understanding. In *Artificial Intelligence in Education, Proceedings of AIED-99,* edited by S. P. Lajoie and M. Vivet, 199-206. Amsterdam: IOS Press.

Anderson, J. R., F. G. Conrad, and A. T. Corbett, 1989. Skill Acquisition and the LISP Tutor. *Cognitive Science,* 13, 467-505.

Anderson, J. R., A. T. Corbett, K. R. Koedinger, and R. Pelletier, 1995. Cognitive tutors: Lessons learned. *The Journal of the Learning Sciences,* 4, 167-207.

Burton, R. R., and J. S. Brown. An Investigation of Computer Coaching for Informal Learning Activities, 1982. In *Intelligent Tutoring Systems,* edited by D. H. Sleeman and J. S. Brown, New York: Academic Press.

Chi, M. T. H., M. Bassok, M. W. Lewis, P. Reimann, and R. Glaser, 1989. Self-Explanations: How Students Study and Use Examples in Learning to Solve Problems. *Cognitive Science,* 13, 145-182.

Conati, C., and K. VanLehn, 1999. Teaching Meta-Cognitive Skills: Implementation and Evaluation of a Tutoring System to Guide Self-Explanation While Learning from Examples. In *Artificial Intelligence in Education, Proceedings of AIED-99,* edited by S. P. Lajoie and M. Vivet, 297-304. Amsterdam: IOS Press.

Katz., S., A. Lesgold, E. Hughes, D. Peters, G. Eggan, M. Gordin, and L. Greenberg, 1998. Sherlock II: An Intelligent Tutoring System Built Upon the LRDC Tutor Framework. In *Facilitating the Development and Use of Interactive Learning Environments,* edited by C. P. Bloom and R. B. Loftin. Mahwah, NJ: Erlbaum.

McKendree, J., 1990. Effective Feedback Content for Tutoring Complex Skills. *Human Computer Interaction,* 5, 381-413.

NCTM, 1989. Curriculum and Evaluation Standards for School Mathematics. National Council of Teachers of Mathematics. Reston, VA: The Council.

Paolucci, M., Suthers, D., and A. Weiner, 1996. Automated Advice-Giving Strategies for Scientific Inquiry. In *Proceedings of the Third International Conference on Intelligent Tutoring Systems (ITS'96),* edited by C. Frasson, G. Gauthier, and A. Lesgold, 372-381. Berlin: Springer-Verlag.

Recker, M. M., and P. Pirolli, 1992. Student Strategies for Learning Programming from a Computational Environment. In *Proceedings of the Second International Conference on Intelligent Tutoring Systems, ITS '92,* edited by C. Frasson, G. Gauthier, and G. I. McCalla, 382-394. Berlin: Springer-Verlag.

Ritter, S., 1997. Communication, Cooperation and Competition among Multiple Tutor Agents. In *Artificial Intelligence in Education, Proceedings of AI-ED 97 World Conference,* edited by B. du Boulay and R. Mizoguchi, 31-38. Amsterdam: IOS Press.

Shute, V. J., and K. A. Cluck, 1996. Individual Differences in Patterns of Spontaneous Online Tool Use. *The Journal of the Learning Sciences,* 5 (4), 329-355.

VanLehn, K., R. M. Jones, and M. T. Chi, 1992. A Model of the Self-Explanation Effect. *The Journal of the Learning Sciences,* 2 (1), 1-59.

Wood, H. A., and D. J. Wood, in press. Help Seeking, Learning and Contingent Tutoring. To appear in *Computers and Education* (special edition, 2000).

Further Results from the Evaluation of an Intelligent Computer Tutor to Coach Self-Explanation

Cristina Conati[1], Kurt VanLehn[2]

[1]Department of Computer Science, University of British Columbia
2366 Main Mall, Vancouver, B.C. Canada V6T 1Z4
email: conati@cs.ubc.ca
[2]Department of Computer Science, University of Pittsburgh,
Pittsburgh, PA, 15260, U.S.A
vanlehn@cs.pitt.edu

Abstract

We present further results on the educational effectiveness of an intelligent computer tutor that helps students learn effectively from examples by coaching self-explanation – the process of explaining to oneself an example worked-out solution. An earlier analysis of the results from a formative evaluation of the system provided suggestive evidence that it could improve students' learning. In this paper, we present additional results derived from a more comprehensive analysis of the experimental data. They provide a stronger indication of the system's effectiveness and suggest general guidelines for effective support of self-explanation during example studying.

1 Introduction

The research presented in this paper represents a step toward exploring innovative ways in which computers can enhance education and learning. While most intelligent tutoring systems support students during problem solving and teach domain specific skills, we have devised a computational framework that supports learning from examples and that coaches the general learning skill known as self-explanation - generating explanations and justifications to oneself to clarify an example solution. Several studies show that self-explanation greatly improves learning from examples (for overviews of these studies see [4] and [10]) and that coaching self-explanation can extend these benefits ([3], [4]). Our framework, known as the SE-Coach, aims to provide the individualized monitoring and guidance to self-explanation that has been proven so beneficial when administered by human tutors. It has been implemented and tested within Andes [11], a tutoring system that helps students learn Newtonian physics through both example studying and problem solving.

Other tutoring systems rely on examples as instructional means, but they use them to support students as they solve problems, not as a specific learning phase prior to and complementary to problem solving. These systems present students with relevant examples as they are solving problems and help students understand the connection between the example and the problems [12], [7], [1]. However, none of these systems monitor how students study and understand the presented examples. Moreover, the systems themselves, rather than the students, generate explanations to help the students understand the examples. The Geometry Tutor [2] explicitly encourages students to explain the solution steps they have used to build geometry proofs, in terms of geometry axioms. However, the explanations are generated during problem solving and consist simply of selecting an item from a list of geometry axioms. The student does not have to explain the content of the axiom. Furthermore, the tutor makes the student explain each solution step, instead of trying to assess if some explanations may be more beneficial for the student than others.

Unlike the systems above, the SE-Coach includes an interface designed to encourage spontaneous, constructive self-explanation of examples. It also includes a help module that explicitly elicits further self-explanation tailored to a student's needs, as assessed by the SE-Coach probabilistic student model, when the interface scaffolding is not sufficient to overcome the natural reticence to self-explain that many students show [4], [10].

Self-explanation is a learning process whose underlying mechanisms are still unclear and under investigation. Since the SE-Coach is built on existing hypotheses about the features that make self-explanation effective for learning, an accurate evaluation of its effectiveness may allow us to shed light on the validity of the hypotheses and possibly suggest new ones. In [6], we presented initial results of a formal evaluation that we performed to test the usability and effectiveness of the system. These results indicated that the SE-Coach's interface is easy to use and generally effective in stimulating self-explanation. They also provided initial support on the SE-Coach's educational effectiveness. In this paper, we present a more detailed analysis of the experimental data that reveals a significant interaction between experimental condition and the learning stage in which students used the system, and provides insights on how the SE-Coach can more effectively bring students to constructively learn from examples.

2 Overview of the System

The SE-Coach's interface includes three different levels of scaffolding for self-explanation, to accommodate the varied propensity to self-explain that different students have, so as to provide each student with the minimum intervention sufficient to trigger constructive self-explanation.

The first level of scaffolding is given by a masking interface that presents different parts of the example covered by grey boxes (see Figure 1). In order to read the text or graphics hidden under a box, the student must move the mouse pointer over it. The fact that not all the example parts are visible at once helps students focus attention and reflect on individual example parts, and allows the SE-Coach to track student's attention [6]. The second level of scaffolding is provided by explicit prompts to self-explain. These prompts go from a generic reminder to self-explain, that appears when a student uncovers an example part, to more specific prompts for self-explanations that have been shown to correlate with learning in the self-explanation studies: (a) justify solution steps in terms of domain principles; (b) relate solution steps to goals in the underlying solution plan.

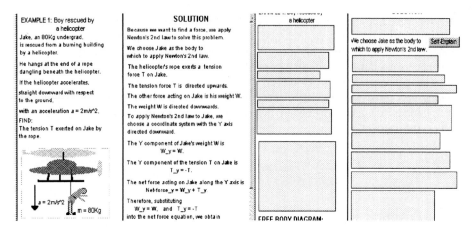

Figure 1: A physics example (left), as it is presented in the masking interface (right)

The third level of scaffolding consists of menu-based tools designed to provide constructive but controllable ways to generate the above self-explanations, to help those students that would be unable to properly self-explain if left to their own devices [10]. If a student selects the prompt to self-explain in terms of domain principles ("This is true because..."), a Rule Browser is displayed in the right half of the window (see Figure 2a), while if the student selects the prompt to self-explain in terms of the solution plan ("The purpose of this step is..."), a Plan Browser is activated instead.

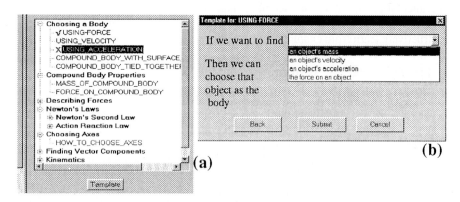

Figure 2: (a) Selections in the Rule Browser and (b) Template filling

The rule browser contains a hierarchy of physics rules, reflecting the content of the SE-Coach's knowledge base. The student can browse the rule hierarchy to find a rule that justifies the currently uncovered part. The SE-Coach will use a green check or a red cross to provide feedback on the correctness of the student's selection (see Figure 2a). To explain more about the actual content of a rule, the student can click on the "Template" button in the rule browser. A dialog box comes up (see Figure 2b) with a partial definition of the rule that the student can complete by selecting appropriate fillers from available pull down menus. The SE-Coach gives immediate feedback on the student's selections.

The plan browser is similar to the rule browser, but it displays a hierarchical tree representing the solution plan for a particular example instead of the SE-Coach's physics rules. The student explains the role of the uncovered part by selecting in the plan hierarchy the step that most closely motivates the fact.

The SE-Coach includes a probabilistic student model based on a Bayesian network. The Bayesian network comprises a model of correct self-explanation for the current example, probabilities estimating the student's physics knowledge and nodes representing the student's reading and self-explanation actions. At any time during the interaction, probabilities in the Bayesian network assess how well the student understands the example solution and how the student's knowledge changes as a result of the interaction with the system [5]. Using this assessment, the SE-Coach prompts the student to generate further self-explanation to fix gaps in the student's example understanding.

Initially, self-explanation is voluntary. However, if a student tries to close the example when the student model indicates that there are still some lines left to self-explain, then the SE-Coach generates a warning and colors pink the corresponding masking interface boxes. It also provides more directive advice as of what interface tool should be used to better self-explain each line. The SE-Coach's tutorial interventions represent a fourth, stronger level of scaffolding for self-explanation, directed to help those students that do not self-explain because they tend to overestimate their understanding [4].

3   Empirical Evaluation of the SE-Coach

To test the system's effectiveness for learning, we performed a formal study with 56 college students. The SE-Coach does not provide any introductory physics instruction, because it is meant to complement regular classroom activities. Therefore, an evaluation of the SE-Coach requires subjects who have the right level of domain knowledge for using the system. Students generally benefit more from examples when they are studying a new topic, whereas as the students' knowledge improves, problem solving becomes more effective for learning [8]. Hence, to evaluate the SE-Coach adequately, subjects need to have enough knowledge to understand the topic of the examples, but not so much knowledge to find the examples not worthy of attention. The ideal evaluation setting for the SE-Coach would be in the context of an introductory physics course, where it is possible to control when students are ready to study examples on a new topic. Unfortunately, we could not coordinate the SE-Coach's evaluation with a specific physics course. Instead, we conducted the study in our laboratory, with students who were taking introductory physics classes at four different colleges: the University of Pittsburgh (20 students), Carnegie Mellon University (14 students), Community College of Allegheny County (5 students) and U.S. Naval Academy (17 students). The best we could do to get subjects at comparable learning stages was to run the subjects after their first class on Newton's Second Law and before they took a class test on the topic.

The one-session study comprised: 1) solving four pre-test problems on Newton's Second Law; 2) studying examples on Newton's Second Law with the system; 3) solving post-test problems equivalent but not identical to the pre-test ones; The study had two conditions. In the *experimental (SE)* condition, 29 students studied examples with the complete SE-Coach. In the *control* condition, 27 students studied examples with the masking interface and Plan Browser only[1]. They had no access to the Rule Browser and Templates, nor feedback or coaching.

3.1. Effectiveness of the SE-Coach

As we reported in [6], the analysis of the log data file from the study shows that the SE-Coach's interface is easy to use and is quite successful at stimulating self-explanation. The gains scores between post-test and pretest were higher for the SE condition, although the difference between gain scores of the two conditions was not statistically significant. Since then, we have sought to better understand the reason behind the above outcome by restricting the analysis to the subgroups of subjects coming from different colleges. We found that the SE condition of CMU (Carnegie Mellon) and CCAC (Community College of Allegheny County) students performed better than the control condition (see Figure 3). The performance difference, as measured by an Analysis of Covariance with post-test as dependent variable, pre-test as covariate and condition as main effect, was statistically significant for CMU students ($p < 0.04$) and nearly significant ($p = 0.0576$) for CCAC students. In contrast, in the Pitt (Univ. of Pittsburgh) and USNA (U.S. Naval Academy) subgroups, students in the control condition performed slightly better than students in the SE condition (see Figure 3), although the difference was not statistically significant

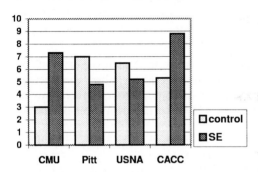

Figure 3: Gains scores for the four subgroups

Figure 4: pretest scores for the four subgroups

The commonality of behavior between CMU and CACC students is quite surprising, because CMU and CCAC are supposed to be, respectively, the best and the worst among the four colleges in the study. This ranking is confirmed by the pretest scores shown in Figure 4. The difference in pretest performance between CMU and CCAC is the only one that approaches significance ($p = 0.0561$), among the pretest performances of the four groups.

---

[1] We let the control students access the Plan Browser because introductory physics courses usually do not address solution planning, therefore control students would have had too much of a disadvantage if they had not been able to see what a solution plan is through the Plan Browser.

To understand what may have caused this different learning behavior, we collapsed and analyzed the data in two subgroups with the same learning outcome, CMU-CCAC and Pitt-USNA. Within the CMU-CCAC group, students in the SE condition performed significantly better than students in the control condition, after covarying out the pretest ($p = 0.021$). Pitt-USNA students in the control condition performed slightly better than those in the SE condition, but the difference is not statistically significant ($p > 0.2$).

3.2. Possible Differences in the Student Populations

One possible explanation for the above results could be a difference in physics and background knowledge between the two subgroups of CMU-CCAC and Pitt-USNA students. However, an ANCOVA with post-test as dependent variable and subgroup and condition as main effects, shows that there is still a significant interaction ($p < 0.01$) of subgroup with condition after covarying out pretest only and both pretest and SAT scores. Although 10 subjects are excluded from the latter ANCOVA (we did not have these subjects' SAT scores), these data still provide a strong indication that physics and background knowledge do not explain the different performance of the two subgroups.

A second explanation for the different learning behavior of the CMU-CCAC and Pitt-USNA subgroups could be that subjects in the two subgroups used the system differently. The one thing that CMU and CCAC have in common, and that distinguishes them from Pitt and USNA students, is that they start the semester more than a week later. Therefore, although all the subjects participated to the experiment after they had their lectures on Newton's laws and before they took a class test on the topic, Pitt and USNA subjects were ahead in the course schedule and had likely spent more time on Newton's laws than CMU and CCAC subjects when they participated to the study. Our data show that this did not significantly influence the pretest performance of the two subgroups. However, it may have caused the students in the two subgroups to have a different attitude toward the example study task we made them perform.

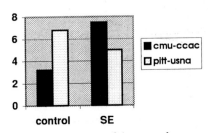

Figure 5: gains scores of the two subgroup in each condition

If we analyse the learning patterns of the two subgroups within each condition, we find that in the SE condition, CMU-CCAC students learned more than Pitt-USNA students (see figure 5), although the difference is not statistically significant ($p > 0.1$). In the Control condition, Pitt-USNA students learned significantly more than CMU-CCAC students ($p < 0.03$). These outcomes could be due to two reasons:

- In the SE condition, Pitt-USNA students did not use the SE-Coach as extensively and effectively as the CMU-CCAC students did.
- In the Control condition, Pitt-USNA students self-explained spontaneously more that the CMU-CCAC students did.

310

We will now verify these two hypotheses by comparing the log data of the two subgroups within the SE and the control condition.

Log data analysis of the two subgroups within the SE condition

To test whether CMU-CCAC students used the SE-Coach better than the Pitt-USNA students in the SE condition, we compared time on task, statistics describing how subjects used the interface self-explanation tools (Rule Browser, Plan Browser and Templates) and how they reacted to the SE-Coach's advice to further self-explain.

Rule Browser	CMU-CCAC (12)	Pitt-USNA (17)	p
Initiated	63.6%	61.4%	0.8
Correct	88%	86%	0.6
Attempts before correct	1.1	1.3	0.35
Max # attempts	7.8	10.2	0.45
Attempts before abandon	4.3	3.7	0.7

Template	CMU-CCAC (12)	Pitt-USNA (17)	p
Initiated	57.6%	53.8%	0.7
Correct	97.2%	96.8%	0.8
Attempts before correct	0.47	0.51	0.8
Max # attempts	2.2	2.7	0.3
Attempts before abandon	3	0.15	**0.011**

Plan Browser	CMU-CCAC (12)	Pitt-USNA (17)	p
Initiated	36.2%	45%	0.55
Correct	92%	81%	0.15
Attempts before correct	1	1	0.9
Max # attempts	3.9	3.8	0.96
Attempts before abandon	1.4	1.1	0.77

Table 1: Statistics on interface tools usage for CMU-CCAC and Pitt-USNA students

	CMU-CCAC (12)	Pitt-USNA (17)	p
Rule prompts followed	41%	37%	0.8
Plan prompts followed	50%	36%	0.36
Read prompts followed	31%	35%	0.88

Table 2: SE-Coach prompts statistics for CMU-CCAC and Pitt-USNA students

For each interface tool, we computed the following data summaries (see Table 1): *Initiated:* percentage of the explanations that students initiated out of all the explanations that could be generated with that tool for the available examples. *Correct*: percentage of the initiated explanations that were generated correctly. *Attempts before correct:* average number of attempts the students made before achieving a correct self-explanation. An attempt is the submission of an incorrect self-explanation. *Max # attempts:* average maximum number of attempts needed to achieve a correct self-explanation. *Attempts before abandon:* average number of attempts before abandoning a self-explanation. We also computed how many of the different prompts generated during the SE-Coach tutorial interventions (prompts to self-explain using the Rule Browser, the Plan Browser or by reading more carefully) the students actually followed (see Table 2). There is no statistically significant difference in the average time on task for the two subgroups ($p > 0.1$). The only significant difference in the way CMU-CCAC and Pitt-USNA students used the system in the SE condition is that CMU-CCAC students performed a significantly higher number of attempts before giving up on a Template explanation (see Table 1, Template data). This suggests that the CMU-CCAC students had a higher level of motivation to learn from the SE-Coach self-explanation tools, consistently with the fact that students in the CMU-CCAC group had started studying Newton's Laws later than Pitt-USNA students and thus they were likely more willing to put substantial effort in learning from examples on the topic.

The CMU-CCAC students' higher level of motivation can explain why they learned more from the SE-Coach than the Pitt-USNA students did, although in general they did not use the system more easily and extensively (as Table 1 and Table 2 show). Selecting items in the browsers and filling templates does not necessarily trigger constructive learning if students do not reflect on what they are doing. Indeed, if students are not motivated to put substantial effort in studying examples, the actions of browsing and Template filling may act as distracters from learning. Students may concentrate their attention on selecting items to get positive feedback on their interface actions, but not actually reflect on the physics behind the actions and behind the worked out solution. Thus, we argue that CMU-CCAC students in the SE condition learned more from the same self-explanation actions than Pitt-USNA students because, being more motivated, they reasoned more constructively on their self-explanation actions and on the physics underlying them.

This argument is supported by the correlation between post-test scores and the number of rules that reached high probability in the student model. The correlation is very low ($r < 0.1$) for Pitt-USNA students and it is higher ($r = 0.33$) for the CMU-CCAC students. Since the probabilities in the student model are driven upward by correct self-explanations conducted on the SE-Coach's interface, the high correlation of the CMU-CCAC group suggests that their self-explanations drove their understanding upward just as they drove the model's probabilities upward, whereas the low correlation of the Pitt-USNA group suggests that their learning was independent of their use of the SE-Coach's self-explanation tools.

Log data analysis of the two subgroups within the control condition

The hypothesis that the learning of Pitt-USNA students in the control condition is due to spontaneous self-explanation is not easy to verify, because in this condition students could not express their self-explanation through the SE-Coach. The only log data file that could indirectly indicate self-explanation in the control condition are: (1) average number of multiple accesses to example lines; (2) standard deviation of the above measure; (3) average time spent on each example line; (4) standard deviation of the above; (5) time on task; (6) number of accesses to the Plan Browser; (7) number of selections in the Plan Browser.

We ran a regression analysis of post-test on the above variables for the Pitt-USNA control group and we found a marginally significant correlation of post-test scores with average and standard deviation of line accesses ($p = 0.083$ and $p = 0.057$ respectively). We found no significant correlations in the same regression analysis for the CMU-CCAC control group. These results support the hypothesis that Pitt-USNA control students were selectively reviewing example lines because they were self-explaining specific example parts, while the CMU-CCAC control students' reviewing actions were not accompanied by effective self-explanation. The hypothesis that Pitt-USNA students self-explained more in the control condition is consistent with the fact that Pitt-USNA students had started studying Newton's Laws earlier and had probably gained more knowledge on the topic. This knowledge was not strong enough to make Pitt-USNA students perform better in problem solving tasks (their pretest performance was comparable to the CMU-CCAC students' one). However, it was sufficient to enable Pitt-USNA control subjects to generate effective self-explanations under the minimal scaffolding provided by the masking interface. We argue that it is indeed the minimality of the scaffolding that allowed Pitt-CMU control students to bring to bear their knowledge at best. Because of their more advanced learning stage, spontaneous self-explanation triggered by the masking interface likely came quite effortlessly to Pitt-USNA control students and therefore was not suffocated by the lower level of motivation that prevented Pitt-USNA students in the SE condition to learn effectively from the SE-Coach self-explanation tools.

4 Conclusions and Future Work

In this paper, we discussed the results of a formal study to evaluate an intelligent computer tutor that coaches the meta-cognitive skill known as self-explanation – generating explanations to oneself to clarify an example worked out solution. The tutor provides different levels of tailored scaffolding for self-explanation, to provide each student with the minimum intervention sufficient to trigger self-explanation while maintaining the spontaneous, constructive nature of this learning strategy.

Formal studies are fundamental to assess why and how a computer tutor does or does not support learning. Understanding how students use and learn from the SE-Coach is especially important, because the SE-Coach focuses on a learning process that no other tutoring system has tackled so far and whose underlying mechanisms are still unclear and under investigation. In particular, different studies have shown that both simple prompting [4] and more elaborate scaffolding [3] enhance self-explanation and learning, but no study has yet addressed the explicit comparison of these different kinds of intervention. The study that we performed provides initial insights on this issue. In this paper, we have presented data analysis results indicating that the stage of learning in which the students use the system influences how much they benefit from versions of the system that provide different amounts of scaffolding for self-explanation. The data suggest the following conclusions on the SE-Coach effectiveness and, in general, on the effectiveness of support for self-explanation during example studying.

- Rich scaffolding for self-explanation, like the one provided by the complete SE-Coach in the experimental condition, can improve students' performance at an early learning stage. At this stage, students are still unfamiliar with the subject matter. Hence, they benefit more from structured help in using domain knowledge to generate effective self-explanations and are more motivated to put substantial effort in exploiting this help.

- As students become more proficient in the subject matter, even minimal prompting, like the one provided by the masking interface in the control condition, can help improve their self-explanations. At this stage, more elaborate scaffolding can actually be less effective, if it requires students to put too much effort in studying examples, because they may lack the motivation to do so.

Of course, more data is necessary to confirm these conclusions. We plan to gather the data by running a study in the context of classroom instruction, where it is easier to control at what stage of learning the students use the system. If the study confirms the results presented in this paper, it may be beneficial to add to the SE-Coach the capability to automatically tailor the available levels of scaffolding depending upon the student's familiarity with the examples topic.

5   References

1.   Aleven, V., & Ashley, K. D. (1997). Teaching case-based argumentation through a model and examples: Empirical evaluation of an intelligent learning environment. In *Proc. of AIED '97, 8th World Conference of Artificial Intelligence and Education*, Kobe, Japan.
2.   Aleven, V., Koedinger, K. R., & Cross, K. (1999). Tutoring answer-explanation fosters learning with understanding. In *Proc. of AIED '99, 9th World Conference of Artificial Intelligence and Education*, Le Mans, France.
3.   Bielaczyc, K., Pirolli, P., & Brown, A. L. (1995). Training in self-explanation and self-regulation strategies: Investigating the effects of knowledge acquisition activities on problem-solving. *Cognition and Instruction, 13*(2), 221-252.
4.   Chi, M. T. H. (in press). Self-Explaining: The dual process of generating inferences and repairing mental models. *Advances in Instructional Psychology*.
5.   Conati, C. (1999). An intelligent computer tutor to guide self-explanation while learning from examples. *Unpublished Ph.D. thesis*, University of Pittsburgh, Pittsburgh.
6.   Conati, C., & VanLehn, K. (1999). Teaching meta-cognitive skills: implementation and evaluation of a tutoring system to guide self-explanation while learning from examples. In *Proc. of AIED'99, 9th World Conference of Artificial Intelligence and Education*, Le Mans, France.
7.   Gott, S. P., Lesgold, A., & Kane, R. S. (1996). Tutoring for transfer of technical competence. In B. G. Wilson (Ed.), *Constructivist Learning Environments* (pp. 33-48). Englewood Cliffs, NJ: Educational Technology Publications.
8.   Nguyen-Xuan, A., Bastide, A., & Nicaud, J.-F. (1999). Learning to solve polynomial factorization problems: by solving problems and by studying examples of problem solving, with an intelligent learning environment. In *Proc. of AIED '99, 9th World Conference of Artificial Intelligence and Education*, Le Mans, France.
9.   Pearl, J. (1988). *Probabilistic Reasoning in Intelligent Systems: Networks of Plausible Inference*. San Mateo, CA: Morgan-Kaufmann.
10. Renkl, A. (1997). Learning from worked-examples: A study on individual differences. *Cognitive Science, 21*(1), 1-30.
11. VanLehn, K. (1996). Conceptual and meta learning during coached problem solving. In C. Frasson, G. Gauthier, & A. Lesgold (Eds.), *ITS96: Proc. of the 3rd Int. Conference on Intelligent Tutoring Systems, Montreal, Canada*. New York: Springer-Verlag.
12. Weber, G., & Specht, M. (1997). User modelling and adaptive navigation support in WWW-based tutoring systems. In *Proc. of User Modeling '97*.

Analyzing and Generating Mathematical Models: An Algebra II Cognitive Tutor Design Study

Albert Corbett, Megan McLaughlin, K. Christine Scarpinatto, William Hadley

Human Computer Interaction Institute
Carnegie Mellon University, Pittsburgh, PA 15213 USA

Abstract. This paper reports a formative analysis of a Math Modeling Tool in the Algebra II Cognitive Tutor. This tutor is designed to support algebraic reasoning about real world problems. This study focuses on reasoning about situations that can be modeled with general linear form expressions ($c = ax + by$). Formative evaluations of an early general linear form lesson showed that it helped students comprehend the underlying problem situations, but was less successful in helping students construct symbolic models of the situations. These evaluations guided design of a new tool to scaffold students' understanding of the componential structure of these symbolic models and the mapping of model components to the problem situation. An empirical evaluation shows that the new tool successfully helps students understand the structure of these mathematical models and learn to construct them.

1 Introduction

This paper reports an empirical evaluation of a Math Modeling Tool recently introduced into the Algebra II Cognitive Tutor [3]. The tool is intended to help students learn to write general linear form models ($ax + by = c$) of problem situations. The tool design was guided by formative evaluations of an initial general linear form lesson and provides students the opportunity to both analyze and write such symbolic models. In the following sections we describe the Algebra II Cognitive Tutor and the problem solving activities that introduce general linear form models. We briefly describe two formative evaluations of these activities and the consequent design of the Math Modeling Tool. We conclude with an empirical evaluation demonstrating the effectiveness of the new tool and a brief discussion of design issues.

2 The Algebra II Cognitive Tutor

The Algebra II Cognitive Tutor builds on a successful collaboration between the Pittsburgh Urban Mathematics Project in the Pittsburgh School District and the Pittsburgh Advanced Cognitive Tutor (PACT) Center at Carnegie Mellon. This collaboration previously yielded the Algebra I Cognitive Tutor [4], now in use in about 150 schools in the United States. The Algebra II Tutor reflects the National Council of Teachers of Mathematics [5] curriculum standards and its design is guided by three goals: (1) to support students in applying algebra to real-world problems, (2) to support reasoning among multiple representations, (tables, graphs, symbolic expressions, and natural language) and (3) to employ modern computational tools.

This study focuses on problems that can be modeled by general linear form equations, $c = ax + by$. This lesson presents problem statements such as:

> You are selling ads for the school yearbook. There are two types of ads, full-page and half-page. Full-page ads sell for $400 each and half-page ads sell for $250 each. We want to sell enough ads for a total income of $15,000.

The dual lesson objectives are to help students learn to answer numerical questions about these situations, such as: "If you sell 20 full-page ads, how many half-page ads do you need to sell?" and to construct a general linear form model of the situation, e.g., $250x + 400y = 15,000$. Such general linear form relationships pose an interesting challenge because they are an early stumbling block for students in the Algebra II curriculum and because they ultimately form the basis for linear programming.

Fig. 1 displays two windows from a general linear form tutor problem. The problem statement in the upper window describes a problem situation and asks five questions about the situation. The worksheet in the lower window is blank at the beginning of the problem (except for row labels on the left side) and students answer the questions by completing the worksheet. Students (1) identify relevant quantities in the problem and label the columns accordingly; (2) enter appropriate units in the first row of the worksheet; (3) enter a symbolic formula for each quantity in the second row; and (4) answer the questions in the successive table rows. In Fig. 1 the student has completed approximately 3/4 of the problem.

The problem situation displayed in Fig. 1 can be represented as an operator hierarchy, as depicted in Fig. 2. In both the equation and the hierarchical representation in this figure, the variable x represents the number of half-page ads that are sold, the product $250x$ represents the income from half-page ad sales, the variable y represents the number of full-page ads that are sold and the product $400y$ represents the full-page ad sales income. The sum $250x + 400y$ represents total income and is set to the constant $15,000$ in this situation.

These worksheet problems are intended to help students understand the underlying hierarchical structure of the problem situation and to learn to construct general linear form math models. Each question in Fig. 1 is formed by assigning a given value to either a variable or product node in the hierarchy and asking students to compute the value of another variable or product node. For example, Question 2 in Fig. 1 asks "If the income from full-page ads [$400y$] is $4000, how many half-page ads [x] do we need to sell?" Students can answer the questions by traversing the operator hierarchy and successively applying the operators (in moving up through the hierarchy) or the operator inverses (in moving down through the hierarchy). The worksheet formula row requires students to write a symbolic model of the situation. In specifying the formula for "Total Income" in Fig. 1, the student is constructing one side of the general linear form relationship $250x+400y$. The other four formula cells in the worksheet essentially scaffold construction of this expression from its hierarchical constituents, x, y, $250x$ and $400y$. The five question values in the "Total Income" column implicitly encode that this algebraic sum is equal to the constant 15,000.

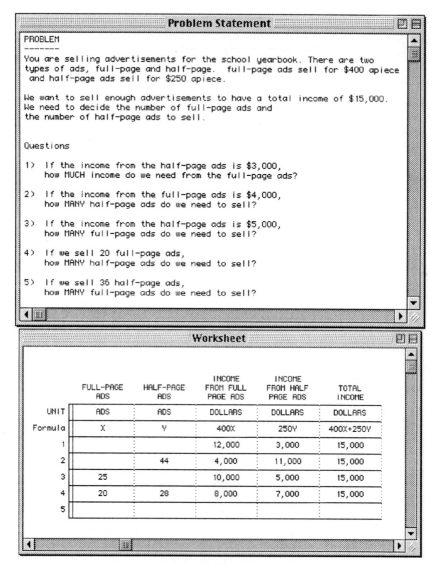

Fig. 1. The PACT Algebra II Tutor interface: A general linear form problem statement and worksheet.

The Algebra II Tutor is constructed around a cognitive model of the problem solving knowledge students are acquiring. The model reflects the ACT-R theory of skill knowledge [1] in assuming that problem solving skills can be modeled as a set of independent production rules. The cognitive model enables the tutor to trace the student's solution path through a complex problem solving space, providing feedback on each problem solving action and advice on problem solving as needed. This *model tracing* process ensures that students reach a successful conclusion to each problem

317

and has been shown to speed learning by as much as a factor of three and to increase achievement levels, in comparison to students solving problems on their own [2].

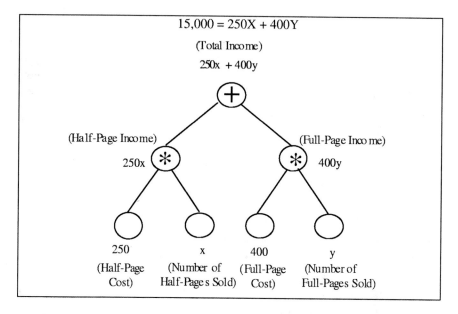

Fig. 2. Symbolic and hierarchical representation of the Fig. 1 problem situation.

The cognitive model for general linear form worksheet problems is tied to the underlying hierarchical structure of the problem situation. In solving each question, the model begins by identifying the given quantity. If the quantity has not yet been labeled, it finds and labels an open column, enters the unit, then enters the given value in the appropriate row. It then follows the hierarchical solution path through the question. For example, in question 2, the cognitive model recognizes it needs to compute the product by, then chains forward to the sum (constant) term, then to the ax product and finally finds the value of the variable quantity x. Students are *not* required to overtly follow these canonical solution paths. The tutor can recognize correct problem solving actions in any temporal order. However, if help is requested, the student is guided along a canonical path as described above.

3   Formative Evaluations

We completed two formative evaluations of the general linear form worksheet lesson. The first focused on students' understanding of the underlying hierarchical problem situations and the second focused on students' success in modeling the situations with a general linear form symbolic expression.

3.1   Understanding the Problem Situation

The first study examined both test data and tutor performance data to evaluate students' understanding of the underlying problem situation. In this study 19 students completed paper-and-pencil tests before and after completing the cognitive tutor lesson. These tests consisted of a problem situation and five numerical computation questions requiring students to traverse different paths through the underlying situation hierarchy. Students only wrote numerical answers. No worksheet was provided, and no algebraic representation of the situation was provided by, or for, the students. Achievement gains from pretest to posttest confirmed the effectiveness of the tutor lesson. Students averaged 44% correct on the pretest and 72% correct on the posttest. This 64 percent achievement gain is significant ($t = 3.08$, $p < .01$).

The order in which students filled in the worksheet cells in the tutor problems provides further evidence on students' understanding of the underlying hierarchical problem structure. The probability that the temporal order in which students fill the worksheet cells follows the underlying hierarchichal pathways rises from 0.46 for the first tutor problem to 0.76 for the final tutor problem. This increase is significant, $t = 2.81$, $p < .05$ and provides compelling evidence that students are learning the hierarchical relations in each problem situation.

3.2   Modeling the Problem Situation

A second study of the worksheet lesson examined how well students can generate symbolic models of problem situations and how well they understand these models. In this study 17 Cognitive Tutor Algebra II students completed two tests following completion of the general linear form worksheet lesson. One test presented a problem situation and five numerical questions, as in the earlier formative study, but also included a sixth question asking students to write a general equation that models the situation, e.g.,

> In this situation we need to earn $15,000 by selling half-page and full-page ads. Please write a general equation that represents this problem situation. Please use variables to represent the half-page ads and full-page ads and write an equation that shows how many of each are required to earn $15,000

The second test examined students' understanding of general linear form symbolic models. This test presented both a problem situation and a corresponding general linear form inequality and asked students to write natural language descriptions of the inequality components. An example test is presented in Fig. 3 with some appropriate answers displayed in italics.

Students in this study averaged 75% correct on the five numerical problem solving questions in test 1, replicating performance posttest performance levels from the first study. More importantly, students only scored 35% correct in writing a mathematical model of the situation, e.g., $250x + 400y = 15,000$. Accuracy rates for each of the five questions on the second test are displayed in Fig. 3. Students are very successful in describing the two constants, averaging 83% correct on questions (a) and (d). However, they are far less successful in describing any terms that include a variable, averaging 41% correct across questions (b), (c) and (e).

Suppose you have $10 to spend on refreshments at a movie theater. A box of popcorn costs $2.00 at the snack bar and a beverage costs $1.50. We can use the following inequality to represent the different snack combinations you can afford.

$$2x + 1.5\, y \bullet 10$$

Please describe in your own words what the following five parts of the inequality represent in the snack bar situation.

    (a) What does the number 1.5 represent in this situation?   (85% correct)
          The price of a beverage

    (b) What does the variable y represent in this situation?   (47% correct)
          The number of beverages you purchase

    (c) What does the term 2x represent in this situation?   (41% correct)
          The total you spend on popcorn

    (d) What does the number 10 represent in this situation?   (82% correct)
          The amount of money you have to spend

    (e) What does the sum 2x + 1.5y represent in this situation?   (35% correct)
          The total you spend on popcorn and beverages

Fig. 3. A symbolic model analysis paper-and-pencil test.

To examine the relationship between success in describing each of the five symbolic components on the second test and success in writing the full general linear form equation in the first test, we computed five chi-square analyses. Two of these tests were at least marginally reliable. Students who were able to describe the variable (y) were more likely to be able to write the equation ($\chi^2 = 10.43$, df = 3, p < .05) and students that were able to describe the product $(2x)$ were marginally more likely to be able to write the equation ($\chi^2 = 6.80$, df = 3, p < .10).

Although this pattern of results does not prove a causal relationship, it is consistent with the hypothesis that helping students understand the mapping from the symbolic expression components to the problem situation will help students learn to write these symbolic models. This hypothesis inspired the design of a mathematical modeling tool, as described in the following section.

4   The Math Modeling Tool

We developed a Math Modeling Tool to scaffold students' understanding of the general linear form symbolic components and the mapping of these components to the problem situation. This tool is inspired by the analysis test described in the previous section. The tutor interface is displayed in Fig. 4. The tool presents a problem situation and a symbolic inequality that models the situation. The tool contains 8 rows for describing the mapping between situation components and symbolic model components. In this figure the analysis tool is seeded with each component in a hierarchical decomposition of the math model and the student fills in natural language descriptions of each component in the corresponding blank. Students select these natural language descriptions from a menu, as displayed in Fig. 5.

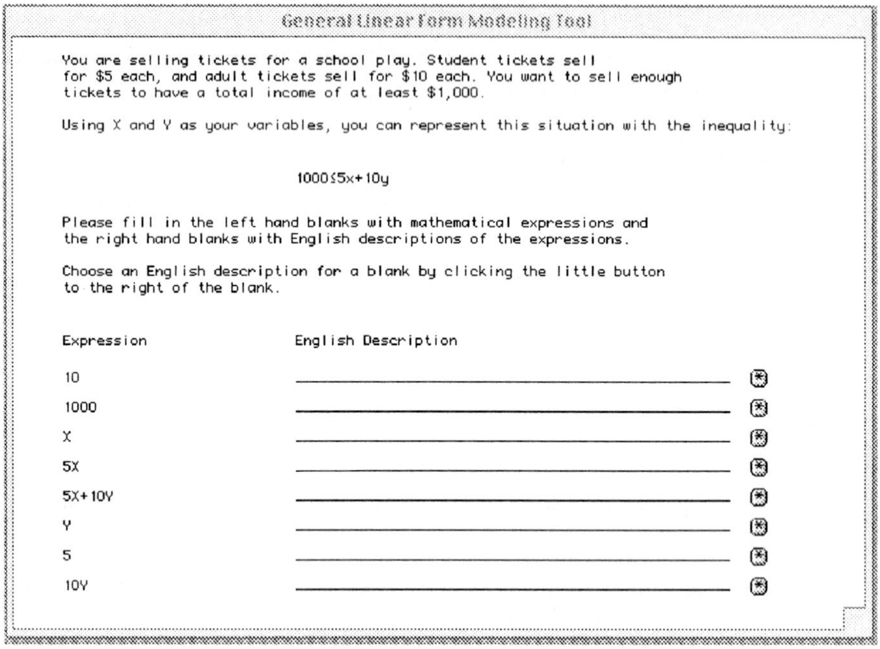

Fig. 4. The Math Modeling Analysis Tool Interface

Fig. 4 displays just one possible initial configuration of the tool. There are 17 slots in the tool that can be seeded or left blank at the beginning of a problem. The problem description is always presented, but the inequality can be seeded (as in Fig. 4) or left blank, each of 8 inequality components can be seeded (as in Fig. 4) or left blank and each of 8 component descriptions can be seeded or left blank (as in Fig. 4). If the inequality is left blank, students are required to fill it first. Students receive immediate accuracy feedback on each action they perform in the modeling tool and can request help in filling any slot. This tool was evaluated in the following study.

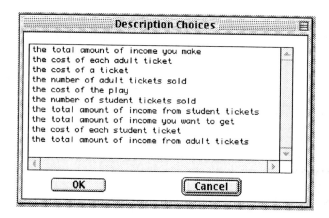

Fig. 5. The natural language description menu.

5   The Study

The Math Modeling Tool was piloted in a 4-day period near the end of the academic year. Eight-three Cognitive Tutor Algebra II students participated in the study. Fifty-six were enrolled in a Pittsburgh high school and 27 were enrolled in a nearby suburban high school.

5.1   Design

Lesson Design. Students completed 8 problems in the lesson. In the first and last problem all 17 slots in the math modeling tool were left blank. In these problems the student was required to type the inequality first, then fill in the remaining 16 blanks (8 inequality components and 8 natural language descriptions) in any order. In the remaining six problems the inequality was seeded. In two of these problems all 8 symbolic expression components were seeded and the student was required to provide the 8 descriptions. In two problems the 8 descriptions were provided and the student was required to type the corresponding expression components. In the other two problems a mix of expression components and descriptions were seeded and the student was required to fill in the missing blank in each pair.

Test Design. The same two tests were employed in this study as in the second formative evaluation described in Section 3.2. A problem solving test presented a problem situation description and students answered 5 numerical computation questions and generated a general linear form symbolic model. A model analysis test presented a problem description and general linear form inequality model and asked students to describe five hierarchical components of the model (as displayed in Fig. 3). Two versions of each test were constructed. Each version was completed as a pretest by one half of the students and a posttest by the other half of the students.

Procedure. Students completed the two pretests during an initial class period. The problem solving test was completed and removed before the analysis test was completed. Students worked through the 8 math modeling tutor problems over the next two days. Students completed the two posttests on the fourth day of the study, again completing the problem solving test before the analysis test.

5.2 Results

Table 1 displays the students' pretest and posttest performance in constructing and in describing components of general linear form symbolic models.

Mathematical Modeling and Numerical Computation (Test 1). Table 1 displays two measures of student accuracy in writing the general linear form symbolic model. The strict criterion requires students to code both sides of the inequality correctly *and* code the correct inequality relation between them, e.g., 1.5x+2y • 10. The relaxed criterion requires students to code both sides of the relationship correctly, e.g., 1.5x+2y and 10, irrespective of the relational operator coded (a correct inequality, equation or incorrect inequality). Student accuracy in writing the general linear form model is reliably higher on the posttest than the pretest, both for the strict criterion, $z = 3.60$, $p < .001$ and the relaxed criterion, $z = 3.83$, $p < .001$).

Table 1. Student pretest and posttest performance (percent correct) in generating general linear form mathematical models and in analyzing model components.

	Test 1 Write a GLF Symbolic Model		Test 2 Write Natural language Description of Symbolic Model				
	Strict Scoring	Relaxed Scoring	Constants		Variable Components		
			a	c	x	ax	ax+by
	%corr	%corr	%corr	%corr	%corr	%corr	%corr
Pretest	7%	40%	86%	47%	64%	54%	45%
Posttest	30%	68%	94%	57%	71%	49%	68%

The mathematical modeling tool did not affect student performance in completing the five numerical computation problems. Students averaged 64% correct on the pretest and 68% correct on the posttest and this difference is not reliable.

Natural Language Descriptions (Test 2). Table 1 also displays the impact of the Math Modeling Tool on students' descriptions of the symbolic expression components. The overall increase in correct descriptions from 59% on the pretest to 68% on the posttest is reliable, $t(82) = 2.81$, $p < .01$. The improvement in describing the sum expression (e.g., 1.5x+2y) is reliable, $z = 3.34$, $p < .001$. The pretest to posttest performance change for the other four individual questions is not significant.

6 Discussion

The Math Modeling Tool significantly improved student success in writing general linear form mathematical models and significantly improved achievement in describing symbolic model components, but did not affect achievement in solving numerical computation problems. This pattern is consistent with our preliminary interpretation of the formative evaluations described in section 3. Students' success in writing symbolic models in the earlier studies was primarily limited by their understanding of the symbolic representations and their mapping to the problem situations, rather than their comprehension of the underlying problem situation. This study helps demonstrate the importance of ongoing formative evaluations and iterative refinements of intelligent tutoring environments.

Note that after using the Math Modeling Tool, students are more successful in generating the two sides of the symbolic inequalities than at encoding the inequality sign relating them. While the problem statements display the inequality sign in the symbolic models, students are not required to actively process this component of the models. Hence this study demonstrates an important design principle: declarative presentation of information is not sufficient to support learning. Students need to actively engage with knowledge structures to learn how to use them. However, this study suggests that actually performing a skill (e.g., writing math models), is not the only activity that supports learning the skill. Other problem solving activities that support understanding of a task can help scaffold performance of the task.

Acknowledgements

This research was supported by NSF grant number 9720359 to CIRCLE: Center for Interdisciplinary Research on Constructive Learning Environments and by grants from the Buhl Foundation, the Grable Foundation, the Howard Heinz Endowment, the Richard King Mellon Foundation and the Pittsburgh Foundation.

References

1. Anderson, J.R.: Rules of the mind. Lawrence Erlbaum, Hillsdale, NJ (1993)
2. Anderson, J.R., Corbett, A.T., Koedinger K.R., Pelletier, R.: Cognitive tutors: Lessons learned. Journal of the Learning Sciences, (1995), 4, 167-207
3. Corbett, A.T., Trask, H.J., Scarpinatto, K.C., Hadley, W.S. A Formative Evaluation of the PACT Algebra II Tutor: Support for Simple Hierarchical Reasoning. In B. Goettl, H. Halff, C. Redfield and V. Shute (Eds). Intelligent Tutoring Systems: 4th International Conference, ITS '98. Springer, New York (1998).
4. Koedinger, K.R., Anderson, J.R., Hadley, W.H., Mark, M.A.: Intelligent tutoring goes to school in the big city. Artificial Intelligence and Education, 1995: The Proceedings of AI-ED 95. AACE, Charlottesville, VA (1995)
5. National Council of Teachers of Mathematics: Curriculum and Evaluation Standards for School Mathematics. The Council, Reston, VA (1989)

A Coached Collaborative Learning Environment for Entity-Relationship Modeling

María de los Angeles Constantino-González [1] and Daniel D. Suthers [2]

[1] Center for Artificial Intelligence, Monterrey Institute of Technology (ITESM), E. Garza
Sada 2501 Sur, Monterrey, N.L. 64849, Mexico
aconstan@cia.mty.itesm.mx
[2] Information and Computer Sciences, University of Hawai'i, 1680 East West Road, POST
303A, Honolulu, HI 96822, USA
suthers@hawaii.edu

Abstract. We discuss the design of an agent for coaching collaborative learning in a distance learning context. The learning domain is entity-relationship modeling, a domain in which collaborative problem solving is regularly practiced, and for which there exist formally interpretable representations of problem solutions known as entity-relationship diagrams. The design of the coach was based on socio-cognitive conflict theory, which states that collaborative learning is effective to the extent that learners identify and discuss conflicts in their beliefs. Students begin by constructing individual entity-relationship diagrams expressing their solution to a database modeling problem, and then work in small groups to agree upon a group solution. The coaching agent leverages learning opportunities by encouraging students to share and discuss solution components that conflict with components of the group solution. Our work shows one way to utilize domain specific knowledge in order to facilitate collaboration.

1 Introduction

Distance Learning has become a very popular educational paradigm due to recent advances in computing and telecommunications, and shifts in the demographics of student populations to include more working or geographically isolated individuals. Unfortunately, distance learning has focused primarily on individual learning and has given little emphasis to the development of collaborative skills. Although students sometimes work in a group, there is little evaluation of the collaboration process and the students' collaborative skills. Yet, "with social and intellectual isolation, students may fail to develop and refine those cognitive an interpersonal skills increasingly necessary for business and professional careers" [1]. The development of these skills should be promoted in distance learning environments.

Studies of collaborative learning in the classroom show that, properly designed, collaborative learning improves students' achievement, critical thinking and cooperative behavior [9, 13]. However, just as simple interaction in the classroom does not equal collaboration [7], it is not sufficient to provide distance learners with only a channel of communication. Individuals may not consider others' opinions, and may give only a final solution without explaining how that solution was obtained [23]. Coaching in a computer-mediated collaborative environment may help distance students to develop collaborative skills.

Several knowledge-based systems have been designed to support the development of group skills. Some of them were developed for general discussion scenarios, typically comparing use of sentence openers to models of dialogue [14, 15, 18, 20]. Some systems track both dialogue and domain actions [4], or provide individual domain specific tutoring in a collaborative virtual environment [10]. Finally, other systems have been developed to support collaboration by pairing students who need help with those who can supply that help [2, 11]. The difference between our software coach and the previous work discussed above is that our coach utilizes domain specific knowledge in order to facilitate collaboration.

Our coach supports computer-mediated collaborative learning of database design. It functions within a "groupware" environment in which students construct solutions to database modeling problems using the Chen diagrammatic notation [8] for Entity-Relationship (ER) Modeling. ER modeling is one of the most commonly used data modeling formalisms for conceptual database design, a collaborative task in which analysts and database users participate to produce a conceptual schema of their global view of data [5, 10]. The performance of the final database system depends highly on the correct design of the conceptual schema, yet data modeling is a difficult task for novices [6, 19].

The coach identifies semantically important differences between students' ER diagrams and, based on neo-Piagetian theory concerning the role of conflict and its resolution in learning, encourages students to address these differences in ways expected to lead to learning. According to Socio-Cognitive Conflict Theory, students learn from controversies when they discuss their different viewpoints, pose alternatives, and request and give explanations [24]. The value of the disagreement does not depend as much on the correctness of the opposing position as on the attention, thought processes and learning activities it induces [12]. Considering the utility of cognitive conflicts, it is important that students confront and discuss their differences. Unfortunately, this kind of interaction may not arise spontaneously [17, 24]. Collaborative distance learning software should provide an environment where students are encouraged to make their ideas explicit to others, be aware of and review their teammates participation, give and request explanations, and address conflicts. Our software is intended to facilitate these kinds of interactions.

2 COLER

COLER is a World Wide Web (WWW)-based computer-mediated Collaborative Learning environment for Entity Relationship modeling. The learning objectives are to improve students' performance in database design using the Entity-Relationship

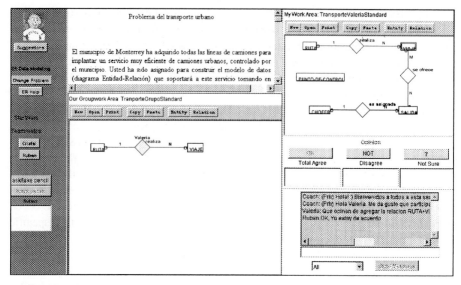

Figure 1. COLER Group Session Interface

modeling formalism, and to help students develop collaborative and critical thinking skills. The design objectives are to promote learning interactions via an intelligent coach, to enable interaction between students from different places via a networked environment, and to not be restricted to a specific platform.

2.1 COLER's Interface

COLER provides four different modes of operation according to the type of user (student/professor) and the selected type of session (individual/group). COLER's student/group interface is shown in Figure 1. The *problem description window* (upper center) presents an entity-relationship modeling problem. Students construct their individual solutions in the *private workspace* (upper right) using the Chen notation. They use the *shared workspace* (lower center) to collaboratively construct ER diagrams while communicating largely via the *chat window* (lower right). They can use a HELP *button* (upper left) to get information about Entity-Relationship Modeling. A *team panel* (middle left) shows which teammates are already connected. Only one student, the one who has the pencil, can update the shared workspace at a given time. The *floor control panel* (bottom left) provides two buttons to control this workspace: ASK/TAKE PENCIL and LEAVE PENCIL. Additionally, this panel shows the name of the student who has the control of this area and the students waiting for a turn. An *opinion panel* (middle right) shows teammates' opinions on a current issue. This area contains three buttons: OK: Total agreement, NOT: Total or Partial Disagreement, and ?: Not sure, Uncertainty. When a button is selected, students have the option of annotating their selection with a justification. Opinion button selections are displayed in both the chat area and the opinion panel. We insert opinion selections (along with any optional justifications) into the chat in order to correlate these opinion-expressing actions with the chronology of the chat discourse. We display selections in the opinion panel to provide students with a persistent summary of their teammates' current opinions. A *personal coach* (upper left) gives advice in the chat area based on the group dynamics: students participation and group diagram construction. Although several suggestions may be computed at a certain time, only one is shown in the chat area. The others may be given on demand by pressing the SUGGESTIONS button, which is disabled if the coach does not have any advice to offer.

COLER is designed for sessions in which students first solve problems individually, and then join into small groups to develop group solutions. The initial problem solving helps ensure individual participation, and provides the raw materials for the negotiation of differences. The private workspace also enables students to try solutions they are uncertain of without feeling they are being watched. When all of the students have indicated readiness to work in the group, the shared workspace is activated, and they can begin to place components of their solutions in the workspace. This may be done either with COPY/PASTE from private workspaces, or by making new structures in the shared workspace. After each change to the workspace, the changed object is highlighted in yellow; then, students are required to express their opinions using the OK/NOT/? buttons before making subsequent use of the shared workspace.

2.2 Implementation Architecture

COLER's implementation is based on an architecture for intelligent collaborative learning systems originally used for the implementation of the Belvedere software for collaborative critical inquiry [22]. The COLER implementation architecture includes Java 1.1 applets that are in charge of the different functions of the system, such as chat, floor control, voting, private and shared ER modeling. It uses Belvedere's diagrammatic classes and components for networking. COLER's applets as well as the personal coach communicate with an mSQL database server via a JDBC Object Request Broker. This broker also informs the Connection Manager of user changes. The Connection Manager is a process on the server that keeps track of the clients using any diagram. It informs other clients via their Listener sockets of the changes to their diagram for "what you see is what I see" updating.

2.3 Coach Modules

The main activity of the coach is to monitor participation and to identify and evaluate differences between diagrams to encourage students to discuss them. Each student's client contains a private coach, which monitors the private workspace of its student - the "currently monitored student" or CMS. Each coach also monitors the shared workspace, and records students' selections of opinion buttons and their participation in the shared workspace and in chat discussions. (No natural language interpretation is attempted.) The Coach utilizes four modules, each contributing distinct expertise, and each implemented as a Java thread.

Differences Recognizer. Opportunities for students to collaborate are detected by finding semantically significant differences between individual and group ER diagrams. The Differences Recognizer can either find differences specifically related to the currently added object, or find all "extra work" that the student can contribute to the group. The differences were identified through a review of database literature and with the guidance of a database expert. A weight is assigned to each difference depending on its impact on solution quality. This weight is considered by the coach to decide when to give advice. Top-weighted differences include Missing entity, Extra entity, Missing relationship, Extra relationship, Missing key attribute, Difference in cardinality, and Difference in optionality.

Diagram Analyzer. This module detects ER diagram anomalies. Currently it is only syntax-based. Later we will check for semantic anomalies.

Participation Monitor. The Participation Monitor attends to the activity in the group diagram. If nobody has worked in the group diagram for a period of time, it reports this event. It also monitors whether each student is participating too much or too little. The monitor tracks each student's number of contributions, incrementing the value each time a student adds something. To evaluate participation, a standard deviation (s.d.) is computed. If the s.d. exceeds a threshold of participation (e.g. 1.5) the monitor assumes there is a problem in participation and individual students are checked. If the difference between a given student's activity and the mean exceeds the s.d., then it is assumed that the student is part of the problem, as follows: Student Contributions - Mean > s.d.: Student has participated too much; Mean - Student Contributions > s.d.: Student has not participated enough.

Personal Coach. The Differences Recognizer, Diagram Analyzer and Participation Monitor communicate their results to the Personal Coach, which generates potentially applicable advice and selects the advice to give, if any. This process is described in detail below.

2.4 Generating Advice

Advice types were defined based on the collaborative learning literature and several observatory studies summarized in a subsequent section. The types (and abbreviations used in Figure 2) are: *Group participation* (encouraging participation and/or allowing others to participate): Contributing to the group solution (GC), Contributing a specific object to the group solution (SC), Giving teammates a chance to participate (LP, LM), Listening to others (LO), Inviting others to participate (IP), Continue working on task (not shown in Figure 2), General Participation (GP). *Group discussion* (suggestions for chat): Ask for or Give explanations or justifications (AE, GE), Analyze alternative solutions (AA), Express disagreement (ED), Express uncertainty (EU). *Feedback* (suggestions for use of opinion buttons): Give feedback by voting (GF), Ask for feedback (AF). *Reflection*: Reflect about a specific issue (RA). *Checking Own Discrepancies:* Review one's contribution (CD). *ER Modeling* (diagram syntax): Connect

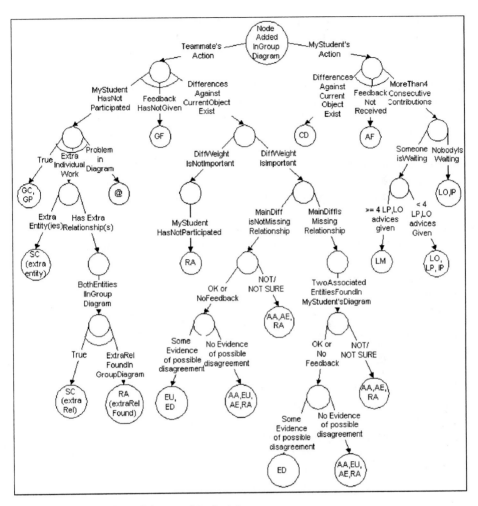

Figure 2. A portion of the coach's decision tree

a disconnected entity, define an entity's key, add a relationship's name, review whether the diagram is complete (not shown in Figure 2).

The coach might generate several suggestions for any given event. For example, a decision tree describing the coach's reasoning for the "Add Object" event is shown in Figure 2. This is an and/or decision tree: as indicated by the "and" arcs, several leaves may be reached at once. Also, each leaf may propose more than one advice type (AA, EU, etc.). The tree has two main "or" branches, depending on who performed the action.

If a teammate added the object (left hand branch of Figure 2), processes to evaluate (1) participation, (2) feedback, and (3) discussion are executed (branches connected by an "and" arc): (1) If the Participation Monitor indicates that the CMS has not participated, the coach generates advice shown in the leftmost subtree: General Contribution, General Participation, Reflection About an issue. Specific Contribution suggestions are computed according to extra individual work done by CMS. ER Modeling suggestions correspond to syntax-based problems found in the group diagram, according to a subtree, not shown, attached at the @ in Figure 2. (2) Feedback evaluation simply checks whether the student has selected one of the **OK/NOT/?** buttons. (3) The discussion evaluation process takes into account the number of differences found, the type of differences and the student's participation. Discussion suggestions are generated by the evaluation of the differences found, as shown in the large subtree in the center of the figure.

If the CMS added the object (right hand branch of Figure 2), processes to evaluate (4) discrepancy checking, (5) received feedback and (6) participation are executed: (4) A suggestion to Check Discrepancies is generated based on an evaluation of the differences found. (5) If opinions from others (OK, NOT, ?) have not been received, then Ask for Feedback is generated. (6) If the Participation Monitor indicates that the CMS has done many consecutive contributions, it generates advice from the following types: Listen to Others, Let Participate, Invite others to Participate.

2.5 Selecting Advice

Sets of advice can potentially be generated by many of the leaves of either the left or right subtree of Figure 2, as well as by trees for other events. If the combined set includes several types of advice for the same category, those that have been previously used are eliminated, implementing a preference to avoid giving the same kind of advice twice. If there is no new type of advice, all the types of advice are considered. Then, for each selected type of advice an advice pattern is randomly chosen and the corresponding text is generated by binding variables from the current situation (e.g. student's name, object's type, object's name). Finally, a preferences-based sort algorithm [21] is run if needed to choose between multiple advice instances. Examples of preferences are New Advice (don't repeat variable bindings), Many Instances (prefer advice of a type that applies more than once), and Category Preferences (e.g. Discussion, Participation). The order of the preferences may change during the collaborative session depending on the group's performance. If the group seems to need more participation advice, this category of advice is promoted. Otherwise, discussion is encouraged.

3. Empirical Studies

The design of both COLER's interface and coaching algorithms has been based on numerous empirical studies, to be described in detail in a future publication. Initially we observed small groups of students solving ER problems using pencil and paper, in both laboratory and classroom settings, in some cases with a database expert monitoring and coaching their work. These studies helped us understand the range of group dynamics and of responses to coach interventions. Once the COLER interface became available, we conducted "Wizard of Oz" studies in which the expert could see students' individual diagrams and send chat messages to both individuals and the group. In these sessions we observed the types of advice given by the expert and students' responsiveness to this advice. Students were usually cooperative, but we also identified the need to enable the coach to take away the pencil from a student who is not letting the others participate. Informed by these paper-based and Wizard of Oz studies as well as by our literature review, COLER's coach was then implemented by the first author.

The automated coach is currently undergoing testing. Five further sessions have been conducted in order to evaluate usability and the coach algorithms. Teams of three students participated in each of these sessions. Some of these students were taking a database course at ITESM; others were graduate students who had already taken this course. Students located in different rooms used COLER to solve a database modeling problem first individually and later in a group. At the end of the two-hour study they answered a survey regarding the performance of the coach.

Two of these sessions were conducted with the human expert present, who was able to comment on the performance of the coach. These sessions helped us to detect some problems in COLER's user interface and coach algorithms. The software coach was pressing students too much to continue working when some time had passed and they had not done any action in the group diagram. Some of these problems were fixed by adjusting the values of parameters.

The other three sessions were conducted with the human coach not present. Instead, he is being shown the information available to the automated coach, and asked to rank the advice types according to their reasonableness for each situation. These judgements will be compared to the advice actually generated and selected by COLER in order to evaluate the advice generation and selection algorithms. This evaluation is underway at this writing.

From the surveys we learned that students think that the presence of a coach during the session is important to motivate them to discuss and help others; that the coach didn't interrupt them too much (after the adjustments); and that some of the advice was useful while some was irrelevant or redundant. They asked for some group advice instead of just personal suggestions and to include some domain-advice. We are conducting further studies to observe how students will use COLER's advice.

4. Conclusions and Future Work

The current version of the coach only has access to the student's private workspace and the shared workspace. If a portion of the student's solution differs in a nontrivial way from the group's solution and the student has not disagreed with the group's solution this coach highlights the difference and suggests that the student discuss it with the others. Thus, this version of the coach helps avoid *"missed opportunities"* for collaborative learning [3]. A planned future version of the coach will differ primarily in its ability to inspect all students' private workspaces as well as the shared workspace. This coach will notice when two students have conflicting solutions, neither of which have been shared with the group. It will be able to suggest that one of the students share his/her solution with the others. If the student does so, the conflict situation that would result can be addressed by the first version of the coach. Thus, this version of the coach will help to *create* opportunities for collaborative learning. Each one of these versions can be improved by adding knowledge in the form of a pre-stored "expert" or correct solution to the problem being solved. This additional knowledge may improve the coach's selection of which collaboration advice to give and to whom, as well as to comment on correctness of solutions [16].

This work is part of a research agenda that seeks to characterize the knowledge needed to facilitate collaborative learning processes. We focus on how domain specific reasoning can guide the coaching of collaborative interactions. (Other work has either coached domain problem solving or provided generic support for collaborative dialogues.) Specifically, we are investigating how much leverage can be gained by a basic ability to detect semantically interesting differences between two representations of problem solutions. This approach is restricted to domains in which students can construct formal representations of problem solutions. Once we have fine tuned this approach for the ER domain and established the range and limits of its educational value, we will be able to test the value of the approach in other domains that have this property.

5. Acknowledgments

We thank our colleagues at the Learning Research and Development Center of the University of Pittsburgh for their support, in particular Alan Lesgold for hosting the first author as a visiting scholar the second as his research associate, Sandy Katz for discussions about collaborative learning, and Kim Harrigal and Dan Jones for their assistance with the implementations. We also thank Jose G. Escamilla of ITESM for his advisorship of the first author, our domain expert Jose I. Icaza of ITESM, Moraima Campbell of ITESM for her support in user interface design, and the Center for Artificial Intelligence of ITESM for facilities for the research. During this research, Constantino-González was funded by ITESM Campus Laguna, and Suthers was funded by the Presidential Technology Initiative (while at LRDC) and by NSF's Learning and Intelligent Systems (while at the University of Hawai'i).

References

1. Abrami, P.C. and Bures, E.M. (1996) Computer Supported Collaborative Learning and Distance Education, Reviews of lead article. The American Journal of Distance Education 10(2): 37-42.
2. Ayala, G. and Yano, Y. (1996). Learner Models for Supporting Awareness and Collaboration in a CSCL Environment. ITS'96, Third International Conference of Intelligent Tutoring Systems, Montreal, June, pp. 158-167.

3. Baker, M. J. and Bielaczyc, K. (1995). Missed opportunities for learning in collaborative problem-solving interactions. *AI&ED 95.*
4. Baker, M.J. and Lund, K. (1996). Flexibly Structuring the Interaction in a CSCL environment., In EuroAIED.
5. Batini, C., Ceri, S. and Navathe, S. B. (1992). Conceptual Database Design: An Entity-Relationship Approach. Benjamin/Cummings, Redwood City, California.
6. Batra, D. and Antony, S.R. (1994). Novice Errors in Conceptual Database Design. European Journal of Information Systems, Vol. 3, No. 1, pp. 57-69.
7. Brown, A. L. and Palincsar, A.S. (1989). Guided, cooperative learning and individual knowledge acquisition. In L. Resnick (Ed.), Knowing, Learning and Instruction: Essays in Honor of Robert Glaser. Hillsdale, NJ: Lawrence Erlbaum Associates.
8. Chen, P. (1976). The Entity-Relationship Model - Toward a Unified View of Data, ACM Transactions on Database Systems, Vol. 1, No. 1, pp. 9-36.
9. Gokhale, A. A. (1995). Collaborative Learning Enhances Critical Thinking, Journal of Technology Education, 7(1), 1995.
10. Gordon, A. and Hall, L. (1998). A Collaborative Learning Environment for Data Modelling, American Association for Artificial Intelligence.
11. Ikeda, M., Go, S., & Mizoguchi, R. (1997, August 18-22). Opportunistic Group Formation. Paper presented at the AI-ED 97: World Conferennce on Artifical Intelligence in Education, Kobe, Japan.
12. Johnson, D.W., Johnson, R.T and Smith, K. A. (1997). Academic Controversy. Association of the Study of Higher Education.
13. Johnson, D.W., Johnson, R. T. and Smith, K.A. (1991). Increasing College Faculty Instructional Productivity, ASHE-ERIC Higher Education Reports.
14. McManus, M. M. and Aiken, R.M. (1995). Monitoring Computer Based Collaborative Problem Solving", Journal of Artificial Intelligence in Education , 6(4) , 308-336.
15. Okamoto, T., Inaba, A. & Hasaba, Y. (1995). The Intelligent Learning Support System on the Distributed Cooperative Evironment, Proceedings of Artificial Intelligence in Education, August, Washington, D.C., p. 588
16. Paolucci, M., Suthers, D., & Weiner, A. (1996). Automated advice-giving strategies for scientific inquiry. Intelligent Tutoring Systems, 3rd International Conference, Montreal, June 12-14, 1996.
17. Rabow, J., et al. (1994). Learning Through Discussion, Sage.
18. Robertson, J., Good, J. & Pain, H. (1998). BetterBlether: The Design and Evaluation of a Discussion Tool for Education, IJAIED.
19. Shanks, G. (1996). Conceptual Data Modelling: An Empirical Study of Expert and Novice Data Modellers. ACIS '96.
20. Soller, A., Goodman, B., Linton, F. & Gaimari, R. (1998). Promoting Effective Peer Interaction in an Intelligent Collaborative Learning System. Proceedings of the Fourth International Conference on Intelligent Tutoring Systems (ITS 98), San Antonio, Texas.
21. Suthers, D. (1993). Preferences for Model Selection in Explanation. Proceedings of the13th International Joint Conference on Artificial Intelligence (IJCAI-93). Chambery, France, August 1993, pp. 1208-1213.
22. Suthers, D. and Jones, D. (1997). An Architecture for Intelligent Collaborative Educational Systems, AI&ED97, Japan.
23. Webb, N. (1985). Student Interaction and learning in small groups: A research summary. Learning to Cooperate, Cooperating to Learn.
24. Webb and Palincsar, A. S. (1996). Group processes in the classroom. Handbook of Educational Psychology. D. Berlmer & R. Calfee Eds. Simon & Shuster Macmillan NY, 1996

Model of an Adaptive Support Interface for Distance Learning

Aude Dufresne

C.P. 6128 Succ. Centre-Ville, Montr al, Canada, H3C 3J7
dufresne@com.umontreal.ca

Abstract. We developed a distributed support model in an interface for distant learning. The support is integrated into the ExploraGraph navigator which makes it possible to navigate through conceptual graphs of activities and knowledge elements. The learner may specify goals using a Control Panel (Explore the calendar, the content, Plan my activities). He may specify his degree of completion of the elements of the course. These are used by the help system to display contextual help, using hypertext, graphical cues, Ms Agents avatars, voice, visual and force-feedback guiding. The graphs are used to display the overlay model of the learner as a feedback to his progression. The system is built in Visual Basic and operates under Windows. The support is described as a rule-based system in the database. A course on the design of learning application was developed using the interface and the support model was evaluated with it.

1 Introduction

The ExploraGraph interface was designed in the context of the Canadian TeleLearning Network of Center of Excellence to facilitate interaction in the distance learning context. After studying learners in various distant learning situations, it became evident to us that existing interfaces were not sufficently supportive of the interaction and of the learning process. Distance learners have to navigate between pages of web documents, search engines and text instructions; they must use various communication tools and organize their activities with little support. They are isolated and asynchronous help is not always efficient in supporting them on critical dimensions of telelearning : technical proficiency, task management, content orientation, motivation in achieving course objectives.

The ExploraGraph interface was developed as an alternative to simple web interaction, in order to increase flexibility, visibility, and structure in the learning environment. Inspired by the Explora interface developed at LICEF [1] we tried to develop a more dynamic and flexible interface for learner access to the Center for Virtual Learning. Inspired by the MISA methodology on the structure of learning environments [2]. With the ExploraGraph interface, the learner navigates in graphic conceptual structures of tasks, knowledge elements and documents, that provide him with a schematic notion of what is to be learned and what he has to do. In the conceptual graphs, various types of nodes (concepts, actions, rules, etc..) and links (composition, precedence, regulation, etc..) not only highlight the structure for the learner, but they also allow an automatic arrangement of elements and facilitate the support system. Graphs may be browsed by the learner, who can either superficially read the description and instructions available at the nodes, or double-click on specific elements to access their content. This interface, which served as a front end to a web course, was used to integrate adaptive support based on the progression of learners and their actions in the environment.

2   Adaptive Interfaces in Support of Distance Learning

The need to integrate adaptive interfaces to learning environments has become an important field of research [3,4,5] especially because of its importance in reducing navigation disorientation and promoting exhaustive learning in hypertext systems, in particular in web learning applications. Adaptation may take many forms, based on modifications of content and/link access and annotations.

One of the main limitations of adaptive interfaces resides in the information obtained by the system on the user s activity and knowledge. In order for adaptive interfaces to increase the salience of some elements, such as which are the next most appropriate elements to be learned, it is necessary to define elements such as the proposed learning structure, the elements already seen, but also, what does the user wish to learn next.

In a closed environment like the one mostly used in AI systems, interesting support systems may be developed to guide the user in the prescribed tasks. The more immersive the simulation, the easier it is to follow and help the learner [6]. But in open environments like in distance learning, it is difficult to know what the learner is trying to do and to support and guide him into efficient learning strategies. In fact, either the system takes control and guides the user in restrictive paths, or it is more remote and the learner needs to have the initiative to fetch and find appropriate help. Very often the support the learner would need is some orientation suggestion, some reminders of how he could improve his strategy, for which he will not ask help. Even when he seeks help, he have trouble finding exactly what he needs and how to formulate it to the system.

If the structure of the content is encyclopedic and easy to chunk, then one can offer direct manipulation, with the learner accessing a graph representative of the structure of concepts to be learned, as in ExploraGraph. Using the learner s navigation path in the graph, an overlay model may be extracted and projected as a feedback: What information has he/she read? For how long? How long ago? In that context the annotation of adaptive links can suffice to support the user s navigation and encourage completion of exploration and understanding. Without such cueing users are more disoriented in hypertextual content [7]. Cueing also makes the environment more dynamic and interactive to the learner, it may incite passive learners to be more active in their exploration of the learning content [8].

However, education and learning theories insist it is better that learning take place in a more active, situated and collaborative setting. In this context, the content has to be organized in a more complex way and this complicates possible support to navigation. In our system, as in the MISA model [2], learning activities are organized around many structures, among others: knowledge structure, activity scenarios and documents structure. In this context there may be many paths to access knowledge and the user needs some coaching and adaptation at a more general level in order to best assimilate content. Part of the activities take place outside the system, which then serves only as a gateway and a guide. For this, a meta-level of support is needed: the system must use strategic information on the structure of group activities, on the user s higher level of intentions and eventually on collaborative interdependence among learners. The present project proposes a model and generic prototype designed to integrate generic support in the telelearning context. Usability evaluations were made at various stages of system development and raise interesting considerations and suggestions for such a generic supportive interface.

3 Research Objectives

We were among the first to experiment with link annotations [9,10] where visited links are generically modified, as the user finishes accessing the information they contain. In the context of activities and distance education, our interest was more proactive: we wanted to attract user attention to tasks or contents that were more relevant at a specific point in time. We were interested in the pacing of the meta-level of information attached to a learning content, in order to track the evolution of learner expertise and to support learner motivation. We were also interested in using different modalities of support (physical and visual guidance, feedback, triggering of shortcuts) and in how to link and integrate those forms of support in context.

To achieve these goals, it proved necessary to enrich the structured representation of the content with a dynamic representation of the different contexts in which help could be displayed, and to integrate both passive and more active forms of support in the environment. We will briefly describe the ExploraGraph environment, before discussing why and how its support system was built and what considerations arose during its development and evaluation.

4 The ExploraGraph Environment

4.1 The ExploraGraph Editor and Navigator.

The ExploraGraph Editor is a generic environment where structures of activities, knowledge elements, documents may be described. The elements used in the representation (nodes, links, icons, shapes, etc.) may be changed easily. Rules for support have to be described directly in the Access database using SQL queries and Forms.

The ExploraGraph Navigator [11] was designed to facilitate the visualization of graphical structures (see figure 1). A physical model of nodes (mass and repulsion), links (elasticity) and of general organization (gravity and friction) is used to simulate the relations between elements of the course. As the learner explores the nodes, these zoom and rearrange themselves in order to maximize visibility and contextual relations, following the focus of interest. Nodes may have different shapes, icons or size. Each one has an attached description and properties like visited and completion levels, which may be displayed graphically (gage). Those properties and Importance (size) may be set dynamically, to highlight areas of the information to be explored. This corresponds to the concept of map adaptation [5].

A Control Panel is incorporated in the Navigator, where the learner may choose a general intention: Explore, Plan, Revise his own progression, Adjust the system (each with various options). Choosing a goal may trigger a set of actions in the system, zooming on a specific graph, opening applications. It also triggers help, especially the first time it is used. Help and actions may be adapted contextually.

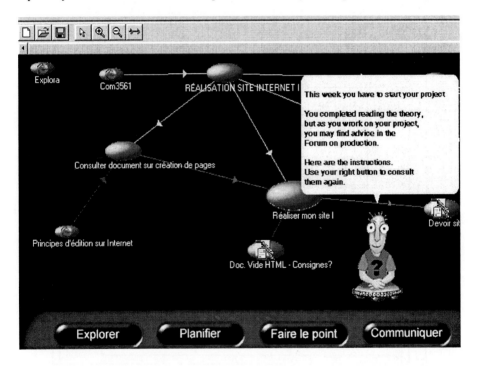

Fig. 1 The ExploraGraph Navigator, showing the graphical structure, the Control Panel and a MsAgent giving a contextual explanation.

In Figure 1 the user have asked what were his tasks. The agent zoom on the main activity of the week and suggest him to consult the description using his right button.

4.2 Structure of the Support System

The support system was developed behind the ExploraGraph system as a rule-based system in Visual Basic using the Access database. Figure 2 shows the functional architecture of the system.

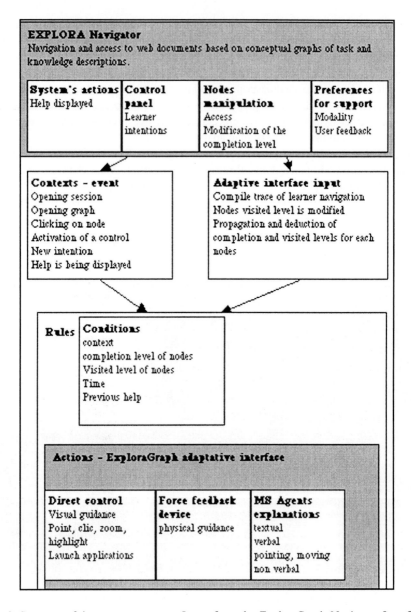

Fig. 2. Structure of the support system: Input from the ExploraGraph Navigator Interface; context recognition and trace analysis; rule-based system to display contextual support.

The learner s model is based first on his navigation in the structured content. Two properties are retained on each content node —was it visited?[1], was it marked as

---

[1] At the present time, we only consider the number of times a node was visited and not the duration of each visit (delay before another node is selected). Although it is difficult to know whether consultation time can be considered a valid measure (user is active and understands); it would be interesting to add this to the learning model. We

completed? It also uses the goals and subgoals specified by the learner using the Control Panel —I want to explore (knowledge, tasks or calendar), to plan, to communicate (with others, technical questions, questions on the course, etc.). Other contextual controls could be added when the learner selects a node —More information on that Who can help me with that ?

The rule-based system is triggered by events in the manipulation of the interface — such as the learner opening a graph, specifying an intention on the Control Panel, clicking on a content, marking an event as completed, asking for more or less help, or when the system displays a help message, etc. For each contextual event, specific rules are examined and more specific conditions are examined —date, traces of user s navigation, earlier help messages. A rule is chosen and triggers a set of actions to support the learner :

- Graphical highlight and links annotation [8], which give a general idea of the structure and which are less intrusive than more formal guiding.
- Avatars animations which are used for graphical demonstrations (attention seeking, pointing, etc.), but also for non-verbal communications and motivational purposes. Avatars audio voices, used to attract attention and more easily combined with visual demonstrations than text.
- Visual guiding to present users with procedures and actions which they may use to realize their intentions.
- Force feedback guiding, which combined with visual demonstration, drag more attention, takes less cognitive concentration, facilitates memorization [12] and ensures that the user gets the full demonstration.

Avatars where introduced in the environment partly °to fulfill the need for social context° when no other learner is on line [13] but also to serve as the interface to the advisory system. They were not presented as omniscient persona, but rather as assistants having specific goals and limited competence. One agent was to support the user in is use of the system, the other was to serve as the tutor assistant in carrying instructions and advice on the learning situation.

4.3   Implementation of the Support System

Support control and events methods are embedded in the objects of the generic interface (Visual basic objects) : Opening of a graph, Control Panel choice.
Rules are described in the relational Access database (with the description of graphs), each rule being an SQL query. The system uses different tables to describe elements and relations of the help system: CONTEXTS, CONDITIONS, RULES, GROUP OF ACTIONS, ACTIONS, TRACE. Events specify a context and, in the CONDITIONS table, each SQL query associated with this context is executed until one is found true. SQL queries use the properties of the tasks (structure of activities and knowledge elements as described in the graphs) and of the learner model which are described in

---

could calculate the ratio of effective duration on prescribed duration in the task model (each element having a duration property).

the database tables.[1] The RULES table then specify, for that condition, the GROUP OF ACTIONS to be launched. The ACTIONS table describes the specific properties of each actions.

5   Usability Evaluation

We experimented using the system for a period of 8 weeks, with 9 students taking a course on the design of telelearning interface. All subjects had avatars explanations at the beginning but for some students the avatars interventions became less frequent . For those the support for activities was limited to the first sessions. The group was also split for the modality of support: some learners had haptic guidance (with a force feedback device) while others had only visual demonstrations.

Evaluation was based on the trace analysis of students and on evaluation questionnaires. We also observed and used grids to describe reactions of learners to the support system. Results were used to qualify the usability of the support system elements: what was appreciated, what appears to be efficient and what should be improved. The visual and haptic conditions were also compared.

The qualitative results suggested that:

- Avatars were appreciated. Though their intervention were found too frequent at the beginning, users were longing to see them more often later in their course.
- Users were asking to be able to review demonstrations and to control avatars when they needed help.
- Users with the haptic guidance later reuse more the demonstrated procedures.
- The haptic guidance should be improved so transition and physical properties of guidance would be easier to follow [14]
- Verbal explanations were too long, users were reading and acting faster than the avatars could explain.
- Movement, gestures and non-verbal signals of avatars were appreciated.

Those are very general results, but we will now examine the model of support behind the interface and discuss the considerations they were addressing and how the support model should be improved.

5.1   The Control Panel — Empowering both Learner and Tutor

Although interfaces generally have menus, following a suggestion of [15], we added to the ExploraGraph system a meta-level menu, where learners may choose among generic intentions. As Norman [16] has shown, difficulties in systems arise because users have complex goals, which are not easily translated into the system s set of actions. He writes about the gulf of execution :

I want to find what I have to do = Open calendar, find this week and next and look for deadlines, compare to what you have already done, determine priorities, find descriptions and documents linked to activities.

---

[1] For now the learner model is embedded in the task model, because the system is used as a standalone, but it will be separate in the networked version.

It is relatively easy to specify a set of plausible generic intentions that the learner may choose from and to support them. The learner model, the task model defined in the conceptual graphs and context may then be used to narrow possibilities: date, ranking and priorities among tasks, relation between tasks and concept elements, degree of exploration and completion of activities, etc.

From the perspective of ITS, the Control Panel plays a very important role, not only in enriching the learner model, but in integrating shared control into the help system. As Crampes [17] have shown, if the support system has too much control, learners rely on the system s intelligence; if more control is given to the learner (with help not proactive but accessible), help is not used sufficiently. They suggest a gaming type of shared control, where the learner may access help or proceed without it, but loses points upon failure. This kind of economist model is interesting, but is not always possible in an open environment such as distance learning.

With the Control Panel, help is not given in parallel to user activity: the latter triggers and accompanies a shortcut to what the learner wants to do.

> You want to know what is more urgent ? Here it is, I open it and zoom it for you and don t forget that it counts for half of your evaluation .

5.2 Conflicting Contexts and Support

The help system is triggered in different contexts, following actions of the user or of the system. Though this tends to limit the help given, it was found natural for learners to be offered help only when they voluntarily changed the context. Even then, pre-experimentation showed that support should be spread out in time. For example, during the usability evaluation, helping was first set at every third opening of a graph, and this was found to be too frequent and disturbing. Delaying support to every fifth opening, produced less negative comments.

As in every distributed support system, conflicts arise among rules when different contexts are triggering actions. Priorities have to be assigned among different types of context —users goal specifications (Control Panel) and actions are the first priorities, then deadlines, followed by learning the interface, interventions to support motivation and social activities come next, when nothing else is more urgent.

5.3 Adjusting the Types and Sequence of Support Actions

Once a context and a specific condition are recognized, a set of actions is triggered. Executing these actions may also cause problems. Since help is given at the level of intentions and complex activities[1], the sequence of explanation or guidance tends to be lengthy, with control having to be shared with the user. In Norman s model of action, this is linked to the gulf of evaluation : How can the user understand and integrate the system s activity within his own?

> Why does the system show me that ? What does it mean ?

---

[1] How should you plan your work ? Why and how should you communicate your questions ?

Therefore, control has to be shared between the user and the system, especially for demonstrations, where the system must turn over control to the learner.

> You should change the Completed control or select this option (do it) . Now look here (pointing), if completed activities have been checked, you can use this Control Panel to find out what to do next.

Some problems arose with this shared control. Although Johnson & al. [6] describe various AI techniques to control agents, they don t seems to address problems of control sharing with the user, as if 3D presence made intervention more natural and accepted by users. Their pedagogical agents advise learners and complement their actions, in a way that seems more continuous and accepted to them. But in an open environment support is more difficult to integrate.

Surprisingly, the force feedback device (computer-controlled mouse) was found less disturbing, even though it was more controlling. At any rate, there were less ambiguities as to who was supposed to do something next. The user was either being physically guided, or loose (completely in control). However, the transition between states was found disturbing: learners found the device surprising . The guiding linkage should be better calibrated in order to smoothen control transitions. They could be proposed to the learner so he would be prepared for them.

5.4   Integrating User Preferences

It is easy to let the user interrupt support or to let him set preferences on its intervention. But for the user caught up in the heat of action, adapting the interface might prove a tedious and bothersome task, so we intend to integrate adaptive functions that will streamline both global and individual users' feedback on the help system, in order to adjust future help functions both in general and individually. Such a mixed adaptive learning environment appears primordial in ensuring system adaptation to longer learning situations, in conformity with his evolving choices [18]. The concept of collaborative adaptation is a very important area of research [19].

References

1.   Paquette, G., Ricciardi-Rigault, C., Paquin, C., Li geois, S., & Bleicher, E. (1996). Developing the Virtual Campus Environment. , ED-Media International Conference, Boston.
2.   Paquette, G., Aubin, C., & Crevier, F. (1997). Design and Implementation of Interactive TeleLearning Scenarios. , ICDE 97   (International Council for Distance Education), Penn State University, USA.
3.   Browne, D., & Totterdell, P. (1990). Adaptive User Interfaces. London: Academic Press, 227p.
4.   De La Passardi re, B., & Dufresne, A. (1992). Adaptative Navigational Tools for Educational Hypermedia. In I. Tomek (Ed.), Computer Assisted Learning (pp. 555-567). Berlin, New York: Springer-Verlag.
5.   Brusilovsky, P. (1996). Methods and Techniques of Adaptive Hypermedia. User Modeling and User-Adapted Interaction, 6, 87-129.

6. Johnson, W. L., Rickel, J. W., & Lester, J. C. (2000). Animated Pedagogical Agents: Face-to-Face Interaction in Interactive Learning Environments. Intern. Journ. of Artificial Intelligence and Education, 11, in press.

7. Brusilovsky, P. (1997). Efficient Techniques for Adaptive Hypermedia. Intelligent hypertext: Advanced technqiques for the World Wide Web. Lect. Notes in Computer Science, 1326, 12-30.

8. Lee, Y. B., & Lehman, J. D. (1993). Instructional Cuing in Hypermedia: A Study with Active and Passive learners. Journal of Educational Multimedia and Hypermedia, 2(1), 25-37.

9. Dufresne, A., & Tremblay, I. (1991). Modelling Distributed Knowledge to Support Learning Environments in Physiology and Computer Science. International Conference on Simulation in Engineering Education. Simulation Series, 24(2), 185-189.

10. Dufresne, A. (1997). From adaptable to adaptive interface for distance education. , Workshop on Intelligent Educational Systems on the World Wide Web, AIED 97, Kobe, Japan(pp. 94-98).

11. Dufresne, A., Cosmova, V., LeTran, T., & Ramstein, C. (1999). EXPLORA: An interface to support the learner with dynamic graphs and multimodal goal driven explanations. , AIED'99, IOS Press, Maine(pp. 660- 662).

12. Arcand, J.-F. (1995). An Artificial Neural Network for the Ergonomic Evaluation of a Human-Computer Interface, International Conference on Tools with Artificial Intelligence, IEEE, New Orleans, Louisiane (pp. 606-608).

13. Pentti, H., & Timo, N. (1998). The Comptence of Learning Companion Agents. International Journal of Artificial Intelligence iin Education, 9, to be published.

14. Boucher S. (2000). valuation de l impact des modalit s visuelle, auditive et haptique d une interface comme support la t che dans un environnement hyperm dia de t l formation. M moire de ma trise. Universit de Montr al.

15. Ruelland, D. (2000). Vers un modele d'autogestion de l'apprentissage dans un environnement de tele-apprentissage. Ph.D thesis. Universit de Montr al.

16. Norman, D. A., & Draper. (1986). User Centered System Design: New perspectives on human-computer interaction. Hillsdale: Earlbaum, 536.

17. Crampes, M. (1999). User Controlled Adaptivity versus System Controlled Adaptivity in Intelligent Tutoring systems. In S. P. Lajoie, & M. Vivet (Ed.), Proceedings of the AIED'99 (pp. 173-180). Amsterdam: IOS Press.

19. Kay, J. (1995). The UM Toolkit for Cooperative user Models. User Modeling and User-Adapted Interaction, 4(3), 149-196.

Acknowledgement

This research was funded within the TeleLearning Network of Centres of Excellence, Canada. The development of an application using ExploraGraph was funded by the Office of Learning Technologies, Canada.

Agent's Contribution for an Asynchronous Virtual Classroom

Kenji Matsuura, Hiroaki Ogata and Yoneo Yano

Faculty of Engineering, Tokushima University
2-1, Minamijosanjima, Tokushima 770-8506, Japan
http://www-yano.is.tokushima-u.ac.jp/
(matsuura, ogata, yano)@is.tokushima-u.ac.jp

Abstract. This paper describes a new idea about the multi-agents that act as classmates of learners in an asynchronous virtual classroom. The environment of this virtual classroom is designed to support asynchronous participants. Some agents in the system are based on learner-model of the past learners, and others are on the educational strategy the teacher has given in advance. In such situation, it is necessary for a learner to filter classmates who are actually software agents in the user interface. Furthermore, the actions of these agents are also to be defined. Therefore, we propose two types of strategies to select well-fitted classmates first things in this paper. Then, we define these agents' action in an agent-based asynchronous virtual classroom.

1 Introduction

It becomes more common for those who design a lifelong learning environment to realize it on computers and networks as the virtual school/classroom [2][6]. These movements make the ordinary learning environment, like classroom-based education in a school, extend to the virtual one via the Internet [3][4][5].

However those environments could have some problems that the system has to compel users to participate in at the same time [8]. Otherwise, if the system allows a user to participate in anytime, all the things she/he can do in that environment is to see static learning materials for the reason why she/he has no way to communicate with others synchronously. The problem is that it is awfully difficult for an asynchronous learner to communicate with others immediately when she/he wants to ask or to make comments on the learning materials in the classroom. For example, concerned with a supporting distance-lecture system, learners have to use the same learning materials at the same time, otherwise the system cannot provide the collaboration space among learners. On the other hand, the approaches to bind software agents to a learner's environment as a companion have been seen recently [1].

The main purpose of the researches to support distance learning is to study how the system provides a collaborative learning environment for learners or makes a learner acquire new knowledge and refine it on network [7]. The learning environments of some ordinary studies propose one-way communication in which the systems show a learner teaching materials. On the other hand, if the system provides a collaborative environment to learners, they have to participate in synchronously, or they may use asynchronous communication tools without any utilization of past learners' action. Therefore, we have been developing AAVC (Agent-based Asynchronous Virtual Classroom) to solve those problems.

AAVC system combines self-instruction with collaboration by agents. A learner in AAVC system uses networked computers to learn or communicate with remote learning resources, including teachers and other learners, but without the requirement to be online at the same time. In the concrete, AAVC has the efficiently visualized learning environment to support distance lecture that uses exposed video images of a teacher and some virtual learners. A learner in this system is able to see some classmates and their actions in the environment. Some of them are software agents of past lectured learners and the others are on behalf of prepared educational agents. In such situation, a learner feels much presence that she/he shares time and space with a teacher and other learners. A learner in this system may also collaborate with other learners or a teacher by using agent communication, while the other real learners don't participate in the same class at the same time. Hence this system links people as well as machines across the time and place.

In this paper, we describe how to select these autonomous agents as classmates for a learner first of all. Then, we also define their action in our AAVC system.

2 Agent-Based Asynchronous Virtual Classroom

2.1 Features of AAVC

It is important for those who learn in an asynchronous learning environment that the system provides a virtual community space for teaching and learning. The environment of AAVC has some comparable advantages shown as follows:

(1) Anytime/Anywhere learning

The system enables a learner to request the resources at anytime on WWW, if the classroom is opened to the public. Then the system sends its learning materials and additional information about the classroom on the educational strategy. The information are may be changed by means of the strategy every time a learner participates in AAVC.

(2) Seamless Learning

Other classrooms linked by the teacher are seen in an information space, and a learner may moves to other classroom at anytime. Due to the teacher's educational linking strategy, a learner can make his own knowledge amplify.

(3) Learning by observing others' interaction

Watching the interaction among other learners or between a learner and the teacher makes to construct effective discussing way for the learner and to be aware of various viewpoints. The system indicates other learners' past action, especially their statements in the past discussion.

(4) Learning through collaboration

This system provides to learners a collaboration space with others. In such situation, a learner can refine his/her acquired knowledge through the discussion. The system prepares synchronous / asynchronous collaborative environments for the continuous discussion.

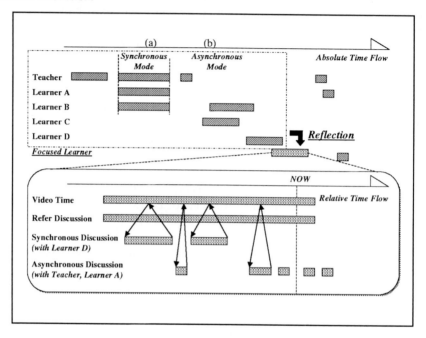

Fig. 1. Time Flow

2.2 Time flow

Fig.1 shows the time flow in AAVC. At first, the lecture is recorded as the video image, which is made into MPEG or simply RA file. When the other teaching materials are ready for the class, the AAVC might be opened to the public on WWW. Then the system enables learners to request to participate in. As we focus on certain learner, she/he can see some agents of the other learners who have participated in at the past time, and some additional agents in the user interface. As the learning time goes on, she/he can also recognize the other learner D. At the beginning of a classroom, the system organizes the classmates, actually agents, who are divided two groups: past learners' agents and educational agents. When the learner D participates in the middle of the classroom, the system indicates the existence of learner D, without any interrupting the learner's lecture.

3 Agents Model

3.1 Types of agents

Table 1. The types of agents in AAVC

Types	Whose Agent?	Each roles or explanations
My-agent	Learner-self	- Managing the learner's individual knowledge
Simu-agent	Other learner	- Managing the other learner's individual knowledge - Imitating other learner's past action
Claque-agent	Teacher (as learner)	- Carrying out an action plan of the claque learner that the teacher have given in advance
Helper-agent	Teacher	- Managing shared knowledge - Answering the learner's questions

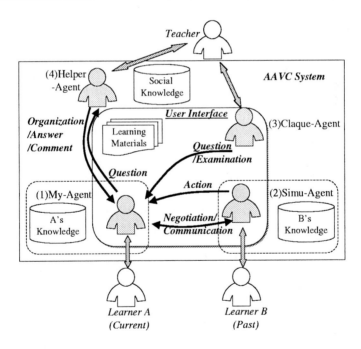

Fig. 2. Agents' conceptual model

The kinds of software agents are shown in Table.1, whose conceptual model is illustrated with Fig.2. My-agent displays some action patterns according to the learner's operation, e.g., clicking a mouse or typing a keyboard. This agent plays a role that monitors the learner's action and manages his/her individual knowledge. Simu-agent acts on the past-attended learner's model, which is constituted by the learner's action log. Simu-agent imitates the past learner's actions and manages the learner's individual knowledge. Claque -agent is a preset-typed educational agent that acts for the learner to give him/her some advice. Since these actions make a learner have his/her own opinion or want to ask some questions to others about shown statements, both actions may also induce collaboration with others. Helper-agent acts on the pedagogical strategy given by the teacher and answer the learner's question. In those types of software agents, the number of claque-agents is adjusted by the system. Each agent has its own action model, implemented on the server-side scripts, of which action is generated on reaction-planning architecture.

3.2 Agent's Action

In order to realize these agents' action, we have defined what kinds of actions are suitable in such environment at some points of view. Concerned with agents action on the client side, two functions are necessary, of which agent simulates the other past learner's action to be aware of other's view points and shoots some questions to the learner to improve the acquired knowledge into stable one.

(1) Simu-agents' simulation

This example of script shows how simu-agents imitate the past learner's action when a learner requests to show certain past discussion. Since AAVC system abbreviates the past discussion, each statement has to go to the tune to the relative time in each lecture. The first statement in a discussion goes at the relative time (RT) from the beginning of the lecture. As to other statements, the system calculates the start time in the way to summate RT plus each statement's calculated interval time.

In that environment, there are some cases that a learner wants to ask some questions or to comment on his/her opinion during watching a discussion. Of course, she/he can, but without stopping its discussion and the statement is added at the end of the discussion at the relative time. If she/he wants to cut into the discussion, she/he must start new discussion with a new title.

(2) Claque-agent's addressing

It is important to fix the acquired knowledge in the lecture to the stable. So the system enables a teacher to establish the claque-agent's addressing with some attributes (relative time in the lecture, what statement to appear, and other flags). The statement belongs to some kinds of question, comment, or a fixed form of an examination. When a learner attends at a lecture, claque addresses to the learner and brings his/her answer to helper on the server-side.

```
While (exists statements) {
  If (first statement of the discussion) {
    Then {
      Define the agents' action as follows:
        Start time: relative time (RT) of the Discussion
        Interval time: calculate time fit for the statement length
      Display: parallel (statement 0) }
  } Else if (statement ID == N) {
    Then {
      Define the agents' action as follows:
        Start time: relative time of the statement
        Interval time: calculate time :(RT + summate later statements time)
      Display: parallel (statement N) }
  }
}
```

(3) Helper-agent's advise

Helper-agent plays two important roles. First role is that helper diagnoses the learner's answer of the claque's question and replies it if a teacher establish the action. The second role is to retrieve candidates to the question of a learner, which is inputted during watching the past discussion, from the shared knowledge base. If topics are not found, helper-agent retrieves from personal knowledge base. In that case, only the candidates from personal knowledge base of which attribute is open to public are shown to the learner.

3.3 Classroom formation

AAVC has two ways of classroom formation that are available in which a learner requests to join the classroom. When the members in the classroom are few at the beginning, the number of the displayed agents is large. But the number of participants who have joined to a classroom increases as time goes on. Then the displayed classmates have to be filtered off on certain criterion as follows.

(1) Regard the communication among learners as important

The system selects simu-agents as classmates at first, who have participated in the classroom and uttered in this model. The system gives high priority to be selected to those who have uttered more times than others. In this way, the system attempt to support an asynchronous encounter and to increase collaborations among learners.

(2) Regard the educational strategy of the teacher as important

The system selects claque-agents as classmates to be given the high priority of selecting. While this type makes a learner collaborate with teacher rather than other learners, a learner may want to collaborate with other learners in order to answer the question from claques.

AAVC changes how to select these criterions automatically. At the beginning of the classroom, the system use (1) because many topics among learners are expected to discuss then. Since the number of discussion occurred in the classroom decreases, the system selects (2) to intervene the learner's study.

4 Implementation

4.1 System Configuration

Fig.3 shows the system configuration of AAVC. AAVC system is built on the WWW with Java. As a fundamental rule, the server is to control and the clients to request. While all available data/files are located on the server side, clients have only viewer and don't have any data. Each data and Modules on the server side are shown as follows:

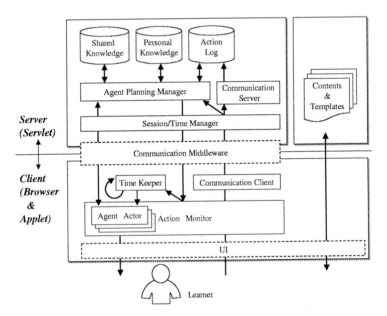

Fig. 3. System Configuration

Video contents: Video images of the lectures, which can be edited by the teacher.

Action log: Action history log files of hold session, which will be processed and made into a learner model, and then deleted when the learning finished. The AAVC system makes into learner model by diagnosing these action logs, which is used for another learner.

Shared Knowledge: Shared knowledge base is constructed of some tables. For example, question and answer about prearranged keywords, monitoring the synchronous communication with chat, and e-mail based asynchronous communication among learners.

Personal Knowledge: Compared with shared knowledge, the AAVC system has the personal knowledge base to storage individual memo. A learner can use memo tool at anytime she/he wants, of which enables to write the memo text and some drawings. They are processed into individual objects in the database on server-side.

Session/Time Manager: is to manage the session-ID, other session variables and relative/absolute time of clients' lecture

Agent Planning Manager: is to control the agent's activity as keep the time

Agent Actor: is to act each action thread in time order unless agent-planning manager gives priority to another thread.

Action Monitor: is to monitor the clients interaction and to propose additional information to a learner

4.2 User interface

Fig. 4. An example of User Interface

There are two factors of technology to give learners the feeling of much presence. One is video image frame, which shows a teacher's lecture with its teaching material, and the other is classmates frame, which shows the other learners' action. Fig.4 is an image of main window. When a learner requests a lecture to watch, she/he goes into the virtual classroom of which mainly components are the lecture video image and learners pictures. In addition, extra information is seen in another windows to show the classroom's properties, real learners' information to participate in, and the other classrooms' information. The video image is embedded at opposite side to the virtual learners in the window. A learner can see the lecture in it and control the streaming as the learner's occasion demands.

Some certain actions, which are carried on table 1, are brought to a learner by clicking the virtual objects and selecting displayed menus. Those menus make learners collaborate with others, who are classified to a teacher, another learner, and the system's educational agent. To collaborate with others, a learner inputs some questions or comments to the WWW server. In some cases, the server rapidly replies at the actions of the learner, but it does not in other cases. That's depends on the teacher's readiness for the classroom. If any candidates of answer-sentences are not retrieved, the system sends a question-message to learners or a teacher by asynchronous tools like e-mail.

5   Conclusion

We proposed the agents contribution in an agent-based asynchronous virtual classroom. Its architecture allows learners to learn anytime and anywhere. To realize that, this paper specially emphasized on how the system selects multi-agents to construct the classmates, when those agents acts, and what kind of actions of them is activated.

As the knowledge demands imposed upon those who teach and learn increase, new technologies are making possible innovative approaches to educating students and employees outside of the academic and corporate classroom. For learners who are geographically remote from tutors and peer students, the AAVC system plays very important role. Due to AAVC, teachers and learners are needless to share time and place. While we have not referred to the membership in the same class, the teacher may confine the member of the class, as she/he wants. However, the teacher has to work hard for initial readiness. So our future work is to reduce the work of a teacher and to evaluate the prototype system through its trial use.

References

1   Frasson, C., Martin, L., Gouarderes, G., Aimeur, E.: LANCA : a distance Learning Architecture based on Networked Cognitive Agents, *Proc. of ITS'98*, U.S.A. (1998)
2   Gerhard F.: lifelong Learning, *NSF Symposium Proc. on Learning and Intelligent Systems* (1997) 7-12

3   Gregory D. Abowd.: Classroom 2000: An experiment with the instrumentation of a living educational environment", *IBM Systems Journal*, Vol.38, No.4 (1999) 508-530

4   Harasim, L., Hiltz, S. R., Teles, L., and Turoff, M.: learning Networks, *The MIT Press*

5   Hiltz, S. and Wellman, B.: Asynchronous Learning Networks as a Virtual Classroom, *Communication of ACM*, Vol.40, No.9 (1997) 44-49

6   Longworth, N., and Davies, W., K.: LIFELONG LEARNING, *Kogan Page*

7   Ogata, H., Matsuura, K., and Yano, Y.: Knowledge Awareness: Bridging between Shared Knowledge and Collaboration in Sharlok, *Proc. of Educational-Telecommunications 1996*, Boston, U.S.A. (1996) 232-237

8   Matsuura, K., Ogata, H., and Yano, Y.: Agent-based Asynchronous Virtual Classroom, *Proc. of ICCE'99*, Vol.1, Japan (1999) 133-140

Theoretical and Practical Considerations for Web-Based Intelligent Language Tutoring Systems[1]

Trude Heift[1] and Devlan Nicholson[2]
[1] Linguistics Department and [2] Natural Language Laboratory,
Simon Fraser University, Burnaby, B.C., Canada V5A1S6,
{heift@sfu.ca},{devlan@cs.sfu.ca}

Abstract. This paper discusses the inherent goals and trade-offs involved in the design of an efficient, robust Web tutor within the context of a working, hypermedia framework. The focus is on the *German Tutor*, an Intelligent Language Tutoring System (ILTS) that implements generality, interactivity, and modularity as contrasted with more traditional computational constraints and architectures. Design and pedagogical goals of Web-based delivery, such as intelligence and efficiency, will also be addressed but again with an emphasis on the special requirements of efficient, adaptive hypermedia systems.

1 Introduction

As Web technologies for adapting existing educational content converge with increased bandwidth, more and more uniquely Web-based applications emerge. But while the Internet's convenient access, currency and variety of material, and integrated multimedia can extend traditional instruction, it also requires a more profound degree of adaptivity and interactivity.

The diversity of users alone, presents a challenge in design. First of all, the system needs to be general enough to suit a variety of competencies, and backgrounds. For example, Intelligent Language Tutoring Systems (ILTSs) have commonly based their error analysis at least partly on the native language of the student [17]. An on-line system, however, must adopt a more general scheme in order to accommodate international access and cases where the native language of the user might not be known.

System performance and efficiency are also central to interactive learning support systems. Any interaction with a visible delay between the browser and the server defeats the purpose of an interactive system and can, in the worst case, distract from the problem solving activity [6]. While efficiency motivates most server arrangements from form-based CGI interfaces [2], to Java technology [16], to a combination thereof [7], we have adopted and will describe a heterogeneous three-tier architecture that integrates multiple servers and several programming languages. A primary Web server interacts with the client machine via CGI scripts and JAVA technology while

---

[1] This research was supported by PR Grant 13 871344.

the intelligent and adaptive components reside on a separate server dedicated to answer processing. This layered design has proven to be efficient and scalable.

Generally, we discuss an ILTS for German which forms the grammar practice component of a Web-based introductory course for German. The *German Tutor* has been specifically designed for Web-delivery emphasizing generality, modularity, and efficiency.

Intelligence is imparted to the system by a grammar and a parser which analyzes student input, and a student model that maintains learner profiles, displays instructional feedback suited to learner expertise, and suggests remedial exercises. Error analysis, however, is not restricted to the grammar and parser. The system implements further answer checking modules to better accommodate multiple native languages while, at the same time, distributing processing load in case of multiple, simultaneous users. The system's design is also highly modular. Answer processing components are kept separate from learner feedback, user modeling, and the actual student task. For example, student exercises are stored in a plain text file which the JAVA code extracts and displays on a Web page. Exercises can be modified quickly, or instructors can change feedback messages to suit their pedagogical needs, creating a more flexible authoring environment.

In the following, we will describe the overall system architecture, the error detecting mechanism, and the student model of the *German Tutor*. In all sections we will make reference to design considerations emphasizing generality, modularity, and efficiency. We will also provide results of a system trial and conclude with further research suggestions.

2 System Description

2.1 System Architecture

The *German Tutor* relies on a three-tier architecture, illustrated in Figure 1. Actual processing of student input is distributed over two computers for reasons of efficiency. The intelligent and adaptive parts of the answer checking process reside on a dedicated UNIX machine running Prolog while the Java and HTML serving and preprocessing is handled by a Web server. The Web server has two main functions:

First, it handles the interaction between the client and Prolog application. JAVA applets, rather than HTML, have proven to be more suitable in providing the student exercises, while communicating reasonably efficiently with the Prolog server. While JAVA applets require initial loading time, Web pages do not have to be reloaded for each exercise.

In addition, navigation within the task is appropriately restricted. Stern [14:1], for example, points to a problem with some hypermedia systems: "the built-in back buttons of a Web browser allow students to see previous exercises which might not always be desirable in a hypermedia system".

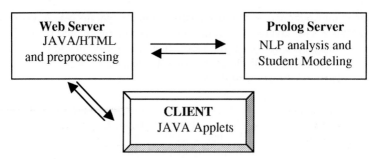

Figure 1: An Interactive Learning Support System

The second task of the Web server is to handle the preprocessing of student input. Figure [2] illustrates the flow of a sentence through the various answer processing modules. All modules except the spell and grammar check reside on the Web server and are implemented in JAVA. These JAVA components, however, share preliminary information from the Prolog server regarding the expected constraints of the exercise, which is provided during the spell check stage detailed below.

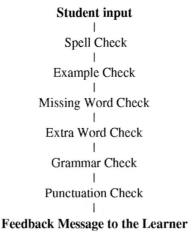

Figure 2: Answer-Checking Modules

The system is organized in such a way that if any module detects an error, further processing is blocked. As a result, only one error at a time will be displayed to the learner which avoids overwhelming the student with extensive error reports in case of multiple errors. Studies have shown [15] that displaying more than one feedback message at a time makes the correction process too complex for the student. From a computational point of view, interrupting the error processing mechanism also assists in distributing the queue for each module in case of multiple, simultaneous users.

The first module in analyzing student input is a spell check for which we use the International Ispell (Version 3.1.2) with our own dictionary. The current dictionary contains approximately 3800 words. During the spell check we also extract the base forms of each word in the user's input. The uninflected words are needed later to determine whether the learner followed the task, that is, whether the student answer contained the words expected. The Example Check compares these base forms with those in the student input.

When defining an exercise, we also pre-store all possible correct answers. For example, for the task given in (5),

> (5) Build a sentence with the following words:
> Er / hören / Musik
> *He / to listen to - to hear/ music*

we store the possible answers, given in 6(a) – (d):

> (6a) Er hört Musik.
> (6b) Er hört die Musik.
> (6c) Musik hört er.
> (6d) Die Musik hört er.

Using a genetic algorithm[2], the system then determines the most likely answer (MLA) intended by the student. Storing multiple answers allows for freer student input and, at an introductory level, involves little extra work.[3]

The Missing Word Check module matches the extracted base forms with those of the MLA. If any of the words in the MLA are not contained in the student answer, the system will report an error.

The following check, the Extra Word Check, handles additional or extraneous words in the student answer. Errors in omission and insertion are commonly handled by the grammar in other systems [4], [13], however, our initial testing showed that system performance is higher if these two error types are treated outside the grammar. Doing so avoids the exponential cost of each additional rule within a declarative grammar, in particular, in accommodating multiple native languages.

The Grammar Check is the most elaborate stage. Here the sentence is sent from the Web server to the PROLOG server, analyzed by the parser according to the rules and lexical entries of the grammar component, and returned. Currently, the grammar component covers the concepts of an introductory course.

The Punctuation Check performs a final string-match of the student answer with the MLA. By this stage, other errors have been eliminated and any failure is reported as an error in punctuation.

Each module is responsible for different error classes and operates independently. This modular design has also advantages with respect to error coverage and efficiency. The Missing and Extra Word Checks, for example, employ algorithms which make no reference to the native language of the student. As a result, the system achieves a wider error coverage by still providing informative feedback. System performance is also improved because the processing load on the Prolog server is reduced. These two error classes are handled by the Web server which, unlike the Prolog server, handles multiple user requests simultaneously. The grammar and the parser cover the remaining grammatical error classes. While the error analysis here is highly detailed, the robustness of the system with respect to multiple native languages remains to be determined.

The system also separates the answer checking mechanisms from the student tasks. Student exercises are extracted from a separate text file. This modular design allows for convenient authoring. Instructors can design their own exercises without any specialized knowledge of the system's sophisticated technology.

---

[2] The genetic algorithm was adapted from Huang and Miller [11].

[3] At an advanced level where exercises become even less constrained, alternatives to pre-storing correct answers can be considered (see also [8]).

In the following section, we will briefly describe the student model of the *German Tutor.*[4]

2.2   Student Model

A number of user modeling techniques have been employed in ILTSs over the past decade [12], [5], [1], but the challenging task in hypermedia systems begins in overcoming the statelessness of the HTTP protocol for identifying students and maintaining user models adaptive to the individual [14]. A number of solutions have been proposed which range from cookies, structured URLs, hidden fields to login screens [14], [6], [17]. The choice depends primarily on the application.

The *German Tutor* keeps a database of users, each entry established by an initial login. The student login and password is sufficient for the design of our system since students do not navigate through different HTML pages during grammar tasks, but access a consistent applet. The student identification is required by the Student Model which has two main functions:

First, for each student the Student Model keeps score across a number of error types, or, nodes such as grammar, vocabulary, punctuation, etc. The grammar node is broken down into more fine-grained categories. For example, it will contain detailed information on the student's performance on subject-verb agreement, case assignment, word order of past participles, etc. At the end of each exercise set, students receive detailed information on the errors they have made. This information is further being used for remediation.

Second, student performance history determines the specificity of the feedback message displayed (see also [3]). The Student Model maintains the learner model update by keeping score for each node. Depending on student input, the score for each node will go up or down. The amount by which the scores of each node are adjusted is specified in a master file and may be weighted to reflect different pedagogical purposes, such as emphasis of an exercise, importance of an error, etc. The messages are then selected according to the current learner level at each error node.

The main strength of the Student Model in the *German Tutor* is that a single errorful message will not drastically change the overall assessment of the student. The grammar nodes indicate precisely which grammatical violations occurred, allowing for a fine-grained assessment of student competency. The consequence is that a student can be at a different level for each given grammar constraint reflecting her performance of each particular grammatical skill. This subtlety of evaluation is desirable in a language teaching environment because as the student progresses through a language course a single measure is not sufficient to capture the knowledge attained and to distinguish among learners. The Student Model aids in directing each student toward error-specific and individualized remediation.

In the final section, we will discuss some of the results of a recent system trial.

---

[4] For a detailed NLP analysis of the system, see [9].

3   System Trial

The system was tested with 19 students during a one-hour class session in the fall semester 1999. In addition, students were able to use the *German Tutor* during a period of one week from their home computer. Students had a choice of working on two different chapters and a total of 244 sentences were analyzed by the system.[5] The system kept a detailed log of user interactions and, in addition, students filled out a questionnaire.

In the questionnaire, students responded that they liked the system for a number of reasons: first, they felt that the immediate feedback and freer grammar practice was very valuable. They stated that they would be using the system for general practice as well as for quiz preparation. Second, in one of the questions students were asked whether they noticed that the feedback adjusts to their level of expertise and whether they prefer receiving feedback of varying specificity. 84% of the participants stated that they noticed and preferred this scheme and found it useful to have feedback messages adjust to their competence level. The remaining participants did not particularly notice the change in feedback but expressed general approval.

3.1   Accuracy of the System

Out of the 244 sentences which were processed by the system, only one was analyzed incorrectly by the parser and the grammar. For the sentence *Ich kaufe Klaus eine neue Krawatte*, the student submitted the correct answer, however, the system incorrectly identified an error with the direct object *eine neue Krawatte*. The problem was traced to the algorithm which selects the desired parse and was subsequently fixed.[6]

The high accuracy of the system is due to at least three factors. First, the language tasks, although allowing for freer input, nonetheless constrain the domain. The system displays tasks in which students select from a given pool of vocabulary and grammatical structures. Second, students' language proficiency is still limited at an introductory level and thus neither the grammatical constructions nor the vocabulary are highly complex. Third, preprocessing the sentence for spelling, omission, and insertion errors undoubtedly increases the accuracy of the grammar and the parser because it eliminates much of the ambiguity of errorful natural language.[7]

---

[5] The total number of exercises students worked on during this time frame was higher. However, for the purpose of this paper, only the data for the type of exercise displayed in Example (5) will be considered. It contains the most elaborate answer checking mechanism which thus requires the most processing time.

[6] Due to lexical and syntactic ambiguities, a parser generates more than one interpretation for a sentence. The system implements two strategies for selecting the desired parse. First, we take into account pedagogical considerations in choosing a parse [10] and subsequently we scan all generated parses for the least number of errors.

[7] Allowing for free input would undoubtedly affect the accuracy of the system. However, the purpose of the system is to provide a highly accurate, meaningful practice environment for second language learners. The system thus takes advantage of the constrained domain given by a beginner learner level.

3.2   System Performance

During the period of the trial, students used the system in class as well as from their home computers. In the questionnaire students were asked whether they thought that the system speed from home or in class was either too slow, too fast, or appropriate. Students were also asked to indicate their Internet connections. Interestingly, 79% of the students felt that the system from home was fast enough despite modem connections of 36k – 58k baud. However, 21% of the participants thought that the system when used during in-class was too slow. Our subsequent investigation revealed that unrelated user traffic on the Web server itself had caused excessive delays during the trial.

Analyzing the time log, we discovered some slight fluctuation in the processing time of sentences, in particular, in the processing time of incorrect vs. correct sentences. For instance, for the incorrect sentence *Ich wohnst in Rom* the processing time of the grammar check was 2883 ms while for the correct sentence *Ich wohne in Rom* it was 1980 ms. However, this response time also depends on the overall activity of the server. For example, in another instance the incorrect sentence *Ich wohnt in Rom* took slightly less time (1947 ms). The overall log, however, suggests that while exceptions occur as traffic varies, incorrect answers require more time.

Multiple users undoubtedly affect the performance of the system. However, in analyzing the logs we did not discover excessive differences. For example, in one instance there were 8 sentences sent within a minute, the processing time per sentence, however differed only slightly (2174 ms, 2138ms, 2831ms, 3125ms, 2438ms, 926ms, 927ms, 513ms)[8]. This is partly because the sentence analysis terminates if one of the modules discovers an error thus distributing the queue for each module.

Again, however, the data and student responses suggest that significant time delay can be caused by unrelated user traffic on the Web server itself. As mentioned, 21% of the students thought that the system during class time was too slow although the internal processing time did not seem to be affected by the number of trial participants. The Web server of the system unfortunately handles a large amount of university Web traffic which, at busy times, undoubtedly affects our results.

We are currently moving the JAVA technology to a dedicated Web server to avoid unrelated user traffic. While the speed of the ILTS itself seems quite reasonable we are, nonetheless, also working on performance improvements there. First, we are making changes to the grammar within the lexical look-up which will speed up the grammar check. With respect to system flow, we are also implementing an initial string match. At the moment, the processing of a correct sentence passes through all answer checking modules. However, the complete answer checking mechanism is unnecessary if it can be quickly determined that the sentence is correct.

---

[8] For the last three processing times listed, the sentences failed with the spell check, i.e. relatively early.

4   Conclusions and further Research

In this paper we discussed an ILTS which emphasizes generality, modularity, and efficiency as essential design criteria for an adaptive and interactive Web-based tutor. The ILTS consists of various answer checking modules to better accommodate multiple native languages while, at the same time, distributing processing load in case of multiple, simultaneous users. The system is highly modular allowing for convenient authoring, as well as ease of maintenance and adaptability. Efficiency is achieved with a three layer architecture: a Web server interacts with the client machine via CGI scripts and JAVA technology and the intelligent and adaptive components reside on a separate server dedicated to answer processing. Our further research will focus on extending the exercise variety while continuing to improving the system's overall performance. With respect to further data collection and analysis, we will also test the system with students of multiple native languages and investigate the pedagogical impact of the system.

References

1. Bailin, A. (1995). AI and Language Learning. *Intelligent Language Tutors: Theory Shaping Technology.* Holland, M. V., Kaplan, J.D., Sama, M.R., eds. Mahwah, New Jersey: Lawrence Erlbaum Associates, Inc.: 327-343.
2. Brusilovsky, P., Ritter, S., and Schwarz, E. (1997). Distributed intelligent tutoring on the Web. In: B. du Boulay and R. Mizoguchi (eds.). *Proceedings of AIED '97*, Amsterdam: IOS: 482-489.
3. Brusilovsky, P., Ritter, S., and Weber, G. (1996). ELM-ART: An Intelligent Tutoring System on the World Wide Web. In: Frasson, C., Gauthier, G. and Lesgold, A., eds. *Lecture Notes in Computer Science.* Springer Verlag: 261-269.
4. Covington, M.A., and Weinrich, K.B. (1991). Unification-Based Diagnosis of Language Learners' Syntax Errors. *Literary and Linguistic Computing*, 6 (3): 149-154.
5. Bull, S. (1994). Student Modelling for Second Language Acquisition. *Computers and Education*, 23 (1-2): 13-20.
6. Eliot, C. (1997). Implementing Web-Based Intelligent Tutors. *Proceedings of the Workshop "Adaptive Systems and User Modeling on the World Wide Web"*, 6th International Conference on User Modeling, Chia Laguna, Sardinia.
   http://www.contrib.andrew.cmu.edu/~plb/UM97_workshop/Eliot.html
7. Faulhaber, S. and Reinhardt, B. (1997). D3-WWW-Trainer: Entwicklung einer Oberfläche für die Netzanwendung.
8. Gerbault, J. Towards an Analysis of Answers to Open-Ended Questions in Computer-Assisted Language Learning. In: Lajoie, S. and Martial, V., eds. *Proceedings of AIED '99*, Amsterdam: IOS: 686-689.
9. Heift, T. (1998). *Designed Intelligence: A Language Teacher Model.* Ph. D. Dissertation, Simon Fraser University, Canada.
10. Heift, T. and McFetridge, P. (1999). Exploiting the Student Model to Emphasize Language Teaching Pedagogy in Natural Language Processing. *Computer-Mediated Language Assessment and Evaluation in Natural Language Processing*, ACL/IALL: 55-62.
11. Huang, X. and Miller, W. (1991). *Advanced Applied Mathematics*, (12): 373-357.
12. Kurup, M., Greer, J. E., and McCalla, G. (1992). The Fawlty Article Tutor. *Intelligent Tutoring Systems.* Frasson, C., Gauthier, G., McCalla G.I, eds. Lecture Notes in Computer Science. Springer Verlag: 84-91.

13. Schwind, C. B. (1995). Error Analysis and Explanation in Knowledge Based Language Tutoring. *Computer Assisted Language Learning*, 8 (4): 295-325.
14. Stern, M. (1997). The Difficulties in Web-based Tutoring, and Some Possible Solutions. *Proceedings of the Workshop "Intelligent Educational Systems on the World Wide Web"*, 8th Conference of the AIED-Society, Kobe, Japan.
    http://www.contrib.andrew.cmu.edu/~plb/AIED97_workshop/Stern.html
15. Van der Linden, E. (1993). Does Feedback Enhance Computer-Assisted Language Learning. *Computers & Education*, 21 (1-2): 61-65.
16. Warendorf, K. and Tan, C. (1997). ADIS – An animated data structure intelligent tutoring system or Putting an interactive tutor on the WWW. In: Brusilovsky, P., Nakabayashi, K. and Ritter, S. eds. *Proceedings of the Workshop "Intelligent Educational Systems on the World Wide Web"*, 8th Conference of the AIED-Society, Kobe, Japan.
    http://www.contrib.andrew.cmu.edu/~plb/AIED97_workshop/Warendorf/Warendorf.htm
17. Yang, J. and Akahori, K. (1997). Development of Computer Assisted Language Learning System for Japanese Writing Using Natural Language Processing Techniques: A Study on Passive Voice. *Proceedings of the Workshop "Intelligent Educational Systems on the World Wide Web"*, 8th Conference of the AIED-Society, Kobe, Japan.
    http://www.contrib.andrew.cmu.edu/~plb/AIED97_workshop/Yang/Yang.html

Adaptive Multimedia Interface for Users with Intellectual and Cognitive Handicaps

Moreno L. [1], González C.S. [1*], Aguilar R.M. [1], Estévez J. [1], Sánchez J.[1], Barroso C.[1]

[1]Centro Superior de Informática. Universidad de La Laguna.
c/Delgado Barreto s/n 38200. Tenerife. España
[1]Instituto de Ciencias de la Educación (ICE). Tenerife. España

Abstract. This paper presents an Adaptive Multimedia Interface embedded in an Intelligent Tutorial System (ITS) for intellectual and cognitive handicapped children. There are many educational programs specifically designed for helping students but in general they do not consider the adaptation of the performed tasks to the individual characteristics of each one of the children. The aim of this work is designing a computer-based environment for supporting a teaching strategy where both the pedagogic aspects and the learning goals were adapted according to the particularities of the pupil. The two fundamental problems that are approached in this paper are: designing the interface that is embedded in an Intelligent Tutorial System and implementing an efficient communication of knowledge.

1 Introduction

This paper describes the implementation of a multimedia interface that takes part in an ITS. The goal of this interface is to adapt the presentation of the contents to the individual needs of the students with intellectual and cognitive handicaps.

Most of the software packages available today do not take into account the individual features of the final receptors of these contents. They do not change the teaching strategies according to the requirements of each user. Another drawback is that the proposed tasks are presented following a repetitive sequence. This fact limits its application to students with learning problems: the motivation of the student along the automatic tutoring is affected negatively and the uncertainty about what the student is learning: the concept or the repetitive pattern showed by the software.

The first goal of this work is to implement a multimedia interface where the presentation of the educational contents is adapted to the individual characteristics and preferences of the children. The second goal is to provide the teachers with a tool that helps them in checking the benefits of different strategies to approach the teaching task of a particular concept. Finally, the multimedia interface gives an important feedback to the ITS where the results of the presented tasks are included.

The benefits of using a tool as this one come from the individualised teaching of the students. The system goes through the concepts of the domain according to the

---

* Corresponding email author: carina@cip.es

framework given by the Spanish Scholar Curriculum, but the teaching strategy changes, following the particular features of each student (cognitive age, chronological age, attention level, ...).

We have based our system in the frame of the General Law for the Spanish Educational System. However, this study has been restricted to the Childhood Educational Period (3 chronological years) in the subject of Physical and Social Environment, more particularly to the theme "Objects from the Near World" and to basic concepts (Inside-Outside, Up-Down, Big-Small). This restriction makes the analysis of the teaching strategies easier, allowing us to recognise common criteria in these strategies. In this way, we can generalise the decision processes making possible their application in other similar situations. It is important to remark that the teaching strategies are used to build the logic flow of the activities presented to children, and they are provided by domain experts.

The two most important problems approached in this paper are:

- The design of an interface that is embedded in an ITS.
- The design of an efficient strategy for knowledge transmission.

This paper has been organised as follows. Firstly, we described the design of an interface embedded in an ITS. Then, we presented a methodology to build an efficient way to transmit knowledge. This methodology takes into consideration the specific contents, how they are taught and the applied instruction model.

2 The Problem of Designing the Interface of an Intelligent Tutorial System

The design of an ITS is closely related to how the ITS presents the domain knowledge to the student. These strategies are given by a type of expert knowledge that considers how the teaching process should be, and how the specific problems that could arise are diagnosed.

Following these goals, the fundamental parts of the ITS are [1]:

- A Knowledge Based System (KBS) where the knowledge of the Student Model, Pedagogical Model and Didactic Model is represented.
- A Multimedia Interface, that is used to present and communicate the concepts to the student. This communication process must be dynamic and fluent.

2.1 The Knowledge Based System

We have followed the KADS methodology for knowledge structuring [2]. This allows us to build the KBS in a comprehensive and systematic way: the Pedagogic, the Didactic and the Student Model are represented in the KBS.

One of the types of knowledge that has to be isolated is the domain knowledge (static knowledge, composed of concepts, relation and facts that are necessary for reasoning in a particular application).

The student model is composed of the student profile and the student record. The profile contains those personal characteristics that are related to motor, cognitive and psychosocial development. Variables considered in the profile are: chronological age, cognitive age, physical capacities (motor functions, ocular contact, auditory capacity), cognitive development (short time memory, attention, capacity to form concepts, capacity to group objects in significant categories, development of language and vocabulary, word understanding, capacity of reaction and initiative), relation with the environment (connection with the environment, level of adaptation, participation in group activities, getting of information from the environment), personality (fear to failure, dynamic - hyperactive or passive), patterns of behaviour (repetitive behaviour, restricted behaviour, stereotyped activities), preferences (colours, personal interests). The student profile will influence the learning style.

The pupil's record comprises: the variables related to concepts already learned by the pupil and the tendencies followed in the learning process (repetition of the exercises, tasks that have not been completed, rhythm of evolution between activities, learning style, cognitive and motivational processes). The student record is parametrised by a set of variables and a function. The vp variables describe progress in learning a concept. The fls functions(f: (vp. Style-Learning)=>R) measure how well the student achieved the learning goal for a particular learning style.

The concepts that have to be learned by the pupil are determined taking into consideration the cognitive age. Each concept is related to a set of learning goals.

In addition, it is necessary to provide the KBS with the pedagogic strategies followed by the teachers in the teaching process. Another fundamental part is the pedagogic model, where both the learning goals and the way they are taught are included. That is, for each student, the activities that are proposed to teach a particular concept are specified taking into account the records of student.

In contrast with the domain knowledge, the control knowledge includes the reasoning processes that are followed in solving specific problems. This control knowledge is divided into knowledge about activities (activities that are carried out to reach the learning goals), and inference knowledge (elemental steps in the general problem solving activity).

Therefore, the Problem Solving Method used by teachers consists of following a planning process. In this process, the nodes of the tree search are the situations at which the student can arrive during learning (they represent the level of achievement of the objectives). Branches between nodes represent the change from a situation to another. A plan is the set of exercises that a pupil has to complete. The goal of this sequence of exercises is to reach a final node as near as possible to the objective node.

At each moment, the student situation can be derived from his record. As was explained above, the learner record is parameterised by a set of progress variables vp and by a function that measures the learning carried out with different sequences of tasks. This sequence of tasks give us the learning style used. We have different types of tasks: explanation, evaluation, motivation and reinforcement task.

Subsequently, one specific sequence of task give us the learning style used. E.g. Mot-Exp-Eval-Re, Mot-Exp-Mot- Re-Eval, Exp-Eval, Mot

The elements to take into account for designing the sequence of activities (plan) are: characteristics of the pupil, objectives of learning and resources available.

2.2 The Multimedia Interface

The interaction with the student is carried out through three different types of activities: motivation, teaching explanation, evaluation and reinforcement [3]. These activities are related to the previously introduced operation modes.

For instance, if the goal is "To identify an object from the near setting", the general features of the different activities are:

- *Motivation activity*: At the beginning and at the end of each session the system presents a motivation task. The system selects a particular activity because it is already known that the user can solve the task without great difficulties. Other kind of motivations are also considered: feedbacks for the student that are presented both previously to the task and when the task has been completed.
- *Explanation activity*: The physical attributes of the object (shape, dimension, colour, etc ...) and another complements determined by its situation are presented.
- *Evaluation activity:* The object has to be recognised when it is embedded in different scenarios. The object appears together with other related objects. In this activity, recording the interaction of the student with the application is a fundamental operation.
- *Reinforcement activity:* The same object is presented with variations of the physical attributes and complements. Learning the concept under study can be reinforced through describing other related concepts by its functionality or physical appearance.

The individualised teaching process consists on determining, from the characteristics of each pupil, which the learning objectives are. Then the sequence of activities that a pupil will have to do to acquire the contents set by the objectives must be determined. Adapting means in many occasions, to eliminate the contents, and in others to sequence. Sequencing means divide the objectives in smaller sub-objectives. The activities are designed according to the characteristics of the student, the learning goals and the available teaching resources.

3   Knowledge Transmission

The problem of finding an efficient way to transmit the knowledge by means of presentations adapted to the particular requirements of each subject is treated here.

The multimedia interface integrates both the verbal language and the visual and sound language. We consider the multimedia communication as a particular type of communication where several media and languages or symbolic systems are taking part. In this type of communication, the message is codified in different ways and requires from the student perceiving through several senses.

In our case, knowledge transmission is carried out through different interactions between the student and a system composed of a computer and all the necessary complements that make possible the interactions. The complex task of achieving an efficient knowledge communication using an intelligent system can be summarised in the following sub-problems.

- Which concepts are going to be taught and how are they going to be represented?
- Which kind of interaction between the student and the computer is necessary and how are these interactions going to be included in the system?
- Using the previously determined interactions, which strategy is going to be followed to reach the proposed pedagogic goals?

3.1 Definition of the Specific Knowledge that is Going to be Transmitted

The contents that this kind of children must learn are defined in the Spanish curriculum, the difference with the other children is that these learn slower, it takes longer to pass from one state to another to them, they have more regressions and they need more individualization in teaching.

We have based our system in the General Law for the Spanish Educational System. This study has been restricted to the Childhood Educational Period (3 chronological years) in the subject of Physical and Social World, more particularly to the theme "Objects from the Near World" and to basic concepts (Inside-Outside, Up-Down, Big-Small).

We start with concepts related with objects with the following characteristics. They can be natural or artificial objects. They are common objects from the most immediate world. They are involved in common and daily activities. The specific goals are: 1-To identify the object ; 2-To learn the characteristics and functionality of the object.

The analysis has been focused on the particular problem of teaching these concepts. Experts provided us with the teaching strategies, in other words, they gave us the logical flow of the tasks. Then, our work consisted extracting common features in these strategies (norms of didactic intervention). This generalisation process makes possible designing systems where a larger number of similar situations could be approached.

Several common objects from the "near world" where chosen. In an early age, the proximity of the object is in general related with activities involved in feeding. Therefore, all the objects where chosen from this area.

From these objects, we extracted the relations with other more basic concepts. These related concepts can be grouped showing a distribution in areas, blocks, subjects and concepts.

3.2 Design of Interactions and Dynamics

3.2.1 Interaction

We considered some previous studies of the diversity of human abilities, backgrounds, motivations, personalities, and workstyles that affect the interactive-system's design. Understanding the physical, intellectual and personality differences among users is vital [4].

It is important for designers of interactive systems a good understanding of the cognitive and perceptual abilities of the users [5,6]. The Journal of Ergonomics proposed this classification of human cognitive processes: short-term memory, long-term memory and learning, problem solving, decision making, attention and set (scope of concern), search and scanning and finally time perception. They also suggest a set of factors affecting perceptual and motor performance: perceptual (mental) load, knowledge of results, monotony and boredom, sensory deprivation, ...

On the order hand, personality differences affect the design of systems. People may have very different preferences for interaction styles, pace of interaction, graphics versus tabular presentations, and so on. There is not a simple taxonomy of user personality types. A popular technique is to use the Myers-Briggs Type Indicator (MBTI), which is based on Carl Jung's theories of personality types [7].

The learning-disabled children education can be positively influenced by designing a special courseware that avoids lengthy textual instructions, confusing graphics, extensive typing, and difficult presentation formats [8]. Neuman's advice to designers of courseware for learning-disabled students is applicable to all users:

- Present procedures, directions, and verbal content at levels and formats that make them accessible even to poor readers.
- Ensure that response requirements do not allow students to complete programs without engaging with target concepts.
- Design feedback sequences that explain the reasons for student's errors and lead students though the processes necessary for responding correctly.
- Incorporate reinforcement techniques.

Shneiderman's studies reinforce the need for direct-manipulation of visible objects of interest [9]. Following these studies, we have selected an interaction style based on direct manipulation of the visual representation of the objects and actions. This has been described previously as the interface object-action model and it is specially recommended for pupils that require a simpler and more immediate interface [10].

An important aspect in designing an interface is building an information tree. The educational contents are transmitted through an environment and a context. The environment has a graphic and conceptual representation, i.e. the metaphor. The events and their related contents are organised following a tree structure. The information tree is a way to represent the guidelines of a program both in its structural and dynamic aspects. The metaphor, the structure, and the functioning dynamic make a coherent universe both from the graphical and conceptual points of view.

Our universe is composed of objects that are representations of concepts. The implementation of the relations among objects and concepts has been carried out through object indexing. Each index represents the belonging of each object to a particular subsets of the universe.

One of the requirements is to represent the object in its more common framework. It is important to choose for each object the more adequate set of media. In addition, we present each object together with a set of words that define the concept (spoken and written).

An important source of stimuli, comes from the inclusion of animated agents. The role of these elements in the presentation is to interact and co-operate with the pupil in order to make more natural the way in that this interaction is performed. The animated agents present the problem, they drive the execution of the presentation and they answer in a positive or negative manner according to the obtained results(Fig. 1). A very important benefit of using this kind of animated agents is that the motivation of the pupil is enhanced.

Other important requirement is to keep the attention of the student (Fig. 2). In order to get this, we have to provide the system with a rich variety of alternatives (different stimuli) for describing each concept. This allows the system to present the same concept in many ways. In other words, it is important to avoid the tedious repetition of presentation patterns because this goes against the attention and motivation of the student.

Fig. 1. Positive stimulus   **Fig. 2.** To keep the attention of the child

3.2.2. Dynamics

The dynamic of the presentation is specified in a stage called construction of the presentation. This stage takes into consideration the characteristics and preferences of the user. Therefore, given a concept to teach, the information about the student and the learning goals, the presentation is composed identifying which media and styles are the most adequate to communicate the concept.

We have systematised the construction of the presentation using a methodology based in the formation of a sentence composed by a subject and a set of complements. The subject is the object under study, and the complements are the external elements related with the object such as the scenario where the object has been embedded or other objects in the proximity. The complexity of the task for the pupil can be controlled by changing these complements. This sentence is built dynamically according to the known specific features of the child and the learning goals. The particular object determines the media (static image, sound, video or animation).

In the dynamic construction of our presentation is necessary to define our primitives (concepts=objects=stimuli) and the relations among them. We have defined different categories in the universe of object that are going to be used to represent the concepts. A category of objects is used to represent a thematic area and all the objects belonging to this category are related with this area. It is necessary to determine which objects are going to be used to teach a concept. It is also necessary to identify the category where these objects are included and the relations with other categories. As a final stage, the system determines the relations between the different elements of the category, the scenario where the object under study is going to be embedded (this selection is carried out taking into account the desired complexity for the task) and the complements that are going to be presented in the proximity of our object under study. Therefore, an object in a presentation belongs to one of the following classes: study object, scenario and object's complements.

Other important feature of this interface is the application of a random mechanism. This mechanism is used to present random positive and negative reinforcement, and combination of different media to represent concepts.

3.3 Reaching the Proposed Pedagogical Objectives

Designing an instructional system consists of sorting sequences of instructions in such a way that they lead to reach a specific learning goal.

The learning goals are defined for a particular student and a sequence of actions to reach these goals is considered. This is a search in a space of states, where only the sequences that leads to reach the proposed goal can be considered.

One of the subsystems drives the sequence of instructions and operates with the interface to guide the student through the set of tasks that are necessary to reach the learning goal.

Following the Gagné's theory [11] we have used in the teaching process the following sequence of events:

Event 1: Calling the attention of the pupil.
Event 2: Giving some information to the student about the learning goals.
Event 3: Giving some information to the student about previously learned concepts.
Event 4: Presenting different stimuli. (images, animations, sounds, video).
Event 5: Guided learning.
Event 6: Reporting the result of the activity.
Event 7: Evaluation of the performance.

These events will be carried out according to the state of the pupil determined by his profile and by his record. Both the sequence of activities and the presentation of contents will vary depending on this state. For example, with a pupil who has as a characteristic of his personality the fear to fail, we intensify the self-confidence using tasks that he has previously made successfully, we lower the difficulty level and we teach him again the concept in which he failed. We increase the maximum interaction waiting time and we present fast tasks. If he is hyperactive, we use short steps, and fast and effective tasks. We will also use this strategy to present a new concept, as a motivating introductory task and every time we want to motivate. If he fails, we stop teaching this concept, we give examples and we explain step by step how to solve it. Then we teach him again but changing the way to do it: we use other activities, or the same activity but changing the organisation and the stimulus. If he fails again, it can be due to problems of previous learning, concepts that he has not acquired properly, and therefore, the application present activities which allow the system to consolidate those concepts.

If he fails another time, the process is stopped because it can cause frustration in the child. It may happen that the difficulty and the handicap are the barriers that make impossible to learn the concept.

Adapting the curriculum to make it suitable for this kind of children means sequencing: divide the objectives in smaller sub-objectives. The learning objective can be still reached, but in smaller steps, although many times this means eliminating contents.

4- Conclusions

In this paper we have described a methodology to construct an adaptable presentation that changes its contents according to the particular needs of each handicapped student (pupils with learning difficulties). The KADS methodology has been chosen for designing the KBS part of the ITS. This had given us a structured way to represent the acquired knowledge.

The structure of the Universe of objects that are going to take part in the presentation has been defined in a compatible way with the guidelines given by the knowledge and functioning patterns included in the KBS. This process has been included in a general methodology, allowing us to work from simpler to more complex ITSs. We have followed the recommendations of previous works in the area for deciding about specific components of the interface, for instance the interaction style. Additional elements as using agents to keep the attention of the children on the proposed task have been included.

With this methodology, we have implemented several prototypes that have been used in a preliminary experimental stage. Specific modules have been tested in the *Acaman Special School* and in the *Asociación de Trisómicos 21* both of them in Tenerife. The presented multimedia interface has had a good acceptation both by children and teachers. Children see the activities presented by the system as a game, and the commentaries of the teachers were positive especially in relation with the possibility of designing their own multimedia materials.

This first stage of the research has provided us with new results and observations that are being used to refine our conceptual models. Especially we hope to improve two models: the student model and the didactic model.

One of the most important problems that has arose is the extraction of the pedagogic knowledge. This type of knowledge takes a fundamental role in deciding the strategies that this interface is going to follow: the pedagogic, didactic and student models can only be extracted using this knowledge. A promising way to refine these important models is through experimentation with the basic prototypes. From this experimentation, we have found that there are other important characteristics that should be included in the student model. For this reason, we are researching the importance of additional features in the basic sets "profile" and "record" that represent the student model.

Nowadays, we are designing software applications that help in the acquisition of the expert knowledge. We have considered two simultaneous goals. a) To make easier for teachers, the construction of their own learning activities. b) To register what activities the teacher carries out in order to explain a particular concept to a specific student, what goals he considers, what kind of media he utilises, and finally, what positive and negative reinforcements he applies after the result of the activity has been obtained. We have found a bigger difficulty in representing the didactic model, but once the mentioned tools work properly the task to find an adjusted didactic model will be facilitated.

5 Acknowledgment

We are indebted to the people of *Acaman Special School* and *Association of Trisomics 21* for their collaboration in this project. One of us, C.S. González wishes to thank financial support from the *Agencia Española de Cooperación Internacional (AECI)*.

References

[1]. Moreno, L.; Aguilar, RM.; González C.S.; Barroso, C.; Estévez, J.I.; Sánchez, J.L.; del Rosario, A.; Díaz, C.; "Intelligent tutorial system for aiding children with intellectual and cognitive handicaps". In *Proceedings in Advanced Research in Computers and communications in Education,* Japan. (1999). 844-846.

[2]. Schreiber G.; Wielinga B.; Breuker J.;"KADS. A Principle Approach To Knowledge-Based System Development". Ed. Academic Press Limited. 1993.

[3]. González C.S., "Sistema tutorial inteligente para la enseñanza en niños con discapacidades intelectuales y cognitivas". Tesis de Licenciatura. Universidad de La Laguna. Santa Cruz de Tenerife. (1999).

[4]. Schiff W., "Perception: An Applied Approach". Houghton Mifflin, New York. (1980).

[5]. Wickens C. D.,"Engineering Psychology And Human Performance". Second Edition. HaperCollins. (1992).

[6]. Edwards A. D.N., "Extra-Ordinary Human-Computer Interaction: Interfaces For Users With Disabilities". Cambridge University Press, Cambridge, U.K. 1995.

[7]. Glinert E., P. ,York, Bryant W. ,"Computers and people with disabilities". Communications of the ACM,35,5 (pp. 32-35). 1992.

[8]. Neuman D., "Learning disabled student's interactions with commercial courseware: A naturalistic study". Educational Technology Research and Development, 39, 1 (pp 31-49). 1991.

[9]. MacArthur C., Shneiderman B., "Learning disabled student's difficulties in learning to use a word processor: Implications for instruction software evaluation". Journal of Learning Disabilities, 19, 4, (pp 248-253). 1986.

[10].Shneiderman B. "Designing The User Interface". Third Edition. Addison-Wesley. (1998).

[11].Gagné R . "The Conditions Of Learning". New York. Holk Rinehart and Winston, 4th Edition. 1985.

Evaluating the Need for Intelligence in an Adaptive Hypermedia System [§]

Tom Murray ♣
Janette Piemonte ♠
Samia Khan ♦
Tina Shen ♣
Chris Condit ♠

♣ Computer Science Department, ♠ Department of Geosciences, ♦ School of Education
University of Massachusetts, Amherst, MA
tmurray@cs.umass.edu, www.cs.umass.edu/~tmurray

Abstract. We described a formative evaluation of Tectonica Interactive, an introductory geology hyper-book that was authored and delivered using the MetaLinks software. MetaLinks is a framework and authoring tool for the creation of adaptive hypermedia documents that support the learner's exploration of richly interconnected material. The formative evaluation involved 19 subjects, and data was collected from navigation traces, a questionnaire, focus-group discussions, and think-aloud interviews. We interpret the results in terms of how the system addresses the issues of disorientation, cognitive overload, discontinuous flow (poor narrative flow or poor conceptual flow), and content non-readiness. We were interested in how features of the current implementation address these issues, and we were looking for evidence for the need of more advanced (adaptive and/or intelligent) features.

1. Introduction

The goal of the MetaLinks project is to provide a framework and authoring tools for the creation of adaptive hypermedia documents (hyper-books) that support the user's exploration of richly interconnected material. Both the potential benefits and the known difficulties with hyper-books have lead researchers to implement a number of adaptive and intelligent software features ([1], [2]). However, empirical evidence informing the design of such software is sparse ([3], [4]), leaving open the question of how much additional effectiveness results from a given infusion of technological power (which adds significantly to the development cost and complexity of the software). After sketching out preliminary designs for a number of advanced or

---

[§] This work was supported by the Office of Naval Research ASSERT grant no. ONR/N00014-97-1-0815, and the National Science Foundation's CCD program grant no. NSF DUE-9652993. We would like to thank Saunders College Publishing for the use of content from their introductory geology text book.

intelligent software features, our approach was to implement a less sophisticated version of the software and evaluate it for evidence that learners would benefit from the more advanced features.

A Hyper-book is a hypermedia document, such as an educational web-site or CD-ROM, that contains a coherent body of subject matter organized and written for educational purposes. A number of potential benefits and problems have been identified in the shift from traditional to electronic books, all stemming from the ability to link (or "jump") from one "location" to another. Hyper-books can be authored to contain alternative structures, content, and navigation paths that emphasize different goals, skill levels, or perspectives ([5], [6]). Potential problems with hyper-books include the following. First is the problem of how the system can best support the new capabilities, since users may become overwhelmed with the options or fail to understand their significance or effect. Second, the ability to jump around in the information space can result in disorientation as to where one is located or has been. Third, navigational jumps can interrupt the narrative and conceptual flow of the material, so that its reading can be disjointed or confusing.

Traditional hyper-books address the above issues in the design of their fixed structure and navigation tools. More advanced hyper-books are adaptive and/or provide explicit guidance to the learner. *Adaptive* hypermedia documents are composed "on the fly," so that the content, style, and/or sequencing of the pages is customized to the needs of the particular learner and situation ([7], [8], [9]). Even more sophisticated (or intelligent) systems provide guidance or feedback regarding the learner's progress or planned learning trajectory. Our software development plan has been to create a "non-intelligent," minimally adaptive framework, and then add more sophisticated features based on the needs of users as measured in formative evaluations. Though the current version of MetaLinks is minimally adaptive, it does include a number of innovative features (described later) and it is actually quite sophisticated when compared to traditional hypermedia. We have used the MetaLinks framework to author a web based hyper-book called Tectonica Interactive in the domain of introductory geology (based on [10]). Tectonica Interactive, with approximately 400 pages and 500 graphics, has undergone three rounds of formative evaluation. We will describe the second round in this paper.

In the remainder of this paper we will describe the options we considered for adding more sophistication to the system. Then we will describe the version of the software as it is currently implemented. Then we will describe a formative evaluation study designed to inform further development of the system. Finally we will describe the results, which indicate that well designed interface features and non-intelligent tools seem to satisfy many of the user needs that we expected we would have to address by adding intelligent software components.

2. Potentials for Adaptation, Intelligence, and Coached Inquiry

Previous research has substantively documented the existence of three hypermedia problems for which adaptivity might provide a solution: disorientation, cognitive overload, and discontinuous flow ([1], [11], [12], [13], [14]). **Disorientation** refers to users not knowing where they are, where they have been, or how to get to where they want to go in hypermedia space. **Cognitive overload** refers to users being overwhelmed or confused by the options available to them in multi-path, multi-tool environments such as hypermedia documents. We separate the problem of discontinuous flow into two issues: narrative flow and conceptual flow. **Narrative flow** refers to the didactic or dialogical flow of the text itself. **Conceptual flow** refers to the flow of ideas or concepts. To this list of issues we add **content readiness**, which is the traditional intelligent tutoring systems goal of tailoring content so that the learner is neither bored because it is too easy, nor overwhelmed because it is too difficult (i.e. remaining within the learner's "zone of proximal development").

Learner's goals in navigating through hypermedia material vary along a spectrum from convergent or "finding" goals through divergent or "exploratory" goals ([15], [16]). Exploratory navigation is appropriate for open-ended questions and/or learning in ill-structured domains in which the richness of the content suggests multiple themes, perspectives, or learning paths [6]. Also, inquiry-based learning methods involve initial stages of articulating and refining the driving question and then exploring potential sources of information before narrowing down an information search (17). To address these problems we considered a number of software features which we list below (see [18] for a description of our interpretation of each method): Adaptive navigation support using history-based and prerequisite-based link annotation (similar to [7]); Adaptive content (using methods similar to [19], [9]); Adaptive sequencing (as in [2]); Adaptive navigation maps (as in [20]); and Coached inquiry (supporting learner goals of broadening, breadth and coverage, completeness, efficiency, and readiness, using path analysis methods similar to those used in [21]).

3. The MetaLinks/Tectonica Software

MetaLinks content is stored in a relational database (using web-enabled FileMaker Pro) and requires only a web browser for delivery (we make heavy use of JavaScript and Dynamic HTML in the implementation). However, before implementing most of the features mentioned above, we decided to implement a less intelligent version of the software that was rich with pragmatic and usability features, and evaluate the software to help us decide which additional intelligent or adaptive features were warranted. We wanted to leave the locus of control and intelligence with the user as much as possible, and supplement this with machine control or intelligence if a need was seen in our users.

MetaLinks has a "full-featured" user interface. Early observations (see [23]) indicated that learners had quite a variety of styles and needs, and that a similar variety of features was needed. In addition to its navigation and orientation features, MetaLinks pages are adapted using features called stretch-text and narrative smoothing. Below we explain the features that are relevant to the issues of disorientation, cognitive overload, discontinuous flow, and content readiness. Figure 1 shows a page from Tectonica Interactive.

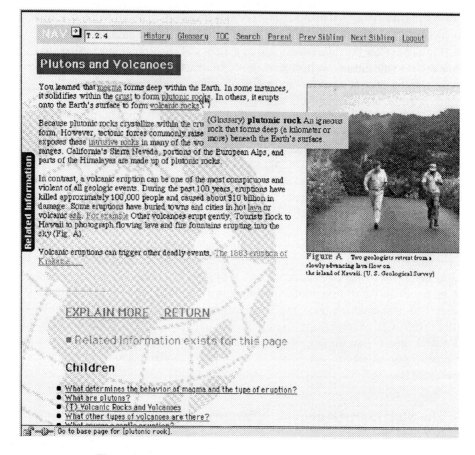

Figure 1: Tectonica Interactive page T.2.4, with a picture showing two geologists running from a lava flow.

1. **Annotated Table of Contents**. Content in MetaLinks hyper-books has a primarily hierarchical organization. The **disorientation** issue is addressed by providing a hierarchical TOC page that shows where learners have visited, and where the current page is. In addition each page lists its "children" pages at the bottom.

2. **Stretch Text**. Non-essential text such as examples and footnotes can be hidden inside "stretch text." We also use stretch-text to imbed the glossary definitions of all glossary terms. This feature addresses the **content readiness** issue. It also helps with the **cognitive overload** issue by reducing the amount of content visible on the page.

3. **Glossary base pages**. The terse definitions that pop up in the stretch text of glossary terms may not be enough to alleviate the learner's ignorance about a concept. If the user *clicks* on a glossary term they navigate to its "base page," which is the page

in the hyper-book that best explains that concept. This feature addresses the **content readiness** issue. It also addresses the **conceptual flow** issues by allowing learners to easily learn about prerequisite concepts.

4. **Custom Depth Control.** The default narrative flow in MetaLinks hyper-books differs from text books and other hyper-books -- it is breadth-first rather than depth-first, and organized for "horizontal reading." The default "next" page is the sibling page. Thus the default is to continue reading at the same level of generality. Horizontal reading sets the stage for an innovation called "custom depth control," which addresses the problem of **cognitive overload.** In MetaLinks the Next and Back buttons in traditional hyper-books are replaced with Explain More and Next buttons. Thus, the user has continuous control over whether they want to continue at the same level or delve into more detail on the current topic.

5. **Narrative smoothing**. We have a simple but elegant partial solution to the **narrative flow** problem. Each page has associated with it an "intro text" paragraph. This paragraph eases the reader into the subject of the page, giving a little background or introduction. If the user jumps to that page in a non-standard way, the intro-text is pre-pended to the main text of the page.

6. **Typed Non-hierarchical Links**. As mentioned, the primary organizational structure for MetaLinks hyper-books is the hierarchy, as reified by the TOC. However, hierarchies do not capture the conceptual richness of most domains. MetaLinks includes (non-hierarchical) links called Related Links in addition to the hierarchical child and parent links between pages. These links are "typed" or categorized to indicate the type of relationship they represent. Here are some of the approximately 20 link types we use in Techtonica Interactive: Where in the world?, Are scientists sure?, Famous catastrophes!, Historical Background, How is it measured? Related Links address the issue of **Conceptual Flow**.

4. Formative Evaluation Method

The MetaLinks software was used to author and deliver Tectonica Interactive (or "Tectonica"), an introductory geology hyper-book. The contents of the text Modern Physical Geology (Thompson & Turk 1996) were obtained in digital form from the publisher, and part of it was significantly transformed and extended to create Tectonica. Tectonica is an incomplete prototype hyper-book. Containing about 400 hypermedia pages, 500 graphics, and 750 glossary items, its content corresponds to one third (about 200 pages) of the contents in the original text book.

At the most general level, the questions we hoped to answer in the formative evaluation were "how well do the current features work?" and "what evidence can we find to support the need for the more sophisticated features?" In addition to the question of additional features we were particularly interested in the use and usability of the unique and innovative features of MetaLinks, including narrative smoothing, custom depth control, and some aspects of our related links feature.

A total of 19 students from an undergraduate introductory Oceanography course participated in the study. They were compensated $15 upon completing the study.

Subjects received one hour of training in a practice session that took place two to seven days before the main trial. In this practice session they were given instruction in the tools and navigation concepts of Tectonica.

Subjects had both an open-task and a closed-task session in which they used Tectonica to answer a question. Their goal was to satisfy their curiosity and be able to explain what they learned to a peer. Closed task questions asked subjects to investigate specific geological phenomenon. For the open task subjects were asked to conceive of a question or topic in geology that interested them and to explore it using Tectonica. Nine subjects were given an open task then a closed one, and 10 were given a closed task then an open one. We collected data from program traces, a post-questionnaire, focus group interviews, and think-aloud interviews. In this paper we summarize the portion of the data and analysis relevant to the success of some features and the need for additional features (see Murray et al. 2000 for more details).

5. Evaluation Results

The evaluation trial was done for formative purposes, not to generate statistically significant or confidently generalizable results. Still, definite trends did emerge, and the data from the various sources (program trace, questionnaire, focus-groups, and think aloud interviews) show significant correspondence. To give a general idea of navigation activity, there were an average of 81 moves per subject in the two task sessions, or an average of 1.1 moves per minute. "Moves" includes going to and from TOC, search, and glossary pages, as well as navigating to content pages. Below we will summarize the results by issue.

Disorientation. Below are the questionnaire questions related to disorientation, along with the average and standard deviations of the answers (n=19):

- #10: Did you visit and learn about topics that were not directly related to your main question? 15 of the subjects answered "yes." This indicates that subjects did in general "explore" the material rather than go directly to an "answer."

- #20: If I diverged from a topic/page of interest, it was easy for me to return to that information. AGREE (ave 2.2 SD .9).

- #63: I felt lost as I navigated through Tectonica. RARELY (ave 3.2 SD .8)

- #87: Which question did you ask yourself most frequently: "Where am I? What should I look for next? How do I go there? Where have I been?" 12 answered "what should I look for next?" and 3 indicated they did not ask themselves any of these questions. This indicates that subjects were predominantly focused on the content rather than trying to figure out the system or the task.

In the focus-groups subjects were also explicitly asked questions about disorientation. Interviews and focus-group data confirm the finding that the great majority of users felt that they knew where they were, where to go next, and how to get there.

Cognitive Overload. Below are the questionnaire questions related to cognitive overload, along with the average and standard deviations of the answers:

- #5: Do you feel that you were able to answer the questions thoroughly? AGREE (ave. 1.8 SD .9)

- #13: There was NOT an appropriate amount of material on each page. DISAGREE (ave. 3.8 SD .9)

- #15: The time needed to use Tectonica was adequate for the material learned. AGREE (ave. 1.9 SD .6)

These answers mostly relate to overload in terms of the content and task, and indicate that students were not overwhelmed or confused with the content or task. Focus-group and interview data did not show significant evidence of cognitive overload regarding use of the MetaLinks features. Answers to question #87 above ("Which question did you ask yourself most frequently") also indicate that users were not overly confused by the software.

Narrative Flow. Below are the questionnaire questions related to narrative flow:

- #84: The text flowed nicely from one page to another. AGREE (ave 1.9 SD .7)

- #85 The presence of introductory text facilitated my understanding of the material on the page. The average was OFTEN (1.9) but this question was confusing and 5 subjects left it blank.

Narrative flow was explicitly addressed in the focus-groups and, in agreement with the questionnaire data above, there was no evidence of narrative choppyness or unevenness.

Conceptual flow and Content Readiness. We neglected to include a questionnaire item that directly addressed these issues. But in focus-groups we did ask whether students ever felt that they had navigated to a page for which they were lacking the prerequisite knowledge and therefore could not understand it. We found no evidence of frustration over the lack of prerequisite knowledge.

Overall Enjoyment and Perceived Learning. There were 10 questions related to overall enjoyment and perceived learning effectiveness. Despite the fact that most learners indicated that they were not particularly interested in geology, the answers to these questions indicated overwhelmingly that subjects found Tectonica enjoyable, easy to use, and productive. Significantly, the two questions that compared Tectonica with book learning favored the hyper-book (standard deviations of about 1, two of the 19 subjects would prefer a text book).

Areas where 3 to 5 subjects expressed frustration included (from focus-group data): not finding content they wanted because the book was incomplete; the TOC, showing all of the 400 pages listed with hierarchical nesting, was overwhelming; subjects were sometimes surprised to find themselves back at a page they had previously been (the software does not provide the classic "Back" button as in most hypermedia); and several subjects were confused with the parent/child/sibling metaphor used for the hierarchical structure of the hyper-book. These will be addressed in future software versions.

Navigation Tool Use. The major disappointment of the trial is that subjects did not use either the Custom Navigation or the Related Links as much as we had hoped. Since these are potentially the most complex features to understand, the low use likely contributed to the positive findings noted above. Of the 18 types of navigation moves tracked, the most common over all subjects were: Go To Child (19% of the total moves), Return (17%), Search (13%), Custom Depth feature (10%), TOC (9%), and History (6%). Navigation using Related Links occurred in just 1% of the moves (it was used a total of 10 times).

Subjects did navigate through the hierarchical content space, maintaining or deepening/expanding topics of interest, but usually they selected particular children rather than selecting Explain More to visit all of the children. Also, they did exhibit exploratory, non-hierarchical navigation, but chose to use the TOC and search engine as jumping off points for their tangential explorations rather than Related links. Use of the Custom Depth feature was, though less then hoped for, respectable, while use of Related links was almost non-existent, in sharp contrast with use of the direct-to-child links. We strongly suspect that the visual salience of these two features effected their frequency of use. A list of a page's children appears at the bottom of each page, while the "Related Info" tab has to be clicked to pull out the Related Pages list. In a future study we will switch the location of these features to measure the effect of salience on use.

6. Conclusions

We have described a formative evaluation of Tectonica Interactive, an introductory geology hyper-book that was authored and delivered using the MetaLinks software. MetaLinks is designed to provide a framework and authoring tools for the creation of adaptive hypermedia documents that support the learner's exploration of richly interconnected material. The formative evaluation involved 19 subjects, and data was collected from navigation traces, a questionnaire, focus-group discussions, and think-aloud interviews. The data (some of which is still being analyzed) is leading to conclusions in several areas, including: differences between open and closed tasks, differences between the first and second sessions due to increased familiarity with the software; the importance of feature salience; factors effecting hierarchical vs. tangential navigation patterns; identifying a set of stereotypical navigation styles; as well as numerous feature improvements indicated from the data. In this paper we focused on the issues of disorientation, cognitive overload, discontinuous flow (poor narrative flow or poor conceptual flow), and content non-readiness. We were interested in how features of the current implementation address these issues, and we were looking for evidence for the need of more advanced (adaptive and/or intelligent) features. We discovered that the current set of features, which leave the locus of control and intelligence solidly with the learner, in general avoid all of these potential problem issues. Learners responded positively to questions regarding the usability and usefulness of MetaLinks. 90% said they would prefer using the hyper-book to a text book. No individual feature stood out as being confusing, but the Related (non-hierarchical) Links and the Custom Depth Control features did not get as much use as we had intended. At this point we have not found any strong evidence for the need of additional adaptivity or intelligence. In particular, by issue:

Content readiness and conceptual flow. Adaptive content has been used in other systems to customize page content to the learner's readiness and goals. With MetaLinks we found that stretch-text for footnotes and details allowed the learner to obtain more elaborate information as needed. Adaptive sequencing has been used elsewhere to ensure that prerequisite pages are given first. In MetaLinks stretch-text glossary word definitions, and the ability to click to go to a glossary word's "base page" enabled learners to easily fill in missing prerequisite knowledge.

Narrative flow. While others have designed sophisticated methods for creating narrative transitions between arbitrary chunks of content, we found that the relatively simple narrative smoothing feature worked to ensure a smooth narrative flow.

Disorientation and cognitive overload. The MetaLinks Annotated TOC and Annotated History features, along with other cues for where each page was situated in the hierarchy, seemed adequate to keep users oriented. There was little evidence of learners loosing track of where they were or how to get where they wanted to go. The design of the user interface and navigation tools seemed to avoid problems with cognitive overload. However, the two most complex features were not used very often.

It is important to note that generalizations from these results are limited in several ways, including: small sample size, possible idiosyncraticies of the geology domain, and the sparse use of the Related Links and Custom Depth Traversal features.

This work supports the notion that good interface design and passive but powerful user features can sometimes provide the benefits that are ascribed to more sophisticated or intelligent features (which can be more presumptive, controlling, or intrusive than passive features). A corollary to this notion, which we did not test but has been proven out in numerous projects, is that no matter how intelligent or sophisticated educational software is, inadequacies in the interface or usability of the software will surely overshadow the benefits of the intelligence. We by no means intend to indicate that sophisticated modeling and intelligence is of no benefit, but rather that non-intelligent, yet full-featured, base-line software should be developed and evaluated before adding intelligence, in order to determine the most effective applications of intelligence.

Our future work will take us in several directions. We will soon be using MetaLinks to author hyper-books in other domains. We will be studying design issues in the process of authoring hyper-books. We will be trying to determine whether Related Links and Custom Depth Control can be made more useful.

References

[1] Conklin, J. (1987). Hypertext: An Introduction and Survey. IEEE Computer, September 1987, pp. 17-41.
[2] Brusilovsky, P. (1998). Methods and Techniques of Adaptive Hypermedia. In P. Brusilovsky, A. Kobsa, and J. Vassileva (Eds), *Adaptive Hypertext and Hypermedia,* Chapter 1, pages 1-44, Kluwer Academic Publishers, The Netherlands.
[3] Eklund, J. & Brusulovsky, P. (1998). The Value of Adaptivity in Hypermedia Leaning Environment: A short review of empirical evidence.

[4] Dillon, A. & Gabbard, R. 1998. Hypermedia as an educational technology: a review of the quantitative research literature on learner comprehension, control, and style. Review of Educational Research, Vol 68 No. 3, pp. 322-349.

[5] Ferguson, W., Bareiss, R., Birnbaum, L, & Osgood, R. (1992). ASK Systems: an approach to the realization of story-based teachers. *J. of the Learning Sciences* 2(1), pp. 95-134.

[6] Spiro, R.J. & Jehng, J.C. (1990). Cognitive Flexibility and Hypertext: Theory and Technology for the Nonlinear and Multidimensional Traversal of Complex Subject Matter. In D. Nix & R. Sprio (Eds.) *Cognition, Education, and Multimedia*. Erlbaum, 1990.

[7] Brusilovsky, P., Schwartz, E., & Weber, G. (1996). A Tool for Developing Adaptive Electronic Textbooks on the WWW. *Proc. of WebNet-96*, AACE.

[8] Vassileva, J. (1994). A Practical Architecture for User Modeling in a Hypermedia-Based Information System. In *4th International Conference on User Modeling*, pages 115-120, Hyannis, MA, 1994.

[9] De Bra, P. & Calvi, L. (1998). AHA: a generic adaptive hypermedia system. Proceedings of he 2nd Workshop on Adaptive Hypertext and Hypermedia, Hypertext '98, Pittsburgh, June, 1998.

[10] Thompson, G.R. & Turk, J.T. (1997). Modern Physical Geology, Second Edition.. Saunders Publishing Co: Philadelphia, PA.

[11] Luckin, R., Plowman, L., Laurillard, D. Straforld, M., & Taylor, J. (1998). Scaffolding Learners' Constructions of Narrative. *Proceedings of Int. Conf. of the Learning Sciences*, 19988.

[12] Beasley, R.E. & Waugh, M.L (1995). Cognitive mapping architectures and hypermedia disorientation: An empirical study. J. of Educational Multimedia and Hypermedia 4(2/3), pp. 239-255.

[13] Plowman, L., Luckin, R., Laurillard, D. Straforld, M., & Taylor, J. (1998). Designing Multimedia for Learning: Narrative Guidance and Narrative Construction. Draft paper available from the authors.

[14] Stanton, N.A. & Baber, C (1994). The Myth of navigating in hypertext: How a "bandwagon" has lost its course! J. of Educational Multimedia and Hypermedia, 3(3/4), pp. 235-249.

[15] McAleese, R. (1989). Navigation and Browsing in Hypertext. Chapter 2 in R. McAleese *Hypertext: Theory Into Action*. Norwood NJ: Ablex Publ.

[16] Heller, R. (1990). The Role of Hypermedia in Education: A look at the research Issues. J. of Research on Computing in Education, Vol 22, pp. 431-441.

[17] Wallace, R.M., Kuperman, J., Krajcik, J. & Soloway, Elliot (2000).Science on the Web: Students Online in a Sixth Grade Classroom. JLS 9(1) 75-104.

[18] Murray, T., Khan, S., Piemonte, J., Shen, T., & Condit, C. (2000). Conceptual and Narrative Flow in Electronic Books and Hypermedia Documents. Working paper available from the author.

[19] Stern, M., & Woolf, B.P. (1998). Curriculum Sequencing in a Web-Based Tutor. In the Proceedings of Intelligent Tutoring Systems-98.

[20] Verhoeven, A. & Waarendorf, K. (1999). External Navigation Control and Guidance for Learning with Spatial Hypermedia. J. of Interactive Media in Education 99(1).

[21] Suthers, D. & Weiner, A. (1995). Groupware for developing critical discussion skills. CSCL '95, Computer Supported Collaborative Learning, Bloomington, Indiana, October 1995.

[22] Murray, T., Condit, C., Piemonte, J., Shen, T.,& Khan, S. (1999). MetaLinks—A Framework and Authoring Tool for Adaptive Hypermedia. Proceedings of AIED-99, pp. 744-746.

[23] Khan, S., Murray, T., & Piemonte, J., (2000). Qualitative Hypermedia Evaluation Methods. A paper presented at the Eastern Educational Research Association, Clearwater, FL.

[24] Brusilovsky, P. & Eklund, J. (1998). A study of user model based link annotation in educational hypermedia. J. of Universal Computer Science, vol. 4, no. 4, pp. 429-448.

Tailoring Feedback by Correcting Student Answers

Brent Martin and Antonija Mitrovic

Intelligent Computer Tutoring Group
Department of Computer Science, University of Canterbury
Private Bag 4800, Christchurch, New Zealand
Telephone: 64-3-304-7733
B.Martin@cosc.canterbury.ac.nz, tanja@cosc.canterbury.ac.nz

Abstract. Constraint-based models [7] represent the domain by describing states into which a solution may fall, and testing that solutions in a state are consistent with the problem being solved. Constraints have a relevance condition (which defines the state) and a satisfaction condition (which tests the integrity of the solution.) In this paper we present a purely pattern-based representation for constraints, and describe a method for using it to generate correct solutions based on students' incorrect answers. This method will be used to tailor feedback, by presenting the student with correct examples that most closely match their attempts.

1 Introduction

Constraint-based modeling (CBM) [7] represents the domain as a set of states, where all solutions that are a member of a constraint's relevance state must also be a member of its satisfaction state. This approach is only interested in states that are considered to be pedagogically significant: it is not concerned with any other states the solution may be in, nor in the path used to arrive at the solution. This dramatically reduces the amount of information required in the model, overcoming the problem of general student model intractability [10]. The definition of constraints in constraint-based modeling in [6] specifies the minimum requirements of a constraint, but leaves open the representation of the constraint conditions. Ohlsson suggests that a variety of methods might be employed, including pattern matching: the important point is that each state constraint is a pair of (possibly complex) tests on problem states.

This work is based upon SQL-Tutor [4], an Intelligent Tutoring System based on CBM, which teaches the SQL database language to second and third year University students. The system has taken four years to build, and now contains around 500 constraints. CBM is used for two purposes: to diagnose student answers, and as a student model. Ohlsson does not describe using CBM for long-term modeling. SQL-Tutor uses an overlay model [1]. Constraints are encoded in LISP, where state definitions are fragments of LISP code. In this paper, we propose an alternative representation for constraint-based models, which allows constraints to be used to generate solutions. We use this feature to build correct solutions to problems that the student has answered incorrectly, where the generated solution is as close as possible to the student's original answer.

We first describe CBM in more detail. Section 3 presents the strengths and weaknesses of SQL-Tutor. Our new representation is introduced, and its features described in section 4. We then explore one of the potential added uses for the new representation, namely tailoring feedback by correcting the students' wrong answers. Finally we draw conclusions about the new representation and feedback generation, and indicate further research areas we are pursuing.

2 Constraint-Based Modeling

CBM is a method that arose from experiments in learning from performance errors [8]. Ohlsson proposes that we often make mistakes when performing a task, even when we have been taught the correct way to do it. He asserts that this is because the declarative knowledge we have learned has not been internalised in our procedural knowledge, and so the number of decisions we must make while performing the procedure is sufficiently large that we make mistakes. By practicing the task, however, and catching ourselves (or being caught by a mentor) making mistakes, we modify our procedure to incorporate the appropriate rule that we have violated. Over time, we internalise all of the declarative knowledge about the task, and so the number of mistakes we make is reduced.

Procedure-tracing domain models [1] check whether or not the student is performing correctly by comparing the students procedure directly with one or more "correct" ones. In CBM, we are not interested in what the student has done, but in what *state* they are currently in. As long as the student never reaches a state that is known to be wrong, they are free to perform whatever actions they please. The domain model is therefore a collection of state descriptions, of the form:

> "If <relevance condition> is true, then <satisfaction condition>
> had better also be true, otherwise something has gone wrong."

In other words, if the student solution falls into the state defined by the relevance condition, it must also be in the state defined by the satisfaction condition.

3 Motivation

In SQL-Tutor, constraints are encoded in LISP (as is the rest of the system,) where a constraint is checked for violation by evaluating the code fragment for the relevance condition, and if true, evaluating the code for the satisfaction condition. The domain model is a flat set of around 500 modular constraint definitions. A student answer is diagnosed by testing each constraint in turn. The student model is an overlay of the domain model, containing a tally of the number of times each constraint has been used, and how many times it has been violated. Another student model has been explored, which takes into account the evolution of each constraint over time, and superimposes a structure over the flat constraint set to allow decisions based on the student model to look more generally at student performance [2]. A probabilistic model has also been proposed [3].

Feedback in SQL-Tutor is applied directly to each constraint in the domain model: when a constraint is violated, it produces a message that describes the underlying domain principle that has been failed. In addition, the student may be shown all or part of a correct solution. Problems are chosen based on the student model: the constraints which are relevant to each question are compared to the student model, to see how they match the student's performance on those constraints. The problem that best matches the currently targeted constraints wins.

SQL-Tutor has been successful in the classroom, and is well liked by the students who use it [5]. However, there are two areas that might be improved if the constraint set could be used to generate SQL. These are now described.

3.1 Feedback can be Misleading

SQL-Tutor selects problems from an authored set of examples. Each problem consists of the problem text, and an "ideal" solution to the problem. In SQL, usually there is more than one correct query for any problem, so the ideal solution represents just one of a (possibly large) set of correct solutions. Because the domain model is state-based, it is able to cope with differences between the student and ideal solutions.

Problems arise, however, when the ideal student solution is presented to the student as feedback. Through a series of in-class evaluations of SQL-Tutor, we have measured the apparent speed of learning while pupils interact with the system. Analysis of the data obtained indicates that differences in the feedback given have a significant effect on the speed of learning. Further, one of the most successful modes of feedback is "partial solution", where the pupil is presented with the fragment from the ideal solution for one of the SQL clauses in which they have made mistakes. The drawback with this approach is that the fragment may sometimes be correct within the context of the ideal solution, but *incorrect* within the context of the student solution. Consider the following example:

Problem:
List the titles of all movies directed by Stanley Kubrick.

Ideal Solution:
```
SELECT      title
FROM        movie
WHERE       director=(select number from director
            where fname='Stanley' and lname='Kubrick')
```

Student Solution:
```
SELECT      title
FROM        movie join director on number = director
WHERE       fname='Stanley' and lname='Kubrick'
```

Submitting this attempt (correctly) yields the following result:

"You have used an attribute in the FROM clause which appears in several tables you specified in the FROM clause. Qualify the attribute name with the table name to eliminate ambiguities."

However, when prompted for a partial solution for the FROM clause, the system returns "FROM movie" which is not correct within the context of the student solution.

3.2 Limited Problem Set

SQL-Tutor contains a set of 82 problems, from which each problem to be presented to the student is chosen. A selection is made based on the best fit between the constraints relevant to each problem, and the target constraints suggested by the student model. Two problems may arise when doing this: (1) there may not be an example which is a good fit for the student's current state, and (2) we may run out of problems to set the student.

4 Constraint Representation

In the new representation, constraints are encoded purely as pattern matches. Each pattern may be compared either against the ideal or student solutions (via a MATCH function) or against a variable (via a TEST function) whose value has been determined in a prior match. An example of a constraint in SQL-Tutor using this representation is:

```
(34
"If there is an ANY or ALL predicate in the WHERE
clause, then the attribute in question must be of the
same type as the only expression of the SELECT clause of
the subquery."

(match SS SELECT '(?* ?a1
  ("<" ">" "=" "!=" "<>" "<=" ">=")
  ("ANY" "ALL") "(" "SELECT" ?a2 "FROM" ?* ")" ?*))

(and (test SS (!type (?a1 ?type))
     (test SS (!type (?a2 ?type)))))

"WHERE"
)
```

This constraint tests that if an attribute is compared to the result of a nested SELECT, the attribute being compared and that which the SELECT returns have the same type. The syntax of the MATCH function is:

```
(MATCH <solution name> <clause name> (pattern list))
```

where <solution name> is either SS (student solution) or IS (ideal solution) and <clause name> is the name of the SQL clause to which the pattern applies. The pattern list is a set of terms, which match to individual elements in the solution being tested. The following constructs are supported:

- ?* - wildcard, matches zero or more terms that we are not interested in
- ?var - variable, matches a single term
- "str" - literal string
- (lit1, lit2, lit3…) - list of possible allowed values for a single term

Variables and literals (or lists of literals) may be combined to give a variable whose allowed value is restricted. For example, (("ANY" "ALL") ?what) means that the term that the variable ?*what* matches to must have a value of "ANY or "ALL". Subsequent tests of the value of a variable may be carried out using the TEST function, which is a special form of MATCH that accepts a single pattern term and one or more variables.

In the previous section we stated that SQL-Tutor uses domain-specific functions to extract features of the solutions, and to make special comparisons between them. In the new representation, this is no longer required. For example, comparisons which test for a relationship between two variables are accomplished using a list of tuples, which enumerates the relationship. The type of an attribute is obtained in this fashion by testing the attribute variable against a list, i.e.

```
(TEST SS ((("director" "INTEGER")
           ("lname" "STRING")…) (?attribute ?type)))
```

Describing all constraints fully in the above format leads to much repetition. *Match templates* are used to reduce the effort of encoding the constraints. For example, the match template for *!type* used previously is:

```
(!type (??a ??t) = (test ((("director" "INTEGER")
                    ("lname" "STRING")…) (??a ??t)))
```

When the constraint set is compiled, the template names are expanded into their corresponding pattern matches. The constraints that are used for evaluation are, therefore, purely pattern matches with no sub functions. It is this property that facilitates generating SQL from the constraint set.

5 Solution Generation

In the new representation, the (expanded) constraints make explicit all of the encoded domain knowledge: for any given constraint, all requirements of the ideal and student solutions are encapsulated in the MATCH and TEST pattern lists, and the logical connectives between them. This means that the relevant constraints plus the variable bindings for each describes all that we know about the solution relevant to the problem, given our current domain knowledge.

Consequently, given a complete domain model, we can rebuild the solution from just the relevant constraints and their bindings. In the following example, we list the match patterns resulting from the evaluation of a correct student solution. Only matches related to the student solution are listed, with variable bindings substituted back in to give bound fragments of the student solution. The resulting list contains many fragments that subsume others, i.e. they are a more specific version of one or more other fragments. In this case, the subsumed fragments are deleted.

Ideal Solution

SELECT	title
FROM	movie
WHERE	director=(select number from director
	where fname='Stanley' and lname='Kubrick')

Student Solution

SELECT	title
FROM	movie join director on director = director.number
WHERE	lname = 'Kubrick' and fname = 'Stanley'

Bound Matches (with subsumed fragments omitted)

SELECT	(title ?*)
FROM	(?* movie JOIN director ON director = director.number ?*)
WHERE	(?* lname = 'Kubrick' and ?*) (?* = 'Kubrick' and fname ?*)
	(?* 'Kubrick' and fname = ?*) (?* and fname = 'Stanley' ?*)

The WHERE clause contains more than one fragment. These are "spliced" together by joining overlapping fragments. Removing the wildcards yields:

SELECT	(title)
FROM	(movie JOIN director ON director = director.number)
WHERE	(lname = 'Kubrick' and fname = 'Stanley')

which is the same as the student solution.

6 Correcting an Erroneous Solution

To provide tailored feedback, we produce a correct solution that is as close as possible to the student's attempt, based on pattern matches from the relevant constraints. The previous example illustrates that the constraints may contain sufficient information about a correct solution to rebuild it. In the case of an incorrect solution, the fragments obtained from satisfied constraints tells us about the correct parts of the solution, while violated constraints indicate parts of the solution that must be corrected. To build a correct solution from a mal-formed one, we correct each violated constraint, and add the resulting fragments to those obtained from the satisfied constraints.

There are three types of constraint violation that may occur: a MATCH against the student solution fails; a MATCH against the ideal solution fails; and a TEST fails. The first failure type indicates that one or more terms are missing from the student solution. This is corrected by adding the fragment for the failed MATCH. The second failure indicates that there are one or more extraneous terms in the student solution, which can be corrected by omitting the match fragment. Finally, a failed TEST indicates that one or more variables in a previous match fragment are incorrect. These are corrected by substituting the expected value for those variables.

The correct solution is built by beginning with the set of solution fragments created by the satisfied constraints, and passing it through a modified version of the constraint evaluator, which accepts bound matches (including wildcards) as valid input. Each time a constraint is violated, action is taken (as indicated above) to remove the violation. The fragment set is then checked for subsumed fragments, and these are removed. The cycle then repeats until no constraints are violated. At this stage the fragments are spliced together, as in the previous section, and wildcards removed, yielding a corrected solution.

7 Example of Solution Correction

SQL-Tutor has been subjected to three evaluation studies [5] where, as well as collecting general statistics about the performance of the system, we logged the students' attempts. There were many cases where the student solution was fundamentally different to the ideal solution, and so the feedback given for a partial solution was not relevant to their answer: Of all partial or full solutions presented to a student, 22 percent were either fundamentally different to the student solution, or differed such that the student made unnecessary alterations to their solution. We now examine the performance of solution generation in one such situation. As detailed in the previous section, generating the correct solution involves testing the solution against the constraints, extracting solution fragments from satisfied constraints, and adding, removing, or modifying fragments for violated constraints. This process is repeated until all fragments are valid, and none are missing. The solution is then built by splicing together the remaining fragments.

In the following example, the student has made one minor mistake: they have omitted a quote. This, however, has several consequences: the expected quoted string is missing (and an incorrect one is instead observed;) the construct of the rest of the clause is rendered syntactically incorrect; and the mal-formed string is identified as an erroneous attribute name. The ideal and student solutions are:

Problem:
List the titles of all movies directed by Stanley Kubrick.

Ideal Solution:

SELECT	title
FROM	movie
WHERE	director=(select number from director
	where fname='Stanley' and lname='Kubrick')

Student Solution:

SELECT	title
FROM	movie join director on number = director
WHERE	lname='Kubrick and fname='Stanley'

On the first assessment, the student solution is passed to the constraint evaluator, which returns the set of correct fragments, and the action list for violated constraints. The fragments returned are:

SELECT	(?* title ?*)
FROM	(?* movie JOIN director ON director = director.number ?*)
WHERE	(?* lname = ?*) (?* 'Kubrick and fname = ?*) (?* = 'Stanley' ?*)

The action list indicates how to correct the violated constraints. Table 1 depicts the actions carried out on this fragment set.

Reason	Failed binding	Remedy	Result
Constants used in comparisons must be compared to an attribute	Where ?* 'Kubrick and fname = 'Stanley' ?*	Replace ('Kubrick and fname) with a valid attribute	The failed match is replaced with a term of the form (?* ~attribute = 'Stanley' ?*)
String constants appearing in the ideal solution must appear in the student solution	Where ?* 'Kubrick' ?*	Add the missing match	Fragment added

Table 1. actions carried out after initial assessment

At this stage the incorrect term ('Kubrick and fname) has been removed from the fragment list, and the missing string 'Kubrick' added, along with a placeholder for the missing attribute. This is a consequence of the modularity of the constraints: a constraint that tests that an attribute is valid and/or present does not know which attribute is the required one. An interim solution is now built from the fragments, and resubmitted. This continues until the solution no longer violates any constraints. At this stage, the WHERE clause consists of two fragments. These are spliced together, and the result retested, until it too does not violate any constraints. At this point wildcards are removed, and the solution is complete. It is a corrected version of the student solution:

```
SELECT      (title)
FROM        (movie JOIN director ON director = director.number)
WHERE       (lname = 'Kubrick' AND fname = 'Stanley')
```

8 Discussion

In the example described in the previous section, we generated a corrected version of an incorrect student answer, despite the student and ideal solutions being fundamentally different: the ideal solution has used a nested SELECT, while the student solution includes a JOIN. This suggests that the new representation is sufficient for the domain model to be generative. However, there is room for improving efficiency. First, the algorithm described is greedy, in that it performs actions for all failed constraints and their bindings, even though they may be undone by actions for later constraints. In particular, it may generate new fragments that are later deleted again. This is inefficient, and we need to explore ways to reduce the amount of redundant work performed, without adding unnecessary complexity.

Second, each failed constraint results in just one action, based on the first item in the condition that failed. Some constraints are encoded as a MATCH, with either unrestricted or partially restricted variable terms, which are then further restricted by other tests. If the initial MATCH fails, it will generate an action that adds a fragment containing similarly general terms. These terms will remain until they are picked up by another constraint failure (possibly for this same constraint) in a subsequent processing step. It may be possible to perform more work at each action, by incorporating more than just the first failed step in the condition, thereby reducing the number of iterations overall.

Finally, there is no guarantee that the solution being built will converge. Often, there are multiple ways to satisfy a failed constraint, some of which may lead to extraneous constructs being added to the solution. It is important that these are removed, and that the solution does not "oscillate" between two or more solutions. We are currently investigating this behaviour.

9 Conclusion and Further Work

Constraint-based modeling is an "innocent until proven guilty" approach to domain modeling, for which the representation of the constraints has not previously been explicitly designed. We presented a pattern-based representation that can be used to fully encode the required domain knowledge without supporting functions. We have shown that by using this representation, the SQL-Tutor constraint-based model can generate valid SQL queries. We have demonstrated one benefit of this feature: that we can generate corrected versions of student answers, for use as feedback. We now need to verify the approach, by further testing with SQL-Tutor, and by exploring other domains, to see whether the approach can be applied to constraint-based models in general. We are also investigating the following areas.

9.1 Problem Generation

We previously described the limitations of using a fixed problem set. When correcting student solutions we began with bound fragments obtained from the relevant constraints. An extension of this is to generate an ideal solution from *unbound* fragments, obtained from the set of target constraints. In many cases, potential values for unbound variables in the fragments will be enumerated in the constraints themselves (e.g. all valid values for a table name are enumerated in constraints which check that a table name is valid,) while others (such as literals) will need to be provided externally.

9.2 Constraint Authoring

The new representation is a concise language, with a simple structure and few constructs. We intend to produce an editor that facilitates the writing of constraints and match templates.

9.3 Constraint Induction

We have shown that examples can be generated from constraints. An interesting possibility is whether constraints can be induced from examples. Much human intervention would still be required, because: the feedback for each constraint would need to be input; the inducer is unlikely to induce all desired constraints; and some of the induced constraints may be fortuitous or incorrect generalisations. We are currently investigating using the MARVIN algorithm [9] to induce constraints in partnership with a teacher.

References

1. Holt P., Dubs S., Jones M. and Greer J. The State of Student Modeling. *Student Modeling: The Key to Individualized Knowledge-Based Instruction.* pp 3-39, Springer-Verlag, 1994.
2. Martin, B. Constraint-based Student Modeling: Representing Student Knowledge. *Proceedings of the Third New Zealand Computer Science Research Students' Conference.* pp 22-29 Hamilton NZ, 1999.
3. Mayo, M., Mitrovic, A. Estimating Problem Value in an Intelligent Tutoring System using Bayesian Networks. *Proc. 12th Australian Joint Conf. on AI*, pp. 472-473, Sydney, 1999.
4. Mitrovic, A. Experiences in Implementing Constraint-Based Modeling in SQL-Tutor. *Proceedings of ITS'98*, pp. 414-423.
5. Mitrovic, A. and Ohlsson, S. Evaluation of a Constraint-Based Tutor for a Database Language. *International Journal of Artificial Intelligence in Education*, 1999.
6. Ohlsson, S. & Rees, E. The function of conceptual understanding in the learning of arithmetic procedures. *Cognition & Instruction*, 8. pp 103-179, 1991.
7. Ohlsson, S. Constraint-Based Student Modeling. *Student Modeling: The Key to Individualized Knowledge-Based Instruction.* pp 167-189, Springer-Verlag, 1994.
8. Ohlsson, S. Learning from Performance Errors. *Psychological Review*, Vol 3. No 2, 241-262, 1996
9. Sammut, C. and Banerji, R.B. Learning concepts by asking questions. *Machine Learning: An Artificial Intelligence Approach,* volume II, 1986, Morgan Kaufmann, San Mateo, CA
10. Self, J. A. Bypassing the Intractable Problem of Student Modeling. In *Intelligent Tutoring Systems: At the Crossroads of Artificial Intelligence and Education*, C. Frasson and G. Gauthier, eds, pp 107-123, Ablex Publishing Corporation 1990

Design Principles for a System to Teach Problem Solving by Modelling

Gérard Tisseau[1], Hélène Giroire[1], Françoise Le Calvez[2],
Marie Urtasun[2], and Jacques Duma[3]

[1] Equipe SysDef - LIP6, Université Paris6, Boîte 169, Tour 46-0 2° étage,
4 Place Jussieu, F-75252 Paris Cedex 05.
e-mail: <Surname>.<Name>@lip6.fr
[2] CRIP5, Université René Descartes, 45 rue des Saints Pères,
F-75270 Paris Cedex 06.
e-mail: <Surname>.<Name>@math-info.univ-paris5.fr
[3] Lycée technique Jacquard, 2 rue Bouret, F-75019 Paris.
e-mail: dumajd@club-internet.fr

Abstract. This paper presents an approach to the design of a learning environment in a mathematical domain (elementary combinatorics) where problem solving is based more on modelling than on deduction or calculation. In this approach, we want to provide the student with a presentation which is close to the natural language formulations that she tends to give spontaneously, while ensuring a rigorous mathematical reasoning. To do so, we have introduced three modelling levels : first a mathematical formalisation of the students' intuitive process, then a conceptual and computational model allowing mathematical reasoning as well as communication with the student, and finally a presentation consisting in several interfaces, each one grouping problems of some class. These interfaces are viewed as nondeterministic "machines" that the student uses to build a configuration satisfying some constraints.

1 Introduction

Classically, the activities offered by an intelligent tutoring system (ITS) are centred on problem solving. In the domain of mathematics, proposed problems are often solvable by a deductive method: starting from the given facts, considered as a set of axioms, the learner can apply inference rules to get new facts and so find a way to the property to prove or to the result of the requested calculation. While this kind of process is promoted in such domains as transformation of algebraic expressions [9] and proof of geometric properties, it is not suitable to all domains. In other domains such as combinatorics (counting the number of ways of arranging given objects in a prescribed way), this unsuitability is apparent in the pupils' reactions to the problems: "I can't represent the problem", "I understand the solution given by the teacher but I don't understand why mine is wrong", "I'm proposing a solution but I have no way of finding out if it is right or wrong". We interpret these reactions as representational difficulties: the main part of the solving process does not come from a clever chaining of inferences or calculations, but from the elaboration of a suitable representation and from the transformation of one representation into another equivalent one. The importance of representations in problem solving is studied for example in [1], [3], [11].

We are particularly interested in these domains because they offer a good opportunity to acquire some important abilities, such as the ability to elaborate models. But because of the difficulties they present and of the particular processes they require, they are not given much attention to in the official curriculum. In France, combinatorial mathematics in secondary school is very little developed. There is a deficiency here and we think that an ITS approach can help to fill the gap.

This paper presents an approach to the design of a learning environment in elementary combinatorics at secondary school level (final year), taking into account the characteristics of this kind of domain. We first present the "COMBIEN?" project within which this approach takes place, then we describe the activities proposed to the learner and the related interaction mode: the interfaces are viewed as nondeterministic "machines" that the student uses to build a configuration satisfying some constraints. We then discuss the modelling choices we made to offer the student a presentation close to the natural language formulations that she tends to give spontaneously, while ensuring a rigorous mathematical reasoning.

2. The COMBIEN? Project

Our project, called "COMBIEN?" ("how many?" in French) is to design and implement a learning environment allowing a student to familiarize herself with the mathematical concepts necessary to rigorously solve combinatorics problems.

2.1 Project Review

Since the beginning of the "COMBIEN?" project, we have carried on simultaneously theoretical reflections and implementation experiments. From our experience of teaching combinatorics in the classroom, we have defined the mathematical bases of a solving method, which we will call "the constructive method" in the rest of this paper. It is adapted to the usual student's conceptions and gives access to the mathematical theory of the domain [8]. We have defined a classification of the domain problems and solution schemata associated with the different classes. This classification has been used as a basis for an IA system that solves combinatorics problems [7]. We have defined a language to represent a problem and a solution according to the constructive method and we have implemented an IA system that can verify a solution written in this language. This language proved difficult to use because of its generality and abstraction, so we have defined a conceptual object-oriented model better suited to an interactive use. This model has been implemented in experimental data input interfaces [2]. In the same time, we have implemented different interface prototypes to explore various interaction possibilities [5]. From this, we selected a certain kind of interface that we called "configuration building machines" [8].

The paper presents the design principles that lie at the basis of these machines.

2.2 Pedagogic Objective

The combinatorics problems that we consider have all an analogous form: given a set or sets (e.g. a pack of 32 cards), count within some "universe" of configurations (e.g. the set of all possible five-card hands) the elements satisfying some constraints (e.g. including two spades and two hearts). Rigorously solving this kind of problem requires an appropriate, often abstract and complex representation using the concepts of set theory (e.g. sets, mappings, sets of sets). For a beginner, this approach is inaccessible because the representation is very different from the usual mental image.

However, some students are able to solve these problems [6]. Their answer, though correct, is not a real mathematical proof and they are generally unable to justify every aspect of it. Our objective is to introduce some basic concepts (e.g. sets, lists, mappings from a set to another, equality of sets defined by constraints) and some reasoning schemata that can be applied to them. The point is to acquire representations and practices of the domain in order to prepare a subsequent theoretical course, so that abstract theorems become understandable and can be effectively used. To reach this goal without excessive formalisation, we give the learner the possibility to express herself in terms similar to those of the usual student's answer.

To achieve our project, we first carried out a theoretical study of the domain in order to specify what we wanted the student to learn and what activities could help her to reach this goal. We have elaborated a mathematical formalisation of the method corresponding to the typical answer given by students [8]. We have called this method "a constructive method for counting", as it is based on a dynamic perspective describing a sequence of actions. Let us start from what the learner knows to bring her progressively to the awareness of the underlying abstract structures and of the rigorous methods of mathematical reasoning that apply to these structures.

The aim is not so much to make counting experts, as to train students to a modelling task and to make them able to represent a situation by a complex structure. This ability is essential in modelling and design activities, as shown by the increasing importance attributed to modelling methods in software engineering. We think that counting problems are a good starting point for that and that similar processes can be found in other domains like probabilities and algorithmics. Moreover, solving counting problems does not request only to know how to describe a structure, but also to reason about such a description.

3 The Student's Activities

The activities that we offer to the learner do not consist in counting but in describing. Before asking "how many?", it is necessary to first ask "what?", in order to give a precise representation of the configurations that must be counted. In the course of an activity, the student must fulfil three requirements, that we specify in this section: she must produce some result, she must use some specific resources to produce this result and the process that she follows must be generic.

The *result* that the student must produce at the end of each activity is an example of a configuration satisfying some constraints. For example, a five-letter word including two occurrences of the letter A. A possible answer is "ALPHA". But we do not ask her to simply write an example, we force her to use certain resources to build it, in order to make her aware of the structure of the configuration.

The *resources* offered to the student look like a "machine" to which the student must give instructions so that it produces the desired result. We have chosen the instruction set and the inner workings of such a machine to familiarise the learner with the underlying representations and principles. For example, an instruction can be something like "select 3 positions and fill them with letters taken randomly in the set of the letters different from A". The machine carries out this task and replies something like: "I have selected the positions 2, 4 and 5. At the position 2, I put an L, at the position 4, I put a P, and at the position 5, I put an H". This presentation suggests the mathematical concept of a mapping from the set of the possible positions (1 to 5) into the set of letters. In order to solve the above problem, the learner will have to say something like:

1. I declare I am going to use 5 positions, from 1 to 5.
2. I declare I am going to use the usual alphabet with 26 letters.
3. At the start, all positions are free.
4. First, I want the machine to select 2 free positions and to fill them with "A".
5. Next, I want the machine to select 3 free positions and to fill them with letters taken randomly in the set of the letters different from A, with possible repetitions.
6. After that my work will be done: the generated word will be a solution.

The learner's activity is thus a kind of *programming*, with declarations and instructions. But, unlike classical programming, programs here can include nondeterministic instructions. It is not the learner who selects positions or letters, it is the machine that does it randomly, according to the specifications of the learner.

The *process* followed by the learner must be generic: she must write instructions so that, if the machine executed them in all possible ways, it would produce all solutions, nothing but solutions and each solution exactly once. This rule is what we call the *basic principle of counting*. Note that the machine does not actually execute the instructions in all possible ways, but only in one way, randomly chosen.

4 Interface and Interaction

A machine appears on the screen in a window like a form including interaction elements (widgets) of a classical type: buttons, menus, fields. Each machine concerns a particular problem class, but all machines have the same use pattern: the learner selects a problem to solve, she gives a model of this problem and then she gives a construction of a solution, i.e. a program. Problems are stored inside each machine not only as texts, but also in an internal representation.

The student selects the text of a problem in natural language by a selection device (a menu and a text field). She must then specify some elements in order to model the problem. For example, for the problems of the type "build a five-card hand with two hearts and two spades", she must specify how many elements she wants and in which set the machine must select them. The possible sets are predefined in a menu, each answer being connected to her usual experience. The student can for example ask: "I want to build a set of [five] elements, taken from [a pack of 32-cards]" (the words in brackets are chosen from menus). This first modelling stage is thus very short while bringing an awareness of representation choices.

The student then describes her construction in the form of an instruction sequence. In this example, all instructions have the same type, like the following example: "I want [two] elements whose [suit] [is] [spades]".

The presentation is like a text written in natural language, with blanks to fill in. The syntax and the type of words suggest the role of each element, so it is not necessary to label them with abstract concepts like "attribute", "comparator", "value". In the internal representation, these labels exist and the elements that look like strings are in fact composed objects ("suit" is an instance of an Attribute class, and is related to its possible values and to the sets to which it can be applied). The menus' item lists are dynamic: for example the last menu to the right (possible values) has been updated when the student selected the attribute "suit".

The learner then asks the machine to execute the instruction, which provides a set of elements (for example a seven of spades and a queen of spades) that are automatically added to the current configuration, which always stays visible on the screen. This automatic addition makes what would be the final instruction of the construction implicit: form the reunion of all generated pieces. The resulting configuration could be for example: {seven of spades, queen of spades, ten of hearts, eight of hearts, king of diamonds}.

The machine restricts the learner's possibilities in order to guide her through her progression and to prevent mistakes caused by inconsistencies or confusions without pedagogic interest. However, the machine leaves her the possibility to make mistakes concerning combinatorics concepts and signals them. But the most interesting errors are the violations of the basic principle of counting: "I refuse to execute the instruction 'select two spades' because you already asked 'select three spades' in a preceding instruction. If I accepted, certain configurations would be generated more than once, for example ...". The machine is specialised in a particular program schema, so it possesses the necessary knowledge to make this diagnostic.

5 Modelling Issues

The above interfaces are based on an internal representation implementing a model of the domain and of the problems. We discuss here modelling issues, the choices we made and the lessons that can be learned.

5.1 Problem Classes and Program Schemata

As the learner's activity is a kind of programming, it is necessary to define the concepts involved in this type of programming as well as a language to express them. We first defined a language based on basic set theory, which uses such concepts as interval, cartesian product, reunion, complement, subset, combination, function, injection, singleton and others. A program to build a configuration is composed of a sequence of declarations of set and declarations of mappings. These mappings are nondeterministic instructions to build pieces of the result, the building of the result being a reunion of pieces. We implemented a prototype using this language, but it became clear that it could not be proposed to a student. Although all instructions are elementary, it is not easy to understand how they are arranged to produce the result, and it is even less easy to invent this arrangement from scratch. The language is then like an assembly language: powerful and general, but unstructured and at too low a level. This phenomenon is likely to happen in most of the domains where problem solving relies on a modelling phase: a general mathematical theory that can represent the problems may be unsuited as a communication mean with the student. We then abandoned this approach and introduced the idea of a program schema, which we present below.

In fact the program has a structure: it first includes declarations of fixed sets necessary to the construction, then non deterministic instructions (mapping between two sets) using auxiliary instructions for selecting subset of former sets and finally the building of the result as a reunion of the pieces. Moreover this structure naturally results from a plan according to which it is possible to build a configuration as an union of mappings.

But asking a beginner to invent such a plan from scratch is too demanding. For an expert, this structure and this plan correspond to a classical resolution schema associated with a certain problem class. An expert knows different classes and their related resolution schemata, and this helps him to solve classical problems: he first analyses the problem to identify its class and then, he applies an associated resolution schema. In fact, using a classification to solve problems is a general method. J.G. Dubois [4] proposes a classification for simple combinatorial configurations, but it does not exactly cover the problems that we consider and it was not conceived to be used in a learning environment. We have defined our own classification of the problems of the domain allowing to solve the major part of the problems that are posed at the considered level. This classification served as a basis for Syrclad-Combinatorics, a system that automatically solves combinatorics problems [7].

The existence of classes on the screen, is suggested by the existence of different windows, each showing a "machine to build configurations". Each machine is associated with a problem class and a resolution method (a program schema to build a configuration). Each machine proposes problems that can be modelled according to the class and solved by the associated method. The important idea is that this class and this method are embedded in the look and the inner workings of the machine.

The program structure is predetermined: first declaration schemata, then a sequence of instructions having all the same schema. The learner does not have to reinvent this structure, but she has still choices to make to reach her goal.

What can be remembered from this discussion is the idea to classify problems and to present each class in an appropriate way, rather than to use a unique general formalism.

5.2 Domain and Problem Modelling

A machine must build configurations according to the learner's instructions and reason about these instructions, for example to verify that they respect the basic principle of counting cited above. It must include a computational model of the domain that allows mathematical reasoning. On this point, we agree with [9] when he stresses the importance of models explicitly described at knowledge level, and the necessity to elaborate a "resolution theory" of the domain. Despite the anticipated variety of the machines (about fifteen), this model must be the same for all machines to reflect the internal consistency of the domain. It must allow to represent not only mathematical concepts, but also the problems and the learner's activity, which is centred on a specific method (our constructive counting method [8]).

We have defined such a model as an object-oriented conceptual model in the sense of software engineering. The higher level classes are Problem and Construction, thus reflecting the learner's activity: she is given a problem and she must represent it and solve it by providing a construction (a program). Each machine represents a certain construction type associated with a problem type. The definition of the conceptual model is based not only on the logical structure of the main concepts (problem, construction), but also on a concern that the student can use a representation close to her usual language. This has been made possible by the fact that the underlying theoretical method (the constructive counting method) has been itself elaborated from the students' usual answers.

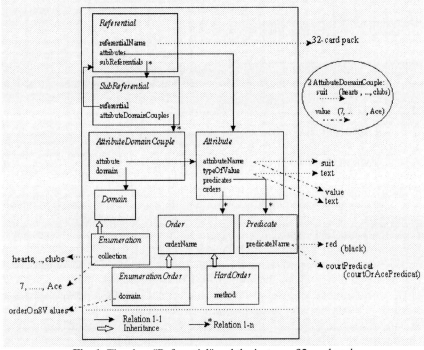

Fig. 1. The class "Referential" and the instance 32-card pack.

To compensate for the excessive generality of mathematical language, where every structure can be assimilated to a set, we have assigned different *roles* to the structures involved in counting, and namely to those involved in the constructive method. For example, the sets of objects (a pack of cards, the letters of the alphabet, tokens) used to form configurations have been called "referentials" and the set of configurations in which the solutions are selected has been called "universe" (it is similar to the possibility space in probability theory). This vocabulary and these concepts do not appear, to our knowledge, in usual courses on combinatorics, but they have proved helpful. A referential (Fig.1 above) is the union of subreferentials, each of them being defined as a set of couples attribute-domain. The "suit" attribute (for a card-pack) derives its values from the domain composed of the values hearts, spades, diamonds, clubs. A domain is defined as an enumeration of values or as an interval of numerical values or alphabetical values. To each attribute, we can associate predicates applying to values (for instance the "being red" predicate applies to suits of cards).

There are 2 types of universe: PartUniverse (used to model a set of parts of a referential, for instance the set of the 5-card hands from a 32-card pack) and AssociationUniverse (used to model a set of mappings from a set into another, for example the set of 5-letter words, each word seen as a mapping from the set of 5 places into the set of letters).

Some concepts do not concern directly mathematical objects (sets, elements, universe) but the means of expression offered to the learner. This introduces a metalevel, which we discuss below.

5.3 Metamodelling

To communicate with the machine, the learner must speak of objects included in referentials, such as playing cards and tokens that can be coloured and numbered. It is often heard that combinatorics does not require to know the nature or the properties of the involved objects, because the only goal is to count them. This is not quite true. In order to count configurations including playing cards, it is necessary to know that each card has a suit and a value, and what the possible values of these attributes are. Likewise, it is necessary to know what an even number is or what it means for a letter to be a vowel. The interface must therefore offer the learner some means of expression to refer to these objects, these attributes and these properties, and the conceptual model must include the related concepts.

In fact, the only important aspects are that the objects have attributes, that these attributes take their values in predefined lists and that it is not necessary to interpret or decompose these values: they are merely atomic. However, these values can have unary properties (a number can be even, a letter can be a vowel) and can be compared to each other. We have restricted the representation of objects to these modelling primitives, which are close to those of the relational model for databases.

To define a subset of a set of objects, the learner can use a declarative *selection formula*. The set of spades in the pack can be designated by: "the cards whose 'suit' attribute has the value 'spades'". This concept of selection simplifies the constructions that the learner must write. Instead of defining in advance the auxiliary sets that she will need for her construction (and to do it for example with cartesian products, which is not very natural), she can introduce them only when she needs them, as a selection and without naming them. This comes close to a formulation in natural language: "I want two cards whose suit is spades". The student can introduce such a selection formula, called "filter" in the model. It is a conjunction of properties, each of them being a comparison, (the suit = spades), a membership (the suit is in {spades, clubs}) or an assertion using a predicate (the number being even).

Finally, our choice consists in introducing a metalevel: instead of including predefined classes (e.g. the Card class, the Token class), we explicitly represent a representation formalism. The model includes for example the classes Attribute, Predicate, Domain, Comparison, Comparator. One benefit of this approach is to allow a teacher (or even a student) to introduce himself new types of objects without having to modify the conceptual model or to program the computer. Through the interface, the student uses this formalism to express her solutions, but the presentation hides the details of the formalism.

Problem Modelling: this formalism is used to model the problem. For each exercise, a wording in natural language is stored as well as an internal representation (class Problem). A problem is defined by a universe describing the type of configurations (for instance: the set of all possible five-card hands) and a set of constraints defining the relevant configurations (for example: the hands including two spades and two hearts). Three classes of constraints are defined: NumberConstraint, RestrictionConstraint, DistributionConstraint. An example of NumberConstraint is "with exactly 2 elements whose suit is spades". An example of RestrictionConstraint is "the letters at the positions 1 and 3 are vowels". An example of DistributionConstraint is "with exactly 2 cards of the same card-value and 3 cards of another card-value ".

Solution Modelling : In the constructive method, the solution of a problem is given in the form of a program of construction (class Construction), as defined in Sections 5.1 and 5.2. There are 2 types of constructions corresponding to the two types of universe: PartConstruction and AssociationConstruction. An example of partConstruction is : "choose 2 cards whose suit is hearts and 3 cards whose suit is spades". An example of associationConstruction is: "choose 2 places, fill them with the letter A, then fill the other places with distinct letters all of them other than A".

A construction is composed of subconstructions, so that the final construction (a 5-card hand) is the union of the sets given by the subconstructions (2 hearts, 3 spades). The constructive method demands that the constructions satisfy some mathematical properties in order to be valid. For example, for a part construction (choose 2 hearts then 3 spades), the subsets from which the choices are made (hearts, spades) must be disjoint. For each exercise the system has a complete model of the exercise (class Problem) and an associated solution (class Construction).

6 Conclusion

This paper shows the approach we are proposing within the "COMBIEN?" project for elementary combinatorics, a mathematical domain where problem solving presents difficulties that are more of a modelling and representation kind than of a deduction or calculation kind. The implementation of an ITS in such a domain must take this specificity into account with regard to the activities offered to the student, the conceptual model used by the system, the presentation of the interface and the mode of interaction. We propose activities that require the student to model the problem and to carry out a construction with the help of nondeterministic machines.

402

Two obstacles are avoided: the first is to be too abstract, with an excessive mathematical technicity, and the second is to be too concrete and not to lead to a real learning of mathematical concepts. To reduce abstraction, we introduce several machines associated with different problem classes and corresponding to methods that are effectively used by students. To link the student's activities with a rigorous mathematical reasoning, we have introduced two intermediary conceptual levels between the basic combinatorics theory and the interface presentation: first a constructive counting method and then a conceptual model that can be used in the reasonings as well as in the interface presentation.

We have implemented several prototypes to test these ideas and we are now beginning to integrate them in a running system. In order to implement different machines more easily, we have devised a general declarative formalism to specify the interfaces [10], and we have implemented a code generator that generates most of the interface code from specifications in this formalism. Our next work will be to specify and generate different machines with this generator, and to test them with students.

References

1. Abidin B., Hartley J.R., Developing mathematical problems solving skills, Journal of Computer Learning (1998) 14, 278-291.
2. Annell M., Malthet V., Giroire H., Tisseau G., Construction d'interface de saisie d'un problème de dénombrement. Rapport interne Lip6 janvier 99.
3. Cox R., Brna P., Supporting the use of external representations in problem solving: the need for flexible Learning Environments. JAIEd, 6, 2/3, 1995, p.239-302.
4. Dubois J.-G., Une systématique des configurations combinatoires simples. Educational studies in Mathematics 15 (1984), p. 37-57.
5. Duma J., Giroire H., Le Calvez F., Tisseau G., Urtasun M., Mise en évidence de styles de résolution, évolution de l'interface dans le projet COMBIEN ?, Actes des 4èmes journées francophones EIAO, ENS Cachan, T.2, Guin, D. & al. (eds.), Eyrolles, 1995, p. 245-256.
6. Fischbein E., Gazit A., The combinatorial solving capacity in children and adolescents. Zentralblatt für Didaktik der Mathematik, 5, 1988, 193-198.
7. Guin N., Changing the representation of a problem in order to solve it : use of classification, in proceedings of AI-ED 97, Kobe (Japan), August 18-22, 1997, p. 583-585.
8. Le Calvez F., Urtasun M., Giroire H., Tisseau G., Duma J., Les machines à construire. Des modèles d'interaction pour apprendre une méthode constructive de dénombrement. EIAO'97, actes des 5èmes journées EIAO de Cachan, Baron, M., Mendelsohn, P., Nicaud, J.-F., (eds), Hermès, 1997, p.49-60.
9. Nicaud J.-F., Building ITSs to be used: Lessons Learned from the APLUSIX Project, Lessons From Learning, Lewis, R & al. (eds), IFIP, North Holland, 1994, p.181-198.
10. Tisseau G., Duma J., Giroire H., Le Calvez F., Urtasun M., Spécification du dialogue et génération d'interfaces à l'aide d'interacteurs à réseau de contrôle. Actes de la 11ème Conférence francophone IHM'99 p. 94-101.
11. White B.Y., Frederiksen J.R., Causal model progressions for intelligent learning environments. Artificial Intelligence, 42, 1990, p.99-157.

Evolution of the Hypotheses Testing Approach in Intelligent Problem Solving Environments

Janine Willms, Claus Möbus

Fachbereich Informatik, Abteilung Lehr-und Lernsysteme,
C.v.O. Universität Oldenburg, D-26111 Oldenburg, Germany
{Janine.Willms,Claus.Moebus}@Informatik.Uni-Oldenburg.de

Abstract. In this paper, we compare different realizations of the hypotheses testing approach in the IPSEs (Intelligent Problem Solving Environments) ABSYNT, PETRI-HELP and MEDICUS and introduce the changes necessary to transfer the hypotheses testing approach to the real world domain of patent applications. Patent-IT is the first IPSE to overcome the limiting aspects of fixed specifications and a black box oracle.

1   Hypothesis Testing and the IPSE Approach

The *hypotheses testing approach* is a core concept of what we call *intelligent problem solving environments* (IPSE) ([8], [9]) and also gives a key qualification having a beneficial influence on the student's knowledge acquisition process. The learner acquires knowledge by actively exploring a domain, creating solution proposals for problems, testing hypotheses about their correctness, during which the system analyzes the proposals and provides help and explanations, making use of an oracle or an expert knowledge base. The IPSEs we developed initially had some limiting aspects such as fixed specifications and a black box oracle. We now present the IPSE Patent-IT, which does not exhibit these limitations. This has become necessary due to the rather demanding domain of inventions and patents. The novice should learn how to transform an inventive idea into a legal patent.

The IPSE approach is psychologically based on the ISP-DL theory of knowledge acquisition and problem solving [8], which is influenced by theoretical assumptions of van Lehn [13], Newell [11], Anderson [1] and Gollwitzer [5]. It briefly states that new knowledge is acquired as a result of problem solving by applying weak heuristics in response to impasses. Furthermore, existing knowledge is optimized if applied successfully. The learner encounters four distinct problem solving phases namely deliberation, resulting in marking a goal as an intention, planning how to satisfy the intention, execution of the plan and evaluation of the result. Several design principles for IPSEs [8] could be drawn from the following assumptions:

- The system should not interrupt the learner but offer help on demand. According to the theory, the learner will look for and appreciate help at an impasse.
- Feedback and help information should be available on request at any time, taking the actual problem solving phase of the learner into account.

- Help should be tailored to the learner's pre-knowledge as much as possible. The best method to fulfill this requirement is to let the learner freely state hypotheses of the solution.

1.1 The Scope of our IPSEs so far and what is to come

We have developed several IPSEs in variable application domains. The one common characteristic is that, the hypothesis testing process is fixed and hidden in a black box. The IPSEs ABSYNT and PETRI-HELP each define a closed world in which the learner explores a domain. MEDICUS defines the next step towards a non-closed world application, because real-world scenarios may act as a source for modeling. The modeling task is left to the learner, and MEDICUS is able to evaluate the equivalence of two different representations (specification, bayesian belief networks) of the real world scenario by an internal and fixed diagnostic process.

Patent-IT is an IPSE, which supports the application of a patent by assessing critical aspects. The learner needs *evaluation, judgement and argumentation skills* to perform this task. He has to construct a model of his invention and is supported by the IPSE in his critiquing process. In this connection, the domain of patents serves as a kind of *metadomain,* which *incorporates the hypothesis testing process.* Neither a task specification nor the model are fixed in Patent-IT. The patentability of an invention is dependent on the state of the art. It is necessary that the model is *not* a derivative from the state of the art. This differs from previous IPSEs, where the model was to be equivalent to a specification or its logical conclusion. The state of the art for an invention is a *real world concept.* It is defined by a research in real world patent and literature databases and consists of a set of documents. By changing the model of the invention the state of the art also changes. This dynamic behavior of the domain makes a diagnostic process quite difficult and is realized in Patent-IT as a dialogue based cooperation of the system and the learner, which makes the process transparent and understandable for him. The critical dialogue depends on the modeled invention, the domain ontology known to the system, the results of the search for the state of the art and the user's statements and arguments. By defending his invention, the learner may use his pre-knowledge as much as possible. In impasse situations where he needs support, Patent-IT is able to control the evaluation process, direct the learner and offer argumentative hints. Patent-IT is therefore the next consequent step on the evolutionary line of IPSEs.

1.2 ABSYNT ("Abstract Syntax Trees")

The ABSYNT [8] problem solving environment supports learners by offering help and proposals for functional programming in a graphical tree representation of pure LISP. The learner is given a fixed set of tasks. The programming task is internally represented as a symbolic goal, which triggers a set of transformation rules developed in the Munich CIP project ([2], [12]). In a diagnosic, hypotheses and help environment, the learner may visually state the hypothesis in a tree-like representation, that his solution proposal (or a boldly marked part of that proposal) to a programming task is correct. The system then analyzes this part of the solution proposal. One reason for the hypotheses testing approach is that, in programs, bugs cannot be absolutely localized. Therefore, the decision, which parts of a buggy

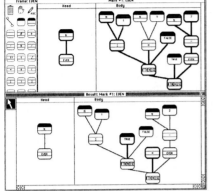

solution proposal are to be kept, is left to the learner. This results in the system giving help and error feedback on the implementation level by synthesizing complete solutions, starting from the learner's hypothesis. If the hypothesis is embeddable within a complete solution, the learner may ask for completion proposals.

The hypotheses testing is a hidden process, based on a set of hundreds of diagnostic rules, defining a "goals-means-relation", which analyzes and synthesizes several millions of solution proposals for 40

programming tasks. The rules, which are not shown to the user, generate complete solutions, recognize and complete incomplete proposals. The learner works in a closed world, defined by the tasks and the internal rules of the IPSE.

1.3   PETRI-HELP

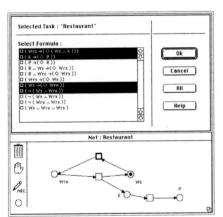

PETRI-HELP [8] supports novices in learning to model dynamic systems with condition-event petri nets. Tasks are stated as a set of temporal logic formulas, which describe the behaviour of a dynamic system. The learner is asked to construct a petri-net model that fulfills the given formulas. He may test hypotheses based on his solution by selecting those formulas he believes to be fulfilled by his model. The system checks the hypotheses through model checking ([3],[7]) by interpreting the temporal logic formulas on the case graph of the learner's petri net. This model

checking mechanism is a domain-independent method for dynamic systems. We adapted it for an IPSE in the domain of pneumatic (PULSE) [14] and electronic circuits (MSAFE). The model checking process is normally hidden from the learner.

1.4   MEDICUS

MEDICUS [4], [9] is designed as a problem solving tool for modeling uncertain domains. Diagnosis in domains of complex, fragile and uncertain knowledge is quite a difficult reasoning and problem solving task. Therefore, the training of diagnostic strategies will be supported by the system qualitatively (i.e., what information is necessary to support or differentiate between given hypotheses?) as well as quantitatively (i.e., how does information gathered affect my diagnostic hypotheses? Which information should be acquired next?). The learner may state hypothetical conclusions of a given situation and the resulting strategic actions.

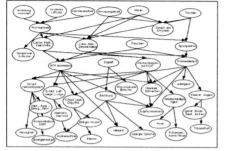

The learner may construct bayesian belief networks (BBN) as explanatory models, evaluate their consequences qualitatively and quantitatively and revise the models with support from the system. The learner asserts the dependence or independence of multiple variables in a diagnostic dialog. He then states the hypothesis that his BBN is consistent with this information. The system analyzes this hypothesis using the d-separation criterion. If the dependence and independence assertions are not given by the modeled BBN, a new BBN is constructed internally from the dependence and independence assertions and compared to the modeller's graph. The hypotheses testing method is a mathematical method, external to the "learn domain". It always leads to a correct answer and allows explanations for a redesign of the modeled BBN. This may lead to the result that edges have to be removed from and/or added to the graph in order to be consistent with the dependencies and independencies.

2 Elaboration of a Taxonomy of Different Hypotheses Used in our Prior IPSEs

On a high level viewpoint all those IPSEs share the characteristic, which enables the learner explore a domain, state hypotheses after which the system assesses the correctness of the solution proposal by a domain-independend diagnostic process. Even in those systems, different types of hypotheses can be found depending on task formulation and solution proposal. On taking a closer look, at least two different dimensions of hypotheses are used in the initial IPSEs. In ABSYNT, a hypothesis is actually (a part of) the *solution proposal*, whereas in PETRI-HELP, the hypothesis is a selection of the *task specification*. For many domains it is possible to offer those two dimensions of hypotheses.

MEDICUS is slightly different, because no specific task is given. Instead, the learner himself models two different representations (dependence/independence statements and BBNs) of the same domain with the hypothesis that both representations are equivalent. The independence statements play the role of a specification and the BBNs, the role of the solution model.

We will show that hypotheses testing in Patent-IT still allows another approach. Like in MEDICUS, there is no task given, but several criteria mentioned in the patent law must be fulfilled by the learner's invention.

The learner constructs a model of his invention. This model may be divided into several parts and each combination out of these may serve as a hypothesis. This is similar to hypotheses testing in ABSYNT. It is also possible to state different hypotheses according to the criteria of the patent law. Some of these criteria are independent, hence the possibility of checking them separately. Others depend on each other, e.g. it is impossible for an invention to be inventive if it is not novel. The opportunity to state hypotheses according to the criteria which have to be proven is similar to the approach followed in PETRI-HELP.

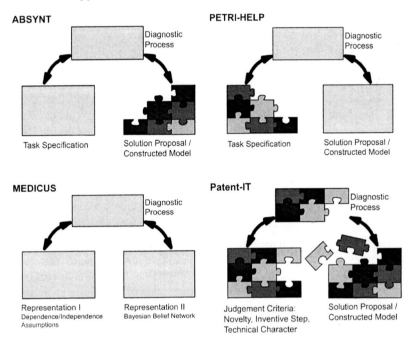

Fig. 1. Overview of different hypothesis selection opportunities

Patent-IT offers a further opportunity of stating a hypothesis. The diagnostic process of an IPSE is embedded in the *metadomain* of patent application examination. This examination process was elicited by empirical studies by the first author at the German Patent Office (DPMA)[1] and the European Patent Office (EPA) and integrated into Patent-IT. The process is made transparent to the inventor in order to familerize him with the patent law and the processes in the patent offices. In comparison to prior diagnostic processes in our IPSEs, the analysis method in Patent-IT is neither complete nor correct. The process heavily depends on heuristics and ontological knowledge of the invention domain. The diagnostic process is therefore carried out as a sequential process in cooperation with the system and the learner. It is possible to enter this process at different entry points, i.e. under different assumptions. Everything before the entry point forms a theoretical basis, which may or may not be

[1] Grateful acknowledgements are due to the DMPA and the EPA for having given us the opportunity to participate in the work carried-out in these patent organizations.

true. This is a hypothesis testing approach, which was not available in the initial IPSEs, due to the diagnostic process being hidden in a black box.

We can see that the hypotheses testing approach may be applied in many different domains leading to different forms of realization (Fig. 1). In the next section, we will describe the IPSE Patent-IT in greater detail.

3   Patent-IT

Patent-IT is designed to help an inventor to evaluate the acceptability of his invention as a patent. The goals of Patent-IT are to:
- explain basic concepts of the patent domain "just in time",
- introduce the judgement criteria and judgement processes which are applied by the patent researchers and patent examiners,
- lower the inhibition level of applying for a patent by offering simulated trial applications,
- gain more detailed information before an expensive patent application process is started,
- stimulate the systematic structuring of the invention,
- discover a strategic combination of invention features,
- help the inventor search for the state of the art,
- offer an argumentation testing ground to defend the patentibility of his invention,
- find and emphasize the critical aspects of his patent application.

In this case, the evaluation process is difficult because many undefined factors are influencing the result. Usually, the inventor is unable to tell if his invention is patentable or not. Moreover, the details of the current state of the art are unknown to him. One of the most important steps in the evaluation process is therefore to find the relevant state of the art. The inventor does not even know the best level of abstraction to describe his invention and which linguistic form he should use. The use of *natural language texts* to describe an invention is another factor of uncertainty. Usually, words, terms or phrases can be understood differently. Many words have two or more meanings and misunderstandings are normal. Even if two people agree on the same meaning of a concept, they may have a *different ontology*, leading to the fact that, one says that the invention is not novel compared to a document of the state of the art whereas the other rejects this point of view.

We designed a new cooperative form of the hypotheses testing method as a result of these uncertainties. The user, in this case the inventor, is included in the evaluation process. The evaluation process itself is not domain independent any more but a simulation of the processes in the patent organization.

The examination process can be divided into several subtasks (Fig. 2). Usually, the inventor prepares the application for patent with or without the help of a patent attorney, after which the application is examined by the patent organization. The initial step involves the classification of the invention according to the International Patent Classification (IPC). The application is then transferred to a research department, where the search for the state of the art is performed resulting in a search report which is transferred to the patent applicant.

The search report is the foundation for further examination. A patent examiner compares the documents in the state of the art with the invention. At the EPA he

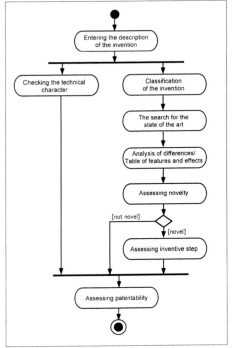

decides the novelty and inventiveness of the patent application in a process called the "Problem-Solution-Approach".

According to the patent law a condition to be fulfilled by the invention is its technical character. This is difficult to decide especially if the application refers to a software-related invention.

Patent-IT is designed to assess the patentability of an invention *before* the application process is started and *before* the actual features to be claimed are determined by writing down the application for a patent. This means that the whole process of examination must be simulated by the system. The system acts as classifier, researcher and examiner and represents the public by attacking the user's invention but at the same time it supports the user when necessary. Unfortunately, the method to evaluate the users inventive idea has become domain-specific and uncertain.

Fig. 2. A model of the evaluation process

We will now describe the *cooperative process of evaluation* between the inventor and the IPSE Patent-IT. As stated earlier, the evaluation process heavily depends on environmental factors, heuristics and ontological knowledge.

When Patent-IT is started, the user is asked in a html-based dialogue to describe his invention, i.e. the topic, a title, features and special characteristics of features, effects and advantages as well as disadvantages of the invention. These phrases are analyzed to extract keywords to be searched for, and stopwords which are neglected. The system is designed to allow easy access to a common but limited ontological network called Wordnet [15] in order to expand each keyword to a set of synonyms, super- and sub-terms. The search is performed in the IBM-Patentserver [6] and the results are presented to the user. Now it is the user's task to select the most relevant documents. These documents define the state of the art for this special invention. The next step is to generate the table of differences. Usually, the inventor is convinced that his invention is novel and inventive. It is now important to assess the similarities of the invention and the state of the art in the most objective way. In a critical dialogue, the system tries to find a justification for the belief that the feature in focus is already given in the state of the art. The inventor has to defend his invention. This dialogue game results in a filled table of differences, in which an indication is made for each feature or effect of the invention found in each of the documents of the state of the art. This table is used by the system to trigger empirical rules about novelty and inventiveness. In spite of the inventiveness of the user's idea, it could be rejected because of the lack of technical character. It is therefore necessary to assess the technical character of the invention. Patent-IT uses a database of arguments on the technical character of several inventions taken from legal proceedings in order to attack the user's invention or to give him advice on how to present his case.

As already stated, the user engages in a cooperative process with the system, both having distinct tasks and skills. Two parts are needed in order to assess the patentability of the invention in this dialogue based evaluation process: a) The user's knowledge about the domain of the invention, his ability to understand the content of documents and to generate arguments and b) the system's knowledge about how to perform searches and how to decide whether an invention defined by a set of features and effects is inventive or not.

3.1   Hypothesis Testing in Patent-IT

Hypothesis testing is made possible by choosing a *set of features* as defining elements for the invention.   If the result of the evaluation process poses a question of the novelty and inventiveness of the application, the user may adjust his hypothesis by adding more detailed features and therefore reducing the claimed scope of the protection.

Furthermore, it is possible to state a *hypothesis based on certain judgement criteria*. For example, the user may state that his invention is patentable according to the criteria novelty and inventiveness under the assumption that the technical character of the invention is given.

Due to the stepwise process of evaluation, a third kind of hypothesis is possible. The user is able to define an *entry point and a stopping point for the evaluation process*. This allows partial tests of the invention, which are not directly related to the judgement criteria. One example may be the evaluation of an invention given a set of predefined documents as the state of the art.

The methods used by Patent-IT to perform the evaluation processes are based on a cooperative dialogue between the system and the user. Patent-IT makes use of multiple knowledge bases in order to find justifications for a critical dialogue. The user is however always able to state that the system's conclusions are wrong in this special case. The knowledge bases are adapted according to the user's statements. New synonyms and ontological relationships are saved in a separate user-wordnet. They may be transferred to the original wordnet after review. New legal proceedings may be integrated into the case base in order to introduce new arguments. Incorrect results of the hypothesis testing are possible, because a user is able to tell lies to the system or to define meaningless inventions. But Patent-IT is designed as a system to support the applicant by providing a testing ground for a real patent application. Therefore telling lies to the system would not make sense.

Even though the dialogue based evaluation process may still produce incorrect results because Patent-IT is an open system, and the evaluation process depends on the chosen state of the art. In reality, even if two different examiners examine the same application resulting in a different state of the art, the overall result concerning the patentability of the application is mainly the same. We are therefore confident that the systematic process simulated by the system will be able to at least give hints about critical aspects concerning the patent application.

Patent-IT is designed as a distributed web-based system. The main actions are controlled by a production-system architecture, which includes rule bases for the different parts of the evaluation process. Some of these rules cause the establishment of a connection to a patent server in the internet in order to find relevant documents, while others retrieve ontological related terms to a keyword from an online ontology. Patent-IT is still under development, but main parts have already been realized. Further work includes the integration of the case based argumentation framework and the production system as well as the evaluation of the whole system with sample patent applications.

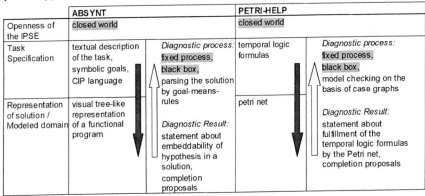

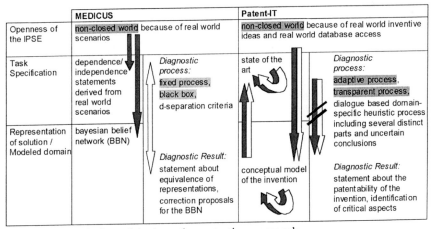

Fig. 3. The evolution of the hypotheses testing approach

4 Summary of the Hypotheses Testing Approach in Different IPSEs

Different domains have led to different realizations of the hypotheses testing approach. Fig. 3 summarizes the differences between IPSEs realized in our working group. The dark arrows indicate the users actions, the white ones, processes of the system. The hypothesis testing approach chosen for Patent-IT is the result of the desire to improve evaluation skills in a real world domain with all its uncertainties. Supported by the IPSE, the learner develops a model of his invention and searches for the relevant state of the art. The next step is for the learner and the system to engage in a critical dialogue in order to cooperatively find clues that the invention was derivable from the state of the art and therefore is not patentable. This conclusion would make it necessary to adjust the model and to restart the process.

References

1. Anderson, J.R. (1993). Rules of Mind. Hillsdale: Erlbaum.
2. Bauer, F.L., Ehler, H., Horsch, A., Möller, B., Partsch, H., Paukner, O., Pepper, P. (1987). The Munich Project CIP, Vol. II: The Program Transformation System CIP-S. Berlin: Springer (LNCS 292).
3. Clarke, E.M., Emerson, F.A. & Sistla, A.P. (1986). Automatic Verification of Finite-State Concurrent Systems Using Temporal Logic Specifications. ACM Transactions on Programming Languages and Systems, Vol. 8, No. 2, 244 - 263
4. Folkers, J., Möbus, C., Schröder, O., Thole, H-J., (1996). An Intelligent Problem Solving Environment for Designing Explanation Models and for Diagnostic Reasoning in Probabilistic Domains, in: C. Frasson, G. Gaulthier, A.Lesgold, Intelligent Tutoring Systems, Proceedings of ITS'96, Montreal, Berlin: Springer, LNCS 1086.
5. Gollwitzer, P.M. (1990). Action Phases and Mind-Sets. In E.T. Higgins, R.M. Sorrentino (eds): Handbook of Motivation and Cognition: Foundations of Social Behavior, 2, 53-92.
6. IBM-Patentserver: http://patent.womplex.ibm.com/
7. Josko, B. (1990). Veryfying the correctness of AADL modules using model checking, in: J.W. de Bakker, W.P. de Roever, G. Rozenberg (eds.), Proceedings REX-Workshop on stepwise refinement of distributed systems: models, formalisms, correctness. Berlin: Springer, LNCS 430, 386-400.
8. Möbus, C. (1995). Towards an Epistemology of Intelligent Problem Solving Environments: The Hypothesis Testing Approach I, in: J. Greer (ed.), Artificial Intelligence in Education, Proceedings of AI-ED 95, Washington, D.C., August 16-19, 1995, Charlottesville: AACE, 138-145.
9. Möbus, C., (1996). Towards an Epistemology on Intelligent Problem Solving Environments: The Hypothesis Testing Approach II, in: Proceedings of EuroAIED 96, Lisbon, Portugal, Sept. 30 - Oct. 2.
10. Möbus, C., Schröder, O. (1997). Building Domain Models by Novices in Stochastics: Towards the Probabilistic Semantics of Verbalized Stochastic Relations, in: B. du Boulay, R. Mizoguchi, Artificial Intelligence in Education: Knowledge and Media in Learning Systems, Amsterdam: IOS Press, pp. 394-401.
11. Newell, A. (1990). Unified Theories of Cognition, Canbridge: Harward Press.
12. Partsch, H.A. (1990). Specification and Transformation of Programs: A Formal Approach to Software Development. Berlin: Springer.
13. Van Lehn, K. (1988). Toward a Theory of Impasse-Driven Learning. In H. Mandl, A. Lesgold (eds): Learning Issues for Intelligent Tutoring Systems. Springer, 19-41.
14. Willms, J., Göhler, H., Möbus, C., (1997). Testing Hypotheses in an Engineering Domain: Combining Static and Dynamic Analysis of Pneumatic Circuits, in: B. Boulay, R. Mizoguchi (eds.): Artificial Intelligence in Education, Amsterdam: IOS-Press, 680-682.
15. Wordnet: http://www.cogsci.princeton.edu/~wn

The Impact of Representation on Coaching Argument Analysis

Violetta Cavalli-Sforza

Center for Biomedical Informatics, University of Pittsburgh
Suite 8084 Forbes Tower, 200 Lothrop Street, Pittsburgh, PA. 15213
violetta@cbmi.upmc.edu

Abstract. Graphical representations have long been associated with more efficient problem solving. More recently, researchers have begun looking at how representation may affect the information that students attend to and what they learn. In this paper we report on a study of how graphical representation may influence interaction between a human coach and a student engaged in analyzing argument texts. We compared coaching interaction with subjects working with a predefined graphical representation to subjects who developed their own representation. The predefined representation, with a better "cognitive fit", to the task, allowed subjects to do more work on their own. Coaching was more systematic and both more efficient and more effective.

1 Introduction

Understanding scientific arguments and scientific controversies is an important aspect of science education even for the non-scientist, and one that has largely been neglected in science school curricula. The Belvedere project, at the University of Pittsburgh's Learning Research and Development Center, sought to develop a computational environment in which students could analyze and construct arguments using a database of short texts drawn from selected scientific debates [1, 2]. Significant attention was devoted to constructing graphical representation for arguments [3] and research was conducted on the use of coaching strategies to help students generate their own arguments [4, 5]. More recently, Suthers [6] began investigating how representations may bias the information attended to, the knowledge expressed, and the learning outcomes in collaborative critical inquiry.

Using an early version of the Belvedere environment, we examined how choice of graphical representation impacts learning of target argument concepts and coaching interaction between a human coach and learners engaged in an argument analysis task. The graphical representations, experimental design, and overall results of the study are discussed in [7]. Here, after briefly reviewing the design and results of that study, we present a detailed analysis of the impact of representation on coaching and conclude by discussing the relevance of the findings to intelligent tutoring systems.

2 Study Design and General Results

Four subjects, non-science major college undergraduates, participated in an extended experiment in which they studied several concepts pertaining to the description, support and critique of causal theories. They analyzed short texts drawn from a historical scientific debate. They drew diagrams representing the information in the texts, either the description of a causal theory or arguments in support of and/or against such a theory. They received coaching from the experimenter throughout diagram construction.

Two subjects (in the FIXED condition) used a predefined box-and-arrow graphical representation that specifically encoded important concepts of scientific argument. Distinct shapes, enclosing text, represented scientific propositions with different statuses (e.g., rectangle = observation, rounded rectangle = explanation). Links with specific names, directionality, and arrowheads provided different types of relationships between propositions and/or other links. The remaining two subjects (in the FREE condition) had similar graphical primitives available but could use them and label them at will, thereby effectively constructing their own graphical representation. FIXED condition subjects studied sample analyses of texts that used the predefined graphical representation. FREE condition subjects viewed the same analyses through a schematic text-based representation in which sentences were labeled by their role (e.g., "premises", "conclusion", "claim", "grounds", and "warrant").

Subjects in the FIXED condition adapted rather easily to the representation they were given. Subjects in the FREE condition went down very different representational paths. One subject (Free-1) developed, rather laboriously, a representation similar to that used in the FIXED condition, although it remained plagued by inconsistencies and other problems throughout the experiment. The other subject (Free-2) drew the causal theory diagrams using a curious mix of analogical and abstract representation (e.g., using 7 shapes to represent 7 continents). Since the chosen representation could not be easily extended to express more abstract content, for texts containing primarily arguments Free-2 fell back on a labeled text strategy similar to the one used in the instructional materials.

Consonant with Suthers' [6] hypotheses, only subjects who used a box-and-arrow abstract representation, (Free-1 and FIXED condition subjects) expressed in their diagrams some of the more complex relational concepts (e.g., multi-step support, dialectical argument patterns), which were realized with distinctive linkage patterns. There was also a link between subjects' use of the concept in the diagram and the ability to give a good definition. The crucial factor underlying these results appeared to be whether the representation used by subjects was *relation-centered*, as box-and-arrow representations are, or *role-centered*, as the labeled-text schema adopted by Free-2 is. These findings point out that it is risky to let students develop their own representation for a task, though it may lead to deeper processing. At best, like Free-1, students will develop a sufficiently expressive representation, but at a significant cost in time, clarity of the resulting work, and attention that could be focused on target instructional concepts. At worst, like Free-2, they may fail to find an adequate representation and consequently may not learn to apply the target concepts.

The second finding of the study, and the focus of this paper, was that a predefined task-appropriate representation, in addition to emphasizing and supporting important instructional concepts, also significantly facilitates coaching. We begin by describing the general coaching approach and the methodology used to code the interaction data for five diagrams, roughly one fourth of the diagrams that subjects drew. We then present results from quantitative and qualitative analyses of coaching, pointing out the key differences between interaction with subjects in the two representation conditions.

3   Coaching Approach

Coaching was provided by the experimenter based on a general mental model of the argument contained in the texts being analyzed. Because there was usually more than one way of representing — and sometimes even interpreting — the content of the text, this approach was deemed more flexible and appropriate than comparing a subject's work to a specific "expert" diagram. For similar reasons, we applied a generally non-interventionist coaching philosophy. The coach waited for the subject to produce at least a partial draft of the analysis before beginning to comment on it, unless the subject appeared to need assistance or specifically requested it. Working from a model was particularly effective with FIXED condition subjects, whose diagrams showed significant overlap with a model that used the same concepts expressed in Belvedere's graphical primitives. With FREE condition subjects, the model had to be even more flexible, in order to allow the coach to map between the subject's representation and the desired analysis and to avoid overly influencing the subject to represent things in a specific way. As a consequence, some of the final FREE condition diagrams deviated more from an ideal analysis than the final diagrams of FIXED condition subjects.

Scaffolding Strategies (SS)	Coaching Strategies (CS)
• Remind subject of goal and progress (L)*	Positive (+): Praise subject's work (L)
• Ask question about a step in the solution (L)	Negative (-): Critique subject's work:
• Suggest a high-level solution plan. (M)	• Signal potential problem (L)
• Provide a limited number of choices (M)	• Suggest information to consider / Signal missing information (M)
• Give hint(s) about solution path(s) (M)	• Criticize subject's work (tell what's wrong) (H)
• Suggest crucial step(s) in solution (H)	• Correct subject's work (give right answer) (H)
• Perform parts of the solution plan (H)	• Explain correction to subject (VH)
• Lead subject through plan steps by asking questions (H)	• Argue with subject (VH)
• Model task for the student (VH)	

* Level of Coach Engagement/Knowledge Required (L – low; M – medium; H – high; VH - very high)

Fig. 1. Summary of scaffolding and coaching strategies

Two classes of strategies were used in providing assistance. Scaffolding strategies were applied when the subject seemed unable to proceed on a task without receiving assistance. Coaching strategies were applied after the subject had produced a (partial) analysis. The strategies employed are shown in Figure 1. The application of scaffolding and coaching strategies was interwoven. For example, a coaching strategy would be used to evaluate the subject's analysis, which would lead the subject to attempt improving the analysis. This would call for a scaffolding strategy to help the subject carry out the improvement. Within the two general classes, individual strategies differ in the amount and type of knowledge required, as well as in the degree of coach engagement in the task. The coach always attempted to begin with low engagement/low knowledge strategies, which require the subject to do more work, and to progress to more demanding strategies only when necessary.

4   Analysis and Coding Methodology

Our approach to analyzing the coaching interaction data overlaps with those developed by Pilkington [8] and Katz *et al.* [9], but reflects the needs of our application. For each diagram, the raw protocol of the interaction (transcribed from videotapes and indexed to the diagrams) was synthesized into an *interaction summary*. First, the protocol was segmented into groups of related utterances by the subject and/or the coach. Each utterance group represents a self-contained thought by one person and abstracts away interruptions and simultaneous speech by the other person that were not extending the original thought in a significant way. The utterance group was then summarized into a *summary utterance*, a single statement that reflects the essential content of the utterance group. One or two summary utterances, taken together, form one *interaction unit*. An interaction unit can include:

- a summary utterance by the subject and one that represents the coach's response
- a summary utterance by the coach with a verbal response or action by the subject
- a summary utterance by the coach alone, for example a comment praising the subject's work.

An example of an interaction unit composed of two summary utterances corresponding to the protocol excerpt in Figure 2 is the following:

S: I'll use an *and* to show the relation between items 1, 2, 3.
C: You should be more specific than *and*. It has to do with time sequence.

S: Okay huh (thinks)   Okay now I wanna say that this *(points to shapes 1, 2, and 3)* broke up, do I just well okay I guess I'll just do another *and*.
C: The fact that the c- the big c- supercontinent broke up S: Hm hm
C: Right and how to link it to the previous one? S: Hm hm
C: Huh is there huh there is yeah there can be an 'and' relationship and I think in this case there can be something a little more specific huh that has to do with the with the time sequence in which the two events happened in which the time relative to...*(subject interrupts)*

Fig. 2. Protocol fragment corresponding to an interaction unit

The summary utterance for the coach abstracts away the two intermediate utterances by the coach, which are only making sure that the coach knows what the subject is referring to. Although the subject is speaking in terms of graphical links (e.g. *and*), the coach is hinting that simple conjunction is not the correct relationship among the statements..

Several interaction units may be grouped into a single interaction group to indicate that they all pertain to a specific issue or topic of discussion. Interaction groups may be nested to show the overall structure of the interaction. The top-level group has a heading describing the main topic of the interaction, with nested interaction group headings giving the various subtopics addressed.

Each interaction unit was also classified on the basis of the primary *content* as well as the communicative *form* of the interaction. The content categories include: rhetorical structure (**Cs**), representation (**Cr**), scientific domain (**Cd**), graphical interface (**Cg**), and meta-topics (**Cm**, mostly concerning general ways of carrying out a task). An interaction unit dealing primarily with the interrelationship of two statements in the domain text was coded as rhetorical structure; an interaction unit dealing primarily with the appropriate link, link name, or linkage pattern to use to represent that relationship in the graph was coded as representation. For example, the interaction unit corresponding to Figure 2 was analyzed as having content "rhetorical structure" and form "hint". The communicative form categories represent different communicative actions used by the coach to help the subject improve his or her graphical analysis of a text. A partial list of categories used is shown in Figure 3.

Fd: remind of prior action	**Fq**: ask question
Fe: explain why	**Fr**: review (progress, definition, etc.)
Fh: hint at characteristics of answer	**Fs**: suggest what, how
Fi: draw attention to	**Ft**: tell what, how
Fn: criticize by saying no/bad/wrong	**Fv**: verify what subject /diagram means
Fp: praising, agreeing	**Q** : question (information seeking, not coaching)

Fig. 3. Coding of Communicative Form of Interaction

5   Quantitative Analysis of Coaching Interaction

The goal of the quantitative analysis of coaching interaction was to characterize differences in the content and form of coaching interventions required by subjects in the two experimental conditions. Differences were noted in both the content and the communicative form of the interaction.

5.1 Content of the Interaction

Table 1 shows the distribution of interaction units over content categories. For each subject, the first row gives the absolute number of interaction units in each category. In the second row, in *italics*, the TOTAL column shows the partial total of interaction units over the three most salient categories: rhetorical structure, representation, and domain. The remaining columns show the percentage of interaction units in each of the three categories with respect to this partial total. There is significant variation among subjects in the number and proportion of interaction units.

Table 1. Distribution of Interaction Units Over Content Types

Subject	Structure	Representation	Domain	Belvedere	Meta	TOTAL
Free-1	81	47	14	18	6	166
	57.0%	33.1%	9.9%	—	—	142
Free-2	101	24	2	17	15	159
	79.5%	18.9%	1.6%	—	—	127
Fixed-1	66	11	8	17	7	109
	77.6%	12.9%	9.4%	—	—	85
Fixed-2	83	17	2	24	1	127
	81.4%	16.7%	1.9%	—	—	102
TOTAL	331	99	26	76	29	561
	72.6%	21.7%	5.7%	—	—	456

The proportion of interaction units for rhetorical structure is similar for all subjects except Free-1, for whom it is lowest, since it competes with other content categories and especially representation. The proportion of interaction units concerned with representation is higher for subjects in the FREE condition than subjects in the FIXED condition. In particular, the number of interaction units is significantly above expected for Free-1, who was actively developing a graphical representation, and below expected for Fixed-1 who, with few exceptions, adapted well to the use of the FIXED representation conventions. Free-2 also has a sizeable proportion of interaction units on the topic of representation, although given the total number of interaction units it is actually below expected value. The results for this subject are skewed by the large number of interaction for one diagram, which account for about one third of the total interaction units, are mostly in the rhetorical structure category, and are caused by an unsuccessful coaching interaction. If that diagram is disregarded, the percentage of interaction units on representation climbs to 32.9% of interactions (23 interactions) in the three main categories.

5.2 Form of the Interaction

Table 2 gives a summary of the interaction units for each subject grouped by form of communicative action and content. The numbers are not large, but this data suggests a number of differences across subjects and conditions.

Subjects in the FREE condition were asked many more questions by the coach (category **Fq**) in the course of coaching, in order to elicit from them the relationships in the rhetorical structure of the text they were trying to represent. Questions in this category were usually related to the implementation of one of the scaffolding strategies. In addition, the coach needed to ask Free-2 a number of questions in order to understand what the diagrams meant (**Q**). Subjects in the FREE condition were also told what to do (**Ft**) more often than subjects in the FIXED condition, who received suggestions (**Fs**) more often. Both are examples of scaffolding strategies. Subjects in the FREE condition received more reminders (**Fd**) about their previous work, mostly regarding the use of the representation. Reminders implemented both coaching (criticizing) and scaffolding (hinting) strategies.

Table 2. Interaction Unit By Subject, Content and Communicative Action

Encoding	Fr-1			Fr-2			Fx-1			Fx-2			Tot
	Cs	Cr	Cd	Cs	Cr	Cd	Cs	Cr	Cd	Cs	Cr	Cd	
Fd	1	4		1									6
Fe	3	6		6	7		3	3		9		1	38
Fh	2	1		6			3		1	7	1		21
Fi	8	5	2	4			6	1	2	8	1		37
Fr	3			9			1			2			15
Fq	22	2	5	23	2		7			10	1		72
Fs	4	9	1	3			4	1		7	4		33
Ft	7	4		9	2	1	3	1	1	1	2		31
Fv	2			6	4		7			9			28
Q	3	3		10	5		4		1	4			30
Tot	81	47	14	101	24	2	66	11	8	83	17	2	456

LEGEND: Cs = rhetorical structure, **Cr** = representation, **Cd** = domain

The coach verified (**Fv**, coaching) subjects' intentions more often in the FIXED condition, asking the subjects if what they drew was really what they meant and signaling, in a non-directive low-engagement way, that there was a problem with the diagram. A similarly low-engagement way of signaling a problem was just to draw attention to a point in the diagram (**Fi**, coaching). It was often sufficient to get the subject to correct the problem, and was used more frequently and successfully with subjects who had drawn detailed diagrams (Free-1, Fixed-1, and Fixed-2).

The general picture painted by Tables 1 and 2 is that the FIXED representation required less interaction, allowed subject and coach to focus on rhetorical structure, and resulted in more coaching of subject work and less scaffolding to get the work done. Both scaffolding and coaching strategies used with subjects in the FIXED condition were less directive and required lower coach engagement. This conclusion was supported by a qualitative analysis of the coaching interaction.

6 Qualitative Analysis of Coaching Interaction

In addition to the detailed quantitative analysis of coaching actions described above, we examined more qualitatively the interaction over a larger number of diagrams and compared the characteristics of the interaction between subjects in the same experimental condition and between experimental conditions.

6.1 Coaching in the FIXED Condition

Although not all the final diagrams for subjects in the FIXED representation condition were error-free, the diagrams were mostly quite good. The fault for lingering imperfections rested with the coach who either forgot to or chose not to pursue problems further. One feature of the coaching interaction that was striking and common to FIXED subjects was the overall efficiency of the communication, especially when compared to the interaction with Free-1. In all but one instance for each subject, diagrams had only very localized problems, requiring changes to individual elements of the diagram and little coaching. The coach could usually just point out that there was a problem, or indicate the general nature of the problem (is that shape right, should the link start there?), and the subject could fix the problem quickly, often without further help. In some cases, subjects found the problem on their own simply by reading over the diagram. If further coaching was needed, it mostly required hinting.

The interaction with Fixed-1 was very synthetic and to the point. Coaching tended to be very non-directive, hinting at the existence and nature of a problem but leaving most of the changes up to the subject. Fixed-2 was a little more hesitant and exhibited more trouble with applying some of the instructional concepts. However, although the interaction with this subject was somewhat longer, it was characterized by the same overall efficiency and effectiveness.

6.2 Coaching in the FREE Condition

Subjects in the FREE condition differed from each other as much as, if not more than, they differed from Fixed-1 and Fixed-2. They were, however, similar in that they both required significant interaction to clarify the representation they were developing. Unstable and insufficiently expressive representations made coaching more difficult and not always effective.

For Free-1, the coaching interaction was less clearly separable into short distinct episodes and mostly occurred during construction of the initial diagram. Although Free-1, like the FIXED condition subjects, used a box-and-arrow type of representation, many of the links did not correspond to FIXED representation links (especially in causal theory diagrams), nor were shapes used in the same way. This subject was not always explicit or consistent in his use of the representation, so the coach could not always evaluate and correct the diagrams by referring to a canonical model. Free-1 encountered substantial difficulties in choosing the level of representation (choosing the primary objects to represent as shapes), especially in diagramming causal theories, and appeared to be resistant to coaching. On several occasions, when the coach was trying to explain or suggest something, Free-1 interrupted to propose one or more alternative solutions, disregarded interventions from the coach or insisted on a particular way of doing things, and read the diagram over and over to check the representation. As a result, the coaching process was less effective, the protocols were very extensive, and each diagram took a relatively long time to construct. Protracted interactions were, at times, extremely frustrating for the coach, although the subject did seem to genuinely enjoy the task.

Free-2 mixed direct and abstract representations in diagrams describing a causal theory. In these diagrams, interaction often concerned representation and was necessary in order for the coach to understand the representation and verify that the diagram correctly represented the content of the text. In diagrams of texts containing primarily arguments, Free-2 stopped using box-and-arrow graphics altogether and coaching addressed rhetorical structure almost exclusively. With two notable exceptions, coaching interactions with Free-2 tended to be brief; this was due, in large part, to the low level of detail in this subject's analysis of texts. Free-2's diagrams were very synthetic relative to the ones drawn by other subjects. The coach attempted to induce this subject to show information at a greater level of detail, especially information that showed the relationship of different texts and portions of texts to each other. In some cases, however, Free-2 had difficulty diagramming rhetorical relationships due to the limitations of the representation.

FREE condition subjects ran into serious problems only at a few points in the construction of their diagrams. However, unlike for FIXED condition subjects, coaching was not always successful. For Free-1, a coaching failure occurred while trying to develop a representation for describing causal theories; for Free-2, coaching failed catastrophically when this subject was unable to capture the argument structure of a text by applying and extending the representation.

7 Summary and Conclusions

In the last few years computational environments for teaching argumentation and critical inquiry skills have been developed (e.g., [3, 10, 11]). In some of these environments, the argument is represented in an external artifact, using a graph or some other type of representational scheme (e.g., containers, matrix). Suthers [6] hypothesizes that these external abstractions provide: 1) cognitive support, by helping learners "see", internalize, and keep track of complex relations; 2) collaborative support, by providing shared objects of perception that coordinate group work by serving as referential objects and status reminders; and 3) evaluative support for mentors, by giving a basis for assessing learners' understanding of scientific inquiry, as well as of subject matter. He further proposes that representation may bias the information attended to, the knowledge expressed, and learning outcomes.

In this paper, we have presented some findings concerning the impact of representation choice on coaching argument analysis. Our findings support Suthers' hypotheses. Representations with a good "cognitive fit" for the task provide cognitive support, resulting in analyses of arguments that apply instructional concepts, are clearer and more correct, and express information at the right level of detail for the task. They provide collaborative and evaluative support, even when the collaborators are a learner and a coach, by supporting a more efficient and effective coaching interaction, allowing the learner to do more of the work and requiring less engagement from the coach. Such representations are also not easy to develop, and the deeper understanding that learners may gain by trying to develop a suitable representation is likely to be offset by the increased difficulty in communicating with another agent, be it another learner or a coach, a human being or a machine.

These findings are important for computer-assisted coaching of argumentation, since the capabilities of automated coaches, especially in complex and hard-to-formalize domains, are still well behind those of a human coach. Even an automated coach, with limited domain knowledge but with a good knowledge of argument and communicating with a learner through an adequately expressive and mutually well-understood representation, has some chance of providing useful advice. In contrast, a computer coach that shares with a learner a poorly understood or inadequate representation, be it natural language or a diagrammatic representation, is even less likely than a human coach to achieve a successful coaching interaction.

Acknowledgments

This research was funded under National Science foundation grant MDR-9155715. We gratefully acknowledge the supervision of Dr. Alan Lesgold and the contributions of J. Connelly, M. Paolucci, D. Suthers and A. Weiner.

References

1. Cavalli-Sforza, V., Moore, J.D., Suthers, D.D.: Helping students articulate and criticize scientific explanations. In: Brna, P., Ohlsson, S., Pain, H. (eds.): Proceedings of AI-ED 93, World Conference on Artificial Intelligence in Education (1993) 113-120
2. Suthers, D., Weiner, A, Connelly, J., Paolucci, M.: Belvedere: Engaging students in critical discussions of science and public policy issues. In: Proceedings AI-ED 95, World Conference on Artificial Intelligence in Education (1995)
3. Suthers, D.D., Cavalli-Sforza, V.: Issues in graphical media for evaluating and debating scientific theories. In: Cox, R., Petre, M., Brna, P., Lee, J. (eds.): Proceedings of the Workshop on Graphical Representations, Reasoning, and Communication. AI-ED 93, World Conference on Artificial Intelligence in Education. (1993) 5-8
4. Paolucci, M., Suthers, D.D., Weiner, A.: Automated advice-giving strategies for scientific inquiry. In: Frasson, C., Gauthier, G., Lesgold, A. (eds.): Intelligent Tutoring Systems, Third International Conference. Lecture Notes In Computer Science. Springer-Verlag, New York, NY (1996) 372-381
5. Toth, J.A., Suthers, D.D., Weiner, A.: Providing expert advice in the domain of collaborative scientific inquiry. In: du Boulay, B., Mizoguchi, R. (eds.): Proceedings AI-ED 97, World Conference of the Artificial Intelligence in Education Society. IOS Press, Amsterdam (1997)
6. Suthers, D.D.: Representational bias as guidance for learning interactions: A research agenda. In: Lajoie, S.P., Vivet, M. (eds.): Proceedings of AI-ED 99, World Conference of the Artificial Intelligence in Education Society IOS Press, Amsterdam (1999) 121-128
7. Cavalli-Sforza, V.: Constructed vs. received representations for scientific argument: Implications for learning and coaching. In: Proceedings of The Twenty-First Annual Conference of the Cognitive Science Society (1999) 108-113
8. Pilkington, R.M.: Analyzing educational discourse: The DISCOUNT scheme. Technical Report No. 019703, Computer Based Learning Unit, University of Leeds, Leeds, UK (1997)
9. Katz, S., O'Donnell, G., Kay, H.: An approach to coding educational dialogues for descriptive and prescriptive purposes. In: Proceedings of the AI-ED 99 Workshop on Analyzing Educational Dialogue Interaction: Towards Models that Support Learning. IOS Press, Amsterdam (1999) 22-32
10. Pilkington, R.M., Hartley, J.R., Hintze, D.: Learning to argue and arguing to learn: An interface for computer-based dialogue games. Journal of Artificial Intelligence in Education 3(3) (1992) 275-295
11. Bouwer, A.: ArgueTrack: Computer support for educational argumentation. In: Lajoie, S.P., Vivet M. (eds.): Proceedings of AI-ED 99, World Conference of the Artificial Intelligence in Education Society. IOS Press, Amsterdam (1999) 121-128

Bringing Scrutability
to Adaptive Hypertext Teaching

Marek Czarkowski and Judy Kay

Department of Computer Science
University of Sydney
AUSTRALIA
marek,judy@cs.usyd.edu.au

Abstract. There is considerable appeal in using adaptive hypertext for teaching. It should provide the teacher with the possibility of creating teaching materials which can be customised to match the individual student's background and preferences.

This paper describes ADAPT-Tutor, a scrutable adaptive hypertext system. This enables the learner to scrutinise the system to determine how the document was adapted. They are also able to control the adaptation by altering the student model at any time in the interaction. The student can see which parts of the student model have been used to control aspects which appear in the document.

The system has three major parts: ADAPT for authoring; Tutor for the student interface; and ATML is the language used for adaptive hypertext source documents. This paper describes the student view, in Tutor, especially the scrutability support.

We describe the use of ADAPT-Tutor in a large first year course. The paper discusses the use made of the scrutability support.

1 Introduction

There has been considerable interest in using adaptive hypertext for teaching, for example [2] [17]. There are many dimensions of individualisation in adaptive hypertexts [4] since they can be individualised in content as well as navigation. There have also been some positive evaluations of their teaching effectiveness [9].

From the point of view of a teacher creating hypertext material, the appeal of adaptivity is that one can provide material that is well suited to some students but not to others. At the same time the multiple paths for different students are managed within a single framework. For example, consider the case where we teach the programming language C. If some students know Pascal, we might wish to point out, and build upon, the similarities between the two languages. Importantly, we might point out conceptual clashes between the languages and particular problems for Pascal programmers learning C. On a quite different level, some students may prefer to learn C in terms of mathematical examples, while others would prefer text handling examples and yet others might like examples relating to unix system internals. The author of an adaptive hypertext can take advantage of all these possibilities. Moreover, system support for building adaptive documents makes this more manageable and elegant than conventional hypertext can be [13]. In particular, we may wish to perform adaptations at any level of granularity from the word or link up to larger blocks of a document.

Previous work on adaptive hypertext has provided learners with customised learning materials. However, when the learner sees an arbitrary page of the hypertext, they have no way of knowing how it was customised. This paper addresses the learner's question,

– How was this teaching material adapted to *me*?

Continuing our example, above, the detailed set of questions a student might ask includes:

– Which aspects are based on my knowing Pascal?
– How would the teaching material look if the system believed I did not know Pascal?
– What other things might it have shown me, but it did not because it treated them as irrelevant to me?

We describe a hypertext as *scrutable* if the learner can explore the interface to find answers to questions such as these.

Why bother with scrutability? There are several reasons which motivate us to explore ways to build scrutable systems. First, there is merit making systems available to the user. As Fischer argues, there is good reason to make complex systems comprehensible [10]. In a teaching context, it has been argued that this can give the learner a greater sense of control [11]. It is also closely related to the arguments for making a learner model accessible to student. This has been discussed by many researchers including, for example, Self [16], Bull and colleagues [1], and others [8] [6] [15].

Our focus on scrutability of adaptive hypertext is a logical extension of our work on um, a toolkit for scrutable user and student modelling [12]. In um, we took care to represent the learner model in a form which enables the learner to scrutinise it, seeing what the system believes about them and how those beliefs were derived.

The ADAPT-Tutor system is an exploration of scrutable adaptive hypertext. The hypertext author uses ADAPT-Tutor's editing tools to create adaptive lessons. The ADAPT editor supports the author creating hypertext pages in the language ATML, a markup to HTML 4.0 which conforms to XML 1.0. Later the student can use the Tutor interface to make use of the teaching materials. The ADAPT-Tutor tools and the teaching materials implemented by Czarkowski are described in more detail in [7]. The work, especially the interface design, has been strongly influenced by the ELM-ART system [17] [3] which teaches LISP.

2 Addition of Adaptive Elements

As a first stage in exploring scrutable adaptive hypertext, ADAPT-Tutor was used to create an enhanced form of a single chapter of material used for a first year computer science course [14]. Since the author of that chapter had to commit to paper, they had to settle for a single form of the material. The material was important for one of the two major practical tasks of the semester. The main sections from the first part of the material are shown in Fig. 1, a course map which we will discuss in the next section.

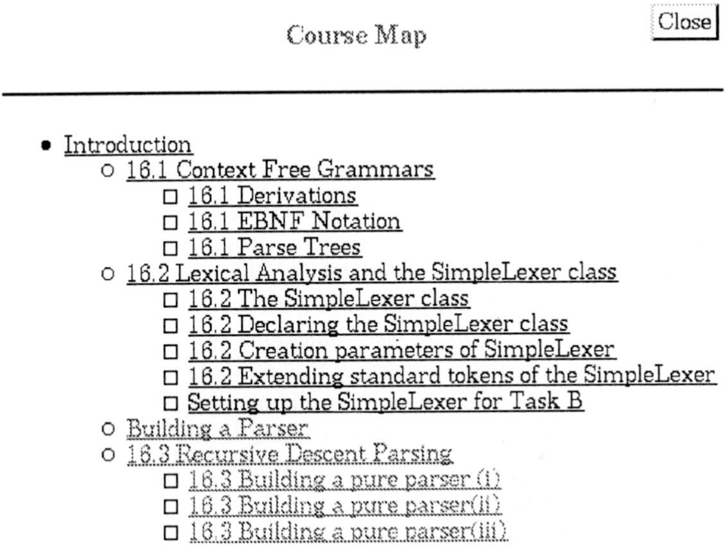

Course Map · Close

- Introduction
  - o 16.1 Context Free Grammars
    - □ 16.1 Derivations
    - □ 16.1 EBNF Notation
    - □ 16.1 Parse Trees
  - o 16.2 Lexical Analysis and the SimpleLexer class
    - □ 16.2 The SimpleLexer class
    - □ 16.2 Declaring the SimpleLexer class
    - □ 16.2 Creation parameters of SimpleLexer
    - □ 16.2 Extending standard tokens of the SimpleLexer
    - □ Setting up the SimpleLexer for Task B
  - o Building a Parser
  - o 16.3 Recursive Descent Parsing
    - □ 16.3 Building a pure parser (i)
    - □ 16.3 Building a pure parser (ii)
    - □ 16.3 Building a pure parser (iii)

Fig. 1. Course map

This paper describes our experiments in creating an interesting class of adaptive hypertext document. This is the translation of paper-based teaching materials to hypertext, with enhancements based on the possibility of adding optional parts to the text. The original author of the text had to decide on their compromise audience. This is based upon their own model of the 'average' student's background and preferences. With an adaptive hypertext, we could accommodate a broader range of students, catering to their differences. The material had the following adaptive enhancements:

- self-test questions;
- suggestions for exercises;
- gentler lead in material for each of the major ideas;
- customisation based on which of the practical tasks the student was doing (the course offered some choice);
- additional references or background.

These represent a very interesting range of optional additions which characterise classes of adaptivity that seem promising for improved teaching. Some allow for gentler presentations. Others support students in doing self-assessment as they read material: these could well feed into a student model. The customisation to the student's task means that examples and text can be made to fit the student's learning context better. Also, the student's choice of task may reflect a preference to learn within the domain of that task: this is the reason for offering students such as choice of tasks. Fortunately, our level of adaptivity has quite modest student modelling requirements. In fact, we decided to keep the current series of experiments simple, by making use of a student model which was purely based on user answers to a small set of questions about these factors.

3   Overview of **ADAPT-Tutor**

Students interact with the Tutor interface of ADAPT-Tutor. They first register with Tutor and they can work through a familiarisation tutorial which explains the facilities of Tutor. On starting a new teaching unit, they are asked questions which establish their initial student model (profile). The questions asked are determined by the definitions created by the hypertext author, who provides questions like: *Would you like to be asked questions to test your understanding?* and corresponding the possible answers, in this case, *Yes* or *No*.

Next, students see an interface with teaching material like that shown in Fig. 2. The icons across the top offer various facilities, including the course map shown in Fig. 1. The others give a teacher's news page, a notes editor, glossary, the personal profile, discussion room, log out and, at the far right, help.

The bulk of the material on the page is the text of the section that the student has just accessed, which is Section 16.2 in the example of Fig. 2.

3.1   Navigation

The user can proceed through the material by selecting the right arrow at the end of each page. This takes the student through the default route. Alternately, the student can select the course map and then click on any of the topics to move to it. This follows the general approach of systems like ELM-ART [5] by using colour to indicate recommended parts of the hypertext. Green is used to code pages which the student is ready to read and red for those the student is not ready for. The difference is determined by preconditions for each page. Pages which have already been visited are shown in black. Since the map appears in its own window, the student can keep it on the screen while they work through the hypertext document.

3.2   Explanation of adaptation

At the very bottom of each page of teaching material is a link, *How was this page adapted to you?*. As in Fig. 2 this is below the navigation arrows and a horizontal line. The message appears in blue, distinguishing it from other links on the page. When the student selects it, the bottom of the page expands to

16.2 The SimpleLexer class

The SimpleLexer class is used perform lexical analysis, that is, to read characters from input and group these characters into tokens like

```
left-par, String, plus, left-par, Integer, mul, Real, right-par, left-par
```

All you then have to do is to use these tokens to build an expression tree. Using a technique called Recursive descent parsing this turns out to be quite straight forward.

However, we first need to learn how to create and set up an instance of the SimpleLexer class.

How was this page adapted to you?

Fig. 2. Example of adapted teaching material

summarise the adaptations on that page. If there has been no adaptation, this is indicated with the message *There was no adaptation of this page.*

Where there has been adaptation, the bottom of the screen expands to show a screen like that in Fig. 3. In this case, there are two sets of adaptation on the page. The first caused material to be excluded because the student answered *no* to the question *Would you like to see suggestions for exercise questions?*. The second caused material to be *included* because the student had answered *yes* to the question *Would you like to be asked question to test your understanding?*. The line *Inclusion value* indicates the answer that was required for a part of the material to be included. The next line, with *Your value*, shows what the student answered. In general, each adapted aspect of the page causes a separate entry in the adaptation explanation section.

If the user clicks on the text *[highlight]* the interface indicates the part of the page controlled. If the adaptation involved omission of material, as in the first case in Fig. 3, Tutor moves the display to the point where the additional material might have been placed and shows the message *...content removed here....* Although it would have been quite feasible to show the actual content that had been omitted, this was not necessary: it is easy for the user to alter their profile and see how that affects the document. If the user selected *[highlight]* for an aspect that was included, as in the second case in Fig. 3, Tutor highlights the background of the relevant material in yellow. (This has been done in Fig. 3 - it appears as the subtle, hatched grey background in this paper.)

How was this page adapted to you?   (see help)

- **excluded** [highlight] [un–highlight]
  Condition: Would you like to see suggestions for exercise questions?
  Inclusion value: yes
  Your value: no
- **included** [highlight] [un–highlight]
  Condition: Would you like to be asked questions to test your understanding?
  Inclusion value: yes
  Your value: yes

[hide explanation]

Fig. 3. Example of adaptation explanations expanded

Your profile

Would you like to be asked questions to test your understanding of the material?
⦿ yes
◯ no

Would you like to see suggestions for exercise questions?
⦿ yes
◯ no

Would you like to be shown easy/lead up material?

(Lead up material will prepare you for the textbook material, hopefully making it easier
to understand)
⦿ yes
◯ no

Which TaskB project are you doing?
◯ B1: A spreadsheet
⦿ B2: A query interface to tabular data
◯ other

Fig. 4. Example of a profile display

Once the user has examined the explanations of the adaptations, they can select *[hide explanation]* at the bottom of the screen, causing the display to revert to the usual form as in Fig. 2. This reduces the clutter of the explanations and the distraction from the main learning task.

At any stage, the user can see their profile and alter it via a screen like that in Fig. 4.

4 Trials with ADAPT-Tutor

The main trial of ADAPT-Tutor has been in the second semester of a large first year course. The whole class of about 600 students was mailed an invitation to try Tutor. The system encouraged them to use their system login name for Tutor but there was no checking possible. In all 113 users registered, ostensibly 108 as students in the course and 6 as teaching staff. Note that the web interface suggested that students use their normal login name. We had no way to check if they did so and some certainly chose humorous and other odd names that were not those for any account. It mat be that they wanted to maintain anonymity.

A summary of log data is shown in Table 1. The first row indicates that the average number of logins per user was 3.5, with the median being 2 and the standard deviation 3.4. The range of logins was 0 to 18 and 65% of users used it more than once. Inspection of the log indicates some of this activity was due to problems with the browser where cookies were not enabled. Also, some students were regularly checking the *Discussion Room*. The zero values correspond to users who registered but never logged in (mainly because of browser problems or disabled cookies). The second row of the table shows corresponding levels of use for the course map.

Table 1. Summary of log data

	Average	Median	STD	range	%age of larger use
logins	3.5	2	3.4	0 - 18	65 > once
use course map	4.8	0	17.2	0 - 125	34 > once
open profile	1.4	1	1.1	0 - 7	28 > once
expand adapted	1.0	1	3.0	0 - 22	29 >= 1

The third row shows the number of accesses to the student model. Entry to a Tutor teaching document takes the student to this page. So all students who made use of the teaching material had at least one access to it. The log indicates that 28% of users returned to the profile at least once more. Analysis of the student profiles indicates that 84% answered *yes* to the question, *Would you like to be asked questions to test your understanding of the material?*, 85% answered *yes* to the question, *Would you like to be shown easy/lead up material?*, and to *Would you like to see suggestions for exercise questions?* and 80% answered *yes* to the question, *Would you like to see references to background material or other teaching resources?*. Overall the picture that emerged was of two types of student: the majority matched a stereotype which preferred all the optional material, while a minority stereotype elected for the basic minimum form of the material. So, although in theory, there were 48 (2 x 2 x 2 x 2 x 3) different models, these two stereotypes dominated.

The final row of the table shows the level of use of the explanations of the adaptation. This facility was clearly not used heavily. However, 29% of users made at least once use of it. Examining the logs, it turns out that many of these selections were for pages which had no adaptation. Even so, of those who sought explanations, 27% went on to select a *[highlight]* link to see what had been adapted.

The Tutor interface also allowed users to leave free-form comments. Overall, these were few but very positive about Tutor, the teaching materials, the adaptivity and the support for scrutability.

5   Discussion and conclusions

Adaptive hypertext is a promising teaching medium because it offers the author a chance to cater for the different needs of students. It means that an author can create a single meta-hypertext which will be combined with an individual student model to produce an individualised hypertext learning document.

Our trials of Tutor indicate that a substantial minority of students explored the explanations of adaptation: 29% examined the adaptivity and 27% of these users went further, checking the actual parts of the hypertext page affected by the adaptation. This level of interest is quite high, given that the students saw Tutor as offering additional assistance for a challenging part of the current course work. Their focus was, naturally, on learning. Any time devoted to exploring the adaptation was a distraction from that main task.

The student model in our trial was quite modest. It had just five components. Even, so, this is actually an interesting model. It includes components which select optional extra material: questions to test understanding; suggestions for exercises; easy/lead up material; and additional references. It also includes alternate material, based upon which of the tasks the student is doing. For the material in the lesson of the trial, we did not feel the need for different material based upon the student's previous knowledge. Even so, this would operate in the same ways: either as optional additional material or as a set of alternate versions of the material. Perhaps more important, the author of a meta-hypertext has a challenging task in managing the intellectual load of the many possible versions of their hypertext. We can expect that in any small but coherent teaching document, it will be possible to achieve interesting and useful adaptation with a quite modest student model.

One simplified element in our trial was that the system only defined the student model values from the actual input given by the student. This means that the student is in very strict control of the student model. It may be interesting to update the student model on the basis of the student's answers to self-assessment questions. This option would have violated the spirit of other self-assessment material in the course. In future, we will explore including this source of student modelling information, perhaps optionally.

The Tutor interface adapts at several levels:

- The course map uses colour to indicate parts of the hypertext that the student has visited (black), parts they are deemed ready to visit (green) and parts that involve concepts the student seems not to have met yet (red). As the student moves through the hypertext document, the map dynamically changes to reflect the current situation.
- Parts of the text are hidden from the student, based on the values in the student profile.
- Parts can be displayed under the control of the student profile.
- Links from the current material can also be displayed or not, on the basis of the student profile.
- Alternative teaching material can be set up (in our case, this was done to make the text mesh with the task the student had selected).

The granularity of adaptation can operate at the finest details, such as a word or phrase, up to large blocks of teaching material.

The student cannot scrutinise the red-green definitions in the course map: the current implementation does not enable the student to see the conditions which control the colour selection. However, the simple highlighting mechanism does enable the student to scrutinise all the other adaptations listed above. It is mainly useful for the scrutiny of adaptation at the fine-grain.

Tutor also allows the student control these adaptations by altering the student profile. This approach can be used for *what-if* experiments, enabling the student to see what Tutor would do if they answered questions differently. When a student does this, they can scrutinise the effect of the large grain-size.

The notion of scrutable, adaptive hypertext has considerable appeal. It offers learner control well beyond that available in conventional hypertext. At the same time, it offers the advantages of adaptivity, where the learner can set their student model and see a consistent set of hypertext teaching resources, generated from that model. It also makes the learner aware of the adaptation, at a global and detailed level. It offers a coherent and elegant structure for the author of the adaptive, individualised teaching material. The current trial of ADAPT-Tutor demonstrates interesting, useful, though modest adaptation and represents a foundation for continuing work in supporting and delivering scrutable, adaptive hypertext.

References

1. Bull, S., Brna, P., Pain, H.: Extending the scope of the student model. User Modeling and User-Adapted Interaction. **5**:1 (1995) 44–65
2. Brusilovsky, P., Pesin, L., Zyryanov, M.: Towards an adaptive hypermedia component for an intelligent learning environment. In: Bass, L., Gornostaev, J,

Unger, C. (eds.): Human-Computer Interaction, Lecture Notes in Computer Science. Springer-Verlag, Berlin (1993) 348–358

3. Brusilovsky, P., Schwarz, P., Weber, G.: ELM-ART: an intelligent tutoring system on the World Wide Web. In: Frasson, C., Gauthier, G., Lesgold, A. (eds.): Proceedings of the Third International Conference on Intelligent Tutoring Systems, ITS-96. Springer, Berlin (1996) 261–269

4. Brusilovsky, P.: Methods and techniques of adaptive hypermedia. User Modeling and User-Adapted Interaction. 6:2-3. Kluwer (1996) 87–129

5. Brusilovsky, P.: Adaptive hypertext: an attempt to analyse and generalise. In: Brusilovsky, P., Kommers, P., Streitz, N.: Multimedia, Hypermedia and Virtual Reality Models, Systems and Applications. Springer (1996) 288-304

6. Corbett, A.T., Anderson, J.: Knowledge tracing: modeling the acquisition of procedural knowledge. User Modeling and User-Adapted Interaction. 4 (1995) 253–278

7. Czarkowski, M.: An adaptive hypertext teaching system. Honours Thesis, Basser Dept of Computer Science, University of Sydney (1998)

8. Crawford, K., Kay, J.: Metacognitive processes and learning with intelligent educational systems. In: Slezak, P., Caelli, T., Clark, R., Perspectives on Cognitive Science, Ablex (1993) 63-77

9. Eklund, J., Brusilovsky, P.: The value of adaptivity in hypermedia learning environments: a short review of empirical evidence. Proceedings of the the Ninth ACM Conference on Hypertext and Hypermedia. ACM, Pittsburgh (1998) 11–17

10. Fischer, G., Ackerman, D.: The importance of models in making complex systems comprehensible. In: Tauber, M.: Mental models and Human-computer Interaction 2. Elsevier (1991) 22–33

11. Höök, K., Karlgren, J., Waern, A., Dahlbeck, N., Jansson, C.G., Lemaire, B.: A glass box approach to adaptive hypermedia. User Modeling and User-Adapted Interaction 6:2-3 Kluwer (1996) 157–184

12. Kay, J.: The um toolkit for cooperative user modelling. User Modeling and User-Adapted Interaction. 4:3 Kluwer (1995) 149–196

13. Kay, J., Kummerfeld, R.J.: User models for customized hypertext. In: Mayfield, J., Nicholas, C.: Advances in hypertext for the World Wide Web. Springer Verlag (1997) 47–69

14. Kingston, J.: An introduction to computer programming with Blue, second edition. Basser Department of Computer Science, University of Sydney, Australia (1998)

15. Paiva, A., Self, J., Hartley, R.: Externalising learner models. Proceedings of World Conference on Artificial Intelligence in Education. AACE, Washington (1995) 509–516

16. Self, J.: Bypassing the Intractable Problem of Student Modelling: Invited paper. Proceedings of the 1st International Conference on Intelligent Tutoring Systems. Montreal (1988) 18–24

17. Weber, G.: Adaptive learning systems in the World Wide Web. In: Kay, J. (ed.): Proceedings of UM99: Seventh International Conference on User Modeling. Springer-Verlag, Wein, New York (1997) 371–378

ITS Tools for Natural Language Dialogue: A Domain-Independent Parser and Planner

Reva Freedman, Carolyn Penstein Rosé, Michael A. Ringenberg, and
Kurt VanLehn*

Learning Research and Development Center
University of Pittsburgh
Pittsburgh, PA 15260
{freedrk, rosecp, mringenb, vanlehn}@pitt.edu
http://www.pitt.edu/~circle

Abstract. The goal of the Atlas project is to increase the opportunities for students to construct their own knowledge by conversing (in typed form) with a natural language-based ITS. In this paper we describe two components of Atlas—APE, the integrated planning and execution system at the heart of Atlas, and CARMEL, the natural language understanding component. These components have been designed as domain-independent rule-based software, with the goal of making them both extensible and reusable. We illustrate the use of CARMEL and APE by describing Atlas-Andes, a prototype ITS built with Atlas using the Andes physics tutor as the host.

1 Motivation

The goal of the Atlas project is to enable the involvement of students in a more active style of learning by engaging them in a typed dialogue with an ITS. This dialogue can include both natural language and GUI actions. In this paper we motivate the use of dialogue in intelligent tutoring. We also describe resources developed on the Atlas project that are available for use on tutoring projects interested in including dialogue capabilities in their applications. The two key domain-independent components described here are APE, the Atlas Planning Engine, and CARMEL, the natural language understanding component. APE is a "just-in-time" planner specialized for easy construction and rapid generation of hierarchically organized dialogues. CARMEL is a general purpose engine for language understanding composed of robust and efficient algorithms for parsing, semantic interpretation, and repair. We explain how we used these components to build a prototype for a new tutor, Atlas-Andes, that adds a dialogue capability to the existing Andes physics tutor.

---
* This research was supported by NSF grant number 9720359 to CIRCLE, the Center for Interdisciplinary Research on Constructive Learning Environments at the University of Pittsburgh and Carnegie-Mellon University.

Collaborative dialogue between student and tutor is a well-documented prominent component of effective human tutoring [1–3]. A recent corpus study of reflective follow-up dialogues [4] demonstrates the potential for natural language
dialogue to enhance the ability of tutoring systems to effectively diagnose student misconceptions. Furthermore, recent research on student self-explanations
supports the view that when students express their thinking in words it enhances their learning [5, 6]. Students learn more effectively when they are forced
to construct knowledge for themselves.

Without natural language dialogue, the best remediation tools available to
tutoring systems are hint sequences. Hints are a unidirectional form of natural
language: the student can't take the initiative or ask a question. In addition, there
is no way for the system to lead the student through a multi-step directed line of
reasoning or to ask the student a question, except via a list of pre-coded answers.
As a result, there is no way to use some of the effective rhetorical methods used
by skilled human tutors, such as analogy and *reductio ad absurdum*. Thus, the
use of natural language dialogue allows us to extend the tutor's repertoire to
include the types of remediation subdialogues seen in corpus studies.

An elevator slows to a stop from an
initial downward velocity of 10 ms in
2 sec. A passenger in the elevator is
holding a 3 kg package by a string.
What is the tension in the string?

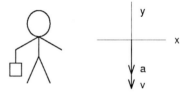

Fig. 1. Sample problem from the Andes physics tutor

2   Natural Language Dialogue in Atlas-Andes

Atlas-Andes is a dialogue-extended version of the Andes [7] tutoring system using
the capabilities offered by the Atlas tool set. Andes is an ITS whose domain is
first-year college physics. It tracks the student as the latter attempts to solve
a problem. If the student gets stuck or deviates too far from a correct solution
path, it provides hints and other assistance. The left-hand side of Fig. 1 shows
a typical Andes problem with its accompanying drawing. On the right is seen
the student's partially completed free-body diagram, or sketch of the vectors
involved.

In this example, the elevator is decelerating, so the acceleration vector should
face the opposite direction from the velocity vector.[1] Andes responds to this
frequent student error by turning the incorrect item red. If requested, it will

---

[1] If the acceleration vector went in the same direction as the velocity vector, the
elevator would speed up and smash into the ground.

provide the first hint of a sequence, in this case "Think about the direction of the acceleration vector." Follow-up hints include further information about the direction of acceleration and, eventually, the answer. The prototype Atlas-Andes system replaces these hints by a choice of generated subdialogues, such as the one shown in Fig. 2.

```
S: <draws acceleration vector in same direction as velocity>
T: What is the definition of acceleration?
S: I don't have any clue.
T: OK, let's try this. If a car was driving along east, which way would
   you have to push on it to make it stop?
S: West.
T: Exactly, the opposite direction. What does that tell you about the
   direction of acceleration?
S: It goes west too.
T: Right. The net force goes the opposite direction, and so does the
   acceleration. Try to draw the acceleration vector again now.
S: <draws acceleration vector correctly>
```

Fig. 2. Example of generated dialogue

This example shows some prominent features of both APE and CARMEL. From the planning point of view, after the student's initial response, Atlas-Andes was able to drop an unpromising line of attack and try a different one. Later, it was able to give specific responses to statements by the student. From the language understanding point of view, we can see that Andes-Atlas can effectively interpret student responses, even idioms like "I don't have a clue."

3   Implementation of a Prototype Tutor

In this section we describe how a pre-existing tutoring system can be extended to offer dialogue capabilities using Atlas. Figure 3 illustrates the architecture of the resulting extended system. While we focus our discussion on the prototype Atlas-Andes system, the same approach could be used to add dialogue capabilities to a wide range of tutoring systems. In Fig. 3 we see that students interact with the dialogue-extended system through the User Interface Manager, which interprets mouse clicks and key presses. GUI actions are then channeled through the GUI Interpreter which interprets them and stores a representation of the interpreted input for the Tutorial Planner (APE), described in Section 4. Natural language input is channeled through the Input Understander (CARMEL), which interprets the student's input. Just as the GUI Interpreter does, it stores a representation of the interpreted natural language input for the Tutorial Planner. The Tutorial Planner then uses the input representation, as well as data from the host system (in this case Andes) and other sources, to formulate a response which it sends back to the student via the User Interface Manager.

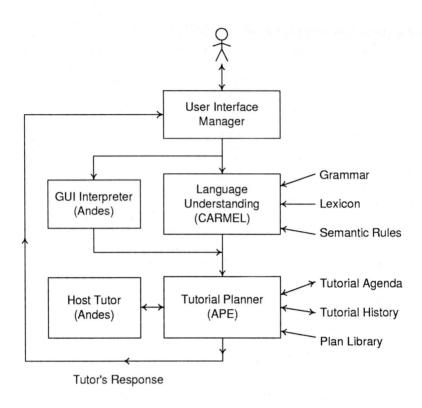

Fig. 3. Architecture of Atlas-Andes

Two domain-specific knowledge sources are required to apply the Atlas tools (APE and CARMEL) to a new domain, namely a plan library to guide the Tutorial Planner and semantic mapping rules to guide the Input Understander. A corpus of transcribed, spoken human-human dialogues using two experienced tutors and 20 students attempting to solve physics problems informed the development of the prototype Atlas-Andes system. The prototype system contains 21 semantic mapping rules and a plan library of approximately 100 plan operators, including roughly equal numbers of operators for dialogue creation, responding to specific student misconceptions, and handling domain-independent dialogue issues. In addition to API and GUI handling, the latter category includes general tutoring policies such as whether the student should be allowed to take the initiative and return to the GUI without finishing a subdialogue in process. With this knowledge the system can generate a large number of variations of the dialogue in Fig. 2 as well as selected examples of other ways of teaching about the direction of acceleration, such as the mini-*reductio* in Fig. 4. Thus the resulting system has the ability to tailor its approach to a wide variety of student inputs. Operators are selected based on historical information gathered by the tutor (discourse/interaction history), information about the current situation (the tutor's current goal and the student's latest response), and domain knowledge. As an example of the latter, if a student draws an acceleration vector which is incorrect but not opposite to the velocity vector, a different response will be generated.

In the remainder of the paper, we will discuss the APE tutorial planner and the CARMEL input understander in greater depth.

4 APE: The Atlas Tutorial Planner

Planning is required in dialogue-based ITSs in order to ensure that a coherent conversation ensues as the tutor's pedagogical goals are accomplished. If the system just responds to student actions, the resulting conversation will not necessarily be coherent, and the tutor has no way to ensure that its own teaching goals are met. Although Wenger [8] wrote in 1987 that using a global planner to control an ITS would be too inefficient, developments in reactive planning have made this goal a realistic possibility.

One cannot plan a conversation in advance unless the student's responses are classified into a small number of categories, and even then it would be wasteful. Furthermore, depending on the quality of the student's answers, one might need to change the plan during the conversation. For these reasons we work with partial plans that are expanded and refined only as needed. This style of planning is often called *reactive planning* [9, 10].

For adding dialogue to ITSs, we have developed a reactive planner called APE (Atlas Planning Engine) that is specialized for dialogue. In a previous study [11], we showed how modeling human-human tutorial dialogues according to the hierarchical structure of task-oriented dialogues [12] can make them tractable for plan-based generation. In the tutoring dialogues we have studied, a main building block of the discourse hierarchy, corresponding to the transaction level in Conversation Analysis [13], matches the *tutoring episode* defined by VanLehn [14]. A tutoring episode consists of the turns necessary to help the student accomplish one correct problem-solving step, e. g. to make one correct entry on a graphical interface. Our planner makes it convenient to satisfy local goals without disturbing the basic hierarchical structure.

Figure 4 shows a sample plan operator from Atlas-Andes. For legibility, we have shown the key elements in English instead of in Lisp.

To initiate a planning session, the user invokes the planner with an initial goal. The system searches its operator library to find all operators whose goal field matches the next goal on the agenda and whose filter conditions and preconditions are satisfied. Goals are represented by first-order logic without quantifiers and are matched using full unification. Since APE is intended especially for the generation of hierarchically organized task-oriented discourse, operators have multi-step recipes. When a match is found, the matching goal is removed from the agenda and replaced by the steps in the recipe. This operation is repeated until a primitive (non-decomposable) step is reached. If the primitive step corresponds to a question, the tutor asks the question and ends its turn. If the

438

```
(def-operator handle-same-direction
  :goal (...)
  :filter (...)
  :precond (...)
     ; We have asked a question about acceleration
     ; ... and the student has given an answer
     ; ... from which we can deduce that he/she thinks acceleration and
           velocity go in the same direction
     ; and we have not given the explanation below yet
  :recipe (...)
     ; Tell the student: "But if the acceleration went the same direction
           as the velocity, then the elevator would be speeding up."
     ; Mark that we are giving this explanation
     ; Tell the student that the tutor is requesting another answer
     ;   ("Try again.")
     ; Edit the agenda so that tutor is ready to receive another answer
  :hiercx ())
```

Fig. 4. Sample plan operator

primitive step corresponds to a statement, the tutor utters the statement but continues to plan, allowing the generation of multi-sentence turns.

To tailor the tutor's responses to the student as much as possible, one needs the ability to change plans during a conversation. This ability is provided in APE through the use of three types of recipe steps that can update the agenda. APE can skip the remainder of a strategy if circumstances have changed; it can replace a strategy with another strategy that has the same goal; and it can replace a sequence of goals at the top of the agenda. The last type is especially useful for responding to a student utterance without disturbing the global plan. In this way our approach differs from that of Vassileva [15]. Her work, based on AND-OR graphs, uses a separate set of rules for reacting to unexpected events.

A second way to tailor the tutor's response to the student is to take context into account before choosing a response. APE provides this ability in two ways. The "hierarchical context" or *hiercx* slot of an operator, shown in the last line of Fig. 4, provides a way for the planner to be aware of the goal hierarchy in which a decomposition is proposed. Additionally, operators can update and test predicates in a dynamic knowledge base.

APE communicates with the host system via an API. It obtains information from the world—the GUI interface, the natural language understanding component (CARMEL), and the host tutoring system—through preconditions on its plan operators. It returns information and action requests through recipe steps that update its knowledge base and execute external actions. Further details about the APE planner can be found in [16], and a deeper treatment of the role of reactive planning in dialogue generation can be found in [17].

Many previous dialogue-based ITSs have been implemented with finite-state machines, either simple or augmented. In the most common finite-state model, each time the human user issues an utterance, the processor reduces it to one of a small number of categories. These categories represent the possible transitions between states. There are several problems with this approach. First, it limits the richness of the student's input that can be appreciated. With APE, on the other hand, the author can write arbitrarily complex predicates, evaluable at run time, to define a class of input. Second, one can only take history and context into account by expanding the number of states, putting an arbitrary restriction on the amount of context or depth of conversational nesting that can be considered. Third, the finite-state approach misses the significant generalization that tutorial dialogues are hierarchical: larger units contain repeated instances of the same smaller units in different sequences and instantiated with different values. Finally, the finite-state machine approach does not allow the author to drop one line of attack and replace it by another without hard-coding every possible transition, thus limiting the tutor's ability to tailor its responses.

The prototype Atlas-Andes system described above shows that APE permits one not only to build more sophisticated ITSs but to build them faster. Since the domain-specific tutorial strategies are built from a small vocabulary of lower-level operators, there is a considerable economy of scale when expanding such a prototype to a full-scale tutoring system. Additionally, many of the operators that express general tutoring policies and conversational strategies are domain-independent and do not need to be repeated when expanding domain coverage.

5 CARMEL: The Atlas Input Understander

The task of the Atlas input understander is to extract relevant information from student explanations and other natural language input to pass back to the planner. This information can take the form of single atomic values or collections of flat propositional clauses, depending upon what the planner requires in specific contexts. In either case, CARMEL, the Core component for Assessing the Meaning of Explanatory Language, is used to parse the student input onto a feature structure representation that contains both syntactic and semantic information. Domain specific pattern matchers called semantic mapping rules are then used to match against particular patterns of features in order to identify and extract the needed information.

The overarching goal behind the design of the Atlas input understander is to facilitate the rapid development of robust natural language understanding interfaces for multiple domains. While interest in language understanding interfaces for tutoring systems has grown in recent years, progress towards making such interfaces commonplace has been greatly hindered by the tremendous time, effort, and expertise that is normally required for such an endeavor. Our long term goal is to build a tool set to semi-automate the process by applying machine learning techniques that require system developers only to annotate corpora with information pertinent to tutoring, thus insulating them from the underlying linguistic aspects of the development. At the heart of our design is the CARMEL core language understanding component, which is available for use on other tutoring projects.[2] Its underlying robust understanding technology [18–20] has already proven successful in the context of a large scale multi-lingual speech-to-speech translation system [21, 22].

CARMEL provides a broad foundation for language understanding. It is composed of a broad coverage English syntactic parsing grammar and lexicon; robust and efficient algorithms for parsing, semantic interpretation, and repair; and a formalism for entering idiomatic and domain-specific semantic knowledge. Current dialogue-based tutoring systems, such as CIRCSIM-Tutor [23] and AutoTutor [24], rely on shallow processing strategies to handle student input. This technology has so far proven effective for efficiently processing short student answers and for evaluating content based on inclusion of relevant vocabulary. In contrast, the goal of CARMEL is to support a deeper level of analysis in order to identify arbitrarily complex relationships between concepts within longer student answers.

Our approach is to achieve the most complete deep analysis possible within practical limits by relaxing constraints only as needed. CARMEL first attempts to construct analyses that satisfy both syntactic and semantic well-formedness conditions. A spelling corrector [25] is integrated with the lexical look-up mechanism in order to robustly recognize the student's intended input in the face of typos and spelling errors. The robust parser [19] has the ability to efficiently relax syntactic constraints as needed and as allowed by parameterized flexibility settings. For sentences remaining beyond the coverage of its syntactic knowledge, a repair stage [18], relying solely on semantic constraints compiled from a meaning representation specification, is used to assemble the pieces of a fragmentary parse. Thus, robustness techniques are applied at each stage in processing student input in order to address the wide variety of phenomena that make language understanding challenging.

In a recent evaluation of CARMEL's syntactic coverage, we measured the parser's ability to robustly analyze student input by testing it on a subset of our corpus of tutoring dialogues that had not been used for development of the prototype. The test corpus contained 50 student sentences and 50 multi-sentence student turns randomly extracted from the full corpus. The utterances ranged in length from 1 to 20 words, with an average length of 8 words per utterance. The parser was able to construct analyses covering 87% of the corpus when a high flexibility setting was used, taking on average .1 seconds per sentence.

When the parser is unable to construct an analysis of a sentence that deviates too far from the grammar's coverage, a fragmentary analysis is passed on to the repair module that quickly assembles the fragments [18]. Our approach to repair is unique in that no hand-coded repair rules are required as in other approaches to recovery from parser failure [26, 27]. A recent evaluation demonstrates that CARMEL's repair stage can increase the number of acceptable interpretations produced by between 3% (when using a high flexibility setting) and 9% (when a restricted flexibility setting is used), taking on average only .3 seconds per sentence.

---

[2] Interested parties should contact Carolyn Rosé at rosecp@pitt.edu.

6 Conclusions

One goal of the Atlas project is to develop reusable software for implementing natural-language based ITSs. In this paper we described CARMEL and APE, the parser and planner, respectively, for Atlas. We illustrated this work with an example from Atlas-Andes, a prototype physics tutor built using the Atlas framework. We showed how using these components could enable not only better tutoring but reduced authoring time as well.

7 Acknowledgments

We are grateful to Abigail Gertner for her generous assistance with the Andes system. Mohammed Elmi and Michael Glass of Illinois Institute of Technology provided the spelling correction code. Pamela Jordan provided constructive commentary on the manuscript.

References

1. Merrill, D.C., Reiser, B.J., Landes, S.: Human tutoring: Pedagogical strategies and learning outcomes (1992) Paper presented at the annual meeting of the American Educational Research Association.
2. Fox, B.A.: The Human Tutorial Dialogue Project: Issues in the design of instructional systems. Hillsdale, NJ: Erlbaum (1993)
3. Graesser, A.C., Person, N.K., Magliano, J.P.: Collaborative dialogue patterns in naturalistic one-to-one tutoring. Applied Cognitive Psychology **9** (1995) 495–522
4. Rosé, C.P.: The role of natural language interaction in electronics troubleshooting. In: Proceedings of the Energy Week Conference and Exhibition, Houston (1997)
5. Chi, M.T.H., Bassok, M., Lewis, M.W., Reimann, P., Glaser, R.: Self-explanations: How students study and use examples in learning to solve problems. Cognitive Science **13** (1989) 145–182
6. Chi, M.T.H., de Leeuw, N., Chiu, M.H., LaVancher, C.: Eliciting self-explanations improves understanding. Cognitive Science **18** (1994) 439–477
7. Gertner, A., VanLehn, K.: Andes: A coached problem solving environment for physics. In: Proceedings of the Fifth International Conference on Intelligent Tutoring Systems (ITS '00), Montreal (2000)
8. Wenger, E.: Artificial Intelligence and Tutoring Systems: Computational and Cognitive Approaches to the Communication of Knowledge. San Mateo, CA: Morgan Kaufmann (1987)
9. Georgeff, M.P., Ingrand, F.F.: Decision-making in an embedded reasoning system. In: Proceedings of the Eleventh International Joint Conference on Artificial Intelligence (IJCAI '89), Detroit (1989) 972–978
10. Wilkins, D., Myers, K., Lowrance, J., Wesley, L.: Planning and reacting in uncertain and dynamic environments. Journal of Experimental and Theoretical Artificial Intelligence **7** (1995) 121–152
11. Kim, J., Freedman, R., Evens, M.: Responding to unexpected student utterances in CIRCSIM-Tutor v. 3: Analysis of transcripts. In: Proceedings of the Eleventh Florida Artificial Intelligence Research Symposium (FLAIRS '98), Sanibel Island, Menlo Park: AAAI Press (1998) 153–157

12. Grosz, B.J., Sidner, C.L.: Attention, intentions, and the structure of discourse. Computational Linguistics **12** (1986) 175–204
13. Sinclair, J.M., Coulthard, R.M.: Towards an Analysis of Discourse: The English Used by Teachers and Pupils. London: Oxford University Press (1975)
14. VanLehn, K., Siler, S., Murray, C., Baggett, W.: What makes a tutorial event effective? In: Proceedings of the Twenty-first Annual Conference of the Cognitive Science Society, Madison (1998) 1084–1089
15. Vassileva, J.: Reactive instructional planning to support interacting teaching strategies. In: Proceedings of the Seventh World Conference on AI and Education (AI–ED '95), Washington, D. C., Charlottesville, VA: AACE (1995)
16. Freedman, R.: Using a reactive planner as the basis for a dialogue agent. In: Proceedings of the Thirteenth Florida Artificial Intelligence Research Symposium (FLAIRS '00), Orlando (2000)
17. Freedman, R.: Plan-based dialogue management in a physics tutor. In: Proceedings of the Sixth Applied Natural Language Processing Conference (ANLP '00), Seattle (2000)
18. Rosé, C.P.: A framework for robust semantic interpretation. In: Proceedings of the First Annual Conference of the North American Chapter of the Association for Computational Linguistics (NAACL '00), Seattle (2000)
19. Rosé, C.P., Lavie, A.: Balancing robustness and efficiency in unification augmented context-free parsers for large practical applications. In Junqua, J.C., Noord, G.V., eds.: Robustness in Language and Speech Technologies. Dordrecht: Kluwer (1999)
20. Rosé, C.P.: Robust Interactive Dialogue Interpretation. PhD thesis, School of Computer Science, Carnegie Mellon University (1997)
21. Woszcyna, M., Coccaro, N., Eisele, A., Lavie, A., McNair, A., Polzin, T., Rogina, I., Rosé, C.P., Sloboda, T., Tomita, M., Tsutsumi, J., Waibel, N., Waibel, A., Ward, W.: Recent advances in JANUS: a speech translation system. In: Proceedings of the ARPA Human Languages Technology Workshop, Princeton, NJ (1993)
22. Suhm, B., Levin, L., Coccaro, N., Carbonell, J., Horiguchi, K., Isotani, R., Lavie, A., Mayfield, L., Rosé, C.P., Dykema, C.V.E., Waibel, A.: Speech-language integration in a multi-lingual speech translation system. In: Proceedings of the AAAI Workshop on Integration of Natural Language and Speech Processing, Seattle (1994)
23. Glass, M.S.: Broadening Input Understanding in an Intelligent Tutoring System. PhD thesis, Illinois Institute of Technology (1999)
24. Wiemer-Hastings, P., Graesser, A., Harter, D., the Tutoring Research Group: The foundations and architecture of AutoTutor. In Goettl, B., Halff, H., Redfield, C., Shute, V., eds.: Intelligent Tutoring Systems: 4th International Conference (ITS '98). Berlin: Springer (1998) 334–343
25. Elmi, M., Evens, M.: Spelling correction using context. In: Proceedings of the 17th COLING/36th ACL (COLING-ACL '98), Montreal (1998)
26. Danieli, M., Gerbino, E.: Metrics for evaluating dialogue strategies in a spoken language system. In: Working Notes of the AAAI Spring Symposium on Empirical Methods in Discourse Interpretation and Generation, Stanford (1995)
27. Kasper, W., Kiefer, B., Krieger, H., Rupp, C., Worm, K.: Charting the depths of robust speech parsing. In: Proceedings of the 37th Annual Meeting of the Association for Computational Linguistics (ACL '99), College Park (1999)

Cooperative Agents to Track Learner's Cognitive Gap

G. Gouardères[1], A. Minko[1 2], L. Richard[2]

[1]Equipe MISIM - Laboratoire d'Informatique Appliquée –
IUT de Bayonne, 64100 Bayonne – France
Guy.Gouarderes@iutbay.univ-pau.fr
[2]Interactive STAR Rue Marcel Issartier 33700 Mérignac - FRANCE
Anton.Minko@STAR-IMA.com, Luc.Richard@STAR-IMA.com

Abstract : This paper presents the earlier results of the CMOS project including an embedded multi-agents ITS to efficiently help the learner faced with troubleshooting maintenance tasks. This environment carry on dedicated responses for aeronautical training sessions according to a three-step principle : first «introduce», next «convince» and at least «get to do». We emphasize on two main characteristics : a real-time full simulation of the technical domain, and it works with an tutoring multi-agents architecture, ASITS. ASITS is supplied with reactive and cognitive agents to track the learner performance, detect inherent negative effects (the learner's "cognitive gaps"), and as a feedback issue, to identify some deficiencies that current training simulator lack. Therefore, as measuring gap values with quantitative rules keeps sometimes hazardous, the concept of simulation has to be extended to a Qualitative Simulation approach.
Key Words: Interactive Learning Environments, Real-time Simulation, Intelligent Tutoring Systems, Multi-agentss Systems, Graphical Interface, Diagnostic Reasoning.

1. Introduction

This paper describes why « intelligent » desktop simulators for individual learning and/or team training rely on social aspects of distributed artificial intelligence. This reflection leads us to study computationally intelligent behavior using specifically tailored architecture for multi-agents ITS (ASITS, Actor System for ITS). This architecture has been applied in a simulation-based learning environment in order to allow the instructors to perform anytime assessment [2] by tracking the learner in real time (Progressive Assessment). As a feedback issue, we show how specialized cognitive agents can contribute to model the interaction design of a learning session in an Intelligent Desktop Trainer. Such systems are dedicated to train the learner in immersive condition not only by adding of Virtual Reality interface but mainly by anytime merging of «introducing the learner» sequences in CBT mode, combined with FBS procedure operations to «convince» and «get to do» with FFS to confirm.
We have also begun to identify some crucial points that current training desktop simulator lack in order to detect inherent negative effects (i.e. the learner's"cognitive gaps") brought into the learning process both by imperfect or incomplete immersion in simulation and by insufficient learner expertise for pedagogical strategy in ITS[6].

By introducing new key concepts from Degani & Wiener in the design [4] of task-oriented activities, we have shown that the learner cannot be considered as a simple "executant". He has to be trained to take real time decisions from concurrent activities: understanding of checklists and correct execution of prescribed operations. They have to be mastered in reverse mode as a dual control of each other by a specific ITS strategy, the "reverse assessment" : free learner's interaction with the real time kernel of the simulator in fact, is tightly coupled with an evolutive checklist window which traces and monitors the learner in ITS mode (and vice versa).

To verify these assumptions, we have developed a prototype[1] as a fully runnable maintenance simulator [11]. In this system, the "full-simulation" principle is supported by an embedded architecture built on three simulation layers: Real-time Kernel (free-play mode), distributed simulation (individual or team teaching of procedure) and qualitative simulation (evaluating cognitive gaps from the learner). Consequently, software agents within the ASITS architecture have to support learner and instructor inter-activity, traceability and ITS strategy through the three layers.

This architecture outperforms simply guessing the advantages of traceability of both the knowledge evolution in ITS and the simultaneous detection of change in the cognitive profile of the learner. This aspect can be estimated (positively or no) depending on three learning mode identified as a, b, c mechanisms (§4.3) and with a primitive cognitive gaps typology (tunnel effect, dropping or context gaps), we have shown what aspects of a user's behavior can be monitored by a gap evaluator agent.

2. New Concepts for Simulation Training in Aeronautics

2.1. Key Concepts for the Design of Task-Oriented Activities

Degani & Wiener [4] have focused on the manner in which pilots use checklists in normal situations. In addition. Boy [3] has completed this research by studying the use of the checklists in abnormal and emergency situations both carrying out an exhaustive analysis of pilots' cognitive activity. As new research issues from this previous work we emphasize on first, the search for tools more adapted to human operators, destined to improve the reliability of the human-system tandem and second, if users do not apply procedures as expected, it is important to ask if it should be considered as an error (i) if the non application is an attempt to adapt procedures because the operational situation is rarely identical to the expected situation or (ii) if the non application is a result of improper procedure design.

In these conditions, the human operator cannot be considered as a simple "executant" and he has to be trained to take real time decisions from both concurrent activities for anytime assessing of (i) the valid understanding of checklists, (ii) the correct execution of prescribed operations. This is why classical desktop simulators have to be changed for more realistic and intelligent ones.

---

[1] CMOS (Cockpit Maintenance Operation Simulator) supported by Airbus Training.

2.2. Different Approaches for Training Simulation

At Rolls Royce, the initial stage of maintenance training is made with an Active Mock-Up which simulates the control boards of a Turbine Engine according to the ALARP process (As Low As reasonably Possible). This strategy consists, using the case-based slow down in functioning, of initiating, understand and "get to do" in the same environment. On the other hand, at Delta AirLines, each training stage has dedicated simulation devices: FFS (Full Flight Simulators), FBS (Fixed based simulator) et CBT (Computer Based Training). The practice courses begin by using the CBT then passing on the FBS where low level tasks are integrated in the operations and, finally, learners access to the FFS where they practice the flight procedures and manoeuvres. The philosophy consists in having always an instructor behind the learner in order to validate the three stages on CBT, FBS and FFS. In fact, the role of instructor is paramount in the training as he plans the activities for each learner, chooses strategies for linking the simulator's using with the procedures' follow-up (and vice versa). Finally, he establishes an evaluation protocol for certification exam assessment. These pedagogical activities aren't automated at all in the cabin simulators. However, they have been developed and largely automated in traditional learning environments and, particularly, in the intelligent tutoring systems (ITS) [7]. A fair model of classical ITS simulator is Sherlock II, a learning-by-doing system for electric fault diagnosis for F15 fighter aircraft [8]. Nothing in Sherlock architecture depended upon an assessment of the student. This was made intentionally because of the many ways a problem can be solved and the lack of any body of expertise that was complete and closed. But in a debriefing session, an expert coach can always take what the student has done so far and give advice on how to proceed toward a solution, but it cannot always decide that a student's approach was wrong. Today, most of ITS systems for training are similar to Sherlock and lack of the progressive assessment of learner's competency . In order to solve this problem, we have first introduced the concept of "full-simulation" which has integrated the last performances in desktop trainers [11] by merging the following three paradigms:

- Full Fidelity Simulation targets at a quality insurance given by a very fine grain for represented knowledge issued from simulation modules, each one is devoted to a specific aircraft system (Hydraulics, Engines, Electricity ...) and they act together as reactive agents in the Real Time Kernel of the simulator,
- Distributed Simulation dynamically split on different stations zooms processes of the previous modules allowing the learner to focus on precise point with an important cognitive unballasting,
- Qualitative Simulation monitors interactions between the learner and the simulator in terms of positive or negative effects when assessing the learner's performance.

When the previous functions act together, the issued realistic feed-back can be qualified of "Full-Simulation" in spite of the lack of an effective immersive interface.

3. A Prototype for "Full-Simulation"

The CMOS prototype is a learning environment advanced prototype (fully runnable) dedicated to aeronautical maintenance operators (Airbus A340). The constitutive characteristic of this learning environment is the "full-simulation" principle supported by en embedded architecture built on three simulation layers:

- First layer – Real-time kernel, as in FFS2.
- Second layer – knowledge base of prescribed tasks. Aeronautical procedures are composed of strictly defined tasks.
- Third layer – reasoning analysis on tasks performed by tutoring system – Qualitative Simulation

Equipped with software agents, that support traceability of interactivity through the three layers, this prototype intends to cope with cabin simulator efficiency.

3.1. Human Factors in Aeronautical Training

Trainers' developers usually seek to minimize human information processing and cognitive demands on the user when they work for learning on simulators, and more often in safety-critical sequences or procedures. However, the way of achieving this goal differs greatly with respect to avoid different classes of cognitive difficulty (task load, cognitive gaps…). For this primary work, we have used a reduced framework for classifying the different cognitive task loads:

1. Concurrent mastering of three layers of simulation: kernel, checklists, ITS
2. Splitting learner activity into two alternate but equivalent interactions between hypertext document and window simulation; and
3. Possibility of joint interaction from multiple learners acting on networked station as in the simulator.

The methods we used to perform task analysis in # 1 are HCI related ones adapted to man-machine interaction [3], in which reactive agents for detecting cognitive task loads and learner's misses will be paramount. Detecting gaps into task analysis for # 2 needs methods for recording the distributed design process and replaying portions of it if necessary. This will require creation of novel methods and interfaces for real-time tracking of learner's activity with adaptive agents operating at any time.

For # 3 we have developed tools and techniques to assess how users will work and perform with cognitive agents in distributed engineering environments [7].

3.2. Qualitative Monitoring of the Learner's Operations

The learner can operate in free-play mode (as in an immersive FFS) but the real-time kernel of the simulator cannot assume a quantitative comparison of the value of expert solution with the value of student solution. It can just signalize if «cockpit» equipments and indicators run properly or not. This is why the qualitative simulation is necessary (but not sufficient) to monitor the progressive assessment of the learner.

4. Multi-Agent ITS

In multi-agent based ITS, this perspective raises three major problems: (i) the definition of the communication standards for exchanging real-time information between the agents, (ii) the indexing of expertise to facilitate 'know-how' tracking within all the relevant domains and (iii) the cognitive interaction design.

---

[2] Full Flight Simulator –simulators which are used in the aircraft companies like Boeing or Airbus to train pilots. These devices are real scale 1-cabin simulators.

In order to resolve the problems raised before, agents must integrate adaptable strategies to monitor the user's actions when mastering two concurrent activities: understanding of checklists and correct execution of prescribed operations. This two basic activities has to be managed in reverse mode as a dual control of each other by a specific ITS strategy, the "reverse assessment" : a- free learner's interaction with the real time kernel (pseudo free play) in fact, it is tightly coupled with b- an evolutive checklist window (aeronautical procedures) which monitors the learner in ITS mode. This strategy must be applied to study maintenance procedures (AMM tasks) together with the practice of tracking and troubleshooting procedures (TSM tasks). A relevant selection of significant procedures is based on their frequency of use or on their specific structure. Consequently, defining the curriculum consists mainly in choosing a precise set of "key-tasks" in order to give the learner a general knowledge of the structure of the complete course and a documentation handling experience. The structure of the meta-help window is an hypertext active document identical to the AMM paper form (see "Layer2" fig. 1). The content is enhanced with graphical icons, and underlined texts are links to other hypertext documents.

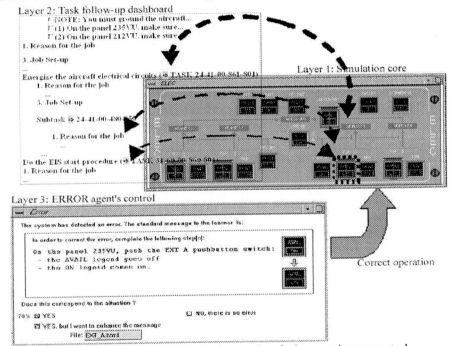

Figure 1. Three-layered learner's interaction during a maintenance task

The interaction between the three layers is not strictly planned before. During the practice of the task, the trainee could choose between acting directly on a flight-deck pushbutton (layer 1, fig. 1), checking an item on the checklist (top left window layer 2, in fig. 1) or even ask the ITS to trace step by step this task (layer 3).

Problem can occur when analyzing conflicts in reasoning steps and attempts to track possible issues to bridge the gap between the ITS and learner reasoning. In agent-based simulation, different agents play specific roles to achieve these goals [7]: at a first level, pedagogical agents (learner, tutor…) play simulated learning scenarios, at a second level, gap detector agents trace their reasoning and at a third level, cognitive and evaluator agents detect and solve conflicts to improve new strategy.

4.1. General Presentation of Multi-Agent ITS

Three main components of an ITS (the student model, the knowledge model, and the pedagogical model) have been formerly built in the form of intelligent agent architecture as in the Actor's agent [6]. It is possible to limit the number of actors and the casting of roles by (i) viewing learning as a reactive process involving several partners (human, simulated functions, pedagogical agents…), (ii) adapting each advising agent to various learning strategies co-learner, advisor,…[7].

4.2. Typology of Pedagogical Agents in the Simulation-Based Multi-Agent ITS

According to the "users in the loop" concept [7], general characteristics of different agents used are following:
- Cognitive Agents: consider different strategies and learning styles, establish learning objectives, create, locate, track and review learning materials, e.g., diagnostic and assessment instruments, learning modules, mastery tests, etc…,
- Adaptive Agents: register changes and review/track students' progress and manage student-tutors communications both asynchronously and synchronously,
- Reactive Agents: assign appropriate materials to students, manage student-ITS communications synchronously (when desired/required),evaluate student needs.
The remaining problem is how to classify cognitive interactions amongst a society of cognitive agent acting together in shared initiative (or not) with the learner(s).

4.3. Classification of Cognitive Interactions

We need to have agents which mimic human behavior in learning situations. From previous multi-agent ITS experiments, we have emphasized on the potential of agent to carry on end-user's mechanisms. We have classified three levels of abstraction depending on the functional aspects of learner's practice:
  - *(a-mechanism): learning as replication, where agents can provide instructional data, representation of pedagogical strategy, and one of them, the Tutor, is devoted to mimic the teacher acting in the classroom (learning can be embedded as a reactive mechanism),*
  - *(b-mechanism): learning by tautology, where demonstrations can be designed to guide the learner through the learning process with the help of specialized agents as Tutor, Companion, Adviser… (learning process can be embedded as an adaptive mechanism),*
  - *(c-mechanism): learning by dynamic interactions and shared initiative, where the computer is more active and information is not only provided by the courseware, but can be modified and generated by the learner (learning can be embedded as a cognitive mechanism).*
At a second stage, which is the related current phase of the work, the ASITS architecture allows to detect in real-time the emergence of deviant behaviors and cognitive misses from the learner. What we call cognitive gaps of the learner.

4.4. Cognitive Gaps Typology: Dropping Gap & Context Gap

However, the success of pure multi-agent based tutoring system depends on a learner's motivation and self-discipline. We intend to profile such behavior by just using three types of cognitive gaps: -the 'context gap' at the points of divergence between the purpose of the tasks performed within an ITS and the purpose of the predicted solutions expected by the pedagogue (that needs a b-mechanism - the 'dropping gap' (i.e., the rate of renunciation due to the lack of motivation and help) which implies a c-mechanism approach. Thereby, this method for weakening the "dropping gap" inevitably introduces the 'context gap' restraint jointly with the shared initiative problem between the learner and the system. The solution to reduce the dropping gap by agents' auto-adaptation introduces often the context gap, which brakes the initiative share between the learner and the system. Such conflict limitation needs a specialized type of actor - the gap evaluator agent.

4.5. Cognitive Agents as Gap Evaluators:
The "instructor assistant" plays the role of a collaborator and his helps are more and more useful because he observes, captures and generalizes decision helps made by other agents. The learning of activities by agents was limited to two simple mechanisms: (i) learning by needs satisfaction (individual), such as the agents of two levels (reactive and planned) [2] with the planner agent for beliefs and presupposes, (ii) learning by satisfaction of contradictions (collective), which uses a genetic algorithm in the aim to resolve antagonist constraints between the evolution of each agent and the operation of the whole system.

5. Architecture of the Multi-Agent System

The following scheme displays the organization of different agents, which form all together the general architecture based on ASITS principles. This learning environment evolves permanently and independently from agents' objectives.

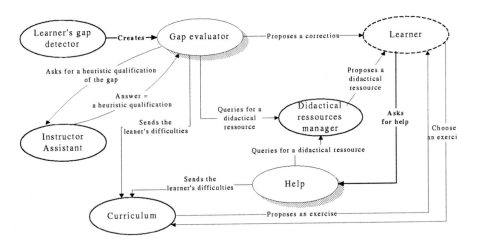

Figure 2: Cognitive agents managing interactions with the learner

5.1.   Human Agents

The Learner and Instructor agents are the two human agents of the system and they are absolutely free in their interactions. All interactions of the learner and of the instructor are mediated by a graphical interface.

5.2.   Cognitive Agents Role

Cognitive agents are present permanently in the environment: They are created at the launch of application and "live" until its end. It is represented by one exemplaire.

Learner's gap detector agent supervises the interactions of the learner with the system. It is based on the know-how model in order to detect each gap of the learner. This gap detection does not evaluate the gap (severity level of the error).

Curriculum agent controls the progression of the learner in the whole course. Synthesizing different problems encountered by the learner, he is responsible of organizing learning sessions and of individualizing the progression in difficulties. After recognizing learner's profile, it proposes the sessions of activities.

Depositor of Instructor's Experience agent collects preferences in order to guide the learner according to the personal instructor's style. It must, by the demand of Gap Evaluator agent, analyze this gap and propose a heiristical qualification.

5.3.   Reactive Agents Role

Reactive agents are the different lifetime. They are created by another agent (cognitive or reactive) and are killed after their objective is completed. Depending on situation, each type of reactive agents is represented by 0 to n exemplaires.

Gap evaluator agent is created by Learner's gap Detector agent in order to find the real signification of the gap (negligible gap, notable, important, major error...)

Learner Assistant agent offers the requested help when the learner demands it. The only interaction of this agent with the environment is produced when the learner, after numerous indexes or helps, can not correct his/her error. In this case, Assistant agent realizes, step-by-step, a demonstration of the correction.

Observator of Instructor's Heuristics agent is created by the Learner's Gap Evaluator agent. It uses machine learning techniques in order to collect the precise and heuristical interventions of the instructor but it stores also the acquired knowledge.

6. Experimenting with KQML and CIAgent Agents [1]

6.1.   Agent classes

The ASITS architecture support autonomous agents by the definition of a generic class of agent-supervisor named CIAgent[3] which monitors six principal agents:

-    Ag.I: initialization agent (not presented in fig.2) because it is not permanent
-    Ag. LGD: Learner's Gap Detector
-    Ag.DRM : Didactical Ressources Manager
-    Ag.IA : Instructor's Assistant
-    Ag.C : Curriculum
-    Ag.GE#n : Gap Evaluator

---

[3] CIAgent = Constructing Intelligent Agent.

In addition, these five agent types are cognitive, they are represented by an unique instance. The last agent is reactive, the whole system can have dynamically from 0 up to n agents of this type, and it perish (Dead state) at the end of their script.

6.2. Results

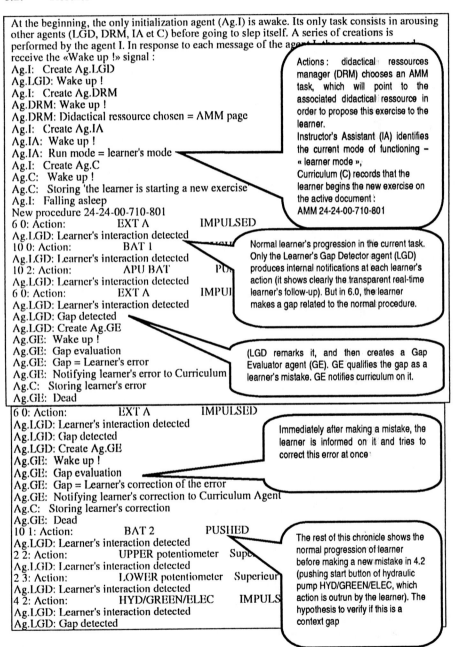

At the beginning, the only initialization agent (Ag.I) is awake. Its only task consists in arousing other agents (LGD, DRM, IA et C) before going to slep itself. A series of creations is performed by the agent I. In response to each message of the agent I, the agents concerned receive the «Wake up !» signal :

Ag.I: Create Ag.LGD
Ag.LGD: Wake up !
Ag.I: Create Ag.DRM
Ag.DRM: Wake up !
Ag.DRM: Didactical ressource chosen = AMM page
Ag.I: Create Ag.IA
Ag.IA: Wake up !
Ag.IA: Run mode = learner's mode
Ag.I: Create Ag.C
Ag.C: Wake up !
Ag.C: Storing 'the learner is starting a new exercise'
Ag.I: Falling asleep
New procedure 24-24-00-710-801
6 0: Action: EXT A   IMPULSED
Ag.LGD: Learner's interaction detected
10 0: Action: BAT 1
Ag.LGD: Learner's interaction detected
10 2: Action: APU BAT   PU
Ag.LGD: Learner's interaction detected
6 0: Action: EXT A   IMPUI
Ag.LGD: Learner's interaction detected
Ag.LGD: Gap detected
Ag.LGD: Create Ag.GE
Ag.GE: Wake up !
Ag.GE: Gap evaluation
Ag.GE: Gap = Learner's error
Ag.GE: Notifying learner's error to Curriculum
Ag.C: Storing learner's error
Ag.GE: Dead

Actions: didactical ressources manager (DRM) chooses an AMM task, which will point to the associated didactical ressource in order to propose this exercise to the learner.
Instructor's Assistant (IA) identifies the current mode of functioning – « learner mode »,
Curriculum (C) records that the learner begins the new exercise on the active document : AMM 24-24-00-710-801

Normal learner's progression in the current task. Only the Learner's Gap Detector agent (LGD) produces internal notifications at each learner's action (it shows clearly the transparent real-time learner's follow-up). But in 6.0, the learner makes a gap related to the normal procedure.

(LGD remarks it, and then creates a Gap Evaluator agent (GE). GE qualifies the gap as a learner's mistake. GE notifies curriculum on it.

6 0: Action: EXT A   IMPULSED
Ag.LGD: Learner's interaction detected
Ag.LGD: Gap detected
Ag.LGD: Create Ag.GE
Ag.GE: Wake up !
Ag.GE: Gap evaluation
Ag.GE: Gap = Learner's correction of the error
Ag.GE: Notifying learner's correction to Curriculum Agent
Ag.C: Storing learner's correction
Ag.GE: Dead
10 1: Action: BAT 2   PUSHED
Ag.LGD: Learner's interaction detected
2 2: Action: UPPER potentiometer   Sup
Ag.LGD: Learner's interaction detected
2 3: Action: LOWER potentiometer   Superieur
Ag.LGD: Learner's interaction detected
4 2: Action: HYD/GREEN/ELEC   IMPULS
Ag.LGD: Learner's interaction detected
Ag.LGD: Gap detected

Immediately after making a mistake, the learner is informed on it and tries to correct this error at once

The rest of this chronicle shows the normal progression of learner before making a new mistake in 4.2 (pushing start button of hydraulic pump HYD/GREEN/ELEC, which action is outrun by the learner). The hypothesis to verify if this is a context gap

```
Ag.LGD: Create Ag.GE
Ag.GE:  Wake up !
Ag.GE:  Gap evaluation
Ag.GE:  Gap = Learner's error
Ag.GE:  Notifying learner's error to Curriculum Agent
Ag.C:   Storing learner's error
Ag.GE:  Dead
4 2: Action:          HYD/GREEN/ELEC       IMPULS
Ag.LGD: Learner's interaction detected
Ag.LGD: Gap detected
Ag.LGD: Create Ag.GE
Ag.GE:  Wake up !
Ag.GE:  Gap evaluation
Ag.GE:  Gap = Learner's correction of the error
Ag.GE:  Notifying learner's correction to Curriculum Age
Ag.C:   Storing learner's correction
Ag.GE:  Dead

1 0: Action:          Ecam            C
Ag.LGD: Learner's interaction detected
3 2: Action:          Ecam            C/B
Ag.LGD: Learner's interaction detected
2 0: Action:          Ecam            HYD
Ag.LGD: Learner's interaction detected
0 0: Action:          Low air press BLUE    Non affic
Ag.LGD: Learner's interaction detected
0 1: Action:          Low air press GREEN   Non affich
Ag.LGD: Learner's interaction detected
0 2: Action:          Low air press YELLOW  Non aff
Ag.LGD: Learner's interaction detected
4 2: Action:          HYD/GREEN/ELEC       IMPUI
Ag.LGD: Learner's interaction detected
4 2: Action:          AC ESS BUS SHED
Ag.LGD: Learner's interaction detected
```

The same mecanisms as in the action 6.0 are launched in order to always guide the learner as efficiently as possible. But in this time, this doesn't work, because the learner is "displaced". He needs to re-establish the context of 4.2.

After he sees that it doesn't work, the learner tries to make a series of actions (10, 3.2, 2.0,) which guides him to a new attempt by trying 4.2 after 02 and... this time, it is correct: bus access is trusted (ACCES BUS SCHED) because the spontaneous precedent actions replaced him in the good context

Error indication just retired. It can be classified as a "context gap". This fact may be validated by the instructor during the debriefing.

7. Conclusion

We have begun different experiments using this prototype, previously with senior engineers and instructors all along the development cycle and nowadays with novice learners: students from the Institut de de Maintenance Aéronautique at Bordeaux and others from the Institut Universitaire de Technologie at Bayonne with the aim of classifying the different cognitive tasks load during learner's interactivity.

Depending on three functional aspects of learning identified as a, b, c mechanisms and with a rather primitive cognitive gaps typology (Tunnel Effect, Dropping, and Context Gaps), we have shown what aspects of a user's behavior can be monitored by a gap evaluator agent.

Implemented with a Java repository of agents (CIAgent), the deliberately limited actor's architecture, the Gap Evaluator agent. This Gap Evaluator agent is responsible for qualifying the gap: from "nothing important" to "major misunderstanding" for a given type of gap – dropping, context or tunnel – in a, b, c mechanism).

the major scientific obstacle consists in identifying behavioral aspects of the learner which can be captured, controlled and learned by different cognitive (or not) agents in shared initiative between learner and system.

Our plan is to extend the rather poor capabilities of learning within the current cognitive agents. Another promising way to investigate is the improvement of man-machine interaction by immersing the learner in virtual reality interfaces. This may originate a new spread of influent cognitive discrepancies or shifts that need to identify new types of distinctive gaps.

References

1 Bigus J.P., Bigus J., « Constructing intelligent agents with Java», Wiley Computer Publishing, 1997.

2 Beck J.E., Woolf B. Park, « Using a Learning Agent with a Student Model», Fourth International Conference on Intelligent Tutoring Systems -ITS'98- San Antonio. USA-August 1998., Lecture Notes in Computer Science, 34, Springer.

3 Boy G., « Cognitive Function Analysis. Ablex, Stanford», CT, 1998.

4 Degani A., Wiener E.L. "Cockpit Checklists : Concepts, Design and Use" Human Factors, Ashgate, 35, 327-365, 1993

5 Forbus K.D., « Qualitative process theory: twelve years after», Artificial Intelligence 59 , pp. 115-123, 1993

6 Frasson C., Mengelle T., Aïmeur E, Gouardères G., « An Actor-based Architecture for Intelligent Tutoring Systems», Third International Conference ITS'96, Montreal, Lecture Notes in Computer Science, June 1996, Springer

7 Gouardères G., Frasson C., « On effectiveness of distance learning using LANCA», Workshop on Pedagogical Agents. Fourth International Conference on Intelligent Tutoring Systems -ITS'98- San Antonio. USA- 1998.

8 Katz, S. Lesgold, A. Eggan, G. Greenberg, L., « Towards the Design of More Effective Advisors for Learning-by-Doing Systems», Lecture Notes in Computer Science, Springer. Intelligent Tutoring Systems, Third International Conference, ITS '96, pp. 641-649, Montréal, Canada, 1996.

9 Kuipers B.J., « Reasoning with qualitative models», Artificial Intelligence 59, pp. 125-132, 1993.

10 Munro A., Surmon D., Johnson M., Pizzini Q., Walker J. «An open architecture for simulation-centered tutors 9th Int. Conf. on AIED -Le Mans, pp. 578-585, - ISSN: 0922-6389- IOS Press - Amsterdam- The Netherlands, 1999

11 Richard L., Gouarderes G., « An Agent-operated Simulation-based Training System», Proceedings of the 9th Int. Conf. on AIED -Le Mans, pp. 578-585, - ISSN: 0922-6389-IOS Press - Amsterdam- The Netherlands, 1999

Agent-Mediated Language-Learning Environment Based on Communicative Gaps

Hiroaki Ogata, Yuqin Liu, Youji Ochi, and Yoneo Yano

Department of Information Science and Intelligent Systems, Tokushima University
2-1 Minamijosanjima, Tokushima 770-8506, Japan
E-mail: {ogata, yu, ochi, yano}@ is.tokushima-u.ac.jp
URL: http://www-yano.is.tokushima-u.ac.jp/ogata/

Abstract. This paper focuses on the problem of language transfer in foreign language learning. The transfer caused by the difference between learner's mother language and target language, often leads a communicative gap. This paper first analyzes the semantic relations between learner's mother language and target language. Then proposes a CGM (Communicative Gap Model) due to language difference. We have developed a communicative language-learning environment called Neckle (Network-based Communicative Kanji Learning Environment) to support foreign language learning through communication with native speakers. Neckle has a software agent that observes the conversation between the learner and the native speaker, checks up the communicative gap according to CGM, and notices the gap for the support of language learning congenial to each learner. Learners can not only be aware of the language difference but also acquire its cultural background from the native speakers.

1 Introduction

With the fast development of computer networking, people around the world have more chances to communicate directly. By applying computer networking to language learning, it is now possible for learners to communicate with native speakers in foreign languages. In fact, many approaches, which are intended to improve exchange among different cultures and language learning by e-mail, have been proposed [7,17,16]. Hanson et al. [7] used the Internet for improving international cooperation and comprehension among university students around the world. Through the exchange of e-mail, the learner's ability to comprehend and express themselves in foreign languages has been highly improved. Saita et al [16] examined the variation of learners' language misuse and corrected usages while learners communicated with native speakers by e-mail. Saita et al. reported that through the exchange of e-mail, the percentage of language misuse gradually declined, learners came to use sentences with more complicated structure, and the ability of the learner to use the language was improved. They also pointed out that to communicate directly with native speaker was very important for foreign language learning. These approaches that emphasize the foreign language study through communication, are known as a communicative approach [11, 14]. A communicative approach is a foreign language learning method, which emphasize communication primarily. Grammatical rules and vocabularies are secondly. Recently, it has attracted much interest in CALL (Computer Assisted Language Learning). We apply this approach to support the acquisition of Japanese Kanji meaning with communication tools [12].

Cross-linguistic influences have also been identified as important factors influencing second language acquisition [15]. Language transfer means that one's mother language previously learnt tends to influence the learning a foreign language and have both negative and positive effects. It can be observed in conversation, semantics and phonemics. If a transfer takes place with no difference between the mother language and target language resulted it is called "positive transfer". If a transfer happens with different results it is called a "negative transfer". The "negative transfer" is a serious problem on foreign language learning usually causes a communicative gap [13, 15, 18]. Therefore, it is necessary to focus on the language difference in foreign language learning. In this paper, the system supports Chinese learners to study Japanese Kanji focusing on the meaning difference between Japanese Kanji and Chinese Kanji.

As for related researches, an intelligent CALL system called Mr.Collins [4, 5] was developed. It focused on language transfer that is caused by the grammatical difference between learner's mother language and target language. The system facilitated the acquisition of pronoun placement in Portuguese learning. 'Cross Talk' [10] is a CALL environment using multimedia based on cross-cultural pragmatics. It tackles on the issues of pragmatic transfer in the conversation between learner and native speaker. However, there are few approaches focusing on communicative gaps in CALL.

This paper proposes an agent-mediated language-learning environment called Neckle (Network-based Communicative Kanji Learning Environment) that focuses on the meaning difference between learner's ML (Mother Language) and TL (Target Language). In Neckle, a software agent that supports Chinese people learning Japanese Kanji is named Ankle (Agent for Kanji Learning).

2 Languages Difference and Communication

The "negative transfer"(hereafter sited as transfer) often leads communicative gaps. Contrastive linguistics is worthwhile work for predicting and preventing language transfer [20]. In this section, first, we analyze the relation of vocabulary meaning between learner's ML and TL. Then we consider the communicative gap due to the meaning difference.

2.1 Meaning Relation between ML and TL

The research of contrastive linguistics has been carried out on the relation between language's vocabulary meanings. Andou [1] classified the relation into 3 groups. (1) "Same", (2) "Overlap", (3) "Different". In this study, we furthermore subdivided the "(2)Overlap" into "Inclusion" and "Overlap-different" from the point of view of foreign language learning. Figure 1 shows the relationship and some examples between Japanese and other languages.

456

(I) Same: both of learner's ML and TL are signify the same or have common meaning. e.g., in Japanese, "春 (Haru)" means "Spring" only.

(II) Inclusive: (IIa): The meaning scope of ML is a subset of TL; (IIb): The meaning scope of ML is wider than that of TL. e.g., in Japanese, "着る(Kiru)" means "put the clothes on "only such as coats , jacket, not including such as pants, skirt , so "着る(Kiru)" belongs to (IIa). One the other hand, "兄弟(Kyodai)" in Japanese means not only brothers, but also sisters. So "兄弟(Kyodai)" belongs to (IIb).

(III)　　Overlap-different: while ML and TL have common meaning, they also have different meaning. For instance, in Chinese, "単位(Tan'i)" has no meaning of "credit" like Japanese, it means "place of employment" instead. However, a common meaning of "a unit" exists, so "単位(Tan'i)" belongs to (III).

(IV)　　Different: The vocabularies of ML and TL hav no common meaning because of different culture. For example, "鳥居(Torii)" is a symbol of Japanese culture. So the "鳥居(Torii)" is peculiar to Japanese language.

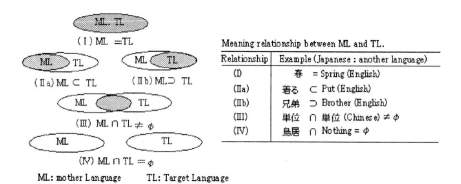

Fig. 1. Meaning relation between mother language and target language.

2.2 CGM (Communication Gap Model)

We have analyzed the factors of communicative gaps in conversation as follows:

(1) Difference in meaning between learner's ML and TL: Learners may make misunderstanding of a word of TL because of the difference between ML and TL language[15]. When the meaning relationship is (II)"inclusion" or (III) " they have common meaning and different meaning each other, a communicative gap may occur to learners.

(2) Learner's position of the communication: Two positions exist in communication, one is a "sender" and the other is a "receiver". Even if meaning is different, a communicative gap might not occur depending on the learner's positions (sender or receiver).

(3) Written form of learner's ML and TL (characters or letters): this system provides a text-based communication, therefore, it is possible that language transfer may occur even with the same written form. For example, if written form was different, there would be no gap. But, if the written form was the same, gap will occur. For example, "走" means "walking" " in Chinese, but it means "running" in Japanese.

Table 1. Communicative gap model

Meaning relation \ Position	Written form: Same		Written form: Different	
	Receiver	Sender	Receiver	Sender
I ML = TL	×	×	×	×
II(a) ML ⊂ TL	○	×	○	×
II(b) ML ⊃ TL	×	○	×	○
III ML ∩ TL ≠ φ	○	○	○	○
IV ML ∩ TL = φ	○	○		×

Considering the three above factors, we propose CGM (Communicative Gap Model) based on the different meaning (see Table 1).

- In (I), because the meaning is same, there will be no gap.
- In (IIa), when the student's position is a receiver, the student will take the TL's meaning with a narrower view than the TL, so a gap will occur. When the student's position is a sender, a gap will not occur because the native speaker is able to understand the meaning by the context.
- In (IIb), when the student is a receiver, it is not easy to understand native speaker intentions. When the student is a sender, a gap can occur if the native speaker takes the student's meaning into a narrower scope than the student intended.
- In (III), depending on a common meaning, a gap can occur at both student and the native speaker.
- In (IV), if the written form is different, a gap caused by language transfer will not occur. However, if written form is the same, a gap can occur at both the sender and the receiver.

3 Communicative Foreign Language Learning Environment

In this section, we present an agent-oriented framework, which focuses on the difference in the meaning between learner's ML and TL.

3.1 Design Strategies of Learning Environment

The design strategies of the framework are as follows:

(1) Communicative approach: learners study TL through communication with native speakers.
(2) Focusing on the language difference: this system mainly supports to acquire the knowledge where there is a difference between learner's ML and TL.
(3) Learner-centered design: knowledge of TL is based on learners' needs and depends on the contents of the conversation. An agent supports language

learning according to the communication contents and the status of student's understanding.

3.2 Diagram of Agent's Support

The agent's behaviors are as follows:
(1) Agent observes the communication between learners and the native speaker.
(2) Agent analyzes the conversation at real time using the "Dictionary of knowledge", and looks for the difference between learner's ML and TL.
(3) Agent judges the communicative gap according to the CGM.
(4) Agent notifies the knowledge difference according to the student model.
(5) Agent constructs the intervening timing asking whether the student has already understood.
(6) Agent decides the "teaching strategy" according to the response of learners. If a student's answer was wrong, the agent would notice the difference of knowledge according to certain teaching strategies.

3.3 Student Model and Intervention, Teaching Strategies

This study applies a communicative approach and supports students to learn foreign language through communication with a native speaker. The principles are as follows:
(1) To avoid interrupting communication, the agent doesn't frequently intervene in the conversation.
(2) Knowledge teaching does not interrupt conversation for a long.
We suggest the strategies of the system intervention and teaching based on the above principles.

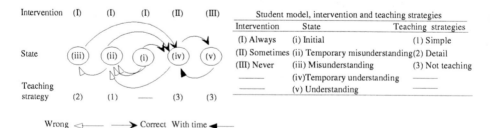

Intervention	State	Teaching strategies
(I) Always	(i) Initial	(1) Simple
(II) Sometimes	(ii) Temporary misunderstanding	(2) Detail
(III) Never	(iii) Misunderstanding	(3) Not teaching
————	(iv)Temporary understanding	————
————	(v) Understanding	————

Fig. 2. Relation of intervention, student model and teaching strategies.

3.3.1 Student Model
In this system, we examined the state of student's knowledge by question. We classified the state of knowledge into "understanding" and "misunderstanding", then divide it further into "temporary understanding" and "temporary misunderstanding."
The status of student's understanding changes as in Figure 2.
(i) Initial: Agent has not checked any Kanji words for meaning difference.

(ii)Temporary misunderstanding: Learner's answer to a question was wrong, but only once.
(iii)Temporary understanding: Learner's answer to a question was correct once.
(iv)Misunderstanding: Learner's answer to a question was wrong again.
(v)Understanding: Learner's answer to a question was correct again.
Each knowledge state will change acording to the following rules.It will change to the state in writen inside the < >symbols. when learer's answer was wrong.(see Figure2)
(i)→(iv) <(ii)> :"Initial" moves to "Temprary understanding" if learer's answer was right. Otherwise, it moves to "Temprary misunderstanding".
(ii)→(iv) <(iii)>: "Temprary misunderstanding" moves to "Temprary understanding" if learer's answer was right. Otherwise it moves to "misunderstanding".
(iii) → (iv) <(iii)>: "Misunderstanding" moves to "Temprary understanding" if learner's answer was right. Otherwise, "misunderstanding"is repeated.
(iv)→(v) <(ii)>: "Temprary understanding" moves to "Understanding" if learner's answer was right. Otherwise, it moves to "Temprary misunderstanding".
(v)→(iv): don't intervene in conversation if state is "Understanding". However, "Understanding" moves to "Temporary understanding" with time.

3.3.2 Intervention Strategies
If there is any gap, the agent will intervene into the conversation as following, according to the student's model.
(1) Always: The agent always intervenes if student's knowledge state was "initial", "temporary misunderstanding", or "misunderstanding".
(2) Not always: Agent intervenes when "temporary understanding" appears several times.
(3) Never: Agent does not intervene when the knowledge state is "understanding".

Table 2. Teaching strategy.

Simple teaching	Detailed teaching
Relation among the ML & TL	Relation among the ML & TL
Meaning of the TL	Meaning of the TL
———	Meaning of the ML
....	Relevant Knowledge of TL

3.3.3 Teaching Strategies
In order to do not interrupt the communication for along time, we propose teaching strategies into "simple" and "detail" (See Table 2).
(1) Simple: showing the diagram of relation between learner's ML and TL intended for "temporary not-understanding ".
(2) Detailed: teaching knowledge of meaning, spelling, grammar, and usage, etc. about TL intended for "misunderstanding".

4. Neckle

A system called Neckle (Network-based Communicative Kanji Learning Environment Focusing on the Difference between Japanese and Chinese Kanji Meaning) has been developed. Neckle has an agent interface called Ankle (Agent for Kanji Learning). In this environment, learners whose ML is Chinese learn Japanese Kanji through conversations with Japanese native speakers. This section we explain the development and user interface of Neckle.

4.1 System Architecture

Neckle has three parts: communication tool, Ankle and server. Communication tool uses text-based chat.

4.1.1 Ankle
Ankle always stays in learner's environment, supporting Kanji learning. It is composed of modules as following.
(1) Monitor: it is used for recording a dialogue between the learner and the native speakers. It finds Kanji in the conversation and then, determines whether these Kanji have meaning difference consulting the "Dictionary of knowledge"
(2) Agent interface: it is used for supporting knowledge learning.
(3) Student model: it is used for recording the learners' status of knowledge, last attending date and attending times.
(4) Mechanism of intervention strategy: if Kanji with meaning difference was used in conversation, the agent checks the gap existence according to CGM, notices a gap based on the learner model, and then determines intervention timing.
(5) Mechanism of teaching strategies: Ankle intervened in the conversation with question. If the learner's answer was wrong, the agent will decide the teaching strategy by referring to the student model.

4.1.2 Server
The server is composed of the following modules.
(1) Morpheme analyzer: a Japanese morpheme analyzer system. It analyzes the morphemes in a conversation and replays the result to Ankle.
(2) Dictionary server: the Kanji knowledge of Chinese and Japanese is recorded in this base. It is used for Ankle to judge any difference and teach the Kanji knowledge.

4.2 User interface

The user interface is shown in Figure 3. It has five windows: "chat", "Ankle", "question", "teaching" and "dictionary".
a)   Chat window: the learner can engage in a real time dialogue with a native speaker through the Chat system. For example, a Chinese learner "YU" and a

Japanese student "MORI" talk about a major at the University. Their conversation is as follows:

YU:Hi. I'm yu. Are you ready?

MORI:Ok. Let us talk about our study! What's your major?

YU:My major is Japanese literature.

MORI:Are you interested in Japanese language?

YU:Yes . I want to be a Japanese translator (翻訳)

"翻訳" in Japanese means "Translator" only. However in Chinese, its meaning is not only "Translator" but also "Interpreter". Therefore, Japanese people might understand into "Translator" only. So communicative gap might occur.

b) Agent window: the agent Ankle has an interface of personification, which starts with the Chat window. It monitors the dialogue and intervenes when different knowledge is involved in the dialogue. Ankle provides the learner with the message and transmits the intention to the learner using a prepared dialogue template.

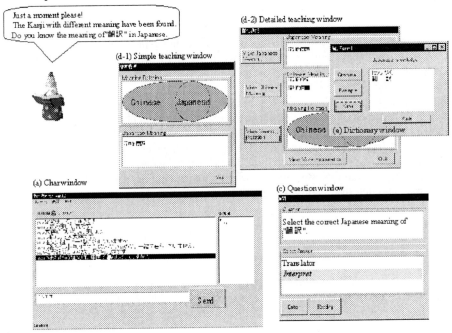

Fig. 3. User interface of Neckle.

c) Question window: Ankle provides learner with a question. Checks the answer and informs leaner about its correctness, with sound. Learner chooses from the choices. For example, about Japanese "翻訳(honyaku)", it is correct if learner chooses "Translator", and the conversation can continue without Ankle's intervention. However it is not correct if leaner chooses "Interpreter", then window (d-1) or (d-2) appears for teaching correct knowledge.

d) Teaching window:

  (d-1) Simply teaching window: for "temporary misunderstanding", the system gives operates with a diagram of the relationship of the Japanese-Chinese Kanji meanings. When the learner clicks a Japanese area, the meaning window will be popped up.

  (d-2) Detailed teaching window: for "misunderstanding", the system compares the learner's Chinese with the Japanese meaning to support the understanding of Japanese meaning. If the student requests to know other knowledge, a dictionary window will be showed.

e) Dictionary window: in addition to the Kanji meaning, Grammar, spelling and so on are also provided.

6. Conclusions and Future Work

This paper deals with the problem of language transfer in foreign language learning and analyzes the meaning relation between learner's ML and TL. We propose a communicative gap model based on meaning difference and suggest an environment for foreign language learning called Neckle. We also described an agent support that is a different approach from [2, 3]. Finally, we present the development of Neckle, which uses the agent Ankle, and show the experimentation about Neckle. Neckle was developed on the Windows NT using Visual Basic 6.0. Access 97 was used for the Database. Chasen [8] is the morpheme analyzer of Japanese, and the Microsoft Agent [9] was used as our agent interface. In the future work, we will make Ankle to consider more learners' state of knowledge understanding, especially for advanced learners, and let the agent take part in conversation between learner and native speaker in a natural way. Secondly, we will try to apply Neckle to other languages.

Acknowledgments

This research was supported in part by the Grant-in-aid for scientific research No. 09558017, No.09480036, No.11878032 and No.11780125 from the Ministry of Education, Science, Sports and Culture in Japan.

References

1. Andou, S.: *The logic behind English and Japanese,* daisyukan (1986) 28-37. (in Japanese)
2. Ayala, G. & Yano, Y.: GRACILE: A Framework for Collaborative Intelligent Learning Environments, *Journal of Japanese Society for Artificial Intelligence*, Vol.10, No.6 (1995) 988-1002.

3. Ayala, G.: Modeling Software Agent for a Japanese Language Lifelong Learning Environment, *Proc. International Conference on Computer Processing of Oriental Languages 99,* (1999) *509-514.*

4. Bull, S.: Promoting Effective Learning Strategy Use in CALL, *Computer Assisted Language Learning,* Vol.10, No.1 (1997) 33-39

5. Bull, S., Pain, H. and Brna, P.: Student Modeling in an Intelligent Computer Assisted Language Learning System: The Issues of Language Transfer and Learning Strategy, *Proc. International Conference on Computers in Education 93* (1993) 121-126.

6. Bunkacho: *The Kango equivalent for Chinese,* research material of Japanese education (1978) 85-143 (in Japanese)

7. Hanson, J., Ribold, M. and Weber, P.: Cross Cultural Awareness, *Proc. World conf .on Educational Multimedia, Hypermedia & Telecommunications* (1998) 1900-1901.

8. Matumoto, Y., Kita, N., Yamashita, T., Hirano, Y., Ima, K. and Imamura, T: *System of Japanese morpheme analyzer – Chasen, Version1.0* (http://cactus.aist-nare.ac.jp/lab/nlt/ chasen.html) (1997) (in Japanese)

9. Microsoft Corporation: *Microsoft Agent Documentation,* (http://msdn.microsoft.com/ workshop/imedia/ agent/documentation.asp) (1999)

10. Mike Levy: Theory and Design in a Multimedia CALL Project in Cross - Cultural Pragmatics, *Computer Assisted Language Learning,* Vol.12, No.1 (1999) 29-57.

11. Keith Johnson and Keith Morrow: Communication in the classroom: applications and methods for a communication approach London: Longman. (1981)

12. Liu, Y., Ogata, H., Ochi, Y., and Yano, Y.: Agent based Computer Supported Language Learning Environment focusing on Languages Distinction, *Proc. International Conference on Computer Processing of Oriental Languages 99* (1999) 261-264.

13. Lado, R : *Linguistics across cultures: applied linguistics for language teachers.* Ann Arbor: Michigan University Press. (1957)

14. Okazaki, T., Okazaki, H.: *Communicative approach in Japanese education,* Bonjinsya (1990) (in Japanese)

15. Odlin, T.: *Language Transfer, Cross-Linguistic Influence in Language Learning,* Cambridge University Press. (1989)

16. Saita, I., arruson, R., Itoman, D., Otubo, K., Mtuzaki, H., Kawazoe, Y.and Iguti, N.: Designing Japanese Language Learning using Email, *Journal of Japanese Language Teaching Society* (1996) 49-54 (in Japanese)

17. St. Olaf : College Intercultural E-Mail Classroom Connections (1989) http://www.stolaf.edu/network/iecc/.

18. Tanaka, S., Abe, H.: The Language transfer in the foreign language learning -historical background and present-, *English education,* No, 1 (1989) 78-81, Taisyukan (in Japanese)

19. Tobita, Y., Ro, Y.: *Dictionary of Japanese and Chinese meaning,* Nan'undo (1987) (in Japanese)

20. Wardhaugh, Ronald: *The Contrastive analysis hypothesis,* Teachers of English to Speakers of Other Languages Inc. Quarterly 4 (1970) 123-30.

TEATRIX: Virtual Environment for Story Creation

Rui Prada*, Isabel Machado** and Ana Paiva*[1]

*IST-Technical University of Lisbon and INESC
Rua Alves Redol 9, 1000 Lisboa - Portugal
Rui.Prada@gaiva.inesc.pt
Ana.Paiva@inesc.pt
**INESC and CBL, University of Leeds
Rua Alves Redol 9, 1000 Lisboa - Portugal
Isabel.Machado@inesc.pt

Abstract. This paper describes TEATRIX; a learning environment designed to help children, and their teachers, in the whole process of collaborative story creation. TEATRIX provides an environment where both drama and story creation are merged into one medium providing a form of collaborative make-believe for children. While creating a story TEATRIX allows the children to interact with each other in a distributed 3D environment, by means of their chosen characters. Each character is an intelligent software agent living in the world of the story: the theatre stage. Characters that are not controlled by children act autonomously according to the actions and goals set up by their role in the story. The roles in the story are based on the work by Vladimir Propp on folk tales and can be chosen from a set that includes a villain, a hero, a princess, a helper, etc. Children not only set up the scene for the development of the play and its characters, but also do the whole performance. TEATRIX is being evaluated in a Computer Integrated Classroom (CiC) environment which is part of an EU funded project (the NIMIS project).

1. Introduction

Drama is part of our lives since early childhood. Children as young as three engage in the art of make-believe exploring the boundaries of the real and the fantastic [13]. One of the most important aspects of drama is that it provides a type of activity where children engage in the play actively, with several senses. Aristotle refers to this as "enactment": which means to act rather than to read. Enacted representations involve direct sensing as well as cognition [5].

However, due to its physical grounding, acting is often seen as activity done separately from the creation of stories and the writing process. Merging acting, reading and writing into one single environment, and supporting it, was one of the main goals of the research here presented. Such environment aimed at providing effective support for children developing: their notions of narrative, through the

---

[1] Ana Paiva is currently an academic visitor at the Intelligent and Interactive Group, Depart. of Electrical and Electronic Engineering, Imperial College of Science Technology and Medicine, London, UK.

dramatization of several situations; and, their ability to take a 2nd and 3rd person perspective across the experience of a wide range of situations.

To achieve such pedagogical goals, we relied strongly on the experiences that a school (O Nosso Sonho[2]) has with their *"Dramatic room"*. The *"Dramatic room"* is a special room where children choose to go to play dramatic games. There, they dress up, choose their story, choose their characters and act.

Based on this experience and evaluations conducted in the school [8] we designed TEATRIX, which is like a game where children, collaboratively, create their own stories, by choosing the scenes, the characters, acting and writing. In TEATRIX children create the stories using a set of pre-defined scenes and a set of pre-defined characters. These characters may act on behalf of the children or autonomously. Each child will expect the story to evolve in reaction to her character's actions. So, their characters must act in a believable way, in order for the story creation environment to engage the children in an entertaining experience, which can meet the child cognitive needs to interpret, understand and interact with the world in term of stories [1].

In this paper we will describe TEATRIX, its underlying architecture, and the role of the autonomous agents (as synthetic characters in the stories) and present some steps taken in the evaluation process.

This paper is organized as follows: first we will provide a description of what is TEATRIX, describing the several phases in the story creation process. Then, we will present the architecture used for the story creation environment and the agents there embedded. We show how such architecture fulfils the needs of TEATRIX story creation aims. Finally we will present the evaluation set up where TEATRIX is being used and tested.

2. Teatrix: General Description

TEATRIX is part of a large project **NIMIS** (Networked Interactive Media In Schools) [4], an **ESE** (Experimental Schools Environments) project in the i^3 (Intelligent Information Interfaces) area. The main goal of the **NIMIS** project is to develop a virtual classroom where the current activities, as well as new ones, can be carried out by children and teachers. TEATRIX is one of the applications within NIMIS. Others include "Today's Talking Typewriter"[15] and "T'rrific Tales". The first step in the development of TEATRIX was to experience and to gather information from collaborative story creation situations in real classrooms by children of target ages. The findings have shown that these activities are performed in well-defined phases [9]. In the first place the teacher together with his pupils chooses the story to be played, then each child chooses which character he wants to play. When everybody is happy with his role in the story, the stage set-up and the characterization of the young actors is made. The class is ready for the performance and the play begins.

---

[2] O Nosso Sonho is a school in the suburbs of Lisbon situated in a deprived area. The school's pedagogical approach, since it is not a curricular school, aims at promoting free choice and mature decisions by the children. So, everyday children have the freedom to choose which "room" to go, either, the drama room, the intellectual room or the studio room. The CiC environment is set up in one side of the intellectual room.

Aiming at the recreation and expansion of this activity in a virtual interactive learning environment. TEATRIX transposes the story creation process of a real classroom into a virtual classroom and merges the writing with the playing. We've recognized from the real world experience that the whole process can be divided into three different phases, for each we've defined a different module: story set-up, story creation and story writing.

2.1 Phase 1: Story Set-up - Backstage

In this module a child can shape the story to be created by describing its main components: scenes, characters and items.

A scene is a spatial location where the characters can perform and interact; it has some décor objects that enrich its definition and has several exits, which allow the connection of different scenes. The characters can use these exits to move between scenes. For instance, in *Hansel and Gretel* possible scenes are: the house of the children, through the forest, a path in the forest, the wicked witch house, etc.

 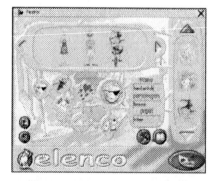

Fig. 1. Story set-up. On the left is the scenes set-up and on the right is the characters set-up.

Characters are defined by their name, their type, which defines their social stereotype (e.g. a little girl, an old lay, etc.), and their role in the story. A role, according to Barbara Hayes Roth [3], is the class of individuals, whose prototypical behaviours, relationships, and interactions are known both to the actors and to the audience. TEATRIX only allow six different roles for its characters: *villain, hero, helper, magician, beloved one and beloved relatives*. The choice of these roles is based on the seminal work done by the Propp [11] on folk and fairy tales. Our *Hansel and Gretel* example will have four actors: a boy, a girl, an old lady and a bird. The boy will be "Hansel" and he'll be a *hero*, the little girl will be "Gretel" and also a *hero*, the old lady will be a "wicked witch" and will be the *villain* and the bird will be the *helper*.

Throughout the play characters may need some items to support their performance. Items extend the base behaviour of a character as they give it new forms of interaction (e.g. with a magic wand a wicked witch can bewitch the little boy Hansel).

The story set-up is only completed when every character and item is placed on its starting scene (the place where they will first appear when the story creation starts) and the desired connections between the scenes as established. Figure 1 shows two application snapshots of the backstage module.

Finaly, the whole set-up is saved for future use or used immediately for a performance.

2.2. Phase 2: Story Creation - On stage

Once the initial set up is done, children can then play the prepared story. Note that one story set-up can be used for creating many different stories. The set-up only defines the initial situation (scenes, charcters and items), and it is not difficult to see that from the same starting point several stories may emerge.

This story creation module is a multi-user module where several children can work together on the same story giving life to the characters. A child may have two roles in this phase: to be the owner of the story or just be one of its players. The owner is the one who took the initiative of the story creation. He chooses the story he wants to create from the set of stored set-ups and then waits for other children to join in. The owner sees every character that is chosen and has the power to initiate the story performance.

When everything is ready, the curtain is raised. The initial situation is narrated and a three-dimensional representation of the story world will appear (see figure 2 that shows a scene in a forest featuring a witch, a girl and a big cooking pot). Each child gets a view of the scene where his character was first placed. The child can control his character by choosing a specific action chosen from set of defined actions, which can change according to the character's type and role.

All characters that were not chosen by any child are system controlled and act in a goal oriented manner based on their type and role. For example, a villain will have the major goal to harm the hero.

Fig. 2. Creating a story. The central area show a 3D representation of the scene our controlled character is currently in, we can see other characters and items that are also there.

The children interact with each other and with the world, by means of their characters, being able to talk to the others, pick up and use items. The story emerges from this interaction. However, not all interactions lead to a coherent story. Thus, to support the achievement of a coherent structure in the performance, guaranteeing that the characters perform according to their roles a director may be put in charge. We will discuss this element in more detail later in this paper.

When the story is considered finished, usually by the director (can also be finished by some children giving up), it will be stored for future replay or writing.

2.3 Phase 3: Story Writing - The audience

In this module children can see the stories they've performed as a recorded movie and reflect upon the work done. The movie can be stopped at any time, rewound or forwarded as desired. A montage process can also be done on the original story. As a child watches the movie she can write about it or even criticize it. A child can write more than once about the same story. All written stories are stored to be read later or shared with other children.

3. The Agents in the Fantasy Worlds of TEATRIX

When the play starts all characters in the story creation environment must act in order for a story to emerge. To achieve that, they were built as intelligent agents living in a synthetic 3D world. The use of intelligent agents as synthetic characters has had an increase of interest in the past few years. Works such as [2], [6], [12], [14] are good examples of how intelligent agents can improve the communication between learning environments and learners. Such agents can have life-like properties in order to help the learner, explain concepts, and demonstrate tasks. But the use of synthetic characters in learning situations does not necessarily fall into a tutor or a companion role. For example, recently a synthetic character was used as a learner avatar in a 3D world to teach microprocessor concepts [7]. In TEATRIX the intelligent agents will be the actors in a play.

To support the development of these agents we've elaborated an architecture with two main concepts: the world and the agents.

3.1 The World

The world is the space where objects and agents exist. In TEATRIX the world is a three-dimensional stage divided into several locales (the scenes referred in section 2.1). The world objects are classed according to an ontology that divides the world entities into animated, that can change the world (e.g. agents), and inanimated. The inanimated entities can be portable and/or usable. The usable entities that are portable are items. Each different story will have a different ontology, based on the previous definition, depending on the world objects it may have. E.g. a story that takes place in a forest scene and has a magic wand on it needs a magic wand class and other classes that describe the décor objects in a forest (e.g. a tree class) in the ontology.

3.2 The Agents

The characters in the story are implemented as agents "living" in the world of the story, its stage.

The agent architecture has five components (see figure 3): (1) the mind, responsible for the agent's behaviour; (2) the body, responsible for the representation of the agent in the world; (3) the effectors, responsible for the execution the agent actions in the world; (4) the sensors, responsible for the information acquisition; and (5) the inventory which keeps track of the agent's possessions.

Not every component is needed in a TEATRIX agent. For example, the body and the inventory can be undefined, which means that the agent can not be placed in a world locale, because it's "physical" representation is defined in his body, and cannot pick up items from the world (since it does not have a way of keeping them). The mind, sensors and effectors are essential.

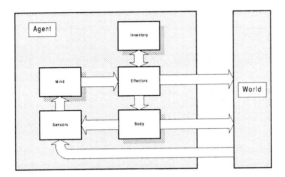

Fig. 3. Agent Components.

Next, we present a more detailed description of each agent component.

Mind. The mind keeps the agent's knowledge about the world (the world model) and about himself: the actions he can perform, their consequences, his goals and his emotional state. The decision-making process is based on this knowledge. The agent can react to a perception or just act because it wants to change the world to according to its goals. Figure 4 shows the mind components and the links between them.

Five components manipulate the mind information: (1) the Perception Filter determines if a perception received from a sensor is relevant to the agent at that particular moment (similarly to [10]); (2) the World Model Update assures that the internal World Model is coherent with the perceptions received; (3) the Emotional Reaction change the Emotional State as the World Model or agent Goals change; (4) the Goal Update revise the agent Goals as his World Model or Emotional State change; (5) the Action Planning is responsible for the planning of the agents' actions. Planning takes into account the current Goals, World State, the Actions that can be performed and the Emotional State. The Emotional State allows the agent to have preferences between Actions in certain circumstances.

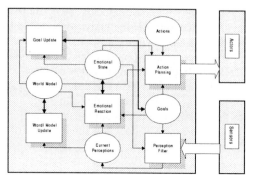

Fig. 4. Mind Components. Boxes represent mind processes and ellipses mind knowledge.

When the mind decides which action to perform it informs the corresponding effector to start the execution of that action. However, the agent's behaviour is conditioned by the its type and role. Two agents of the same type act differently if they have different roles and two agents with different types perform differently the same role. The character role defines some goals for the agent. For instance a "hero" has a predefined goal that is defeating the "villain" [9].

When a child controls a character, the mind of such agent has a passive role. The agent will not act by itself and therefore the action planning will be inactive. However, all other components will still be active as the agent will continue to have an emotional state and its own goals. For example, the child may force her character to do something against its current goals, and although it performs such behaviour, its emotional state will change into a more negative one.

Body. The body represents the agent in the world. Such representation is not only the agent's appearance to others, but also its "physical" state, which includes properties such as height, weight, position in the world, etc.

Characters are represented in the world as "sprites" which means they don't have 3D representations but animated 2D representations. For every action there is an animated sequence of images that represents it in the world. The character type reflects its "physical" appearance so the animations vary according to a character type. The emotional state also changes the way the actions are represented.

Effectors. An effector is the component that contains all the information of how to perform an action. The performance is divided in three phases. In the first phase the effector verifies if all preconditions are fulfilled. This verification is necessary because the world model of the agent can be different from the real world, and thus, although the agent believes he can perform an action, that may not possible in the real world. After such verification the action execution starts. Each step in the execution has a partial effect in the world and must be represented; this representation is achieved through the body. When the execution ends, the effector makes sure the action is finalized, performing the correct changes on the world. When an action needs an item to be performed the effector can use the inventory contents for that. In TEATRIX there are some basic actions that are common for all agents: walk, get item, drop item, use item, activate item, interact and talk. The agent can have some specific type and role actions that will enrich this basic set.

Sensors. Sensors are the information translators that gather information from the world changes and inform the mind about such changes. An agent knows the effects of his own actions by means of his sensors. A sensor can filter a world event and not deliver it to the mind. This process simulates the "physical" limitations of the agent. This is different from the perception filtering process of the mind, in that case the process verifies if the agent is interested in the event and not if he is able to "see" it.

Inventory. The inventory can be seen as a backpack where the agent keeps all its possessions. The agent may also have an item in his hand, and it can switch that item with any other in his backpack, only that item (in the hand) can be used.

3.3 Director Agent

The director agent is the one responsible for narrative control of the story. Having no "physical" representation in the world, he has no body or inventory. However, he has some God-like privileges, this means, he can sensor in all world locales, insert some new items or characters in any world locale and is able to know about every action occurring in the world. Further, the director agent can talk to the other agents, giving them performance directives, even control them if need (in behalf of the story coherence). It is the director agent who decides when the story is over. A child can also control this agent and thus becomes the director of the play.

3.4 Distributed Architecture

Since TEATRIX is a co-operative environment we needed to distribute the architecture defined above. As we've mentioned before there is one child who takes the initiative of creating the story. This child will have specific competencies that the other ones don't. The module associated with that child is named the story server.

In each story creation process there will be a story server and zero or more others client modules. The server module is responsible for resolving synchronization conflicts for shared resources (e.g. two characters try to get the same item) and for controlling the system time. The server also controls the director agent and all character agents that were not chosen by any child (system controlled).

The other modules, as well as the server, have complete information about the world and its locales. Each module controls the agent chosen by its child user, but only has clones of the other characters in the world. These clones don't have capability of reasoning (e.g. don't have a mind) and thus only repeat the actions that the agents they clone perform.

The director agent can not be cloned and only acts in the server world. Its actions are then transferred from world to world.

4. Evaluation

To ground the development of TEATRIX we've performed some studies on how stories arise and are developed in the *dramatic room* of the school "O Nosso Sonho". These results will, in the future, be used for the evaluation that is being carried out at the different schools within the project. The NIMIS classroom [15] (see Figures 5) is already in use in three different schools: one in Duisburg, Germany, one in the Leeds, UK, and one in Lisbon, Portugal. A first prototype of TEATRIX is installed in the Portuguese school and has started to be used by the children and the teachers.

Our plans for evaluation include the study of the conditions where the NIMIS classroom and its applications lead to the improvement of literacy, narrative skills and the ease of collaboration between children.

Fig. 5. NIMIS Classroom. Photos taken in the German school during a lesson where the NIMIS software was in use.

5. Conclusions

In this paper we have described TEATRIX a learning environment designed to help children, and their teachers, in the whole process of collaborative story creation. TEATRIX provides an environment where both drama and story creation are merged into one medium providing a form of collaborative make-believe for children. We've described the underlying architecture of TEATRIX focusing on the role of the autonomous agents (as synthetic characters in the stories). We've discussed the diverse elements that form part of the agent's architecture showing how these elements are combined to achieve the behaviour of the characters playing roles in the story.

TEATRIX is already in use in the school integrated in a Computer Integrated Classroom Scenario (CiC) developed within the NIMIS project. The next step is to evaluate its use and find out how the system is helping the students and the teachers in their learning activity, in particular in literacy.

References

1. Dautenhahn, K.: "Story-Telling in Virtual Environments". Working Notes Intelligent Virtual Environments, Workshop at the 13th biennial European Conference on Artificial Intelligence, Brighton, UK, 1998.

2. Frasson, C., Mengelle, T. and Aimeur, E.: "Using pedagogical agents in a multi-strategic intelligent tutoring system", in Proceedings of the AI-ED workshop on Pedagogical Agents, Kobe, 1997.

3. Hayes-Roth, B.: "Acting in Character", in Creating Personalities for Synthetic Actors, Eds R. Trappl and P. Petta, Springer, 1997

4. Hoppe U. et al: "The NIMIS Project" technical report, The NIMIS project, 1999.

5. Laurel, B. Computers as Theatre, Addison-Wesley, 1993.

6. Lester, J., Converse, S., Kahler, S., Barlow, S., Stone, B. and Bhoga, R.: The Persona effect: Affective Impact of Animated Pedagogical Agents. In CHI'97 Electronic Publications, 1997

7. Lester, J., Zettlemoyer, L., Gregoire, J. and Bares, W.: "Explanatory Lifelike Avatars: Performing User Centered Tasks in 3D Learning Environments, in Autonomous Agents'99, ACM Press, 1999

8. Machado, I., Martinho, C. and Paiva, A.: Once upon a time... In Proceedings of the AAAI Symposium on Narrative Intelligence, Ed. P. Sengers and M. Matheas, AAAI Press, 1999.

9. Machado, I. and Paiva A.: "Heroes Villains, Magicians...: Believable Characters in a Story Creation Environment". In Proceeding of the AIED workshop on Life-like Pedagogical Agents, Le Mans 1999.

10. Martinho, C. and Paiva, A.: "Pathematic Agents: Rapid development of Believable Emotional Agents in Intelligent Virtual Environments", in Autonomous Agents'99, ACM Press, 1999.

11. Propp, V.: Morphology of the folktale. Austin: University of Texas Press, 1968.

12. Rickel, J. and Johnson, L.: Integrating Pedagogical Capabilities in a Virtual Environment Agent. In W.L. Johnson & B. Hayes-Roth (ed.): Autonomous Agents'97, ACM Press (1997).

13. Singer, D and Singer, J.: The House of Make-Believe, Harvard University Press, 1990.

14. Swan, E., Johnson, L. and Ganesham, R.: Pedagogical Agents on the Web. In Autonomous Agents'99, ACM Press, 1999.

15. Tewiseen, F., Lingnau, A. and Hoppe,U.: "Today's Talking Typewriter" Supporting Early Literacy in a Classroom Environment. To be published in the proceedings of Intelligent Tutoring Systems 2000 Conference.

Fading and Deepening: The Next Steps for Andes and other Model-Tracing Tutors

Kurt VanLehn[1], Reva Freedman[1], Pamela Jordan[1], Charles Murray[1], Remus Osan[1],
Michael Ringenberg[1], Carolyn Rosé[1], Kay Schulze[3], Robert Shelby[2], Donald Treacy[2],
Anders Weinstein[1], and Mary Wintersgill[2]

Abstract. Model tracing tutors have been quite successful in teaching cognitive skills; however, they still are not as competent as expert human tutors. We propose two ways to improve model tracing tutors and in particular the Andes physics tutor. First, tutors should fade their scaffolding. Although most model tracing tutors have scaffolding that needs to be gradually removed (faded), Andes' scaffolding is already "faded," and that causes student modeling difficulties that adversely impact its tutoring. A proposed solution to this problem is presented. Second, tutors should integrate the knowledge they currently teach with other important knowledge in the task domain in order to promote deeper learning. Several types of deep learning are discussed, and it is argued that natural language processing is necessary for encouraging such learning. A new project, Atlas, is developing natural language based enhancements to model tracing tutors that are intended to encourage deeper learning.

[1] University of Pittsburgh, Learning Research and Development Center, Pittsburgh, PA, 15260 (vanlehn@cs.pitt.edu)
[2] United States Naval Academy, Department of Physics
[3] United States Naval Academy, Computer Science Department

1   Model Tracing Tutors

This paper considers how to improve an already successful type of intelligent tutoring system, the model-tracing tutor (MTT). Although Anderson, Boyle and Reiser (1985) coined the term, MTT refers to a relatively broad class of intelligent tutoring systems, namely those that contain a model of the cognition that one would like students to engage in and a means of encouraging students to reason in that fashion. An MTT usually has three modules: an expert model, a graphical user interface and a pedagogical module. After describing these modules below, we describe in the following sections the two main problems that MTT face and our proposed solutions to them. We conclude with a short comparison of the proposed MTT and human tutors.

An MTT contains an *expert model* which models how the designers would like students to reason. It has problem solving strategies that are coherent, precise, complete, and often quite simple. Sometimes the strategies are designed to enhance learning rather then accurately replicate expert strategies. They may require doing steps that students and even some instructors do not usually do, such as solving algebra word problems by writing arithmetic equations before writing algebraic ones (Aleven, Koedinger, Sinclair, & Snyder, 1998).

Most MTT have a *high bandwidth graphical user interface* (GUI). A GUI has high bandwidth if it has students display most of their reasoning, typically by requiring them to enter more information than they would if they were working as normal on a sheet of paper (VanLehn, 1988). For instance, students might have to define variables, as in the Andes physics tutor (Gertner & VanLehn, 2000), or provide coherent labels for columns in tables and axes in graphs (Aleven, Koedinger, & Cross, 1999; Aleven et al., 1998). Some GUI even have students maintain a goal tree (e.g., Koedinger & Anderson, 1993; Reiser, Beekelaar, Tyle, & Merrill, 1991; Singley, 1990). Many MTT designers claim that explicating such information increases learning, and there is some evidence for that claim (e.g., Merrill & Reiser, 1994; Singley, 1990).

An MTT also contains a *pedagogical module* that can provide immediate feedback and hints. Feedback is given whenever the student's action does not match the expert model's action. Help is usually provided via a hint sequence. A hint sequence starts with a general hint, then allows the student to try again. If the student's new action is also incorrect or the student ask for more help, then the tutor gives the next hint in the sequence, which provides more information about what the target action should be. The hints become more specific until the student enters the target action correctly. If the tutor runs out of hints, it either tells the student exactly what to enter or does the action for the student. Clearly, the pedagogical module is based on the hypothesis that immediate feedback and hint sequences facilitate learning. There have been several studies of this hypothesis (e.g., Anderson, Corbett, Koedinger, & Pelletier, 1995; Mark & Greer, 1995).

2 Fading

Although MTTs have an enviable track record (e.g., Anderson et al., 1995; Koedinger, Anderson, Hadley, & Mark, 1995; McKendree, Radlinski, & Atwood, 1992; Reiser, Copen, Ranney, Hamid, & Kimberg, in press; Shelby et al., in prep.), they are sometimes criticized as being too rigid. Below, we review such claims then discuss "fading," which is an obvious solution to the rigidity problems. However, the bulk of this section concerns some non-obvious problems that fading causes, how they emerged in the Andes tutoring system, and what we propose to do about them.

MTTs are sometimes criticized for allowing only one strategy for problem solving when many are possible. For instance, Anderson and Corbett's Lisp tutor has been criticized for forcing students to enter code top-down (e.g., Reiser, Kimberg, Lovett, & Ranney, 1992). The critics argue that when the tutor keeps students on the solution path of a single strategy, it prevents the students from inventing their own strategies, testing them and refining them.

A second complaint is that the tutor often forces students to enter information that they often try to hold in their working memory. This could prevent students from learning how to manage their use of memory. For instance, when solving complex algebra equations, some students try to write down fewer intermediate steps then expert mathematicians (Lewis, 1981). Such students need to learn to write more down and trust their memory less, but the rigid scaffolding of MTT GUIs thwarts such learning because it controls how much they must write down.

A third criticism is that the tutor provides too much scaffolding of error handling. Because the tutor detects errors for the student and hints at how to correct them, when students of MTTs are tested with the tutor absent, they are often worse at detecting and correcting their own errors than students who covered the same material without the tutor (Reiser et al., in press).

As Collins, Brown and Newman (1989), McArthur (1990) and others have noted, expert human tutors often start with large amounts of scaffolding, then *fade* it as students exhibit more competence. Similarly, MTTs should fade the procedural restrictions on problem solving, thus allowing students to solve problems any way they want, to experiment with strategies and to manage their use of memory. MTTs should also fade their support for error handling, thus allowing student to learn how to detect and correct errors by themselves.

2.1   Andes is Already Partially Faded

Although most MTTs should fade their scaffolding, our MTT, Andes (Gertner & VanLehn, 2000; VanLehn, 1996) has the opposite problem. It has turned out to have too little scaffolding. Although Andes flags incorrect entries by turning them red, it allows students to enter steps in any order and to omit almost any step. This gives Andes' students the freedom to discover strategies and manage their use of memory. On the other hand, the lack of procedural restrictions has caused 2 pedagogical problems.

First, some students failed to develop effective problem solving strategies, and Andes' hints about what step to do next only frustrated and confused them. The log files indicate that many Andes students do not follow a single strategy. They often mix steps from multiple strategies, probably without knowing that they are doing so. When a student asks for advice on what to do next, Andes uses probabilistic reasoning to guess the step the student might be trying to do next and construct a hint sequence leading up to it (Gertner, Conati, & VanLehn, 1998; Gertner, 1998). The students sometimes can't figure out why that step should be next. Indeed, there usually is no good explanation because their strategy wasn't coherent. Some students felt quite frustrated by the apparent randomness of Andes' advice, not realizing that it was caused by their own random behavior.

Second, when students received hints on errors, they often could not fix the errors themselves. Instead, they proceeded all the way to the last hint in the sequence, which would tell them exactly what to enter. Andes hint sequences are no different in design from those used successfully by other MTT, which suggests that it is the *context* of the hints which is causing them to fail. For instance, a common error was to omit a negative sign that was introduced by projecting a vector. Andes' first hint on a sign error is to "check your signs." If the student has drawn the appropriate vector and is working on projecting it (e.g., entering an equation such as $V_x=-V*\cos\theta$), then this hint would probably work fine. However, the students who make this error have often skipped both drawing the vector and writing the projection equation down. When they receive the "check signs" hint, they can't figure out where the negative sign should have come from because they did the calculations in their head. Many hints fail not because they are bad hints, but because Andes let student do so many critical steps in their head that the students cannot reconstruct their reasoning in order to find the error.

From these observations during formative evaluations, it has become clear that although Andes' faded scaffolding allows students to invent their own strategies, repair their own errors, and manage their use of memory, some students seem to need more scaffolding. They should be constrained to use a single strategy and to not skip key steps. That is, some students need the rigid, procedural scaffolding that most MTT have but Andes lacks.

2.2   Micro-Adaptive Fading

A straightforward approach to fading is to equip the MTT with different levels of scaffolding. Novice students start with a high level of scaffolding. As their competence increases, the tutor reduces (fades) the level of scaffolding. This is a *macro-adaptive* approach to fading (cf. Shute, 1993). The tutor changes its level of scaffolding in between problems, but during a problem's solution, the level remains the same. Inspired by our analysis of human tutors, we are revising Andes to use a *micro-adaptive* approach to fading. The scaffolding only occurs at the moment the student seems to need it.

The key idea is that although Andes will be able to recognize a wide variety of strategies, skipped steps, etc., it will only give advice and help on a single strategy. The strategy to (a) select a quantity whose value is sought, (b) decide which major physics principle is appropriate for finding it, (c) execute the procedure for that principle, (d) figure out which quantities still need to be found, then repeat the cycle from step (a). This strategy is well known in physics, and the procedures often appear in textbooks. Some tutoring systems (e.g., Reif & Scott, 1999) constrain students to follow this strategy. The physicists on the Andes project have designed the specific strategy to be taught by determining which physics principles are the major ones and designing procedures for them. For instance, Newton's second law (F=m*a) is a major principle, but the weight law (W=m*g) is not. Instead, it is included in the Newton's law procedure. The physicists also determined which steps in the procedures must be entered by student on the Andes GUI, and which can be done mentally if the student wishes.

The new Andes will not constrain students to follow the strategy. Just as before, students can enter steps in any order, skipping as many as they like. As long as they enter a correct step, it will turn green. Moreover, if they can fix their incorrect (red) steps without help, then they will see no signs of the target strategy. However, if they ask for help, then Andes will try to get them to follow the target strategy.

More specifically, if they are stuck and ask for a hint on what step to do next, Andes will start by asking them, "What quantities are you seeking?" and offering a menu. Incorrect menu selections evoke feedback and a hint sequence. When the student has selected a quantity that is actually sought in this problem, then Andes asks, "What principle should be used to find it?" and offers a menu. Again students get feedback and hints until they have chosen a principle appropriate for the problem and the sought quantity. Andes then matches the principle's procedure to the student's entries and determines the first step that the student has not yet done. It gives hints on that step. When the student finally does the target step, this help episode is over, and the student resumes solving the problem. If the student immediately asks for another hint on what to do next, then Andes may skip some of the dialog and just give hints on the next step in the principle's procedure. In other words, the procedural scaffolding is there if the student wants it, but they have to ask for it.

When the student asks "what's wrong?" with an incorrect step, then the new Andes will not always given them help on that step. If the student has skipped some critical steps, then Andes will identify which one should be done first and hint it by saying, "Your errors are probably caused by skipping <step>. If you do it, you'll probably figure out what your errors are. If not, ask me for help again." If the student does ask for help again, they will get it in a context which allows the hints to succeed. For instance, they won't actually get hints on fixing a sign error until they have first drawn the relevant vector.

This approach to fading is micro-adaptive in that scaffolding is done only on the part of the strategy whose absence is causing errors or confusion. As students become more competent, they ask for less help and thus receive less scaffolding. Thus, Andes fades the scaffolding without even maintaining a student model.

Andes' micro-adaptive fading should cause more transfer than macro-adaptive fading. If students are forced to follow a specific procedure, then they will only learn how to do the procedure. They won't learn about the errors and confusions that happen if they don't follow it. With Andes' micro-adaptive fading, students learn the value of the procedure the hard way, by making errors and getting lost. This increases the chance that they will use the target strategy when working on their own, thus increasing transfer.

3   Deep Learning

MTTs have sometimes been criticized for failing to encourage deep learning. The following are probably only a few of the criticisms that fall under this category, but they are certainly enough to set a challenging research agenda:

1. If students don't reflect on the tutor's hints, but merely keep guessing until they find an action that gets positive feedback, they can learn to do the right thing for the wrong reasons, and the tutor will never know such shallow learning occurred (Aleven et al., 1999; Aleven et al., 1998).
2. Since the tutor does not ask students to explain their actions, students may not learn the domain's language. Our verbal protocols are replete with domain language misuse. Educators have become increasingly concerned that students learn to "talk science," as that appears to be part of a deep understanding of the science, as well as facilitating scientific writing, working collaboratively in groups, and beginning to participate in the culture of science.
3. The high bandwidth GUI, which asks students to display many of the details of their reasoning, doesn't promote stepping back to see the "basic approach" one has used to solve a problem. Even students who have gotten high grades in a physics course can seldom describe their basic approaches, nor tell when two problems have similar basic approaches (Chi, Feltovich, & Glaser, 1981).

4. Students of quantitative skills, such as algebra or physics problem solving, are usually not encouraged to see their work from a qualitative, semantic perspective, so they fail to induce versions of the skills that can be used to solve qualitative problems and to check quantitative ones for reasonableness. Even physics students with high grades often score poorly on tests of qualitative physics (e.g., Hestenes, Wells, & Swackhamer, 1992).

Many of these objections can be made to just about any form of instruction. Even expert tutors and teachers have difficulty getting student to learn deeply. Therefore, these criticisms of MTT should only encourage us to improve them, not reject them.

There are two common themes in the list above. First, all four involve integrating problem-solving knowledge with other knowledge, namely: (1) principles or rationales, (2) domain language, (3) abstract, basic approaches and (4) qualitative rules of inference. Second, the kinds of instructional activities that are currently used to tap these other kinds of knowledge make critical use of natural language. Although one can invent graphical or formal notations to teach these kinds of knowledge on a computer, they might be more confusing to the students and instructors than the knowledge that they are trying to convey. Moreover, students and instructors are likely to resist learning a new formalism, even a graphical one, if they will only use temporarily.

3.1 Atlas: a Natural-Language Enhancement for Model-Tracing Tutors

We believe that if MTTs are to become more effective at encouraging deep learning, they must use natural language. Therefore, we have begun building *Atlas*, a module that can be added to Andes or other MTT in order to conduct natural language dialogs that will promote deep learning. Atlas uses natural-language generation technology originally developed for CIRCSIM tutor (Freedman & Evens, 1996), the LC-FLEX parser (Rose & Lavie, in press), and the COCONUT model of collaborative dialog (DiEugenio, Jordan, Thomason, & Moore, in press). See (Freedman, Rose, Ringenberg, & VanLehn, 2000) for a description of the system architecture.

Initially, Atlas will support only a simple form of interaction. Most of the time, the students interact with Andes just as they ordinarily would. However, if Atlas notices an opportunity to promote deep learning, it takes control of the interaction and begins a natural language dialog. Although Atlas can ask students to make Andes actions as part of the dialog (e.g., it might have the student draw a single vector), most of the dialog is conducted in a scrolling text window. When Atlas decides the dialog is complete, it signs off and lets the student return to solving the problem with Andes.

The dialogs are called *knowledge construction* dialogs, because they are designed to encourage students to infer or construct the target knowledge. Like a Socratic tutor (Collins & Stevens, 1982), Atlas tries to avoid telling the student what the student needs to know, but it may do so as a last resort.

3.2 Knowledge Construction Dialogs to Teach Principles

So far, Atlas conducts just one kind of knowledge construction dialog. The dialogs are designed to teach a domain principle. They occur when the student has made an error or gotten stuck, and has asked Andes for help. Atlas takes over when Andes would have given its final hint. Instead of telling the student the target principle, it conducts a dialog designed to teach the principle in a Socratic fashion.

The specific dialogs we are implementing were observed in transcripts of human tutors (VanLehn, Siler, Murray, & Baggett, 1998; VanLehn, Siler, Murray, Yamauchi, & Baggett, in press). For instance, consider the target principle "When an object is moving in a straight line and slowing down, its acceleration is opposite its velocity." VanLehn et al. (in press) observed 15 knowledge construction dialogs for this rule. However, they can be reduced to three basic types. One derives the target principle from the definition of acceleration, another uses analogy, and a third shows that the students' belief (that acceleration is in the same direction as velocity) leads to contradictory and absurd conclusions.

Knowledge construction dialogs are often nested. For example, suppose the tutor starts by asking the student for the definition of acceleration. Most students will say, "velocity divided by time," which is almost right, so the tutor corrects it in a subtle way (Graesser, Person, & Magliano, 1995) by splicing in the missing information "Yes, it's *the change* in velocity divided by time." However, if the student's response indicates greater confusion than that (e.g., "It's the derivative of time."), then the tutor may drop into a knowledge construction dialog on the definition of acceleration. Empirically, human tutors seldom nest knowledge construction dialogs more than two deep. If the student seems hopelessly confused, then the tutor may abandon the top level knowledge construction dialog and start a different one by saying, e.g., "Well, forget about the definition of acceleration. Let's try an analogy. Suppose...."

Implementing even one knowledge construction dialog strategy is a major endeavor. Not only must the dialog strategy itself by developed, but types of student responses must be anticipated, each with an appropriate tutorial response. Moreover, the knowledge mentioned in the dialogs must be represented in such a way that the natural language processing modules can both recognize it in the students' contributions to the dialog and render it as fluent, easily understood text for the tutor's contributions. Our progress has been slow thus far, but should pick up as we develop more and more knowledge construction dialog strategies, because we expect them to share many parts.

3.3 Other Knowledge Construction Dialogs

We are in the process of collecting examples of other types of knowledge construction dialogs from a public archive of tutorial dialogs (see http://www.pitt.edu/~circle/Archive.htm) and designing Atlas dialog strategies to encourage deep learning of several different kinds. The following list indicates our plans and is numbered to correspond to the list of deep learning types mentioned earlier:

1. *Avoiding superficial learning.* Critics say that MTT students often learn how to do the right thing for the wrong reasons. That is, they induce conditions for their operators that have roughly the same extension as the correct conditions. To detect such shallow learning, Andes-Atlas should periodically ask students to describe and justify their actions. For instance, if the student enters $F-W-m*a=0$, Atlas-Andes should ask, "What are you doing here?" Hopefully, the

student will answer, "I'm applying Newton's law along the vertical axis." However, if they say, "I'm solving F−W=m*a," then the tutor should probe deeper to see if there is any knowledge behind the algebra.

2. *Using the domain language.* Critics say that MTTs should teach students how to use the language of the domain. For example, if the students, when asked the question above, fail to give a recognizable answer, they should be coached on how to use physics language more accurately. For instance, the tutor might say, "I didn't understand your explanation. Could you say something like, 'I applied <a principle> to <objects> because I wanted <goal>.'? For example, you might say, 'I applied Newton's Second Law to the car because I wanted to find its acceleration.'"

3. *Inducing and using abstract plans.* Critics say that MTTs should encourage students to see the basic approach behind their problem solving and abstract plans from the details. For instance, after students have finished the classic Atwood's machine problem (two blocks hung from either end of a string that is draped over a massless, frictionless pulley), Atlas-Andes could ask them: "What was your basic approach to this problem?" They will hopefully say something like, "I applied Newton's law twice, once for each block."

4. *Connecting qualitative and quantitative reasoning.* MTTs should teach students how to reason qualitatively and how to connect that qualitative reasoning with their quantitative reasoning. For example, the tutor could interject qualitative questions into the student's work, such as "If the acceleration and the tension force are both upward, then increasing the tension should increase the acceleration, right? Is your equation consistent with that fact?" After the problem is solved, the tutor can ask the student to indicate what will happen under other conditions specified qualitatively. For instance, a common question that textbooks ask after students have solved the Atwood's pulley system is, "What would you expect to happen if the two blocks had the same mass? What do your equations say? What would happen if the left block's mass were zero? What do your equations say?"

Andes-Atlas is intended to close the gap between human tutors and MTTs. It provides enrichments to the usual MTT dialog in the form of knowledge construction dialogs. Although it might be possible to provide these enrichments with a GUI solution, the nature of the enrichments makes that unlikely. They clearly call for a language-based solution and that is what Andes-Atlas will provide.

Acknowledgements

This research was supported by Grant N00014-96-1-0260 from the Cognitive Sciences Division of the Office of Naval Research and by Grant 9720359 from the LIS program of the National Science Foundation. We gratefully acknowledge the contributions of the "Andes Alumni," Abigail Gertner, Cristina Conati, Patricia Albacete, Stephanie Siler, Ellen Dugan, Zhendong Niu and David Correll.

References

1. Aleven, V., Koedinger, K. R., & Cross, K. (1999). Tutoring answer-explanation fosters learning with understanding, *Artificial Intelligence in Education* (pp. 199-206). Amsterdam: IOS Press.
2. Aleven, V., Koedinger, K. R., Sinclair, H. C., & Snyder, J. (1998). Combating shallow learning in a tutor for geometry problem solving. In B. P. Goettle, H. M. Halff, C. L. Redfield, & V. J. Shute (Eds.), *Intelligent Tutoring Systems, Proceedings of the Fourth International Conference* (pp. 364-373). Berlin: Spring-Verlag.
3. Anderson, J. R., Boyle, C. F., & Reiser, B. J. (1985). Intelligent tutoring systems. *Science, 228*, 456-462.
4. Anderson, J. R., Corbett, A. T., Koedinger, K. R., & Pelletier, R. (1995). Cognitive Tutors: Lessons Learned. *The Journal of the Learning Sciences, 4*(2), 167-207.
5. Chi, M. T. H., Feltovich, P., & Glaser, R. (1981). Categorization and representation of physics problems by experts and novices. *Cognitive Science, 5*, 121-152.
6. Collins, A., Brown, J. S., & Newman, S. E. (1989). Cognitive apprenticeship: Teaching the craft of reading, writing and mathematics. In L. B. Resnick (Ed.), *Knowing, learning and instruction: Essays in honor of Robert Glaser* (pp. 543-494). Hillsdale, NJ: Lawrence Erlbaum Associates.
7. Collins, A., & Stevens, A. (1982). Goals and methods for inquiry teachers. In R. Glaser (Ed.), *Advances in Instructional Psychology, Vol. 2* . Hillsdale, NJ: Lawrence Erlbaum Associates.
8. DiEugenio, B., Jordan, P. W., Thomason, R. H., & Moore, J. D. (in press). The agreement process: An empirical investigation of human-human computer-mediated dialogues. *International Journal of Human-Computer Studies*.
9. Freedman, R., & Evens, M. W. (1996). Generating and revising hierarchical multi-turn text plans in an ITS. In C. Frasson, G. Gauthier, & A. Lesgold (Eds.), *Intelligent Tutoring Systems: Proceedings of the 1996 Conference* (pp. 632-640). Berlin: Springer.
10. Freedman, R., Rose, C. P., Ringenberg, M. A., & VanLehn, K. (2000). ITS Tools for natural language dialogue: A domain-independent parser and planner. In C. Frasson (Ed.), *Proceedings of ITS 2000*. . Berlin: Springer-Verlag.
11. Gertner, A., Conati, C., & VanLehn, K. (1998). Procedural help in Andes: Generating hints using a Bayesian network student model., *Proceedings of the 15th national Conference on Artificial Intelligence* .
12. Gertner, A. S. (1998). Providing feedback to equation entries in an intelligent tutoring system for Physics. In B. P. Goettl, H. M. Halff, C. L. Redfield, & V. J. Shute (Eds.), *Intelligent Tutoring Systems: 4th International Conference* (pp. 254-263). New York: Springer.
13. Gertner, A. S., & VanLehn, K. (2000). Andes: A coached problem solving environment for physics. In C. Frasson (Ed.), *Proceedings of ITS 2000* . New York: Springer.
14. Graesser, A. C., Person, N., & Magliano, J. (1995). Collaborative dialog patterns in naturalistic one-on-one tutoring. *Applied Cognitive Psychology, 9*, 359-387.
15. Hestenes, D., Wells, M., & Swackhamer, G. (1992). Force concept inventory. *The Physics Teacher, 30*, 141-158.
16. Koedinger, K., & Anderson, J. R. (1993). Reifying implicit planning in geometry: Guidelines for model-based intelligent tutoring system design. In S. P. L. a. S. J. Derry (Ed.), *Computers as cognitive tools* . Hillsdale, NJ: Lawrence Erlbaum Associates.
17. Koedinger, K. R., Anderson, J. R., Hadley, W. H., & Mark, M. A. (1995). Intelligent tutoring goes to school in the big city. In J. Greer (Ed.), *Proceedings of the 7th World Conference on Artificial Intelligence and Education* (pp. 421-428). Charlottesville, NC: AACE.
18. Lewis, C. (1981). Skill in algebra. In J. R. Anderson (Ed.), *Cognitive skills and their acquisition* (pp. 85-110). Hillsdale, NJ: Lawrence Erlbaum Associates.

19. Mark, M. A., & Greer, J. E. (1995). The VCR tutor: Effective instruction for device operation. *The Journal of the Learning Sciences, 4*(2), 209-246.
20. McArthur, D., Stasz, C., & Zmuidzinas, M. (1990). Tutoring techniques in algebra. *Cognition and Instruction, 7*(3), 197-244.
21. McKendree, J., Radlinski, B., & Atwood, M. E. (1992). The Grace Tutor: A qualified success. In C. Frasson, G. Gautheir, & G. I. McCalla (Eds.), *Intelligent Tutoring Systems: Second International Conference* (pp. 677-684). Berlin: Springer-Verlag.
22. Merrill, D. C., & Reiser, B. J. (1994). Scaffolding effective problem solving strategies in interactive learning   environments. In A. R. a. K. Eiselt (Ed.), *Proceedings of the Sixteenth Annual Conference of the Cognitive Science   Society* (pp. 629-634). Hillsdale, NJ: Lawrence Erlbaum Associates.
23. Reif, F., & Scott, L. A. (1999). Teaching scientific thinking skills: Students and computers coaching each other. *American Journal of Physics, 67*(9), 819-831.
24. Reiser, B. J., Beekelaar, R., Tyle, A., & Merrill, D. C. (1991). Gil: Scaffolding learning to program with reasoning-congruent   representations. In L. Birnbaum (Ed.), *The International Conference of the Learning Sciences: Proceedings of the 1991 Conference* (pp. 382-388). Charlottesville, NC: Association for the Advancement of Computers in Education.
25. Reiser, B. J., Copen, W. A., Ranney, M., Hamid, A., & Kimberg, D. Y. (in press). Cognitive and motivational consequences of tutoring and discovery learning. *Cognition and Instruction.*
26. Reiser, B. J., Kimberg, D. Y., Lovett, M. C., & Ranney, M. (1992). Knowledge representation and explanation in GIL, an intelligent tutor for   programming. In J. H. a. C. Larkin, R.W. (Ed.), *Computer Assisted Instruction and Intelligent Tutoring Systems: Shared Goals   and Complementary Approaches* (pp. 111-150). Hillsdale, NJ: Lawrence Erlbaum Associates.
27. Rose, C. P., & Lavie, A. (in press). Balancing robustness and efficiency in unification-augmented context-free parsers for large practical applications. In J. C. Junqua & G. V. Noord (Eds.), *Robustness in Language and Speech Technology* : Kluwer Academic press.
28. Shelby, R. N., Schulze, K. G., Treacy, D. J., Wintersgill, M. C., Gertner, A. G., & Vanlehn, K. (in prep.). The Andes Intelligent Tutor: an Evaluation .
29. Shute, V. J. (1993). A macroadaptive approach to tutoring. *Journal of Artificial Intelligence in Education, 4*(1), 61-93.
30. Singley, M. K. (1990). The reification of goal structures in a calculus tutor: Effects on problem   solving performance. *Interactive Learning Environments, 1*, 102-123.
31. VanLehn, K. (1988). Student modeling. In M. Polson & J. Richardson (Eds.), *Foundations of Intelligent Tutoring Systems* (pp. 55-78). Hillsdale, NJ: Lawrence Erlbaum Associates.
32. VanLehn, K. (1996). Conceptual and meta learning during coached problem solving. In C. Frasson, G. Gauthier, & A. Lesgold (Eds.), *ITS96: Proceeding of the Third International conference on Intelligent Tutoring Systems.* . New York: Springer-Verlag.
33. VanLehn, K., Siler, S., Murray, C., & Baggett, W. B. (1998). What makes a tutorial event effective? In M. A. Gernsbacher & S. J. Derry (Eds.), *Proceedings of the Twentieth Annual Conference of the Cognitive Science Society* (pp. 1084-1089). Hillsdale, NJ: Erlbaum.
34. VanLehn, K., Siler, S., Murray, C., Yamauchi, T., & Baggett, W. B. (in press). Human tutoring: Why do only some events cause learning? *Cognition and Instruction.*

An Intelligent Learning Environment for Novice Users of a GUI

Maria Virvou, Katerina Kabassi

Department of Informatics,
University of Piraeus,
Piraeus 18534, Greece
{mvirvou, kkabassi}@unipi.gr

Abstract. This paper describes an intelligent learning environment for novice users of a GUI. The learning environment allows users to work in a protected way; it monitors their actions and reasons about them so that it can make hypotheses about what their real intentions have been and examine whether these have been met. In case the system believes that the user has made an error it informs him/her about the error and suggests alternative actions that would have met his/her real intentions. In this way, a novice user can learn from his/her mistakes. The system performs student modelling which is based on an adaptation and implementation of a cognitive theory called Human Plausible Reasoning. The theory is used to simulate a novice user's correct or incorrect thinking as long as this is plausible according to the theory.

1   Overview

Novice users of software products lack the experience and knowledge about how to use a software product. Therefore they often experience problems while interacting with the product even if the user interface is considered user friendly, as is the case for Graphical User Interfaces. For example, McGraw [1] points out that even graphical user interfaces may prove difficult to traverse and use.

In this paper we describe an intelligent learning environment for novice users of a GUI that manipulates files, such as the Windows 95 Explorer [2]. The learning environment allows students to work in an uninterrupted way as they would in a standard explorer. However, it constantly reasons about their actions and intervenes to offer advice when it diagnoses an error. Therefore, if a user makes a mistake s/he will see the system's advice and thus learn from this mistake without having to suffer the consequences of it. An example of a possible mistake could be clicking the mouse on the command "copy" twice instead of clicking on "copy" and then on "paste".

The system needs to perform diagnostic reasoning in order to generate hypotheses about the students' incorrect actions. As Cerri and Loia [3] point out diagnostic reasoning is complex since intermediate states may be uncertain and human reasoning is influenced by many variables. Therefore, they suggest that a diagnosis of incorrect task performance by humans can only be achieved via a model of the human reasoning that gave rise to that performance.

For the diagnostic reasoning, which is part of the student modelling of the intelligent learning environment, we have adapted and implemented a part of a theory called Human Plausible Reasoning theory [4]. Human Plausible Reasoning theory (henceforth referred to as HPR) is a domain-independent theory originally based on a corpus of people's answers to everyday questions. HPR formalises the plausible inferences based on similarities, dissimilarities, generalisations and specialisations that people often use to make plausible guesses about matters that they only know partially.

One problem associated with the application of HPR to student modelling for the GUI is that there may be many plausible explanations about user's errors. The selection of a plausible explanation among the hypotheses generated can be improved if the context of a user's command is taken into account. Therefore, we have introduced the notion of "instability", which is used to imply the initiation of a user goal. For example, a user may create a new folder. This would add an instability to the file store because the system would expect the user to put some content to the new folder. Later, if the user issues a command that assigns content to this folder the instability introduced earlier is removed and the system considers the command as expected.

2 Related Work

2.1 Human Plausible Reasoning

HPR is based on analysis of people's answers to everyday questions about the world [4; 5; 6]. The theory consists of a formal representation of plausible inference patterns that are frequently employed in answering everyday questions, a set of parameters that affect the certainty of people's answers to such questions and a system relating the different plausible inference patterns and the different certainty parameters.

The theory represents an attempt in formalising plausible inferences that occur in people's responses to different questions. For example, if the question asked was whether coffee is grown in Llanos region in Colombia, the answer would depend on the knowledge retrieved from memory. If the subject knew that Llanos was in savanna region similar to that where coffee grows, this would trigger an inductive, analogical inference, and generate the answer yes [7].

According to the theory a large part of human knowledge is represented in "dynamic hierarchies", which are always being updated, modified or expanded. In this way the reasoning of people with patchy knowledge can be modelled. Table 1 illustrates an example of the patchy knowledge a person may have. The matrix illustrated in Table 1 is a collection of statements about geographic data. An example of a statement is: precipitation(Egypt) = very-light, which means that the precipitation of Egypt is very light. Precipitation is the descriptor, Egypt is the argument and very-light the referent. A descriptor is applied to an argument and together they form a term. For example, precipitation applies to Egypt and they form the term precipitation(Egypt). Descriptors, arguments and referents are organised into isa and ispart type hierarchies.

Table 1. Experimental Matrix of Geographic Data [6]

Location	Climate	Water supply	Has river?	Precipitation
Angola	?	Moderate or Abundant	Yes	Abundant
Egypt	Dry climate	Moderate	Yes	Very light
Florida	Subtropical	?	?	Moderate
Italy	Mediterranean	Moderate	Yes	?

There are four kinds of relation between objects in hierarchies: generalisation (GEN), specialisation (SPEC), similarity (SIM) and dissimilarity (DIS). Statement transforms, the simplest class of inference patterns, exploit the 4 possible relations among arguments and among referents to yield 8 types of statement transform. Statement transforms can be affected by certainty parameters. For example the degree of similarity (•) affects the certainty of any SIM or DIS inference.

2.2 Intelligent Tutoring Systems and Intelligent Help

The intelligent learning environment for a GUI has the architecture of Intelligent Tutoring Systems. It is widely agreed that the major functional components of an ITS architecture are the domain knowledge, the student modeller, the advice generator and the user interface [8; 9; 10].

However, the system itself is based on previous systems developed for providing intelligent help. One of them is called RESCUER [11; 12]. RESCUER is meant to operate on top of a UNIX shell and it silently monitors users interacting with UNIX. In case the system diagnoses an error of a user, it provides spontaneous help. The reasoning mechanisms of RESCUER are very similar to those of the system described in the present paper. However, the domain of UNIX commands is very different from the domain of a GUI where user actions are associated with mouse events and similarities of actions may involve the geographical position of objects on the screen.

A first attempt of adapting the reasoning mechanisms of RESCUER into a GUI resulted in a system called IFM [13]. This system served as a first prototype that could be evaluated by real users. Indeed the evaluation of IFM together with an empirical study conducted on users of a standard explorer resulted in the specification of major improvements, which are incorporated in the present work. In addition, further research has resulted in extending the adaptation and implementation of HPR to a much larger extent than IFM.

A similar approach to the student modelling of the intelligent learning environment is that of Calistri – Yeh [14], who has developed a model of plan recognition that addresses plan-based misconceptions. However, Calistri – Yeh assumes that the user must have explicitly stated his/her goal whereas in our case the system infers users' goals through monitoring and interpreting their actions. Another difference is that we use HPR transforms to provide a classification of misconceptions, instead of causal logic.

Finally, Eller and Carberry [15] describe a similar approach in a different domain (natural-language dialogues). They present meta-rules for hypothesising the cause of dialogue ill-formedness and for relaxing the plan inference process. Our approach of transforming a user's action can be considered close to the relaxation of the semantic interpretation of a user's utterance. However, in our case such "relaxation" of a user action can be achieved by the HPR statement transforms. The advantage of our method is that it provides a relatively domain-independent method of relaxation. Indeed, we have used HPR transforms in a different domain, such as UNIX, which is different from the domain of a GUI.

3   Operation of the System

The intelligent learning environment for novice users allows them to issue commands as they would in a standard explorer. The user issues a command (e.g. selects an icon or a command from a menu) and then the system reasons about it in order to categorise it in one of four categories, namely "expected", "neutral", "suspect", "erroneous". A command is categorised as expected if it is compatible with the user's hypothesised goals. It is considered suspect if it contradicts the system's hypotheses about the user's goals and erroneous if the command is wrong with respect to the user interface formalities. The command is considered neutral if it cannot be assigned to one of the former categories.

If the action is categorised as expected or neutral, it is executed normally. However, if the action is categorised as suspect or erroneous then it is transformed based on HPR.

The transformation of the given action is done so that similar alternatives can be found, which would not be suspect or erroneous. Therefore, the system reasons about every alternative action found so that it can categorise it in one of the four categories in a similar way as the actual command issued by the user. If an alternative action is categorised as neutral or expected then it is added to the list of alternatives to be presented to the user. As Mitrovic et al. [16] point out there may be different explanations of observed incorrect user's actions. Therefore, there is a need to attach priorities to different explanations so that some may be preferred over others. Expected actions have priority over neutral ones. There is also a degree of certainty associated with each command so that these may be sorted in a priority order. If no better alternative can be found, then the user is only notified about the diagnosed problem but s/he is not given any further advice.

An example of an interaction of a novice user with the intelligent learning environment is the following: The user's initial file store state is shown in Fig.1. Folders are represented as boxes and files in plain text.

The user intends to move A:\program1.pas into A:\project1\. However, s/he accidentally attempts to move A:\program1.pas into A:\project2\. In this case, not only does s/he move the file into the wrong folder but s/he also runs the risk of overwriting the file A:\project2\program1.pas, which is a destructive action.

The intelligent learning environment would suggest the user to move the file into A:\project1\ instead of A:\project2\ for two reasons:

1. A:\project1\ is empty whereas A:\project2 is not.

2. If the command issued by the user is executed it will result in the destruction of an existing file.

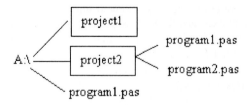

Fig. 1. Initial file store state of a novice user.

4   Domain Representation

Domain representation is one of the most important components of the system, since HPR transforms are based on hierarchies of objects. Domain Representation consists of two kinds of knowledge: knowledge about the file store and knowledge about GUI operators. The first part of the domain representation constitutes knowledge about objects of the file store, the file store itself and its properties, and the second one constitutes knowledge about commands: how they affect the file store as well as their other properties.

In order to identify the commands, which the system expects to be issued for the completion or the continuation of a plan, we introduce instabilities. Instabilities are important properties of the file store, since they are used for recognising the users' goals.

4.1   Instabilities for Goal Recognition

The system tries to assign meaning to command sequences by keeping track of the user's actions. A meaning to command sequences can be assigned by checking whether the user's goal of removing instabilities is satisfied.

Instabilities are introduced in order to check how stable the file store is. They are used extensively by the system for the comparison of alternative commands, generated to serve as possible corrections of the given command. The existence of a property such as instability implies a transition of the current state of the file store to another file store state (e.g. from a file store state that contains multiple copies of a certain file to the file store state that some of those copies are deleted).

In the current implementation, a file store is considered to be absolutely stable if it does not contain:

1. empty directories
2. directories with only one child
3. multiple copies of a certain file
4. folders with the name 'New Folder'

5. files with the name 'New File'
6. a file placed in clipboard by a cut or copy command but not used since.

Empty directories are considered to render the file store unstable because they do not have any purpose of existence if they have no contents. One would expect the user to fill the folder with some other objects or delete it. Similarly, a directory with only a child, is expected to either have more contents or to be deleted and its contents to be moved to its parent directory. There is no use for someone to have multiple copies of a certain file. People tend to have at most two identical copies of a certain file, so in any other case we expect them to delete or modify them. When someone creates a new folder we expect him/her to give it a name different from the one given by the computer. In case the user keeps the original name, s/he will end up having a disk full of folders with the same name. This situation is similar for files. Finally, an instability is introduced when a cut or copy command is executed and is not followed by a paste command. There is no purpose for placing a file or folder in the clipboard if not for pasting it somewhere on the disk.

Of course, there may be a case that one has a good reason for doing one of the actions described above, such as having a folder with only one object. Instabilities are only used to indicate the users' goal. An action that leads to an unstable file store cannot be considered as erroneous but that it may be in a middle of a plan. The system expects actions that remove an instability and is alerted by actions that only add new instabilities, when there are still others pending.

4.2 HPR in the System

When applying HPR to the domain of a GUI, certain problems arise, such as the fact that no explicit question is asked to the user. HPR presumes that explicit questions are asked to the user. Therefore, the system makes the assumption that users ask questions to themselves. The questions a user asks himself/herself are relevant to his/her effort to form the command, so that it would be acceptable by the GUI and the result of the action would meet his/her goal.

When a user performs an action we assume that the user believes that the action is acceptable by the GUI and that it meets his/her goal. This assumption is called the basic principle. The particular questions that the user is assumed to have asked himself/herself are:

What is the syntactic structure of the command?
Is the execution of the command acceptable to Windows?

The HPR terms that correspond to the above questions are the following:

```
internal-pattern(action)=typed-pattern

Windows-acceptable(typed-pattern)=yes
```

One of the main problems identified during the evaluation of the first prototype was that sometimes the system produced too many alternative commands to show them to the user. However, novice users could not choose the command they really wanted to execute and they ended up executing a command different from the one they intended. In order to solve this problem, alternative commands should be presented in some order of priority. One way for ordering the alternatives was to enhance the Student Modeller by adding a calculation of the degree of certainty for each alternative. This degree was calculated by using the certainty parameters of HPR.

We have used five certainty parameters: degree of certainty (γ), degree of typicality of an error set in the set of all errors (τ), degree of similarity of a set to another set (σ), frequency of an error set in the set of all errors (φ) and dominance of a subset in a set (δ).

The first certainty parameter described is the degree of similarity. This parameter is used to calculate the similarity of two commands or two objects. The similarity between two commands of the hierarchy is pre – calculated. The value of similarity is based on the result of the commands, for example cut and copy command that have a similar result, have high similarity where as cut and paste command have lower degree of similarity. Moreover, the degree of similarity is based on the relative distance of the two commands in the user actions hierarchy. Two commands that are neighbours in the user actions hierarchy, such as mktxt and mkdoc, have greater similarity than those having a long distance between them. Finally, similarity depends on the relative geographical position of two commands in the screen, because novice users tend to entangle such commands. The degree of similarity is used not only for the commands but for the objects as well. The similarity between two objects is dynamically calculated. The value of similarity depends on how similar their names are and if they are neighbouring files or folders.

Another certainty parameter used is the degree of typicality. The value of the typicality of a command is based on the frequency of execution of the command, estimated by the user model and the estimated frequency of execution of the particular command by all users in general.

It has been observed that users tend to repeat the same errors. In order to recognise those errors we keep the user model. The categorisation of user's errors is not enough; one has to know how often a user makes a particular error. The degree of frequency of an error, represents the frequency the user had done the specific error.

All users have a weak point. This point can be recognised by the dominance of an error in the set of all errors. This parameter shows the percentage of a category of errors in the set of all errors. For example, if the dominance of the deletion errors is 0,7, we can easily conclude the particular user does mainly deletion errors. All parameters are combined in order to calculate the probability of each alternative command. This probability is called degree of certainty and determines whether this command is to be proposed to the user and in what priority.

4.3   The System's Algorithmic Approach

In this section we present the algorithmic approach of the intelligent learning environment in pseudocode.

```
PROCEDURE ADVICE GENERATOR
   Initialise model-of-file-store to current file store
   FOR EACH user-action DO
      Set add-instability FALSE
      Set delete-instability FALSE
      Update copy of model-of-file-store with effect of
       user-action
      initialise alternatives to nil
      argument_transformation(user_action)
      FOR each alternative DO
         CATEGORISE alternative
         IF (alternative is EXPECTED) OR (alternative is
             NEUTRAL) THEN add_to_alternatives
         FOR EACH alternative DO
           Calculate certainty parameters
         ENDFOR
         Sort alternatives -> sorted-alternatives
      ENDFOR
   ENDFOR
ENDFUNCTION
```

5   Evaluation

The intelligent learning environment was evaluated in terms of how useful it was for novice users and how successful it was in reproducing advice similar to human experts. Therefore, during the evaluation, 8 novice users were video recorded while working with a standard manipulation program, such as Windows 98/NT Explorer. The protocols collected were given to 10 human experts to comment them. All of the human experts possessed a higher degree in Computer Science and had teaching experience in file manipulation programs.

The comments were studied carefully and served as a usability testing of a standard explorer. It was found that novice users have indeed a lot of problems while interacting with such a program [17]. Furthermore, the protocols collected were also given as input to the intelligent learning environment. In this way we could compare the comments of the human experts to the reactions of the learning environment. The results of the evaluation showed that the learning environment was quite successful at achieving a high degree of compatibility with the majority of the experts' advice. However, some problems were also identified. For example, sometimes it generated a lot of alternative commands.

6   Conclusions

In this paper we have described an intelligent learning environment for novice users of a GUI. Users are monitored while working in a protected mode. The system tries to identify problematic situations and diagnose the cause of the problem, so that it can offer appropriate advice. Novice users can benefit from the system's advice and thus they may learn from their own errors.

The system combines two reasoning mechanisms; a simulator of human error generation, which is based on HPR that is a domain independent cognitive theory, and a limited goal recognition mechanism. These mechanisms have proved quite successful at producing advice similar to human experts. However, what is most important is that these mechanisms are quite domain independent and can be used in similar intelligent environments. Indeed, the domain of GUI described in the current research served as a second case study for the adaptation of the underlying mechanisms; the first one was for the domain of UNIX command-language shell, which is very different from a GUI.

However, the evaluation of the learning environment also showed some limitations of it, such as the generation of many alternative commands. Addressing these limitations is among the future plans of this research. This can be done by extending the adaptation and implementation of HPR in order to include more features that may be quite useful.

References

1. McGraw, K. L.: 'Performance Support Systems: Integrating AI, Hypermedia and CBT to Enhance User Performance'. In Journal Of Artificial Intelligence in Education, Vol. 5. No. 1. (1994) 3-26
2. Jennings, R.: 'Unveiling Windows 95', Que Corp. (1994)
3. Cerri, S. A. & Loia, V.: 'A Concurrent, Distributed Architecture for Diagnostic Reasoning'. In User Modeling and User-Adapted Interaction, Vol. 7. No. 2. (1997) 69-105
4. Collins, A., Michalski R.: 'The Logic of Plausible Reasoning: A core Theory'. In Cognitive Science 13, (1989) 1-49
5. Burstein, M.H. & Collins, A.M.: 'Modeling a theory of Human Plausible Reasoning'. In Artificial Intelligence III: Methodology, Systems, Applications, T.O'Shea, T. and Sgurev, V. (eds.), Elsevier Science Publishers B.V. (North Holland) (1988) 21-28
6. Burstein, M.H., Collins, A. & Baker M.: 'Plausible Generalisation: Extending a model of Human Plausible Reasoning'. In The journal of the Learning Sciences, 3 and 4, (1991) 319-359
7. Carbonel, J.R. & Collins, A.: Natural semantics in artificial intelligence. In Proceedings of the Third International Joint Conference on Artificial Intelligence, Stanford, California, (1973) 344-351
8. Hartley, J.R. & Sleeman D.H. 'Towards intelligent teaching systems'. In International Journal Man-Machine Studies, Vol. 5, (1973) 215-236
9. Burton, R.R., & Brown, J.S.: A tutoring and student modeling paradigm for gaming enviroments. Computer Science and Education, Colman, R. and Lorton, P.Jr. (eds.), ACM SIGCSE Bulleting, Vol. 8, No. 1, (1976) 236-246
10. Wenger, E.: 'Artificial Intelligence and Tutoring Systems'. Morgan Kaufman, Los Altos, CA (1987)
11. Virvou, M.: 'RESCUER: Intelligent Help for Plausible User Errors'. In Proceedings of ED-MEDIA/ED-TELECOM 98, World Conferences on Educational Multimedia and Educational Telecommunications, Vol. 2, (1998) 1413-1420.
12. Virvou, M. & Du Boulay, B.: 'Human Plausible Reasoning for Intelligent Help'. In User Modeling and User-Adapted Interaction, Vol. 9, (1999) 321-375

13. Virvou, M.& Stavrianou, A.: 'User modelling in a GUI'. In Proceedings of the 8th International Conference on Human-Computer Interaction (HCII 99), Munich, Germany, Vol. 1, (1999) 262-265

14. Calistri-Yeh, R. J.: 'Utilizing User Models to Handle Ambiguity and Misconceptions in Robust Plan Recognition'. In User Modeling and User-Adapted Interaction, Vol. 1, No. 4, (1991) 289-322

15. Eller, R. & Carberry, S.: 'A Meta-rule Approach to Flexible Plan Recognition in Dialogue', In User Modeling and User-Adapted Interaction, Vol. 2, No. 1-2, (1992) 27-53

16. Mitrovic, A., Djordjevic-Kajan, S. & Stoimenov, L.: 'INSTRUCT: Modeling students by asking questions'. In User Modeling and User Adapted Interaction, Vol. 6, No. 4, (1996) 273-302

17. Virvou, M. & Kabassi K.: 'An Empirical Study Concerning Graphical User Interfaces that Manipulate Files'. To appear in Proceedings of ED-MEDIA 2000, World Conferences on Educational Multimedia and Educational Telecommunications (2000)

A System for
Concerned Teaching of Musical Aural Skills

Geraint A. Wiggins[1,3] and Shari Trewin[2,3]

[1] Department of Computing, City University, London, Northampton Square,
London, England, EC1V 0HB, geraint@city.ac.uk
[2] Institute for Communicating and Collaborative Systems, University of Edinburgh,
80 South Bridge, Edinburgh EH1 1HN, Scotland, shari@dai.ed.ac.uk

Abstract. We present *teaching concerns*, a domain-independent mechanism for controlling the content and form of automated teaching interactions. Concerns represent commonsense teaching requirements such as challenging a student. Concerns have been implemented in **Tapper**, a new system for musical ear training. We describe and give real examples of concerns in action within **Tapper**. We claim that this approach produces sensible and explicable individualised interactions within a loosely structured curriculum.

1 Introduction and Overview

In this paper, we describe the teaching strategy applied in **Tapper**, a new system for musical ear training, and give examples of teaching in progress in experimental sessions with children.

A particular contribution of this work is the inclusion in **Tapper**'s control mechanism of the notion of *teaching concern*. A teaching concern is a particular governing aspect of the teaching process, on which a teacher might be focussed at a particular time. For example, teaching concerns implemented in the current system include boosting the confidence of a beginner and broadening the coverage of the student's knowledge. Not all concerns are active at all times, and their changing strengths interact to control the behaviour of the system. **Tapper** chooses a path through the curriculum based on the teaching concerns and on the performance of the student, giving a more natural and precisely tailored learning experience than would be otherwise possible.

2 Related Work

Our work is set in context of several well-known ITS architectures, all of which encode a notion of *teaching strategy*, though none of these is exactly the same as that in **Tapper**.

Sokolonicki [2] gives a good survey of ITS architectures; there is little point in reiterating his work here. In summary, many existing ITSs support reasoning systems

---

[3] This work was mostly carried out while the first author was working at the Division of Informatics, University of Edinburgh. The second author is now working in the Accessibility Research group, IBM T J Watson Research Center. Correspondence should be addressed to the first author.

of some kind which guide the teaching process in terms of *strategy*. In most cases in this survey, a strategy is a high-level decision to which an ITS strictly adheres, often for an extended period. For example, the decision to use the Socratic method, or choosing the balance between teaching and assessment, is the level of strategy discussed. However, Major [1] cites evidence that in human teaching situations, strategy is also continually reassessed at a lower level, adjusting individual aspects of a lesson when appropriate, so that "a complete strategy change would happen gradually in a series of smaller steps" (p. 121). This view is corroborated by our education consultant, Joanne Armstrong (personal communication).

DOMINIE [3] also features explicit reasoning for teaching strategy selection. It has strategies at the level of (*e.g.,*) "cognitive apprenticeship" and "practice". DOMINIE makes its strategic decisions according to several heuristic factors, such as "achieving a balance between teaching and assessment". These heuristic factors do not, as they stand, encode a teaching behaviour – rather, they ensure that whatever strategy is chosen is used coherently. DOMINIE was the first system to automate selection from several different strategies, and Spensley *et al.* note that "It is not clear what theoretical basis exists for this choice because current teaching practices do not often involve extended one to one interactions" (p. 199). Our work addresses this issue: musical ear training is an example of one to one interaction; and we are studying the emergent properties of just such a multi-objective strategy selection procedure.

GTE [5] and PEPE [6] also reason about instructional strategy. Further, Van Marke, quoted by Wasson (p. 301), notes that teachers' "instructional knowledge" allows them to "adapt their teaching strategy according to the situation", and both systems are very knowledge-rich in this respect. However, as with DOMINIE, their knowledge is expressed in terms of how to teach a given curriculum, or particular aspects of it, rather than in terms of an over-arching, on-going detailed analysis of the student's behaviour within that curriculum.

The work to which ours owes most is that of Major [1], who has designed an ITS construction system, COCA. COCA constructs multiple-strategy systems, and the user specifies the strategy selection reasoning. COCA-built systems have a fixed operating cycle: decide which concept to teach next; decide which tutorial activity and style to use; choose the content of the next interaction; and act on student assessment. COCA has two levels of strategy, high, as above, and low level, which decides what kind of concept (*e.g.,* easier, harder or new) to proceed to next. COCA uses a set of rules to make these decisions, which are hard-wired by the ITS designer. The rules may encode heuristics, but apparently do not have a mutually coordinated response to the current situation: they respond only disparately to data in the student model, and there is no means of describing a unified response mechanism. It is this gap that the present work aims to fill.

3   Architecture

To set the context in which concerns are applied, we describe the architecture of **Tapper**, as illustrated in Figure 1. The blocks in the diagram are explained below. In a paper of this length, we cannot give the full detail of a complex system such as this; readers needing more detail are referred to [4]. However, this overview is enough for the reader to understand §4, which introduces our central topic: using *teaching concerns* to direct the student's course of study.

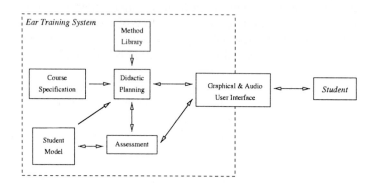

Fig. 1. The Architecture of the Experimental System, **Tapper**

Course Specification The *course specification* is a logical description of the material to be taught in the ear training course. Each section of the material is associated with an indication of which *methods* (see below) the system could use to teach it, and how the material maps on to the variables in the method.

The curriculum is specified in terms of *topics*, *examples* and *questions* to use in teaching the topics. The current curriculum, biassed towards musical ear training, consists of topics such as "pulse", "beats in a bar" and "rhythm". Examples are frames which will be instantiated by the system with one of a set of musical examples of equivalent difficulty.

Each topic is uniquely named, and has a difficulty level and a set of methods appropriate for teaching it, ordered by difficulty. Each topic also has *pre-requisites*, which must be achieved by the student before it is first introduced.

Method Library The *method library* is a logical description of *methods* by which material may be taught, specified in the abstract. The curriculum contains no information about how to present the material to students; presentations are generated on the fly. This avoids the need to encode individual lessons for each topic: one simply specifies which methods are appropriate and the system does the rest.

Eleven methods are available in the current version, some general and some ear-training-specific. They include: demonstrating a topic; asking different kinds of question; and asking the student to improvise to fill in a gap in an example.

Each method specifies the class of teaching examples for which it is appropriate. Most examples fit into several classes.

New methods may be added to the system in a standard way; so long as they conform to **Tapper**'s representation, they will be integrated automatically with existing methods and curricula.

Student Model The *student model* records information about the student's progress through the curriculum. It provides information for other modules in the system to use when making decisions. Other modules can query the student's standard or exposure to specific elements in the course specification, or their overall performance.

Students are also assigned a specific skill level (1-3) according to their performance. Skill levels are used by the *assessment module* (see below) and the *didactic planner*.

Didactic Planning The highest level of control in **Tapper** rests with the *didactic planner*. Having loaded a student profile, or started a new one, it executes sequences of cycles, like those in COCA [1]. Each cycle consists of presenting material to the student, gathering their response, analysing it, providing feedback, and then updating the student model and session records.

As in COCA, **Tapper**'s overall behaviour is governed by a high-level strategy. In **Tapper**, the strategy module makes broad and fairly simplistic suggestions, for example suggesting a change when things are getting too easy for the student, or repeating a cycle when a student has done very poorly. When these strategies do not fully specify the content (topic, method and example) of the next cycle, *teaching concerns* are used to make the necessary decisions. These concerns interact with the low-level strategies to produce a behaviour which is coordinated, but which is potentially more responsive to the needs of the particular student than is possible in a domain-independent system without multi-level strategy. This interaction is explained in §4.

Assessment The *assessment module* is an inference system which uses information from the student and the course specification to assess the student's knowledge, in ways specified by library methods. The assessment of the student's musical input is by no means trivial, but will be discussed elsewhere [4].

Graphical & Audio User interface The user interface of the system is currently geared towards the application with which we have been experimenting: musical ear training. It is capable of displaying music in various ways, both visually and aurally, and is able to read input from the student in the form of text typed on the computer keyboard and rhythms tapped out on one of several input devices.

4 Using Concerns to Guide Teaching

4.1 The Concern Mechanism in Tapper

Tapper's high level teaching strategies do not usually fully dictate the contents of the next interaction. **Tapper** also uses a set of *teaching concerns* to make the necessary decisions, sometimes overriding the high level strategy altogether.

There are four primary teaching concerns in the current prototype: boosting student confidence; challenging the student; reinforcing material already taught; and increasing coverage of the curriculum. More concerns could be easily added in future. All concerns are assigned numerical values. 0 indicates that **Tapper** is unconcerned about the property in question. The maximum concern in **Tapper** is currently 7, though this is arbitrary.

In the current version, teaching concerns are initialised by examining five variables:

- the student's performance in the previous cycle of this session;
- the average of the student's performances in the previous four cycles;
- the current activity (try a topic for the first time, practice, recap or revise);
- the student's performance with the current topic, if a topic is defined; and
- the student's overall performance for all cycles attempted.

For each concern, a set of *influences* is defined in terms of the above variables. Each influence has a positive or negative strength in the range 1-3. For example, if the average of the student's recent performances is very poor, this has a positive influence of strength 3 on concern for boosting the student's confidence, and a negative influence of strength 3 on concern for increasing coverage within the curriculum. The influences of all the variables on each concern are combined by summing the total influences and limiting the result to the permissible range.

Concerns are used identically for all **Tapper**'s main didactic planning, whether choosing topics, methods or examples. The mechanism is domain- and curriculum-independent, and allows addition of new topics, methods or examples to the curriculum, so long as the existing curriculum representation is adhered to. Concerns are used to choose appropriate *low level strategies* for choosing the contents of the next cycle. Existing low level strategies include:

- choose something of similar/higher/lower difficulty to/than the last one;
- choose something easy/hard/average;
- choose something the student is strong/average/weak at;
- reuse the previous choice;
- go to something which builds on the last choice;
- choose something new to the student;

Each low level strategy is related to the four teaching concerns, either being a good strategy to address the concern, a reasonable strategy, indifferent, or bad. For example, the strategies of choosing a new or harder topic, or a topic the user is weak on, are good for addressing concern about challenging the user. Strategies which choose easy topics, or topics the user is good at, are bad strategies for that concern.

All of the available low level strategies are scored according to the current set of concerns, ordered, best first, and tried, in order, until a solution is found. Several strategies may be tried, since not all strategies are applicable in every situation. For example, the strategy *harder* cannot be applied when the student is already on the hardest option.

When updating the teaching concerns after choosing one aspect of the next interaction, **Tapper** decides how well each concern has been addressed by the strategy applied. If it has been addressed, its strength will be reduced. At the same time, new concerns will be introduced, if appropriate.

The rest of this section uses a real interaction sequence to illustrate how teaching concerns and low level strategies are used to choose the contents of an interaction.

4.2 Example: A Student Performing Well

In this example, a capable student, L, is having her first lesson with Tapper. She is studying her second topic: tapping the accented beat of a tune, and has performed three cycles well on this topic. Throughout the session, she has used a single, easy method, and easy examples. Now, high level teaching strategy dictates that she should be given more practice with the current topic, but should move on to a new method. The teaching concerns are used to choose the method and then the example for the next cycle.

L's recent performance has been rated as 'good', her performance in the previous cycle was 'very good', her overall performance is 'good', her performance on the current topic is 'good', and her activity is 'practice'. Using this information, **Tapper** examines the influences for each concern. L's recent good performance has a negative influence on concern for boosting her confidence, level 1, so the overall level of concern for boosting confidence is limited from -1 to 0. None of the influencing variables affects concern for increasing coverage of the curriculum, or for reinforcing the material already taught, so those concerns are also set to 0. L's overall good performance has a positive (level 1) influence on concern for challenging her, so that concern total is 1.

Given the single concern of challenging the student, the system orders the set of known strategies as shown below, from the strategy most likely to choose a challenging method, to the least likely.

- weak – choose a method the student is weak on;
- harder – choose a harder method than the previous one;
- average – choose a method the student is average at;
- different – choose a different method to the last one;
- next – choose the next method (a suggested order in which to use methods is given for each topic, and a general default ordering is also defined);
- hard – choose a hard method;
- previous – choose a method used before the most recent;
- strong – choose a method the student is good at;
- easier – choose an easier method;
- easy – choose an easy method.

So **Tapper** first tries to find a method L is weak on. This fails, since she has only tried one method, and is doing well with it. **Tapper** then tries to choose a method harder than the current one. Since a topic has already been chosen, it does so by referring to the ordering for methods provided for that topic in the curriculum. In this way, it finds a more difficult method: *fillin*, in which the student is asked to perform without having heard the example in advance.

Having chosen a method, an example is needed. First, **Tapper** adjusts the set of concerns to take into account the method chosen. The strategy *harder* is good for addressing concern about challenging the student. So, the level of concern for challenging the student is reduced, and returns to 0.

At this stage, **Tapper** has no particular teaching concerns, so the default strategy ordering is used to choose an example. The first strategy tried is *same* – use the same kind of example as the previous cycle. In this case, the kinds of example required by the two methods are identical, so the strategy succeeds, and chooses an example of the same form and difficulty as the previous cycle (though not the same tune), and so the session proceeds.

5   Concerned Teaching in Action

Formative evaluation of the **Tapper** system as a whole has been carried out in a school environment with four eight year old and four twelve year old children. The children used **Tapper** for three 20 minute sessions, each subsequent session building on progress made previously.

The children responded positively to **Tapper**, and found it easy to use. They experienced some difficulty with some parts of the curriculum, prompting revision of the demonstrations and explanations provided in the original curriculum. Further development of the feedback given on each cycle is also in progress, in consultation with the children's own music teacher, who acted as consultant on this project. This work will be reported elsewhere. The rest of this section gives an example session recorded in this evaluation, focussing on the way in which concerns interact with the higher level teaching strategies to control the contents of each cycle. Less interesting parts of the session are abridged. A further example is given by Wiggins *et al.* [7]

5.1   Case Study: A Student's Second Session

Our case study is taken from the second session with **Tapper** for G_2, a girl of 12 years old. G_2 was a capable musician and **Tapper** responded well. She passed the easy sections quickly, and soon reached areas where **Tapper**'s advanced features can be seen.

G_2 had been playing the violin for four years. She was a competent musician. She reported that, although she had found a problem with the user interface, she enjoyed working with **Tapper** (particularly the way the exercises got harder with time – see below), and that felt that she had made progress.

With all the subjects' second sessions, teaching follows on from the first session, as recorded in the student model. We join this session after cycle 3; the current topic is *accented beats*. G_2 is doing well, so current concerns are with challenging her and broadening her coverage of the curriculum. Method-choosing strategy *new* addresses both these concerns, but there is no appropriate new method, so **Tapper** chooses a *harder* method.

```
Cycle 4:

High level teaching strategies: Stick with the same topic,
    change method to avoid boredom.

Choose a method:
    Concerned with challenging the student at level 6.
    Concerned with broadening the student's coverage at level 3.
    Strategy "new" failed.
    Strategy "harder" succeeded. Choice made: methodName(fillin)

Choose an example:
    No concerns.
    Strategy "same" succeeded. Choice made: accentFrame(easy)

The student responded, and the result was very good, scoring 94.
```

Following this strong score, high level strategy is to stick with the same topic and method in cycle 5, but concerns are still to challenge and broaden. A harder example is chosen, and this time G_2 does less well, scoring only 65. The resulting concerns in cycle 6 are changed: the challenge has gone, and the level of concern for broadening is reduced.

Broadening coverage is less appropriate to examples than to topics and methods, but the selection here is still logical – **Tapper** has chosen a harder exercise to broaden the student's ability within the set of examples appropriate for that topic and method.

```
Cycle 6:

High level teaching strategies: stick with the same topic and
      method, but choose a new example.

Choose an example.
      Concerned with broadening the student's coverage at level 1.
      Strategy "new" failed.
      Strategy "next" failed.
      Strategy "harder" succeeded. Choice made: accentFrame(hard)

The student responded, and the result was very good, scoring 96.
```

Cycle 7 sees the concerns being assessed twice, once for a change of method, and once for a change of example. Here, the concerns are supporting the high level strategy, and would do so even more effectively with a fuller method set, where a high-scoring strategy (*e.g., new*) would have been successful. However, *different*, though normally a good strategy for challenging, can only find a method which is in fact easier than the current one.

```
Cycle 7:

High level teaching strategies: Stick with the same topic,
      change method and example to avoid boredom.

Choose a method.
      Concerned with challenging the student at level 2.
      Concerned with broadening the student's coverage at level 1.
      Strategy "new" failed.
      Strategy "harder" failed.
      Strategy "next" failed.
      Strategy "weak" failed.
      Strategy "average" failed.
      Strategy "different" succeeded.
          Choice made: methodName(followcue)

Choose an example:
      Concerned with broadening the student's coverage at level 1.
      Strategy "new" failed.
      Strategy "next" failed.
```

```
Strategy "harder" failed.
Strategy "same" succeeded. Choice made: accentFrame(hard)
```

The student responded, and the result was very good, scoring 100.

In the final cycle of this case study, G_2's excellent score in cycle 7 has led again to concern for challenge and broadening. The high level strategy is anyway to change topic, so **Tapper**'s components are unanimous in trying the *new* strategy. G_2 has already met the prerequisites of a new topic, and this is selected and demonstrated.

5.2 Discussion

The case studies demonstrate the effect of the concerns on the teaching process, and how they respond to the student's performance. In particular, two points should be noted. First, there is a dynamic balance between the concerns of boosting confidence and of challenging Second, **Tapper**'s low-level response to the concerns can produce a very reasonable emergent behaviour over time, as exemplified in cycles 5-7 of G_2's case study, where the material taught gets progressively – but smoothly – harder as G_2 learns.

This behaviour arises exclusively from the concerns and their effect on the low-level strategies and is not hard-coded into the system. As such, it is very general and readily extensible.

Also, the study suggests several ways in which **Tapper** could be improved, notably in its ability to understand the nature of errors, and in the coverage of its curriculum, whose poverty restricts the power of the concern mechanism to respond to the user.

6   Conclusion and Further Work

This project has shown that the emergent behaviour of an ITS, based not on pre-programmed transition through a curriculum, but rather on a mixture of high- and low-level localised reasoning, can lead to a natural and precisely tailored learning experience for each student. In this paper, we have demonstrated this behaviour *via* two examples of our system's operation.

Note that the mechanism we have described is domain- and high-level strategy-independent, and so may be expected to generalise to other areas of education seamlessly. This means that the architecture on which **Tapper** is based can form an effective framework for comparing different aspects of teaching systems, to a high degree of granularity, because of the independence of its various modules.

A particularly important aspect of this work is that real teachers tend to think in terms like our concerns. This means that a system based on this way of thinking is more likely to be amenable to use by teachers for contstructing their own ITSs (though **Tapper** in its current form is not appropriate for this).

We expect that this work will continue in several directions: extending the curriculum; building better high-level strategies; improving the understanding of student input; and increasing the range of modalities by which the student can interact with **Tapper**.

In future versions of **Tapper**, we anticipate that the basic strategy would be extended with more sophisticated strategies. For example, when a student has performed badly on a long example, an appropriate strategy would be to split the example into parts, teach each part separately, then reconstruct the original example.

Finally, further experimental work is required, to verify **Tapper**'s response to a wider range of children of different musical backgrounds.

Acknowledgements

This work was supported by UK Engineering and Physical Sciences Research Council research grant number GR/L99029 and by City University, London.

We are enormously grateful to Joanne Armstrong, of Fettes College Junior School, Edinburgh, who was educational consultant to this project, and who designed the educational content of **Tapper**'s curriculum and methods. We also thank Luke Phillips, who helped with the evaluation of student input, and Márcio Brandão, who, with Luke, helped to run the experiments and to process the results.

References

1. N. Major. Modelling teaching strategies. *Journal of Artificial Intelligence in Education*, 6(2/3):117–152, 1995.
2. T. Sokolonicki. Towards knowledge-based tutors: a survey and appraisal of intelligent tutoring systems. *Knowledge Engineering Review*, 6(2):59–95, 1991.
3. F. Spenseley, M. Elsom-Cook, P. Byerley, P. Brooks, M. Federici, and C. Scaroni. *Using multiple teaching strategies*, pages 188–205. Ablex Publishing Corp., Norwood, New Jersey, 1990.
4. S. Trewin, J. Armstrong, L. Phillips, and G. A. Wiggins. An intelligent teaching system supporting music education research, prep. In preparation.
5. K. van Marcke. GTE: An epistemological approach to instructional modelling. *Instructional Science*, 26(3/4):147–191, 1998.
6. B. Wasson. Facilitating dynamic pedagogical decision making: PEPE and GTE. *Instructional Science*, 26:299–316, 1998.
7. G. A. Wiggins and S. Trewin. A system for concerned teaching of musical aural skills. Research paper, Department of Computing, City University, London, Northampton Square, London EC1V 0HB, England, 2000. Extended version of paper published in ITS 2000.

Broader Bandwidth in Student Modeling:
What if ITS were "Eye"TS?

Kevin A. Gluck[1], John R. Anderson[2], and Scott A. Douglass[2]

[1]Air Force Research Laboratory, 6030 South Kent St., Mesa, AZ 85212-6061, USA
kevin.gluck@williams.af.mil
[2]Department of Psychology, Carnegie Mellon University, Pittsburgh, PA 15213 USA
ja+@cmu.edu; sd3n@andrew.cmu.edu

Abstract. The ability of an ITS to develop an accurate student model is inherently limited by the bandwidth of information available. We have completed an exploratory research project showing that eye movement data provide a means of broadening this bandwidth. This paper describes three examples in which more information about cognitive process is available from having access to a student's eye movements than is available simply from key presses and mouse clicks.

1 Introduction

More than 25 years ago, Hartley and Sleeman [1] described the characteristics that instructional software must possess if it is to be considered an intelligent tutoring system (ITS). In their words, these characteristics included: (i) a representation of the teaching task, (ii) a representation of the student, (iii) a set of teaching operations, and (iv) a set of means-ends guidance rules. In more contemporary vernacular, these have come to be known as (a) the expert module, (b) the student model module, and, integrating (iii) and (iv) from Hartley and Sleeman's list, (c) the tutor module. As Shute and Psotka [2] point out, this basic list of requirements has changed very little in the last quarter of a century, and there is even increasing consensus among researchers in the ITS field regarding what are the important components of ITS. They queried 20 experts for opinions on what is meant by the "I" in ITS. The most common response was that "intelligent" tutoring requires real-time diagnosis of the student, also called a *student model*.

The student model module of an ITS is meant to serve as an analogue to the representation of a student's knowledge and skill level that a human tutor develops while they are working together. Bloom [3] emphasized the striking instructional advantage that one-to-one human tutoring has over traditional classroom instruction. However, few ITS can claim to have achieved a level of instructional effectiveness on par with that of a good human tutor, and the question remains why it is that one-to-one tutoring between a student and a *computer* tutor is not generally as effective as one-to-one tutoring between a student and a *human* tutor. After all, great care is taken in establishing the domain knowledge, the pedagogical strategies, and the student models for these ITS. They should arguably have the upper hand.

One hypothesis regarding why this problem persists is that computers continue to have a significant perceptual disadvantage compared to humans. Computer tutors, as they currently are designed, do not have access to as wide a range of information about the student. Consider that a human tutor can see facial expressions and gestures, hear verbalizations, perceive the passage of time, and determine the direction of gaze. "Human teachers have a much wider variety of cues to work with than have computerized learning systems. An 'eureka' look, a puzzled expression, or a hesitant tone of voice may all shape remedial action" [4, p. 26]. These sources of information allow human tutors the possibility of determining whether the student is on-task, how much difficulty the student is having, what the current frustration level is, and whether to intervene in some way in order to improve the learning experience. Contemporary computer tutors, however, take advantage of none of these potentially informative sources of information about the student. They rely merely on key presses and mouse clicks to develop a student model for each learner. VanLehn [5] referred to this issue of the amount of information about the student that is available to the computer as one of "bandwidth" and similarly noted that bandwidth is highly constrained in ITS.

This leads to the question of what technologies are available that could broaden the bandwidth of information available to an ITS's student model. There are a number of possibilities, including speech recognition, facial expression monitoring, and eye tracking. It is the last of these, eye tracking, that was chosen for exploration in this project [6]. As separate technologies, eye tracking and student modeling are not new ideas. It really is the marriage of the two that we consider to be the innovation. We know of no previous research project that has explored the combination of these two technologies for education. The goal so far has been to explore and describe the instructional opportunities that are afforded by having access to a student's eye movements, in anticipation of a future ITS that is informed by data coming out of an eye tracker in real time. This paper describes three examples in which more information about cognitive process is available from having access to a student's eye movements than is available simply from key presses and mouse clicks. These examples demonstrate how eye movement data broaden the bandwidth of information available to the student model.

2 Method

2.1 Participants

A total of 18 middle-school and high-school students completed this study. Half of the participants were female and half were male. The students ranged in age from 12 to 15 years old (6th to 9th grade). All of the participants had progressed at least as far as Pre-Algebra in their mathematics studies, and 13 were taking or had completed an Algebra class. One student was currently enrolled in an Algebra 2 class. All participants were paid $50 for completing the study.

2.2 The EPAL Algebra Tutor

EPAL stands for Eye Point-of-regard Analysis Laboratory. The EPAL Algebra Tutor is a streamlined recreation of the Worksheet tool, as it existed in the Algebra Tutor used by Koedinger and Anderson [7]. The Worksheet is a tabular spreadsheet interface that holds a problem statement and questions. The student's task is to fill in the column labels and units, enter a variable and an expression written in terms of that variable, and then answer two questions. There were 16 different EPAL Algebra Tutor problems. Completion of the problems proceeded from top to bottom, which was important for testing for an effect of inductive support. With respect to that manipulation, the important thing to know is that in the Non-Inductive Support condition, students did the symbolization *before* answering result-unknown questions, and in the Inductive Support condition, students did the symbolization *after* answering result-unknown questions. Please see Koedinger and Anderson [7] or Gluck [6] for a more complete description of the inductive support effect.

2.3 Design and Procedure

Upon arrival at the laboratory on Day 1, there was a brief eye-tracker calibration test, to confirm that we would be able to acquire a reasonably accurate and stable image of the student's eye. With this confirmed, the student completed a short demographic survey, then a paper-and-pencil pretest. The final activity on Day 1 was an introduction to the EPAL Algebra Tutor, to familiarize the student with the interface and the type of problems to be encountered on subsequent days. Day 2 started with the completion of a second introductory problem, then there were four tutor problems while calibrated on the eye tracker. These were randomly selected (without replacement) from the pool of 16 problems. Days 3 and 4 simply involved the completion of four more problems each day. Day 5 started with the completion of four problems (the last 4 in the set of 16), followed by the posttest and debriefing.

3 Instructional Opportunities

In this section we offer three examples of how eye movements can be used to provide a student model with additional information regarding the fine-grained details of a student's cognitive processes. The additional bandwidth allows for instructional opportunities that would not otherwise be available.

3.1 Error Prediction: Cognitive Attention Shifts and Other Errors

Normal computer-based tutoring systems are *reactive* to students' responses. For instance, when a student commits an error and the tutor recognizes it, the tutor will often react by displaying a bug message. An eye-tracking ITS, however, allows for the possibility of being *proactive* to students' responses. That is, sometimes a student's eyes reveal the cognitive processes the student is engaged in at that moment, and sometimes those cognitive processes suggest that the student is about to commit an error. An eye tracking tutor could intervene and help prevent the error altogether. The goal in this section is to explore the utility of eye movements for use in predicting students' errors before they happen. We have divided the error space into two broad error types: cognitive shift errors and "other" errors.

Shift Errors. Shift errors occur when the student indicates an intent to work on some particular goal(s) then shifts cognitive attention and begins working on a different goal, without indicating the change in the tutor interface. An example of this that occurs in the Algebra Tutor is that the student selects one of the columns but gives the answer for the other column. For instance, the student might click the cell for entering the given value for Question 1 (Q1-Left) and then calculate the solution instead. "Shift" errors of this sort account for 55% of the errors in Given cells for the result-unknown questions and 24% of the errors overall.

Not surprisingly, students tend to display different eye movements when they are entering the given versus calculating the solution. Figure 1 shows a successful episode in which the student does *not* shift attention after selecting the cell. Note how brief and direct the eye movements are.

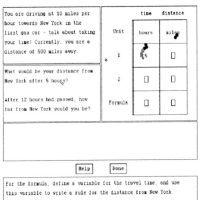 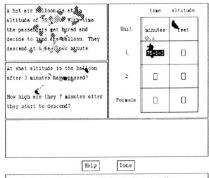

Fig. 1. Example of eye movements during a correct response in cell Q1-Left (the Given cell for Question 1).

Fig. 2. Example of eye movements during a cognitive attention shift error in cell Q1-Left (student tried a solution instead of the given).

The paint traces on the image in Figures 1 and 2 represent fixation points, and they progress from dark to light over time. In Figure 1, the student first looks in cell Unit-Right to confirm that "miles" was accepted as an answer. Then there is a long fixation in Q1-Left, as the student selects the cell. The eyes then dart briefly to the "5 hours" in Question 1, and to the keyboard to type the response. There is a final fixation (in Q1-Left) as the student enters the answer

By contrast, in Figure 2 the student chose the cell for entering the given but has gotten ahead of himself and calculated the altitude rather than simply entering the time. Note all the eye movements over the problem statement — an indicator that the student is calculating the result and not entering the given. This is just one example of a shift error. They also can occur across rows, and they occur in all of the cells.

"Other" Errors. All errors that are not shift errors are grouped as "other" errors. These are all cases in which the student is working on a problem solving goal congruent with the intent indicated in the interface, but the student commits a procedural error of some sort. For instance, a common error in the expression cell is to switch the intercept and the slope. If the answer is supposed to be 12+4x, the student types 4+12x. The student was working on the correct goal (symbolization), but did it incorrectly. Given such a broad definition, "Other" errors are more common than shift errors, but as will now be revealed, they are harder to detect in students' eye movements.

Error Prediction Results. Somewhat of a shotgun approach has been adopted in this analysis. The predictor variables are fixation counts and gaze time in every point-of-regard (POR) region, as well as response latency, from the beginning of the part-task to the first key press. There are 23 POR regions, roughly corresponding to cells in the worksheet. Gaze time in a POR region is computed as the sum of the fixation times for all of the fixations in that region.

The dependent variable is whether or not there actually was an attention shift. This is easily determined. On any particular part-task, if a student entered a response that was identifiable as an attempt at the solution, it was considered a shift. Otherwise, that part-task is coded as a No Shift. All of the predictor variables are entered into a forward stepwise logistic regression predicting Shift/No Shift. This creates a regression equation for the sample of data in that analysis. Predicting whether an attention shift error is occurring is accomplished by feeding the data for that part-task into the equation, to produce a regression score. The score then undergoes a logistic transformation to produce a predicted probability that the error is about to occur. Probabilities above .50 indicate that the model predicts an attention shift.

How accurate is this technique at predicting errors? It depends on the *type* of error you're trying to predict, as well as on the characteristics of the subset of students used in the analysis. Averaging over all subjects and across correct no and correct yes predictions, we found that shift errors can be predicted with 69% accuracy, while other error types average only about 55% accuracy. The accuracy of the predictions can increase substantially, however, in certain subsets of the data. For instance, using just the data from six students who were shift-prone in cell Q1-Left raised the accuracy of the regression model to 84%.

Instructional Implications. Although not perfect, we are encouraged by the fact that such a simple model does rather a good job at predicting errors before they occur. This model *only* has access to the student's eye movements, and their eye movements clearly are revealing regularities in visual search patterns that separate correct from incorrect upcoming responses. While these results are encouraging, the utility of eye movements for predicting errors differs across different cells of the spreadsheet, across different error types within those cells, and across students. A tutor that is designed to intervene proactively based on a student's eye movement data should be designed to intervene only in cases of very high certainty that an error is about to be committed.

3.2 Disambiguation of Solution Method

Solving the First Result-Unknown (Q1-R). Students do not all solve these problems in the same way. One interesting contrast is between students who use the algebra expression to calculate the answer to a result-unknown and students who go back to the verbal problem and reason from that. Koedinger and colleagues [7, 8] have found that students often find it easier to reason about word problems, and Koedinger and MacLaren [9] have proposed a model where there are both algebraic and verbal methods for solving problems. Our eye movement research clearly validates that distinction and allows us to tell which method a particular student used to produce an answer. Figure 3 shows a student using the expression and Figure 4 shows a student using the problem statement.

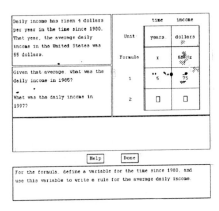 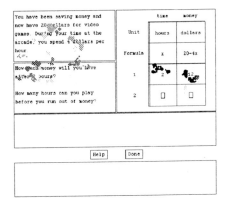

Fig. 3. Eye movement paint trace showing use of the expression to solve the first result-unknown.

Fig. 4. Eye movement paint trace showing use of the problem statement to solve the first result-unknown.

In the case where the expression is used the student shows repeated fixations of the expression. In the case where it is not used the student never fixates the expression but rather fixates the problem statement while reasoning verbally through the problem.

Performance Comparison Across Solution Strategies. Figures 3 and 4 are examples of two very different solution strategies for result-unknowns – one that relies on the expression and one that relies on the problem statement. Now we address the question of how often students are using these two sources of information to arrive at an answer to a result-unknown. We also investigate whether there is a performance advantage for either strategy.

To address these questions, we looked at fixation frequencies in the problem statement and the expression while participants were working on their 1st attempt at Q1-Right. Again, only the nine students in the high formula row condition were used in this analysis, because low formula row students would not have an expression to fixate. Each part-task was labeled as to the presence of fixations in the two regions of interest. If there were one or more fixations in the expression, but not in the problem statement, the part-task was labeled "Expression." If there were one or more fixations in the problem statement, but not in the expression, the part-task was labeled "Problem Statement." Part-tasks were also labeled as "Both" or "Neither," as appropriate. Table 1 shows the percentage of part-tasks, the proportion of correct part-tasks, and the average completion time for all 1st attempts within each fixation pattern.

Table 1. Distribution of fixation patterns during Q1-Right 1st attempts

Fixation Pattern	% of Part-Tasks	Prop. Correct	Time (sec)
Expression (but not PS)	30.1	.88	13.2
PS (but not Expression)	12.6	.50	21.2
Both	23.8	.76	21.1
Neither	33.6	.71	7.7

At the aggregate level, these data indicate that students looked at the expression 54% of the time on their first attempt at solving Question 1, and they ignore the expression on 46% of first attempts. The accuracy data show an advantage for using the expression over using the problem statement. There is a main effect of fixation pattern on accuracy ($F(3, 140) = 3.68$, $p < .02$), and a post-hoc Scheffe's test indicates that those who attended to the expression (but not the PS) while solving the result-unknown responded more accurately than those who looked at just the problem statement ($p < .02$). The other differences are not significant. There is also a main effect of fixation pattern on part-task completion time ($F(3, 140) = 19.69$, $p < .001$), with attending to neither region significantly faster than all of the other fixation patterns and attending only to the expression faster than attending to just the problem statement or to both.

One might hypothesize that these results could be due to differences in behaviors by students of different ability levels. It turns out that, although the high ability students do have a tendency towards reading the expression while working on the result-unknown and the low ability students tend towards reading the problem statement, this does not account for the performance advantage for attending to the expression. The more accurate interpretation seems to be that using the available expression facilitates the process of solving result-unknowns.

Instructional Implications. One goal of the curriculum is to help students understand the value of mathematical expressions. With respect to solving result-unknown questions, the expression is useful in that it provides external memory for the computations required to arrive at a solution, and our performance data do indeed show an advantage for those part-tasks in which students looked at the expression. These strategies cannot be distinguished on the basis of answer alone, but they *can* be distinguished by a tutor that has access to a student's eye movements. The data clearly suggest that the appropriate instructional intervention during part-tasks in which a completed expression is on the screen and the student is ignoring it is to bring the expression to the student's attention. For students who persist in ignoring the expression, probably it would be justified to include some remediation on what the expression represents and its utility in the context of solving result-unknowns.

3.3 Failure to Read Bug Messages

Students often fail to read the bug messages that appear on the screen. We saw examples of this during data collection, and became interested in how often this actually happened. To investigate that we extracted data from only those part-tasks that immediately followed a part-task where an error occurred and led to the display of a bug message. So in all of the part-tasks used in this analysis, the student has just committed an error and there is a bug message on the screen. There are a total of 416 part-tasks that meet these criteria. We also have used only the data from the beginning of each part-task to the first mouse click. This is because mouse clicks clear the message window. Students failed to fixate the message window in 172 part-tasks, meaning that they completely ignored the bug message in 41% of the part-tasks in which a bug message was present.

Bug Messages and Error Recovery. The percentage of messages that are ignored (41%) seems high given that these messages are supposed to help students recover from the error that has just been committed. The messages should presumably be considered to be of high utility. The critical assumption here is that the bug messages actually are facilitating the error recovery process. Is this true? Among part-tasks in which students completely ignored the bug message (the 172 part-tasks mentioned above), the error rate is .38 ($\underline{SD}$ = .49). Averaging over all of the other part-tasks (the 244 part-tasks with at least one fixation in the message window while a bug message is present), the error rate is .50 ($\underline{SD}$ = .50). This is a statistically significant difference ($F(1, 414) = 5.55$; $p < .02$) that indicates no performance advantage, and in fact suggests a *disadvantage*, for attending to the bug messages.

What might explain the surprising, and somewhat disturbing, performance advantage for ignoring the bug messages? One hypothesis might be that individual differences in ability level explain this result – if high ability students are more likely to ignore the bug messages. Analyses to test this hypothesis showed non-significant results. A second hypothesis is that this is a function of cell difficulty – and it appears this is the better explanation. Students read the bug message on 54% of the 96 part-tasks from easy cells and they read the bug message on 60% of the 320 part-tasks from hard cells. This is not a statistically significant difference, but the fact that the overwhelming majority of the part-tasks with bug messages come from hard cells is striking (although predictable). Table 2 shows the error rates for attending vs. ignoring the bug messages, separately by cell difficulty.

Table 2. Error rates for attending vs. ignoring the bug messages, separately by cell difficulty

| | Bug Message | | | | | | |
| | Ignored | | | Attended | | | |
Cell Difficulty	M	(SD)	n	M	SD	n	% Attended
Easy	.30	(.46)	44	.35	(.48)	52	54
Hard	.41	(.49)	128	.54	(.50)	192	60

There is a significant main effect of cell difficulty ($F(1, 414) = 7.42$; $p < .01$), with hard cells showing higher error rates. The effect of attention to the bug message on error rate disappears, and the interaction is not significant either. This analysis goes a long way towards explaining why performance is worse in part-tasks where students attended to the bug message. Students are slightly more likely to attend to the bug message on the hard cells, and despite attending to the bug message, they are more likely to commit an error, because it is a difficult cell.

Instructional Implications. Cell difficulty provides an explanation for the result that error recovery performance is worse when students read the bug messages. Nevertheless, it is tempting to conclude from these results that one should abandon the idea of intervening in cases where the student is ignoring the bug message, on the basis that attending to the message doesn't seem to help. Should we conclude that it is not beneficial, and perhaps is even detrimental, to draw a student's attention to the bug message if that student is ignoring it? No. That would be an unfair conclusion. If there is a bug message on the screen and the student has not attended to it after some period of time, it seems perfectly reasonable to draw attention to the message. It's not likely to hurt, and it might even help.

The next question is when should an intervention take place? When a student is ignoring the bug message, how long should the tutor wait before intervening? Our data show that 20 seconds is a justifiable proposal for a deadline, because this is roughly the point after which continuing to ignore the message no longer shows a performance advantage. In the first 20 seconds after an error is made, students are more likely to self-diagnose the error and get the next response correct when they don't look at the bug message than if they do. After 20 seconds, there is an advantage in error recovery for students who have seen the bug message. Thus, it seems likely that if more than 20 seconds have passed, and the student has not seen the bug message, chances are that another error is about to be committed. The tutor might as well draw attention to the message and hope that does the trick.

4 Summary

The goal in the first phase of this research has been to characterize the instructional opportunities that present themselves if one were to broaden the bandwidth of information available to an ITS by including eye movement data. This paper has described three different uses for eye movements within ITS: predicting impending errors, detecting undesirable solution processes, and identifying students who are ignoring bug messages. In each of these cases, the eye movements provide additional detail regarding cognitive processes, beyond what is available from key presses and mouse clicks alone. In our opinion, the use of eye movements is a promising direction in which to expand the bandwidth of information that is available to an ITS.

Acknowledgements

Funding for this project has been provided by the Air Force PALACE Knight Program and by NSF grant number CDA-9720359 to the Center for Interdisciplinary Research on Constructive Learning Environments (CIRCLE).

References

1. Hartley, J. R., & Sleeman, D. H. (1973). Towards more intelligent teaching systems. International Journal of Man-Machine Studies, 2, 215-36.
2. Shute, V. J., & Psotka, J. (1996). Intelligent tutoring systems: Past, present, and future. In D. Jonassen (Ed.), Handbook of research on educational communications and technology. Scholastic Publications.
3. Bloom, B. S. (1984). The 2-sigma problem: The search for methods of group instruction as effective as one-to-one tutoring. Educational Researcher, 13, 3-16.
4. Holt, P., Dubs, S., Jones, M., & Greer, J. (1994). The state of student modeling. In J. E. Greer & G. I. McCalla (Eds.), Student modeling: The key to individualized knowledge-based instruction (pp. 3-38). New York: Springer-Verlag.
5. VanLehn, K. (1988). Student modeling. In M. C. Polson & J. J. Richardson (Eds.), Foundations of intelligent tutoring systems (pp. 55-78). Hillsdale, NJ: Erlbaum.
6. Gluck, K. A. (1999). Eye movements and algebra tutoring. Unpublished doctoral dissertation, Carnegie Mellon University, Pittsburgh, PA.
7. Koedinger, K. R., & Anderson, J. R. (1998). Illustrating principled design: The early evolution of a cognitive tutor for algebra symbolization. Interactive Learning Environments, 5, 161-179.
8. Koedinger, K.R., & Tabachneck, H.J.M. (1995). Verbal reasoning as a critical component in early algebra. Paper presented at the annual meeting of the American Educational Research Association, San Francisco, CA.
9. Koedinger, K.R., & MacLaren, B. A. (1997). Implicit strategies and errors in an improved model of early algebra problem solving. In Proceedings of the Nineteenth Annual Conference of the Cognitive Science Society, (pp. 382-387). Hillsdale, NJ: Erlbaum.

Accretion Representation
for Scrutable Student Modelling

Judy Kay

Basser Department of Computer Science
University of Sydney
AUSTRALIA 2006
judy@cs.usyd.edu.au

Abstract. This paper describes the *accretion* representation for *scrutable* student modelling. Essentially, the representation maintains a timestamped collection of the evidence about each component of the student model. This is interpreted by a *resolver* at the time that a teaching program needs to determine the value of parts of the model.

The accretion representation treats *external* evidence as ground assumptions which are normally kept long term. By contrast, the student modelling system's *internal* inferences are handled quite differently. This approach supports long-term modelling of the learner's knowledge and other characteristics. It was used in large scale modelling and coaching experiments for knowledge of a text editor.

An important concern for the representation is to support *scrutability* of the student model. This notion is explained in the paper and linked to the design of the accretion representation.

1 Introduction

There are typically many sources of information about the components of a student model. The sources are varied on many dimensions, most notably reliability. As Motro and Smets [8]:245 observe, there has been little work on the problem of combining diverse sources of evidence. This problem is especially important for long term, reusable student models which might be used by a number of teaching systems.

This paper describes the *accretion* representation for student modelling. It was designed to take account of just this problem at the same time as supporting *scrutability* of the student model. This means that the student should be able to scrutinise the details of the student model, its meaning, values of the components, details of the evidence which determines those values, as well as details of the processes used to reason about the student. Scrutability is especially important in student modelling since it enhances learner control and may support metacognition.

The accretion representation was used as the foundation for um [5] which has been used in large scale experiments involving modelling the knowledge of over two hundred users over several years. In these experiments, we used monitor data to construct detailed individual models of each user's knowledge of a text editor called sam. The um toolkit includes interface tools which assist the user in scrutinising their user model, gaining an overview of the model as well as digging deeply into the details of the meanings of parts of the model. This paper takes examples from that domain.

2   Overview of the accretion representation

To introduce the accretion representation, we use the example in Figure 1. This shows the evidence from a student model component for the sam text editor command called xerox. (This creates multiple windows on a file.)

Source	Time (week number)												
	1	2	3	4	5	6	7	8	9	10	11	12	13
xan	–	–	–	–	–	–	–	±	±	+	+	+	+
coach						+							

Fig. 1. Hypothetical example of evidence list

The top line in the figure shows the progression of time over 13 weeks, from left to right. The second line shows that each week, a program called xan analysed logs of the user's interaction with sam. If it found any error-free uses of the command in that week, xan provided a piece of evidence with the value true, shown in the figure as +. This happened in the last six entries in Figure 1. Where there were no uses or any incorrect uses, a negative piece of evidence was created for that week. We can see this in the first nine cases in the figure.

The last line of the figure shows evidence from a coaching program run in week 7. When it coached the student, it provided the evidence indicating the student knew that aspect.

Now consider an intuitive approach to dealing with this collection of information about a component of a student model. One reading of the evidence in the figure is:

– there were 7 weeks where there were no error-free uses, suggesting the student either did not need xerox in this period or did not know it;
– in week 7, the coach taught the student about xerox;
– then there were two weeks with a mixture of error-free and incorrect uses, suggesting that the student is in the process of learning xerox;
– and from week 10 on, there were exclusively correct uses suggesting the student has learnt it.

This sequence of evidence characterises the type of information one might expect for a system which needs to deal with the student's changing knowledge as they learn. The um representation needs to be able to manage such information

516

and conclude about the value of the component. In addition, um must be able to support student scrutiny. So, for example, if the student were to explore this component up to the end of week 7, they should be able to find information enabling them to see the value of this component and the evidence about it at that time.

We note that this example is very simple. It has only external evidence. A typical component of a um model may have evidence which has been derived by various internal inference tools as well as multiple external sources of information.

3   Basic operations: accretion, resolution, destruction

We now describe the three high level accretion operations.

Accretion. This means the addition of a new piece of evidence to the list for a component. Each piece of evidence in Figure 1 was added as one accretion operation. Because it is the the most basic operation, accretion gives the representation its name. Any source can volunteer information about a component. If the source is authorised to contribute to this component, its evidence is added to the component's evidence list.

Resolution. When an accretion operation adds new evidence to a component list, there is no associated interpretation of that evidence. The addition of a piece of evidence does not trigger any conflict assessment or resolution. It is only when a teaching system needs to know the value of a component that it is necessary to decide how to interpret a collection of possibly inconsistent evidence. That interpretation is called *resolution*.

Consider resolution in relation to the example of Figure 1. We see that new evidence arrived each week. Suppose that the value of the component was only needed at weeks 6 and 13. In week 6, we may suppose it was needed by the coach so it could decide whether to coach the student on xerox. Examining the evidence to the end of week 6, each item of evidence has the value false. Note that the student may well have known xerox but simply not needed it in those weeks: this case illustrates some of the difficulty in determining a component's value from the evidence available.

Now consider the resolution of a value by the end of week 13. At that point there are 9 pieces of false evidence and 7 pieces of true evidence. Yet if we take account of the temporal information, we see that the last 4 weeks of evidence were exclusively true. Intuitively, we might resolve that the component is now true. There are many other ways to reason about this information. For example, the fact that true evidence began after the coaching might be important for concluding that the component is true at week 13.

However, if we are very conservative about concluding that the student knows the component, we might conclude a component is true only after 8 weeks of correct use. This case illustrates the flexibility that may be required by different teaching systems when they resolve a component's value.

The um scrutability requirements mean that the process of resolution of a component value must be available to the student. This means that the student should be able to access an explanation of it. For example, if resolution was based upon just the last four weeks of evidence, then at week 13, the explanation should convey the following information:

- the value of the component was determined on the basis of the information available over the last four weeks;
- in that period, the weekly analysis of your use of sam showed correct uses of xerox in each week;
- so it was concluded that you know the xerox command.

The accretion representation is based on the premise that there can be many different resolvers. Intuitively, these correspond to the way that different people assess a collection of evidence differently. For example, some people would conclude that a component was true whenever there was any evidence for this where other people would be more conservative in making such a conclusion.

In summary, there can be many resolution operators so that they can support a range of different reasoning about the component value indicated by its evidence list.

Destruction. To this point, we have described only accretion operators that make the evidence list grow monotonically over time. This may be unacceptable both in terms of the modelling processes and scrutability. Resolution will become increasingly slow as the lists of evidence grows. Any other inference processes that deal with whole lists will also become slower. At the same time, it will become harder for the student to scrutinise the list: the student, like the resolvers, will need to study increasingly long lists of evidence to find those that actually affect the current value of the component. This could be a serious problem if some sources can potentially provide huge amounts of very low grade information as, for example, in the case of monitor data from the sam text editor.

Destruction operations selectively remove evidence. In the case of Figure 1, suppose we knew that all resolvers only made use of the last 4 weeks of evidence. In that case, we can guarantee that all the earlier evidence can play no role in determining the value of the xerox component. So, we could remove all the earlier evidence without affecting the value of the component.

In general, destruction is dangerous from the point of view of scrutability. For the example in Figure 1, suppose we deleted all but the last 4 weeks of evidence. The student is then unable to scrutinise the value of the model as it was at weeks 6 or 7. Since those weeks were important for determining and recording the actions of the coach, the student might well want to scrutinise that part of the model.

Destruction may also pose problems for future flexible use of evidence. For example, analysis of the evidence in Figure 1 suggests the student learnt xerox from the coach. Similar analyses of the evidence for other components which were coached might show a similar pattern. This would then support a high level conclusion that the student learns from this coach.

Although we need to acknowledge the problems with destruction of evidence, efficiency may demand it. No representation can be allowed to grow continuously.

4 Accretion representation

The primitive objects in the representation are called *components* . We refer to a component as $Comp_N$ when it has a list of N items of evidence. We define a function *elist* which returns the list of evidence associated with a component:

$$elist(Comp_N) = \begin{cases} \{\}, if N = 0 \\ \{evidence_e\}, 0 < e <= N \end{cases}$$

Each *evidence_e* in $Comp_N$ has the following attributes:

- value: $\in \{true, false\}$ is the component value supported by this piece of evidence;
- source type: which describes the type of the evidence source (in Figure 1, all are external);
- source identifier: defines the source of the evidence (in Figure 1 these were xerox and coach);
- time stamp: records when evidence was added (in Figure 1 this is the week number);
- extra information: allows arbitrary additional information to be included in the evidence where this is to interpreted outside the accretion model (none appears in Figure 1);
- scrutability information: enables a student to determine the meaning of the evidence in terms of the component meaning, the source identifier, the extra information (in the case of Figure 1, scrutability information is explanations of the meaning of the component xerox as well as the xan and coach sources);

4.1 Resolution operators

There are two types of resolver. Differences between them involve the balance between efficiency and richness of interpretations.

Primitive resolvers. These are the simplest resolvers. They determine the value of a component by taking the value of the most reliable piece(s) of evidence in the list. Typically, this will be determined by characteristics of evidence: the time stamp; the source type; the source identifier. So, for example, in Figure 1, one primitive resolver takes the most reliable evidence as that added most recently. In each of weeks 1 to 6, this is false and so the value of the component would also be false. In weeks 10 to 13, the same metric returns the value true.

For each of weeks 8 and 9, there are two pieces of evidence of opposite value. So the value returned would be conflict.

A primitive resolver requires a function $maxrel_e$ which maps from a list of evidence $\{evidence_e\}$ to a sub-list containing the evidence with highest reliability: $\{evidence_M\}$ with M elements. Then, the resolver must determine the value from these. For example, one that returns a value for the component using a four-value logic:

$$resolver(Comp_N) = \begin{cases} true & if \; \forall \; i, 1 <= i <= M, value(e_i) = true \\ false & if \; \forall \; i, 1 <= i <= M, value(e_i) = false \\ NoEvidence & if \, M = 0 \\ conflict & otherwise \end{cases}$$

A primitive resolver provides an exceptionally simple mechanism. It should be very fast and low cost. It should be straightforward to explain to the student in terms of its process and the details of the metric for assessing reliability. We used a primitive resolver for our large scale trials of um.

Compound resolvers. Against the benefits of a primitive resolver is its lack of power. A major benefit of an evidence-based representation is that many items of low grade evidence should be able to collectively contribute to conclusions about a component. The multi-evidence resolvers determine the component value as a more complex function of the evidence list.

Consider Figure 1. A compound resolver tool might conclude the student knew the component only if they had used xerox correctly for at least 5 consecutive weeks and they had not made any incorrect uses in that period. By week 13, we can see that the last 5 weeks do indeed reflect that the student has made 5 consecutive weeks of correct use. However, there was also some incorrect use. So this resolver concludes the student does not know xerox.

In general, there may be many rich ways to reason about lists of evidence. A compound resolver can use arbitrarily complex reasoning. For example, it could reason from several components' evidence.

4.2 Accretion sources and operators

We now discuss the classes of sources of accretion evidence and the associated operators.

External Sources. Evidence from external sources has to be accepted by the reasoning system as a fait accompli: there may be a complex process involved in collecting the evidence and determining its value, but this is not available to the student modelling system.

From the point of view of scrutability, an external evidence source is a black-box. Because the system does not have access to the processes internal to the source of external evidence, it can only require an ontological description of the evidence source. In our sam experiments, we provided canned text explanations for external evidence sources.

The external beliefs are *ground* beliefs because they act as foundations for the internal inference. It is common for student modelling researchers to make essentially this distinction although the terms used vary. For example, Self [11] uses *basic* and *derived* beliefs and describes systems with other terms like *explicit* and *implicit*.

Internal sources. These come from within the student modelling system. They should support student scrutiny of their processes. They create a new piece of evidence reasoning from the resolved values of arbitrary components. For example, suppose the student is a sam-novice and an expert in vi, an editor in the same family as sam but without a facility like xerox. We may have an internal inference, which we express as a production:

$$\text{sam-novice and vi-expert} \rightarrow \text{not xerox}$$

This means that if the left-hand-side is true, the inference creates a piece of evidence for xerox:

value	source type	source name	week
false	internal	vi expert sam novice	1

Metamophosis (internal) sources. This may be considered a specialisation of the internal operation. A metamorphosis inference builds from several pieces of evidence giving a new piece of evidence with higher reliability. So, for example, in Figure 1 the early evidence showed no correct uses of xerox. Any one of these alone is a weak basis for concluding that the student does not know xerox. However, six consecutive weeks of this evidence may collectively constitute quite strong evidence that the student does not know xerox.

The metamorphosis process can be extremely simple. It may have a threshold for the number of positive evidence items required and the number of negative ones allowed and if this condition is passed, the new evidence is added to the component. For the example in Figure 1, a metamorphosis mechanism might use the last 5 weeks of evidence as follows. If at least three positive pieces of evidence occur in the last five weeks and at most one piece of negative occurs evidence in that time, it adds a piece of evidence like this:

value	source type	source name	week
true	metamorphosis	ok3 in 5 nok 1	13

Primitive resolvers are related to metamorphosis. This is because the representation offers two equivalent mechanisms:

- metamorphosis followed by use of a primitive resolver;
- a compound resolver which determines the value of an evidence list by aggregating evidence within the list.

For heavily used student models, which must operate in real time, the former approach is preferable. This is why we used it in our large scale sam experiments.

4.3 Destruction operators

There are two destruction operators, one applying exclusively to external evidence and the other to evidence lists containing internal evidence.

Destruction of external evidence by compaction. The compaction operation replaces a component's evidence list with a shorter one where:

- only external evidence is deleted;
- and that only if already metamorphosed;
- deleted evidence has no effect on the outcome from any of the resolvers applied to this component.

For example, suppose metamorphosis was used at week 13 giving a piece of evidence like this:

value	source type	source name	week
true	metamorphosis	xan metam	13

Suppose we know that that all resolvers treat this single piece of evidence as more reliable than any or all the xan evidence. Now, basic external xan evidence can have no effect.

Essentially, compaction enables the component to forget about external evidence that has been coalesced into other, more reliable evidence. At the same time, compaction being a destruction operation, is dangerous as it involves loss of information.

Deletion of internal evidence as undo and redo. The undo is another operation that enables the student model to remove irrelevant information, this time, information from internal inferences. Essentially, it relies upon the fact that the modelling system can re-apply its internal inference processes at arbitrary times. The undo removes all internal inferences (except metamorphosis evidence). Then internal inference tools can be rerun. This is a simple mechanism for dealing with complex chains of internal inference that have been affected by changes in external evidence.

For example, suppose that we had run an internal inference tool on the evidence in Figure 1 in week 5. For this discussion, the details of that internal inference are unimportant. Suppose it produced a piece of evidence like this:

value	source type	source name	week
false	internal	xerox infer	5

Then suppose we use a resolver which treats this as the most reliable evidence to that point in time. This single piece of evidence would then be used to conclude the component was false.

Now suppose that in week 13, we again want to assess all the evidence available to that point. The undo operation would remove the internal inference above. We could then rerun the internal inference mechanism which might now produce a piece of evidence like this:

value	source type	source name	week
true	internal	xerox infer	13

Intuitively, this corresponds to reasoning about evidence as needed, keeping internal inferences only until we are ready to review the reasoning about the external evidence available.

The undo operation is trivial to implement. It deletes all internal inferences. The redo operation requires re-execution of all the relevant internal inferences. In comparison with approaches like truth maintenance and belief revision, this is a low cost operation. Moreover, it produces evidence lists which are simple: this is important for efficient management of the model and for the student scrutinising their model.

5 Related work

Our representation is a similar to endorsements [2]. Endorsement-based representations have been used for student modelling, for example, by Murray [9], and for modelling student preferences [1]. Endorsements have also been applied in belief models [3]. The accretion representation is intended to support long-term student modelling, rather like TAGUS [10], THEMIS [6] [7] and SMMS [4] but our concern for supporting scrutability made it natural to develop a representation which holds the details of the evidence for scrutiny by the student.

6 Summary

Accretion is a representation for scrutable student modelling. At its core, it maintains the list of evidence which is the basis for defining the value of a component. It has three basic operations:

- *accretion*, be it external, internal and its specialisation, metamorphosis;
- *resolvers*: *primitive* and *compound*;
- *destruction*: compaction of external evidence for use with primitive resolvers; and undo for internal inferences where this will typically operate in conjunction with the redo;

This representation provides simple mechanisms for dealing with many interesting problems that arise in student modelling: changes in the student due to learning and forgetting, erratic student behaviour as well as noise in evidence sources, short term changes in the student due to effects like moods, stereotype inferences where more reliable inferences override default inferences due to the stereotype and inconsistency in the student's beliefs.

References

1. Elzer, S., Chu-Carroll, J., Carberry, S.: Recognizing and utilizing user preferences in collaborative consultation dialogues. In: Kobsa, A., Litman, S. (eds.): Proceedings of the Fourth International Conference on User Modeling, UM94. MITRE, User Modeling Inc, Hyannis, Massechusetts, USA (1994) 19–24

2. Cohen, P.: Heuristic reasoning about uncertainty: An artificial intelligence approach. Pitman (1985)
3. Galliers, J.R.: Autonomous belief revision and a theory of communication. Technical Report 193, Computer Laboratory, University of Cambridge (1990)
4. Huang, X., McCalla, G., Greer, J., Neufeld, E.: Revising deductive knowledge and stereotypical knowledge in a student model. User Modeling and User-Adapted Interaction. Kluwer, 1:1 (1991) 87–116
5. Kay, J.: A scrutable user modelling shell for user-adapted interaction, PhD Thesis, Basser Department of Computer Science, University of Sydney, Australia (1998)
6. Kono, Y. Ikeda, M. Mizoguchi, R.: To contradict is human: student modelling of inconsistency. In: Frasson, C., Gauthier, G., McCalla, G. (eds.): Intelligent tutoring systems. Springer-Verlag (1992) 451–458
7. Kono, Y. Ikeda, M. Mizoguchi, R.: THEMIS: a nonmonotonic inductive student modeling system. Journal of Artificial Intelligence in Education. 5:3 (1994) 371–413
8. Motro, A., Smets. P: Uncertainty management in information systems. Kluwer, Boston London Dordrecht (1997)
9. Murray, W.R.: An endorsement-based approach to student modelling for planner-controlled tutors. Proceedings of the International Joint Conference on Artificial Intelligence. Morgan Kaufman (1991) 1100–1106
10. Paiva, A., Self, J.: TAGUS - a user and learner modeling workbench, User Modeling and User-Adapted Interaction Kluwer, 4:3 (1995) 197–228
11. Self, J.: Formal approaches to student modelling. In: Greer, J McCalla, G. (eds.): Student Modelling: The Key to Individualized Knowledge-Based Instruction. Springer-Verlag, Berlin Heidelberg New York (1994) 295–352

Using a Probabilistic Student Model to Control Problem Difficulty

Michael Mayo and Antonija Mitrovic

Intelligent Computer Tutoring Group
Department of Computer Science, University of Canterbury
Private Bag 4800, Christchurch, New Zealand
mmayo@cosc.canterbury.ac.nz, tanja@cosc.canterbury.ac.nz

Abstract. Bayesian networks have been used in Intelligent Tutoring Systems (ITSs) for both short-term diagnosis of students' answers and for longer-term assessment of a student's knowledge. Bayesian networks have the advantage of a firm theoretical foundation, in contrast to many existing, ad-hoc approaches. In this paper we argue that Bayesian nets can offer much more to an ITS, and we give an example of how they can be used for selecting problems. Similar approaches may be taken to automating many kinds of decision in ITSs.

Keywords: instructional design; student modeling; evaluation of instructional systems

1 Introduction

Our research is aimed towards developing a general methodology for using the student model to solve decision problems in an ITS. There has been much research in the field of student modeling, and student models that can reasonably accurately predict student post-test performance have been developed (e.g. the ACT Programming Tutor [5]). However, to be truly adaptive, an ITS must make optimal use of the information contained in the student model to tailor its actions to the specific needs of the student. Actions include selecting an appropriate problem if the student asks for it, next topic selection, feedback selection, and selective highlighting/hiding of information. We have developed an approach to adaptive decision-making based on Bayesian probability theory. For each alternative, simple Bayesian networks are used to make multiple predictions about student performance on atomic domain elements called constraints. These multiple predictions are then combined heuristically to give an overall measure of the value of the alternative. The approach is demonstrated in a problem selection module for SQL-Tutor [8,9], an ITS for teaching the database language SQL.

Section 2 briefly introduces SQL-Tutor. In section 3 we describe an approach to selecting problems of appropriate complexity via Bayesian networks. The results of a preliminary evaluation study are discussed in section 4, followed by a comparison of this approach to others section 5. Section 6 is conclusions and future research.

2 SQL-Tutor

SQL-Tutor is a practice environment for undergraduates enrolled in database courses. There are three functionally identical versions for Solaris, MS Windows and the Web. Here we give only a brief description of the system, and the interested reader is referred to other papers [8,9] and the system's Web page[1] for details.

The architecture of the system is illustrated in Figure 1. The system contains definitions of several databases, a set of problems for each database and the ideal solutions to them. The solutions are necessary because SQL-Tutor evaluates student solutions by comparing them to the correct ones. Each problem is assigned a difficulty level, which depends on many features, such as the wording of the problem, the constructs needed for its solution, the number of required tables/attributes etc.

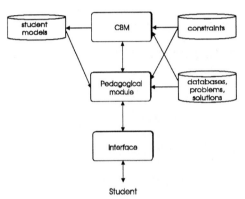

Fig. 1. Architecture of SQL-Tutor

Each student is given a level of mastery, which dynamically changes in accordance with student's performance.

The basic components of the system are the interface, the pedagogical module and the CBM student modeler. The pedagogical module (PM) observes every student's action and reacts appropriately. At the beginning of he session, a problem must be selected for the student. When the student enters the solution, the PM sends it to the student modeler, which analyzes the student's solution in order to identify possible errors. If any errors exist, the PM generates appropriate feedback messages. After the first attempt a student is only told whether his/her solution is correct or not. The level of detail increases if the student is not able to correct the solution.

SQL-Tutor uses Constraint-Based Modeling [10] to diagnose students' solutions. The conceptual domain knowledge is represented in terms of over 500 constraints. A student's solution is matched to the constraints to identify any that are violated. Long-term student knowledge is represented as an overlay model that tallies the percentage of times the constraint has been satisfied (i.e. used correctly). Both students and problems in SQL–Tutor are assigned a level. The student's level is incremented if he/she solves two or more problems consecutively at or above the student's current level, within three attempts each.

There are three ways to select the next problem in SQL-Tutor. Students can work through a pre-specified sequence of problems by clicking *next problem*, they can select a practice problem directly from a menu of problems, or they can turn problem selection over to the system by clicking *system's choice*. In the third case, SQL-Tutor examines the student model and selects the first problem whose level is within +1 or –1 of the student's level, which is also relevant to the constraint that the student has

---

[1] See http://www.cosc.canterbury.ac.nz/~tanja/sql-tut.html

violated most frequently. The rationale for this rule is that if the student has violated the same constraint several times, it is appropriate to target that constraint for instruction. This problem selection strategy is overly simple. In a real classroom, it was often the case that selected problems were too complex or simple for the student, or they jumped to another part of the domain seemingly not connected to the previous problem. We set out here to explore other possibilities for problem selection.

3 Problem Selection Using Bayesian Networks

Bayesian networks [2,11] are tools for representing and reasoning with uncertain knowledge using Bayesian probability theory.

3.1 The Probabilistic Student Model

Before Bayesian networks could be applied to the task of problem selection, SQL-Tutor's student model had to be reformulated in probabilistic terms. The new student model consists of a set of binary variables $Mastered_1$, $Mastered_2$,...,$Mastered_n$, where n is the total number of constraints. Each variable can be in the state *YES* or *NO* with a certain probability, indicating whether or not the student has mastered the constraint.

Initial values for P(*Mastered$_c$* = *YES*) were determined by firstly counting the frequencies with which c was both satisfied and relevant (i.e. either satisfied or violated) in SQL-Tutor logs from previous evaluation studies, and then by dividing the former frequency by the latter. The logs were only analysed up to the point where the user gets the first constraint-specific feedback about c. This ensured that the effects of learning did not bias the initial probabilities. Some constraints did not appear in past SQL-Tutor logs either because they were new or they had never been used. For these constraints, P(*Mastered$_c$* = *YES*) was initialised to 0.5.

If constraint c is satisfied, then P(*Mastered$_c$* = *YES*) increases by 10% of (1-P(*Mastered$_c$=YES*)).
If constraint c is violated and no feedback about c is given, then P(*Mastered$_c$* = *YES*) decreases by 20%.
If constraint c is violated but feedback is given about c, then P(*Mastered$_c$* = *YES*) increases by 20% of (1-P(*Mastered$_c$=YES*)).

Table 1. Heuristics used for updating the student model

The student model is updated after the student submits his/her solution to a problem and receives feedback. The system currently uses the heuristics in Table 1 to update the probabilities. This heuristic approach was chosen over Bayes' rule, because we do not make the assumption that constraints in the SQL domain are probabilistically independent, whereas many other models (e.g. Reye's model [12]) do. Therefore, applying Bayes' rule would result in a calculation that would be impractical to perform on-line. Dependence between constraints in SQL-Tutor arises at least because each violated constraint generates an error message, and so mastery of a constraint depends to some extent on how many other errors were made at the same time. This point is discussed further in sections 3.3 and 5. Constraints may also be dependent because of semantic overlap, syntactic proximity in problems, and pre- and co-requisite relationships. We believe that models where probabilistic independence between all knowledge items is assumed are unrealistic (e.g. Reye's model [12]).

3.2 Predicting Student Performance on Single Constraints

We use a simple Bayesian network (Figure 2) to predict the performance of a student given a problem p on a single constraint c. $Mastered_c$ is from the student model. Both $RelevantIS_{c,p}$ and $RelevantSS_{c,p}$ are *YES/NO* variables. $RelevantIS_{c,p}$ is *YES* if constraint c is relevant to problem p's ideal solution. Because this can be determined from the problem database, $RelevantIS_{c,p}$ is always known with certainty. $RelevantSS_{c,p}$ is *YES* if constraint c is relevant to the student's solution to problem p. $Performance_{c,p}$ is a three-valued node taking values *SATISFIED, VIOLATED* or *NOT-RELEVANT*. The arcs indicate that $RelevantSS_{c,p}$ is dependent on $RelevantIS_{c,p}$. $Performance_{c,p}$ is dependent on whether or not the student has mastered c, and c's relevance to the student solution.

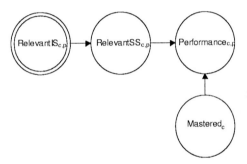

Fig. 2. A Bayesian network for predicting student performance on a single constraint.

A full specification of this Bayesian network requires prior and conditional probabilities. P($Mastered_c$) and P($RelevantIS_{c,p}$) are the prior probabilities, which are already available from the student model and problem database respectively. In Table 2, α_c and β_c are properties of the constraint c. α_c (β_c) is the probability of a constraint being relevant to the student's solution if it is (not) relevant to p's ideal solution. Effectively, α_c and β_c provide a measure of the "predictive usefulness" of the ideal solution. For example, when $\alpha_c = \beta_c = 0.5$, the relevance of c to the ideal solution tells us nothing about the relevance of c to a potential student solution. However, if $\alpha_c = 0.9$ for example, there is a high probability that constraints relevant to the ideal solution will also be relevant to a student solution.

	RelevantIS$_{c,p}$	
	YES	**NO**
YES	α_c	β_c
NO	$1-\alpha_c$	$1-\beta_c$

RelSS$_c$ labels the rows.

Table 2. P($RelevantSS_{c,p}$|$RelevantIS_{c,p}$)

Like the initial probabilities of mastery, we determined values for α_c and β_c from past SQL-Tutor logs. However, these conditional probabilities were not available *directly* from the data. All that can be determined from the logs was the frequencies with which constraints were relevant to the ideal and student solutions, or both. Derivation (1) shows how α_c was calculated using the chain rule. A similar calculation was done for β_c. For new or previously unused constraints, α_c and β_c were initialised to 0.5.

$$\alpha_c = P(RelevantSS_{p,c} = YES \mid RelevantIS_{p,c} = YES)$$
$$= P(RelevantSS_{p,c} = YES \ \& \ RelevantIS_{p,c} = YES) \ / \ P(RelevantIS_{p,c} = YES)$$

(1)

= # times c is relevant to both SS and IS in the logs / # times c is relevant
  to IS in the logs

	RelevantSS$_{c,p}$ Mastered$_c$			
	YES **YES**	**YES** **NO**	**NO** **YES**	**NO** **NO**
SATISFIED	$1-Slip_c$	$Guess_c$	0	0
VIOLATED	$Slip_c$	$1-Guess_c$	0	0
NOT-RELEVANT	0	0	1	1

Perf$_{c,p}$ labels the rows.

Table 3. P($Performance_{c,p}$|$RelevantSS_{c,p}$,Mastered$_c$)

Table 3 is the conditional probability distribution of *Performance$_{c,p}$* given its parent variables *RelevantSS$_{c,p}$* and *Mastered$_c$*. Slip$_c$ (Guess$_c$) is defined as the probability of a student who has mastered (not mastered) c slipping (guessing) and violating (satisfying) the constraint. In the third and fourth columns of Table 3, P($Performance_{c,p}$ = NOT-RELEVANT) = 1.0 and the other entries are 0, because these represent the two scenarios where $RelevantSS_{c,p}$ = NO (i.e. c is not relevant to the student solution). The four columns represent situations where the values of the parent nodes are known with certainty. In practice, the values of the parents will not be known with certainty.

The Bayesian network is used to predict the probabilities of the student violating, satisfying or not using c in his/her solution to p. A simple example will illustrate the evaluation process. Let us take the following constants: $\alpha_p = 0.9$, $\beta_p = 0.1$, $Slip_c = 0.3$, $Guess_c = 0.05$. Now, suppose that c is relevant to problem p's ideal solution (i.e. P($RelevantIS_{c,p}$ = YES) = 1) and the student is not likely to have mastered c (e.g. P($Mastered_c$ = YES) = 0.25). An evaluation of the network yields the probability distribution [P(*Performance$_c$* = *VIOLATED*) = 0.709, P(*Performance$_c$* = *SATISFIED*) = 0.191, P(*Performance$_c$* = *NOT-RELEVANT*) = 0.1].

3.3 Evaluating Problems

A single problem requires mastery of many constraints before it can be solved. The number of relevant constraints per problem ranges in SQL-Tutor from 78 for the simplest problems, to more than two hundred for complex ones. It is therefore necessary to select an appropriate problem for a student on the basis of his or her current knowledge.

We determine the value of a problem by predicting its effect on the student. If the student is given a problem that is too difficult, he/she will violate many constraints. When given a simple problem, they are not likely to violate any constraints. A problem of appropriate complexity is the one that falls into *the zone of proximal development*, defined by Vigotsky [14] as "the distance between the actual development level as determined by independent problem solving and the level of potential development as determined through problem solving under adult guidance or collaboration of more capable peers". Therefore, a student should be given a problem that is slightly above their current level but not so difficult as to discourage the student.

Let us discuss the strategy we propose for selecting problems. Each violated constraint triggers a feedback message. If the system poses a problem that is too difficult, there will be many feedback messages coming from various violated constraints, and it is unlikely that the student will be able to cope with them all. If the problem is too easy, there will be no feedback messages, as all constraints will be satisfied. A problem of appropriate complexity will generate an optimal number of feedback messages. This is the basis of the evaluation function we propose.

The algorithm for evaluating problems is given in Figure 3. The function takes two parameters, the problem *p* to be evaluated and an integer, *OptimalFeedback*. It returns the value of *p*. *OptimalFeedback* is an argument specifying the optimal number of feedback messages the student should see regarding the current problem. Its value is currently set to the student's *level* + 2, reflecting the fact that novices are likely to cope well with a small number of messages at a time, while advanced students are able to resolve several deficiencies in their solutions simultaneously.

```
int Evaluate(problem p, int OptimalFeedback) {
    int Feedbacks:=0;
    For every constraint c {
        Evaluate the Bayesian network;
        If P(Performance_{c,p} = VIOLATED) > 0.45
            Then Feedbacks := Feedbacks + 1; }
    Return (- |OptimalFeedback - Feedbacks|); }
```

Fig. 3. The problem evaluation function.

The evaluation function assumes that feedback will be generated for every constraint where P(*Performance$_{c,p}$* = *VIOLATED*) > 0.45. This heuristic is used because it is intractable to calculate the exact probability of a problem producing the optimal number of feedback messages. The 0.45 value was chosen because initial tests showed that it gave best the results. The problem with the highest value is selected from the pool of unsolved problems within 1 level of the student's level.

4 Evaluation

We performed an evaluation study in October 1999, with second year students enrolled in an introductory database course. The students were randomly assigned to a version of the system with and without the probabilistic student model/problem selector (the control and experimental group respectively). The study consisted of one 2-hour session in which students sat a pre-test, interacted with the system, and then completed a post-test. Timing of the study was a constraint, as students needed to get some overall understanding of databases prior to the study. The only possible time for the study was the last week of the school year, which had a negative effect of the number of participating students.

4.1 Appropriateness of Selected Problems

All student actions performed in the study were logged, and later used to analyse the effect of the proposed problem-selection approach on learning. Both groups had access to the problem selection methods described in section 2: clicking *next problem*, selecting the problem from a menu, or clicking *system's choice*. In the case of the control group, clicking *system's choice* lead to a problem being selected using the simple heuristic discussed in section 2, while the Bayesian approach was used for the experimental groups.

Average attempts	Exper. group	Control group
Next problem	3.18	2.10
System's choice	2.69	4.55

Table 4. Average number of attempts per solved problem.

In order to evaluate the proposed problem selection method, we identified the logs of students who used *system's choice* in both groups. Six students from the experimental group attempted 36 problems selected by *next problem* and 38 problems selected by *system's choice* using the new Bayesian approach. Thirteen students from the control group worked on 106 and 79 problems selected by *next problem* and the original *system's choice* respectively. We counted the number of attempts it took to solve each problem, the averages of which are given in Table 4. The problems selected for the control group by the heuristic were most difficult for students, requiring 4.55 attempts on average to solve. The students in the experimental group were able to solve problems selected by the Bayesian approach in 2.69 attempts on average, compared to 3.18 attempts when problems were visited in turn. The proposed problem selection method compares favourably with the heuristic approach used by the control group.

The new *system's choice* method is only slightly better on average than the *next problem* option for the experimental group, but its advantages are clearer when we observe what happens during the problem solving session. The students start with simple problems, and progress to more complex ones. Figure 4 illustrates the average number of attempts students in the experimental group took to solve the *i*th problem. It can be seen that the initial problems selected by *next problem* are easier for students than those selected by the Bayesian approach. This is explained by the fact that the Bayesian approach progresses faster to more complex problems. However, later problems selected by the Bayesian approach are more adapted to the student and therefore require fewer attempts to be solved.

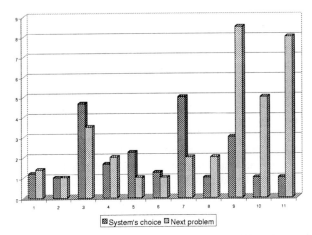

Fig. 4. The average number of attempts to solve *i*th problem by students in the experimental group.

4.2 Pre/post Tests

Pre- and post-tests consisted of three multi-choice questions each, of comparable complexity. The marks allocated to the three questions were 1, 5 and 1 respectively. Nine out of fourteen students in the experimental group and sixteen out of eighteen in the control group submitted valid pre-tests, the results of which are given in Table 5.

Question	Exper. group	Control group
1	0.22	0.25
2	2.67	2.73
3	0.62	0.73
Total	3.44	3.50

Table 5. Means for the pre-test

The mean scores in the pre-test for the two groups are very close, showing that the control and experimental groups contained a comparable cross-section of students. However, a number of factors, such as the short duration of the user study, the holding of the study during the last week of the year etc, conspired to result in a very small number of post-tests being completed. Because some students did not log off, they did not sit the post-test which was administered on a separate Web page. Only one student from the control group and four from the experimental group sat the post-test. As the result, we can draw no conclusions from the post test results.

5   Related Work

Other researchers have proposed the use of Bayesian networks in ITSs. ANDES [4,6,7], an ITS for teaching Newtonian physics, uses Bayesian networks for predicting student performance and problem solving behaviour. The ANDES network has a dynamic component, comprising nodes specific to the current problem, and a static component, comprising nodes representing the student's knowledge. The dynamic component is constructed on-line when a new problem is started. However, this approach relies on the system knowing *a priori* which rules can be relevant to the problem's solution. This is not the case in the SQL domain where the ideal solution is only one example of a correct solution. The usefulness of the ideal solution in predicting the student's actual solution is determined by the α_c and β_c parameters. Thus, in the SQL domain, we are forced to model the entire domain for each problem.

One approach that does model the entire domain is Collins et al.'s [3] hierarchical Bayesian network model for student modeling and performance prediction on test items. A similar hierarchical model was initially intended for our probabilistic student model. However, the key difference between our domain and Collins' example is that SQL-Tutor contains more than 500 constraints whereas Collins' example consists of only 50 questions. Initial investigations showed that it was infeasible to evaluate on-line a traditional Bayesian network modeling all the 500 constraints. Furthermore, Collins' example domain of elementary arithmetic divides neatly into 10 categories (e.g. addition theory, subtraction theory etc) that can be easily organised into a hierarchy, whereas in SQL there is no such simple classification of constraints.

Finally, Reye [12] has proposed a dynamic Bayesian network model for student modeling. Each variable, corresponding to a single knowledge item, is dynamically updated over time using Bayesian probability theory as the student's performance is observed. Again, this is a similar scheme to our student model where single constraints are represented by single nodes. However, Reye's model makes each knowledge item probabilistically independent. This simplification makes Bayesian student modeling tractable, but for solving decision tasks such as problem selection the probabilities need to be combined in some way. Reye does not show how this can be done, whereas this is the main emphasis of our paper.

6   Conclusions & Future Work

One of the vital tasks an ITS has to perform is to provide problems that are of appropriate complexity for the student's current knowledge. In this paper we looked at an existing system for teaching SQL and proposed an improved method for selecting such problems. We use Bayesian networks to predict student performance. Problem value is dependent on the predicted the number of errors the student is likely to make. Each error results in a feedback message. Novices are unable to deal with many feedback messages, while advanced students can, and therefore an optimal number of feedback messages can be established based on the current student's level. Of all available problems, we select the problem that is most likely to generate the optimal number of feedback messages.

Initial evaluations indicate that the proposed solution is promising. However, we have implemented several heuristics due to the inefficiencies of evaluating large

Bayesian networks on-line. For example, both Table 1 and Figure 3 depict heuristics used by the system. Ideally the system should use theoretically sound rules based on probability theory and/or decision theory. Future work will look at developing this further. Use of new technologies such as qualitative Bayesian networks [1], which are known to be much faster in their evaluation time than traditional Bayesian networks, may also make the development of large-scale Bayesian networks feasible.

Future research will also focus on other decision tasks that an ITS must solve. Problem selection is only one, and other tasks include topic selection, adapting feedback, hint selection, and selective highlighting of text. We are working towards a general framework for solving these type of problems.

Acknowledgments

The work presented here was supported, in part, by the University of Canterbury research grant U6242.

References

1. Chao-Lin Liu & Wellman M. 1998. Incremental Tradeoff Resolution in Qualitative Probability Networks. *Proc UAI-98*, pp. 338-345.
2. Charniak E., 1991. Bayesian networks without tears. *AI Magazine*, Winter 1991, 50-63.
3. Collins J. et al. 1996. Adaptive assessment using granularity hierarchies and Bayesian nets. *Proc. ITS'96*, pp. 569-577.
4. Conati C. et al. 1997. On-Line Student Modeling for Coached Problem Solving Using Bayesian Networks. *Proc. UM97*, pp. 231-242.
5. Corbett A. & Bhatnagar A. 1997. Student Modeling in the ACT Programming Tutor: Adjusting a Procedural Learning Model With Declarative Knowledge. *Proc. UM97*, pp. 243-254.
6. Gertner A. et al. 1998. Procedural help in Andes: Generating hints using a Bayesian network student model. *Proc AAAI-98*, pp. 106-111.
7. Gertner A. 1998. Providing feedback to equation entries in an intelligent tutoring system for Physics. *Proc ITS '98, 254-263.*
8. Mitrovic A. 1998. Experiences in Implementing Constraint-Based Modeling in SQL-Tutor. *Proc. ITS'98, 414-423.*
9. Mitrovic A. & Ohlsson, S., 1999. Evaluation of a constraint-based tutor for a database language, *Int. J. Artificial Intelligence in education*, 10, 3-4, to appear.
10. Ohlsson S. 1994. Constraint-based Student Modeling. In: Greer, J.E., McCalla, G.I. (eds.): *Student Modeling: the Key to Individualized Knowledge-based Instruction.* NATO ASI Series, Vol. 125. Springer-Verlag, Berlin, 167-189.
11. Pearl J. 1988. *Probabilistic reasoning in intelligent systems: networks of plausible inference* (revised 2nd edition). Morgan Kauffman, USA.
12. Reye J. 1998. Two-Phase Updating of Student Models Based on Dynamic Belief Networks. *Proc ITS '98, 274-283.*
13. Schäfer R. & Weyrath T. 1997. Assessing temporally variable user properties with dynamic Bayesian networks. In Jameson A., Paris C. and Tasso C. (Eds.) *Proc. UM'97*, pp. 377-388.
14. Vigotsky L.S. 1978. *The development of higher psychological processes*, Cambridge, MA: Harvard University Press.

Adaptive Bayesian Networks for Multilevel Student Modelling

Eva Millán, José Luis Pérez-de-la-Cruz & Eva Suárez

Departamento de Lenguajes y Ciencias de la Computación
Facultad de Informática, Campus de Teatinos, 29071.
Universidad de Málaga, Spain
eva, perez@lcc.uma.es

Abstract. In this paper we present an integrated theoretical approach for student modelling based on an Adaptive Bayesian Network. A mathematical formalization of the Adaptive Bayesian Network is provided, and new question selection criteria presented. Using this theoretical framework, a tool to assist in the diagnosis process has been implemented. This tool allows the definition of Bayesian Adaptive Tests in an easy way: the only specifications required are a curriculum-based structured domain (together with a set of weights) and a set of questions about the domain (the item pool), which will be internally converted into a Bayesian Network. In this way, we intend to make available this theoretically sound technology to educators, minimizing the knowledge engineering effort required.

1. Introduction

It has been widely recognized that the key component in any tool that intends to help a student in the learning process is the *student model* [1]. Without a student model, a system is not able to adapt to the learner, and therefore its capability to provide guiding and assistance is greatly limited. The adaptive capabilities of tutors (human or not) is what makes them really effective, because, as shown in the study by Bloom [2], the best results are obtained when the learning process is individualized for each particular student. Although a student model can be useful even without being very accurate [3], it is clear that the more accurate it is, the better job it can do. The fundamental task in student modelling is *diagnosis*, which is the process used to infer what the student knows from a set of observable facts, that can be answers to posed problems/questions or records about his/her behavior. Obviously this is a hard task, not only because of the difficulty of explaining student behavior, but also because the uncertainty inherent in it.

The main idea underlying an Adaptive Test is well described by Wainer in [4]: *"The basic notion of an adaptive test is to mimic automatically what a wise examiner would do"*. Adaptation in this context means that questions are selected according to the performance shown by the examinee with the goal to diagnose student's state of knowledge as quickly as possible without loss of accuracy. The psychometric theory underlying most Computer Adaptive Tests (CATs) is Item Response Theory (IRT), where it is assumed that the knowledge level of the student is measured with a single variable θ that is called the *trait*. This unidimensional model is enough for evaluation purposes, but in order to build a student model we need to know which parts of the domain knowledge he/she is having trouble with. To this end, we propose to use Bayesian Networks (BNs) instead of IRT as a theoretical basis for Adaptive Tests.

The main advantage of CATs is a *significant decrease* in test length, with *equal or better estimations* of the student's knowledge level, as reported by Wainer, Dorans, Flaugher and other authors in [4]. Also, the use of computers opened up new possibilities: large databases of questions can be stored and managed, question selection algorithms can be performed efficiently, a great number of students can be evaluated at the same time (even in different geographical locations) and multimedia content can be included in questions/answers (like video, sounds, etc).

The main contributions of the work presented here are: a) the mathematical definition of an integrated model that allows the development and updating of a multilevel student model; b) new question selection criteria for the testing algorithm and c) a tool that allows the development of Adaptive Bayesian Tests with minimum knowledge engineering effort. The paper is structured as follows: in the next section we briefly discuss related work; in Sections 3 and 4 we describe the Adaptive Bayesian Network and Testing Algorithm, and finally some conclusions and future directions are presented.

2. Related Work

BNs have been applied successfully to build student models in several systems. We briefly review some of them. There are a number of other interesting works (like for example [5]) about the use of BNs in student modelling. An excellent discussion can be found in [6].

- HYDRIVE [7] models a student's competence at troubleshooting an aircraft hydraulics system. Student's knowledge is characterized in terms of general constructs (dimensional variables), and a BN is used to update these student model dimensional variables, using as evidence student´s actions.
- ANDES [8] is an Intelligent Tutoring System that teaches Newtonian Physics via coached problem solving. This system evolves from OLAE and POLA, and uses BNs to do long-term knowledge assessment, plan recognition, and prediction of student's action during problem solving.
- The work performed by the ARIES Research Group is the most directly related to the approach presented here. In [9], BNs are applied together with granularity hierarchies. Test items are used as evidence to determine if the student masters the learning objectives defined. Three different structures for the BN are compared in terms of the knowledge engineering effort required, test length and test coverage.

3. The Adaptive Bayesian Network

In this section, we define the BN that will support Adaptive Testing. First, we describe the nodes or variables that will be used in the network, and then we discuss relationships and parameter specifications.

3.1. Nodes

Two types of nodes are considered: nodes to measure student's knowledge, that we will call *knowledge variables*, and nodes to gather evidence, that we call *evidential variables*.

3.1.1. Knowledge Variables

We use different variables that allow to measure student's knowledge at different levels of granularity. These variables will represent knowledge in a wide sense, that is, they can represent from declarative knowledge about certain domain to abilities or skills that the student must acquire during the learning process. To simplify the terminology, we call the different types of variables *concepts*, *topics* and *subjects*.

- *Concepts* are the basic units of knowledge, that is, a concept is a part of knowledge that cannot be decomposed in smaller parts. To represent an elementary concept, we will use a random variable C with a Bernouilli distribution, that is, C takes the value 1 if the student knows the concept and 0 otherwise:

$$P(C = x) = p^x (1-p)^{1-x}, \text{ where } p = P(C=1) \text{ and } x \in \{0,1\}. \tag{1}$$

- A *topic* T_i is a pair (C^i, w), where:
  - C^i is a set of mutually independent elementary concepts $C^i = \{C_{i1}, ..., C_{i n_i}\}$,
  - $w = (w_{i1}, ..., w_{in_i})$ is a normalized weight vector that measures the relative importance of each concept in the topic to which it belongs.

To represent student's knowledge about a topic we use a random variable T_i defined as $T_i = \sum_{j=1}^{n_i} w_{ij} C_{ij}$. The probability law of T_i will then be:

$$P(T_i = \sum_{j \in S_i} w_{ij}) = \prod_{j \in S_i} p_{ij} \prod_{k \notin S_i} (1 - p_{ik}), \text{ for each } S_i \subseteq \{1,2,...,n_i\}, \tag{2}$$

where $p_{ij} = P(C_{ij}=1)$, for $i = 1, ..., n$.

- A *subject* is a pair (T, α), where:
  - T is a set of mutually independent topics $T = \{T_1, ..., T_s\}$.
  - $\alpha = (\alpha_1, ..., \alpha_s)$ is a normalized weight vector that measures the relative importance of each topic in the subject that to which it belongs

To represent knowledge about a subject A, we use the random variable $A = \sum_{i=1}^{s} \alpha_i T_i$.

Then the probability law of A is given by equation 3, where $S_i \subseteq \{1,2,...,n_i\}$.

$$P\left(A = \sum_{i=1}^{s} (\alpha_i \sum_{j \in S_i} w_{ij})\right) = \prod_{i=1}^{s} \left(\prod_{j \in S_i} p_{ij} \prod_{k \notin S_i} (1 - p_{ik})\right). \tag{3}$$

3.1.2. Evidential Variables

These variables will be used to gather information about the student. In Adaptive Testing, the evidential nodes are typically multiple choice questions but, in fact, information could be gathered also by means of problems, questions, or tasks provided that the system has the capability of evaluating the correctness of the responses. To represent a question, we use a random variable Q with a Bernouilli distribution, that is, Q = 1 will mean that the student's answer to question Q is correct and Q = 0 that it is incorrect. The probability law of Q is given in equation 4, where where p = P(Q=1) and x ∈ {0,1}.

$$P (Q = x) = p^x (1-p)^{1-x} . \tag{4}$$

3.2. Links and Parameters

Once the nodes of the network have been described, we have to define the relationships among them: aggregation relationships among knowledge variables, and relationships among knowledge and evidential variables.

3.2.1. Aggregation Relationships

To discuss these relationships, we use the generic expression *knowledge item* to refer either to a subject, a topic, or a concept (or, as described earlier, to a skill, an ability, a subskill, etc.). Let us consider a knowledge item I that can be divided in a finite collection of more specific items I_1, ..., I_n. Aggregation or part-of relationships are the relationships established between them. To model the relationship that exists between mastering item I and items I_1, ..., I_n, we have two alternatives: 1) mastering I_1, ..., I_n has causal influence in mastering I, and 2) mastering I has causal influence in mastering I_1, ..., I_n. These alternatives are depicted in Figure 1:

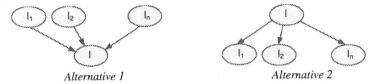

Alternative 1   *Alternative 2*

Fig. 1. Different alternatives to model aggregation relationships

To compare them, we will study the number of parameters needed and the independence relationships implied by each structure. In alternative 1, the parameters are: a priori probabilities {P(I_i), i = 1,...,n} and conditional probabilities P(I/I_1, ..., I_n) ($n+2^n$ values), and the structure means that the I_i (for i = 1,...,n) are mutually independent a priori. In alternative 2, the parameters are: a priori probability P(I) and conditional probabilities P(I_i/I) for i=1,...,n ($1+n^2$ values) and the structure means that the I_i (for i = 1,...,n) are mutually independent given I. It is also interesting to analyze the change in the probabilities as new evidence is gathered. In alternative 1, positive evidence about mastering an item I_j increases the probability of mastering item I, and positive evidence about mastering I increases the probabilities of each of the I_i, i = 1,2,...,n. In alternative 2, positive evidence about mastering an item I_j increases the probability of mastering I, which in turn increases the probabilities of every I_i with i≠j and positive evidence about mastering I increases the probabilities of each of the I_i, for i = 1,2,...,n.

It does not seem clear which of the two alternatives models aggregation relationships better. Perhaps this is the reason that we can find examples of both of them in the literature. Alternative 1 was chosen by VanLehn and his team for ANDES [8] and also by the ARIES Research group in their research about Adaptive Testing [9]. Alternative 2 was chosen by Mislevy and Gitomer in their HYDRIVE system [7], and also by Murray [10]. In our model we have chosen alternative 1. The main reasons for our choice are:

1. Alternative 1 models well the fact that students learn in an incremental way. That is, in order to learn about a topic, students must learn (usually in the order

suggested by the instructor) all the concepts that form part of it. But in alternative 1, the way that evidence is propagated implies that studying a concept increases our knowledge about other independent concepts that belong to the same topic. The underlying assumption in alternative 2 is the same than in IRT theory: there is a single variable (θ = I) that explains student's behavior. Assuming binary nodes, knowing I means to know each and every part of I. However, in our model, knowledge is measured in terms of a discrete variable, meaning that knowledge about I is evaluated considering different degrees of knowledge, that is, the more parts of I we know, the better our knowledge about I is.

2. As for parameter specification, alternative 1 could seem more complex, because it requires an exponential number of parameters instead of the polynomial number required by alternative 2. However, we will show that the definition of the knowledge nodes allows the use of an equivalent network whose parameters can easily be computed using the set of weights defined.

Therefore, the structure of our BN is as depicted in Figure 2.

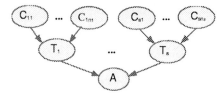

Fig. 2. BN for aggregation relationships

where the concept nodes are binary, and the topic and subject nodes are discrete. The parameters of this network are:

- A priori probabilities $\{p(C_{ij}=1) = p_{ij}, i =1,...,s; j = 1,...,n_i\}$.
- Conditional distributions $P(T_i/\{C_{ij} j =1,2,...,n_i \})$ given by:

$$P(T_i=x/\{C_{ij}=1 \text{ for } j \in S_i, C_{ik} = 0 \text{ for } k \notin S_i\}) = \begin{cases} 1 & \text{if } x = \sum_{j\in S_i} w_j , \\ 0 & \text{otherwise}. \end{cases} \quad (5)$$

- Conditional distribution $P(A/\{T_i i =1,2,...,n \})$ given by:

$$P(A = x/\{T_i = \sum_{j\in S_i} w_j , i =1,...,n\}) = \begin{cases} 1 & \text{if } x = \sum_{i=1}^{s} \alpha_i \sum_{j\in S_i} w_j , \\ 0 & \text{otherwise}. \end{cases} \quad (6)$$

From this set of probabilities, the probability law for A can be computed as:

$$P\left(A = \sum_{i=1}^{s} (\alpha_i \sum_{j\in S_i} w_{ij}) \right) = \prod_{i=1}^{s} \left(\prod_{j\in S_i} p_{ij} \prod_{k\notin S_i} (1-p_{ik}) \right). \quad (7)$$

To reduce the complexity of this network, we are going to show that the behavior of the BN in Figure 2 can be emulated with a much simpler BN. This BN is constructed as follows: new binary nodes $T'_1,...,T'_n$ and A' substitute the corresponding discrete nodes, as shown in Figure 3:

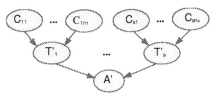

Fig. 3. Equivalent BN for aggregation relationships

The parameters for this BN are:
- A priori probabilities of mastering each concept C_{ij}, $\{p_{ij}, i =1,...,s; j = 1,...,n_i\}$.
- Conditional distributions of T'_i given the corresponding C_{ij}, defined as:

$$P(T'_i | C_{i1},..., C_{in_i}) = \sum_{j \in \{k/C_{ik}=1\}} w_{ij} \, .$$

- Conditional distribution of A' given the corresponding T'_i that we define as

$$P(A'|T'_1,...,T'_s) = \sum_{i \in \{k/T'_k=1\}} \alpha_i \, .$$

Then, the behavior of the two BNs is equivalent in the following sense:

Proposition
For each $i = 1,...,s$ the random variable T_i takes certain value x if and only if the probability that the random variable T'_i takes the value 1 is x. The random variable A takes certain value x if and only if the probability that the random variable A' takes the value 1 is x.
A proof can be found in [11]. The importance of this proposition lies in that it allows us to use a BN with only binary nodes in which the parameters are easily computed from the set of weights.

Example
In order to get a better understanding of aggregation relationships, we present a simple toy example: Let us suppose that a student is learning how to identify vegetable species. Knowledge of the subject domain can be divided in being able to identify vegetables belonging to three different species, that we will call species 1, 2 and 3. The teacher assigns weights $w_1 = 0.2$, $w_2 = 0.5$, and $w_3 = 0.3$ to model the importance of being able to identify each one of the three different species. This can be interpreted in the following way: the teacher thinks that a *balanced* exam about the subject should contain 20%, 50% and 30% of questions relative to the identification of species 1, 2, and 3, respectively. The probabilities that certain student identifies correctly species 1, 2, and 3 are set to 0.8, 0.6 y 0.7. We want to determine which is the knowledge level reached by this student in the subject, that can be measured in terms of the percentage of right answers in a balanced exam. This value can be computed by a simple application of total probability law: let A be the event "the student gives a correct answer to a question about the domain" and let B_i be the event "the question is about the identification of a vegetable of species i", i =1,2,3. Then P(A) can be computed as $\sum P(A/B_i)P(B_i) = 0.8 \ 0.2 + 0.6 \ 0.5 + 0.7 \ 0.3 = 0.73$, meaning that in a balanced exam, the student will answer correctly to a 73% of the questions posed. This kind of behavior can be emulated with an Adaptive Bayesian Network of the type defined: Let I represent knowledge about identification of vegetable species,

and let S_i represent knowledge about identification of vegetables of Species i, i=1,2,3. Then $I = 0.2 S_1 + 0.5 S_2 + 0.3 S_3$, and the equivalent network with binary nodes is shown in Figure 4, together with the conditional distribution $P(I'=1/S_1S_2S_3)$, that is computed as shown in this section. For this particular student, the a priori probabilities for the nodes S_i are $P(S_1 = 1) = 0.8$; $P(S_2 = 1) = 0.6$; $P(S_3 = 1) = 0.7$. Then, if we initialize this network, we have that $P(I'=1) = 0.73$, which means that the knowledge variable I takes value 0.73, or that the percentage of right answers in a balanced exam would be 73%.

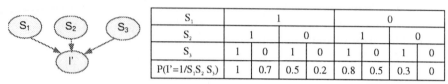

S_1	1				0			
S_2	1		0		1		0	
S_3	1	0	1	0	1	0	1	0
$P(I'=1/S_1 S_2 S_3)$	1	0.7	0.5	0.2	0.8	0.5	0.3	0

Fig. 4. Adaptive BN and conditional probabilities for the example

3.2.2. Evidence-Knowledge Relationships

Let I_1, I_2, ..., I_n be generic knowledge items (typically, concepts) and E_1,...E_s generic evidential nodes. To model the relationship between evidential and knowledge variables we have again two alternatives, that are depicted in Figure 5:

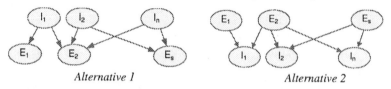

Alternative 1 *Alternative 2*

Fig. 5. Alternatives to model the evidential-knowledge relationship

We have chosen Alternative 1, after an analysis about independence structures, parameters, and knowledge propagation similar to the one presented in Section 3.2.1. This one is also the choice taken by VanLehn in [12].

As for the parameters, we have modified the approach described in [12]. This approach considers that the probability that a situation (evidential node) is solved correctly is 1-s if *all* the knowledge items necessary to solve it are mastered (s is a slip factor) and g/n otherwise (g is a guessing factor, and n is the number of possible answers). We have considered that this probability should depend on the number of items mastered, that is, that it should be greater if the student has only one item missing that if he/she masters only one of the concepts needed. This is specially true when the evidential nodes are multiple choice questions, since the student could choose his/her answer by discarding the incorrect ones. Our proposal consists in using a logistic function to compute the probabilities of giving the correct answer. We have used the IRT 3-parameter logistic function, which "connects" in a smooth way the probability of choosing the correct answer when the student does not know any of the items (1/n, guessing factor) and the probability of giving the correct answer when he/she knows all the items involved (1-s, where s is a small number that represents the possibility of a random slip), as depicted in Figure 6.

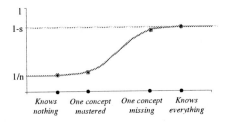

Fig. 6. Logistic function to compute the conditional distribution

So, adding the evidential nodes, the final aspect of our BN is shown in Figure 7, where the nodes A' and T'$_j$ have been renamed A and T$_j$, (j = 1,...,s), respectively, and now the evidential nodes are multiple-choice questions so they have been renamed Q$_i$.

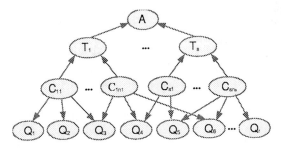

Fig. 7. Adaptive Bayesian Network

Now that the structural model has been defined, we describe the basic elements of our Adaptive Testing algorithm.

4. The Adaptive Bayesian Testing Algorithm

To describe the Adaptive Bayesian Testing algorithm, we will follow the classical description of the basic elements in the development of a CAT, that are: (a) an item response model (b) a scoring method (c) an item pool, (d) an entry level (e) an item selection rule, and (f) a termination criterion. Some of these basic elements are provided by the BN model, others have still to be defined. The *response model* associated to each question is given by the conditional distribution of the question given its parents. Bayesian propagation algorithms constitute a sound *scoring method*. With regard to the *item pool*, the use of the logistic function gives an easy way to specify the parameters (that is, to callibrate questions) that takes into account not only unintentional slips or guessing, but also the fact that the probability of giving the correct answer increases as knowledge is more complete. By the moment, we are using an uniform distribution for the *entry level*, that is, at the beginning of the test and in absence of any other information, we consider that it is equally probable that a student masters or not an elementary concept. If more information about the particular student that is going to take the test is available, this assumption could be changed and the a priori probabilities determined according to this information.

Regarding to the *item selection rule*, we have modified the question selection method reported in [9], that defined an utility measure for each pair (question Q, knowledge item I) as $U^*(Q, I) = |P(I=1/Q=1) - P(I=0/Q=0)|$. In our opinion, this utility measure does not make much sense, since ideally both $(P(I=1/Q=1)$ and $P(I=0/Q=0))$ should be maximized. We have defined the utility in terms of the expected gain of information (i.e. in terms of the expected change in the probability of the knowledge item) $U(Q, I) = (P(I=1/Q=1) - P(I=1)) P(Q=1) + (P(I=0/Q=0) - P(I=0)) P(Q=0)$. This is a weighted combination of the expected information gain for a correct and incorrect answer. The *more informative* question for a given item I is the question Q with maximum utility. Then, to compute the utility measure for every question in the network means to update the network twice for each question in the network, which can be a computationally expensive process. To reduce this complexity, we have defined a simpler utility measure: $U'(Q, I) = P(Q=1/I=1) P(I=1) + P(Q=0/I=0) P(I=0)$, that preserves the ranking when ordering the questions from more informative to less informative (for a detailed proof see [11]). $U'(Q, I)$ can be seen as the probability that Q and I take the same value. Another interpretation for this measure can be given using two concepts inherited from medicine: $P(Q=1/I=1)$ and $P(Q=0/I=0)$ are, respectively, the *sensivity* and *specificity* of the "test" Q for the "illness" I and consequently, both measures should be maximized.

Note that the advantage of using U' instead of U is that the network must be updated twice for each knowledge item instead of twice for each question and the number of knowledge items in the network is much smaller than the number of questions. Moreover, the procedure of computing the utility measures for all questions in the network can be performed when the BN is created, since when new evidence is added to the network we will only need to recompute the utility measures of its sibling nodes (the others are not affected), making the question selection procedure computationally tractable.

As for the *termination criterion*, we have chosen to finish the test when the probabilities of all the concepts are above or below certain instructor-specified level. At this moment, concepts will be considered mastered (non mastered) if their probabilities are above (below) the upper (lower) level fixed. Once the test has finished, the probabilities that A and T_j, $j = 1,...,s$ take the value 1 can be interpreted as a measure of how well a student knows the particular topic or subject. Of course, tests whose purpose is to determine whether the student knows every elementary concept in the network will be very long, but, in return, the information obtained will be very detailed. If the evaluation is performed with less ambitious purposes, for example, if we are only interested in knowing whether the student knows or not a target set of concepts, we use Goal Oriented Algorithms to identify the set of relevant nodes, reducing in this way the complexity of the updating and question selection procedures. With this kind of algorithms, if the evaluation system is integrated within a Tutoring System, we can quickly test if the student knows the particular target concept or set of concepts. Other termination criteria can be defined in terms of the maximum test length or maximum time the test should take.

5. Conclusions

The work presented in this paper provides a mathematical framework to perform Bayesian Adaptive Testing. This framework can be used to develop sound student models that diagnose knowledge at the different levels of granularity required. Also, we have proposed new question selection criteria based on the expected gain of information that are computationally tractable. In order to make this technology available to the educational community, we have implemented a tool (in Java) that supports the development of Bayesian Adaptive Tests with a minimum knowledge engineering effort. Further research is planned in two directions:

1. First, prerequisite relationships should be modeled and included in the BN in a mathematically sound way. Including these relationships will help to get quicker diagnosis (for example, if a prerequisite node is not known, neither will be any of his descendants). Once the whole model has been implemented, we plan to evaluate the testing algorithm using simulated students as described in [9] & [12].

2. Our final goal is to develop a web-based evaluation system similar to our SIETTE system [13], which will have two different uses: (a) with the help of a test editor, teachers will be able to define their tests on line easily. These tests will be stored in a database, where they can be accessed and (b) once the tests have been developed, students will be able to take a predefined test on line. The testing algorithm will compute estimations of student's knowledge and select the next best question to ask in real time as the student answers the questions in the test.

Acknowledgments. We would like to thank the anonymous referees for their valuable comments.

References

1. Shute, V. J. (1995). Intelligent Tutoring Systems: Past, Present and Future. In D. Jonassen (ed), *Handbook of Research on Educational Communications*. Scholastic Publications.
2. Bloom, B. (1984). The 2 sigma problem: The search for methods of group instruction as effective as one-to-one tutoring. *Educational Researcher, 13*, 4-15.
3. Stern, M., Beck, J., & Woolf, B. P. (1996). Adaptation of problem presentation and feedback in an intelligent mathematics tutor. In C. Frasson, G. Gauthier, & A. Lesgold (eds), *Intelligent Tutoring Systems*. New York: Springer Verlag.
4. Wainer, H. (ed.). (1990). *Computerized adaptive testing: a primer*. Hillsdale, NJ: Lawrence Erlbaum Associates.
5. Reye, J. (1998). Two-phase updating of student models based on dynamic belief networks. *Lecture Notes in Computer Science, Vol. 1452*. Springer Verlag.
6. Jameson, A. (1996). Numerical uncertainty management in user and student modeling. *User Modeling and User-Adapted Interaction, 5*, 193-251.
7. Mislevy, R., & Gitomer, D. H. (1996). The Role of Probability-Based Inference in an Intelligent Tutoring System. *User Modeling and User-Adapted Interaction, 5*, 253-282.
8. Conati, C., Gertner, A., VanLehn, K., & Druzdzel, M. (1997). On-line student modelling for coached problem solving using Bayesian Networks. *Proceedings of the 6th International Conference on User Modelling UM'97*. Wien, New York: Springer Verlag.
9. Collins, J. A., Greer, J. E., & Huang, S. H. (1996). Adaptive Assessment Using Granularity Hierarchies and Bayesian Nets. In *Lecture Notes in Computer Science: Vol. 1086*. Berlin Heidelberg: Springer Verlag.
10. Murray, W. (1999). An Easily Implemented, Linear-time Algorithm for Bayesian Student Modeling in Multi-level Trees. In. *Proceedings of the 9th World Conference of Artificial Intelligence and Education AIED'99*. Amsterdam: IOS Press.
11. Millán, E., & Pérez-de-la-Cruz, J. L. (2000). Test adaptativos bayesianos. Technical Report. Dpt. Lenguajes y Ciencias de la Computación, Universidad de Málaga.
12. VanLehn, K., Niu, Z., Siler, S., & Gertner, A. S. (1998). Student modeling from conventional test data: A Bayesian approach without priors. In *Lecture Notes in Computer Science: Vol. 1452*. Berlin Heidelberg: Springer Verlag.
13. Ríos, A., Millán, E., Trella, M., Pérez-de-la-Cruz, J. L., & Conejo, R. (1999). Internet Based Evaluation System. In *Proceedings of the 9th World Conference of Artificial Intelligence and Education AIED'99*. Amsterdam: IOS Press.

Inspecting and Visualizing Distributed Bayesian Student Models

Juan-Diego Zapata-Rivera and Jim E. Greer

ARIES Laboratory, Department of Computer Science,
University of Saskatchewan,
Saskatoon, Canada
Diego.Zapata@usask.ca

Abstract. Bayesian Belief Networks provide a principled, mathematically sound, and logically rational mechanism to represent student models. The belief net backbone structure proposed by Reye [14,15] offers a practical way to represent and update Bayesian student models describing both cognitive and social aspects of the learner. Considering students as active participants in the modelling process, this paper explores visualization and inspectability issues of Bayesian student modelling. This paper also presents ViSMod an integrated tool to visualize and inspect distributed Bayesian student models.

1 Introduction

Ideas such as open student models and the active role of students in the modelling process have led several authors in the student modelling field to consider visualization and inspection of student models as two significant research areas [18]. When student models are presented to students and teachers various questions arise, such as:

- Are students able to understand their student model?
- What kind of representation is more appropriate –textual, graphical, etc. – and in which conditions?
- How does the student model information support students' reflection? Is it possible to use student feedback to build more accurate models?
- What kind of information is it possible to acquire by interacting with the model? Which components of the model should be available to students to visualize and manipulate?
- To what extent can information given by students, teachers and the system be combined to improve the modelling process?

Several authors have been working on some of these questions and interesting results have been found. In a preliminary study, Bull and Pain [2] found that students seem to understand textually presented models. Bull and Shurville [3] show how students and the system can co-operate for the construction of writer models improving the model and accuracy of their predictions. Morales et al. [11] show a graphical representation of the model for a sensori-motor task where modularity and interaction with the model are presented in a complementary way. Dimitrova et al. [6] explore a collaborative construction of student models promoting student's reflection and knowledge awareness. Mühlenbrock et al. [12] propose a teacher assistant which allows teachers to inspect student models in order to assess student's current state of knowledge, arrange students in groups, and suggest appropriate peer helpers. Paiva et al. [13] externalise the student model to the teacher, in order to test the modelling process, support self-assessment, and promote reflection and interactive diagnosis.

Most of the student models in the systems mentioned above are easily inspectable because the modelling approaches are relatively simple to understand. The models are slots and values, feature vectors, simple overlays or rules. More complicated representational formalisms, such as Bayesian belief networks can be effectively used to construct student models, but these representations are harder to inspect.

Several authors in different areas have explored the use of Bayesian belief networks to represent student models [4, 5, 8, 10, 14, 15, and 17]. Martin & VanLehn [10] propose a special interface (assessor's interface) that allows a human (The assessor) to create a Bayesian network of rules and factors. Using this interface the assessor can get an overview of the student's competence and manually increase the probability of a rule when new information is available. Although Bayesian belief networks provide a solid framework for student models in a computationally tractable fashion, understanding the status of a Bayesian network can be difficult. In previous work, we developed VisNet [7, 19] to experiment with how to visualize Bayesian networks.

In this paper, we extend our previous work to permit learners and teachers to inspect student models represented as Bayesian networks. We present a multiple-view application, ViSMod, that has been designed and built to allow students and teachers to experiment with creation of Bayesian what-if scenarios; providing not only a visualization tool, but also an interactive tool for inspection of and reflection on Bayesian student models. In addition, ViSMod has been adapted to visualize and inspect distributed Bayesian student models, allowing the use of student model information from different sources.

2 Visualizing Bayesian Student Models

One of the main advantages of Bayesian belief networks is that they provide an inspectable cause and effect structure among their nodes and direct specification of probabilities in the model [17]. BBNs offer a mathematically sound mechanism to represent uncertainty. Using such a technique (BBNs), assessment of students' knowledge can be carried out effectively. Visualizing and inspecting Bayesian student models becomes an interesting and challenging task that opens not only the internal representation of the student's knowledge, but also the mechanisms to update it to the human interested in knowing more about their representation on the system.

Previous work on how to visualize Bayesian students models showed how a graphical representation of the model in conjunction with different visualization techniques facilitates understanding of cause-effect relationships among nodes, marginal probabilities, changes in probability, and propagation of beliefs throughout the model. Figure 1 shows a screen shot from VisNet, an environment for experimenting with different visualization techniques for Bayes Nets.

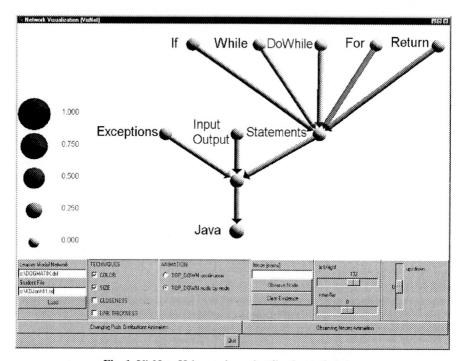

Fig. 1. VisNet– Using various visualization techniques

ViSMod, an extended version of VisNet, provides a flexible architecture where students and teachers can create their own views of a student model by choosing nodes they want to inspect from the Bayesian network representing the student model. Our system assumes the belief net backbone structure for student models proposed by Reye [14, 15], which covers content and social attributes in a three-level structure. The first level covers a prerequisite structure of nodes (e.g. student-knows(topic)), the second level consists of a set of topic clusters directly related to each of the nodes from the first level (e.g. student-claims-to-know(topic)), and the third level holds global nodes that represent general characteristics of the student that affect his/her learning process (e.g. eagerness).

ViSMod offers several widgets to visualize and inspect the model. For example, using the widgets "scrolling up-down", "left-right", and "near-far", it is possible to navigate throughout the model and focus on specific regions. The widgets "observe node" and "clear evidence" allow students to suppose that a specific node has been observed (believed to be true) and visualize how this change on belief is propagated throughout the model. Figures 2, 3, and 4 show a sample of the general three-level backbone structure and two different possible views of the model. A multiple-view platform is particularly useful to determine what components of the model are interesting for students and teachers and which components should be available to students for further visualization or inspection.

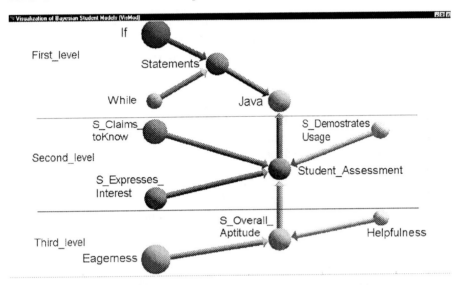

Fig. 2. ViSMod. A sample three-level backbone structure

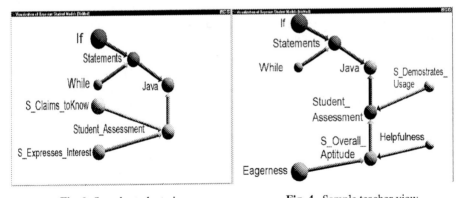

Fig. 3. Sample student view   **Fig. 4.** Sample teacher view

3 Using ViSMod

An initial Bayesian student model organized according to Reye's belief backbone structure [14,15] must be provided to ViSMod. Such a model consists of nodes representing concepts of interest in the domain and directed links indicating influence of one node on another. Probabilities are associated with nodes and strengths of relationships are associated with links. Propagation of probabilities among the nodes, based on observed evidence, is computed according to Bayes rule. For a particular domain, the initial Bayes belief network can be created by the teacher as an overlay on a prerequisite relationship structure or concept map. New nodes and links can be added on any level according to students' or teachers' interests. This model (structure information and evidence) can be derived from the student model of a single ITS or from distributed models of a students from various ITSs.

Students and teachers can visualize the student model using visualization techniques where influence of one node on another or likelihood of a node being known are represented by such things as: colour, size, proximity (closeness), link thickness, and animation. Using ViSMod, it is possible to inspect the model of a single student, compare several students by comparing their models, navigate throughout the model changing focus according to students' and teachers' interests, and use several sources of evidence to animate the evolution of a new model.

Students and teachers can create their own views in order to visualize and inspect the model without changing the internal representation. Using their own views, it is possible to change probability values and add or remove nodes graphically. These views can be used as an important element to promote reflection and engage students and teachers in interesting discussions about their models and to use the results to refine their models.

Besides the obvious goal of continuous student assessment, teachers can also be interested in knowing what kind of evidence is being collected in order to detect possible inconsistencies, misconceptions, or gaps in student knowledge. By using ViSMod, it is possible to visualize and distil distributed student models into a single model, to find causes for inconsistencies and refine the model by changing the structure or adjusting probabilities values of the student model.

In a typical ITS, students are modelled according to their interactions with the system. Using this information, several decisions are taken inside the system in order to adapt the curriculum to the student. Although this approach has been used in many real applications, traditional student models do not differentiate students' and teachers' points of view about the model. Visualization and inspection of student models provide a means of capturing this information and allows for the creation of collaborative student models. By opening the student model, students, teachers, and the system collaborate to improve the accuracy of the model and the quality of help provided by the system.

Some of the benefits that ViSMod provides to students and teachers are:

- A graphical representation of the student model makes it easier for students to understand Bayesian student models.
- A tool that supports multiple views of the student model makes it possible to inspect, modify and create interesting representations of the learning process.
- By allowing inspection of student models and the creation of what-if scenarios, ViSMod supports students' reflection, knowledge awareness, and refining of student models.

- Finally, ViSMod allows visualization of distributed Bayesian student models with different levels of granularity using several sources of evidence.

4 Inspecting Bayesian Student Models

When the model maintained by the system differs in some way to the model that the student or teacher expects, the capabilities of ViSMod to support the creation of what-if scenarios allow students and teachers to interact with the model and refining it.

One of the main problems found when using Bayesian networks is the intense knowledge engineering effort of specifying prior and conditional probabilities [17]. In order to facilitate inspection and understanding of Bayesian belief student models by students and teachers, custom interfaces have been implemented. Using such interfaces, it is possible to avoid direct manipulation of prior, conditional probabilities and integration of new evidence.

Using their own views, students and teachers can create what-if scenarios by choosing nodes, changing probabilities, and adding new evidence without changing the internal state of beliefs. Students and teachers can adjust and experiment with their views in order to create a model that reflects their perception of the learning process with high fidelity. Those scenarios are an important element to find conflicts between what the student and the system may believe about the student's knowledge state.

Working with ViSMod, students and teachers can discuss the student's knowledge state and thus actively engage in knowledge reflection. These discussions can result on changes to the underlying structure of the system's representation of beliefs and a more accurate version of the student model

5 Distributed Bayesian Student Models

Data for student models can be obtained and processed using software tools from widely diverse sources distributed across the Internet. In fact, a student model can itself be distributed. This requires a modelling technique that can store student model data in a distributed fashion and at the same time provide a common inference mechanism. ViSMod provides a flexible architecture for visualizing distributed Bayesian student models. Figure 5 shows how ViSMod is organized to use student's information from three software applications derived from the matchmaker component of I-Help [16], an online testing system named Dogmatix [9], and a web-based discussion forum named CPR [1]. ViSMod allows visualization of student models using different levels of granularity, and integrating several sources of evidence.

A Bayesian student model can integrate information from any telelearning system that has a model of the learner. It is especially useful in systems like I-Help, which integrate student model information form several sources. With ViSMod, students and teachers can visualize and inspect aggregate models maintained by the system.

VisMod can be used to create and maintain different kinds of student model views, to determine the effectiveness of a particular application in maintaining an accurate representation of the student, and to integrate evidence from various sources to be used for various purposes.

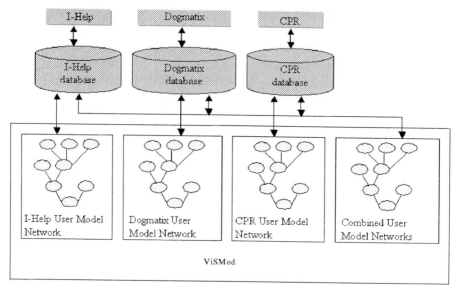

Fig. 5. ViSMod – Visualizing student models from several information sources

Figures 6, 7, and 8 show a fragment of a student model from three different applications –CPR, IHelp, and Dogmatix. Figure 9 shows how ViSMod combines student model information –structure and evidence- from all three applications in a single structure for further visualization and inspection.

Using ViSMod it is possible to integrate evidence from several sources into a single model. The combination of student models relies on the assumption that there is a common ontology among the various student model fragments (segments of a general

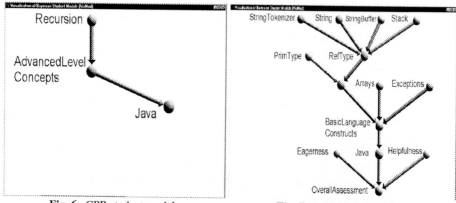

Fig. 6. CPR student model   **Fig. 7.** Ihelp student model

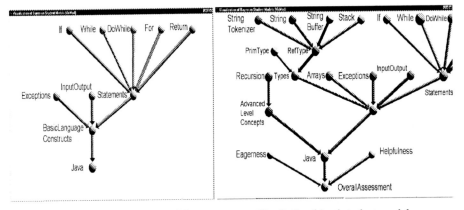

Fig. 8. DogMatix student model   **Fig. 9.** Combined student model

model with some degree of overlapping) and that all of the distributed models were represented as Bayesian belief nets. This process is done by connecting the segments of the network based on the common nodes. That is, per each common node a new link is added and the conditional probabilities of the common node are changed to reflect the new evidence that comes from the new segment.

6 Evaluation

A usability study was conducted with the visualization features of ViSMod. Spatial order, colour, size, proximity (closeness), link thickness, and animation were the visualization techniques evaluated by the participants. After a short explanation about cause-effect relationships and directed acyclic graphs (DAG), ten graduate students were asked to perform a sequence of tasks to determine the efficacy of each of the visualization techniques.

Some of the results found in this study are:

- Spatial order was chosen as an appropriate way to show cause-effect relationships; participants preferred size over colour to represent marginal probability.
- Combinations of techniques appear to be clearer than a single technique; participants chose size and colour as a good combination to represent marginal probability (size) and strength of a relationship (colour).
- For large networks, which are very sensitive to changes in size and position of the nodes, colour is a better alternative.
- Closeness of nodes proved to be an interesting and powerful way to show probability propagation and changes in probability.
- Finally, animation was useful for representing probability propagation; especially node by node animation, which was preferred because it shows both the sequence of Bayesian belief updating and probability propagation.

Future evaluation efforts will be designed to examine scaling up issues, such as:

- expanding and collapsing nodes when using bigger graphs (containing over 50 nodes)
- changing focus to specific regions of the model,
- using different visualization techniques on specific areas of the model, and
- comparing models by showing each model on a transparent layer.

7 Conclusions

ViSMod provides a flexible architecture where students and teachers can create their own views by choosing nodes from a Bayesian student model with a general backbone structure. Using ViSMod, students can understand, explore, inspect, and modify Bayesian student models.

The creation of what-if scenarios in ViSMod promotes students' reflection and knowledge awareness. ViSMod offers a practical tool to determine which components of the model are interesting to students and teachers. Students and teachers create, share and discuss interesting representations of learning process. ViSMod facilitates the evolution of student models by capturing and reflecting the information given by students and teachers during their explorations. Finally, ViSMod allows visualization of distributed Bayesian student models using different levels of granularity, and several sources of evidence.

One future goal will involve refining ViSMod into an authoring tool for creating, tuning and maintaining distributed Bayesian student models. Our aim is to employ this tool to visualize and inspect Bayesian student models in conjunction with different software applications that make use of student model information.

Acknowledgements

We would like to acknowledge the members of the ARIES group for many productive discussions as well as the Government of Columbia and the Canadian TeleLearning NCE for financial support.

References

1. Bishop A. A Case Study of System-Generated Help Responses for the Cooperative Peer Response System [M.Sc. thesis]. University of Saskatchewan, Department of Computer Science. (1998).
2. Bull, S. & Pain, H. 'Did I say what I think I said, and do you agree with me?': Inspecting and questioning the student model, *Proceedings of World Conference on Artificial Intelligence in Education*, Washington DC, (1995) 501-508.
3. Bull, S. & Shurville, S. Cooperative Writer Modelling: Facilitating Reader-Based Writing with Scrawl, in *Proceedings of the workshop 'Open, Interactive, and other Overt Approaches to Learner Modelling' at AIED'99*. Le Mans, France July, (1999).

4. Collins, J. A., Greer, J. E., and Huang, S. X. Adaptive Assessment using Granularity Hierarchies and Bayesian Nets. In Frason, C., C., Gauthier, G. and Lesgold, A., (eds.), *Proceedings of Intelligent Tutoring Systems ITS'96*. Berlin: Springer. (1996) 569-577.

5. Conati, C., Gertner, A.S., VanLehn, K., Druzdzel, M.J. Online student modeling for coached problem solving using Bayesian networks. In Jameson, A, Paris, C., and Tasso, C., (eds), *Proceedings of the sixth International Conference on User Modeling*. New York: Springer-Verlag. (1997) 231-242.

6. Dimitrova, V. et al. STyLE-OLM – an interactive diagnosis tool in a terminology learning environment, in *Proceedings of the workshop 'Open, Interactive, and other Overt Approaches to Learner Modelling' at AIED'99*. Le Mans, France July, (1999).

7. Greer, J., Zapata, J. D., Ong-Scutchings, C., Cooke, J. E. Visualization of Bayesian Learner Models, in *Proceedings of the workshop 'Open, Interactive, and other Overt Approaches to Learner Modelling' at AIED'99*. Le Mans, France July, (1999).

8. Horvitz, E., Breese, J.S., Heckerman, D., Hovel, D., Rommelse, K. The Lumiere Project: Bayesian user modeling for inferring the goals and needs of software users. *Fourteenth Conference on Uncertainty in Artificial Intelligence*. San Francisco: Morgan Kaufmann. (1998) 256-265

9. Kumar V.S., & Yellanki L. Dogmatix: A constraints-based online generative testing system on WWW. Version-1: http://www.cs.usask.ca/grads/vsk719/dogmatix/FinalReport (1997).

10. Martin, J. & VanLehn, K. (1995) Student assessment using Bayesian nets. *Int. J. Human-Computer Studies* 42, (1995) 575-591. Also available on-line: http://www.pitt.edu/~vanlehn/distrib/journal/HCS95.pdf

11. Morales, R. et al. From Behaviour to Understandable Presentation of Learner Models: A Case Study, in *Proceedings of the workshop 'Open, Interactive, and other Overt Approaches to Learner Modelling' at AIED'99*. Le Mans, France July, (1999).

12. Müehlenbrock, M. et al. A framework system for intelligent support in open distributed learning environments. *International Journal of Artificial Intelligence in Education. IJAIED'98*. 9, (1998) 256-274.

13. Paiva, A. et al. Externalising learner models. *Proceedings of World Conference on Artificial Intelligence in Education*, Washington DC, (1995) 509-516.

14. Reye, J. Student Modelling based on Belief Networks. International Journal of Artificial Intelligence in Education. Volume 11 (1999).

15. Reye, J. A Belief Net Backbone for student modelling. In frasson, C., Gauthier, C. and Lesgold, A. (eds.) *Intelligent Tutoring Systems. ITS'96*, Montreal, Canada. Berlin:Sringer-Verlag (1996) 596-604.

16. Vassileva, J., Greer J., McCalla, G., Deters, R., Zapata, D., Mudgal, C., Grant, S. A Multi-Agent Approach to the Design of Peer-Help Environments, in *Proceedings of Artificial Intelligence in Education AIED'99*, Le Mans, France, July, (1999) 38-45.

17. Villano, M. Probabilistic Student Models: Bayesian Belief Networks and Knowledge Space Theory. In Frasson, C., Gauthier, C. and McCalla, G. (eds.) *Intelligent Tutoring systems (Proceedings of the Second International Conference, ITS'92, Montreal, Canada)*. Berlin: Springer-Verlag. (1992) 491-498.

18. Workshop on Open, Interactive, and other Overt Approaches to Learner Modelling. *AIED'99*. Le Mans, France July, 1999. Also available on-line: http://cbl.leeds.ac.uk/ijaied/

19. Zapata-Rivera, J.D., Neufeld, E., Greer, J. Visualization of Bayesian Belief Networks. *IEEE Visualization 1999 Late Breaking Hot Topics Proceedings*. San Francisco, CA. October, (1999) 85-88.

The Explanation Agent

Amal Zouaq, Claude Frasson, Khalid Rouane

Département d'informatique et de recherche opérationnelle
Université de Montréal
C.P.6128, Succ. Centre-ville
Montréal, Québec Canada H3C 3J7
{zouaq,frasson,rouane}@iro.umontreal.ca

Abstract. The problem of judging the effectiveness of a course in general, and of explanations in particular, is certainly one of the most sensible areas in intelligent tutoring systems. In this paper, we present an explanation agent, whose aim is to evaluate the quality of explanations presented to learners. He has two objectives : discovering the source of learner's misunderstandings by taking into account his student model, and helping the course designer to adapt his explanations according to these observations. We use the conceptual graph theory to structure our explanations into a formal representation. This representation is used by the explanation agent to make his deductions about learners misconceptions

1 Introduction

One of the most promising application area for autonomous agents is probably education and training. The term "pedagogical agent" is used to refer to agents created to help the human beings in the process of learning, by the mean of interacting with the learners.

Pedagogical agents exhibit lot of characteristics : They can adapt their interactions to the learner's needs, and to the environment current state, by helping learners to bypass their learning problems. They can collaborate with learners and other agents, and are capable of providing a continuous feedback to the learner. Finally, they can appear as lifelike characters, thus introducing emotions and social aspects in their interaction and relation with learners [6].

In this context, many projects have been developed like the Steve project [11] [12] which consists of a pedagogical agent acting in a virtual environment, who helps the learner to accomplish manual and procedural tasks. This agent can also take the place of a team member, and work with real learners. Adele [7] is another pedagogical agent, designed to help learners in exercise resolution in the medical field. Herman the bug [9], Cosmo [8][1], the Giant [13] and OWL [10] are also pedagogical agents, designed to help the learner in his learning process.

In most of the situations, the assistance is based on explanations given to the learner. Consequently, the quality of this help is related to the quality or usefulness of the explanations. It is for this reason that we have developed an **explanation agent**, whose mission is to present the best explanations to learners, as they encounter problems in the course process or in the exercise resolution. The explanation agent has also to discover learner's misunderstandings related to the explanations presented. Thus, he can identify "good" and "bad" explanations, and inform the course designer of these misunderstandings. The theory of conceptual graphs is used to produce these results.

The understanding process is generally perceived in the resolution of problems. Indeed, in problem solving situations, the learner tries to link various knowledge, normally acquired through a course presentation and structured in his memory. If he fails, we need to know the origin of this misunderstanding, which is related to a lack of knowledge integration. Our ambition is to detect this faulty integration. However, the problem seems to be very complex, especially if we try to deal with the whole course. It appears that the problem is more obvious if we take into consideration a small part of knowledge : explanations. We will focus on this point with the hypotheses that analyzing why an explanation fails can contribute to the comprehension problem in general. Our approach aims to decompose the explanation problem into two steps :

- In order to help the teacher (course designer) to produce and store efficient explanations, we provide him with a set of tools able to structure the explanation into concepts and links between them, resulting in a visual representation based on conceptual graphs.
- In order to detect the problems and misconceptions in the learner understanding, we provide him with the capability to give his own interpretation of the interrelations between concepts, also using conceptual graphs.

Then, an explanation agent is able to use these conceptual graphs structures, and to provide feedback to the designer in order to improve both the quality of explanations and the course content. In this paper, we first present the global learning environment architecture in which the explanation agent and the learner interact, detailing the main components. We then focus on the explanation agent characteristics and architecture, with precision on the quality of explanations. We detail the means to structure the explanation and extract a conceptual graph. Finally, we discuss how this architecture can contribute to learning improvement and we indicate future directions for this research.

2 The Learning Environment Architecture

The global architecture is presented in Fig. 1. It is a client-server architecture, divided in two parts :

- An editor on the server where a course designer can create his courses, exercises and explanations;
- A learning environment where the explanation agent evolves.

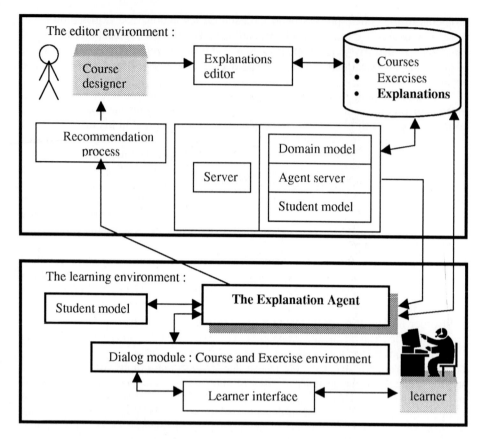

Fig. 1. The learning environment architecture

We briefly detail the main components of this architecture.

2.1 The Editor Environment

It contains the following components :
- **The domain model :** it is composed of all the available courses and exercises. Each course can be represented in the form of a semantic network, with its prerequisites and its constitutive parts. The smallest unit of data in our representation is called a concept. Each exercise is composed of a label, possible answers, and a set of predefined mistakes.
- **The agent server :** the explanation agent is stored on the server. On each learning session, he is sent on the learner's machine.
- **The student model :** The student model is a perturbation model and more precisely, a bug model. A perturbation model combines the standard overlay mode with a representation of faulty knowledge. The common technique for implementing a perturbation model is to represent the expert knowledge and then augment this representation with explicit knowledge of likely misconceptions [5].

In our system, the designer has to elaborate a bug library for each exercise, by enumerating a set of bugs that he has noticed through his courses (experience). The student model is composed of all the statistics related to the learner : his performances, the explanations presented, the non predefined errors, his own conceptual graphs for misunderstood explanations (this point will be detailed later) and the learner score

- **The knowledge base :** it is used to store courses, exercises and explanations.
- **The explanations editor :** It is used to produce explanations in the form of texts or web pages. These pages can contain images, videos, and virtual simulations. This last point makes the explanation more concrete, more understandable. After designing an explanation in the form of texts or web pages, the course designer has to decompose it into key concepts and semantic links between these concepts, resulting into a conceptual graph.

2.2 The Learning Environment

Courses, exercises, and explanations are presented in the learning environment. It is composed of :

- **The dialog module :** this module interacts with the learner through a learning session : initializing the dialog, creating or updating the student model and handling the communication process. In fact, our ITS takes the approach of asking the learner about his level in the different topics that will be treated in the course. In this way, the agent has initial beliefs, that evolve according to the learner's performance. It is a sort of a cooperative student model in the initialization phase. The dialog module is composed of the course and the exercises environment. The explanation agent is loaded on the learner machine at the beginning of a session .
- **The explanation agent :** in a learning session, the explanation agent presents explanations adapted to the learner's model. He sends to the server information related to the learner performances, and all information necessary to detect learner's incomprehension. The explanation agent can present explanations in the course presentation process as well as in the exercises resolution. He has a reactive behavior in the course presentation as he appears when a request for explanation is clearly formulated by the learner, while he has an autonomous behavior in problem solving situations, appearing to provide an explanation when an expected error occurs, to apologize if the error has no explanation, and to express his sadness or happiness, according to learner's actions.

The next section presents the explanation agent in detail.

3 The Explanation Agent Architecture

The explanation agent is a an intelligent agent who has the characteristics of reactivity, mobility, autonomy, learning , deduction and believability.

Reactivity: The explanation agent reacts to user's actions via the learning environment interface. The perception layer clearly shows how this characteristic is implemented.

Mobility : At the beginning of a learning session ,the explanation agent moves from the course server to the student machine. Thus the learner has the last version of the explanation agent code, and consequently the agent's updated behavior.

Autonomy : The explanation agent is completely autonomous in the explanation process.

Learning and deduction : The explanation agent possesses a learning layer.

Believability : The explanation agent is presented as a lifelike and talkative character. He adapts his expressions and actions according to the learner's actions, thus achieving believability.

The explanation agent architecture is based on cognitive agents [2] [3] [4] . They have been defined as reactive, instructable, adaptive and cognitive agents : they react to the activity of others and are able to learn.

Fig.2 presents our explanation agent architecture.

C: The cognition layer

B : The explanation layer

A : The perception layer

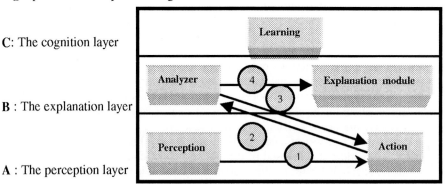

Fig. 2. The explanation agent architecture

- The perception layer

The perception layer is related to reactivity and is used to detect learner's actions : request for explanation, submission of an answer, end of reading, etc. It is composed of two components :
- The perception component : it indicates that the system has an entry, which means that the learner has performed an action, and fires the action component (1);
- The action component : it determines the type of action which has been performed, depending on the learner's context (course or exercise). It then calls the analyzer (2).

- The explanation layer

It is composed of two components :
- The analyzer : When an action is detected, the analyzer is fired to search an explanation if the learner is in a course context, or to compare the submitted solution to the exercise solution if the learner is in the context of resolving an exercise. If the action is correct, the agent congratulates the learner (3). Otherwise, if the solution is incorrect but no explanation is available, the agent informs the

learner of his incapacity to help him (3). If the solution is incorrect, and one or more explanations are existing, the explanation module is fired (4).

- The explanation module : it manages all the process of explanations, and the way they are presented to the learner. Explanations must be situated to create a believable agent. For this reason, when an error occurs, the agent doesn't try to discover implicitly the cause of the error. He rather proposes to the learner a list of possible causes of the error , ordered according to the observed errors frequency for his learner profile. Without this additional information and because sources of error can be numerous, the explanation can be totally inaccurate. The related explanation is presented after the learner choice. If he has no opinion, the most probable cause of error is chosen and the corresponding explanation presented.

• The learning layer

In the learning layer, two main characteristics of the agent are implemented : observation and deduction. The agent observes the most frequent causes of errors made by learners with a certain profile, and creates beliefs based on his observations. He is then able to present the most probable causes of the error, ordered by their frequency. Moreover, the explanation agent has to find, when he is told to do so, the matching between the designer's conceptual graph and the learners conceptual graphs, thus identifying the learner's misconceptions (see section 4 : explanations structure). He is then able to detect their differences and identify the precise sources of misunderstanding. Finally, he can detect new patterns of behaviors for a student profile, regarding to the types of errors, which makes the explanation system more powerful.

The learning layer takes also care of evaluating the quality of explanations. The explanation agent can deduct what explanations are good or bad for a learner profile, by using the Explanation Quality Index. Bad explanations must then be removed by the designer from the knowledge base, and new ones created.

Explanations Quality : Based on the principle that more an explanation is presented to the same learner, more the explanation appears useless, the quality of an explanation is judged according to the number of times it has been presented. This leads to the following rule :

$$EQI = Le / E .$$ (1)

Where :
EQI : Explanation Quality index   **EQI $\in$ [0,1]**
Le : Number of learners who have read the explanation e
E : Number of presentations of the explanation e

the lower the ratio is, the more the explanation is judged of bad quality .
By this rule, we want to show that an explanation cannot be considered as a good explanation if it doesn't solve learners problem, despite the fact that learners read it several times.
The next section presents our way of structuring explanations.

4 Explanations Structure

To structure an explanation, we have looked at a way to extract the main concepts of the explanation and then represent the interrelations between these concepts. The idea was to represent the general meaning of the explanation, focusing on its main components and leaving aside details. We then thought that a visual representation was necessary for the course designer to have an overview of the concepts network. This idea led us to the conceptual graph theory, because of its expressiveness, its representation efficacy and its notational efficacy. Moreover, we needed a formal representation schema, based on a solid formal foundation.

Conceptual graph theory has been described, by Sowa [14] as a universal formalism of knowledge representation : Conceptual graphs are known to be relevant to a broad spectrum of problems in knowledge representation, including modeling of knowledge in intelligent tutoring systems.

The advantages of this approach are :

- To provide the designer with a complete view about what he wants to explain;
- To make the learner capable of expressing its own interpretation of the explanation, and by this way, to give him the possibility of thinking of its main meaning. Moreover, and this is the most important, conceptual graphs make the agent capable of discovering learner's misunderstandings.

So, for the same explanation, the explanation agent has to possess two conceptual graphs : the designer's conceptual graph, and the learners conceptual graphs.

We will now detail how conceptual graphs are created for both sides : from the designer side and from the learner side.

4.1 Explanations Conceptual Graphs : Designer Side

The designer can extract the main concepts of the explanation. So we provide him with a tool for automatically extracting concepts, according to a database of concepts. The steps to construct an explanation conceptual graph are the following :

1. The designer selects the explanation that he wants to structure into a conceptual graph;
2. He then asks the system to analyze the explanation and extract concepts automatically, thus obtaining a list of extracted concepts;
3. If he isn't completely satisfied by the system results, he can add concepts, delete concepts, or modify their rank in the list according to his own perception;
4. After that, the designer has to determine the links between concepts. So a link editor has been implemented. The designer has to match the concepts that he has previously defined, but he can also create a link between a concept already in the database and a concept that he has just defined. We want to underline that there is a classification of some main links, which means links frequently used by course designers. We can quote the link "syn" which designate a synonym, or the link "has-a" which indicates a composition. However, the designer is also free to create new types of links, if he considers that they are necessary to the explanation meaning.

5. Finally, the designer can ask the system to generate a conceptual graph with all the concepts and links that he has previously defined. He then obtains a conceptual graph.

Until now, we have described the different steps the designer must follow to structure his explanations. Let's look at the learner side.

4.2 Explanations Conceptual Graphs : Learner Side

As we have said, the learner can help the agent by drawing graphs for the misunderstood explanations at the end of a learning session. An explanation is misunderstood if it was presented in an exercise where the final learner's score is very low. To determine if the learner's score is low, we compare it with a fail threshold defined by the designer for each exercise. So, for each misunderstood explanation, the learner has to draw a conceptual graph to present his own understanding of the explanation. This will make the agent capable of determining where the chunking of information has been defective if there are wrong or missing links between concepts, or missing concepts. We have implemented a graphical tool, where the learner can easily build his conceptual graphs, by simple drag and drops, and by using lists of concepts and links proposed by the designer. These lists are provided in order to give the learner a starting point, and an idea about what he has to do. Moreover, if learners could use their own concepts and links, it would be very difficult to analyze knowledge not already stored in the system.

Finally, some learners can be discouraged and bored by the necessity of building conceptual graphs. So they can be encouraged by lot of messages of sympathy emanating from the agent, and by receiving rewarding points for their collaborative behavior.

5 Interpretation

We have built a tool that can launch the different processes of the learning layer. This tool is still under development.

The processes of the learning layer are activated when sufficient amounts of data are collected. The explanation agent can then calculate explanations quality index and search typical errors in learners conceptual graphs. We have developed a machine learning algorithm to compare learners conceptual graphs and the designer conceptual graph.

The following results can be presented :
- Concerning the quality of explanations, we can present the "good" and "bad" explanations to the designer;
- Explanations are "bad" if they are not understandable. The agent can determine the causes of misunderstanding of an explanation by comparing the designer's conceptual graph and all the conceptual graphs drawn by learners. Thus, some conclusions can be made by the agent according to a general observation:
  - Some concepts can be missing

- Some links can be missing
- Some links can be wrong

In the three cases, the explanation agent has to determine the frequency of the errors. The results of the analysis are presented in the form of conceptual graphs, with different colors to indicate missing concepts and links, or erroneous links. Some options exist to display only erroneous links, or only non existent links.

The explanation agent can then present his conclusions :

In the first case, the agent can search if the explanation concepts figure in the course followed by learners, by taking into account their profile. If it isn't the case, the agent can advise the designer to build his explanation by using concepts known by learners, to bind these concepts to others already known by learners, or to define the explanation concepts in the course.

If all the explanation concepts are known by learners, the problem is normally in the links between concepts. So, the designer has to elaborate his explanations by emphasizing on the problematic links, and by demonstrating the reasons of the existence or non existence of these links.

- The agent can also present the most frequent errors that weren't initially foreseen by the designer, thus discovering new patterns of behavior. The designer can then elaborate explanations on these problematic areas.
- Finally, the good explanations can also be displayed to the designer, to let him think about the difference between them and "bad" explanations.

6 Conclusion

We have built an agent whose functions are multiple :
- He presents explanations according to learners profile
- He discovers new types of errors, so the bugs library can be extended, and the knowledge base enriched, as new explanations are created to deal with these new errors
- He evaluates explanations quality
- He detects learners misunderstandings by using the theory of conceptual graphs
- He advises the designer to deal with these problems

In general, the knowledge used in the system is constantly re-evaluated according to learners, which insures its quality.

The theory of conceptual graphs is used to obtain the source of misunderstanding from the learner, by comparing his conceptual graph with the designer's conceptual graph.

The agent is presented as a lifelike and talkative character. We think that his expressiveness will have a positive impact on learners motivation.

This work will make us discover the weaknesses in the learner understanding, and thus will facilitate the discovery of the reasons of this misunderstanding.

Finally, it is important to underline that empirical data are necessary to test the effectiveness of the agent's intervention. Our next goal in this research is to observe the student-agent interaction to have a deeper knowledge about what actions, expressions and explanations strategies are effective and which ones are not.

References

[1] Elliot J. L. Coordinating speech and actions for animated pedagogical agents. Internet URL : http://www.csc.ncsu.edu/degrees/undergrad/Reports/jlelliot/thesis97.html

[2] Frasson C., Martin L., Gouardères G. and Aimeur E.(1998). LANCA : a distance learning architecture based on networked cognitive agents. In ITS-98 Conference, Fourth International Conference on Intelligent Tutoring Systems, San Antonio, Texas, August.

[3] Frasson C., Mengelle T. and Aimeur E.(1997). Using pedagogical agents in a multi-strategic intelligent tutoring system. In the Proceedings of Workshop V, AI-ED(97), Pedagogical agents, Kobe, Japan, August 19.

[4] Frasson C., Mengelle T., Aimeur E., and Gouardères G. (1996). An actor-based architecture for intelligent tutoring systems. In ITS'96 Conference, lecture notes in computer science, N1086, Springer-Verlag, pp 57-65, Montreal, June 1996.

[5] Holt P., Dubs S., Jones M., Greer J. (1991) The state of student modeling. In J. E. Greer and G. I. McCalla (eds). Student modeling : the key to individualized knowledge-based instruction, pp 3-35, Vol. 125, NATO ASI series.

[6] Johnson W. L. (1998) Pedagogical agents. Invited paper at the international conference on computers in education, China, October 1998. Internet URL : http://www.isi.edu/isd/VET/vet.html

[7] Johnson L. W., Shaw E. and Ganeshan R. (1998). Pedagogical agents on the web. In ITS'98 Workshop on pedagogical agents, San Antonio, Texas, August 16, Internet URL http://www.isi.edu/isd/ADE/papers/its98/ITS98-WW.htm

[8] Lester J. C., Callaway C. B. and Towns S. G. (1998). Creating lifelike behaviors in animated pedagogical agents. In ITS'98 Workshop on pedagogical agents, San Antonio, Texas, August 16.

[9] Lester J. C., Callaway C. B., Stone B. A. and Towns S. G. (1997). Mixed initiative problem solving with animated pedagogical agents. In the Proceeding of Workshop V, AI-ED 97 Pedagogical agents Kobe, Japan, August 19.

[10] Linton F., Charron A. and Joy D. (1998) The OWL pedagogical agent In ITS'98 Workshop on pedagogical agents, San Antonio, Texas, August 16.

[11] Rickel J. and Johnson L.W. (1998). Animated pedagogical agents for team training. In ITS'98 Workshop on pedagogical agents, San Antonio, Texas, August 16.

[12] Rickel J. and Johnson L.W. (1997). Intelligent tutoring in virtual reality : a preliminary report. In the Proceeding of Workshop V, AI-ED 97 Pedagogical agents, Kobe, Japan, August 19.

[13] Reichherzer T. R., Cañas A. J., Ford K. M., Hayes P. J. (1998). The Giant : a classroom collaborator. In ITS'98 Workshop on pedagogical agents, San Antonio, Texas, August 16.

[14] Sowa, J. F., ed. (1992) Knowledge-Based Systems, Special Issue on Conceptual Graphs, vol. 5, no. 3, September 1992.

The Conceptual Helper: An Intelligent Tutoring System for Teaching Fundamental Physics Concepts

Patricia L. Albacete[1] and Kurt VanLehn[2]

[1] Intelligent Systems Program, University of Pittsburgh, Albacete@isp.pitt.edu
[2] LRDC, University of Pittsburgh, VanLehn@cs.pitt.edu

Abstract. This paper describes an intelligent tutoring system designed to help students solve physics problems of a qualitative nature. The tutor uses a unique cognitive based approach to teaching physics, which presents innovations in three areas. 1) The teaching strategy, which focuses on teaching links among the concepts of the domain that are essential for conceptual understanding yet are seldom learned by the students. 2) The manner in which the knowledge is taught, which is based on a combination of effective human tutoring techniques, successful pedagogical methods, and less cognitively demanding approaches. 3) The way in which misconceptions are handled. The tutor was implemented using the model-tracing paradigm and uses probabilistic assessment to guide the remediation. Some preliminary results of the evaluation of the system are also presented.

1 Introduction

Several studies conducted during the past fifteen years revealed that students in traditional elementary mechanics classes can master problem solving of a quantitative nature, but perform poorly in solving qualitative problems [Halloun & Hestenes, 1985; Hake, 1998]. (An example of a quantitative problem is "A 2kg create slides down a frictionless inclined plane. Determine the acceleration of the crate given that the angle of the plane is 30 degrees." An example of a qualitative problem can be seen in Figure 1.) Moreover, students' naïve conceptions of physics remain intact after finishing their classes, having not been modified or replaced by the newly acquired scientific knowledge.

A few approaches have been proposed to improve this situation, though none has met with great success [Hake, 1998]. Considering that elementary mechanics is a required course for almost all science majors, the above results make it clear that there is a need to improve the instruction of the subject. Toward this end, we developed an intelligent tutoring system, called the Conceptual Helper, which presents a novel cognitive-based approach to teaching conceptual physics. The Conceptual Helper coaches students through homework problems in the area of Newtonian mechanics that deals with linear motion and projectile motion in kinematics and dynamics.

The Conceptual Helper is part of a larger enterprise called Andes [VanLehn, 1996; Gertner et al., 1998]. Andes is basically an immediate feedback model-tracing tutor designed to coach first year physics students through problem solving. It has three help systems. A Procedural Helper that provides procedural help during quantitative problem solving. A Conceptual Helper [Albacete, 1999] that teaches conceptual knowledge of the subject matter to students and tries to get them to abandon misconceptions (this system is described herein). And a Self-Explanation coach that guides students through example studying. At present, each help system works in isolation; however in the future the Conceptual Helper and the Procedural Helper will work cooperatively in an attempt to integrate conceptual and quantitative problem solving.

Two steel balls, one of which weights twice as much as the other, roll off of a horizontal table with the same speeds. In this situation:
a) both balls impact the floor at approximately the same horizontal distance from the base of the table.
b) the heavier ball impacts the floor closer to the base of the table than does the lighter.
c) the lighter ball impacts the floor closer to the base of the table than does the heavier.

Fig. 1. Example of a qualitative problem.

2 The Conceptual Helper from a Technical Point of View

The Conceptual Helper follows the model-tracing paradigm. In its simplest form a model-tracing tutor contains a cognitive model that is capable of correctly solving any problem assigned to the student. Then the technique basically consists of matching every problem-solving action taken by the student with the steps of the expert's solution model of the problem being solved. This matching is used as the basis for providing ongoing feedback to students while they progress through a problem. In the Conceptual Helper when the students make a correct action, the input is turned green to emulate the typical confirmation given by human tutors. On the other hand, when the action is incorrect the input is turned red and some specific feedback is provided.

One tool that the tutor uses to decide what knowledge to teach the student when he makes a mistake is the student model. The student model is represented by a Bayesian network. Each node in the network represents a piece of conceptual knowledge that the student is expected to learn or a misconception that the tutor can help remedy. For example, a node in the network is "if the velocity of an object is constant, then its acceleration is zero." Each node in the network has a number attached to it which indicates the probability that the student has mastered it. In the case of misconceptions the probabilities represent the likelihood that the student holds such a misconception. As the student solves a problem, the probabilities are updated according to the actions taken by the student and the feedback provided by the tutor.

The Conceptual Helper makes use of the student model in deciding which pieces of knowledge it should try to teach to the students and when it should do so. When the student makes a mistake while solving a problem, and the probability of his knowing the corresponding piece of correct knowledge is higher than 0.8, then the tutor will not try to teach it. It will just turn the entry red and then store a short explanation as to what was incorrect. This explanation could be accessed by the student by selecting, "what is wrong with that?" from a help menu. However, if the probability of the student's knowing the corresponding piece of knowledge is lower than 0.8, then the Tutor will try to convey the corresponding knowledge to the student. In the case when the mistake is most likely attributed to a known misconception, the helper just tutors the student on it. The logic behind this decision is that misconceptions are rarely encountered more than once; hence regardless of the probability of the student harboring such a misconception, it is safer to clarify it.

3 The Teaching Strategy Followed by the Conceptual Helper

The Conceptual Helper has two main goals: to teach qualitative physics, and to try to get the students to abandon common misconceptions.

To accomplish its first goal, the Conceptual Helper follows a novel teaching strategy that concentrates on teaching students the *links* that connect the domain's concepts of interest rather than the concepts in themselves. This strategy is based on the cognitive science theory which describes the knowledge base of experts as well structured and *highly connected* (e.g., Chi & Koeske 1983). Several studies (e.g. Van Heuvelen, 1991) suggest that the knowledge of students when they begin an introductory physics course typically consists of a small number of unstructured, disconnected facts and concepts, and they leave the courses with more facts and concepts but their knowledge is equally disconnected and unstructured. Hence the teaching strategy tries to build the students' knowledge bases akin to that of experts.

The links between the concepts of any domain can be of various different types. The word "links" has been traditionally used in Semantic Networks to describe two-place predicates such as "is-a" or "part-of". However, we use the word "links" to describe rich qualitative rules that integrate pieces of knowledge. The kinds of links that the Conceptual Helper focuses on are those which can be inferred from the principles or from the definitions of the concepts of the domain. For example, one of the target links is "the direction of the net force applied to an object is the same as the direction of the object's acceleration." This connection between the concept of acceleration and the concept of net force can be inferred from Newton's second law. Likewise, the link "if the acceleration of an object is zero, then the object's velocity is constant" can be inferred from the definition of the concept of acceleration. These types of links are not evident to the students, in the sense that, even if students can repeat without hesitation the definition of acceleration and Newton's second law, by and large, they are generally not able to assert the links between concepts that follow from those definitions [Reif, 1995]. However, these types of links are essential for reasoning qualitatively about the motion of objects and for solving the qualitative problems. Additionally, the tutor helps students understand some concepts in themselves, such as the concepts of normal force and friction force.

The second goal of the Conceptual Helper is to help students replace their misconceptions with scientifically correct knowledge. The word "misconception" is taken to mean the knowledge that the students bring to the class, having acquired it through interaction with the world's physical phenomena, but that does not agree with scientific knowledge. For example, in Figure 1 the problem is designed to uncover the misconception that weight influences the horizontal motion of an object. The Conceptual Helper handles misconceptions by presenting students with the basic line of reasoning underlying the correct interpretation of the phenomena that are the base of the misconception. This is as opposed to using discovery environments or computer-simulated experiments, which are the two common ways in which teachers have tried to correct misconceptions. We believe that it is not setting up the (simulated) equipment, making the runs, recording the data, and inducing a pattern that convinces a student of a certain piece of knowledge, but rather the line of argument itself. Knowing the correct line of reasoning enables the student to self-explain the phenomenon. An example can be seen in Figure 6.

4 The Libraries of Lessons and Dialogues to Convey Knowledge to the Student

According to the teaching strategy that the Conceptual Helper follows, its main goal is to make sure the student both learn the links that connect the concepts of interest of the domain and abandon common misconceptions. To accomplish this task, it uses two different kinds of interactions with the student, namely dialogues and mini-lessons. Both of these were intended to emulate human tutors as closely as possible, to incorporate some pedagogical techniques that have proven to be effective and to present the knowledge in a way that is less cognitive demanding. To clarify their use the examples given will refer to the problem shown in Figure 2.

Mini-lessons and dialogues were automatically generated from templates where objects, motion directions and graphics were instantiated as needed.

A coin is tossed upward. Considering that there is no effect of air resistance, draw a motion diagram[1] for the coin from the time it is released until it reaches its apex.

Fig. 2. Example of a qualitative problem requiring an explicit solution.

4.1 The Dialogues

When the student makes a mistake while solving a problem, which is judged as not coming from applying a misconception (see definition of misconception in section 3), the tutor will try to correct this mistake by helping the student build the *link* between a known concept and the concept corresponding to the correct action. One of the ways in which the tutor does this is by engaging the student in a short dialogue, emulating the behavior of human tutors when they use hints and leading questions [Fox, 1993].

The dialogue consists of two statements. Each statement is incomplete, but has a menu from which the student can select a completion. The first statement in the dialogue is aimed at eliciting from the student the value of the antecedent of the target link. Conversely, the second statement is aimed at getting the student to provide the consequent of the link. An example of a dialogue can be seen in Figure 3. In the example, the link of interest is: "if (in a linear motion) the velocity of an object is decreasing then the object's velocity and its acceleration have opposite directions."

This is how the dialogues are used. Suppose that a student is solving the problem shown in Figure 2 and that he draws the velocities correctly as pointing up and decreasing, but then he draws the acceleration with an upward direction. Then the tutor turns the input red and verifies that it does not correspond to a misconception. If it does not, the Conceptual Helper finds in the solution graph of the current problem the rule that the student should apply to correct its error and which is on the most likely solution path[2] that the student is following. If the probability of the student

---

[1] A motion diagram consists of describing the position, velocity and acceleration of the system of interest at regular time intervals. The description is achieved through drawing the corresponding vectors.

[2] The system has a program capable of estimating the most likely solution path that the student is following.

knowing the piece of knowledge is lower than 0.8, as revealed by the student model, the tutor presents to the student the first statement of the dialogue.

The velocity of the coin is: *menu choice*:	increasing decreasing constant I don't know
Therefore, the coin's acceleration and its velocity have:	opposite directions equal directions none of the above

Fig. 3. Example of a dialogue used by the Conceptual Helper.

If the student completes the first statement incorrectly the Tutor will try to teach an alternative rule, if such a rule exists. To this end it will present a dialogue corresponding to this second rule. On the other hand, if the student completes the first statement correctly, the second statement comes up. If the student gives the correct completion, he is informed of it and nothing else happens. On the other hand, if the student answers it incorrectly the Conceptual Helper evaluates what further intervention it will pursue as it is explained in the next section.

4.2 The Mini-Lessons

The main way in which the tutor explains knowledge to the student is through the use of short lessons, which are called mini-lessons. There are four kinds of mini-lessons.

Mini-lessons that explain a particular link or a concept. Suppose that a student solving the problem of Figure 2 draws the velocity correctly at two time points but then he draws the acceleration incorrectly pointing upward. Moreover, suppose the Conceptual Helper has already tried to help the student by hinting with the dialogue shown in Figure 3 but that the student has completed the second statement incorrectly. At this point, the tutor will try a more directive intervention, like a human tutor would do [McArthur et al., 1990] by presenting the student with an explanation of the knowledge of interest through the mini-lesson shown in Figure 4.

Most mini-lessons consist of a short piece of text and a graphic or animation, which illustrates what the text describes. The textual part of the mini-lesson begins with a general definition of the concept or principle that constitutes the theoretical basis for the existence of the link of interest. For example, in Figure 4, the definition of acceleration is given as the theoretical basis for explaining the relationship between acceleration and velocity. When appropriate, this abstract definition is followed by an anthropomorphic interpretation. In this example, for instance, the definition of acceleration is brought to life by making the acceleration an agent in changing the velocity. Next, a general definition of the link of interest is presented as well as its application to the particulars of the problem. In the example, this comprises the second paragraph. Additionally, when there is an animation or graphic, a brief explanation is included to highlight the knowledge of interest. Furthermore, the text has some words or phrases, such as the question at the bottom of Figure 4, that are hyperlinks. By clicking on them, the student can find information or pursue a further dialogue with the tutor regarding the underlined topic.

The graphics and animations of the mini-lessons were designed with two main ideas in mind: a) people tend to reason with objects belonging to the material ontology [Chi, 1992], and b) people tend to provide anthropomorphic explanations of how the physical world works [diSessa, 1993; Rochelle, 1992]. Additionally, a microscopic view of matter was used when appropriate [Murray et al., 1990].

Acceleration is a vector defined as the rate of change in velocity with time. You can think of the acceleration vector as what changes the velocity vector. Acceleration can change the velocity's magnitude, its direction, or both.

In this case, the magnitude of the velocity of the coin, i.e., its speed, is decreasing. The acceleration is making it shorter. For that to happen in a linear motion, the velocity vector and the acceleration, have to have opposite directions.

In the animation below, you can see the acceleration vector, with an imaginary arm, making the velocity vector shorter. Notice that the velocity and the acceleration have opposite directions.

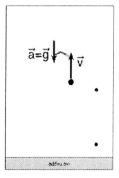

Why is the speed of the coin decreasing?

Fig. 4. Example of a mini-lesson explaining one relationship between the concepts of velocity and acceleration for the problem shown in Fig. 2.

To implement the first of these ideas, it was decided that the tutor would use vectors as much as possible when presenting graphical explanations of the abstract concepts whose connecting links it is trying to teach. Vectors are the correct scientific representation of the concepts and their representation as arrows is concrete, amenable to direct manipulation and has all of the characteristics of material objects. Hence this may facilitate the understanding of the knowledge.

In addition, since people spontaneously use anthropomorphism to explain how objects behave we believe that incorporating this technique into the explanations that the Conceptual Helper gives would make learning the target knowledge less cognitive demanding. Furthermore it may facilitate the production of explanations that the students generate to themselves, which has been argued [Chi, 1996] to be an effective means for learning.

Reminder lessons. The reminder lessons are aimed at refreshing the student's memory of a piece of knowledge. They consist of a textual explanation of the target knowledge which is presented at a more general level. Also, there is no detailed tailoring to the particulars of the problem as there is with explanatory mini-lessons. An example of this kind of lesson can be found in Figure 5 (this is the reminder mini-lesson corresponding to that presented in Figure 4).

> Acceleration is a vector defined as the rate of change in velocity with time. You can think of the acceleration vector as what changes the velocity vector. Acceleration can change the velocity's magnitude, its direction, or both.
>
> In this case, the magnitude of the velocity is decreasing. For that to happen in a linear motion, the velocity vector and the acceleration, have to have opposite directions.

Fig. 5. Example of a reminder mini-lesson.

Reminder lessons are used by the tutor when it has already presented the corresponding detailed mini-lesson, but the student has made a mistake which involves applying the same piece of knowledge. The belief is that, if the student has already received a detailed explanation of the knowledge of interest while solving a problem, but he fails to use it properly in a further step, then a reminder of the knowledge should suffice to get the student to correct his mistakes. This models human tutors as they progressively fade away the support they give to students [Collins et al., 1989].

Mini-lessons that summarize knowledge. When students finish solving a problem, they click on a *done* button. When this happens, the Conceptual Helper presents to the student a mini-lesson that summarizes the most important pieces of knowledge that were used to solve the current problem. The summary mini-lessons were designed to include only a few main ideas based on studies which suggest that very detailed explanations after completion of problem solving can be confusing for the students [Katz & Lesgold, 1994].

There are three main reasons why the tutor uses summary mini-lessons. The first is that, because the student in not engaged in problem solving anymore, he may be more receptive to thinking about specific pieces of conceptual knowledge than while trying to finish the problem [Katz et al., 1996]. The second is that the student could have solved parts of the problem by just guessing. Hence going through the pieces of knowledge that he should know might help rectify the guessing. The third reason for using summary mini-lessons is that, if the student made several mistakes while solving the problem, he may not recall all the corrections made by the tutor and which were really relevant and worth remembering (students may make mistakes that are related to the use of the interface and not to their knowledge of physics). The summary of knowledge presented in the mini-lesson may help in this respect.

Mini-lessons that address misconceptions. Misconceptions are addressed both during regular problem solving and through multiple choice questions. The explanations presented in this kind of mini-lesson are aimed at replacing the student's misconception. They follow the philosophy presented in the teaching strategy (section 3). They consist of a line of reasoning that is based on the scientific knowledge that the student should follow to self-explain the phenomenon of interest. An example of this kind of lesson can be seen in Figure 6. It is the mini-lesson a student would receive if, for example, he clicked on answer b) of the problem presented in Figure 1.

In the case of multiple-choice questions, the tutor will present a mini-lesson regardless of whether the student's answer choice is correct or not. The only difference is in the introductory sentence which states the correctness of the answer.

Your answer is incorrect. Here is why.

We will begin by analyzing the vertical motion of both balls. The only force acting on each ball, on the vertical direction, is its weight. If you apply Newton's second law $F=ma$, in the vertical direction, you get $w_1=m_1g$ for the first ball and $w_2=m_2g$ for the second ball. Therefore, the acceleration of both balls, in the vertical direction, is g, even if the weight of one ball is twice the weight of the other ball.

You may recall that acceleration is what changes velocity. In this case, the acceleration will make the vertical velocity of the balls increase. And since both balls have the same acceleration, their velocities will vary at the same rate. This means that at any instant, on their trip down, they will have the same vertical velocity. Hence, both balls will cover the distance in the same amount of time.

Now, let's analyze the horizontal motion of the balls. The only <u>force</u> acting on the balls is their weight, which is straight down. Hence, if we apply Newton's second law in the horizontal direction for each ball we find that the acceleration is zero because the total force in that direction is zero. Additionally, the problem states that both balls have the same horizontal velocity. And since the acceleration is zero, the velocity of both balls is constant. Additionally, we know from the analysis of the vertical motion of the balls that it takes both balls the same amount of time to get to the ground. Hence if both balls fly with the same horizontal velocity for the same amount of time they will travel the same horizontal distance. In other words, both balls will hit the ground at approximately the same horizontal distance from the base of the table.

Fig. 6. Mini-lesson addressing the misconception "Influence of weight on horizontal motion"

5 Preliminary Analysis of the Evaluation of the System

An evaluation of the system was conducted to test its effectiveness. To this end 42 students taking Introductory Mechanics classes were recruited and randomly divided into a Control group and an Experimental group. Both groups took a paper-and-pencil pre-test that consisted of 29 qualitative problems, 15 of which belonged to the Force Concept Inventory test[3]. Then they solved some problems with the Andes system receiving appropriate feedback according to the group they belonged to. The students in the Control Group had their input turned green or red depending on the

---

[3] The Force Concept Inventory test has become the standard across the US to measure conceptual understanding of elementary mechanics [Hake, 1998].

correctness of the entry. Then, in the case of an incorrect action, the students could ask for help making a choice from a help menu. The kind of help they received consisted of simple hints such as "the direction of the vector is incorrect" or just telling them the answer. On the other hand the students in the experimental group received the green/red feedback depending on whether their action was correct but when the input was incorrect the Conceptual Helper intervened as explained above. After the students finished solving the problems with the system they took a post-test which was the same as the pre-test with the exception of a few changes in the cover stories of some problems.

A preliminary analysis of the data found that the mean gain score (the subject's post-test score minus his or her pre-test score) of the control group was 4.12 with a standard deviation of 5.33, while the mean of the experimental group was 7.47 with a standard deviation of 5.03 -a statistically significant difference $(t(40)=2.094, p=0.043)$. Before this calculation was made, a comparison of the pre-test scores was performed and no statistically significant difference was found between the two groups $(t(40)=0.965, p=0.34)$. The statistically significant difference found between the means of the gain scores suggests that the intervention of the Conceptual Helper had a positive impact on the students' understanding of the concepts as well as on their ability to abandon common misconceptions.

Additionally the effect size was calculated. Effect size is a standard way to compare the results of one pedagogical experiment to another. One way to calculate effect size, used in Bloom (1984) and many other studies, is to subtract the mean of the gain scores of the control group from the mean of the gain scores of the experimental group, and divide by the standard deviation of the gain scores of the control condition. That calculation yields $(7.47-4.12/5.33 = 0.63)$. The effect size of 0.63 was comparable with peer and cross-age remedial tutoring (effect size of 0.4 according to Cohen et al., 1982). Some better results have been obtained with interventions that lasted a whole semester or academic year. For example, Bloom (1984) found an effect size of 2.0 for adult tutoring in replacement of classroom instruction and Anderson et al. (1995) reported an effect size of 1.0 for their tutoring systems. However, the results reported here were achieved with only two hours of instruction.

6 Conclusions

An intelligent coach was described which presents a novel cognitive-based approach to teaching conceptual physics. Moreover, the manner in which the desired knowledge is presented embeds many successful human tutoring techniques, such as providing hints and supporting post-problem reflection, as well as effective pedagogical techniques, like the use of a microscopic view of matter, and techniques that seem to be less cognitively demanding such as the use of anthropomorphism.

A preliminary analysis of the evaluation of the system is encouraging since it seems to reveal that the proposed methodology can be effective in accomplishing the task it was designed to perform.

References

Albacete, P.L. (1999). An Intelligent Tutoring System for teaching fundamental physics concepts. Unpublished doctoral dissertation. Intelligent Systems Program, University of Pittsburgh. Pittsburgh, Pennsylvania.

Anderson, J.R., Corbett, A.T., Koedinger, K.R., & Pelletier, R. (1995). Cognitive tutors: Lessons learned. The Journal of the Learning sciences, 4(2) 167-207.

Bloom, B.S. (1984). The 2 sigma problem: The search for methods of group instruction as effective as one-to-one tutoring. Educational Researcher, 13, 4-16.

Chi, M.T.H. (1992). Conceptual change within and across ontological categories. In Gier, R. (Ed.) Cognitive models of science: Minnesota studies in the philosophy of science. University of Minnesota Press, Minneapolis, MN.

Chi, M.T.H. (1996). Constructing Self-Explanations and Scaffolded Explanations in Tutoring. Applied Cognitive Psychology, Vol. 10, S33-S49.

Chi, M.T.H. & Koeske, R.D. (1983). Network Representation of a Child's Dinosaur Knowledge. Developmental Psychology 19(1), 29-39.

Cohen, P.A., Kulik, J.A., & Kulik, C.C. (1982). Educational outcomes of tutoring: A meta-analysis of findings. American Educational Research Journal, 19, 237-248.

Collins, A., Brown, J.S., & Newman, S.E. (1989). Cognitive apprenticeship: Teaching the crafts of reading, writing, and mathematics. In L. B. Resnick (Ed.), Knowing, learning, and instruction: Essays in honor of Robert Glaser (pp. 453-494). Hillsdale, NJ: Lawrence Erlbaum Associates, Inc.

diSessa, A.A. (1993). Toward an Epistemology of Physics. Cognition and Instruction, 10(2&3).

Fox, B.A. (1993). The Human Tutorial Dialogue Project: Issues in the Design of Instructional Systems. Lawrence Eribaum Associates, Hillsdale, NJ.

Gertner, A.S., Conati, C., & VanLehn K. (1998). Procedural help in Andes: Generating hints using a Bayesian network student model. Proceedings of the 15th National Conference on Artificial Intelligence. Madison, Wisconsin.

Hake, R.R. (1998). Interactive-engagement versus traditional methods: A six-thousand-student survey of mechanics test data for introductory physics courses. American Journal of Physics, 66(64).

Halloun, I.A., & Hestenes, D. (1985). The initial knowledge state of college physics students. American journal of Physics 53 (11) 1043-1055.

Katz, S., Lesgold, A., Eggan, G., Greenberg, L. (1996). Towards the Design of a More Effective Advisors for Learning by Doing Systems. Proceedings of the Third International Conference on Intelligent Tutoring Systems, ITS'96. Montreal, Canada. Springer-Verlag.

McArthur, D., Stasz, C., & Zmuidzinas, M. (1990). Tutoring techniques in algebra. Cognition and Instruction, 7(3) 197-244.

Murray, T., Schultz, K., Brown, D., & Clement, J. (1990). An Analogy-Based Computer Tutor for Remediating Physics Misconception. Interactive Learning Environments 1(2), 79-101.

Reif, F. (1995). Understanding and Teaching Important Scientific Thought Processes. American Journal of Physics, January 1995.

Roschelle, J. (1992). Learning by Collaborating: Convergent Conceptual Change. The Journal of the Learning Sciences, 2(3), 235-276.

Van Heuvelen, A. (1991). Learning to think like a physicist: A review of research-based instructional strategies. American Journal of Physics, 59(10), 891-896.

VanLehn, K. (1996). Conceptual and Meta learning during Coached Problem Solving. In Proceedings of the Third International conference on Intelligent Tutoring Systems. Montreal, Canada. Springer-Verlag.

Acknowledgements

This research was supported by a grant from the Cognitive Science Division of ONR, N00014-96-1-0260.

Macroadapting Animalwatch to Gender and Cognitive Differences with Respect to Hint Interactivity and Symbolism

Ivon Arroyo[1,2], Joseph E. Beck[1,2], Beverly Park Woolf[1,2], Carole R. Beal[3], and Klaus Schultz[2]

[1] Department of Computer Science, University of Massachusetts, Amherst, MA 01003, U.S.A.
[2] School of Education, University of Massachusetts, Amherst
[3] Department of Psychology, University of Massachusetts, Amherst
{Ivon, Beck, Bev}@cs.umass.edu, cbeal@psych.umass.edu

Abstract. We have built empirical models of elementary-school students' behavior from analyzing student interaction with a mathematics tutor with the objective of building teaching policies for individually different students. This model incorporates external information about the student, namely cognitive development and gender. It also incorporates hint features, namely the degree of interactivity and symbolism of each hint given. We found that boys benefit better from non-interactive and low-intrusive hints, while girls benefit better from highly interactive hints. We found that low symbolic hints are more effective for low cognitive ability students than highly symbolic ones, and the opposite happens for high cognitive ability students.

1 Introduction

Plenty of research effort has been devoted to finding optimal teaching strategies for *all* students while making tutoring decisions in ITS. For example, the PACT algebra tutor has been evaluated with two alternative teaching strategies. In an experimental version of PACT students had to explain their reasoning in addition to entering solutions to problems, while students in a control version just entered a numeric answer. The former version of PACT was found to be more effective than the latter one [1]. As can be seen, research on teaching strategies has been aimed at finding effective teaching strategies for all students. However, there is evidence that some specific teaching strategies are only effective for specific groups of students. For example, [9] concluded that their ISIS inquiry-based science tutor was most effective for high aptitude students, and less effective for low aptitude students.

We want to go beyond these single-teaching-strategy findings by looking at strategies that are effective for *individually different students*. [8] proposes a multiple-method approach to individualization, which involves the design of alternate treatments that engage different groups of students through alternative educational stimula. This is called *macroadaptation*, as opposed the usual *microadaptation* that consists of a generic and fine-grained kind of adaptivity that depends on the student's progression in the tutor [12]. The traditional microadaptation in an ITS generally consists of a higher estimation of the student's proficiency as the person shows mastery of the topics being tutored.

There has been some work on macroadaptation in Tutoring Systems. In [11] a battery of IQ questions was submitted at the beginning of the SMART tutoring session and four different empirical student models were derived which depended on these IQ scores. These student models provided a high predictive value in determining students' state of knowledge. However, there were no *qualitatively* different treatments for these groups of students. We want to extend this work in four aspects:

1. We want to macroadapt our system to new populations of users. Our population of students is young children instead of adults;
2. Shute's pre-tests were pencil and paper while our pre-tests are computer-based, shown at the beginning of the first session, so that the data are ready for the ITS to be used in tutoring decisions;
3. We are looking at other individual differences instead of IQ. We follow on the cognitive abilities differences by giving cognitive development tests which we consider relevant for students of this age, and also extend it to incorporate gender differences in learning;
4. The alternative treatments we propose are qualitatively different. We have built hints that differ in two dimensions: formalism of the feedback hints (low symbolism vs. high symbolism), and interactivity of hints (high interactivity vs. low interactivity).

In this paper, we want to transmit two main ideas. The first is that macroadapting a tutoring system to individually different students increases the effectiveness of the tutoring system. The second is to show that the specific partitioning of students and hints that we have chosen is a valid and important one.

2 Methodology

We chose to work in the context of a mathematics ITS for elementary-school children, which has proven to be an effective tutoring system. The methodology that we use consists of classifying hints and students along two dimensions, to then analyze the effectiveness of types of hints against groups of students. This section describes the ITS, the classification of hints and students and how we measured hint effectiveness.

2.1 The domain

Animalwatch is an Intelligent Tutoring System that teaches arithmetic to elementary school students. Animalwatch integrates mathematics with the biological sciences. Specifically, math problems are designed to motivate students to use mathematics in the context of practical problem solving, embedded in an narrative related to endangered species. Animalwatch teaches fractions and whole numbers at a 4th-6th grade level. It provides mathematics instruction for each student based on a dynamically updated probabilistic student model. Problems are dynamically generated based on inferences about the student's knowledge, progressing from simple one-digit whole-number addition problems to problems that involve fractions with different denominators.

2.2 Hints and student categorizations

When a student has trouble solving a problem, Animalwatch initiates a tutoring interaction that helps the student work through the problem. We have built multiple hints to aid on each topic, that were classified along two dimensions. Those dimensions are the degree of hint symbolism and interactivity, which are discussed in section 3.

We have chosen to categorize students along two dimensions: gender and cognitive development. Both these categorizations and the reasons for selecting them are discussed in section 4. Gender is easy to diagnose, but cognitive development is not. We built a computer-based Piagetian test to obtain estimates of cognitive development. A detailed description of this test is given in [2].

2.3 Measuring hint effectiveness: The experiment and data processing

Within an Animalwatch tutoring session, each student goes through a succession of problems. Whenever a wrong answer is entered, a hint is shown. Hints progressively increase the amount of information given. The first hints provide little information, but if the student keeps entering wrong answers, Animalwatch gives hints that will ultimately guide the student through the whole problem-solving process. Hints are given randomly along the two dimensions discussed before, i.e. regardless of the interactivity or symbolism level. Thus, if there were four hints to be picked that could be categorized as: highly interactive-highly symbolic, highly interactive-low symbolic, low interactive-highly symbolic, low interactive-low symbolic, Animalwatch picks randomly one of these four hints.

We analyze how the number of mistakes the student has made changes from problem to problem after seeing a particular kind of hint. Suppose some student gets a subtraction problem. The student answers incorrectly and after a sequence of unsuccessful hints and re-trials is finally given a hint of type Z. Immediately after that, the student enters the correct answer having made a total of X mistakes in this problem. The student then gets a new problem on subtraction of whole numbers. In this new problem, the student makes a total of Y mistakes. We take the difference X-Y as a measure of the effectiveness of hints of type Z, which represents how the number of mistakes is reduced after seeing a hint of type Z (see figure 1).

We look for main and interaction effects for gender, cognitive development, hint interactivity and hint symbolism in predicting hint effectiveness via an

Fig. 1. A case with X-Y difference of mistakes, which is our measure of hint effectiveness

ANOVA. However, it is important to note that other variables could affect our measure of hint effectiveness. For example, a hint would have different effects depending on the difficulty of the before-hint and after-hint problem. In addition, our measure could vary depending on the proficiency of the student at the skill when she saw the hint. The hint could also produce different effects depending on the amount of information that it provides (which also implies that it would be selected at a very specific moment with respect to other hints). We thus perform an analysis the variance with these last variables as covariates, in order to account for their effect.

3 Categorization of hints

Hints were classified along two dimensions: their degree of interactivity and their degree of symbolism. This section discusses this partitioning.

Hint interactivity. We categorize each hint as being highly interactive or low interactive. A synonym of highly interactive hints is "learning-by-doing" hints and a synonym for low interactive hints is "learning-by-being-told" hints (see table 1). Both high and low interactive hints provide plenty of information. However, while a highly interactive hint asks the student for numerous and various kinds of input at each step (dragging and dropping, large amounts of textbox input, etc.), the low interactive hints' interaction involves at most pressing a button to step through an animation, or entering one single number into a text box, or just reading a message. Low interactive hints are also less intrusive and faster to go through, as they require less input from the student. Figure 2 gives examples of high and low interactive hints.

Hint symbolism. The second dimension is the level of numerical symbolism that each of the hints has. We found a way to explain each problem-solving process with two alternative hints: a highly numeric (highly symbolic) one and a concrete (low symbolic) one. Concrete hints involve the use of base-10 blocks for whole number problems and bars that can be partitioned for fraction problems, while highly symbolic hints involve a more abstract procedure that involves direct operations over numerals. We consider operations over numerals as being of a higher level of abstraction because each numeral represents one or more of the concrete objects that are manipulated in the concrete hints. Symbolic hints do not make a connection with real life objects, while concrete hints do. Symbolic hints provide students with powerful tools to reach solutions that can

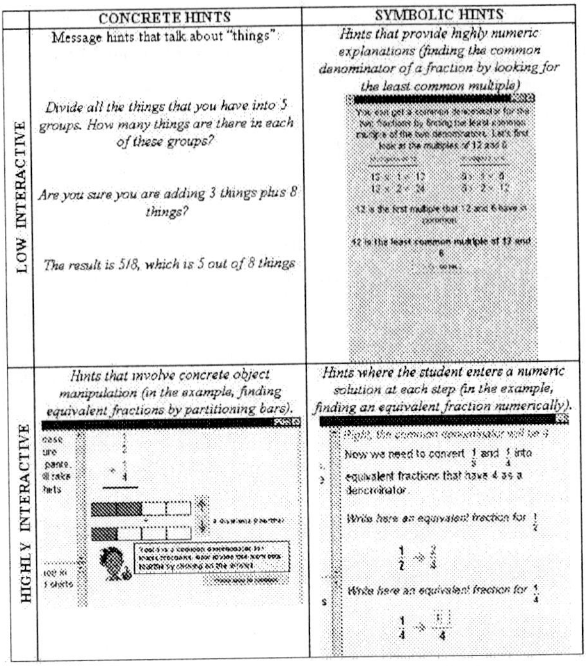

Fig. 2. classification of hints into four categories

be generalized easily to problems with big numbers. Low symbolic hints will be referred as "concrete hints", while we will refer to highly symbolic hints as just "symbolic hints" (see figure 2).

4   Categorization of students

Students were classified along two dimensions: their gender and their level of cognitive development. This section discusses this partitioning.

4.1   Cognitive development

It is known that 5th grade students are at an age of transition from handling concrete to formal operations [10]. It is known that although students develop specific cognitive abilities at an average age, not all students do it exactly at the same time [5]. All this made us believe that we are very likely to be tutoring students that can handle different levels of abstraction in our math domain although they have the same age. We hypothesized that the concreteness or abstractness of the ITS's help system could make a difference in how much they understood and learned. We built a computer-based cognitive development pre-test to diagnose students cognitive ability [2]. This test evaluates students mastery of concrete operations (conservation, serializing, reversing, etc.) and formal operations (proportions, experiment design, combinatorial analysis) through a battery of computer-based Piagetian tasks [13]. In various previous experiments we found that this measure was a good predictor of mathematics ability (R=0.513, p<0.000).

4.2 Categorizing across gender

Extensive research makes us believe that socio-cultural factors can contribute to gender differences in learning when considering students of the age of our population of students. Much research has shown that at the beginning in early adolescence, gender differences exist in math self concept and math utility [6]. Some studies indicate that girls experiences in the classroom contribute to their lower interest and confidence in math learning by the middle school period [4]. Moreover, there is starting to be evidence that girls and boys have different approaches to problem solving [7]. In one of our Animalwatch trials in 1998, we found that girls who were given a version of the tutor with highly interactive and information rich hints performed better than in a version which had only short messages as hints. Meanwhile, the complete opposite happened for boys (they preferred and did better in a version that only gave short messages with scarce information as hints) [3].

5 Experiment and results

In spring of 1999, we experimented with Animalwatch and 60 fifth grade students from a rural area. Students were exposed to 3 one-hour sessions of Animalwatch in the following way: At the beginning of the first session, students went through the cognitive pre-test, and then they started using Animalwatch.

Luckily, girls and boys did not differ significantly in our measure of cognitive development (two-tailed t-test, $p<0.2$), so we could compare girls and boys without their cognitive ability being an intervening factor.

We gathered 5272 cases like the ones discussed in section 2.3. Each case represented a problem that a student couldn't solve correctly from the start, which was finally solved immediately after seeing the hint whose effectiveness we are measuring.

As discussed in section 2.3, we analyzed the effectiveness of different hints for different students by using an ANOVA with four variables as covariates: difficulty of the before-hint problem, difficulty of the after-hint problem, proficiency of the student when she saw the hint, and amount of information/order of selection of the hint. These four variables predicted 64% of the variance of our hint effectiveness measurement. The variable "amount-of-information/order-of-hint-selection" was the best predictor ($F(1,5270)=3352$, $p<0.000$), followed by the difficulty of the first problem ($F(1,5270)=27.66$, $p<0.000$) and the difficulty of the second problem ($F(1,5270)=22.68$, $p<0.000$), and last by the proficiency of the student ($F(1,5270)=15.41$, $p<0.000$).

580

5.1 Gender main effects and interactions

We performed a 2-way ANOVA for interactivity and gender in predicting difference of mistakes with the four covariates discussed above, and found the following results. First, interactivity by itself did not make a difference in predicting
our hint effectiveness measure ($p<0.9$). However, gender did by itself. It seems
that girls in general tended to improve more than boys did ($F(1,5270)=21.81$,
$p<0.000$). We also found an interaction between hint interactivity and gender
in predicting hint effectiveness ($F(1,5270)=17.57$, $p<0.000$). Figure 3.a shows
the predictions of our model after accounting for the four variables discussed in
previous sections. It seems that boys tended to do a lot worse with highly interactive hints, while girls did better with highly interactive hints. We thus found
consistent evidence with our 1998 study: girls again seemed to benefit more from
highly interactive hints, while boys didn't, this time regardless of the amount of
information provided.

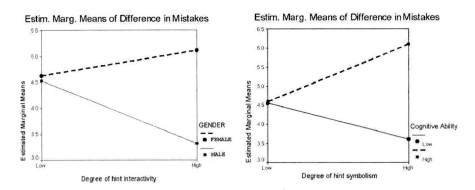

Fig. 3. a) Effects for gender and degree of hint interactivity (left) b) Effects for cognitive
development and hint symbolism (right)

5.2 Cognitive development effects and interactions

We analyzed the relationship between symbolism and our cognitive development
estimates. We performed a 2-way ANOVA for cognitive ability and hint symbolism in predicting the difference of mistakes with the four covariates. We found no
main effect for hint symbolism alone. That is, the degree of hint symbolism was
not a significant predictor of our hint effectiveness measure ($p<0.2$). However,
cognitive ability was ($F(1,5270)=37.35$, $p<0.000$). This did not surprise us, as
we thought it was obvious that higher cognitive ability students could in general
benefit more from any kind of help that we gave them. We also found an interaction effect between symbolism and cognitive ability ($F(1,5270)=35.48$, $p<0.000$).
Figure 3.b shows how both students with low and high cognitive ability do as
well with low symbolic "concrete" hints, but high cognitive ability students do

better with highly symbolic hints while low cognitive ability students do worse with highly symbolic hints.

5.3 Three way interaction effects

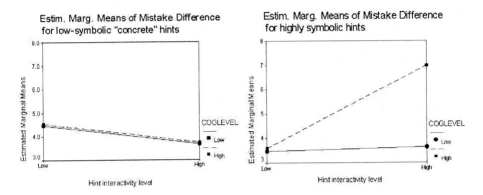

Fig. 4. 3-way interaction effects for interactivity, gender and cognitive ability

Analyzing three-way interaction effects helped us predict 10% more of the remaining unpredicted variance. We found that students of high cognitive ability get excellent results when the high symbolism of a hint is aided by a high interactivity than when it is not. Meanwhile, students of low cognitive ability cannot get to those levels of effectiveness when they are given the same interactive and symbolic condition $(F(2,5269)=5.59, p<0.018$, see figure 4).

We also found 3-way interaction effects when taking into account both gender and cognitive ability with respect to hint symbolism.

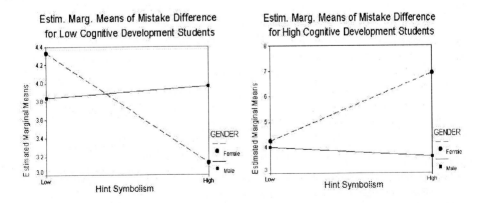

Fig. 5. 3-way interaction effects for symbolism, gender and cognitive ability

In these last graphs we can see how girls behave according to the behavior that we expected. Low cognitive ability girls do better with low symbolic hints and the opposite happens for high cognitive ability girls ($F(2,5269)=10$, $p<0.002$, see figure 5). Meanwhile, the degree of symbolism doesn't seem to affect boys at all compared to girls. One possible explanation is that maybe girls and boys have different goals while using the system. We are assuming that everyone is trying to minimize the number of errors when they get a problem. This way, if a hint were helpful, students would make fewer mistakes in the following similar problem. However, this doesn't necessarily happen if students don't have that objective in mind. Boys might be an instance of such a case. This is an issue that we want to investigate in future trials.

6   Summary and conclusions

In this paper, we have extended the idea of trying to find a correspondence between student types and teaching strategies, expressed as variations of hint features. In this particular case, we considered two specific individual differences and two hint classifications: gender and cognitive differences in the exposure to hints that differed in degrees of symbolism and interactivity.

We build on the philosophy that empirical data is a good source for finding teaching strategies. We introduced a concept of hint effectiveness measured by the decrease of mistakes from one problem to another one after seeing a specific hint type. We found interactions between cognitive development and symbolism that suggest low symbolic hints are more effective for low cognitive ability students than highly symbolic ones, and viceversa for high cognitive ability students. We found interactions between gender and hint interactivity which suggest boys do better with low interactive / low intrusive hints, and that the opposite happens for girls. We also found more sophisticated interactions that involved gender and cognitive abilities mixed together: Boys didnt seem to be very much affected by the degree of symbolism of a hint while girls did. We conclude that when these rules are applied to a tutoring system, its effectiveness should be higher.

We are aware that adaptation implies an exponentially bigger effort than non-adaptation. The more individual differences and hint features we take into account, the exponentially more variations of hints we may need to generate. This could make our tutoring system exponentially larger. However, we also think there are variables that are best differentiators of students' behavior and needs. Those are the variables that we are looking for, which represent important trends of behavior. Moreover, this type of research has two main consequences. It has the descriptive effect of understanding students' thinking better, and the prescriptive effect of deriving successful teaching methods [1].

[1] We acknowledge support for this work from the National Science Foundation, HRD-9714757. Any opinions, findings, and conclusions or recommendations expressed in this material are those of the authors and do not necessarily reflect the views of the granting agency.

References

1. Aleven, V. et al.: Tutoring answer explanation fosters learning with understanding. In Proceedings of the ninth international conference of Artificial Intelligence in Education (1999).
2. Arroyo, I.; Beck, J.; Schultz, K.; Woolf, B.: Piagetian Psychology in Intelligent Tutoring Systems. In the Proceedings of the Ninth International Conference on Artificial Intelligence in Education. (1999) pp. 600-602.
3. Beck, J., Arroyo, I., Woolf, B., Beal, C.: Affecting Self-confidence with an ITS. In the Proceedings of the Ninth International Conference on Artificial Intelligence in Education. (1999) pp. 611-613.
4. Beal, C.: Boys and girls: The development of gender roles. New York: McGraw Hill (1994).
5. Case, R.: The mind's staircase: Exploring the conceptual underpinnings of children's thought and knowledge. Hillsdale NJ: Erlbaum. (1992)
6. Eccles, J.S., Wigfield, A., Harold, R.D., Blumenfeld, P.: Age and gender differences in children's self and task perceptions during elementary school. Child development, 64, (1993) 830-847.
7. Fennema, E., Carpenter, T. P., Jacobs, V. R., Franke, M. L., Levi, L. W.: A longitudinal study of gender differences in young children's mathematical thinking. Educational Researcher, 27, (1998, June-July) 6-11.
8. Jonassen, D.; Grabowski, B.: Handbook of Individual Differences, learning and Instruction. Lawrence Erlbawm (1993).
9. Meyer, T.N. et al.: A multi-year, large-scale field study of a learner controlled ITS. In Proceedings of the Ninth International Conference on Artificial Intelligence in Education (1999).
10. Piaget, J.: The Child's Conception of Number. Routledge and Kegan (1964).
11. Shute, V.: SMART: Student Modeling Approach for Responsive Tutoring. In User Modeling and User-Adapted Interaction (1995), 5, pp. 1-44.
12. Snow, R. E.: Individual differences and Instructional Theory. Educational Researcher (1977), 6, 11-15.
13. Voyat, G. E.: Piaget Systematized (1982).

High-Level Student Modeling
with Machine Learning

Joseph E. Beck and Beverly Park Woolf

Computer Science Department
University of Massachusetts
Amherst, MA 01003
U.S.A.
{beck,bev}@cs.umass.edu

Abstract. We have constructed a learning agent that models student behavior at a high level of granularity for a mathematics tutor. Rather than focusing on whether the student knows a particular piece of knowledge, the learning agent determines how likely the student is to answer a problem correctly and how long he will take to generate this response. To construct this model, we used traces from previous users of the tutor to train the machine learning agent. This agent used information about the student, the current topic, the problem, and the student's efforts to solve this problem to make its predictions. This model was very accurate at predicting the time students required to generate a response, and was somewhat accurate at predicting the likelihood the student's response was correct. We present two methods for integrating such an agent into an intelligent tutor.

1 Introduction

AnimalWatch is an intelligent tutor for teaching arithmetic to grade school students[3]. The goal of the tutor is to improve girls' self-confidence in their ability to do math, with the long-term goal of increasing the number of women in mathematical and scientific occupations. AnimalWatch has been shown to increase the self-confidence of girls who use it[3]. The tutor maintains a student model of how students perform for each topic in the domain, and uses this model to select a topic on which the student will work, to construct a problem at the appropriate level of difficulty for the student, and to determine which feedback is best for the student.

Most student models are concerned with representing the student's ability on portions of the domain. Although useful, it is not always obvious how to map this low-level knowledge to higher level teaching actions. Given that the main purpose of student models for intelligent tutors is to support such decision-making, this is an odd situation.

To overcome this difficulty, we have implemented a machine learning (ML) architecture that reasons at a coarser grain size. We are not interested in low-level cognitive information, rather, we want something that can directly apply to the tutor's decision-making. Specifically, the agent learns to predict the probability the student's next response will be correct, and how long it will take the student to generate that response.

An advantage of this framework is that it permits the centralization of the tutor's reasoning. All of the teaching decisions of AnimalWatch (which makes similar decisions to many intelligent tutors) can be made via this module. First we will discuss related research. Next we describe how our ML agent is constructed. We then discuss specific implementation details for using the agent with our tutor. Finally we conclude with a discussion of the results of our tests, and probable future work.

2 Background

Most intelligent tutors track how well a student is doing on each element in the domain to be taught (for simplicity, we will refer to these elements as "topics"). This is a good starting point, and many ITS have used this framework. Unfortunately, not much progress has been at modeling higher-level information about the student.

It is possible to use the tutor's beliefs of the student's abilities to make higher level predictions. For example, if there are 4 steps required to solve a problem, the probability the student will produce the correct response can be found by multiplying together the probabilities that he knows each rule. This model can be enhanced by accounting for correct guessing and "slips" by a proficient student[1]. However, it does not account for information about how the student has performed on this problem. If he has made 10 prior mistakes, the probability the next answer is correct would probably differ from that of a student who has yet to make his first response. Furthermore, the difficulty of the problem must be considered. A student is more likely to answer a question that (in arithmetic) has small numbers. It is difficult to see how these types knowledge could be embedded in the tutor's beliefs of the student's ability on a topic. Some means of extending "student" modeling[1] to the domain must be made.

Work on the ANDES system[8] has addressed some of these issues. ANDES constructs a Bayesian network representing potential solutions to the current problem. The student's proficiencies and actions are used with this network to determine on which steps the student will need help, and his probable method for solving the problem. This combination of reasoning about problem structure and student knowledge is powerful.

Other work at abstracting higher level information about the student includes NeTutor[11], which determined under which teaching conditions a student best performed. For example, the system determined whether the student learned best with a directed or exploratory learning tasks, and used that information to guide its teaching decisions.

There has also been research in automatically constructing executable models of student behavior. Input-output agent modeling (IOAM) examines student solutions to problems, and constructs a set of rules that describe the student's behavior. This requires a detailed description of the state, but produces an agent that makes similar mistakes (and correct answers) as the actual student[7].

3 Architecture

Given our goal of learning whether a student will generate a correct response, and how long he will take to generate this response, it would be nice to find a low-cost method for doing this. It is certainly possible to explicitly model how students generate their

---

[1] Finding a good term is problematic. For the tutor to better reason about the student, it needs to model information beyond what the student knows/believes..

answers, but this would be time consuming. Therefore, we have constructed a machine learning agent that acts as a "black box" when making predictions. The exact mechanism used by the learning agent is secondary[2]. Any machine learning method for performing function approximation will (in theory) work. The critical issues are what are the model's inputs/outputs, and how the model can be integrated into an ITS.

3.1 What are the inputs/outputs?

When the student is presented with an opportunity to provide an answer, the system takes a "snap shot" of its current state. This picture consists of information from 4 main areas:

1. **Student:** The student's level of proficiency and level of cognitive development
2. **Topic:** How hard the current topic is and the type of operand/operators.
3. **Problem:** How complex is the current problem.
4. **Context:** Describes the student's current efforts at answering this question, and hints he has seen.

After the student makes his next response, the system records the time the student required to make this response and whether it is correct. These two items of information are what the learning agent is trying to predict.

A useful feature of this model is that it is executable. That is, when presented with a problem, it returns characteristics of the student's response. This information is enough for the tutor to make a teaching decision (in the current example, presenting a hint). Information about the student's response and the hint presented are used to generate a new set of context features (see Section 4.2 for more detail). This represents the student seeing a problem, attempting to answer it, and the tutor providing feedback. At this point the new context information is fed back to the ML agent, and the new prediction represents the student's second attempt at answering the problem. Combining the ML agent with the tutor in this manner results in a simulated student[14].

Figure 1 provides an overview of this process. The student, topic, and problem information are assumed to be fixed (but can be initialized with arbitrary values). The predicted student performance in this situation is combined with the resulting teaching action to produce a new set of context features. Since the context describes all of the information about what the student has seen and done, this is the only information that needs to change. If the ML-agent predicts the student will solve the problem, that terminates the simulation cycle.

3.2 How to use the model?

Simply having a model that predicts properties of the student's next response is of limited use unless there is some method for utilizing these prediction by a decision making agent. There are several possibilities for using model we have described. One is simply to construct the tutor with a set of "if-then" rules that use this model for additional accuracy. For example, a rule could be of the form "if the student has spent

---

[2] We have successfully used naive Bayesian classifiers, decision trees, and linear regression.

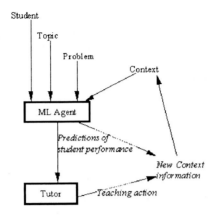

Fig. 1. Schematic for simulated student.

more than 90 seconds on the problem, provide a hint that makes it very likely he will get the problem correct." (as opposed to providing a small amount of information).

One problem with this is the tutor does not take any proactive steps to ensure the student does not approach a bad situation. E.g. the above rule implies taking a long time per problem is not the desired goal, but none of the previous teaching decisions (what problem to present, which topic to work on, etc.) took this knowledge into account.

To overcome this difficulty, we have integrated this model of the student with a reinforcement learning[13] agent whose goal is to learn a teaching policy that keeps the student in "good" learning situations. More details about this agent are available at[6]. This learning agent takes a learning goal and an executable model of the student as input. To follow the above example, the agent could be told it will receive a high reward if the student takes less than 90 seconds to solve a problem, and a low reward otherwise. The agent then uses the simulation of student behavior to experiment with different teaching actions in different contexts. Eventually (hopefully) the agent finds a teaching policy that makes it likely the student will stay in desired states.

4 Implementation issues

Section 3 gives a high-level description of the learning architecture that could be implemented in several ways for a variety of tutors. We now discuss specific implementation details with integrating a learning agent into AnimalWatch.

4.1 AnimalWatch background

AnimalWatch has a series of *topics*, which are items about which it can ask questions. *Operators* include addition, subtraction, multiplication, and division. *Operands* are wholes and fractions. There are also topics on "pre-fraction" skills that do not fit this hierarchy well. Each topic may have a number of *subskills* which are optional steps that may be needed to solve a problem[4]. For example, simplifying the result is a subskill of add fractions. Subskills have a level of difficulty associated with them. Borrowing across several columns in a subtraction problem is more difficult than borrowing from the column directly to the left.

The tutor provides feedback when students make an incorrect response. There are a variety of types of hints it can provide: message hints, interactive hints that demonstrate the procedure involved, and interactive hints that emphasize the underlying concepts.

4.2 Training data and features

Since the tutor records the state of the system every time the student enters a response, it is easy to gather large amounts of training data. Approximately 120 students have used AnimalWatch in two local elementary schools. This yielded 11,000 training instances[3].

All of the data collected were from rural/suburban schools. One class was in the fourth grade, the other in the fifth grade. A question is how well these data generalize to other populations, such as older/younger students, and students in an urban setting.

There are several (48 with the most recent implementation) different features provided to the learning agent. As outlined in Section 3.1, these features can be broken down into several broad categories. Table 1 itemizes these features.

As is typical for machine learning, the design of the features is dependent on the type of learning algorithm used. For example, the operator and operand were initially stored as simple integers. E.g. 1 for addition, 2 for subtraction, 3 for multiplication, and 4 for division. For ML techniques that reason by categories (e.g. naive Bayesian classifiers) this is sufficient. But for simple linear techniques, it is necessary to create 4 separate inputs only one of which is active at a time (i.e. a "one-hot" encoding scheme). The first inputs would be on for addition (while the other three are off), for a subtraction problem the second input would be on and the first, third, and fourth off, etc.

More generally, this is a tradeoff between complexity of the learning algorithm and complexity of the feature space. General techniques can learn with weaker sets of features. Limited techniques, such as linear regression, require a more explicit encoding scheme. Another example of this is the set of combination features. Since regression, the technique we decided to use, cannot handle interactions between inputs, it is necessary to create these interaction features by hand. In this case, we had data indicating that particular Piaget cognitive development questions were relevant to certain topics[2]. Our eventual goal is to migrate to more powerful learning techniques so this lower level engineering is not required. However, this is a more difficult task.

4.3 Function approximator

Given a set of features to describe a state, some means of predicting what will happen next is needed. We settled on using linear regression for the simple reason that it is quick

---

[3] Certain data were removed. Specifically, students with learning disabilities (e.g. unable to read the problems without the help of a proctor) were not considered in the analysis. We also trimmed response times in excess of 6 minutes. There were very few responses in this range, and these data are likely confounded by students needing to leave the room for a few minutes.

Feature type	Information
Student	– Gender – Performance in 9 tasks of Piagetian level of cognitive development[2] – Combined score for Piaget tasks – Proficiency at current topic
Topic	– Operator (one-hot encoding) – Operand (one-hot encoding)
Problem	– Problem difficulty[4] – Size of operands/answer – Number of subskills required[4] – Difficulty of subskills
Context	– Is this student's first attempt? – Number of prior mistakes – Best hint seen – Current hint depth (hints can create subhints) – Maximum hint depth on this problem – Best hint seen – Has student seen a "strong" hint? – Time spent on this problem
Combination	– Particular piaget tasks X topic type

Table 1. List of features for learning agent

and easy to determine if your model is accurate or not, and has a fast execution speed to learn and make predictions. This is a non-trivial concern. AnimalWatch is written in Java, and since we will be integrating the learning components into the system it would be very useful if they were also written in Java. Most ML schemes either use gradient descent (e.g. linear function approximators, neural networks) or use categorical data (e.g. decision trees, naive Bayesian classifiers). Given that we have a long-term goal of learning online, a simple, fast technique such as regression is a good fit.

Our technique of using a simple function approximator to predict observable variables has the advantage of being straightforward to construct. There is not a large computational or research cost of building our model, and no need to try to understand the student's mental state. This is in keeping with Self's[12] recommendations.

Linear regression was used to construct two equations. One equation used the features described in Section 4.2 as dependent variables to predict the amount of time required, the other equation predicted whether the student's response would be correct. Whether a response is correct is a binary value, and in a sense it is odd to apply regression to this situation. However, we are interested in the probability a student will generate a correct response. Consider a situation where 51% of the time the student has no difficulties with a problem, while 49% he makes a mistake and has a difficult time with the problem. We would not want to use a technique that ignored the second possibility. Therefore we use the regression model to predict the mean correct score (incorrect is 0, correct is 1), and compare this with a random number. I.e. if the model predicts an average correctness of 0.8, 80% of the time the system assumes the student provides a correct response, 20% of the time the system assumes an incorrect response.

5   Results

To evaluate the accuracy of the regression models, we correlated the predicted and actual results. The model for predicting the amount of time correlated with the actual times at 0.629. A 2-fold cross validation resulted in a correlation of 0.619, so the regression model learned something other than statistical noise in the data as it was able to predict times for instances which it had not seen. Figure 2 shows the model's performance.

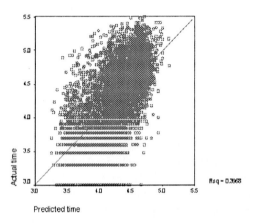

Fig. 2. Predicted vs. actual time for a student's response.

The x-axis is the predicted log-time (measured in milliseconds) by the regression model; the y-axis is the actual log-time[4]. The best-fit linear regression gave an r-square of 0.397. I.e. this model reduces the squared error by approximately 40% when compared to guessing randomly.

The linear regression model was less accurate at predicting whether the student would generate a correct response. The correlation was only 0.496, which gives an r-squared of 0.243. A model that always guessed the student would give a correct response would be correct 60% of the time, while this model's predictions are correct 74% of the time. This does not seem overly encouraging. However, Figure 3 shows the model's performance from a different perspective. The model's predicted values were broken into 101 bins (0, 0.01, 0.02, ... , 0.99, 1.0), the student's probability of generating

---

[4] The logarithm of time was used as this linearized the data.

a correct response for all of the cases in each bin was computed, and the resulting set of
< *predicted, actual* > pairs scatterplotted[5].

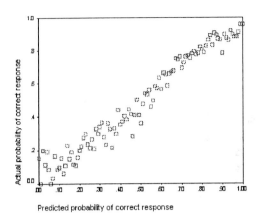

Fig. 3. Accuracy of predicting student responses.

The x-axis is the model's predictions for the probability the student's response will
be correct. The y-axis is the actual probability the student's response was correct. For
example, when the model thought there was a 100% chance the student would generate
a correct response (the right most dot in the graph), the student in fact had roughly a
95% chance of generating a correct response.

According to this graph, the model appears to be very accurate. As it believes the
student is more likely to give a correct response, the student is in fact more likely to do
so. The disparity between the correlation coefficient, which seems fairly weak, and the
graphical display of the model, which seems quite strong, is striking. For an explanation, consider the cases in the middle of the graph (say predicted values of 0.4 to 0.6).
Even if the model is correct, and students have a 40% to 60% chance of generating
correct responses, the model *cannot* have a high degree of accuracy. Assume the model
is deterministic, and always guesses the most likely category (the fact that it in fact selects randomly random does not effect the following results, but would complicate the
argument). For cases in the 40% correct range, the model will guess the student will
make a mistake, and will be correct 60% of the time. For cases in the 50% range, the
model will be right 50%. For cases in the 60% range, the model will guess the student's
response is correct, and will be right 60% of the time. Assuming an even distribution of
cases, this is an accuracy of 56.7%.

Considering all possible probability values from 0 to 1, such a model would have a
maximum accuracy of 75%. Since there are no cases where a student answers a questions with a particular probability (he gets it right or he doesn't, there is no in between),

---

[5] We are not trying to perform a statistical sleight of hand. We cannot simply graph a scatterplot
of predicted vs. actual values since the actual value has only 2 possible values.

it is an interesting question as to whether such a model is useful or useless. As we discuss later, this depends on how the model will be used.

6 Conclusions and future work

We have constructed a model of the student at a coarse grain size and are using this executable model as a simulated student. Our belief is that there is much to be gained by modeling higher level descriptions of students. This has a more natural mapping onto rules describing teaching decisions, and can be used as a simulation to train an agent how to teach students.

The ML agent has done a good job at modeling how long the student will require to generate a response. Accounting for 40% of the variance of time data is difficult, and performance should improve if a more complex function approximator is used. The data for each individual student were not critical for this performance. Each student comprised less than 1% of the training data and could not have a large impact on the model. A question is whether attempting to learn online about each individual would significantly improve accuracy. Prior work[5] found a benefit from learning about individual students to predict time to solve a problem.

It is unclear if the equation for predicting whether the student will answer a question correctly is accurate enough. If the goal is to predict whether the current student will generate a correct response, and the decision is high stakes, then the model is probably not accurate enough. If instead, the goal is to provide a simulation of a student for another learning agent[6], the model is probably accurate enough "on average". As seen in Figure 3 the regression equation generally agrees with the observed data for how often a student will generate a correct response. If a model can determine that for a certain class of situations, the student has a 50% chance of answering correctly, then this should be sufficiently accurate (even though the model is right only half of the time). This is a subtle issue, and needs to be further explored. Intuitively, it is seems likely that online learning would give large increases in accuracy of predicting the student's correctness of response. Informal observation reveals that students have widely varying thresholds for how conscientious they are before providing a response: some recheck their work, others are willing to guess wildly.

We will use more complex machine learning techniques in the future. One possibility is non-linear regression. This is very good for offline learning, but if the model is to be improved it is necessary to store every piece of the data used to construct the model. This is a large drawback if learning is to continue online while the student uses the tutor. Neural networks learn slowly, but incrementally, and can be represented with much less storage space than a comparable non-linear regression and datapoints. As an abstract AI problem, this issue is not important. For deploying a tutor on Pentium and PowerMac class computers in the typical classroom, this is important. To date there has been little discussion of the tradeoffs of lab vs. classroom AI technology.

Although this framework has been presented in the context of AnimalWatch, the architecture is general. Only the details in Section 4 would need to be updated for use with a different tutor. The concept of using a large population of student data to directly train a learning agent is widely applicable. With the scale up in evaluation studies[9, 10], this technique becomes more feasible.

Acknowledgements

We acknowledge the support for this work from the National Science Foundation, HRD-9714757. Any opinions, findings, and conclusions or recommendations expressed in this material are those of the authors and do not necessarily reflect the views of the granting agency.

References

1. J. Anderson. *Rules of the Mind.* Lawrence Erlbaum Associates, Hillsdale, NJ, 1993.
2. I. Arroyo, J. E. Beck, K. Schultz, and Woolf. Piagetian psychology in intelligent tutoring systems. In *Proceedings of the Ninth International Conference on Artificial Intelligence in Education,* 1999.
3. Carole R. Beal, Beverly P. Woolf, Joseph Beck, Ivon Arroyo, Klaus Schultz, and David M. Hart. Gaining confidence in mathematics: Instructional technology for girls. In *Proceedings of International Conference on Mathematics/Science Education and Technology,* 2000.
4. J. E. Beck, M. Stern, and B.P. Woolf. Using the student model to control problem difficulty. In *Proceedings of the Seventh International Conference on User Modeling,* pages 277–288, 1997.
5. J. E. Beck and B. P. Woolf. Using a learning agent with a student model. In *Proceedings Third International Conference on Intelligent Tutoring Systems,* 1998.
6. Joseph E. Beck and Beverly P. Woolf. Learning to teach: A machine learning architecture for making teaching decisions. In *Proceedings of the Seventeenth National Conference on Artificial Intelligence,* 2000.
7. Bark Cheung Chiu and Geoffrey I. Webb. Using decision trees for agent modeling: Improving prediction performance. *User Modeling and User Adapted Interaction,* 8(1-2):131–152, 1998.
8. A. S. Gertner, C. Conati, and K. VanLehn. Procedural help in ANDES: Generating hints using a Bayesian network student model. In *Fifteenth National Conference on Artificial Intelligence,* pages 106–111, 1998.
9. K. R. Koedinger, J. R. Anderson, W. H. Hadley, and M. A. Mark. Intelligent tutoring goes to school in the big city. *International Journal of Artificial Intelligence in Education,* 8:30–43, 1997.
10. Thomas N. Meyer, Todd M. Miller, Kurt Steuck, and Monika Kretschmer. A multi-year large-scale field study of a learner controlled intelligent tutoring system. In *Proceedings of the Ninth International Conference on Artificial Intelligence in Education,* pages 191–198, 1999.
11. M. Quafafou, A. Mekaouche, and H.S. Nwana. Multiviews learning and intelligent tutoring systems. In *Proceedings of Seventh World Conference on Artificial Intelligence in Education,* 1995.
12. J.A. Self. Bypassing the intractable problem of student modelling. In C. Frasson and G. Gauthier, editors, *Intelligent Tutoring Systems: at the Crossroads of Artificial Intelligence and Education,* pages 107–123, Norwood, NJ, 1990.
13. R.S. Sutton and A.G. Barto. *An Introduction to Reinforcement Learning.* MIT Press, 1998.
14. K. VanLehn, S. Ohlsson, and R. Nason. Applications of simulated students: An exploration. *Journal of Artificial Intelligence in Education,* 5(2):135–175, 1994.

Individualized Recommendations for Learning Strategy Use

Susan Bull

ARIES Lab, Dept. of Computer Science, University of Saskatchewan,
Saskatoon, Saskatchewan, S7N 5A9, Canada.
bull@cs.usask.ca

Abstract. This paper describes LS-LS: a system to raise awareness of language learning strategies to help students become more effective learners. The focus is the student model, which contains representations of learning style and current strategy use: information provided explicitly by the learner. LS-LS infers additional strategies of potential interest to an individual, based on the contents of their student model. It also suggests computational learning environments that a student might find useful to practise these new strategies, based on information provided by the (human) tutor about locally available software.

1 Introduction

Linton observes that intelligent tutoring systems (ITS) are often judged by their ability to make tutoring decisions for the learner, despite the fact that self-directed learners actually possess a valuable skill [1]. Learner autonomy is also important in foreign language learning [2]. Much research has indicated that appropriate use of language learning strategies can contribute to autonomy and success in learning a second language [3]. There are various definitions of language learning strategies: some relate to conscious application of techniques to help a learner [4]; others allow the possibility of unconscious strategy use [5]. Kohonen states learners can be made aware of their strategy use, and that they may modify it with 'conscious effort' [5].

Early work suggested there are successful language learning strategies, and teaching these strategies to less successful students might help them improve their performance [6]. Later research found some unsuccessful learners actually use many of the same strategies as more successful peers [7]. Such students need to learn how to apply strategies *appropriately*. Further, it is not the case that all good learners use the same strategies [8]. Strategy choice may depend to some extent on learning style [9]. It seems that while tailored application of learning strategies is useful, there is no single set of strategies appropriate for recommendation to all learners [10]. Indeed, Oxford recommends "strategy training should be somewhat individualized" [3]. However, this is difficult in the typical language learning situation, where there is a single teacher working with a foreign language class, for a limited time period.

A few tutoring systems encouraging the use of a variety of language learning strategies have been implemented [11,12], to foster the kind of self-direction proposed by Linton [1] for an ITS. Nevertheless, these systems are tied to their own contexts.

Implementation of a more widely applicable system to foster the acquisition of language learning strategies has also been undertaken [13]. However, this requires expensive hardware often not available in student Language Centres.

This paper introduces LS-LS (learning style–learning strategies): an environment to raise student awareness of language learning strategies, to help them become more autonomous learners. LS-LS recommends potentially useful additional strategies to an individual, according to their learning style and current strategy use, and suggests ways students may practise these new strategies. It is designed primarily for use in contexts where resources are restricted, and where individualised, teacher-led strategy training programmes are infeasible. LS-LS runs on most Macintosh computers.

LS-LS is centred around a student model constructed with the help of explicit student contributions, following a recent trend in student modelling [14-19]. In addition to providing information for the student model, in LS-LS this approach has the function of promoting learner reflection on both the student's own specific approaches to learning, and on different ways of learning in general. Thus, even before receiving strategy suggestions, students are thinking about their learning.

LS-LS is unusual in the sense that the student model is not part of a larger tutoring system. The suggestions made by LS-LS refer in the main to activities *outside* the LS-LS system. Some of these recommendations will include suggestions for computer-based interaction to practise strategy application. This requires some additional information about the local situation, which must be provided by the teacher.

2 Theoretical Basis of LS-LS

LS-LS aims to help learners become more self-directed by introducing new learning strategies which fit with their learning style and current strategy use. These two types of information form the student model. The initial representations are provided directly by the student, by indicating which aspects of learning style descriptions are applicable to their own learning, and which learning strategy descriptions apply.

Various learning style inventories have been developed [20-22]. That used in LS-LS is adapted from the *Myers-Briggs Type Indicator* (MBTI) [22], as the MBTI was found to correlate with students' choice of language learning strategies [9]. The MBTI is based on Jung's theory of psychological types [23]. It describes people in terms of four characteristics: introversion/extraversion; sensing/intuitive; thinking/feeling; perceptive/judging. However, the MBTI questionnaire is extensive, and in the context of LS-LS learners may not be prepared to spend much time. Therefore a much simplified adaptation is used, whereby students select amongst brief descriptions of learning style components [24]. To compensate for the lack of detail, students may indicate that two poles (e.g. thinking/feeling) are both applicable. This results in a less precise learning style descriptor, but it does ensure that students are not forced into providing information about which they are unsure. Indeed, lack of preference in any of the four descriptor pairs is not necessarily negative. It may indicate that the student does not lie at either extreme of the continuum: their individual learning style may encompass both aspects of the paired descriptors. Allowing this possibility in LS-LS ensures that potentially useful learning strategy suggestions are not suppressed by the system as a result of forced selection of one aspect of learning style over another.

The language learning strategy classification system used in LS-LS is adapted from Oxford's *Strategy Inventory for Language Learning* (SILL) [25]. The SILL has been used extensively by researchers, and has been found to have high validity, reliability and utility [26]. It is administered to students as a questionnaire, and measures the frequency with which a student uses *memory, cognitive, compensation, metacognitive, affective* and *social* language learning strategies, giving the result: low, medium or high use, for each category. As with learning style, in LS-LS students identify their current strategy use from short strategy descriptions. As results have shown, information about individuals' use of strategies from different strategy classes can be very useful for research purposes. However, this kind of information is less meaningful to learners. For example, what does it mean to a student to be told that they have 'a medium use of compensation strategies'? Thus LS-LS requires additional information to be overlaid on Oxford's classification scheme. This is provided by a *Strategy Similarity Measure* (based on [11]). This similarity measure is a theoretical construct indicating conceptual similarities amongst strategies. This allows new strategies to be introduced with reference to strategies already used, so suggestions are more meaningful to learners. It also enables strategies to be considered individually, rather than only in the six strategy groups identified by Oxford.

This approach requires learners to be able to identify their current strategy use, as LS-LS obtains initial representations by self-report. A previous study found adults were indeed able to identify their strategy use in a manner similar to that used to acquire the LS-LS student model. Furthermore, most were interested in doing so [27].

In summary, LS-LS is based on four areas of previous research:
- learning strategy classification [25];
- the ability of students to identify their learning strategy use through self-report in a computational environment [27];
- relationships between learning style and strategy choice [9];
- conceptual similarities between learning strategies [11].

The first area concerns the representations for the student model. The second relates to the method of obtaining this information. Points 3 and 4 form the knowledge base: representations used by LS-LS to infer appropriate strategies to recommend to an individual, according to the contents of their student model.

3   Individualised Suggestions of Learning Strategies

As stated above, to build the LS-LS student model learners provide information about their learning style and currently used learning strategies. This is accomplished by viewing descriptions (for an example see part 3 of Figure 1), and selecting the options which apply. The resulting contents for the student model are illustrated in Table 1.

Table 1 shows the student model of an adult male Mainland Chinese learner of English (advanced level), studying English in the U.K. This is presented in full to illustrate a plausible range of learning strategies an individual may use, and the kinds of strategy that might be suggested to others. This includes 26 of the 62 strategies in Oxford's classification [25]. The student model representations are in Prolog:

learning_style([Style_Components]).
learning_style([extravert, sensing, thinking, perceptive]).
learning_strategies(Strategy_Group, [Strategy_List]).

learning_strategies(cognitive, [skimming, analysing_expressions, translation, notes]).
It can be seen that the student model is quite straightforward, both in terms of its contents and, as discussed above, in the model acquisition process.

Table 1. Representations in the LS-LS student model

Learning Style	Strategy Group	Strategy Name
extravert sensing thinking perceptive	cognitive	skimming, analysing expressions, translation, notes.
	metacognitive	overviewing/linking with known, delaying speech to focus on listening, setting goals, planning, seeking practice opportunities, self-monitoring, self-evaluation.
	memory	grouping information, associating/elaborating, structured reviewing, mechanical techniques.
	compensation	using linguistic cues, language switching, getting help, circumlocution/synonyms.
	social	requesting correction, cooperation with peers, cultural understanding, awareness of others' feelings.
	affective	using relaxation/deep breathing/meditation, using music to relax, using a checklist about feelings.

Once representations for the student model are completed, students may receive suggestions of additional strategies that may be useful. Suggested strategies must fulfil two conditions: (1) they may not conflict with the student's learning style; (2) they must have something in common with at least one used strategy. The former is based on Ehrman and Oxford's finding that learning style appears to influence strategy choice [9]. LS-LS therefore contains representations of permitted learning style–learning strategy links. For example, an ISTJ (Introvert, Sensing, Thinking, Judging) learner will be primarily recommended strategies from the groups metacognitive, cognitive and memory. This is because Ehrman and Oxford's data suggested Introverts and Thinkers are generally uncomfortable with social strategies; Sensers and Judgers disliked compensation strategies; Introverts did not like affective strategies. On the positive side: Introverts were very much in favour of metacognitive strategies; Sensers liked cognitive, metacognitive, and in particular, memory strategies; Thinkers were very positive about cognitive strategies, and also liked metacognitive strategies; Judgers liked social, and especially metacognitive strategies.

Point 2 above fulfils the requirement that strategy recommendations be made with reference to something the learner can readily understand. This is accomplished through a database of strategy links based on the *strategy similarity measure*. Table 2 shows excerpts from the database of strategy links in three of the six strategy groups. The first two examples of Table 2 indicate that there is some similarity between the concepts of the memory strategies *representing sounds in memory* and *imagery*. Thus, a student who uses one of these strategies but not the other, will probably appreciate the potential utility of the new strategy due to the similarity of the function of the pair.

The next two entries in Table 2, *analysing expressions* and *contrastive analysis,* show a similar bidirectional relationship, but in the cognitive group. The fifth entry, also concerning cognitive strategies, illustrates how the suggestion of a new strategy may be based on more than one currently used strategy. If a student uses *contrastive analysis* and *deduction*, but not *analysing expressions*, the latter will be suggested with reference to both *contrastive analysis* and *deduction* (assuming there are no objections from the learning style component). The link between *deduction* and *analysing expressions* is also bidirectional, as indicated by entry number 6, as is the link between *contrastive analysis* and *deduction* (not shown).

Table 2. Excerpt from database of strategy links

Used Strategy	Strategy Suggestion
mem: representing sounds in memory	mem: imagery
mem: imagery	mem: representing sounds in memory
cog: analysing expressions	cog: contrastive analysis
cog: contrastive analysis	cog: analysing expressions
cog: deduction	cog: analysing expressions
cog: analysing expressions	cog: deduction
cog: making notes	mem: grouping
comp: avoiding communication	comp: selecting the topic
comp: avoiding communication	comp: adjusting the message

The next entry illustrates that links, and hence recommendations, occur not only between strategies within a strategy group, but also occur *across* groups. *Making notes* is a common cognitive strategy. However, some students do not organise their notes effectively. For such learners, the memory strategy *grouping* may be suggested.

The last two entries show that a single strategy may be used as support for recommending more than one new strategy. This example also illustrates that links are not always bidirectional. Some students *avoid communication*, a compensation strategy, when a topic is problematic. Alternatives may be suggested, e.g. *selecting the topic* or *adjusting the message*. However, the reverse does not occur: a student who uses one or both of these will not receive the suggestion to *avoid communication*.

---

1 You already use *visual imagery* to help you remember vocabulary. There may be times when imagery is difficult. This might occur, for example, when you need to learn abstract words.
2 You may find using *sound* a good substitute for imagery, as these strategies have the same function of using the senses to learn vocabulary. They are both memory strategies.
3 *Representing sounds in memory* involves creating an association between new and known material by using sound. For example, there may be a word in your native language that sounds similar to the new word you are trying to remember. Or the new word may sound similar to another word that you already know in the target language.

Fig. 1. Example of a strategy recommendation

Figure 1 illustrates a strategy recommendation (generated from templates). It first refers to a strategy the student already uses. It then links this to the new strategy. Finally, the new strategy is described. Note that there is no implication that the suggested strategy should *replace* any strategy already used. It is simply stated that it might be a useful strategy when it is difficult to use an existing one. It is up to the learner to decide whether the new strategy is, in fact, more helpful than any they currently apply in a particular situation.

It may be that a new strategy is not suitable: it will not always hold that a visual learner will benefit from *sound* to the extent other learners might. Hence words like 'might' and 'may' in the recommendation. However, recall only those strategies which do not conflict with learning style pass the 'strategy suggestion threshold'.

Once new strategies have been experienced, the learner may return to LS-LS for further suggestions, which can take recently acquired strategies into account.

4   Recommending Computer-Based Environments

Thus far discussion has centred on the first set of suggestions received by students: general recommendations which may be applicable to a variety of language learning contexts. The second set of proposals concerns these new strategies, but includes suggestions of specific computer assisted language learning (CALL) software available *at their institution*, where some of these strategies can be practised.

Jones explains how the institutional context is a major factor in the design of the majority of CALL programs [28]:

> *Most CALL programs are developed at universities... CALL software is usually intended for a particular course at a particular institution with a particular sort of student with particular needs. This exact matching of needs is what makes computer-based courseware so successful for its intended audience, but which can impair its marketability.* [28]

This implies that LS-LS would be severely restricting its applicability if it were not to take into account potentially numerous in-house developments when suggesting CALL activities for a student. Because much of the courseware may have been developed by language teachers, in many situations this will not include intelligent CALL. Nevertheless, because of its design focus on local students, and its recommendation by LS-LS to students because of the potential for them to practise the application of learning strategies which are *appropriate for them*, any lack of individualisation in the CALL software will be less crucial. The 'intelligence' in this approach is found in LS-LS's inferring suitable programs to recommend, depending on characteristics (learning style and current strategy use) of the individual learner.

Including local information requires input from the local tutor. It must be assumed that the tutor is aware of the CALL options available at their institution as, indeed, a good teacher should be. However, it is not assumed that tutors will already be aware of Oxford's language learning strategy classification system: they may learn about these strategies by reviewing the strategy descriptions in LS-LS (as does the student). Figure 2 shows how tutors provide information about available CALL opportunities. This method of inputting information covers a range of CALL types: e.g. concordancers (cognitive–*recognising forms and patterns, analysing expressions, contrastive analysis, deductive reasoning, resourcing*); traditional drills (cognitive–*repetition, recognising forms and patterns, deductive reasoning*); foreign language chat rooms (cognitive–*practising naturalistically*; compensation–*selecting the topic, adjusting the message, coining words, circumlocution/synonyms*; metacognitive–*seeking practice*; affective–*risk-taking*; social–*cooperation*). It can be seen that for a single strategy, there might be several different kinds of program that may be used to experience it. Therefore learners will often be able to select the kind of software they prefer, or use more than one type of CALL to consolidate the use of their new skill.

Strategies expected to be useful in many implementations are listed for two reasons: (1) to make it easy for teachers to input required information; and (2) to encourage tutors to consider the applicability of the most likely strategies (i.e. not overlook them). Further strategies may be entered if the local situation encompasses them. Space is also available to describe *how* learning strategies may be applied. Specific instances of CALL can also be referred to. Recommendations of CALL environments are presented to students exactly as described by the tutor: the relevant strategies are listed, followed by the teacher's textual description. A few examples of CALL programs are given below, to demonstrate the value of this practice facility.

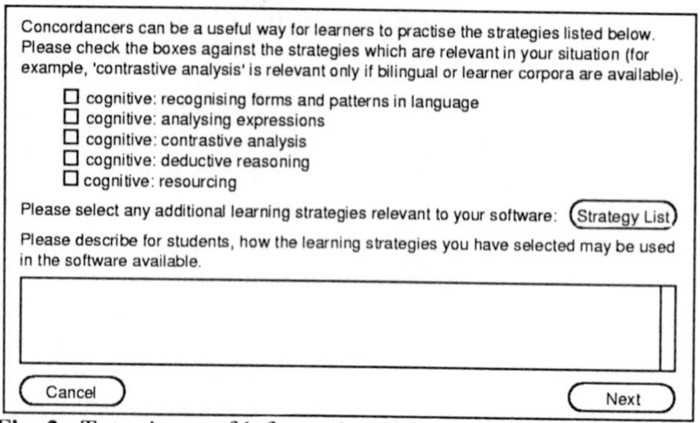

Fig. 2. Tutor input of information about available CALL options

Milton's Electronic Learning and Production Environment aims to help students write appropriately by using a concordancer together with error recognition tasks, a hypertext grammar and databases of underused phrases [29]. Thus it has the potential of encouraging the above-mentioned strategies connected with concordancing, but the *resourcing* and *deduction* opportunities are broader than with many concordancers.

In the context of translation, Metatext is a HyperCard development which has links from the main card containing the source text to datacards where learners may view or send information [30]. Therefore, in addition to improving translation skills, it can be used to explicitly practise the cognitive strategies of *noting* and *resourcing*; and the memory strategies of *grouping* and *using mechanical techniques*.

Sawada et al describe a system with which students may practise writing Japanese Kanji characters and phrases [31]. They can also test their sequencing of strokes in a character, to help them understand the structure of Kanji patterns. Thus learners may extensively practise the cognitive strategy of *formally practising with writing systems*.

Some ITSs contain a model of the target language rules, and also the equivalent rules from a learner's native language, allowing explicit reference to both languages during an interaction [32-35]. Such systems provide opportunities for learners to consider the cognitive strategies of *contrastive analysis* and *language transfer*.

Despite the potential for students to practise a variety of strategies in CALL environments, it is clear they may need guidance on how this might be accomplished– although systems have been designed to foster such skills, they are for the most part not designed with the aim of explicitly tutoring the strategies concerned. Chapelle and Mizuno recognize that much CALL assumes learners are already able to regulate their learning effectively, whereas, in fact, they often do not use the most appropriate strategies [36]. Hence the importance of allowing tutors the space to describe for students, the use of these strategies in the particular CALL contexts (see Figure 2). An advantage students who have used LS-LS might have when using these CALL systems, is that they are by then already aware of the variety of strategies that exist.

Using the student from Table 1, the learner was identified as having the personality attributes ESTP (Extravert, Sensing, Thinking, Perceptive). The rules for generating the sequence of strategy presentations for student selection of used strategies are based on these attributes. Mapping personality attributes to the strategy presentation sequence ensures that learners identify first the strategies they are most likely to use, in case they choose not to complete the full sequence of strategy identification. In our example, cognitive strategies were presented first, as the style components STP each view cognitive strategies positively (and E is neutral) [9]. Second came metacognitive strategies, typically viewed positively by EST, but negatively by P, and so on.

Strategy suggestions were presented, ranked according to personality attributes and strategy similarity measure. In our example, *contrastive analysis* was recommended early, because of the personality component Perceptive, and the used strategies *requesting correction, using linguistic clues, translation* and *analysing expressions*. In contrast, *repetition* was suggested based only on the descriptor Sensing, and came last. This recommendation according to constraints imposed by learning style and the strategy similarity measure, and the ranking of suggestions, ensures that strategies are presented in a sequence reflecting understandability and relevance for the individual.

CALL programs are then suggested, which also fit the constraints of learning style and the strategy similarity measure. These are similarly ranked according to expected utility. For our learner, a bilingual concordancer might be useful, since it allows practice of *contrastive analysis* (a strongly suggested strategy) and also *deduction* (recommended based on one personality attribute and two used strategies). Lower on the list come drills to practise *deduction* and *repetition*. The range of strategy suggestions, and hence CALL suggestions, are likely to vary since even in a small sample of students (5), total suggested strategies ranged from 6 to 16 [24].

An interesting situation has occurred, whereby an intelligent learning environment (LS-LS) will be recommending largely 'unintelligent' programs to students. LS-LS starts from a quite simple student model, performing some complex inferencing [24], to then recommending less adaptive systems. Although these less flexible programs are often criticised for their inability to take into account learner differences, when recommended by LS-LS, such differences have already been catered for.

5   Summary

LS-LS aims to raise student awareness of ways to make their learning more effective, by fostering learner autonomy in a manner that suits their learning style, and is easily understandable according to their current strategies. This occurs as in Figure 3.

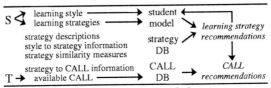

Fig. 3. CALL recommendations

LS-LS prompts students for information about their learning style and approaches to learning, offering descriptions from which they select those aspects they believe apply to their learning. The resulting representations form the two components of the student model. LS-LS also contains a learning strategy database: one part containing strategy descriptions; a second detailing information about strategies typically liked and disliked by learners with different learning styles; a third measuring similarities between pairs of strategies. LS-LS compares information from the student model to the constraints implied in the strategy database (parts 2 and 3), and makes recommendations of potentially helpful strategies to an individual. These recommendations are general: they describe strategies, with examples, but no specific learning materials are suggested. Strategy suggestions are fed back into the student model to be used should the learner later return for a further interaction with LS-LS.

A second database contains representations relating to other CALL systems. This has two parts: a general one detailing kinds of CALL program that can be used to experience different learning strategies; and a specific part describing software available locally. This second part is input by the tutor. LS-LS combines information about strategies it suggested with information in the CALL database, to suggest specific CALL programs a learner might access to try out recommended strategies.

References

1. Linton, F. (1997) Learning to Learn from an ITS, in B. du Boulay & R. Mizoguchi (eds), *Artificial Intelligence in Education*, IOS Press, Amsterdam.
2. Broady, E. & Kenning, M-M. Eds. (1996) *Promoting Learner Autonomy in University Language Teaching*, AFLS/CILT, London.
3. Oxford, R. (1994) Language Learning Strategies: An Update, *ERIC Clearinghouse on Languages and Linguistics*.
4. Fox, J. & Matthews, C. (1991) Learner Strategies and Learner Needs in the Design of CALL Help Systems, *Proceedings of EUROCALL*, Helsinki, 127-132.
5. Kohonen, V. (1992) Experiential Language Learning, in D. Nunan (ed), *Collaborative Language Learning and Teaching*, Cambridge University Press, 14-39.
6. Rubin, J. (1975) What the 'Good Language Learner' Can Teach Us, *TESOL Quarterly* 9(1).
7. Vann, R.J. & Abraham, R.G. (1990) Strategies of Unsuccessful Language Learners, *TESOL Quarterly* 24(2), 177-198.
8. Stevick, E.W. (1989) *Success with Foreign Languages: Seven who achieved it and what worked for them*, Prentice Hall, London.
9. Ehrman, M. & Oxford, R. (1990) Adult Language Learning Styles and Strategies in an Intensive Training Setting, *The Modern Language Journal* 74(3), 311-327.
10. Gillette, B. (1987) Two Successful Language Learners, in C. Faerch & G. Kasper (eds), *Introspection in Second Language Research*, Multilingual Matters, Clevedon, Philadelphia.
11. Bull, S. (1997) Promoting Effective Learning Strategy Use in CALL, *Computer Assisted Language Learning* 10(1), 3-39.
12. Meskill, C. (1991) Language Learning Strategies Advice: A Study on the Effects of On-Line Messaging, *System* 19(3), 277-287.
13. Rubin, J. (1996) Using Multimedia for Learner Strategy Instruction, in R. Oxford (ed), *Language Learning Strategies around the World: Cross-Cultural Perspectives*, Technical Report 13, Second Language Teaching and Curriculum Center, University of Hawaii.
14. Beck, J., Stern, M. & Woolf, B.P. (1997) Cooperative Student Models, in B. du Boulay & R. Mizoguchi (eds) *Artificial Intelligence in Education*, IOS Press, Amsterdam, 127-134.
15. Bull, S. & Pain, H. (1995) "Did I say what I think I said, and do you agree with me?": Inspecting and Questioning the Student Model, in J. Greer (ed), *Proceedings of World Conference on Artificial Intelligence in Education*, AACE, 501-508.
16. Dimitrova, V., Self, J. & Brna, P. (1999) The Interactive Maintenance of Open Learner Models, in S.P. Lajoie & M. Vivet (eds), *Artificial Intelligence in Education*, IOS Press.
17. Kay, J. (1999) Learner Control, submitted for publication.

18. Morales, R., Pain, H. & Conlon, T. (1999) From Behaviour to Understandable Presentation of Learner Models: A Case Study, *Proceedings of Workshop on Open, Interactive and Other Overt Approaches to Learner Modelling*, AIED'99, Le Mans, France, 15-24.

19. Specht, M., Weber, G. & Schöch, V. (1997) ADI: Ein adaptiver Informations-und Lehragent im WWW, in R. Schäfer & M. Bauer (eds) *ABIS-97: 5 GI-Workshop, Adaptivität und Benutzermodellierung in interaktiven Softwaresystemen*, Universität des Saarlandes, 53-60.

20. Felder, R.M. (1993) Reaching the Second Tier: Learning and Teaching Styles in College Science Education, *Journal of College Science Teaching* 23(5), 286-290.

21. Kolb, D. (1984) *Experiential Learning: Experience as the Source of Learning and Development*, Prentice Hall, Englewood Cliffs NJ.

22. Myers, I.B. & McCaulley, M.H. (1985) *Manual: A Guide to the Development and Use of the Myers-Briggs Type Indicator*, Consulting Psychologists Press, Palo Alto.

23. Jung, C.G. (1971) *Psychological Types*, Princeton University Press.

24. Bull, S. & Ma, Y. (submitted) Raising Learner Awareness of Language Learning Strategies in Situations of Limited Resources, submitted for publication.

25. Oxford, R.L. (1990) *Language Learning Strategies: what every teacher should know*, Heinle and Heinle Publishers, Boston MA.

26. Oxford, R.L. & Burry-Stock, J.A. (1995) Assessing the Use of Language Learning Strategies Worldwide with the ESL/EFL Version of the Strategy Inventory for Language Learning (SILL), *System* 23(1), 1-23.

27. Bull, S., Pain, H. & Brna, P. (1993) Student Modelling in an Intelligent Computer Assisted Language Learning System: Language Transfer and Learning Strategies, in T-W. Chan (ed), *Proceedings of International Conference on Computers in Education*, Taiwan, 121-126.

28. Jones, C. (1998) Multimedia and Vocabulary Learning: A Marriage Made in Heaven?, in K. Cameron (ed), *Multimedia CALL: Theory and Practice*, Elm Bank Publications, Exeter.

29. Milton, J. (1998) Exploiting L1 and Interlanguage Corpora in the Design of an Electronic Language Learning and Production Environment, in S. Granger (ed), *Learner English on Computer*, Addison Wesley Longman Limited, London, 186-198.

30. Gillespie, J.H. & Gray, B. (1992) HyperCard and the Development of Translation and Vocabulary Skills, *Computer Assisted Language Learning* 5(1-2), 3-11.

31. Sawada, S., Higashigawa, L., Bandoh, H. & Nakagawa, M. (1997) A CAI System for Overseas Students to Learn Reading and Writing of Japanese Text, in B. du Boulay & R. Mizoguchi (eds) *Artificial Intelligence in Education*, IOS Press, Amsterdam, 653-655.

32. Bull, S. (1995) Handling Native and Non-Native Language Transfer in CALL: Theory and Practice, in R. Wakely, A. Barker, D. Frier, P. Graves & Y. Suleiman (eds), *Language Teaching and Learning in Higher Education: Issues and Perspectives*, CILT, London.

33. Catt, M. & Hirst, G. (1990), An Intelligent CALI System for Grammatical Error Diagnosis, *Computer Assisted Language Learning* 3, 3-26.

34. Schuster, E. (1986) The Role of Native Grammars in Correcting Errors in Second Language Learning, *Computational Intelligence* 2, 93-98.

35. Wang, Y. & Garigliano, R. (1995), Empirical Studies and Intelligent Language Tutoring, *Instructional Science* 10, 225-240.

36. Chapelle, C. & Mizuno, S. (1989) Students' Strategies with Learner-Controlled CALL, CALICO Journal, Dec 1989, 25-47.

An Empirical Approach to On-Line Learning in SIETTE

Ricardo Conejo, Eva Millán, José-Luis Pérez-de-la-Cruz, Mónica Trella

Departamento de Lenguajes y Ciencias de la Computación
Universidad de Málaga. Campus de Teatinos s/n, 29079 Málaga. SPAIN
{conejo, eva, perez, trella}@iaia.lcc.uma.es

Abstract. SIETTE is a web-based evaluation tool that implements CAT theory. With the help of a simulation program, different empirical experiments have been performed with SIETTE with two different goals: a) to study the influence of the parameters of characteristic item curves and selection criteria in test length and accuracy; and b) to study different learning strategies for these parameters. The results of the experiments are shown and interpreted.

1 Introduction

One of the subtasks in an ITS is the evaluation of student's knowledge. SIETTE system [3] has been proposed as a general-purpose web based evaluation system. SIETTE implements *Computer Adaptive Test* (CAT) [5] methodology to improve its performance by reducing the number of questions needed to estimate student's level of knowledge, and is based upon the classical *Item Response Theory* (IRT). SIETTE has been designed as a reusable component to implement a *generic task* [1] for evaluating the knowledge level of a student about certain domain.

Teachers can continuously update the contents of SIETTE question database. This *open architecture* allows the system to evolve and improve its performance over the years. On the other hand, this *on-line* development of question databases is just the opposite of the desired scheme for classical item calibration. Fortunately, the potential great number of students that take the tests provides valuable information that can be used to successively improve teacher's estimations of item parameters.

The main contribution of this paper is an empirical analysis of two issues, namely, the behaviour of SIETTE when using incorrectly calibrated item pools and the feasibility of *on-line* methods for item calibration in SIETTE. The empirical method proposed and implemented uses a program that simulates the behaviour of teachers and students using Monte Carlo techniques.

Item Response Theory (IRT), also known as Latent Trait Theory, was originated in the late 1960s [2]). In a testing context, the *latent trait* is an attribute (*knowledge level*) that accounts for the consistency of test responses. Each question or item is assigned a function (*Item Characteristic Curve*, ICC) that represents the probability of answering to it correctly given the student's knowledge level $\theta \in (-\infty, +\infty)$. Let us represent this probability by the expression: $P(U_i = 1 | \theta)$ or simply by P_i. One of the main problems in IRT theory is to find out the ICCs. It is usually assumed that ICCs belong to a family of functions that depend on one, two or three parameters. These functions are constructed based on the normal or the logistic distribution function. In the three-parameter logistic model the ICC is described by:

$$P_i(\theta) = c_i + (1 - c_i) \frac{1}{1 + e^{-1.7a_i(\theta - b_i)}},$$ (1)

where c_i is the guessing factor, b_i is the difficulty of the question and a_i is the discrimination factor. The guessing factor is the probability that a student with no knowledge at all answers the question correctly. The difficulty represents the knowledge level in which the student has equal probability to answer or fail the question, besides the guessing factor. The discrimination factor is proportional to the slope of the curve. If the discrimination factor is high then students with level lower than b will probably fail and students with lever higher than b will probably give the right answer. Assuming that the ICC belongs to this family, the problem of calibrating questions can be formulated as finding the best estimations for the parameters.

Section 2 of this paper describes the implementation of IRT used in SIETTE and the simulator program, and presents some empirical results obtained for correctly and incorrectly calibrated item pools. Section 3 describes a new on-line learning procedure that improves the behaviour of the system by learning item parameters. Finally some conclusions and open issues are addressed.

2 Simulating the Behavior of SIETTE

In this section, we will describe the techniques that we have used to emulate the behavior of the SIETTE system. First, we will describe how to simulate a correctly calibrated item pool.

2.1. Student, Item and Test Simulation

SIETTE implements the IRT model assuming that student's knowledge can be represented as a random variable θ that takes integer values between 0 and K_{max}. This simplification implies that only a fixed and finite number of states of knowledge are considered. Simulated students as proposed in [4] are used. Every student is represented by his/her value for θ. The simulation begins with the random generation of a population of N students, i. e., with the generation of N random concrete values for θ. These values are considered constant during the test (that is, no student learning occurs while taking the test). In the simulations described here the population has been generated to be uniformly distributed in 0, ..., K_{max}. However, other distributions have also been used, not yielding significant differences in the outputs.

Each item is represented by its ICC. An ICCs is also given by K values, corresponding to the conditional probabilities of giving the correct answer to the question given that the student belongs to each of the K classes. The simulator uses a set of Q void questions (ICCs), that are assumed to be correctly calibrated. These ICCs are generated by assigning values to the parameters a, b, and c in a continuous logistic function, and taking the corresponding values for the K percentiles. The simulator allows changing these parameters or to assign them random values, in order to obtain different item pools.

At the beginning of the test, the student is assigned an a-priori probability of belonging to each of the K classes in which the students can be classified. The posterior probability is computed applying Bayes' rule. The final result of a test is a distribution of probabilities that the student belongs to each class. The test finishes (in the general case) when the probability of belonging to certain class reaches a fixed threshold p (close to 1). This criterion is equivalent to setting a maximum threshold for the standard deviation, which is the one widely used in IRT. Then, we can say that the student belongs to this class with a confidence factor greater than p. Other termination criteria can be used, as for example the maximum number of question to be posed.

The simulator successively poses a question to the virtual student and updates his/her probabilities of belonging to each class. This question can be selected randomly or using CATs criteria. The procedure is repeated until the termination criterion is met. Student's behaviour is determined according to his/her estimated knowledge level and the conditional probability that a student of this knowledge level solves the question correctly. That is, if the virtual student has a knowledge level k and the value of the question ICC for knowledge k is p, a semi-random uniformly distributed value q in [0,1] is generated. If $q>p$, the system will consider that the student gave a correct answer to the question.

2.2. Simulating a Correctly Calibrated Item Pool

The first empirical analysis carried out concerns how the accuracy of student's classification and the average number of questions posed T depend on the number K of knowledge levels considered and on the confidence factor p. The percentage of correctly classified students has been computed for an item pool of $Q = 103$ randomly generated questions (ICCs), where b is uniformly distributed in $[1, K_{max-1}]$, $a=1.2$, and $c= 0.0$ The simulation generates $N = 105$ students. Table 1 shows the results.

The interpretation is that, even with a correctly calibrated item pool, it is not easy to classify "all" the students correctly. This is due to the IRT model itself, that assumes that it is possible (but with a low probability) that a student with a low knowledge level will answer a difficult question correctly and viceversa. The results also show that the percentage of correctly classified students depends more on the confidence factor required that on the number of classes used. On the other hand, the number of questions posed is strongly related to the number of classes considered. For practical reasons, the test should have as few questions as possible, because long tests would be too boring for real students. This practical consideration leads to a compromise between the number of questions and the number of classes.

Table 1. Accuracy of IRT approximation

Number of classes K	Confidence factor $\rho = 0.75$		Confidence factor $\rho = 0.90$		Confidence factor $\rho = 0.99$	
	% of correctly classified students	Average number of questions posed T	% of correctly classified students	Average number of questions posed T	% of correctly classified students	Average number of questions posed T
3	84.05	2.00	95.82	3.58	99.46	5.65
5	81.61	6.23	92.76	10.38	99.37	19.27
7	80.96	11.11	92.85	18.16	99.38	33.12
9	80.86	16.15	92.93	26.39	99.42	47.27
11	80.52	21.19	92.92	34.54	99.26	60.85

The second empirical analysis studies how the accuracy of student's classification and the average number of questions posed T depend on the quality of the item pool, i.e., on the parameters a, b and c. If a increases, the percentage of correctly classified students increases, and the average value of T decreases. If c increases, this percentage decreases a little, but the number of questions posed is much bigger. Tables 2 and 3 show the results obtained by using different values for a and c, (ρ=0.90 and K=7).

Table 2. Guessing factor influence

Guessing factor c	% of correctly classified students	Average number of questions posed T
0.00	92.85	18.16
0.10	92.37	25.34
0.25	92.11	36.05
0.33	91.73	43.37
0.50	91.49	63.37

Table 3. Discrimination factor influence

Discrimination factor c	% of correctly classified students	Average number of questions posed
0.20	90.4	174.9
0.50	91.5	35.2
0.70	91.9	26.3
1.20	92.8	18.1
1.70	93.8	15.3
2.20	95.4	14.8

These results show the great influence of c in the number of questions needed. The discrimination factor, a, does not have such a great influence in the number of questions if it is bigger than certain threshold. For values smaller than that threshold, the number of questions needed grows very fast. That means that items with low discrimination factor are not informative enough and therefore yield too long tests.

The third empirical analysis carried out concerns how the accuracy of student's classification and the average value of T depend on the number K of knowledge levels considered and the selection criterion for posing the next question.

It is known that a CAT procedure can be introduced to improve the performance of the classical IRT model. Two different criteria to select the next best question to ask have been implemented in our simulator: a) *bayesian criterion,* that selects the question that minimises the posterior variance of the student knowledge distribution and b) *adaptive criterion,* that selects the question which difficulty equals the average knowledge of the student. Both criteria are equivalent for logistic ICC, as proved theoretically. Table 4 shows the empirical result obtained with the simulator (with ρ=0.90). It is interesting to compare these results with those obtained in the central files of Table 1, that correspond to selecting the items randomly:

Table 4. Accuracy of the CAT approximation

Number of classes K	Bayesian *Selection criterion*		Adaptive *Selection criterion*	
	% of correctly classified students	*Average number of questions posed T*	*% of correctly classified students*	*Average number of questions posed T*
3	96.06	3.58	95.62	3.58
5	93.31	6.87	94.67	7.37
7	92.75	8.70	94.43	9.03
9	92.53	9.85	94.23	10.14
11	92.10	10.71	94.14	11.02

The number of questions needed is almost half of the number needed using random selection. These results encourage the use of a CAT procedure, but, as it will be shown later, it is very important to assure that the item pool is correctly calibrated. The adaptive criterion has been chosen over the bayesian one because it gives similar results, but its computational cost is much smaller (this is not surprising, since our ICCs are a discretizations of the logistic model). Similar results are obtained with other discrimination and guessing factors.

2.3. Simulating an Incorrectly Calibrated Item Pool

In Section 3.1, we have assumed that the item pool was correctly calibrated. This is not a fair assumption. In fact it can never be perfectly calibrated, because there is a hazardous component that leads to a known bounded error. To simulate the behaviour of an incorrectly calibrated item pool, let us consider that each question in the database has two ICCs: the *real* ICC and the *estimated* ICC. This is the usual situation when the item pool has been calibrated by a human teacher/expert. Our goal is to study the influence of incorrect calibration in the results of the test. To this end, the simulator uses the real ICC to simulate the answer of the question as described in Section 3.2 and the estimated ICC for any other task.

First, we will assume that the teacher has correctly calibrated the difficulty parameter, but not the discrimination factor a. Table 5 shows the results obtained assuming that each question has a discrimination factor randomly distributed between 0.7 and 1.7 and that the teacher has assigned a fixed value a_e to all of them ($\rho=0.90$ and $K=7$). Compare the results with the ones shown in Tables 1 and 3:

Table 5. Discrimination factor incorrectly estimated

Estimated discrimination factor a_e	Random *Selection criterion*		Adaptive *Selection criterion*	
	% of correctly classified students	*Average number of questions posed T*	*% of correctly classified students*	*Average number of questions posed T*
0.2	60.5	67.1	96.6	146.5
0.5	83.2	36.0	96.2	28.0
0.7	93.2	26.6	96.2	16.8
1.2	92.1	18.4	93.9	8.9
1.7	86.1	14.7	86.7	6.4

If discrimination factor estimated a_e is bigger than certain lower bound, the percentage of students correctly classified and the number of questions needed do not change very much. For any reasonable estimation of the discrimination factor, the percentage of correctly classified students depends more on the number of questions posed that on the exact value of the estimated discrimination factor.

In a second experiment, we assume that some estimations of the difficulty parameter are erroneous, but the error is not biased. That is, sometimes the estimated difficulty is higher and sometimes lower than the real difficulty, but this error is normally distributed around the real difficulty. The same assumption will be made for the discrimination factor. We will call this an *equilibrated item pool*. The justification for this assumption is that, in fact, the knowledge level assigned to a student has not a real meaning by itself: it is only a relative value, like the IQ used in psychology. There is a degree of freedom that is commonly solved in the classical MML parameter estimation procedures by assuming that, for the students in the testing group, the knowledge level has certain distribution. The assumption of an equilibrated item pool reduces this degree of freedom by linking test results to teacher's wishes. If the item pool is prepared by a group of teachers, this hypothesis can be interpreted as a consensus in the meaning of each of the classes (levels) considered. Table 6 shows the results obtained from an equilibrated item pool (randomly constructed) with around 35% wrong assigned difficulty factors, $p=0.90$, and $K=7$ classes:

Table 6. Equilibrated item pool ($p=0.90$)

Estimated discrimination factor a,	Random *Selection criterion*		Adaptive *Selection criterion*	
	% of correctly classified students	Average number of questions posed T	% of correctly classified students	Average number of questions posed T
0.2	55.4	78.2	85.4	186.8
0.5	83.1	32.1	82.4	33.3
0.7	85.4	25.8	81.1	18.3
1.2	83.1	16.0	78.4	8.6
1.7	73.7	12.0	71.4	6.1

Logically, the percentage of correctly classified students has decreased, but the discrimination factor and the selection criterion applied play a very important role. The most significant conclusion is that, if the item pool is incorrectly calibrated, better results are obtained when applying the random criterion instead of the adaptive, which seems very logical. The second is that the lower the estimated discrimination, the higher the accuracy of the classification. Unfortunately, when the discrimination decreases the number of questions posed increases, and, if it is too small (smaller than 0.5) the accuracy decreases very quickly.

The good behaviour of small discrimination factors is due to the smaller distance between the estimated and the real ICCs. If the question is incorrectly calibrated, it is better to assume it is not too informative. The fact that the random method shows a better behaviour is explained by the number of questions posed.

In Table 7, the hypotheses are the same as in 6, but we use tests with a fixed number of questions (confidence factor changes accordingly):

Table 7. Equilibrated item pool (fixed number of questions)

	Random *Selection criterion*		Adaptive *Selection criterion*	
Estimated discrimination factor a,	*% of correctly classified students*	*Average number of questions posed*	*% of correctly classified students*	*Average number of questions posed*
0.7	85.6	25	85.1	25
1.2	85.3	25	85.4	25
1.7	83.6	25	80.2	25

Note that the results are similar (sometimes even better using the random criterion) due to the fact that the main advantage of the adaptive criterion (the smaller number of question it usually needs) was lost when fixing the number of questions. Different results but similar conclusions are obtained with other values for ρ and K.

3   On-line Learning

Taking into account that the results of the test are mainly correct if it can be assumed that the questions set is equilibrated and enough questions are posed to the student; it would be possible to use the results of the test get a better estimation for the ICCs. This has been called *on-line calibration* in IRT literature [5]. None of the methods described for on-line calibration, like the EM or BIMAIN are used in our simulator. However it would be possible to improve the behaviour of the learning mechanism if some extra information could be added, for example if we know that some questions are correctly calibrated and some of them are new (as proposed by Mislevy, cited by Wainer in [5]). A bootstrapping learning procedure can also be used.

In SIETTE, it is possible to learn the probability of each value θ of the ICC array directly from the responses of an examinee that has been classified as belonging to certain class θ. After an examinee has finished a test, all questions that compose the test are fed with the global result obtained and the response (correct/incorrect) to that question. A new *learned ICC* (ICC_L) can be obtained by just dividing the total number of positive cases $C^+(\theta)$ by the total number of cases $C(\theta)$. The better the results of the test, the better the quality of the learning process.

3.1.   Incremental and Non-Incremental Learning

Learning takes place when the *current estimated ICC* (ICC_E) is replaced by the new *learned ICC* (ICC_L) This could be done a) incrementally, that is each time a test is completed and keeping all the information from previous examinees; b) by packages, that is, after a fixed number of examinees has completed the test. The new ICC is learned only from the most recent examinees' data without previous information; c) non-incrementally, that is after a complete set of examinees has passed the test.

In the incremental and package modes there could be a problem if the number of examinees in the package is small, because some values of the ICC could be out of experimental cases. This problem is even more serious at the beginning of the incremental mechanism, because there is only one case available. The solution to this problem is to include a small amount M of initial experimental cases that makes the learned ICC be initially equal to the current estimated ICC. In the simulator, this contour condition has been included only in the incremental mode, so in this case the ICC_L is obtained by

$$ICC_L(\theta) = \frac{M \times ICC_E(\theta) + C^+(\theta)}{M + C(\theta)}. \tag{1}$$

In the learning mechanism described below, the number of examinees needed for a calibration depends on the number of questions in the database L, the average number of questions in each test $\overline{N}$, the number of classes or knowledge levels that has been considered K, and the total number of examinees n. The average number of singleton cases that are available to learn the value $ICC_L(\theta)$ is:

$$\overline{C(\theta)} = \frac{\overline{N}}{L \times K} \times n. \tag{2}$$

It has to be taken into account that to estimate a probability from $C(\theta)$ random event observations the following expression applies:

$$p_e = \frac{C^+(\theta) \pm a\sigma}{C(\theta)}, \tag{3}$$

where p_e is the estimated probability, p is the real probability, σ is the standard deviation of the binomial distribution $\sigma = \sqrt{C(\theta) \times p \times (1-p)}$ and a is a constant. So, for example to be 95% sure that the real probability is estimated with an error of $p \pm 0.05$, if p is in the neighborhood of 0.5 (worst case) we should take a sample of $C(\theta)=400$. On the other hand, in this problem not all cases observed come from the right population, because there are also can be errors in the classification process. Our working hypothesis is that the errors present in an equilibrated item pool are compensated. The examinee is sometimes classified higher and sometimes lower.

3.2. Measuring the Learning

The great advantage of using a simulator is that there is complete control over all of the variables that influence the system performance, and that the behaviour of the examinees is only conditioned by their a-priori-known knowledge. So a direct way to measure of the goodness of the learning mechanism could be to measure the improvement in the test performance: the percentage of correctly-classified examinees should increase. Another way of measuring the learning is to define a distance between the real ICC (ICC_A) and the learned ICC (ICC_L). We have selected the simplest distance function:

$$d(ICC_L, ICC_A) = \frac{\sum_{k=0}^{K_{max}} |ICC_L(\theta) - ICC_A(\theta)|}{K} \tag{4}$$

The goodness of the calibration of an item pool can be measured by the average distance among its elements. Table 8 shows the results obtained with each learning mode, at the end of a set of 10^2, 10^3, 10^4 and 10^5 tests, where $p=0.90$, $K=7$, and the initial question database is an equilibrated item pool of $L=116$ questions, with around 50% incorrectly estimated difficulty parameters. The true value for the discrimination factor of all questions in the set is 1.2 but all of them have been estimated initially to be 0.7. The selection criterion was random.

Table 8. Non-incremental, package and incremental learning with random selection

Learning procedure	Examinees learning sample size	% of correctly classified students	Average number of questions	Average cases for learning $C(\theta)$	Average distance to the correct set	% of questions with correctly estimated difficulty
Non-incremental learning	0	75.9	23.8	0	0.090	51.7
	100	74.0	24.7	2.8	0.089	49.1
	1000	74.9	23.6	28.9	0.042	94.8
	10000	75.9	23.8	294.6	0.035	100
	100000	75.8	23.9	2945.1	0.033	100
Packages of 1000 learning	0	75.9	23.8	0	0.090	51.7
	1000	76.1	23.7	29.1	0.046	89.7
	10000	77.2	16.8	18.3	0.045	94.8
	100000	71.8	13.7	13.7	0.061	71.5
Packages of 10000 learning	0	75.9	23.8	0	0.090	51.7
	10000	76.0	23.9	293.8	0.035	100
	100000	87.3	19.2	232.3	0.012	100
Incremental learning	0	75.9	23.8	0	0.090	51.7
	100	73.0	21.9	2.1	0.079	58.8
	1000	81.4	20.8	25.2	0.041	94.8
	10000	88.1	19.4	238.4	0.017	100
	100000	90.2	19.1	2360.8	0.009	100

It should be noted that the upper bound of learning is given by the results obtained with a correct set. Table 1a shows that for $p=0.90$ and $K=7$, the correct set will classify the 92.8% of examinees correctly, requiring an average of 18.1 questions with the random criterion. The percentage of correct classified student shown in Tables 8 are the average during the experiment, including the initial cases when questions have not been modified yet.

Non-incremental learning exhibits good results for approximately more than 10^4 examinees. Package learning is not so good if the package size is smaller than that size. The reason is that there are not enough values to estimate the ICC probabilities for each class. In fact, table 8 show that, if the package is small, there is no convergence. The explanation of this behaviour is that there is a great variance in the learned ICC from just 1000 examinees, and if a poor quality ICC replaces the current estimation the following generation will not be evaluated correctly. Table 8 shows that the incremental learning mode has a better behaviour. ICCs are updated continuously, so both the performance of the test and the quality of the learning process are better. Table 9 shows the results of the same experiment but applying the adaptive criterion to select the question. The criterion to finish the test has been turned off and replaced by a fixed number of questions posed to every examinee, around the same figure that has been used in previous experiment. The results are now even better than those obtained with random criterion. The explanation is that with the same number of questions, the adaptive test classifies better than the random test, so learning is also improved.

Table 9. Incremental learning with adaptive selection and a fixed number of question posed

Examinees learning sample size	% of correctly classified students	Average number of questions	Average cases for learning C(θ)	Average distance to the correct set	% of questions with right estimated difficulty
0	80.9	20	-	0.090	51.7
100	82.0	20	2.0	0.079	55.2
1000	90.2	20	24.2	0.045	94.8
10000	95.1	20	245.9	0.019	100
100000	96.1	20	2462	0.009	100

3.4. Parametric and Non-Parametric Models

SIETTE is designed to be a non-parametric IRT model and it is not necessary to assume any shape for the ICCs. Unlike others non-parametric models, SIETTE does not attempt to approximate a continuous function for the ICC from a sparse set of points, but it deals directly with those points. The above learning mechanism does not make any assumption about the shape so it is appropriate for the non-parametric approach. Another point of view could be that SIETTE deals with $K-1$ parameters that are the conditional probabilities of each knowledge level. However, there are also some disadvantages in the non-parametric approach. First of all, the classical 1, 2 and 3-parameter models need much less information to be calibrated than the SIETTE model for any $K-1$ greater than 3. But a non-parametric learning mechanism can be converted in a more efficient parametric mechanism simply by approximating the just learned ICC by a member of the family of functions considered. This approximation can be done by different methods. In our simulator the sum of weighted minimum squares between the ICC_L and the isomorphic discrete transforms of the logistic family is computed, and the more similar logistic curve is selected. Tables 10 show the results of parametric learning using random selection criterion for 10^3, 10^4 examinees. It should be compared to Table 8.

Table 10 Non-incremental and incremental parametric learning with random selection

	Examinees learning sample size	% of correctly classified students	Average number of questions	Average cases for learning C(θ)	Average distance to the correct set	% of questions with right estimated difficulty
Non incremental parametric learning	0	75.8	23.9	-	0.090	51.7
	100	77.0	22.2	2.1	0.101	44.8
	1000	76.5	23.4	27.4	0.044	92.2
	10000	76.9	23.9	293.4	0.034	100
	100000	75.8	23.9	2949.5	0.033	100
Incremental parametric learning	0	75.8	23.9	-	0.090	51.7
	100	83.0	25.8	2.8	0.074	60.3
	1000	85.1	22.4	27.3	0.037	96.5
	10000	91.2	20.7	255.6	0.012	100
	100000	92.5	20.3	2509.8	0.007	100

Another interesting point is that there seems to be a limit in the approximation that can be achieved with non-incremental learning, either parametric or non-parametric. The explanation of this residual error probably lies on the variance of the random selection of questions from the equilibrated set. The original 116 question set is equilibrated, but the subsets of questions used in the test are not necessary equilibrated.

4 Conclusions

Using a simulator program and applying Monte Carlo methods, we have studied the behaviour of IRT and CAT in the SIETTE system in order to know the quality of the information that can be extracted from a single test and the expected number of questions needed.

For most applications in ITS it is enough to deal with 5-7 knowledge levels about the domain. Less than 10 questions are needed (if they are correctly calibrated). It is desirable to initially calibrate the question set, but it is also possible to trust in the criterion of the teacher(s) that defines the test, and improve its performance by the on-line learning mechanism described. On-line calibration of the ICCs could be done directly, according to the responses of the student and the final result obtained at the end of the test. It also can be done more efficiently if it can be assumed that the ICCs shapes can be described by a family of functions.

If the test is not supposed to be correctly calibrated (i.e. many new questions have been added recently) the best policy to follow is to assign a reasonable low discrimination factor to the incoming questions. It will also be necessary to turn off the adaptive behaviour or even better, keep the adaptive behaviour but force it to increase the number of questions needed to complete the test. This constraint should be eliminated once the question set has been self-calibrated.

The results presented in this paper are obtained from empirical experiments in a simulated environment. It would be also necessary to develop some experiments with real world data. On the other hand, we are currently working in a formalisation of the concept of *equilibrated item pool* and in a theoretical demonstration of the results obtained empirically with the simulator.

References
1. Chandrasekaran, B. (1992). Generic Task: Evolution of an idea. *Technical Report. Laboratory for AI Research. Ohio University. Columbus OH.*
2. Lord, F. M. &. N. M. R. (1968). *Statistical theories of mental test scores.* Reading, MA: Addison-Wesley.
3. Ríos, A., Millán, E., Trella, M., Pérez-de-la-Cruz, J. L., & Conejo, R. (1999). Internet Based Evaluation System. In *Proceedings of the 9th World Conference of Artificial Intelligence and Education AIED'99* (pp. 387-394).
4. VanLehn, K., Ohlsson, S., & Nason, R. (1995). Applications of Simulated Students: An Exploration. *Journal of Artificial Intelligence and Education, 5*(2), 135-175.
5. Wainer, H. (ed.). (1990). *Computerized adaptive testing: a primer.* Hillsdale, NJ: Lawrence Erlbaum Associates.

Cooperative Problem-Seeking Dialogues in Learning

John Cook

University of North London, School of Informatics and Multimedia Technology,
2-16 Eden Grove, London N7 8EA.
j.cook@unl.ac.uk

Abstract. It is proposed in this paper that interactions relating to cooperative problem-seeking can be seen as revolving around a cooperative problem-seeking dialogue model of 'find-predict-explain-refine'. We describe Meta-Muse, a pedagogical agent that was designed to 'structure interactions' and hence facilitate problem-seeking dialogues. The paper describes results from a detailed analysis of the transcribed corpus of the interactions that took place between cooperating students when engaged with MetaMuse. The main empirical results were an elaboration of our cooperative problem-seeking dialogue model and some general results. The paper concludes with a brief discussion of how our empirical findings can be generalized to a re-implementation of MetaMuse.

1 Introduction

Unlike more formalised domains, e.g. physics and mathematics, the nature of dialogues that result from cooperative learning in open domains remains unclear. The fundamental problem is this: when we want to be creative there is often an initial stage where we pick the problem that we want to solve. When we learn this ability to seek out a problem, dialogue with a teacher or with other learners can play an important role as part of an interactive learning mechanism [10]. As well as articulating and explaining a creative intention to peers and tutor (i.e. cooperative learning), the learner will also internalise these dialogues as they become better able to problem-seek. Self-reflection on these creative intentions can be fine-tuned by reference to a history of external dialogues that the learner has been exposed to. Furthermore, newly devised creative intentions can be 'tested-out' by exposing them to further external dialogue. However, such problem-seeking dialogues — that relate to creative intentions — have in the past been little studied. Furthermore, attempts to build computer-based tools to support cooperative learning in such open, problem-seeking domains are few and far between.

One approach to researching cooperative learning has been termed the "interaction paradigm" [7]. The interaction paradigm aims to understand and model the relationship between different types of learning and types of communicative interactions involving learners. The research described in this paper is particularly interested in developing models of interaction that can be used as a basis for the design of Intelligent Tutoring Systems (ITSs). A model of an educational process, with its attendant theory, can be used to form the basis for design of a computer tool for education [2]. For example, Baker and Lund [3] describe a model of task-oriented dialogue that forms the basis of design and implementation of tools for computer-mediated communication between learners and teachers in a computer-supported collaborative learning environment. In this case, a computational model is not directly linked into a system component. However, if we accept Baker's [2] argument that models are not, by their nature, necessarily computational, this opens up a wide range of possible ways in which theories and models can form the bases of design of educational artefacts. As Baker [2] also points out, what is required of such an endeavor is that the specific nature of the relations between theory, corpus, 'model' and design of ITS be made as explicit as possible as legitimate objects of scientific discussion and as means of generalizing findings towards re-design. The author's previous work [5, 6] describes precisely such a principled relation for the case of an ITS for learning musical composition. This previous work by the author explored the systematic relationships involved when moving from theory, to an analysis of corpus data, to the instantiation of computational model, and then on to computational implementation.

In the paper we propose that interactions relating to problem-seeking can be seen as revolving around an interactive learning mechanism of 'find-predict-explain-refine' *(theory,* described in Section 2). We briefly describe a pedagogical agent called MetaMuse that was designed to 'structure interactions' in such a way that would, it was predicted, facilitate problem-seeking dialogues *(computational implementation,* Section 4). However, although the users in an initial evaluation of Meta-Muse [4] reacted favorably, the initial evaluation of the pedagogical agent did not give much insight into the following question: what are the interactive means by which learning agents engage in cooperative problem-seeking? This paper addresses this question by describing results from a recent detailed analysis of a transcribed *corpus* of the face-to-face interactions that took place between cooperating students when engaged with the pedagogical agent MetaMuse (described in Section 6). The paper concludes with a brief discussion of how our analysis findings can be generalized to a re-implementation of our *computational implementation* (MetaMuse).

2 Problem-Seeking

The need for dialogue is especially relevant in open-ended, problem-seeking domains such as musical composition learning [5]. Although we shall use music as the example domain in this paper, we claim that the idea of problem-seeking has implications for other open domains.

Given the open-endedness in music, both in the sense of the problems that could be addressed, and in the sense of the space of possible 'solutions', any educational intervention must be similarly open. A teacher can not simply be directive and "transfer" knowledge because, in problem-seeking domains, there is no "correct" body of knowledge. Teaching interventions can not be restricted to the giving of feedback on simple correct or incorrect response. Like knowledge in the humanities [9], for example, in the domain of musical composition knowledge is essentially problematical: it is not just a question of solving a problem, it is more a question of *seeking out the nature of the problem* and then devising an approach to solving it.

Baker [1] has proposed that argumentation between students is not really about anyone convincing anyone else, nor just about co-constructing knowledge: it is also about defining what it is we are talking about, about clarifying and differentiating concepts (the "co-elaboration of meaning and knowledge" as Baker [1] puts it). Consequently, in this paper we are proposing that if two student peers are engaged in a problem-seeking, cooperative dialogue then the interactions will not focus on 'winning the argument' or 'persuading your partner', it will involve an acceptance by both participants that they will attempt to *'find and refine'* a problem specification; where a problem specification is a description of a problem that is 'interesting' or novel.

Empirical work by Cook [6] shows that in the domain of musical composition, problem-seeking and creative problem-solving interactions had the underlying goals of *'probing, target, clarify* and *give reasons'*. The learner goals of 'clarify' and 'give reasons' have some similarities with Baker's proposal that argumentation involves a process of "clarifying and differentiating concepts" (Baker, personal communication, April 1999). In particular we agree that clarifying concepts is an important component of argumentation. We will now describe the underlying goals observed in Cook [6] in more detail. Specifically, the results of early empirical work [6] indicate that the most frequently used teaching interventions related to problem-seeking were 'critical *probing'* (focused questions were used by a teacher which were based on observations of a student's musical phrase; these questions had the goal of helping the learner 'find' a problem specification) and *'target* monitoring or reflection level' (open-ended questioning that involved the teacher's attempts to elicit verbal self-explanations from the learner about their own attempts at specifying a problem). Learner problem-seeking involved 'critical *clarification'* (elaboration and refinement of some point may be requested or given because (i) a previous attempt was unclear or (ii) a response was required) and 'critical *give reasons'* (any interaction that involves the giving of criteria as a reason). Interaction relating to problem-seeking, therefore, was seen to revolve around a process of find-predict-explain-refine; this process was achieved (by the interacting agents) primarily through the adoption of the goals 'probing, target, clarify and give reasons'.

3 Example of Cooperative Problem-Seeking

Table 1 shows a short face-to-face interaction that is taken from session 5 of the study described below. 'L' and 'C' are study participants and are engaging in what we are calling cooperative problem-seeking (the first part of creative problem-solving). Table 1 shows us how the two study participants cooperate to 'seek' out an idea that they want to work on. What evolves is a joint musical intention to use large interval leaps to create a dramatic effect. Towards the end of the extract shown in Table 1 there is some 'clarification' of what it is that is being talked about, i.e. that the music will sound like a "horror theme".

Table 1. Example of cooperative problem-seeking interactions

L: Do you want to try a different one?

C: Okay then [CLICKS OPTION 1] okay, so this time [CLICKS DATA ENTRY AREA] we need an idea.

C: [LAUGHS] So what, so what can we do?

L: I don't know. [PAUSE WHILE THEY BOTH LOOK AT THEIR OWN HANDOUTS] Large leap, leaps.

C: Umm, I suppose.

C: [GLANCES AT L] Did you say large leaps? Yeah we could do something, something ah, something dramatic, so I mean the idea is that it just changes a little bit and then suddenly it jumps and then it goes down again, and so we, we would we expect some kind of dramatic effect.

L: Like [PAUSE] haunted. [L LAUGHS]

C: Like what?

L: You know when you watch, movie, haunted movies.

C: Yes, yes we're making a horror theme.

L: Right. [BOTH L AND C LAUGH]

---

4 MetaMuse: Computational Implementation

MetaMuse is a pedagogical agent that has been designed to structure interactions [3, 11] between pairs of cooperating learners. An example of the interface for the Meta-Muse is show in Figure 1 ('MetaMuse MainScreen'). The MetaMuse interface structures the interactions between the MetaMuse agent routines and the learner(s) by providing a series of menu options and buttons which are intended to support collaborative problem-seeking dialogue. For example, at an appropriate point MetaMuse will put up a message (not shown in Figure 1) encouraging pairs of learners to predict to each other how a new musical phrase will sound when it is eventually played back by MetaMuse. The design of the pedagogical agent was partially based on the results of a previous analysis of empirical data. For example, one outcome of our previous interaction analysis [6] was prescriptive models of interactions described at the level of participants' goals and communicative acts (the latter being seen as a way of achieving goals). These prescriptive models, which were represented as State Transition Networks (STNs), were used as the basis for the planning of interactions. The pedagogical agent has a preference for the adoption of the goals 'probing and target' (described above); the implicit intention behind the adoption of these goals being to get the learners to (i) make a prediction about their creative intentions before hearing their short musical composition played back to them, and (ii) explain the musical outcome when matched to their prediction.

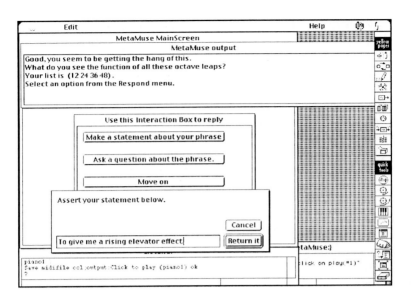

Figure 1. MetaMuse.

A sample interaction with MetaMuse is shown in Figure 1. When a learner clicks on a button, further text windows or dialogue boxes for input are displayed. The 'MetaMuse output' window in Figure 1 contains communicative acts from MetaMuse (which in Figure 1 is giving the learner some encouragement, asking a question about the learner's musical phrase and giving a recommendation to the learner). The learners construct utterances using menus, buttons and dialogue boxes. The interface supports only simple text-based user-system interactions. However, MetaMuse does use a 'preference mechanism' and 'appropriateness conditions' [5] to dynamically generate its intervention. MetaMuse also analyses the learners' phrase and uses the results as the basis for some of its interventions (as is the case in Figure 1).

Above we have suggested (on the basis of an earlier analysis of teacher-learner interactions) that interaction relating to problem-seeking can be seen to revolve around an interactive learning mechanism of 'find-predict-explain-refine'. We have also described an agent that was constructed to promote this type of learning. The remainder of this paper describes empirically based dialogue analysis and modelling that explored the question: what are the interactive means by which learning agents engage in cooperative problem-seeking?

5   The Study

Six sessions were conducted that involved pairs of cooperating learners interacting with each other and MetaMuse. The twelve participants ranged from undergraduate students, postgraduate students, research fellows and members of staff (teaching and support). Seven students were male and five female. Each learner-learner-MetaMuse session lasted between 30 and 40 minutes and was recorded on two video cameras. One camera focused on the computer monitor and the second camera was pointed at the study participants (dyads).

Each session involved the participants being asked to work together (the face-to-face) in order to carry out a small composition task. Briefly, the compositional task was for the participants to attempt, using MetaMuse, to create a phrase by the repeated chromatic transposition of an initial four note motive (C C# F# G). Participants were not given any instructions on how to cooperate on the task other than being requested to "work together on the task". Following each session the observers of the session compared notes and decided on which post-experimental cues to use. Following the completion of a task, cueing distinct 'thought episodes' is a useful way to approach to gathering retrospective verbal reports [8, p. xlix]. This involves constraining the retrospective report by the subject to the recall of distinct thought episodes. Each participant was then individually interviewed for 10 to 15 minutes. Approximately three hours of learner-learner interactions were gathered. Three hours of post-experimental interview data was also collected and extracts incorporated into the analysis. The dialogue analysis described below was performed with the assistance of computer-assisted qualitative methods (NVivo).

6 Results and Interpretations

The main results are reported below with a brief discussion given in the context of the relevant result. An account of users' views of MetaMuse, which were generally positive, can be found in [4]. The main empirical results are an elaboration of our cooperative problem-seeking dialogue model and some general results (scores of the occurrence of problem-seeking sub-categories in the interaction data).

6.1 Elaboration of Cooperative Problem-Seeking Dialogue Model

The cooperative problem-seeking model shown in Figure 2 emerged as a result of our analysis of the interaction data (i.e. if a sub-category appeared to be required it was added to the model). As we noted in the introduction, the research described in this paper is particularly interested in developing models that can be used as a basis for the design of ITSs (models being interpreted in the widest sense of the word). Figure 2 gives us an empirically derived model of the cooperative problem-seeking processes. If taken with its attendant theory (described in Section 2), the above model can be used to form the basis for the re-design of MetaMuse (we will return to this point in the Conclusions).

The categories shown in Figure 2 provide an elaboration of the model of cooperative problem-seeking dialogue, described in Section 2. Several points are worth making about the sub-categories shown in Figure 2.

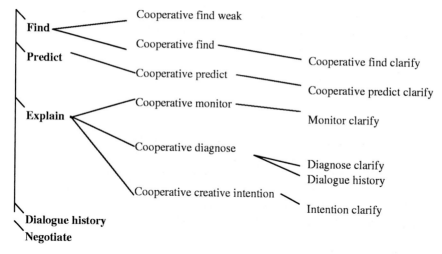

Figure 2. Cooperative problem-seeking dialogue model

Cooperative-find-weak (at the top of Figure 2 as a sub-category of 'find') is just initial experimentation by the pairs, and is mainly task oriented. Cooperative-find is where the pairs are starting to come up with some novel idea; find-clarify (see the end of Table 1 for an example) is an elaboration of that creative intention. Note that some attempts at clarification may include the giving of criteria as reasons.

With Cooperative-predict pairs work together to make a verbal prediction of how their musical phrase will sound when played back. Cooperative-predict-clarify is a refinement of that prediction.

Cooperative-monitor and Cooperative-diagnose occur when learners appear to be working together to explain aspects of their attempts to problem-seek. Cooperative-monitor may involve attempts at clarification. Cooperative-diagnose is further subdivided into attempts to clarify what was meant by a diagnosis and may also draw on a dialogue history. The latter is where a learner makes use of dialogue (external) that the learner has previously been exposed to in order to explain the current context. Cooperative-creative-intention happens when pairs work together to verbalise their ideas; this may also involve the sub-category intention-clarify, where further elaboration of some point with respect to what is intended is provided.

Negotiate, shown at the bottom of Figure 2, has a specific meaning in the context of this work; it is an exchange between learners about how to proceed from a particular point; it may also be an exchange between the learners and one of the experimenters about how to proceed. It may make reference to what has gone before (e.g. it may overlap with the dialogue-history). Negotiation also tends to take place implicitly in other categories, e.g. what problem specification to adopt in 'cooperative-find'. If the negotiation is not related to dialogue about how to proceed, then it is not coded as 'negotiate'.

If there was no evidence of cooperation between pairs then dialogue was coded as either find, predict or explain (i.e. the categories shown on the left of Figure 2). Dialogue history is shown twice in Figure 2 because, although it occurred mainly in the context of a diagnose (where it was identified five times) it could potentially have occurred in the context of other categories shown in Figure 2 (in fact it only occurred once in another context, i.e. negotiate).

6.2 General Results

The scores in Table 2 below were generated by an analysis of the interactions from the six sessions using the model shown in Figure 2. For example, if an occurrence of interaction related to 'Cooperative monitor' were located in the corpus, then the total score for that category would have 1 added to it. Table 2 shows the scores for all categories in our model for all six sessions. Categories shown in bold in Table 2 relate to the left-hand side of the model shown in Figure 2. Some preliminary, general findings relating the interactive means by which learning agents engaged in cooperative problem-seeking are reported below.

Table 2. Problem-seeking sub-category scores by session (S = session)

Category	S1	S2	S3	S4	S5	S6	Total
Find	0	0	1	0	0	5	6
Cooperative find weak	1	1	2	1	0	0	5
Cooperative find	1	2	6	4	4	1	18
Cooperative find clarify	1	0	0	2	1	0	4
Predict	0	0	0	0	0	2	2
Cooperative predict	2	1	6	3	3	1	16
Cooperative predict clarify	1	1	4	2	1	0	9
Explain	0	0	0	0	0	2	2
Cooperative monitor	0	3	5	5	3	1	17
Monitor clarify	2	2	1	5	0	1	11
Cooperative diagnose	2	1	5	5	3	2	18
Diagnose clarify	0	0	4	1	2	1	8
Dialogue history	0	0	3	1	0	1	5
Cooperative creative intention	3	4	3	4	4	3	21
Intention clarify	4	4	1	4	4	1	18
Dialogue history	0	0	0	1	0	0	1
Negotiate	14	13	8	7	14	12	68

MetaMuse encouraged cooperative problem-seeking, which we have defined as a mechanism of 'find-predict-explain-refine'. Earlier work [5] found that a human tutor in UK undergraduate tutorials tended to focus on providing a critique of a student's musical idea. The tutor observed did not support problem-seeking. We can support the claim that MetaMuse encouraged problem-seeking if we total the following scores: Cooperative find (score = 18) + Cooperative predict (score = 16) + Cooperative monitor (score = 17) + Cooperative diagnose (score = 18) + Cooperative creative intention (score = 21), this gives us a total of 90 occurrences when cooperative problem-seeking was identified in the dialogue data. If we combine the non-cooperative category scores Find (score = 6) + Predict (score = 2) + Explain (score = 2) then we get a low score of 10 occasions which were identified as occurrences in the dialogue data of non-cooperative problem-seeking. Indeed, most of this 'non-cooperation' took place in session six (score = 9).

The fourth aspect of our model of problem-seeking is 'refine'. What emerged from our analysis was that part of refine, i.e. clarifying and differentiating concepts, took place as 'clarify' in the context of the relevant process (i.e. in the context of either find, predict, monitor, diagnose or creative intention). The total score for this type of cooperative clarification was the sum of Cooperative find clarify (score = 4) + Cooperative predict clarify (score = 9) + Monitor clarify (score = 11) + Diagnose clarify (score = 8) + Intention clarify (score = 18); the total score for clarify being 50.

We conclude our interpretation of the results by pointing out that the above discussion has empirically validated our model of cooperative problem-seeking. We claim that the phenomenon of cooperative problem-seeking exists in at least one case (i.e. the empirical study), and that this is a possible behaviour that a system could have to deal with.

7 Conclusions

In this paper we have proposed that interactions relating to cooperative problem-seeking can be seen as revolving around a dialogue model of 'find-predict-explain-refine'. We described MetaMuse, a pedagogical agent that was designed to 'structure interactions' and hence facilitate problem-seeking dialogues. We then went on to describe the results from a detailed analysis of the interactions that took place between cooperating students when engaged with MetaMuse. The main empirical results presented in this paper are: (i) an elaboration of our cooperative problem-seeking dialogue model, and (ii) some general results which, amongst other things, show that MetaMuse encouraged cooperative problem-seeking.

The following question now arises: how can our analysis findings be generalized to a re-implementation of MetaMuse? Figure 2 gives us an empirically derived model of the cooperative problem-seeking, interactive learning process. If taken with its related theory (described in Section 2), this model can be used to form the basis for the re-design of MetaMuse. Future work will focus on using our model (Figure 2) to generate STNs that model how pairs of cooperating learners interacted successfully. These prescriptive models of cooperation will be used as the basis for tutoring tactics when MetaMuse is pursuing a goal. For example, the goal 'probing and target' (described above) has one implicit intention of getting the learners to explain if a musical outcome matches their prediction. The new STNs will give MetaMuse a basis for giving learners advice on how work together on a particular aspect of a task. Furthermore, the numerical values presented in Table 2 will be used as weightings (in our agent's preference mechanism) that will allow MetaMuse to make a decision about what exit to take if a choice exists at a state node. Such a re-implementation of MetaMuse will enable our pedagogical agent to be better able to support cooperative problem-seeking. A parallel project is applying the agent development techniques described in this paper to another domain (undergraduate multimedia students' web-site design). Dialogue data from the parallel project will be compared with the results presented in this paper to see if any generalizations can be made about cooperative problem-seeking across different open domains.

Acknowledgements

Thanks to Michael Baker, whose recent discussions with me have helped me to develop some of the ideas presented in this paper. Responsibility for the paper, however, rests entirely with me. The transcription of the corpus was done with the help of Matt Smith. Thanks to Tariq Khan and the three anonymous reviewers for making useful comments on a draft of this paper.

References

1. Baker, M. J.: Argumentation and constructive interaction. In Andriessen, J. and Coirer, P. (eds.): Foundations of Argumentative Text Processing. University of Amsterdam Press, Amsterdam (in press)
2. Baker, M. J.: The roles of models in Artificial Intelligence and Education research: a pro-spective view. International Journal of Artificial Intelligence in Education, 11 (2000) to ap-pear
3. Baker, M. J. and Lund, K.: Promoting reflective interactions in a CSCL environment. Jour-nal of Computer Assisted Learning, 13 (1997) 175-193
4. Cook, J.: Evaluation of a support tool for musical problem-seeking. ED-Media 2000 - World Conference on Educational Multimedia, Hypermedia & Telecommunications. June 26-July 1, 2000, Montréal, Canada (2000)
5. Cook, J.: Knowledge Mentoring as a Framework for Designing Computer-Based Agents for Supporting Musical Composition Learning, Unpublished Ph.D. thesis. Computing Depart-ment, The Open University, UK (1998)
6. Cook, J.: Mentoring, Metacognition and Music: Interaction Analyses and Implications for Intelligent Learning Environments. International Journal of Artificial Intelligence in Educa-tion, 9 (1998) 45-87
7. Dillenbourg, P., Baker, M. J., Blaye, A. and O'Malley, C.: The evolution of research on collaborative learning. In Spada, H. and Reimann, P. (eds.): Learning in Humans and Ma-chines, pp. 189-205. Pergamon, London (1995)
8. Ericsson, K. A. and Simon, H. A.: Protocol Analysis (Revised Edition). MIT Press, Cam-bridge, Massachusetts (1993)
9. Goodyear, P. and Stone, C.: Domain Knowledge, Epistemology and Intelligent Tutoring. In Moyse, R. and Elsom-Cook, M. T. (eds.): Knowledge Negotiation, pp. 69-95. Academic Press, London (1992)
10. Lipman, M.: Thinking in Education. Cambridge University Press, New York (1991)
11. Winograd, T. A.: Language/Action Perspective on the Design of Cooperative Work. Hu-man-Computer Interaction, 3 (1988) 3-30

Course Sequencing for Static Courses? Applying ITS Techniques in Large-Scale Web-Based Education

Peter Brusilovsky

Carnegie Technology Education and
HCI Institute, Carnegie Mellon University
4615 Forbes Avenue, Pittsburgh, PA 15213, USA
plb@cs.cmu.edu

Abstract. We argue that traditional sequencing technology developed in the field of intelligent tutoring systems could find an immediate place in large-scale Web-based education as a core technology for concept-based course maintenance. This paper describes a concept-based course maintenance system that we have developed for Carnegie Technology Education. The system can check the consistency and quality of a course at any moment of its life and also assist course developers in some routine operations. The core of this system is a refined approach to indexing the course material and a set of "scripts" for performing different operations.

1 Introduction

Course sequencing is one of the oldest technology in the field of intelligent tutoring systems (ITS). The idea of course sequencing is to generate an individualized course for each student by dynamically selecting the most optimal teaching operation (presentation, example, question, or problem) at any moment of education. An ITS with course sequencing represents knowledge about the subject as a network of concepts where each concept represents a small pieces of subject knowledge. The learning material is stored in a database of teaching operations. Each teaching operation is indexed by concepts it deals with. The driving force behind any sequencing mechanism is a student model that is a weighed overlay of the domain model – for every domain model concept it reflects the current level of student knowledge about it. Using this model and some teaching strategy a sequencing engine can decide which one of the many teaching operations stored in the data base is the best for the student given his or her level of knowledge and educational goal.

Various approaches to sequencing were explored in numerous ITS projects. The majority of existing ITS can sequence only one kind of teaching operations. For example, a number of sequencing systems including the oldest sequencing systems [2; 14] and some others [8; 12; 15] can only manipulate the order of problems or questions. In this case it is usually called task sequencing. A number of systems can do sequencing of *lessons* that are reasonably big chunks of educational material complete with presentation and assessment [3; 9]. Most advanced systems are able to sequence several kinds of teaching operations such as presentation, examples, and assessments [7; 13].

One could say that sequencing is an excellent technology for distance education. In the situation where students can learn the subject at their own pace, it looks like a great idea to have each student to learn the subject by the most beneficial individualized way. Indeed, sequencing is now the most popular technology in research-level Web-based ITS [4]. However, there is a significant distance between the systems used in large scale Web-based education and research-level systems, even if we only consider research systems that were used to teach real classes like ELM-ART [Brusilovsky, 1996 #732] and 2L670 [De Bra, 1998 #1178]. In a modern large-scale Web-based education context a single course provider operates tens to hundreds of courses that has to be delivered to thousands of students grouped in classes. The biggest concern of a provider is the problem of maintenance. To avoid problems with installing and supporting multiple Web-based education (WBE) systems and teaching the stuff how to use these systems, all serious providers tend to choose one single course management system (CMI). Naturally the providers are choosing modern commercial CMIs such as TopClass [17] or WebCT [18] that can support main needs of a course provider from course material delivery to discussion forums to generation of various course reports. Unfortunately, current CMI systems leave no space for dynamic sequencing. The course model behind all these systems is a static sequence (or a tree) of modules followed by static quizzes and assignments.

Could we find any use for the course sequencing ideas in this rigid context of large-scale Web-based education? The answer is yes. We can suggest at least two meaningful ways to do "sequencing of static courses". First way is dynamic generation of the course before the students hit it. Instead of generating a course incrementally piece by piece, as in traditional sequencing context, the whole course could be generated in one shot. While courses produced by this one-shot generation are not as adaptive as incrementally sequenced courses, they still could be very well tuned for individual students taking into account their individual learning needs and starting level of knowledge. A good example of this approach is DCG system [16]. A similar approach was also described in [1; 10]. Since a course generated with a DCG-like system is static, it could be delivered by a regular CMI system.

While DCG-like approach fits technically to large-scale WBE context, it still has two problems. First problem is that in most places Web-based education is still class-based. Virtual class is still a class. The students from the same class have to learn the same material in about the same time and even take exams at the same date. Naturally, for a class-based WBE an individually generated course will not work. This problem could be solved relatively easy by generating courses that are adapted to the whole class of users. While the product of generation should be rather called customized course than adaptive course, this approach allows a very good level of individualization, especially for the case of reasonably homogeneous classes. We think that in the future systems that can produce courses on demand from the same body of teaching material would be very popular since that will enable a course provider to accommodate to the needs of different customers. A DCG-like approach has, however, another problem – a bootstrapping one. To produce the first customized course a provider need to have a reasonably large database of well-indexed learning material (at least, two to three times larger than the size of a typical course being produced). The startup price of developing such a rich course in addition to the price of the system is a big obstacle to using DCG-like approach.

The second approach to static sequencing suggested in this paper is least ambitious. We suggest to use a course sequencing mechanism as a core of a course maintenance system for static courses developed by a team of authors in a traditional way. The very idea is simple. Since a sequencing mechanism can evaluate several possible options for the "next steps" (i.e., presentation, example, assignment) in a dynamic course and select the best one, it can also check whether the predefined "next step" in a static course is a good one. If the next step is not really good, it can report problems. For example, it can find a situation when an assessment requires knowledge that are not presented yet or, vice versa, when presented knowledge are never assessed. These kinds of course checking are absolutely necessary for any serious course developer team such as Carnegie Technology Education, a WBE "arm" of Carnegie Mellon University. Large-scale modern courses include hundred to thousands of learning items that are produced by a team of developers. Through the life of a course it could be updated and restructured several times. A concept-based course maintenance system is as important for *courseware engineering* as a version tracking system for software engineering.

This paper describes a concept-based course maintenance system developed at Carnegie Technology Education. The system can check the consistency and quality of a course at any moment of course life and also assist course developers in some routine operations. The core of this system is a refined approach to indexing the course material and a set of "scripts" for performing different operations. Next section describes the indexing part and the section after that talks about scripts. We conclude with some speculation about prospects of our work.

2 Content Indexing

There are several possible ways to index the content from very advanced and powerful to very simple. The reported approach supports the functionality that we find essential while being still simple enough to used by course developers.

The simplest indexing approach could be referred as "plain" prerequisite-outcome concept indexing. It is used in systems like Piano-Tutor [9] or InterBook [5]. Plain indexing associate a teaching operation with two sets of concepts - prerequisite and outcome concepts. Plain approach does not distinguish different types of teaching operations and use only two roles in which a concept can be involved in a teaching operation: prerequisite and outcome. It also does not take into account relationships between concepts. Plain indexing has shown to be useful in simple domains or with coarse-grain level of domain modeling (all systems with plain indexing known to the author use about 50 concepts).

The reported approach uses three extensions of plain indexing approach: typed items, advanced concept roles, and links between concepts. Typed items let the system distinguish several types of teaching operations. Advanced concept roles can specify more roles of the teaching operations in regard to concepts. Both mechanisms let the course developer specify more knowledge about the content and support more powerful algorithms. The impact of links between concepts is a more precise student modeling, prerequisite tracking, and richer navigation. Negative side of all three extensions is increased authoring time. In particular, developing a connected concept model of a domain takes considerable time of several domain experts. The increased authoring time could be a problem for a "traditional" (single teacher) context of course development but it is justified in a context of large-scale Web-based education. Here indexing expenses constitute a small fraction of overall course development expenses and are repaid by the possibility to help course designers with developing and modifying courses.

The core of our framework is formed by concepts – elementary pieces of learning material. The size of a concept is not fixed and may depend of a course. We have several kinds of teaching operations in our courses – presentations, examples, assignments, and multiple-choice questions. The type of the item is a part of the index for the item. Concept-role pairs form the rest of the index. We use four kinds of roles (in comparison with only two in InterBook and Piano-Tutor): light prerequisite, strong prerequisite, light outcome and strong outcome. In comparison with "real" or strong prerequisites and outcomes that tells that "deep" knowledge of a concept are produced or demanded by a learning item, the light prerequisites and outcomes deal with surface knowledge about a concept. We have to introduce these four roles to accommodate the needs of real courses.

The course concepts are connected to form a heterarchy. We use one non-typed parent-child link. This link has to express the value usually expressed by "part-of" and "attribute-of" links. Creating a parent-child hierarchy without the need to type links is relatively easy The meaning of this hierarchy is simple – the knowledge of a parent concept is a sum of knowledge of child concepts plus some "integration extra".

3 The Use of Indexing for Courseware Engineering

3.1 Prerequisite Checking

Prerequisite checking is the one of the key benefits of concept indexing. It is important for original course design as well as for a redesign when learning items are moved or changed. With multiple-level indexing we are able to check prerequisites for all learning items. Prerequisite check for linear courses is performed by a sequencing engine that simulates the process of teaching with a student model. It scans learning items in the order specified by the author, updates the student model, and checks the match between the current state of the model and each following item. The following prerequisite problems could be checked:

- **Presentation prerequisites:** a presentation item can be understood because all prerequisite concepts are already presented up to the required level
- **Question prerequisites:** all concepts involved into all questions designed for a presentation page are learned at least up to the advanced level when the page is completed.
- **Example prerequisites:** all concepts involved into an example are learned to the required level right in the section where an example is presented or before; strong prerequisite concepts are learned at least up to the advanced level, weak prerequisite concepts are learned at least up to the surface level
- **Exercise prerequisites:** at the point where an exercise is presented, all strong prerequisite concepts are learned and demonstrated with examples, all weak prerequisite concepts are at either learned or demonstrated with examples.

The prerequisite checking on the level of course items is especially important for programming courses that usually have very few direct prerequisite relationships between concepts. Most of programming concepts could be introduced independently from other concepts. That's why there could be many possible ways to teach the same subject. However, adopting a particular approach to teaching the subject usually results in lots of indirect prerequisites "hardwired" into educational material.

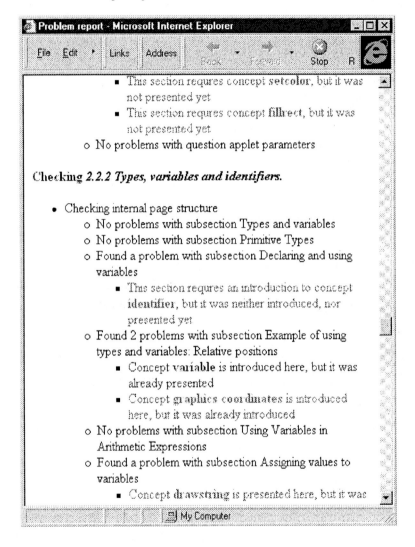

Fig. 1. A fragment of a problem report for a Java course

One example of indirect prerequisites is presentation-level prerequisites: A concept *A* does not depend of concept *B,* but the way of presentation of *A* chosen by the author required understanding of *B.* Another case is example-level or problem-level prerequisites. A concept *A* does not depend of concept *B* and could be learned either before or after *B*. However, in the current course material all available examples or exercises that use *B* also include *A*. As a result, the material requires *A* to be learned *before B*. All these kinds of prerequisites are very hard to keep in mind. The only way to ensure that the course is built or redesigned with no prerequisite conflicts is careful prerequisite checking.

3.2 Finding Content "Holes"

A failure to meet the prerequisites could mean either a problem with structure (the item that could meet the prerequisite does exist in the courses but placed after the checked item) or a problem with content (no item to cover the prerequisite). The system can distinguish these two cases and provide a helpful report of a problem. While the former problem could be often resolved by restructuring the material, the latter indicates a need to expand the course material.

3.3 Consolidation of Presentations

In a well-designed course each concept has to be presented in full in a single place (subsection or section). It is the place where the student will be returning to refill the gaps in his/her knowledge of a concept. This place is called the concept *host section*. A concept could be introduced before its host section (to enable the student to learn or practice other concepts) but hardly more than twice and not after the full presentation. The system can check these rules using indexing. (Note: The same is not true about examples. It's quite desirable to have several examples for each concept).

3.4 Question Placement and Repositioning

Well-designed questions have one or two outcome concepts (question goal). The system can automatically place new questions into the proper place in the course by finding the host section of the question goal. With automatic placement course and question design can be delegated to several authors without the loss of consistency. If the course is re-structured the questions can be automatically repositioned.

3.5 Guidelines for Question Design

By matching concepts presented in a section and concepts assessed by the section question pool it is easy to identify a set of concepts that can never be assessed. The identified deficit could drive the question design process. Same procedure can also ensure that the questions in the pool are reasonably evenly distributed among the section concepts (to avoid the situation where 80% of questions are testing 20% of concepts).

3.6 Matching Presentations with Examples and Exercises

It is possible to check to what extent examples and exercises matches their place in the course and to what extent they cover the presented content. It can be done by matching the set of concepts presented in the section with the joint sets of goal concepts of exercises and examples located in this section. In an ideal situation each section should present, demonstrate (by examples) and assess (by exercises) about the same sets of concepts. If there are too many concepts that are presented but not covered by examples or exercises, the coverage is low. If there are too many concepts that are covered by exercises or examples but not presented in the section (if there is no prerequisite conflict they could be simply presented in previous sections) then the relevance is low. Small mismatch between presentations, examples, and concepts is not a problem, but bigger mismatch in either direction is a sign of poorly designed section and an indication that something has to be redesigned.

3.7 Checking Course Design Against the Real Course

An author could start the course design with a design document that lists all essential concepts to be introduced in each section. The design document could be stored separately from the course. The system can check how the real course matches the original design by comparing where the author planned to introduce the key concepts and where they are really introduced; how the set of target concepts is supported by questions, examples, and exercises.

3.8 Presentation Density and Sectioning

While different concepts may require different amount of presentation, the overall complexity of a content fragment could be measured by the number of concepts presented in it. By controlling the number of concepts presented in each section we can identify two types of problems: presentation density, where too many concepts are presented in a relatively short section, and uneven distribution of content where number of concepts presented in subsections of the same level significantly differs.

3.9 Controlling the Difficulty of Examples and Exercises

Prerequisite indexing of exercises and examples specifies minimal requirements for the concept level that have to be met to make an example or an exercise ready to be taken. Its legal, however that some concepts have *higher* level of knowledge then it is demanded by prerequisites. For example, a strong prerequisite concept of an example has to be learned up to the advanced level. In real life, a student can reach this exercise when he or she has already seen several examples with this concept or even solved an exercise involving this concept. It makes this example easier for that student. Generally, we can estimate difficulty or learning item by measuring a difficulty between the target state of the goal concepts and the starting state. If all goal concepts or an exercise have been already used in earlier solved exercises, the exercise is quite simple. If none of them have even been used in examples, the exercise is very difficult. The difficulty of an exercise is not a constant – it depends on the place of the exercise in the course. It makes sense to control the difficulty of examples and exercises in the course to make sure that none example or exercise is too simple or too difficult.

There is research evidence that there exists an optimal difficulty of a learning item for each individual student (i.e., that the student learns best when he or she is presented with learning items with difficulty closed to optimal. We can't use this finding directly since our courses are static – all students go the same way. But it is quite likely that different groups of users can handle different difficulties. It could be used for making better-targeted courses for special categories of users.

4 Implementation and First Experience

The first version of the system was completed in 1999 and evaluated on one of CTE courses. With a help of the system we were able to find and fix a number of problems in the course. The system is written in Java and supports prerequisite checking, finding content "holes", consolidation of presentations, and question placement and repositioning. Currently the system is not completely interactive. The author has to specify the course structure along with concept tags in a separate file. The situation with question indexing is different - here concept tags are stored as a part of a question. Checking scripts are simply called from a command line. An interactive (GUI-based) version of the system is being developed.

The system was used to check two real courses. While the system turned out to be very useful, we have encountered a problem. In addition to a revealing good number of real large and small hidden problems the system has also reported a number of problems that no real teacher would count as a problem. It turned out that the course consistency rules behind the system are too rigid. In real life teachers can perfectly tolerate a number of small inconsistencies in the course. Moreover, in some cases the course may be formally "inconsistent" with a purpose. A teacher may want to provoke student thinking by presenting an example that is based on a material that is not yet presented but could be understood by analogy with the learned material. Our quick answer to this problem was color coding the course problem report (Figure 1). In particular, the messages that always report a real problem in the course are colored red not to be missed. The messages that report a problem that often may be tolerable are colored green. We use three to four colors in our reports. A real solution to this problem would be a more precise set of checking rules that is adapted to the course "teaching approach" and, probably, a better indexing.

5 Prospects

We plan to continue the work on course maintenance system adding features and checking it with incrementally larger volumes of course material. We see a very important mission in this process. The outcome of this process is not only consistent courses of higher quality, but also a large volume of carefully indexed learning material. Thus we are decreasing bootstrapping cost of more flexible sequencing technologies. We hope that this process will eventually lead to the acceptance of more flexible approaches in large-scale Web-based education: first, to a DCG-like course customization and later to real course sequencing.

References

1. Ahanger, G. and Little, T. D. C.: Easy Ed: An integration of technologies for multimedia education. In: Lobodzinski, S. and Tomek, I. (eds.) Proc. of WebNet'97, World Conference of the WWW, Internet and Intranet, Toronto, Canada, AACE (1997) 15-20
2. Barr, A., Beard, M., and Atkinson, R. C.: The computer as tutorial laboratory: the Stanford BIP project. International Journal on the Man-Machine Studies **8**, 5 (1976) 567-596
3. Brusilovsky, P.: ILEARN: An intelligent system for teaching and learning about UNIX. In: Proc. of SUUG International Open Systems Conference, Moscow, Russia, ICSTI (1994) 35-41
4. Brusilovsky, P.: Adaptive and Intelligent Technologies for Web-based Education. Künstliche Intelligenz , 4 (1999) 19-25
5. Brusilovsky, P., Eklund, J., and Schwarz, E.: Web-based education for all: A tool for developing adaptive courseware. Computer Networks and ISDN Systems. **30**, 1-7 (1998) 291-300
6. Brusilovsky, P., Schwarz, E., and Weber, G.: ELM-ART: An intelligent tutoring system on World Wide Web. In: Frasson, C., Gauthier, G. and Lesgold, A. (eds.) Intelligent Tutoring Systems. Lecture Notes in Computer Science, Vol. 1086. Springer Verlag, Berlin (1996) 261-269
7. Brusilovsky, P. L.: A framework for intelligent knowledge sequencing and task sequencing. In: Frasson, C., Gauthier, G. and McCalla, G. I. (eds.) Intelligent Tutoring Systems. Springer-Verlag, Berlin (1992) 499-506
8. Brusilovsky, V.: Task sequencing in an intelligent learning environment for calculus. In: Proc. of Seventh International PEG Conference, Edinburgh (1993) 57-62
9. Capell, P. and Dannenberg, R. B.: Instructional design and intelligent tutoring: Theory and the precision of design. Journal of Artificial Intelligence in Education **4**, 1 (1993) 95-121
10. Caumanns, J.: A bottom-up approach to multimedia teachware. In: Goettl, B. P., Halff, H. M., Redfield, C. L. and Shute, V. J. (eds.) Intelligent Tutoring Systems. Springer-Verlag, Berlin (1998) 116-125
11. De Bra, P. and Calvi, L.: 2L670: A flexible adaptive hypertext courseware system. In: Grønbæk, K., Mylonas, E. and Shipman III, F. M. (eds.) Proc. of Ninth ACM International Hypertext Conference (Hypertext'98), Pittsburgh, USA, ACM Press (1998) 283-284
12. Eliot, C., Neiman, D., and Lamar, M.: Medtec: A Web-based intelligent tutor for basic anatomy. In: Lobodzinski, S. and Tomek, I. (eds.) Proc. of WebNet'97, World Conference of the WWW, Internet and Intranet, Toronto, Canada, AACE (1997) 161-165
13. Khuwaja, R., Desmarais, M., and Cheng, R.: Intelligent Guide: Combining user knowledge assessment with pedagogical guidance. In: Frasson, C., Gauthier, G. and Lesgold, A. (eds.) Intelligent Tutoring Systems. Lecture Notes in Computer Science, Vol. 1086. Springer Verlag, Berlin (1996) 225-233
14. McArthur, D., Stasz, C., Hotta, J., Peter, O., and Burdorf, C.: Skill-oriented task sequencing in an intelligent tutor for basic algebra. Instructional Science **17**, 4 (1988) 281-307
15. Rios, A., Pérez de la Cruz, J. L., and Conejo, R.: SIETTE: Intelligent evaluation system using tests for TeleEducation. In: Proc. of Workshop "WWW-Based Tutoring" at 4th International Conference on Intelligent Tutoring Systems, San Antonio, TX (1998), available online at http://www-aml.cs.umass.edu/~stern/webits/itsworkshop/rios.html

16. Vassileva, J.: Dynamic Course Generation on the WWW. In: Boulay, B. d. and Mizoguchi, R. (eds.) Artificial Intelligence in Education: Knowledge and Media in Learning Systems. IOS, Amsterdam (1997) 498-505
17. WBT Systems: TopClass, Dublin, Ireland, WBT Systems (1999) available online at http://www.wbtsystems.com/
18. WebCT: World Wide Web Course Tools, Vancouver, Canada, WebCT Educational Technologies (1999) available online at http://www.webct.com

Modelling the Instructor in a Web-Based Authoring Tool for Algebra-Related ITSs

Maria Virvou and Maria Moundridou

Department of Informatics, University of Piraeus,
80, Karaoli and Dimitriou St., Piraeus 185 34, Greece
{mvirvou, mariam}@unipi.gr

Abstract. This paper describes the development of a web-based authoring tool for Intelligent Tutoring Systems and focuses on its instructor modelling capabilities. The tool is called WEAR and aims to be useful to teachers and students of domains that make use of algebraic equations. Specifically, the tool provides assistance to human teachers while they are constructing exercises and it then monitors the students while they are solving the exercises and provides appropriate feedback. The instructor modelling mechanism renders the system adaptable to the specific needs and interests of each individual user (instructor), concerning the construction of new exercises and the retrieval of existing ones.

1 Overview

In the recent years Web-based education has attracted a lot of research energy and has resulted in significant advances concerning distance learning. There are obvious benefits in Web-based education since any student in any place having just a computer and an Internet connection can use a course or educational application developed and installed in some other place. Furthermore, there is a growing need for high quality computer based educational programs that may be used in real school environments [1; 17]. This need can be supported to a large extent by Web-based education. Therefore recently, a large number of educational applications (tutorials, course notes, etc.) have been delivered through the World Wide Web. However, most of them are just electronic books with very limited interactivity. This does not undermine the potential of Web-based education, which can be improved significantly if combined with the technology of Intelligent Tutoring Systems (ITSs). Indeed there have been a lot of successful attempts to either move existing ITSs to the WWW or build from scratch web-based ITSs [2; 4; 13].

Intelligent Tutoring Systems have the ability to present the teaching material in a flexible way and to provide students with individualised instruction and feedback. ITSs have been shown to be effective at increasing the students'-motivation and performance in comparison with traditional learning methods and thus it can be said that ITSs can significantly improve the learning outcomes [9; 14]. However ITSs have often been criticised that they miss the mark in terms of task reality, feasibility and effectiveness [7]. One reason for this has been the difficulty in developing an Intelligent Tutoring System even in small domains. For example, Woolf and Cunningham [19] have estimated that the development of an ITS takes more than 200 hours to produce an hour of instructional material, which in most cases cannot be reused. A possible solution to these problems may be the development of authoring tools, which will help construct cost-effective and reusable ITSs in various domains.

ITSs have been described [5; 3; 18] as having four main components, namely: the domain knowledge, the student modelling component, the advice generator and the user interface. Accordingly, there are systems (authoring tools/shells) that offer the ability to their users to author one and in some cases more than one of these components [11].

The authoring tool described in this paper and in [16] is called WEAR (WEb-based authoring tool for Algebra Related domains). WEAR incorporates knowledge about the construction of exercises and a mechanism for student error diagnosis that is applicable to many domains that make use of algebraic equations. WEAR deals with the generation of instruction, since it offers the ability of problem construction. In that sense it shares the same focus with RIDES [10], an authoring system used for the construction of tutors that teach students how to operate devices through simulations. RIDES generates instruction by providing tools for building graphical representations of a device and for defining this device's behaviour. A system, which adds capabilities to RIDES, is DIAG [15], a tool that simulates equipment faults and guides students through their diagnosis and repair. DIAG is concerned with the creation of domain knowledge and performs student error diagnosis by providing a mechanism that is applicable to many domains that are related to diagnosis of equipment failures. In the same way WEAR performs student error diagnosis by providing a mechanism that can be applied to many algebra-related domains. Furthermore, WEAR gives instructors the ability to control the order by which students solve exercises, by assigning to each exercise a "level of difficulty". Therefore, WEAR beyond generating student problems is also concerned with managing their sequence. The latter is a characteristic that can likewise be met in a system called REDEEM [8], which does not generate instruction but rather focuses on the representation of instructional expertise. REDEEM expects the human instructor to categorise tutorial "pages" in terms of their difficulty, their generality, and whether they are prerequisite for other pages and in that way accomplishes to sequence content and learner activities.

WEAR also gives teachers the ability to search for already constructed exercises and make them available to their own class. Thus, teachers can benefit from the database of problems that have been previously created using WEAR and have been stored in its database. However, the problems stored may be relevant to a wide range of algebra-related domains, may be addressed to many different categories of student, may be associated to many several levels of difficulty and so on. These differences in the problems stored, indicate a need for WEAR to be adaptable to each particular instructor's interests so that it may help him/her in the retrieval of the appropriate information from its database. In addition, to avoid the repetition of exercises WEAR must closely monitor the instructor during the construction of a new problem and notify him/her in case a similar problem already exists in its database. For these reasons, WEAR incorporates an instructor modelling component.

This is considered a major issue for WEAR which aims at providing assistance tailored to each individual teacher's needs and interests. In an ITS there is no need of modelling the instructor since the users of such systems are students learning with them. However, the users of an authoring tool for ITSs are mainly instructors who are interacting with the system in order to build an ITS. A user modelling component for these users will be responsible of keeping and modifying their personal user models. Based on the information provided by these user models, the system will be able to adapt itself to the needs and interests of each individual instructor. This is even more important in cases of a Web-based authoring tool that is available to a diversity of instructors spread all over the range of scope of the Web site. Though the instructor modelling component is not part of the ITS that the tool generates, we consider it to be an important part of the tool since it affects the way the instructors interact with the system and consequently the effectiveness of the generated ITSs.

2   System Operation

The main objective of this tool is to be useful to teachers and students of domains that make use of algebraic equations. Such domains could be chemistry, economics, physics, medicine, etc. In particular the tool takes input from a human instructor about a specific equation-related domain (e.g. physics). This input consists of knowledge about variables, units of measure, formulae and their relation.

Table 1. Examples of input to the system from the domain of physics and economics

PHYSICS		ECONOMICS	
Variables:		**Variables:**	
Velocity	v	Income	Y
Initial velocity	v_0	Consumption	C
Acceleration	a	Investment	I
Time	t	Autonomous consumption	a
Force	F	Marginal propensity to consume	b
Mass	m	Autonomous investment expenditure	i
Impulse	J	Interest rate	r
		Sensitivity of investment in interest rates	c
Formulae:		**Formulae:**	
F=m*a		Y=C+I	
J=m*v		C=a+b*Y	
$v=v_0+a*t$		I=i-c*r	

The instructor does not have to provide the complete list of variables and equations that describe the domain, all at once. S/he may only enter the ones that will be used in the problems to be constructed in the current interaction and add more in subsequent interactions. The tool accumulates domain knowledge each time that the human instructor gives new input. This means that the instructor may give information to the tool at the same rate as lessons progress in a course. Examples of input to the system that an instructor could provide from the domain of physics and economics are shown in Table 1.

2.1 Modes of Operation

WEAR can function in two different modes: the instructor's mode and the student's mode. In the instructor's mode the instructor is able to construct new exercises and/or retrieve previously created exercises. In both cases WEAR provides automatic assistance. Since this paper focuses on the system's instructor modelling capabilities, we will discuss in detail the instructor's mode of operation in the following sections and briefly describe the student's mode of operation here.

Each student is assigned a level of knowledge by the system according to his/her past performance in solving problems with the tool. When a student interacts with the tool for the first time s/he is asked to fill in a questionnaire concerning his/her familiarity with the specific domain, his/her ability to solve equations and his/her competence as a computer user. Based on the student's answers the tool assigns to each student an initial level of knowledge, which will then be modified according to the students' progress. The students' "level of knowledge" and the "level of difficulty" that is assigned to each problem are both in the same range. The tool suggests each student to try the problems corresponding to his/her level of knowledge. For example, if a student at a specific session of interaction with the system is considered to be at the third level of knowledge, the tool will suggest to the student problems of the third level of difficulty to be solved next. When a student attempts to solve an exercise the system provides an environment where the student gives the solution step by step. The system compares the student's solution to its own. The system's solution is generated by the domain knowledge about algebraic equations and about the specific domain in which the exercise belongs (e.g. economics). While the student is in the process of solving the exercise the system monitors his/her actions. If the student makes a mistake, the diagnostic component of the system will attempt to diagnose the cause of it.

2.2 Instructors' Assistance at the Construction of Exercises

When the human instructor wishes to create exercises s/he is guided by the system through a step by step procedure. At each step of this procedure the instructor should specify values for some parameters needed to construct an exercise. Such parameters could be for example what is given and what is asked in the exercise to be constructed. After the completion of this procedure the tool constructs the full problem text and provides consistency checks that help the instructor verify its completeness and correctness. In case of redundancies in the given data the tool lets the instructor know. For example, if the instructor assigns a value to both the dependent and independent variables of an equation, s/he will receive a notification by the system concerning this redundancy. After the construction of a problem the tool lets the instructor preview the problem text and the solution of the exercise as formulated by the system. At this point, the instructor is asked to assign to the problem the appropriate "level of difficulty". The system uses this measure in order to suggest to each student (while in student's mode) what problem to try next.

While students are tackling the given problems the system collects evidence about the level of difficulty so that it can provide feedback to the instructor. For example, if the majority of the students of a certain level have failed in solving a particular problem, which has been assigned to this level, then the instructor is informed. In a case like this, perhaps the instructor may wish to reconsider the level of difficulty since there is evidence that the problem may be of a higher level of difficulty. On the other hand, if many students have managed to solve a problem of a higher level of difficulty than the one proposed by the instructor, the level of difficulty may have been overestimated by the instructor. In this case too, the system informs the instructor. In both cases, the tool does not take the initiative to alter the level of difficulty by itself: it suggests the instructor to increase or decrease this measure according to the observed students' performance in a specific problem. In this way an instructor is being assisted by the system in the classification of problems.

There are two types of problem that the system can assist the instructor to construct:

Problems without numbers. In problems without numbers the system displays every variable that the human instructor has entered. The human instructor should specify which variable is the unknown, which one is given and the type of change. For example in the domain of economics the instructor could select as unknown the variable "income", and as given an "increase" at the level of "interest rates". The system would then produce the following problem text: "How will the increase of interest rates affect the level of income?". This kind of problem evaluates the students' knowledge of the equations involved in each of these problems. In addition it evaluates the students' ability to decide about the influence of each variable over the others. In cases like this students are not requested to solve a particular system of equations, but rather working with analogies. In this way, such problems might measure the students' overall understanding in the domain being taught.

Problems with numbers. In problems with numbers the system displays again every variable that the human instructor has entered and requests the unknown (Fig. 1). The system considers automatically all the variables, which depend on the "unknown" (according to the equations), as possible given data. These variables are shown to the instructor who should now enter their values. The system follows the instructor's actions and reports any inconsistencies. For example, if the instructor enters values for fewer variables than those needed for the problem to be solvable then the system points out the error. Finally, the system produces the problem text. An example of problem text is the following: "If the force is 100 Newtons, the mass is 25 kg, the initial velocity is 0 m/sec and the time is 5 secs, then find the impulse." The instructor may change the problem text to make it more comprehensible; for example: "A force of 100 Newtons is acting on a 25 kg object which is initially stable. After 5 secs how much is the impulse?". In such problems, the students are tested over their ability to solve a system of linear equations (mathematical skills) and their knowledge of the equations describing the particular domain.

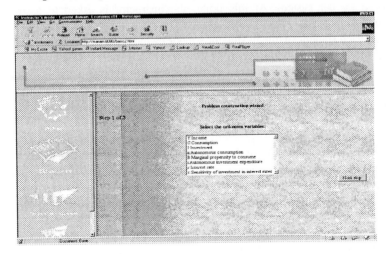

Fig. 1. Problem construction

2.3   Retrieval of Exercises

Beyond constructing an exercise by himself/herself, the instructor has the ability to explore the exercises constructed by others and choose the ones that s/he desires to be accessible by his/her class. The exercises are first categorised according to the domain they belong. At a second level the exercises of each domain are categorised according to the variables they involve and their level of difficulty. Every variable of the domain can possibly form an exercise category. For example, an exercise like: "If the force is 100 Newtons, the mass is 25 kg, the initial velocity is 0 m/sec and the time is 5 secs, then find the impulse." belongs to the broad category "Physics" and in the sub-categories "Impulse", "Velocity" and "Acceleration" due to the variables involved in it. The same exercise could also belong to the sub-category "level of difficulty 1" based on the exercise's level of difficulty (as defined by the instructor).

The categorisation of each exercise (according to the variables involved) is achieved by the system through the following algorithm:

1. Assign the exercise to the categories of every unknown variable in this exercise (In the above example this step results in the category "Impulse" which is the unknown variable).
2. Search the equations that must be solved in order to define the unknown variables' values (in the example, that is the equation J=m*v) for the independent variables that are not "given" in this exercise and assign the exercise to these categories too (in our case that is the variable-category "Velocity"). Consider these variables that

must be given a value by solving an equation as "unknown" variables and repeat this step (this will end in assigning the exercise to the category "Acceleration").

Instructors are allowed either to browse the collection of exercises by selecting the categories and sub-categories that match their needs and interests, or to search the entire collection using some keywords. A user modelling mechanism incorporated in the system is responsible for tailoring the interaction of the instructors with the system to the instructors' needs.

3   Instructor Modelling

The instructor modelling component monitors the instructors' interactions with WEAR and constructs and/or updates a long-term implicit user model [12] for each user - instructor. As we have already mentioned, an instructor either searches for an already constructed exercise or constructs an exercise by himself/herself. WEAR infers from these two actions the users' interest or expertise in something, respectively. This is similar to a system called InfoVine [6], which infers that users are interested in something if they are repeatedly asking the system about it whereas they are expert in something if they are repeatedly telling the system about it. In WEAR, when a user frequently searches for specific categories of exercise then it is inferred that this particular user is highly "interested" in these categories of exercise; whereas when a user often constructs exercises that belong to the same category the inference made is that this user is a "major contributor" in that sort of exercise.

This user model is utilised by the system in order to:

– *Adapt the interaction with its users.* When a user wishes to find an exercise and decides to browse the available categories, s/he will see that in the categories' list the ones that s/he frequently explores are pre-selected for him/her by the system. Of course the instructor is free to select some other categories as well, or even ignore the already selected ones. In addition, if new exercises belonging to the categories that a particular user is interested in are added, the system informs the user when s/he logs in. When a user searches the collection of exercises using some keywords instead of selecting categories, his/her search is saved and the next time s/he logs in and wishes to search the collection s/he is presented with the option to run again the last saved search.

– *Promote co-operative or collaborative work.* Users are offered the choice of seeing what other users have done. When selecting this option, a user is presented with a list of exercises constructed by users who are considered by the system as "major contributors" in the categories that this specific user is considered "interested". A user is considered a "major contributor" in a particular area of s/he has created and/or updated many exercises in this area and these have been solved by a number of students. In addition, when an instructor constructs an exercise by himself/herself and before completing all the steps needed, the system checks if there is any similar exercise already constructed by another instructor who is considered "major contributor". If this is the case, the instructor is offered the choice of seeing the similar exercises and use them instead of constructing his/her own. In that way, the system avoids the repetition of exercises, facilitates the instructors' work and advances the co-operation and collaboration among them.

4   WEAR's Architecture

The system's underlying architecture is shown in Fig. 2. The upper part of the figure (the dimmer part) contains the system's modules dealing with the student. The teacher's input is the domain description in terms of variables, equations and units of measure and all the information needed to construct a problem (known and unknown variables, level of difficulty, etc.). This information is stored and used by the "Problem Solver", a component that interacts with the student while s/he is solving a problem. When the student makes a mistake, the "Error Diagnoser" is responsible of finding out the cause of it. The "Student Model" is updated at every interaction of the student with the system. Using the information kept in that model the system performs individualised error diagnosis when the student solves exercises, builds progress reports and helps the instructor reconsider the level of difficulty s/he assigned to the constructed problems.

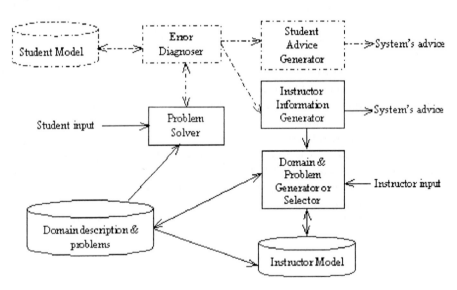

Fig. 2. System's architecture

The "Instructor Information Generator" forms advice for instructors concerning the levels of difficulty of exercises and informs instructors about frequent errors made by students while solving exercises. It also creates student progress reports for instructors. The "Domain & Problem Generator or Selector" helps the instructor construct new exercises and/or retrieve exercises that were previously constructed.

This is done using the "Instructor Model" which is updated at the end of each interaction of the instructor with the system. Finally the "Domain description & problems" contains domain knowledge and problems which have been constructed. The domain knowledge is used by the "Problem Solver" in order to compare the students' solutions to the correct one. The "Domain description & problems" also informs the "Instructor Model" about categories of exercises and provides problems to the "Problem Selector".

The implementation of the system is based on the client-server architecture. Both students and instructors are clients who can use the teaching and authoring services offered by the system using a conventional WWW browser. The system itself resides on a WWW server.

5   Conclusions and Future Work

In this paper we described a web based authoring tool for Intelligent Tutoring Systems in Algebra related domains. We showed that there is a need for an instructor modelling component in order to render the system more flexible and adaptable to particular instructors' interests. The instructor modelling component interacts with other components of the system in order to form an implicit long-term user model of the instructor which is used for tailoring advice to the individual instructors' interests. In this way instructors can easily benefit from the acquisition of domain problems of the system through various users of the web application.

It is within the future plans of this research to evaluate the instructor modelling function of WEAR using a variety of instructors in Algebra-related domains.

Acknowledgements

This work was partially supported by the Greek R&D project MITOS (EPET-II, Greek General Secretariat of Research & Technology). MITOS exploits the technologies of user modelling, information filtering, information extraction and data mining in order to provide users information from financial data, according to their interests. MITOS will be completed by March 2001.

References

1. Alexandris, N., Virvou, M., Moundridou, M.: A Multimedia Tool for Teaching Geometry at Schools. In: Ottmann, T., Tomek, I. (eds.): Proceedings of ED-MEDIA 98, World Conference on Educational Multimedia, Hypermedia & Telecommunications, Vol. 2. AACE, Charlottesville VA (1998) 1595-1597.
2. Brusilovsky, P., Schwarz, E., Weber, G.: ELM-ART: An intelligent tutoring system on World Wide Web. In: Frasson, C., Gauthier, G., Lesgold, A. (eds.): Proceedings of the 3rd International Conference on Intelligent Tutoring Systems, ITS-96. Lecture Notes in Computer Science, Vol. 1086. Springer-Verlag, Berlin (1996) 261-369

3. Burton, R.R., Brown, J.S.: A tutoring and student modelling paradigm for gaming environments. In: Colman, R., Lorton, P.Jr. (eds.): Computer Science and Education. ACM SIGCSE Bulletin, Vol. 8(1) (1976) 236-246

4. Eliot, C., Neiman, D., Lamar, M.: Medtec: A Web-based intelligent tutor for basic anatomy. In: Lobodzinski, S., Tomek, I. (eds.): Proceedings of WebNet '97, World Conference of the WWW, Internet and Intranet. AACE, Charlottesville VA (1997) 161-165

5. Hartley, J.R., Sleeman D.H.: Towards intelligent teaching systems. Int. J. of Man-Machine Studies 5 (1973) 215-236

6. Harvey, C.F., Smith, P., Lund, P.: Providing a networked future for interpersonal information retrieval: InfoVine and user modelling. Interacting with Computers 10 (1998) 195-212

7. McGraw, K. L.: Performance Support Systems: Integrating AI, Hypermedia and CBT to Enhance User Performance. J. of Artificial Intelligence in Education 5(1) (1994) 3-26

8. Major, N., Ainsworth, S., Wood, D.: REDEEM: Exploiting Symbiosis Between Psychology and Authoring Environments. Int. J. of Artificial Intelligence in Education 8 (1997) 317-340

9. Mark, M.A., Greer, J.E.: The VCR tutor: Evaluating instructional effectiveness. In: Proceedings of 13th Annual Conference of the Cognitive Science Society. Lawrence Erlbaum Associates, Hillsdale, NJ (1991) 564-569

10. Munro, A., Johnson, M., Pizzini, Q., Surmon, D., Towne, D., Wogulis, J.: Authoring Simulation-centered tutors with RIDES. Int. J. of Artificial Intelligence in Education 8 (1997) 284-316

11. Murray, T.: Authoring Intelligent Tutoring Systems: An analysis of the state of the art. Int. J. of Artificial Intelligence in Education 10 (1999) 98-129

12. Rich, E.: Users as Individuals: Individualizing User Models. Int. J. of Man-Machine Studies 18 (1983) 199-214

13. Ritter, S.: PAT Online: A Model-tracing tutor on the World-wide Web. In: Brusilovsky, P., Nakabayashi, K., Ritter, S. (eds.): Proceedings of Workshop "Intelligent Educational Systems on the World Wide Web" at AI-ED'97, 8th World Conference on Artificial Intelligence in Education. ISIR (1997) 11-17

14. Shute, V., Glaser, R., Raghaven, K.: Inference and Discovery in an Exploratory Laboratory. In: Ackerman, P., Glaser, R. (eds.): Learning and Individual Differences. Freeman, San Francisco (1989) 279-326

15. Towne, D.: Approximate reasoning techniques for intelligent diagnostic instruction. Int. J. of Artificial Intelligence in Education 8 (1997) 262-283

16. Virvou, M., Moundridou, M.: An authoring tool for Algebra-related domains. In: Bullinger, H.-J., Ziegler, J. (eds.): Human-Computer Interaction: Communication, Cooperation, and Application Design, Proceedings of the 8th International Conference on Human-Computer Interaction - HCI International '99, Vol. 2. Lawrence Erlbaum Associates, Mahwah NJ (1999) 647-651

17. Virvou, M., Tsiriga, V.: EasyMath: A Multimedia Tutoring System for Algebra. In Collis, B., Oliver, R. (eds.): Proceedings of ED-MEDIA 99, World Conference on Educational Multimedia, Hypermedia & Telecommunications, Vol. 2. AACE, Charlottesville VA (1999) 933-938

18. Wenger, E.: Artificial Intelligence and Tutoring Systems. Morgan Kaufman, Los Altos CA (1987)

19. Woolf, B.P., Cunningham, P.A.: Multiple knowledge sources in intelligent teaching systems. IEEE Expert 2(2) (1987) 41-54

Improving Story Choice in a Reading Tutor that Listens

Greg Aist[1] and Jack Mostow[1]

[1] Project LISTEN, 4215 Newell-Simon Hall, Carnegie Mellon University,
Pittsburgh, Pennsylvania 15213, USA
{aist, mostow}@cs.cmu.edu   http://www.cs.cmu.edu/~listen

This abstract summarizes how we improved task choice – picking a story to read – in successive versions of a Reading Tutor that listens to elementary students read aloud. We wanted to motivate children to spend time on the Reading Tutor by giving them some choice in what to read, without spending too much time picking stories. We also wanted them to read plenty of new text, so as to build vocabulary and decoding skills.

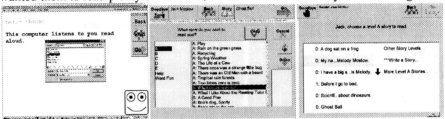

1996: adult-assisted picker   *1998: 2-click picker*   *1999: 1-click picker*

The 1996 Tutor was supervised one-on-one by a school aide, who took ~3 minutes in a generic file picker to help pick stories. To include time spent browsing titles or picking the wrong story by mistake, we measured choice time from the last sentence read in the previous story to the <u>second</u> sentence read in the next story. The mix of new and previously read stories was reflected in the fraction of new sentences, namely ~43%.

The 1998 Tutor aimed at independent classroom use by possible non-readers. It gave spoken prompts on what to do, and read a story title aloud (along with a difficulty estimate based on the percentage of new words) if the child clicked on it. The child clicked *Okay* to pick that story. To pick again, the kid could click on *Story*, or finish the story and answer 1-2 multiple-choice questions like "Was that story easy, hard, or just right?" (Most stories were not finished.) It took ~2 minutes (including questions) to pick stories, with 59% new text – but some children kept rereading the same stories.

To increase this percentage, the 1999 Tutor took turns picking stories, selecting unread stories at the child's reading level (estimated based on assisted oral reading rate). For the child's turn, the simplified "one-click picker" read the list of titles aloud. As soon as a child clicked on a title, the Reading Tutor displayed that story to read aloud. To pick some other story, the child could click *Back* to return to the story picker, which thus replaced 2-click "select and confirm" with "select, then optionally repent." Picking now took 26 seconds, with 66% new text: significantly more than in 1998, p=.003.

Using Computer Algebra for Rapid Development of ITS Components in Engineering

Burkhard Alpers

Aalen University of Technology and Business,
Department of Mechanical Engineering, D-73428 Aalen, Germany
balper@fh-aalen.de

Implementing an Intelligent Tutoring System (ITS) is a costly and time-consuming activity requiring qualifications from many fields like Artificial Intelligence, Instructional Theory, and application expert knowledge. Therefore, ITS are rare and often rather test systems in academic research than wide-spread tools in practical use.

We show how computer algebra systems (CAS) like Maple (TM) or Mathematica (TM) can be used to reduce the development effort for parts of an ITS in engineering considerably. The built-in intelligence of CAS wrt. symbolic computation is exploited for implementing parts of the expert module and diagnostic capabilities for certain assignment types in engineering. This way, a tutored assignment environment can be easily written. As opposed to other approaches which implement so-called "intelligent CAS" with explanatory components from scratch (cf. [Nisheva]), we use an existing CAS and enhance it didactically by implementing tutorial procedures.

Note that we do not claim to provide a "full-fledged" ITS including a student model. Since our learning material is not the only offering but just one part of the overall curriculum (including lectures), this restriction is not problematic. It is the main advantage of our approach, that a tutoring environment for periods of self-study can be implemented with low effort by an instructor in engineering, i.e. by the person who is responsible for making students use it. In order to facilitate this, we set up a sequence of guidelines on how to proceed when writing tutored assignment worksheets for certain classes of engineering problems (cf. [Alpers] for examples on stress analysis) and we implemented generic diagnostic procedures for one of the most frequently occurring underlying mathematical models, i.e. linear systems. These procedures can be used to find faults in linear systems of equations like missing or wrong equations which, for example, occur when students set up equations for equilibrium conditions in mechanics. Moreover, they also give information on certain kinds of errors like wrong symbols, sign errors, wrong terms, or missing terms which (according to [Gertner]) show up frequently. Future work will provide more generic procedures in order to further facilitate the implementation work of an instructor.

Alpers, B.: *Combining hypertext and computer algebra to interconnect engineering subjects and mathematics*, Proc. of the 4th Int. Conference on Technology in Math. Teaching, Plymouth 1999

Gertner, A.S.: *Providing feedback to equation entries in an intelligent tutoring system for Physics*, in: Goettl, B.P. et al..: Intelligent Tutoring Systems, Proc. of 4th Int. Conf. ITS '98, Springer, Berlin 1998 (=LNCS 1452), pp. 254-263

Nisheva-Pavlova, M.M.: *An Intelligent Computer Algebra System and its Applicability in Mathematics Education*, The International Journal of Computer Algebra in Mathematics Education, Vol. 6, No.1, 1999, pp. 3-16

Supporting Discovery Learning in Building Neural Network Models

Safia Belkada, Toshio Okamoto,and Alexandra Cristea

The Graduate School of Information Systems,
1-5-1 chofugaoka, Chofu-shi,the University of Electro-Communications,Japan
{safia,okamoto,alex}@ai.is.uec.ac.jp

1 Introduction

In this paper, we propose a framework based on a hybrid approach to support learning neural networks within an interactive simulation-based learning environment[1], allowing learners to build their neural network simulators by blending the theory with praxis. To diagnose a neural model made by a learner, we construct a script file during the learner's manipulations of objects using a set of inference rules to help determine the network's topology and initial weight values. To this end, we embedded in the system a virtual assistant (VA), which also contributes in the educational stage of neural networks usage. The VA uses the knowledge-based neural network (KBNN) algorithm [2] to translate the script file into a set of nodes represented as an AND/OR dependency tree. From the tree we choose a proper index and examine whether the architecture and the corresponding parameters can be approximated in the knowledge-based neural network (KBNN) space. The VA examines if there is any missing information or wrong conception and points it out to the learner showing him/her where the error or misconception might be. The system has an object-oriented architecture in which an adaptive user interface connected to the learner's skills has the role of a motivator in the learning stage. That is, it allows visualizing neural models as concrete neural objects. In fact, the most of the existing neural networks models have some common components[3], the idea is to implement those simple components and use them to build different and even very complicated systems. The learner builds his/her models in the simulation environment by making use of those components provided by the objects library.

References

1. B.safia, C.Alexandra, O. Toshio: Development of an Intelligent Simulation-Based Learning Environment to Design and Tutor Neural Networks. ICCE99 the 7th international conference, vol.2, (1999) pp.291-298
2. G.G. Towell, J.W. Shavlik, M.O. Noordewier: Refinement of approximately correct domain theories by knowledge-based neural networks. Proceedings of the eighth national conference on AI,Boston, MA. MIT Press, (1990) pp.861-866
3. T. Chenoweth, Z. Obradovic: A multi-component nonlinear prediction system for the Sp 500 Index. Neurocomputing J., vol.3, (1996) pp.275-290

A Cognitive Model for Automatic Narrative Summarization in a Self-Educational System[1]

Laurence Capus and Nicole Tourigny

Département d'informatique, Pavillon Adrien-Pouliot, Université Laval
Ste-Foy (Québec), Canada, G1K 7P4
{capus,tourigny}@ift.ulaval.ca

The use of examples may be a good strategy to learn or to improve one's abilities in a particular field; but the number of educational systems using examples explicitly remains small. The goal of our GARUCAS (GenerAtor of summaRies Using CASes) project is to build an educational system to help users learn text summarization by means of examples. It uses case-based reasoning to build new summaries from old ones. By observing the expert module producing a summary, the system user will learn how to summarize. Thus, the system needs examples of text summarization in order to show how summaries are produced and also to reuse in summarizing other texts. We began with 12 examples of summarization of simple narrative texts.

Summarizing depends on text comprehension and requires identification of important information. Thus, in a context of an educational tool, it is of prime importance that such a tool employs a cognitive model to help the user learn. Indeed, how could people learn from a computer if the methods it uses are incomprehensible?

A narrative text can be represented by using 'plot units' based on affective states of the main character(s), allowing to obtain a highly descriptive structural graph. This is relevant because, from a cognitive viewpoint, a narration is composed of a series of real or fictive events. Furthermore, from this representation, it is possible to compute the product graph of two text structure graphs. GARUCAS must be able to compare the source text of summarization examples with the user's text. In addition, some authors define a text as a set of sequences of the same or different types. One of those is the narrative sequence normally included within a story. It is decomposed into 6 macro-categories with a special function in the logic of the story progress. We used these macro-categories as slots for the summary frame. Each one gives a function of the text segments and then their importance within the summary. In the same way, frames are used for summarizing scientific texts and contained different slots for the objectives, the employed method or still the obtained results. Moreover, the use of frames may offer a solution for avoiding highly disjointed abstracts. Learners will better understand if the system explains them why each text segment is selected to be part of the summary

With this model, the system can then show learners the different segments of the text that should be used to produce the summary. The identification of these text segments is actually the first step in the summarization process. Linguistic rules, such as condensation or syntactic rules, should be then applied in order to generate a more coherent and autonomous final version.

---

[1] This work is supported by the Natural Sciences and Engineering Research Council of Canada (NSERC) with the grant number 155387.

Didactic Situations as Multifaceted Theoretical Objects

Michel Chambreuil, Panita Bussapapach, John Fynn

Université Blaise Pascal – Clermont II, Clermont-Ferrand, France

We will use the term "didactic situation" here to refer to any proposed activity for the learning of a domain. Whatever the learning domain, the type of knowledge to be acquired or the mode in which the learning is conducted, a didactic situation appears to the learner as the central entity of the learning process, the place where the knowledge to be acquired is accessed. Its role as a space where the learner and the knowledge to be acquired come together, turns the didactic situation into a multifaceted and highly complex entity. For individual learning, for example, every facet of this complexity must be taken into account so as to choose and individualize, according to a learning goal, a didactic situation to be proposed to a particular student. These facets must also be taken into account in order to interpret the student's results. It is the analysis of these facets that is at the heart of research being carried out in the framework of the AMICAL project, the theoretical study and development of knowledge-based multimedia computer environments for the teaching and learning of reading. Owing to the limitations of this poster, we can only mention the different facets of a didactic situation, with regard to individual learning. We note here that each of these facets refers to many fields of fundamental theoretical research and that the problems arising in each facet have not yet found definitive solutions. (F1) In relation to didactic planning, a didactic session is a *unit of action* that the tutoring system has at its disposal in order to achieve the goal of a didactic session. This facet refers to the characterization of the knowledge defining this unit of action and to the research at the present time on the theory of action in AI. (F2) In relation to the student, a didactic situation is a *complex problem to be solved*. We refer here to the analysis of the knowledge the student needs to solve the problem. We can mention here three kinds of knowledge: the learning domain knowledge, the knowledge of the problem-solving strategies, and the knowledge of the interface which is the medium of interaction for the problem solving. (F3) In relation to the student and to the tutoring system, a didactic situation is a *space for interaction between the student and the tutoring module*. We analyze here, in the prospect of a pedagogical scenario, the different functional constituents of this space (instruction messages, help, interaction objects...) The analysis of this facet also concerns the design and development methodologies of human-machine interfaces. (F4) In relation to the student and to the tutorial system, a didactic situation is a *space for observation of the student* whose qualitative interpretation will lead to the update of the student representations. In particular, we raise here the problem of filtering, which organizes these observations, in relation to different kinds of interpretations (knowledge of the subject domain, learning behavior...) (F5) In relation to the tutorial system, a didactic situation is a *knowledge structure* taken into account in the decision making process of the tutorial system. We also note that if the directions of the analyses mentioned above correspond to an individual learning situation, many questions concerned are also present in other learning situations. Some of these situations are currently the focus of great attention and relate to some form of collective learning.

The Use of Constraint Logic Programming in the Development of Adaptive Tests

Sophiana Chua Abdullah and Roger E. Cooley

Computing Laboratory
University of Kent at Canterbury
Canterbury, Kent, CT2 7NF, United Kingdom
{sc34,rec}@ukc.ac.uk

This research shows how Constraint Logic Programming can form the basis of a knowledge elicitation tool for the development of adaptive tests. A review of literature reveals that adaptive testing has, in recent years, been used as a student modelling tool in intelligent tutoring systems. Efforts in the construction and delivery of such tests have involved the use of state-space type constructs, such as granularity hierarchies and knowledge spaces, to represent a syllabus. The use of Bayesian probability networks has been proposed as a technique for finding an optimal route through these "spaces" so as to find the shortest sequence of problems to put to the student being evaluated. The research presented here sets out to use "expert emulation" as means of performing the same tasks. The aim is to construct an adaptive test in order to model a student's knowledge, skills and tutorial requirements. The context is the development of such a system to support autonomous revision for examination in a particular domain in elementary mathematics.

When setting tests, human tutors have to set specific problems. This task involves the partitioning of a syllabus or of a range of problem types. This can be done naturally by specifying constraints. Constraint Logic Programming provides a declarative and executable means of describing such specifications. Moreover, software to support this technique can be made sufficiently convenient for it to be used "on the fly" during a knowledge elicitation session involving an expert teacher and an interviewer. Such software facilitates the capture of descriptions of classes of problems and also descriptions of possible responses of a student to those problems. These executable descriptions can be used to generate examples, which can form the basis of further rounds of discussion between the expert and the interviewer.

An Ontological Approach for Design and Evaluation of Tutoring Systems

Stéphane Crozat, Philippe Trigano

UMR CNRS 6599 HEUDIASYC - Université de Technologie de Compiègne BP 20529
60206 COMPIEGNE Cedex - FRANCE
Email : Stephane.Crozat@utc.fr, Philippe.Trigano@utc.fr

People are used to dealing with paper and textual documents. Nonetheless the satisfactory principles for those documents are mostly not transposable to numeric and multimedia ones. Authors do not know **how to design** software and users do not know **how to evaluate** their relevancy. Since the domain is still emerging we do not have rules stating on the characteristics an ITS should fulfil. We quickly understood that computer science was just a small part of the domain, but after having explored several areas such as human-machine interface, multimedia, scenarios, and pedagogy we still can not precisely and totally solve the question. We nevertheless intend to submit an answer, being aware that it would be nothing but a point of view on the problem and not an absolute description. We wanted the knowledge we gathered to be represented and organised so that it could be a statement of the existing reality, sharable by various actors of the domain, effortlessly usable and reusable, easily evolving. These requirements fit with the concept of ontology in AI

Several level of ontology can be distinguished, depending on their level of formalisation. Because our domain is emerging and quickly evolving we could not reasonably propose formal definitions of the concepts. We opted for a **terminological ontology**, *i.e.* an organisation of defined concepts following a conceptual description. Relating to Gruber and Guarino we define the ontology we built as "a partial taxonomy of concepts and relationships between them, depending on the point of view we choose to study the domain, in order to submit the bases for an agreement inside the community". Considering the information we gathered on the domain, we decided to structure the knowledge base with three main kinds of objects: Criteria, questions and rules. Criteria indicate global concepts that characterise a tutoring system, whereas questions and rules allow the formulation of precise and more operational aspects.

In order to validate this ontology and use it in real situation, we developed two applications that exploit the knowledge it represents. Historically the first one is EMPI, an application to assist in the Evaluation of Multimedia Pedagogical Software. The purpose of EMPI is to drive a user into the set of criteria and questions defined in the ontology in order to find the positive and negative aspects of existing software. The second tool, $M \prec^{-1}$, aims to help designers in their choices and specifications. It presents the rules of the ontology to the designer and helps him in determining what will or will not be applied to the piece of software he wants to design.

Our ontology, even if only a restrictive and partial representation of the domain, can bring standardisation and methodology, providing to the actors of the domain a common language and agreeing on what is or should be a tutoring system. Because the terminological ontology we submit remains a human centred knowledge base, it does not aim to impose a too rigid standard, but a flexible description that can be adapted to each situation specificity.

Training Scenarios Generation Tools for an ITS to Control Center Operators

Luiz Faria[1], Zita Vale[2], Carlos Ramos[1], António Silva[1], Albino Marques[3]

[1] Polytechnic Institute of Porto/Institute of Engineering/Department of Computer Engineering
Rua Dr. António Bernardino de Almeida, 4200-072 Porto, Portugal
{lff, csr, asilva}@dei.isep.ipp.pt
[2] Polytechnic Institute of Porto/Institute of Engineering/Department of Electrical Engineering
Rua Dr. António Bernardino de Almeida, 4200-072 Porto, Portugal
zav@dee.isep.ipp.pt
[3] REN-Portuguese Transmission Network (EDP Group)
Rua Cidade de Goa 4, 2685 Sacavém, Portugal

In the last two decades, Intelligent Tutoring Systems (ITS) have proven to be highly effective as learning aids. However, few tutoring systems have made a successful transition to the industrial environment so far. Among the factors that make this transition difficult is the maintenance of such systems. In particular, the preparation of the learning material to the tutoring sessions constitutes a time-consuming task. Usually, in the industrial environment there is not a staff exclusively dedicated to training tasks. This is the case of the electrical sector, where the preparation of training sessions is accomplished with co-operation of the most experienced operators. As this task requires the participation of very busy people that are daily involved in the operation of the power system, it may be difficult to accomplish.

This work presents two tools that allow to generate learning sessions for an ITS, as automatically as possible. This ITS is used to give training to control center operators of the Portuguese Electrical Transmission Network. The main role of these operators is to get the diagnosis of the Power System state through the analysis of the alarm messages arriving to the control center.

The didactic material used in training sessions, conducted by the ITS, is composed by sets of related alarm messages defining a case occurred in the grid, by conclusions that allow to define the case and by a parameter quantifying the difficulty level of the case under analysis. In this context, a case means a set of several incidents related. The alarm messages arriving to the control centre and the analysis of each incident occurred are stored in a database. In this way, a register of the disturbances observed in the electrical grid is maintained. The training scenario generation task consists of looking for the relationships between several incidents and related alarm messages. A last step present in the creation of a training scenario is concerned with the evaluation of the difficulty level of the training scenario. The intelligent tutor will use this parameter to select a study case to present to the learner, according to his needs.

The first application allows to generate and classify training scenarios from real cases previously stored. Nevertheless, the training scenarios thus obtained do not cover all the situations that control center operators must be prepared to deal with. Thus, we have developed another application that allows to create new training scenarios or to edit already existing ones.

Multiple Paradigms for a Generic Diagnostic Proposal

Bego Ferrero, Isabel Fernandez-Castro, and Maite Urretavizcaya

Department of Languages and Computer Systems, University of the Basque Country,
Apdo 649, E-20080 Donostia, Spain

This work concerns the use of multiple diagnosis approaches to build a generic diagnostic system. The main goal of the project is that the teacher can adapt by herself the generic system to several domains in order to detect the student's errors during different problem solving processes. Adapting the generic system requires the teacher analyses thoroughly the domain in order to identify and represent its composing objects, procedures and problems together with their resolution mechanisms. The learning tool constructed with this purpose does not support completely the learning process, since its goal is only to monitor and diagnose the learner's actions. So the other aspects of the teaching activity must be carried out by the teacher or an external (integrated) complementary system (i.e. a tutoring system).

Trying to obtain an exact diagnosis would imply a very deep knowledge representation and such a close relationship to the domain that would be unfeasible in a system proposed as generic. Several diagnostic techniques have been described so far in the ITS literature whose study has established the basis on which our approach is inspired. It combines a variant of the model tracing technique augmented with a set of domain constraints and error libraries. Thus, the diagnostic approach uses the model adequate to the student's activity to determine its errors. Besides it offers short descriptions about the errors and informs of their locations.

This generic diagnostic process is initially based on the model-tracing technique. First the system carries out a supervised diagnosis comparing each student's step with the previously defined problem solving models. However, if the student executes actions that have not been considered in the models, bugs or restrictions (as it is not possible to assure a complete group of solutions), the system is able to determine the possibility of executing this step taking into account the current state of the problem solving process and the domain definition. In addition, the student's resolution processes are recorded in order that the expert can evaluate its correctness and update the solution set and the restrictions when necessary in order to complete the domain model.

This approach has been implemented in CLIPS by means of a general kernel, called DETECTive, and a suitable graphical interface which facilitates the teacher to define the multiple models of the domain. It has been proved with four prototypes in different domains —symbolic differentiation, help for handicapped people in the development of simple tasks, machine tool domain and operation of a photograph camera— obtaining positive results.

A Description Formalism
for Complex Questionnaires

Fabrice Issac and Olivier Hû

fabrice.issac@utc.fr olivier.hu@utc.fr
UTC - UMR CNRS 6599 Heudiasyc - BP 20529 - 60206 Compiegne Cedex

In any educationnal process, evaluation seems impossible to circumvent , and in this context questionnaires are very often used: easy to implement and publishing, modification is largely facilitated... This tool presents nevertheless some limits. We propose a model allowing an implementation of any type of questionnaires to improve the teaching performance while preserving their flexibility and simplicity of implementation. Several aspects can be explored to move up from basic MCQ to advanced questionnaires, and contrary to other existing projects[1], we propose a formalism wich allows these requirements:

- several type of questions: MCQ, multiple answers, open questions...
- several type of structure: tree structure, iteration, random selection...
- several type of results: reinforcement, marks, report, structure adaptation...
- several target: the questionnaire can be exported on paper, Web...
- several results: we can generate several calculs with a same questionaire.

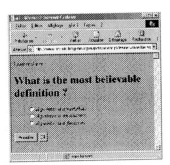

Questionnaire structure   QML Example   Snapshot

The complete system will provide a tool allowing the author to build a questionnaire, and a system which will have to allow the publishing of questionnaires (for the moment only Web and paper, via HTML and LaTeX, are established). An complete example is available at: http://www.hds.utc.fr/˜issac/QML.

[1] M. Sasse and al., *Support for authoring and managing web-based coursework: the TACO project.* Hezami and al. ed., The digital university. Springer-Verlag, 1998.
J. William and al., *The Netquest project: question delivery over the web using TML,* CHEER, 11(2), 1997.

Assisting Planning in Computer-Mediated Explorative Problem-Solving

Kohji Itoh, Makoto Itami, Masaru Fujihira,
Takaaki Kawamura, Kiyoto Kawakami

Science University of Tokyo, Noda, 278-8510, JAPAN

E-mail itoh@te.noda.sut.ac.jp

Abstract. We have been developing a researchers' test bed dubbed CAFEKS (Computer-Assisted Free Exploration of Knowledge Structure) for developing interactive learning environments with coached problem-solving. In this poster, we propose to introduce assistance for the learners planning problem-solving as an extension of CAFEKS.

1 Introduction

CAFEKS is a test bed for developing explorative problem solving environments in which the students are assisted to choose a problem type, to describe their problem and to choose a plan script stack from the plan repertoire provided by the the class, they are assisted in varying degree owing to the system's interpretation of the scripts which usually comprise problem types as subplans again allowing selection of plans of the problem type classes. The system guides them when they get into deadlock.

2 Assisting Planning

In order to give the students more freedom of trying their own planning instead of choosing plans from those provided by the problem type classes refered to from the scripts, we propose to provide the students with a database of problem types and executable scripts from which the student can select problem types and scripts to construct their own plans of problem-solving.

Once constructed, the component problem type classes can provide options of plans for solving the pertaining subproblems. The students are free to follow the pavements or to make detouring.

The principle of tracing the behavior of the students to give advice when they get lost should be observed. For that purpose we need records of the behavior of the students.

In general, however, planning and execution often proceed in interwoven or partially parallel manner. Accordingly we have to distinguish between the records for planning and the records for execution.

For execution we keep recording in the step instance the context, i.e. the record of the so far derived assertions, and the plan stack, i.e. the record of that part of the planning to be executed from that step on.

For planning we will record the parent-child links between the tentative problem type instance (parent) and the tentative problem type, execution instances (children) which are made included in the parent problem type class' plan-assistance script proposed by the students combining the elements from the plan database or selected from the menu of the script stacks of the parent problem type class.

Annotating Exploration History and Knowledge Mapping for Learning with Web-Based Resources

Akihiro Kashihara, Shinobu Hasegawa, and Jun'ichi Toyoda

I.S.I.R., Osaka University, 8-1, Mihogaoka, Ibaraki, Osaka 567-0047, JAPAN
kasihara@ai.sanken.osaka-u.ac.jp

Exploring hyperspace provided by hypermedia/hypertexts often involves constructing knowledge from the contents that have been explored. This would enhance learning. However, learners often fail in knowledge construction since what and why they have explored so far become hazy as the exploration progresses. The main way to resolve this problem is to encourage learners to reflect on what they have constructed during exploration in hyperspace. The reflection also involves rethinking the exploration process that they have carried out since it has a great influence on their knowledge construction. In particular, exploration purposes, which mean the reasons why the learners have searched for the next node in hyperspace, play a crucial role in knowledge construction. For instance, a learner may search for the meaning of an unknown term to supplement what is learned at the current node or look for elaboration of the description given at the current node. Each exploration purpose would provide its own way to shape the knowledge structure. The reflection support accordingly needs to adapt to their exploration activities and the knowledge structure being constructed by the learners.

As a proper reflection support for learning with hypermedia/hypertext based learning resources on the Web, we have developed a reflection support system that encourages learners to annotate their exploration history with exploration purposes that have arisen during exploration. It also transforms the annotated exploration history into a knowledge map that spatially represents semantic relationships between the WWW pages that the learners have visited. Although such semantic relationships, which are not always defined in web-based learning resources, these are specified by the exploration purposes. Using the system, the learners can annotate the exploration history to rethink their exploration process that they have carried out so far. They can also view the knowledge map to reflect on what they have constructed in hyperspace.

Acknowledgements

This research is supported in part by Grant-in-Aid for Scientific Research from the Ministry of Education, Science, and Culture of Japan.

Collaborative Learning Environment which Enforces Students to Induce Ideas

Tomoko Kojiri[1] and Toyohide Watanabe[1]

Nagoya University, JAPAN
Furo-cho, Chikusa-ku, Nagoya 464-8603, JAPAN
Phone: +81-52-789-2735, Fax: +81-52-789-3808
{kojiri,watanabe}@watanabe.nuie.nagoya-u.ac.jp

In order to realize the functionality or environment for collaboration on the information network, the following subjects must be systematically investigated:

1) to organize participating students as a collaborative group,
2) to support effective actions/reactions among students,
3) to not only coordinate the discussion activity successfully but also promote the interactions successively,
4) to enable every student to reach the final discussion goal and encourage the mutual understanding.

At least, many of researches which have been investigated until today are mainly related to 1) and 2), but do not directly address the viewpoints of 3) and 4). The subjects in 3) and 4) are more difficult than those in 1) and 2) because these subjects do not only concentrate on the functionality of system facilities among mechanical interactions attended to each user operations of inter-processes, but also aim to grasp the learning progress and understanding situation for participating students and encourage the complementary discussions and opinion exchanges among them cooperatively. The research viewpoints are very difficult and complex topics in comparison with current technological effects. This paper focuses on 3) with a view to designing the creative framework for being enable to attach to 4).

In order to attain to our objective for developing a framework for the creative learning space, we introduce new collaborative learning support means which monitor learning process according to not only the discussion states but also the progress of deriving answer and suggest advices to the learning group which may resolve inappropriate learning situation. The remarkable aspect of our research is that our proposing system generates advices, based on the following 2 points of view. One is that our supporting entity is a learning group but not individual students. In collaborative learning, students are able to help each other by discussing among the learning group and additionally, such discussion is necessary in order to understand mutually. Therefore, our system grasps the learning situation of group and generates advices that promote the discussion among learning group to solve the exercise, if necessary. The other is encouragement to induce ideas. Mostly, there are more than one answering paths in an exercise and to know other answering paths is meaningful to let students consider the exercise deeply. So, our system aims not only to help students to derive the answer but also to encourage them to derive various ideas.

Adaptive Support for Brain Deficits in Special Education

Jaakko Kurhila[1], Leena Paasu[2], and Erkki Sutinen[3]

[1] Dept. of Computer Science, University of Helsinki, Finland
[2] Dept. of Special Education, University of Joensuu, Finland
[3] Dept. of Computer Science, University of Joensuu, Finland

From the perspective of modern constructivist theories on learning, the large and diverse group of students with learning difficulties and motorical impairments pose a remarkable challenge for software designers. It is obvious that an unlimited hyperspace with free paths in every direction is not the ideal environment for a learner who gets lost even in simple assignments and can neither compose a problem-solving strategy nor uphold attentiveness.

AHMED is a completely domain-independent system to address both learning and motorical deficits. Adaptation to individual learning processes in AHMED is based on the action of the learner during a learning session. The aim is to lead the learner through the *learning space* so that the most suitable learning material is exposed to the learner. To activate the learner, the material typically consists of various tasks with interactive elements, not just information items.

The learning space in our framework has a certain similarity with an n-dimensional hypermedia structure: the learning space has nodes, called *learning seeds*, but not necessarily the links between the nodes. The seeds have their position in the learning space, defined by a numerical parameter for every dimension. The dimensions can be arbitrary, but it is normal to use them as learning objectives, such as 'Subtraction skill' or 'Reading comprehension'. The learner is situated in one of the points in the learning space at a given time, thus representing the learner's situation in respect to the learning material.

Every *action* a learner can make in a seed has an effect for the learner's position in the learning space. The effect can pertain 0 to n dimensions, and the strength of the effect can be arbitrary. The action a learner makes in a seed moves the learner to the seed that matches the learner's previous point in the space added with the effect from of last action. If the learner's position in the space is, for example, $<skill1,skill2> = <3,4>$ and the action the learner makes has an effect of $<skill1> = <+1>$, the learner is taken to a position of $<skill1,skill2> = <4,4>$. This procedure leads to individual learning paths through the learning material. These paths serve as an important basis for evaluation and assessment for the teachers and other learning environment participants.

The learning material in AHMED can be more than traditional frame-oriented computer-aided instruction; seeds in AHMED can be simple multiple-choice questions with right or wrong answers, or they can form more versatile learning objects, such as educational adventures or games. In addition, the learning material can be a hypermedia structure, where the width of the visible hyperspace is the main property to adapt.

Student Modelling and Interface Design in SIAL

A. Martínez[1], M.A. Simón[1], J.A. Maestro[1], M. López[1], and C. Alonso[1]

Dpt. of Computer Science, University of Valladolid, Valladolid, Spain
amartine@infor.uva.es

Abstract. SIAL is an intelligent system for the learning of first order logic. It has been developed as a laboratory tool for Artificial Intelligence courses of Computer Science curricula. Student modelling in this domain is a complex task, but it is necessary if we want to have a good interaction with the student. Interface design has a main role in the system, not only because it configures the environment in which the student works, but also because it becomes part of the error diagnosis process. In this paper we present how we have faced both problems in SIAL.

This paper presents the design principles of the student model and the interface of SIAL.

The diagnosis process is supported by the model tracing [2] and constraint based modelling [3] techniques. SIAL consists of four modules. The *interface* controls the input of the student, which is entered basically by direct manipulation using the mouse. Any expression introduced by the student is filtered through *a lexical-syntactic parser*. User's expressions are represented in a standard notation, and are compared with the output of two *resolution tools*: OTTER, a theorem prover, and SLI, a first order logic resolution system. OTTER is used to detect whether there is a refutation or not, and SLI for finer-grained tests about the clausulation process (resolvents, hyperresolvents, factorizations, subsumptions, and elimination of pure literals and tautologies). Finally, a *constraint base* performs the analysis at a logic level. It applies the solution to a set of constraints, which can detect logical errors, and explain their cause.

Apart of the above mentioned role in the diagnosis process, the interface implements *intelligent selection of expressions* [1], which automatically selects the whole expressions affected by a symbol. This feature fulfils a pedagogical goal, as it helps the student to think always at the subexpression level.

References

1. S. Alpert, M. Singley, and P. G. Fairweather. Deploying intelligent tutors on the web: an architecture and an example. *International Journal of Artificial Intelligence in Education*, 10:183–197, 1999.
2. P. Dillenbourg and J. Self. A framework for learner modelling. *Interactive Learning Environments*, 2(2):111–137, 1992.
3. A. Mitrovic and S. Ohlsson. Evaluation of a constraint-based tutor for a database language. *International Journal of Artificial Intelligence in Education*, 10:238–256, 1999.

A Reification of a Strategy for Geometry Theorem Proving

Noboru Matsuda[1] and Kurt VanLehn[2] *

[1] Intelligent Systems Program, University of Pittsburgh,
[2] Learning Research and Development Center, University of Pittsburgh
3939 O'Hara Street, Pittsburgh PA 15260

This study addresses a novel technique to build a graphical user interface (GUI) for an intelligent tutoring system (ITS) to help students to learn geometry theorem proving with construction – one of the most challenging and creative parts of elementary geometry. Students' task is not only to prove theorems, but also to construct missing points and/or segments to complete a proof (called *auxiliary lines*). The problem space of theorem proving with construction is generally huge, thus understanding a search strategy is a key issue for students to succeed in this domain. Two major challenges in building a GUI for an intelligent learning environment are (a) to build a theorem prover that is capable of construction, and (b) to establish a cognitive model of understanding a complex problem-solving strategy.

So far, we have built a geometry theorem prover, GRAMY, which can automatically construct auxiliary lines when needed to complete a proof. GRAMY utilizes a simple single heuristic for construction, which says that "apply a known axiom or theorem backwards by overlapping the related configuration with the diagram given in the problem while allowing the match to omit segment(s) in the configuration." The auxiliary lines are those which match the omitted segments. Surprisingly, this simple heuristic works very well. This suggests that it might be possible to teach students how to construct auxiliary lines.

In order to develop an ITS based on GRAMY, we need a GUI to display the reasoning in a graphical, manipulable form — to "reify" (make real) the reasoning. Some common techniques for reification have flaws, so suggest a new one. Our basic idea is to reify the search process rather than the structure of the ultimate solution. The resulting GUI shows an intermediate state of proof. It consists of the diagram of a theorem to prove, and applicable axioms (or theorems) in that state. Using tools that look like those of a web browser, the student can select an applicable axiom to proceed a state, or go back and forth between states.

We show how this reification technique can be applied to teach students three basic search strategies; forward chaining, backward chaining, and backing up at dead-ends. We discuss why this reification model should be better than the ones that reifies the entire solution space as trees.

---

* Email: mazda@isp.pitt.edu and vanlehn@cs.pitt.edu   This research was supported by NSF grant number 9720359 to CIRCLE: Center for Interdisciplinary Research on Constructive Learning Environments. http://www.pitt.edu/~circle

VLab : An Environment for Teaching Behavioral Modeling

Elpida S. Tzafestas[1,2] and Platon A. Prokopiou[1]

[1] Institute for Communication and Computer Systems, Electrical and Computer Engineering Department, National Technical University of Athens, Zographou Campus, Athens 15773, GREECE

brensham@softlab.ece.ntua.gr, pplaton@central.ntua.gr

[2] Digital Art Laboratory, Athens School of Fine Arts, Peiraios 256, 18233 Agios Ioannis Rentis,, GREECE

Within the framework of a master in digital art, we have developed a set of educational tools for artificial life and the complexity sciences. These software tools constitute a laboratory curriculum that is used to supplement the theoretical courses on the subject and contain, among other things, an educational tool for behavioral modeling (VLab).

VLab allows the experimentation and control of simulated robotic agents that are Braitenberg vehicle-like (V. Braitenberg, "Vehicles", MIT Press, 1984). The purpose of the lab is to make students familiar with behavioral modeling, albeit of the simple type defined and used by Braitenberg. To better address the target audience of digital art students, we introduce an additional behavioral parameter, the brush, used by the simulated agents to draw/paint while moving around. This arrangement allows us to exploit the users' visual experience and motivation to manipulate and experiment with complex visual forms.

Simulated vehicles move around and draw on a canvas where various stimuli sources are situated (in the relevant literature, stimuli sources are generally thought of as food or light sources). Each vehicle's sensors perceive stimuli sources and are directly connected to its motors that control motion, without elaborate processing. Depending on the connections' properties and topology, a particular phenomenal behavior arises (aggressive, coward etc). In any case, an external observer perceives the vehicle as consciously chasing or escaping the source. In VLab, most of the Braitenberg models are implemented, together with a few variants and synthetic models. The user may modify the various behavioral parameters, including the brush, and exploit the "competition" between vehicles and sources to produce structured patterns (such as lines, ellipses, etc.) or random-like colorful scenes.

Our experience with using the system revealed that the artists show a high motivation for experimenting with the system, which is partly due to the fact that they tend to regard it as a simple abstract art tool that may produce interesting complex forms. Those forms are possible thanks to the versatility of the brush. We have also identified several methodological and theoretical issues that have to be addressed by large-scale educational software tools, for instance by a future expanded version of VLab. Those issues include the balance that has to be found between general- and special- purpose functions and the need for active participation of the user to the system operation so as to ensure high motivation for learning. We also identify the problem of integration of a software-driven educational process to the general educational environment and policy applied, as well as the question of objectiveness of learning. For details, see http://www.softlab.ece.ntua.gr/~brensham/Vlab/

W1 - Modeling Human Teaching Tactics and Strategies

Benedict du Boulay

University of Sussex at Brighton, UK

This workshop explores issues concerned with capturing human teaching tactics and strategies as well as attempts to model and evaluate those tactics and strategies in systems. The former topic covers studies both of expert as well as "ordinary" teachers. The latter includes issues of modeling motivation, timing, conversation, learning as well as simply knowledge traversal.

We see this workshop as a follow-on from the panel discussion at AI-ED'99 that stimulated a debate about the whole issue of how and whether, and with what effect, human teaching tactics can/should be modeled. The description of that panel was as follows:

"According to Bloom, one-on-one tutoring is the most successful form of instruction. [...] Recently, the AI-ED community has been exploring issues of human tutoring in terms of how experts coach novices, when do tutors tutor, how do they tutor in terms of the types of things they say to the learner, and when do they fade their assistance? One issue this panel will address is should computer tutors mimic human tutors or are there special advantages or disadvantages of computers that should be drawn on or avoided? Even if the computer could accurately diagnose the student's affective state and even if the computer could respond to that state [...], there remains one final potential difficulty: the plausibility, or perhaps the acceptability, problem. The issue here is whether the same actions and the same statements that human tutors use will have the same effect if delivered instead by a computer, even a computer with a virtually human voice." (Lepper et al., 1993)

Human-to-human tutoring incorporates mechanisms that are associated with normal conversational dialogue, but rarely incorporate most ideal tutoring strategies. Some of the normal conversational mechanisms can be simulated on computer, whereas others are too difficult to incorporate in current computational technologies. It would be prudent for an ITS to incorporate both ideal pedagogical strategies and some conversational mechanisms that are within the immediate grasp of modern technologies. But this solution is periodically confronted with trade-offs and conflicts between ideal strategies and natural conversation. These issues will be addressed by this panel.

Workshop Program Committee:

Ben du Boulay, University of Sussex, UK (chair)
Art Graesser, University of Memphis, USA
Jim Greer, University of Saskatchewan, Canada
Susanne Lajoie, McGill University, Canada
Mark Lepper, Stanford University, USA
Rose Luckin, University of Sussex, UK
Johanna Moore, University of Edinburgh, UK
Nathalie Person, Rhodes College, USA

W2 - Adaptive and Intelligent Web-Based Education Systems

Christoph Peylo

University of Osnabrück, Germany

Currently, Web-based educational systems form one of the fastest growing areas in educational technology research and development. Benefits of Web-based education are independence of teaching and learning with respect to time and space. Courseware installed and maintained in one place may be used by a huge number of users all over the world. A challenging research goal is the development of adaptive and intelligent Web-based educational systems (W-AIES) that offer some amount of adaptivity and intelligence.

Adaptability with respect to navigation support and presentation helps students to locate and comprehend relevant course material. Intelligent problem solving support and error explanation facilities support their work with assignments. Adaptive collaboration support tools find most relevant helper or collaborator. These are just a few examples implemented in a number of research systems that show how a learner may benefit from adaptive and intelligent technologies. While most commercial courseware systems do not employ intelligent or adaptive technologies, a number of existing research systems have already formed a critical mass for a creative discussion on Web-based adaptive and intelligent educational systems.

The goal of the proposed workshop is to provide a forum for this discussion and thus to continue the series of workshops on this topic held at past conferences, e.g. AIED'97 (http://www.contrib.andrew.cmu.edu/~plb/AIED97_workshop/) and ITS'98 (http://www-aml.cs.umass.edu/~stern/webits/itsworkshop/) workshops. Topics of interest for the workshop include adaptive curriculum sequencing in Web-based educational systems, intelligent problem solving support via the Web, adaptive presentation and navigation support for Web-based education, adaptive collaboration support via the Web, Web-based adaptive testing, porting existing intelligent tutoring systems to the Web, intelligent monitoring of Web-based classes and courses, log mining to improve the performance of Web-based educational systems, authoring tools for developing adaptive and intelligent educational systems on the Web, empirical studies of Web-based adaptive and intelligent educational systems.

Workshop Program Committee:
Christoph Peylo, University of Osnabrück, Germany (chair)
Peter Brusilovsky, Carnegie Mellon University, Pittsburgh, USA
Steven Ritter, Carnegie Mellon University, Pittsburgh, USA
Claus Rollinger, University of Osnabrück, Germany
Mia K. Stern, University of Massachusetts, Amherst, USA
Gerhard Weber, Pedagogical University Freiburg, Germany

W3 – Applying Machine Learning to ITS Design/Construction

Joseph Beck

University of Massachusetts, USA

Machine learning is applicable to many aspects of ITS construction including student modeling, learning tutoring strategies, and providing education partners for a student. With respect to student modeling, learning techniques can be used to induce the student's current state of knowledge. Learning teaching strategies promises to allow the development of more flexible systems that can adapt to the unique requirements of different populations of students, and to differences in individuals within those populations.

A somewhat more general view is that machine learning can be used to automate the knowledge acquisition process of building an ITS. Given the array of knowledge needed (rules on how to teach, provide feedback, update estimates of student knowledge based on his actions, etc.), and the cost of encoding this knowledge, this is potentially a large lever for easing the difficulties of ITS construction.

Adding these capabilities has a price. For unsupervised techniques there is the problem of gathering enough training data to ensure the learning agent can reason correctly. For supervised learning, how much help does the learning agent need? How can it learn to generalize quickly? Also, there is little agreement on what techniques or architectures are most appropriate. Experimenting with different learning paradigms can be very time consuming. Do we know enough to draw general conclusions about the applicability of various techniques? Given that the agent can reason effectively, what do we do now? Does this allow us to construct systems with new capabilities, or only to make existing systems more flexible, and possibly less expensive?

Workshop Program Committee:

Joseph Beck, University of Massachusetts, USA (chair)
Esma Aïmeur, University of Montréal, Canada
Lora Aroyo, University of Twente, The Netherlands
Ken Koedinger, Carnegie Mellon University, USA
Claude Frasson, University of Montréal, Canada
Tanja Mitrovic, University of Canterbury, New Zealand
Vadim Stefanuk, Institute for Information Transmission Problems, Russia

W4 – Collaborative Discovery Learning in the Context of Simulations

Wouter van Joolingen

University of Amsterdam, The Netherlands

In this workshop we aim to explore the cross-fertilization of discovery learning and collaborative learning. Both types of learning are receiving growing interest because they share a vision of learning as a learner-centered, situated and social process. Combining them into collaborative discovery learning opens new possibilities for enhancing learning.

Collaboration during discovery learning can naturally elicit important learning events. For example, explication of one's hypothesis to fellow learners helps the discovery learner make his or her hypothesis more explicit, and encourages justification of and reflection on the hypothesis. Collaboration can be supported by using models of discovery learning to do an automated analysis of the collaboration dialogue and products of collaborative construction. For instance, in learning environments like Belvedere and CSILE, the constructs created by the learner (e.g. argumentation structures) and communication about these constructs can benefit from empirical testing with a computer simulation, and from feedback generated on the basis of an analysis of the simulation domain.

We will address the issues from three stances, a pedagogical stance, a design stance and an architectural stance. Pedagogical issues include the effect of collaboration on discovery and the effect of discovery processes on the communication between learners. The design stance addresses the design of supportive measures for collaborative discovery. The architectural viewpoint concerns the generic design and (re)usability of collaborative discovery environments and their components. A full account of the workshops issues and program can be found at its web site: http://www.ilo.uva.nl/projecten/ITS2000.

The workshop will start with a general introduction by the organizers and possibly other participants based on the position papers. The goal of this opening is to pose the questions that will be the main focus in the second part. The second part will consist of a few interactive demonstration sessions, in which the audience is invited to discuss and make suggestions during the demonstrations given. In the third and final part of the workshop, we will return to the focus questions raised in the first part and try to combine elements of the various demonstrations into the requirements and constraints for a fictitious learning environment that would meet issues raised in the discussion.

Workshop Program Committee:

Wouter van Joolingen, University of Amsterdam, The Netherlands (chair)
Allen Munro, University of Southern California, USA
Daniel Suthers, University of Hawai'i at Manoa, USA

W5 – Case-Based Reasoning in Intelligent Training Systems

Esma Aïmeur

University of Montréal, Canada

The workshop will bring together researchers working primarily in the design and development of intelligent systems in education. Emphasis is on the application of case-based reasoning (CBR) to support computer-based learning. This workshop intends to appraise the current level of development and to identify fruitful avenues of research for the next five years in case-based teaching systems. Important concerns in intelligent tutoring research (ITS) are how to ease implementation effort, enable re-usability of software components, and how to realize the more ambitious objective of self-improvement (e.g., automated acquisition of pedagogical, problem-solving, and planning knowledge). These objectives of intelligent tutoring are commonly stated virtues of CBR. The workshop will examine the latest developments in supporting learning using CBR technology. We are interested in all aspects of CBR as relevant to learning environments. This includes learning environments whose architecture has a CBR component. It also includes systems whose pedagogical approach is case-based, such as a case method or a Socratic method of teaching, as well as systems that focus on selecting, tailoring, and/or presenting examples. Finally, it includes systems designed to teach skills of reasoning with cases. Of particular interest is the use of CBR in instruction and interaction planning. Central to this are strategies for selecting suitable interaction moves and responses, methods for generating explanations, and other techniques for tailoring the interaction between students and the tutor. Software issues are also relevant and the workshop will discuss architectures which include components dedicated to managing the interaction that use CBR. Pedagogical agents, such as dialog generators, and multi-agent systems that co-operate to tailor lessons, explanations, and interfaces in educational systems are of interest too provided CBR is a significant component of the architecture. Submissions in any of the areas discussed above and outlined below are welcome although other relevant topics will be acceptable too. Those papers that cover a cross-section of areas are particularly encouraged. As well as research papers, applications are sought that demonstrate a new technique or a general principle. These may be fully operational industrial systems or research prototypes. In either case, the main contribution of the application to understanding the role of CBR in ITS must be clear and justified.

Workshop Program Committee:

Esma Aïmeur, University of Montreal, Montréal, Canada (chair)
Vincent Aleven, Carnegie Mellon University, Pittsburgh, USA
Tariq Khan, North London University, London, England
Ramon Lopez de Mantaras, Spanish Council for Scientific Research, Spain
Riichiro Mizoguchi, Osaka University, Osaka, Japan
Ian Watson, University of Salford, England

W6 – Learning Algebra with the Computer, a Transdisciplinary Workshop

Jean-François Nicaud

University of Nantes, France

All over the world many researchers are working on the improvement of the learning of algebra with the help of the computer. Activities have various forms including design and development of innovative software, experiments with innovative software like computer algebra systems, reflection about the nature of the algebra to be taught, and theories of algebra learning. These researchers belong to different disciplines, in particular maths education, psychology, and computer science. They do not usually participate in the same conferences and so unfortunately miss the opportunity for collaborative discussions toward their common goals of improving the learning of algebra.

This workshop aims at bringing together researchers interested in algebra learning for a presentation of their recent constructions and results.

Topics of interest for the workshop include formal manipulations, formal problems, functions, multiple representations of functions, applications of algebra in other domains, word problem solving, algebraic models of problem situations, and related topics. Projects may address algebra learning from young children's first exposure to algebraic ideas through college level algebra.

Workshop Program Committee:

Jean-François Nicaud, University of Nantes, France (chair)
Ferdinando Arzarello, University of Turin, Italy
Nicolas Balacheff, CNRS, Laboratoire Leibniz, France
Monique Baron, University of Paris 6, France
Michael Beeson, San Jose State University, USA
Carolyn Kieran, UQAM, Montréal, Canada
Kenneth R. Koedinger, Carnegie Mellon University, Pittsburgh, USA
Anh Nguyen-Xuan, University of Paris 8, France
Steven Ritter, Carnegie Mellon University, Pittsburgh, USA
Rosamund Sutherland, University of Bristol, UK

W7 – Advanced Instructional Design for Complex Safety Critical & Emergency Training

Mike Dobson [1], Mike Spector [2]

[1] CSALT, Lancaster University, UK
[2] Syracuse University, USA

The workshop will bring together expertise in emergency training , intelligent agents, collaborative learning and communication theory. Participants will examine the use of intelligent agents, team based instructional design theories and models of cognition that could contribute to improved learning outcomes such as better,

- shared sense of emergency situations,
- communication between team agents,
- organizational communication for coordination, and
- understanding & management of time critical behavior under jeopardy.

Some early attempts to train operational teams emphasized minimizing error by practice and improving team co-ordination. Limitations of this approach led to instructional strategies that also accept and manage errors trying to mitigate their consequences. Minimizing error and mitigating its consequences imply different training needs and approaches. Group training theory now emphasizes improvement of situation awareness leading to effective communication and co-ordination. Communicating situation information encourages group situation awareness, minimizes the risk of poor communication, and is likely to reduce error.

Distributed high fidelity simulation systems with intelligent agent technology provide a realistic and enormously flexible group training experience for trainees. There are however several outstanding questions for designers and practitioners that will be the subject of this workshop. Participants will discuss factors for optimizing simulations including: fidelity, inter agent and organizational communications; strategies for developing and measuring shared mental models; and the inherent complexity and difficulty of training for this kind of domain.

The goal of the workshop will be the exchange of ideas and experiences on instructional design strategies, communication analysis and advanced technology solutions for performance improvement in safety critical and emergency situations.

Workshop Program Committee:

Mike Dobson, CSALT, Lancaster University, Bailrigg, UK (chair)
Mike Spector, Syracuse University, USA (co-chair)
Frederick Elg, University of Linkoping, Sweden
Dirk Solk, TNO, The Hague, The Netherlands
Jelke van der Pal, NLR, Amsterdam, The Netherlands
Fred Pass, Open University of Netherlands, The Netherlands
Pal Davidsen, University of Bergen, Norway

Young Researchers Track

An Informal Model of Vocabulary Acquisition During Assisted Oral Reading and some Implications for Computerized Instruction
Greg Aist
Carnegie Mellon University, USA

Virtual Hospital Round: A Cognitive Tool for Clinical Teaching
Zahra R. S. Al-Rawahi
University of Sussex, Brighton, UK

The Zone of Comprehension and the Level of Scaffolding in an Exploratory Learning Environments
Saleh S H Al Shidhani
University of Sussex, Brighton, UK

Towards Macro-Adapting an ITS to Individual Differences
Ivon Arroyo
University of Massachusetts, Amherst, USA

Improving the Effectiveness of World Wide Web Delivered Courses.
Tim Barker and Rachel Pilkington
University of Leeds, U.K.

Problem Solving in a Didactic Situation in a Computer Assisted Learning-to-Read Environment: Knowledge Used by the Student
Panita Bussapapach
Université Blaise Pascal - Clermont, France

Performance and Mental Efficiency as Determinants for Dynamic Problem Selection in a Computer-Based Electronic Learning Environment
Gino Camp
Open University of the Netherlands, The Netherlands

A Cognitive Model for Automatic Narrative Summarization in a Self-Educational System
Laurence Capus
Université Laval, Canada

Designing Pedagogical Hypermedia: An Information-Centered Approach
Stéphane Crozat
Université de Technologie de Compiègne, France

Using Pedagogical Hypermedias in Real Situations: Experiments Results.
Stéphane Crozat
Université de Technologie de Compiègne, France

Collaborative and Intelligent Applications in Education
Raquel Díaz Fernández and Yannis Dimitriadis
Universidad de Valladolid, Spain

The Role of Metacognition in Interactive Learning Environments
Claudia Gama
University of Sussex, UK

Adding a Cognitive Model of Human Tutors To an Intelligent Tutoring Systems
Neil T. Heffernan
Carnegie Mellon University, USA

SITS: A Scrutable Teaching System
Sam Holden
University of Sydney, Australia

A Framework For Intelligent Behavior in Agents Systems
Yan Laporte
Université de Sherbrooke, Sherbrooke, Canada

Teamwork Based User Modeling
Michael S. Miller and Jianwen Yin
Texas A&M University, USA

Using XML for the Validation of Tests Resources in Intelligent Tutoring Systems
Azly Nacro and Bernard Lefebvre
Université du Québec à Montréal, Canada

DIVILAB: Distributed Virtual Laboratory a Shared Discussion Space for Scientific Argumentation
Nadège Neau
TRIGONE Laboratory, France

WebCT : A Survey
Martin Pagé and Ruddy Lelouche
Université Laval, Canada

Matching Instructional Conditions to Styles of Users in SMILE Maker
Svetoslav Stoyanov
University of Twente, The Netherlands

Collaborative Learning Environment for Problem Solving: Some Design Solutions
Neli Stoyanova
University of Twente, The Netherlands

The Design of a Multi-Agent Based Two-Domain Tutoring System for PERL
Tiffany Ya Tang and Albert Wu
The Hong Kong Polytechnic University, Hong Kong

Measurement Issues in Student Modeling for Intelligent Tutoring Systems
Mike Timms
University of California Berkeley, U.S.A.

ITS Web-Based Architecture for Hierarchical Declarative Domains
Mónica Trella López
University of Málaga, Málaga, Spain

From CAI Systems to Web-Based Distributed Intelligent Tutoring Systems
Yujian Zhou
Illinois Institute of Technology, USA

YRT Organization

Chair

Roger Nkambou, Université de Sherbrooke, Canada

Seniors reviewers and supervisors

Peter Brusilovsky, Carnegie Mellon University, Pittsburg, USA

Cyrille Desmoulins, Université Paris VI, France

Aude Dufresne, Université de Montréal, Canada

Martha W. Evens, Illinois Institute of Technology, Chicago, USA

Art Graesser, The University of Memphis, USA

Ulrich Hoppe, University of Duisburg, Germany

Claire Isabelle, Université de Moncton, Canada

Wouter van Joolingen, University of Twente, The Netherlands

Judith Kay, University of Sydney, Australia

Bernard Lefebvre, Université du Québec à Montréal, Canada

Heinz-Juergen Thole, University of Oldenburg, Germany

Author Index

Lecture Notes in Computer Science

For information about Vols. 1–1736
please contact your bookseller or Springer-Verlag